FIFTH EDITION

SPORT IN CONTEMPORARY SOCIETY

An Anthology

FIFTH EDITION

SPORT
IN
CONTEMPORARY
SOCIETY

An Anthology

D. STANLEY EITZEN

Colorado State University

St. Martin's Press
NEW YORK

Editor: Sabra Scribner
Manager, publishing services: Emily Berleth
Editor, publishing services: Douglas Bell
Project management: Publication Services
Production supervisor: Joe Ford
Cover design: Patricia McFadden
Cover photos: *(Top and center photos)* Alan Laidman, Uniphoto. *(Bottom photo)* Carl Yarbrough, Uniphoto.

Library of Congress Catalog Card Number: 94-74757

Manufactured in the United States of America.

0 9 8 7 6
f e d c b a

For information, write:
St. Martin's Press, Inc.
175 Fifth Avenue
New York, NY 10010

ISBN: 0-312-11985-2

To My Grandchildren

Christopher, Nicole, Jacob, Zachary, and Cooper

Contents

Part Three
Sport and Socialization: The Mass Media   **98**

Part Four
Sport and Socialization: Symbols   **126**

Part Five
Problems of Excess: Sport and Violence   **153**

Part Six
Sport and Deviance   **183**

Part Seven
Problems of Excess: Big-Time College Sport   **217**

Part Eight
Problems of Excess: Sport and Money   **261**

Part Eleven
Structured Inequality: Sport and Sexuality   **389**

Preface

Most North Americans are at least somewhat interested in sport, and many are downright fanatical about it. They attend games, read the sport pages and sport magazines, participate in fantasy leagues, and talk endlessly about the subject. But even those fans who astound us with their knowledge of the most obscure facts about sport do not necessarily *understand* sport.

Do sport buffs know how sport is linked to other institutions of society? Do they understand the role of sport in socializing youngsters in both positive and negative ways? Do they know that the assumption that sport builds character is open to serious debate? Do they know that racism continues in sport? What about the ways in which sport perpetuates gender-role stereotypes in society? How do owners, coaches, and other sport authorities exercise power to maintain control over athletes? These are some of the issues this book examines.

There are two fundamental reasons for the ignorance of most North Americans about the role of sport in society. First, they have had to rely mainly on sportswriters and sportscasters for their information, and these journalists have typically been little more than describers and cheerleaders. Until recent years journalists have rarely examined sport critically. Instead they have perpetuated myths: "Football helped a whole generation of sons of coal miners escape the mines" or "Sport is an island free of prejudice and racism."

The second reason for our sports illiteracy is that sport has been ignored, for the most part, by North American academics. Only in the past twenty years or so have North American social scientists and physical educators begun to investigate seriously the social aspects of sport. Previously, as with sports journalism, academic research on sport has tended to be biased in support of existing myths. In particular, the early research by physical educators was aimed at proving that sports participation builds character. In this limited perspective phenomena common to sport such as cheating, excessive violence, coaching tyranny, and the consequences of failure were, for the most part, simply ignored.

Today, however, not only academics but also a new breed of sports journalists are making insightful analyses of the role of sport in society. They examine the positive *and* negative consequences of sport for people, communities, schools, and nations. They demystify and demythologize sport. Most significant, they document the reciprocal impact of sport on the various institutions of society: religion, education, politics, and economics. There is no danger that sport will suffer from such examination. Critical reflection leads, sometimes, to positive changes. Moreover, the scholarly scrutiny of sport reveals a subject far more complex and far more interesting than what we see on the fields and arenas and what we read in the sport pages.

This book is a collection of the writings representing this new era of critical appraisal. It includes contributions from both journalists and academics. The overriding criterion for inclusion of a particular article was whether it examined critically the role of sport in society. The praise of sport is not omitted, but such praise, as with condemnation, must be backed by fact, not mythology or dogma. (Occasionally a dogmatic piece has been included to challenge the critical faculties of the reader.) The selection of each article was also guided by such questions as: Is it interesting? Is it informative? Is it thought-provoking? Does it communicate without the use of unnecessary jargon and sophisticated methodologies?

In short, the selections presented here not only afford the reader an understanding of sport that transcends the still prevalent stereotypes and myths; they also yield fascinating and important insights into the nature of society. Thus, this book has several groups of potential readers. First, it is intended to be the primary or supplementary text for courses in the sociology of sport, sport and society, and foundations of physical education. Second, the book can be used as a supplemental text for sociology courses such as the introduction to sociology, American society, and social institutions. A third audience for this book is general readers who wish to deepen their understanding and appreciation of sport.

The fifth edition of *Sport in Contemporary Society* has undergone extensive revision. Two sections have been deleted—sport and religion, and sport and politics. Three sections are new—sport as a microcosm, symbols, and sexuality. The selections have been reorganized around four themes: (1) sport as a microcosm of society, (2) sport and socialization (organized sports, mass media, and violence), (3) problems of excess (violence, deviance, big-time college sport, and money), and (4) structured inequality (social class, race, gender, and sexuality). More than half of the selections are new to this edition. An important improvement in this edition is the inclusion of gender- and race-related articles throughout the collection, not just "ghettoized" in their appropriate sections. The result is a collection of lively and timely essays that will sharpen the reader's analysis and understanding of sport *and* society.

My choices in this revision have been guided by the suggestions of two valued friends and colleagues, George H. Sage and Michael A. Messner. Also very helpful were the reviewers selected by my editor Sabra Scribner. These reviewers include: Beth Shapiro, Rice University; James H. Frey, University of Nevada–Las Vegas; Michael Givant, Adelphi University; Daniel T. Gallego, Weber State University; Peter J. Stein, William Paterson College; and Robert Brustad, University of Northern Colorado.

My greatest debt is to the authors found in this volume. My thanks to them for their scholarship and, most significant, for their insights that help us to unravel the mysteries of this intriguing and important part of social life.

D. Stanley Eitzen

D. Stanley Eitzen (Ph.D., University of Kansas) is the John N. Stern Distinguished Professor of Sociology at Colorado State University. He is a past president of the North American Society for the Sociology of Sport, and has served as editor of the *Social Science Journal*. Professor Eitzen began his career as a high school teacher and athletic coach, and his interest in the sociology of sport has led him to author or co-author numerous books and articles, including *Sociology of North American Sport*, Fifth Edition (Brown & Benchmark, 1993). His most recent publications on subjects other than sport include *Paths to Homelessness: Extreme Poverty and the Urban Housing Crisis*, co-authored by Doug A. Timmer and Kathryn Talley (Westview Press, 1994); *Social Problems*, Sixth Edition, co-authored by Maxine Baca Zinn (Allyn & Bacon, 1994); and *In Conflict and Order: Understanding Society*, Seventh Edition, co-authored by Maxine Baca Zinn (Allyn & Bacon, 1995).

FIFTH EDITION

SPORT IN CONTEMPORARY SOCIETY

An Anthology

Part One

Sport as a Microcosm
of Society

In the following quote, sportswriter E. M. Swift argues that sport is a reflection of society:

> In sports, certainly to North Americans, 1994 was an unusually disheartening year. Greed seemed to go unchecked. A baseball strike led to the cancellation of the World Series. An extended hockey lockout threatens the entire NHL season. It was a year of increasingly shocking violence away from the fields of play: the attack on Nancy Kerrigan by the Tonya Harding camp; the gunning down of a Columbian soccer player who had accidentally scored against his own team in a World Cup loss to the U.S.; the O. J. Simpson indictment for a brutal double murder.
>
> Against this tawdry backdrop we've again been forced to face up to the sad truth that sports isn't a sanctuary. It reflects, often all too clearly, society. And, yes, today greed and violence are a big part of society.[1]

Swift's argument is also mine—sport is a microcosm of society. If we know how sport is organized, the type of games played, the way winners and losers are treated, the type and amount of compensation given the participants, and the way rules are enforced, then we surely also know a great deal about the larger society in which it exists. Conversely, if we know the values of a society, the type of economy, the way minority groups are treated, and the political structure, then we would also have important clues about how sport in that society is likely organized.

The United States, for example, is a capitalistic society. It is not surprising, then, that in the corporate sport that dominates, American athletes are treated as property. In the professional ranks they are bought and sold. At the college level players once enrolled are unable to switch teams without waiting for a year. Even in youth sports, players are drafted and become the "property" of a given team.

Capitalism is also evident as team owners "carpetbag," i.e., move teams to more lucrative markets. At the same time these owners insist that the cities subsidize the construction of new stadiums, thereby making their franchises more profitable. The players, too, appear to have more loyalty to money than to their teams or fans.

Americans are highly competitive. This is easily seen at work, at school, in dating, and in sport. Persons are evaluated not on their intrinsic worth but on the criterion of achievement. As Sage has written, "Sports have consented to measure the results of sports efforts in terms of performance and product—the terms which prevail in the factory and department store."[2]

Athletes are expected to deny self and sacrifice for the needs of the sponsoring organization. This requires, foremost, an acquiescence to authority. The coach is the ultimate authority, and the players must obey. This is the way bureaucracies operate, and American society is highly bureaucratic whether it be in government, school, church, or business. As Paul Hoch has stated, "In football, like business . . . every pattern of movement on the field is increasingly being brought under the control of a group of non-playing managerial technocrats who sit up in the stands . . . with their headphones and dictate offenses, defenses, special plays, substitutions, and so forth to the players below."[3]

Thus, American sport, like American society, is authoritarian, bureaucratic, and product-oriented. Winning is everything. Athletes use drugs to enhance their performances artificially in order to succeed. Coaches teach their athletes to bend the rules (to feign a foul, to hold without getting caught) in order to win. Even at America's most prestigious universities, coaches offer illegal inducements to athletes to attend their school. And, as long as they win, the administrators at these offending schools usually look the other way. After all, the object is to win, and this mentality permeates sport as it does politics and the business world.

These are but some of the ways in which sport mirrors society. In this section we shall examine this relationship through four selections. The first, by sportswriter Bill Stokes, shows the appeal of sport to fans. He describes many elements found in sport—the money, commercialism, social class, race, heroes, the importance of winning, violence, and sacrifice—that are found also in society. Stokes concludes with this admonition to sport analysts who wish to observe and understand the fans of sport: "Perhaps whoever said, 'You can tell a lot about society by the way it plays its games' could have added: 'You can tell a lot, too, by who watches them—and how.'"

The second selection, by D. Stanley Eitzen, illustrates what the structure of two major team sports, football and baseball, tells us about Americans and American society.

The third reading, an excerpt from Mariah Burton Nelson's *The Stronger Women Get, the More Men Love Football,* shows the way sport has separated boys and girls, how it denigrates women, how the media's portrayal of sport shapes our perceptions of women and men, and how sport celebrates manliness and sexy women. In effect, manly sports "comprise a world where men are in charge and women are irrelevant at best." In this context, we better understand the role of sport in shaping traditional gender roles and its responsibility, in part, for sexual violence.

Nelson's excerpt achieves an important goal—to get the reader to be a better analyst of sport, by recognizing the subtle and not-so-subtle messages. She says:

> We live in a country in which the manly sports culture is so pervasive we may fail to recognize the symbolic messages we all receive about men, women, love, sex, and power. We need to take sports seriously—not the scores or the statistics, but the process. Not to focus on who wins, but on who's losing. Who loses when a community spends millions of dollars in tax revenue to construct a new stadium and only men get to play in it, and only men get to work there?
>
> Who loses when football and baseball so dominate the public discourse that they eclipse all mention of female volleyball players, gymnasts, basketball players, swimmers?
>
> Who loses when coaches teach boys that the worst possible insult is to be called "pussy" or "cunt"?
>
> Who loses when rape jokes comprise an accepted part of the game?

The final selection, by sociologist Jay J. Coakley, enhances our understanding of sport and society by elaborating on the two contrasting theoretical approaches—functionalist and conflict—that guide much of the work of sport sociologists. The understanding of both of these perspectives is vitally important to the analyst of society. Each approach offers significant insights about society. However, the theoretical approach guiding the structure of this book and the choice of selections is the conflict perspective. As I stated in the preface to Eitzen and Sage's *Sociology of North American Sport:*

> [The] goal is to make the reader aware of the positive and negative consequences of the way sport is organized in American society. We are concerned about some of the trends in sport, especially the move away from athlete-oriented activities toward the impersonality of what we term "corporate sport." We are committed to moving sport and society in a more humane direction, and this requires, as a first step, a thorough understanding of the principles that underlie the social structures and processes that create, sustain, and transform the social organizations within the institution of sport.[4]

NOTES

1. E. M. Swift, "Giving His All," *Sports Illustrated* (December 19, 1994): 88.
2. George H. Sage, "Sports, Culture, and Society," paper presented at the Basic Science of Sport Medicine Conference, Philadelphia (July 14–16, 1974), pp. 10–11.
3. Paul Hoch, *Rip Off the Big Game* (Garden City, New York: Doubleday Anchor, 1972), p. 9.
4. D. Stanley Eitzen and George H. Sage, *Sociology of North American Sport,* 5th ed. (Dubuque, Iowa: Wm. C. Brown, 1993), p. xi.

1. *Take Me Out to the Crowd*

BILL STOKES

What can you say about sports fans? Try this:

- *Sports fans are losers.* They pay millions of dollars to bottom-line corporations for the privilege of watching pampered, overpaid prima donnas perform routine, robotian feats for which a worshipful society has been training them since childhood. In return, the fans are considered an annoyance by the athletes, are looked upon largely as money fodder by the corporations, and are coerced by politicians into spending millions of tax dollars for athletic facilities.
- *Sports fans are unhealthy.* They sit in the stands or vegetate in front of TV sets stuffing themselves with junk food and watching people play games instead of being active themselves. They drink too much beer, in part because TV sports and on-site advertising convince them it is the way to have a good time. They divert their mental energies from solving their problems and improving their lives and instead become absorbed in meaningless contests between participants who play/work for whoever pays them the most money.
- *Sports fans are a societal liability.* In their intense glorification of winners and preoccupation with competition, fans foster a win-at-all-costs mentality that encourages cheating, violence, and the harming of opponents, all of which carries over deleteriously into daily life on a personal, community, and international level.
- *Sports fans are crazy.* By their own admission, especially in Chicago, the fans themselves say there is no other explanation for behavior that includes sitting out in subzero weather, cheering for perennial losers, paying enough for a couple of hot dogs and two or three beers to buy a pair of shoes, and believing that sporting events matter enough to warrant endless serious conversation, much of it cluttering up the public airways.

  Fortunately, the craziness does not reach the proportions of the hooligan behavior surrounding some European athletic events where, in 1988, a Croydon, England, bricklayer named Harry sucked out and then bit off a policeman's eyeball, after which, according to Bill Buford's book, *Among the Thugs*, Harry was arrested in his blood-stained clothes while sitting with his wife and eating a basket of legs and thighs at the local Kentucky Fried Chicken store.

You could say all of those things about sports fans, and you would be pretty much on the money. Which brings up another thing you could say: Sports fans are gamblers, to the tune of an estimated $120 billion a year— nobody knows what the real figure is—to bookies and gambling syndicates largely controlled by organized crime.

And you could say a lot more. But first, perhaps, it would be appropriate to look at some of the fans in their fan environment, perhaps as a fan in waiting, or a fan-to-be or simply as a rookie fan, which pretty much describes this writer who "arrives in camp" with limited experience and mixed priorities and as a general failure as a sports fan. On rare occasions of spectating I have been unable to generate much emotion for competition between young people who are strangers to me.

SEPT. 17, WRIGLEY FIELD, CUBS vs. PHILLIES

It is a sunny, humid day, and $10 buys a parking spot on a public street from a man in an old station wagon who drives off with a friendly wave.

There is an aura of "picnic" in the air, and there are obviously a lot of people who control their own destiny enough to spend their own or their boss's Thursday afternoon watching baseball. In twos, threes and small groups, they wend their way toward the park, talking and laughing, with the shouts of souvenir vendors echoing everywhere.

A hot lava of noise spills out of the Cubby Bear Lounge at the corner of Clark and Addison. Inside, the incredibly loud rock music makes conversation impossible, so the young fans stare and shout at each other as they crowd together and drink beer.

At first view, the green of the playing field is like a strange welcome mat, greener than it seems on TV, and bigger. The smell of popcorn, the organ music, the neatly uniformed players throwing and batting in pregame warmups, the bustle of the fans, and the panoramic view all combine to produce an ambience that gathers the fans into its center in a maternal-like embrace. It is immediately apparent that this is a very different experience from watching baseball through the knothole of television.

There are many father–son duos in the stands. Gary Heller of Chicago, with his 5-year-old son, Joseph, says: "I have very fond memories of my father bringing me here as a child. So many things in life are in constant change, but the ballpark hasn't changed much, and I like that."

Baseball is oblivious to time and reflects life in rural America as it existed in the not-too-distant past, says D. Stanley Eitzen, Colorado State University sociology professor who is co-author of "Sociology of North American Sport" and "Sport in Contemporary Society." Eitzen says that football, by comparison, emulates contemporary urban society where people have rigid schedules, appointments, and time clocks to punch.

"Baseball is an island of stability in a confused and confusing world and continues to be popular because of our longing for the peaceful past," Eitzen says.

Bill Vlink of Wildwood holds his 4-year-old son, Doug, and sways to the seventh-inning "Take Me Out to the Ballgame" performance of Harry Caray. "I come here to be with my son," Vlink says, "and I like to dream that I am one of the players out there on the field."

Attending a sporting event suspends normal authority roles, puts aside generational differences and eases talk between a boy and his father, says Janet Lever in "Soccer Madness," published by The University of Chicago Press. Lever, now a sociology professor at California State University, Los Angeles, says that there is a suspension of status differentials between fans in a stadium or sports bar, and a cab driver can talk on an equal basis with someone wearing a cashmere coat.

"You're never lonely at the ballpark," Lever says.

The Cubs win 3-0 before 7,743 fans, and on the trip home, these fans can tune in to any number of sports talk shows that seem to go on forever. Lever says that fans can talk longer about sports than about the weather, and even though they may appear to be arguing, they are having fun.

SEPT. 23, COMISKEY PARK, WHITE SOX vs. ATHLETICS

On a cool autumn evening the sun slices down to reflect off the blue and white of the stadium as the fans filter in. There is almost a sterility to the new brightness of Comiskey, but the aroma of frying onions and the organ music lend it the familiar "old" ballpark air.

High up in the stands, after having climbed 84 steep, heart-stimulating steps, Jay Cooper, 22 and his father, Ralph, of Oak Park have cashed in a Father's Day gift of tickets, and they sit together with a blanket across their knees. The Coopers enjoy a genuine bird's-eye view that drastically reduces the size of the playing field and puts them above the cruising pigeons. Jay, a college student, says he would like to be a trainer and work with professional athletes.

"You have to start at the high school or college level, but I think it is a field of growing opportunity," Jay says.

Sociologist Eitzen would agree, speculating that the futuristic extreme of increased technology in sport may take the form of "genetic engineering" in which superior athletes are bred. In the meantime, he says, the deliberate selection of future athletes during their early childhood will become more of a reality, and they will receive even more special training than they already do, thus isolating them even further from the fans.

Among the other fans with a bird's-eye view on this cool autumn night are Doug Cohen of Highland Park and Jim Spear of Arlington Heights, who are with family and friends in one of the skyboxes.

"It's a nice easy way to watch the game," Cohen says of the skyboxes. "You can talk business and still be a part of the action."

Most skyboxes are purchased by corporations that write them off as a business expense because they are used to entertain clients and customers. Their growing presence, however, creates an "upper" and "lower" class distinction in the otherwise generally democratic environment of the fan, and the cab driver is isolated from the cashmere coat with brutal symbolic bluntness.

But the rapidly rising cost of attending games—about 10 percent per year for all sports—is keeping many of the less-affluent fans away from athletic events altogether. Michael and Rita Jedlowski of Chicago, at the game with some of their children and their friends, complain that they cannot afford to come very often.

"I think some of the prices are outrageous," Michael Jedlowski says.

Noah Liberman of Chicago's Team Marketing Report, a newsletter published for sports executives, says that the typical cost for two adults and two children attending a 1992 Sox game was $96.81, up 18.7 percent over the previous year. Cost for a Cubs game was $96.98, up 16.3 percent.

Of all major league baseball teams only the Yankees at $101 and the Blue Jays at $112 cost more.

By comparison, Liberman says the typical cost for a family of four attending a Bears game is $176, and for a Bulls game, $197.91. All of these tabulations assume average purchase of refreshments and souvenirs.

The Sox win 17-6 before 26,279 fans, all of whom head for home to the wail of a saxophone player who has set up his street-musician business beneath a nearby viaduct.

OCT. 31, DYCHE STADIUM, NORTHWESTERN VS. MICHIGAN STATE

Under a gray and white sky, a purple and white homecoming crowd files into the stadium while "The finest band in the land!" plays and marches out on the artificial turf. It is a Saturday afternoon collegiate ritual as old as raccoon coats and roadsters, and it tugs at the hearts of grads young and old.

R.A. and Helen Lenon of Glenview sit close together under a blanket and watch it all as they have since back in the early 1940s when they were at Northwestern as an instructor and student, respectively.

Northwestern has not had a winning football season since 1971, but that doesn't bother the Lenons.

"They keep trying," R.A Lenon says. "I don't think it is so important who wins if the players do their best."

Fans would obviously prefer the pleasure of winning to the suffering of defeat, sociologist Lever says, but adds that even suffering can be appreciated as an indication of loyalty and caring deeply about something.

Allen Guttmann, professor of English and American Studies at Amherst College and author of "Sports Spectators," among other, related books, says that college football has historically provided a regular and socially sanctioned occasion for displays of manly courage, outbursts of drunken revelry, transgressions of the dean's rules and regulations, and the release of whatever impulses these rules and regulations have suppressed.

"And once the student has graduated," Guttmann says, "the force of nostalgia conspires with the calendar—games are played on weekends when middle-class citizens turn from labor to leisure—to give football a special place among the many versions of the emotional 'time-out.'"

In "Sports Spectators," Guttmann quotes a fan who says, "When the team comes running out onto the field and the bank strikes up 'Dear Old Nebraska U,' the tears damn near scald my cheeks. It is life's ultimate experience."

The Lenons are obviously not quite so emphatic about their experience, and they watch decorously as Northwestern loses when a last-minute kick is off the mark by inches.

Meanwhile, over in the student section, the young fans' feet stick to the stairs and the aisles because of the sugary fall-out from an afternoon of throwing marshmallows.

Northwestern loses 27-26 before 31,101 fans, but is has been a party, and a bittersweet homecoming mood prevails. It was so close!

NOV. 14, NOTRE DAME STADIUM, NOTRE DAME VS. PENN STATE

Snow sifts down out of low clouds, the temperature is in the 30s, there are 25 seconds left in the game, Notre Dame is on the short end of a 16-9 score, and God is obviously somewhere in the packed stadium.

As the sun breaks unexpectedly over the snow-covered field for the first time all day, Sister Patricia Jean rises up out of her seat in the stands and, with the helping hands of other fans, laboriously makes her way up the steps toward an exit.

"I've got to go somewhere and pray for our boys," she says, and she is not smiling.

There is a television time-out on the field, and Sister Patricia Jean pauses long enough to tell a little story about Alan Page, the Notre Dame All-American and professional football great who is now a Minnesota Supreme Court justice.

Page was a freshman, she says, and was about to be cut from the team because he wasn't tackling hard enough.

"One of the Brothers and I talked to him," Sister Patricia Jean says, "and Alan told us he was afraid he might hurt someone if he got too aggressive. Well, I said to him, 'Alan, isn't that what football is all about!' and after that he turned into a wonderful player."

Sister Patricia Jean heads off toward the elevator—as good a place to pray as any—and the game resumes. The Notre Dame quarterback is about to be sacked, but he scrambles free and throws a desperation pass that is caught by a diving receiver. Penn State now leads 16-15. There are 17 seconds left. Notre Dame goes for two.

Again the quarterback is chased all over the slippery field, and he finally launches a pass that sails toward a corner of the end zone and is obviously going to land out of bounds. Then, from out of nowhere, a receiver leaps high into the air, stops the flight of the ball with his fingertips and hauls it in as he crashes down onto the snow-covered field.

Sister Patricia Jean and, obviously, God have done it: Notre Dame wins 17-16, and the place is up for grabs.

There was a time, not so long ago, when churches opposed sports and recreation, Eitzen says. But over the last century there has been a complete reversal, and now there is wide use of sports to promote church-supported colleges.

Notre Dame is but one example of the many religious colleges using football and basketball to advertise, Eitzen says, and he points out that, ironically, it was a church college—Southern Methodist University—that received the most severe penalty ever from the NCAA. The college's football program was temporarily abolished after fans and some others connected with the university lied, cheated and generally violated NCAA rules, Eitzen says.

Although religion has suffered a decline of interest and commitment over the last 20 years, according to Eitzen, the powers and influence of sport have increased enormously.

Sport has taken on so many of the trappings of religion that some feel that it is a new religion, Eitzen says. The gods are the superstar athletes; the saints are the likes of Vince Lombardi, whose "Winning isn't everything; it's the only thing" has become the basic commandment of today's sport; the high priests are the coaches; the stadiums are the houses of worship filled with masses of highly vocal "true believers"; and the sport halls of fame are the shrines.

The clergy frequently uses sports metaphors, Eitzen says, quoting one who concluded a recent sermon with, "and one day you will cross the finish line and stand before Jesus Christ." And if "Dropkick Me, Jesus, Through the Goalposts of Life" wasn't the actual title of the country-and-western song, it should have been.

Thousands of euphoric Notre Dame fans mill about on the field for an hour or more after the game, trying unsuccessfully to tear down the goal posts, dancing in the wet snow and finally drifting off, many of them in the direction of "Touchdown Jesus," the figure of Christ with upraised arms that dominates a mosaic on the front of the Theodore M. Hesburgh Library.

DEC. 13, SOLDIER FIELD, BEARS vs. STEELERS

It's cold in Chicago, but not too cold for tailgate socializing, and in a remote parking lot, three young men sit slouched around a barbecue grill. They are passing around a nearly empty fifth of peppermint schnapps, and each holds a can of beer from the case that sits nearby. "We're gonna win today," one of them shouts, and the others wave their beer cans and shout, "Da Bears! Da Bears!"

The Soldier Field turf looks as worn as an old rug, and the odd mix of columns and glass and concrete gives the stadium the ambience of an organized junkyard. Most of the fans are wearing heavy outdoor clothing, complete with winter hats that pull down over their ears.

"You gotta wear seven or eight shirts," says Eric Hanson of Palatine, "and you gotta be nuts to be here when you could be home watching this on TV."

"We had an invitation to a TV party, but we came here instead," says Hanson's friend Eileen Bracci. "It's great."

Hanson has a box of Cracker Jack in one hand and a cup of beer in the other, and he is careful not to spill from either one as he and Bracci embrace near one of the refreshment stands.

Contrary to Hanson's assessment about the necessity of heavy clothing, three young men in the stands strip to the waist and alternate between jumping up and down in their seats and parading up and down the aisles with a banner that says, "McCaskey Sucks," an apparent reference to Bears president Michael McCaskey. The young men apparently keep warm by drinking a lot of cold beer.

"Not all spectators at sports events are sports spectators," author Guttman says, and lists, among others: "dandies of both sexes who strut and preen, hooligans who show up because they want to bash someone, spouses dragged by spouses, and lovers seeking the privacy of a public place."

There is also the matter of voyeurism, according to Guttmann, in which people respond to the "sensual attractiveness of youthful bodies in motion."

Bears coach Mike Ditka does not have a youthful body, but it is in motion as he paces and spits up and down the sideline. But his team is winning, and there are no emotional eruptions from him on this day. Ditka limps as he paces. Most former football players limp, and periodically on this cold afternoon, injured players are helped off the field. Sometimes there is an occasional cheer when a Steeler player goes down.

"With the emphasis on winning, athletes are expected to play with injury," says Dorcas Susan Butt, a professor of psychology at the University of British Columbia and author of "Psychology of Sport."

"It is not only professional athletes who jeopardize their health in the name of winning," Butt says. "We also expect this kind of sacrifice from young people in school."

During an average season, there are some 125,000 knee injuries—30,000 of them requiring surgery—to football players at all levels of competition. An estimated half million football players are injured each fall. Many of these injuries occur on the college and professional level, where millions of fans watch the players' suffering with what seems to be a combination of indifference and impatience.

Butt, a former world-class tennis player who received her doctorate at the University of Chicago, says fans are generally considered naive and bothersome by athletes who are caught up in travel schedules and their own careers.

The athletes need the fans to watch them perform, Butt says, but they do not want a personal relationship with them. In what Butt calls a form of prostitution, athletes are now paid to spend time with fans, usually those in corporate, political or entertainment areas.

Athletes also do not like sportswriters, Butt adds. "Players look down on sportswriters behind their backs and smile to their faces," she says, adding that Joe Namath spoke for most athletes when he once told a writer, "I don't need any of you $100-a-week creeps to go around writing about me."

Cathy Butler, wife of Bears kicker Kevin Butler, does not agree with Butt's assessment of the player/fan relationship. "We love the fans, and Bears fans are the best," she says as she sits in the stands and watches the game with friends. "They support the team no matter what, and they are very nice to us."

Everyone is nice today because the Bears are winning and Bears linebacker Mike Singletary is retiring. It is either a day for a fifth of schnapps and lots of heavy clothes or drinking beer and stripping down to the waist, depending on what kind of a fan you are.

The fact is, of course, that most Bears fans conduct themselves in an orderly manner and appear to be as normal as is possible considering that they are sitting out in a frigid stadium and watching a game of calculated violence.

Just what effect watching this violence has on fans is not totally understood. Research at the University of Wisconsin and other studies have shown that watching football and other aggressive sports increases hostility and aggression in spectators and that the extent of it depends on the degree of aggression of the athletes.

Spokespersons for shelters for battered women report that the day of the Super Bowl has become one of the worst days for domestic violence against women. This year, for the first time, the network carrying the game aired a public service announcement on domestic violence in its pre-game show.

But with the exception of a couple of brief fist fights that are quickly broken up by security workers, the Bears fans do not exhibit any undue violence on this occasion.

The Bears win 30-6 before a full house. It is Ditka's last home game. Three weeks later, after a sycophantical media blitz appropriate to the public stalking and assassination of a president, Ditka is fired for not being a winner.

JAN. 21, CHICAGO STADIUM, BLACKHAWKS VS. WASHINGTON CAPITALS

It is an hour before game time at the big barn-like stadium on Chicago's West Side. The red seats are empty, the ice is very white and clean, and the organist is playing "Moon River." But, like a huge machine coming slowly to life or a thunderstorm gathering itself, the scene begins to build energy.

Beer vendor Dennis Uczen knows that it will be a good night because hockey fans drink a lot of beer. He leans back against a brick wall and waits for the crowd to build, a heavy load of 20 cups of beer suspended from his shoulders and protruding out over his chest. On a good night he will sell 12 to 15 loads, he says.

"The fans can be inconsiderate," Uczen says, "They don't want you in their way, yet they want to be served immediately."

But Uczen has been selling beer at Chicago athletic events for 24 years and he says it is a good job. He pushes away from the wall and shouts, "BEER HERE. BEER HERE," as he moves out into the stands.

Selling beer and a lot of other products to the fans is what it's all about. Beer and tobacco companies attach themselves to sports like leeches, even on the college level, and the irony of this is lost on the fans, who claim one of their thrills is watching outstanding physical specimens with perfect bodies. In the meantime, drink up and light up, the fans are urged, as their lungs and livers turn to garbage.

In another facet of commercialism, professional athletes are paid millions of dollars to endorse shoes and other sports items that are then so overpriced as to make the parents of aspiring athletes faint dead away.

The players are out on the ice, the up-tempo organ music is much louder, and the crowd noise simmers like a huge caldron of audio soup. Then it boils over into a frenzy of shouting and whistling that continues throughout the singing of the national anthem. By the end of the song, the singer's voice is completely lost in the unbridled roar.

"Please use proper language," the loudspeaker blares and tells fans that there is a $100 reward for anyone who turns in someone who throws something.

Seconds into the game, the Blackhawks score, and all of the fans jump to their feet to cheer and whistle. Bill Lee of Palos Hills and his son-in-law Bob Ficht of Burbank are among them.

"It really gets your adrenaline going," Ficht says.

The adrenaline apparently does not flow so much for some female fans. In nearby seats, four young women—Joanne Snyder, Mary Schlichter, Dawn Schroeder, and Pat Ambriz, all of whom live and work in the western suburbs—say the hockey game is an entertaining night out for them.

"We don't get so into records and statistics as men do," Snyder says.

"We hope the Blackhawks win," Schroeder says, "but we don't get all bummed out over a loss like men seem to."

As indicated by these young fans, attending a sporting event is apparently more of a social occasion for many women, while male fans tend to get more into the competition and somehow relate it to their macho identity. So the awesome gender stereotyping that defines values for the sexes from early childhood rears its head in the stands and seems to cheer, *"La difference."*

Out on the ice, penalties are called on various players who are then sent to sit in what seems like one of sport's oddest accoutrements—the penalty box. Some of the fans voice their objection when a penalty is called on a Blackhawk, shouting derisively at the officials.

Sports officials are not respected much by athletes and, therefore, by fans, Butt says. Their status will continue to deteriorate so long as athletes use tactics to downgrade them. An example occurred earlier this year when Charles Barkley of the Phoenix Suns dove over a scorer's table to get at an official. A resulting fine and suspension cost Barkley $40,000, but he dismissed this and told the official he thought had blown the call. "You can't control me with money," Barkley said.

Many of the men in the stands are dressed in suits and ties, and John Gregorio of Glenview and Tony Nasharr of Hinsdale explain that they have stopped off at the game on the way home from their law offices downtown.

"Basketball is boring compared to hockey," Gregorio says, adding that the hockey fans have become more sophisticated and less rowdy in recent years.

"There is less fighting and beer spilling," Gregorio says. "I think one of the reasons is that the hooligans have been priced out of the stadium. It cost us $120 for our two tickets."

Beer sales are cut off at the start of the third period, and as it begins, a cluster of men in an outer aisle gather tightly around 12 large cups of beer sitting on the floor at their feet. The men laugh and drink, while nearby another group of young men engage in friendly roughhousing, pushing each other to the floor and wrestling briefly.

The Blackhawks win 6-2 before a full house, and in spite of hockey's reputation for free-for-alls and fighting, the aggression this night is limited to a number of arguments and some pushing and shoving. Among the cab drivers waiting for the fans outside the stadium is John Terkert, who says the Blackhawks would do a lot better if all of the officials hadn't been bought off.

JAN. 22, CHICAGO STADIUM, BULLS vs. CHARLOTTE HORNETS

It's the hot ticket in Chicago. The little slip of paper that gets you into the Stadium for a Bulls game is currency of the id or the pocketbook, depending on how you want to spend it.

"Everybody is a fan and wants to be here," says Patricia Davis of Chicago, who is at the game with her husband, Hank. "We were offered $175 each for our tickets, but we would never sell them. This is a big night for us."

As usual, there isn't an empty seat in the house. Manipulation of the house lights, loud organ music, and fireworks spitting from a corner of the scoreboard combine to energize the crowd as the players are introduced. Seconds into the game, Michael Jordan scores, and moments later he falls flat as he tries to steal the ball. The fans applaud and cheer his moves wildly.

The athlete, as hero, symbolizes for the spectator his team, his country, and his fantasized fulfillment in sport achievement, psychologist Butt says. The athlete's hobbies, lifestyle, dress, and personality become a banner to follow, particularly for young people who may be deprived of relationships with elders.

That, of course, translates into big bucks, and Jordan is paid millions annually in product endorsements. When the cash register bells ring with such vigor, the point is reinforced that fans are important to athletes largely in their purchase of tickets and products.

"The sport fan is the mark in a fraudulent event," author/psychology professor Butt says. "He or she is led to believe that their presence is meaningful, when it is not, just as the fan is led to believe that what he or she sees has a certain meaning when it has none."

There are some interesting racial mixes in the components of the game here on this cold winter night: Most of the players are black, most of the cheerleaders are white, and the great majority of the fans are white. In a recent year, black athletes dominated basketball (80 percent) and football (55 percent), while 25 percent of professional baseball players were black.

These percentages are increasing, and sportswriter Frank Deford speculates in his book, "The Big Game Is Over: This Way to the Exit, Bwana," that if this trend continues, it may lead to the demise of these three professional team sports. Pointing to the "identity crisis" that occurred in boxing when the sport ran out of white athletes for white ticket buyers to identify with, Deford asks, "How long will white pride—white racism, if you will—support black athletes?"

The next decade will be crucial in determining the future of these sports, professor/author Eitzen says, and will depend on the degree of occupational discrimination and the racial antipathy held by affluent whites.

The game is in the final minutes now and the Bulls are struggling to close in on the leading Hornets. But in the excitement, Kay Jacobsen and Marlene Weinstein, both of Chicago, leave their seats because somebody in the upper decks is throwing something that hurts when it hits.

Security workers peer up into the crowd but are unable to spot the offenders.

"I think they are throwing those cough drops that they were giving away outside the stadium," Weinstein says. "One of our party is on blood thinner, and it could be bad if he got hit on the head and it ruptured a blood vessel."

Most Bulls fans are obviously well behaved, but the championship victories of the last two years have been followed by rioting in the streets. Following the 1992 championship game, hundreds of people were arrested after cabs were overturned, windows smashed, and stores looted. There were no deaths, unlike the rioting in Detroit in 1990 when the Pistons won the championship and seven people died in the ensuing "celebration."

Guttmann says much of this "hooligan"-like behavior is not by sports fans but by young males who feel disadvantaged and shut off from society and who may be looking for an excuse to vent their frustration. There is also the element of crowd behavior in which individuals do things they would not otherwise do, Guttmann says.

There will be no cause for a celebration riot on this night as the Bulls lose 105-97 before a packed house.

JAN. 27, ROSEMONT HORIZON, DE PAUL vs. BAYLOR

The Screaming Demons, De Paul's 25-member pep band, is tuning up near the east basket, and if you want to talk to its director, Greg Fudala, you have to move off to the side and away from the blare of the brass.

"We try to work with the cheerleaders to keep people in the spirit of the game," Fudala says. "The band members are all music majors, and they each get a $500 stipend for playing all year. That helps a little with the $12,000 tuition."

"Sports fans are kind of crazy," Fudala says. "They will support teams that are not doing well, and a lot of them cheer for De Paul when they have nothing to do with the college."

Louis Rexing of Chicago admits to a certain amount of "craziness" in his support of De Paul, but it is based on his having earned undergraduate and master's degrees from the college in the early 1980s.

If you attend a De Paul basketball game, you will hear Rexing. He will be up in the northeast corner of the Horizon with a group of friends, and he will be standing up most of the time with his hands cupped around his mouth, and he will be shouting in a foghorn-like voice that carries out over the stands and playing area like an audio surf.

And sometimes when Fudala directs the De Paul fight song, Rexing will cup his hands closer to his mouth and whistle along with such volume that it seems as if a piece of the pep band has splintered off and landed up in the stands.

"It relieves my tension," Rexing says of his high-decibel cheering. "It is like the release you would get from a primordial scream."

Psychologist Guttmann says that the role of shouting, screaming, arm-waving spectator is an alternative to the more restrained roles of parent, employee and civilized citizen. And although it may not be a catharsis in the sense of purgation that produces calm and tranquility, Guttmann says, it is an outlet for expressing excitement in a society where emotions are tightly controlled in our ordinary lives.

"My wife, Candace, doesn't come to the games with me," Rexing says, "but I took her to a game on our first date, and she told me years later that it was the reason she married me. She said she figured that anyone who could act like that in public must be pretty confident and sure of himself and would be a great partner."

By the end of the game, Rexing cannot talk: He can shout, but he cannot talk.

"It happens all the time," he whispers, and then he turns toward the playing court and bellows in a voice that carries up into the rafters of the Horizon, "GO DEMONS!"

The Demons "go," winning by the slim margin of 72-70, and Rexing is a happy man.

So what can you say about sports fans?

Perhaps whoever said, "You can tell a lot about a society by the way it plays its games" could have added: "You can tell a lot, too, by who watches them—and how." And as the late sportswriter Red Smith was fond of saying, "The oldest building still standing in Rome is the Colosseum." A testament, no doubt, to the fans.

And while spending time with the fans to do this story did not convert me *into* a fan, it made me a fan of the fans. They are the vital and vocal spirit of a youthful country that will never grow up and might self-destruct if it did. So you have to love the fans for their enthusiasm and their friendliness.

Of course, many of us also love them because if they weren't gathered in stadiums and ballparks they would be out cluttering up the trout streams and the hiking trails.

2. *The Structure of Sport and Society*

D. STANLEY EITZEN

An important indicator of the essence of a society is the type of sport it glorifies. The examination of the structure of a society's dominant sport provides important clues about that society and its culture. For example, answers to the following questions will greatly inform the observer about that society: Is the sport oriented toward a group (team) or the individual? Does the outcome depend essentially on strength, speed, strategy, deception, or the mastery of intricate moves? Is the activity cerebral or physical? Is the primary goal to win or to enjoy the activity?

Let us begin by looking at what Americans consider the essence of sport—winning—to show how other societies have a different view more consonant with their culture. Sport, as played in America, is an expression of Social Darwinism—a survival-of-the-fittest approach where everyone competes to be alone at the top. Players are cut from teams even in our schools if they are not considered good enough. Tournaments are organized so that only one team or individual is the ultimate winner. Corporations sponsor contests for youngsters such as "Punt, Pass, and Kick," where winners are selected at the local level and proceed through a number of district and regional contests until a winner is declared in each category.[1]

In cooperative, group-centered societies, such sporting activities would seem cruel, even barbaric, because success is achieved only at the cost of the failure of others. These societies, rather, would have sports where the object is something other than winning. For instance:

> The Tangu people of New Guinea play a popular game known as *taketak,* which involves throwing a spinning top into massed lots of stakes driven into the ground. There are two teams. Players of each team try to touch as many stakes with their tops as possible. In the end, however, the participants play not to win but to draw. The game must go on until an exact draw is reached. This requires great skill, since players sometimes must throw their tops into the massed stakes without touching a single one. *Taketak* expresses a prime value of Tangu culture, that is, the concept of moral equivalence, which is reflected in the precise sharing of foodstuffs among the people.[2]

SOURCE: "The Structure of Sport and Society" by D. Stanley Eitzen. From *Sport in Contemporary Society,* 1st ed., by D. Stanley Eitzen. Copyright © St. Martin's Press.

This example demonstrates that a society's sports mirror that society. Cooperative societies have sports that minimize competition, while aggressive societies have highly competitive sports. This raises a question about the nature of the most popular American sports. What do they tell us about ourselves and our society? Let us concentrate on the two most popular team sports—football and baseball—as they are played at the professional level.[3]

THE DIFFERING NATURES OF FOOTBALL AND BASEBALL

Although there are some similarities between football and baseball, for example, cheating is the norm in both,[4] these two sports are basically different. In many ways they are opposites, and these incongruities provide insightful clues about Americans and American society.

Two fundamentally different orientations toward time exist in these two sports. Baseball is not bounded by time, while football must adhere to a rigid time schedule. "Baseball is oblivious to time. There is no clock, no two-minute drill. The game flows in a timeless stream with a rhythm of its own."[5] In this way baseball reflects life in rural America as it existed in the not-too-distant past compared to football's emulation of contemporary urban society, where persons have rigid schedules, appointments, and time clocks to punch.

The innings of baseball have no time limit, and if the game is tied at the end of regulation innings, the teams play as many extra innings as it takes to determine a winner. Football, on the other hand, is played for sixty minutes, and if tied at the end, the game goes into "sudden death," that is, the first team to score wins. Thus, even the nomenclature of the two sports—"extra innings" compared to "sudden death"—illustrates a basic difference between them. There are other semantic differences. A baseball player makes an "error," but a football team is "penalized." The object of baseball is to get "home" while the goal of football is to penetrate deep into the opponent's "territory." In baseball there is no home territory to defend; the playing field is shared by both teams. There is no analogue in baseball for the militaristic terms of football, for example, "blitz," "bomb," "trap," "trenches," "field general," "aerial attack," and "ground attack."

Such linguistic differences imply a basic discrepancy between baseball and football. Baseball is essentially a calm and leisurely activity while football is intense, aggressive, and violent. Football is foremost a form of physical combat, whereas baseball is one of technique. A baseball player cannot get to first base because of his strength, aggression, or ability to intimidate. His only way to get there is through skill. In football, however, survival (success) belongs to the most aggressive. Former football player George Sauer has suggested that aggression on the football field leads to success just as it gets one ahead in American society:

How does football justify teaching a man to be aggressive against another man? And how does it justify using that aggression for the ends that it has? I think the values of football as it is now played reflect a segment of thought, a particular kind of thought that is pretty prevalent in our society. The way to do anything in the world, the way to get ahead, is to aggress against somebody, compete against somebody, try to dominate, try to overcome, work your way up the ladder, and in doing so, you have to judge yourself and be judged as what you want to be in relation to somebody else all the time. Given the influence football has on young children, the immense influence it has as a socializing force in society, its impact should be rigorously examined. People learn certain values from watching football, from watching aggression, from watching it performed violently and knowing that these guys are going to get a big chunk of money if they do it well often enough.[6]

The two sports require different mentalities of their athletes. Football players must be aggressive, while that is not a necessary ingredient for the baseball player. Also, baseball is a game of repetition and predictable action that is played over a 162-game schedule. The players must stay relaxed and not get too excited because to do so for every game would be too physically and emotionally draining over the six months of the season. Moreover, because the season is so long, players must pace themselves and not let a loss or even a succession of losses get them down. In football, though, losing is intolerable because of the short season (sixteen games). Thus, football players must play each game with extreme intensity. As a result, the incidence of taking amphetamines ("uppers") has been much greater among football players than among baseball players. The intensity that characterizes football resembles the tensions and pressures of modern society, contrasted with the more relaxed pace of agrarian life and baseball.

One of the most interesting contrasts between these two sports is the equality of opportunity each offers. Baseball promotes equality while football is essentially unequal. This difference occurs in several ways. First, football originated among college elites and even today requires attending college to play at the professional level. Baseball has never been closely identified with college. Essentially, the way to make it in baseball is to work one's way through the minor leagues rather than by attending college (although that is one route).

A second way that baseball is more egalitarian than football is that it can be played by people of all sizes. There have been small All Star players such as Phil Rizzuto, Bobby Shantz, Pee Wee Reese, Joe Morgan, and Freddie Patek. Football, however, is a big man's game. In football the good, big team defeats the good, small team, whereas in baseball, the good, small team has an equal chance of beating the good, big team.

Baseball is also more equal than football because everyone has the opportunity to be a star. Each position has its stars. Pay is divided about equally by position. Except for designated hitters, all players must play both offense and defense. Thus, each player has the chance to make an outstanding defensive play or to bat in the winning run. Stardom in football is essentially reserved for those who play at certain positions. Only backs, receivers, and kickers score points while others labor in relative obscurity, making it possible for the "glamour boys" to score. This is similar, by the way, to American society, where the richest "players" score all the points, call the plays, and get the glory at the expense of the commoners. There is also a wide variance in pay by position in football.

A final contrast on this equality dimension has to do with the availability of each of the sports to the masses. The average ticket price for major league baseball is approximately one-third that of professional football. The cheaper tickets for baseball allow families to attend and provide live entertainment for members of all social classes. Football, however, excludes families (except for the rich) and members of lower classes because of the high prices and the necessity of purchasing season tickets.

Another major dimension on which these two sports differ is individualism. Baseball is highly individualistic. Elaborate teamwork is not required except for double plays and defensing sacrifice bunts. Each player struggles to succeed on his own. As Cavanaugh has characterized it:

> Although there are teams in baseball, there is little teamwork. The essence of the game is the individual with or against the ball: pitcher controlling, batter hitting, fielder handling, runner racing the ball. All players are on their own, struggling (like the farmer) to overcome not another human being but nature (the ball). This individualism is demonstrated when the shortstop, cleanly fielding the ball, receives credit for a "chance" even if the first baseman drops the thrown ball. It is demonstrated when a last-place team includes a Cy Young Award-winning pitcher or a league-leading hitter. It is perhaps most clearly manifest in the pitcher-batter duel, the heart of the game, when two men face each other. Baseball is each man doing the best he can for himself and against nature within a loose confederation of fellow individualists he may or may not admire and respect. This reflects a society in which individual effort, drive, and success are esteemed and in which, conversely, failure is deemed the individual's responsibility.[7]

Football, in sharp contrast, is the quintessence of team sports. Every move is planned and practiced in advance. The players in each of the eleven positions have a specific task to perform on every play. Every player is a specialist who must coordinate his actions with the other specialists on the team. So important is each person's play to the whole, that games are filmed and reviewed, with each play then broken down into its components and each player graded. Each player must subordinate his personality for the sake of the team. The coach is typically a stern taskmaster demanding submission of self to the team. The similarity of the football player to the organization man is obvious. So, too, is the parallel between football and the factory or corporation, where intricate and precise movements of all members doing different tasks are required for the attainment of the organization's objective.

CONCLUSION

Sociologist David Riesman in his classic *The Lonely Crowd* noted a shift in American character since World War II.[8] Prior to that war Americans were what Riesman called "inner directed," which fit the demands of an essentially agrarian society. The farmer and the small entrepreneur succeeded on their own merits and efforts. "Rugged individualism" was the necessary ingredient for success. There was the firm belief that everyone was a potential success.

But since the war the United States and Americans have changed. Rural life is replaced by living in cities and suburbs. Individuals now typically are dominated by large bureaucracies, whether they be governments, schools, churches, or factories. In these settings Riesman noted that Americans have become "other directed." Rather than an "automatic pilot" homing the inner-directed person toward an individual goal, the other-directed person has an "antenna" tuned to the values and opinions of others. In short, he or she is a team player and conformist.

Baseball, then, represents what we were—an inner-directed, rural, individualistic society. It continues to be popular because of our longing for the peaceful past. Football, on the other hand, is popular now because it symbolizes what we now are—an other-directed, urban-technical, corporate-bureaucratic society. Thus these two sports represent cultural contrasts (country vs. city, stability vs. change, harmony vs. conflict, calm vs. intensity, and equality vs. inequality). Each sport contains a fundamental myth that it elaborates for its fans. Baseball represents and island of stability in a confused and confusing world. As such, it provides an antidote for a world of too much action, struggle, pressure, and change. Baseball provides this antidote by being individualistic, unbounded by time, nonviolent, leisurely in pace, and by perpetuating the American myths of equal opportunity, egalitarianism, and potential championship for everyone.

Football represents what we are. Our society is violent. It is highly technical. It is highly bureaucratized, and we are all caught in its impersonal clutches. Football fits contemporary urban-corporate society because it is team-oriented, dominated by the clock, aggressive, characterized by bursts of energy, highly technical, and because it disproportionately rewards individuals at certain positions.

The uniquely American sports of football and baseball, although they represent opposites, provide us with insight about ourselves and our society. What will become of these sports as society changes? Will we continue to find football and baseball so intriguing as society becomes more structured? We know that in the future American society will be short of resources. We know that its citizenry will be older and more educated than at present. We also know that society will become more urban. What will these and other trends mean for society and for sport? One thing is certain—as society changes so, too, will its sports. Does this mean that baseball and football will change? Will another sport emerge that is more attuned with the culture and structure of society? Or will baseball become even more popular as we become more nostalgic for the peaceful, pastoral past?

NOTES

1. D. Stanley Eitzen and George H. Sage, *Sociology of American Sport* (Dubuque, Iowa: Wm. C. Brown, 1978), pp. 68-69.
2. George B. Leonard, "Winning Isn't Everything: It's Nothing," *Intellectual Digest* 4 (October 1973):45.
3. Several sources are especially important for the material that follows: Gerald J. Cavanaugh, "Baseball, Football, Images," *New York Times* (October 3, 1976): 2S; George Carlin, "Baseball-Football," *An Evening with Wally Londo* (Los Angeles: Little David Records, 1975); Leonard Koppett, "Differing Creeds in Baseball, Football," *Sporting News* (September 6, 1975):4,6; Murray Ross, "Football Red and Baseball Green," *Chicago Review* (January/February 1971):30-40; Richard Conway, "Baseball: A Discipline that Measures America's Way of Life," *Rocky Mountain News Trend* (October 19, 1975):1; "Behind Baseball's Comeback: It's an Island of Stability," *U.S. News & World Report* (September 19, 1977):56-57; William Arens, "The Great American Football Ritual," *Natural History* 84 (October 1975):72-80; Susan P. Montague and Robert Morais, "Football Games and Rock Concerts: The Ritual Enactment of American Success Models," in *The American Dimension: Cultural Myths and Realities,* William Arens (ed.), (Port Washington, New York: Alfred, 1976), pp. 33-52; and R. C Crepeau, "Punt or Bunt: A Note in American Culture," *Journal of Sport History* 3 (Winter 1976):205-212.
4. Cf. D. Stanley Eitzen, "Sport and Deviance," *Sport in Contemporary Society*, 1st ed. (New York: St. Martin's Press, 1979), pp. 73-87.
5. Crepeau, "Punt or Bunt," p. 211.
6. Quoted in Jack Scott, "The Souring of George Sauer," *Intellectual Digest* 2 (December 1971):52-55.
7. Cavanaugh, "Baseball, Football, Images," p. 25S.
8. David Reisman, *The Lonely Crowd* (New Haven: Yale University Press, 1950). The analysis that follows is largely dependent on Crepeau, "Punt or Bunt," pp. 205-212.

3. We Don't Like Football, Do We?

MARIAH BURTON NELSON

If you grew up female in America, you heard this: Sports are unfeminine. And this: Girls who play sports are tomboys or lesbians. You got this message: Real women don't spend their free time sliding feet-first into home plate or smacking their fists into soft leather gloves.

So you didn't play or you did play and either way you didn't quite fit. You didn't fit in your body—didn't learn to live there, breathe there, feel dynamic and capable. Or maybe you fell madly, passionately in love with sports but didn't quite fit in society, never saw yourself—basketball player, cyclist, golfer—reflected in movies, billboards, magazines.

Or you took a middle ground, shying away at first but then later sprinting toward aerobics and weight lifting and in-line skating, relishing your increasing endurance and grace and strength. Even then, though, you sensed that something was wrong: all the ads and articles seemed to focus on weight loss and beauty. While those may have inspired you to get fit in the first place, there are more important things, you now know, than how you looked. No one seemed to be talking about pride, pleasure, power, possibility.

If you grew up male in America, you heard this: Boys who *don't* play sports are sissies or faggots. And this: Don't throw like a girl. You got this message: Sports are a male initiation rite, as fundamental and natural as shaving and deep voices—a prerequisite, somehow, to becoming an American man. So you played football or soccer or baseball and felt competent, strong, and bonded with your male buddies. Or you didn't play and risked ridicule.

Whether we were inspired by Babe Ruth or Babe Didrikson or neither, and whether we played kickball with our brothers or sisters or both, all of us, female and male, learned to associate sports prowess and sports privilege with masculinity. Even if the best athlete in the neighborhood was a girl, we learned from newspapers, television, and from our own parents' prejudices that batting, catching, throwing, and jumping are not neutral, human activities, but somehow more naturally a male domain. Insidiously, our culture's reverence for men's professional sports and its silence about women's athletic accomplishments shaped, defined, and limited how we felt about ourselves as women and men.

* * *

You may remember. There was a time not too long ago when women in bright tights did not run along highways, bike paths, forest trails. Now they do. "Horses make a landscape look more beautiful," the Sioux medicine man Lame Deer (and, later, Alice Walker) said. You may harbor a similar feeling about this endless stream of rainbow runners: Women make a landscape look more beautiful.

You may have noticed that boys are no longer the only ones shooting baskets in public parks. One girl often joins the boys now, her hair dark with sweat, her body alert as a squirrel's. Maybe they don't pass her the ball. Maybe she grabs it anyway, squeezes mightily through the barricade of bodies, leaps skyward, feet flying.

Or she teams with other girls. Gyms fill these days with the rowdy sounds of women hard at play: basketballs seized by calloused hands, sneakers squealing like shocked mice. The players' high, urgent voices resonate, too—"Here!" "Go!"—and right then nothing exists for them except the ball, the shifting constellation of women, the chance to be fluid, smooth, alive.

What does this mean? What does it mean that everywhere, women are running, shooting baskets, getting sweaty and exhausted and euphoric? What changes when a woman becomes an athlete?

Everything.

On playing fields and in gyms across America, women are engaged in a contest with higher stakes than trophies or ribbons or even prize money. Through women's play, and through their huddles behind the scenes, they are deciding who American women will be. Not just what games they will play, but what role they will play in this still-young nation. Not only what their bodies will look like, but what their bodies can do.

* * *

One recent Sunday my young niece, Teagan, walked past the family room, where her father and brother were watching football on television. Her father's big fist punched the air. Her little brother's small fist made the same gesture. "Touchdown!" yelled her father in his big booming voice. "Touchdown!" yelled Alex in his small child's voice. They did not notice Teagan.

Teagan entered the kitchen, where her mother was preparing dinner. "Mommy," she said, "we don't like football, do we?"

We don't like football, do we?

Oh, some women do. Some of us appreciate the balletic dance between passer and receiver or the impressive speed, skill, or strength of individual athletes. We enjoy rooting for the home team, feeling in tune with a community. We find that by watching—even a few minutes here and there—we can better converse with men at work. Or we take to the fields ourselves, enjoying autumn games of flag football with our friends.

"I happen to love football," says Jamie Zimron, a San Francisco therapist and aikido teacher. "When I'm watching it, I block out all the crashing and violence that goes on. I look at the team play: the timing, the beauty of the quarterback going back and the receiver making the cutting motion, reaching out his hands, taking it in." Quarterback Joe Montana, Zimron's favorite player, "is not a big macho man," she says. "He's humble and understated, with presence, vision, grace, and ease. He doesn't force things, doesn't hurry, doesn't get rattled. When he plays, magic happens."

Carol Galbraith, a Washington, D.C., writer and lawyer, enjoys playing. "What I love is being a tight end. As a kid, I never got to play. It was a very male sport, the kind you're excluded from, and that made it more attractive. I like seeing the ball into my hands and hauling ass and scoring."

But we're also troubled by football. Jamie Zimron is bothered by the high injury rate. "I read in the paper the next day about the torn ligaments, destroyed knees, concussions, broken ankles, separated shoulders." And the steroid use: "It's insane. Sort of like the nuclear arms race: The other team's doing it, so I've got to, even if it's totally toxic and fatal."

Galbraith refuses to watch men play. She refers to football players as "grunty slobs" whose larger-than-life portrayals serve as a "constant reminder that males are bigger than females and that violence is a male province." Men's large bodies and their displays of aggression "are supposed to trigger all this fear and respect," she says. "It's a show of force. A veiled threat in a way."

Many women are angry at football, basketball, baseball, boxing, ice hockey, wrestling, soccer—sports that I call the manly sports; sports that men use to define masculinity. Many women hate the veiled threat. Many resent the time their husbands, fathers, or brothers spend screaming at the tube, slapping raucous high-fives, indulging in loud emotional outbursts that seem misplaced and out of proportion to the drama at hand. Women often feel alienated from their male co-workers when they spend so much time talking sports. Most women lack the nostalgic reference points—Little League did not admit girls until 1973—and the ability to identify with hulks.

Many mothers don't want their sons to play—or want them to play but not get injured, and that omnipresent fear of injury clouds all enthusiasm. They're uncomfortable when the coaches call their sons wimps or sissies. Women don't want sissy sons, but women don't want the opposite either: brutal sons who grow inured to their own pain or to the pain of others.

Women seem to intuit that football and other manly sports hurt women. There's something about the way certain games are played and the way they're worshiped that's injurious to women's mental and physical health. When Patricia Bowman testified that William Kennedy Smith "tackled" her on the lawn, we cringed. When Desiree Washington testified that boxer Mike Tyson "pinned" her to the bed, then raped her, we were furious but not surprised. When a new "sports bar" opens in New York and it features topless dancers, we understand that this seems natural to the bar's owner and its enthusiastic patrons. We sense a connection: there's something about male sports privilege that contributes to the sexual objectification and abuse of women. Given how pervasive and what cultural icons men's sports are, that's a scary thought.

* * *

"Who's your team?" a man asks a boy he has just met in a doctor's office.

"The Atlanta Braves," the boy replies.

"Good choice," says the man. Actually, almost any men's pro or college team would suffice. The important thing is to "have" a team, love a team, follow a team. To identify with successful manly athletes is to feel successful and manly oneself, to feel a part of the dominant male culture. Millions of men affirm their manliness and manly ties by betting on sports, discussing sports, arguing over sports, agonizing over decisions such as, Should I root for Baltimore, where I grew up, or Cleveland, where I live now? These men argue over whether Pete Rose should be admitted into the Hall of Fame. They can become irritable for an entire day if "their" team loses.

To women, this can sound silly, but many men take manly sports seriously. The games become symbolic struggles, passion plays reenacted daily to define, affirm, and celebrate manliness. The games offer men a chance to admire huge bodies, "aggressive play" and "very physical teams," to gossip over who did what and in what year, to compete over statistics: "When did the Boston Red Sox win their last World Series?" "Who scored the most points in a single NBA game?" When discussing sports, men reminisce about their own high school sports "careers." They imagine that they themselves somehow "just missed" becoming famous athletes.

Few men take no interest in the World Series, the Super Bowl, the Final Four, or the latest boxing match. Of those who do abstain from the daily sports dialogue, some have failed at youth sports and retain an antagonism for the arena that injured their egos or their bodies. "I was big, slow, and clumsy," recalls Brent LaFever, a facilities manager from Winston-Salem, North Carolina. "Now I hate watching sports. They're so barbaric. When people come to visit, my wife and I don't let them turn on the television. Often they leave."

Other men develop an antipathy for sports because they did play and didn't like what they saw of the manly sport culture: the cutthroat competition, the cruel coaches, the required "toughness." Numerous men were humiliated by coaches who insisted on "making a man out of them" but ignored the sensitive boys that they were.

Regardless of his reasons, the grown man who pays no attention to male sporting dramas must be, it seems to me, among the most secure and confident of all men, because he relinquishes a daily opportunity to identify with the culture's primary male heroes and in the process risks censure or at least estrangement from other men. Yet even a man who steers clear of the daily barrage of sports events, sports pages, sports television, and sports talk radio shows will often devise ways to fake it. In response to overtures such as, "How 'bout those Redskins!" he may utter an ambiguous, noncommittal exclamation, such as, "They've got quite a quarterback!" Rare is the man who not only opts out of the manly sports system but also criticizes it—who, in response to "How 'bout those Redskins!" will say, "I hate football. It's racist, sexist, and far too violent for me."

Sport has been called the last bastion of male domination. Unfortunately, there are others—Congress, for instance. But sport constitutes the only large cultural institution where men and women are (sometimes) justifiably segregated according to gender. It is one of the few remaining endeavors where male muscle matters.

Women have always been strong. We have carried water, harvested crops, birthed and raised children. Women do two-thirds of the world's work, according to New Zealand economist Marilyn Waring. But as women in the late twentieth century gain increasing economic, political, and athletic strength, many men cling to manly sports as a symbol of "natural" male dominance. The stronger women get, the more enthusiastically male fans, players, coaches, and owners seem to be embracing a particular form of masculinity: toughness, aggression, denial of emotion, and a persistent denigration of all that's considered female. Attitudes learned on the playing fields, or by watching sports on television, leach into the soil of everyday life, where many men view women and treat women with disdain. They call baseball the national pastime—which, in a diverse society, "unites us all." But baseball, football, and other manly sports do not unite Americans. They unite American men in a celebration of male victory. By pointing to men's greater size and strength and by imbuing those qualities with meaning (dominance, conquest), many men justify to themselves a two-tiered gender system with men on top. As University of Iowa sports sociologist Susan Birrell has noted, "It's a short leap from seeing men as physically superior to seeing men as superior, period."[1]

Sports are an escape, men often say. One wonders what they are escaping from. Men who *must* watch The Game seem to me to be escaping from women's demands for freedom, equality, and simple attention—as well as from housework, child-care, and other family responsibilities.

Manly sports are more than a refuge from the reality of women's liberation. By creating a world where masculinity is equated with violence, where male bonding is based on the illusion of male supremacy, and where all of the visible women are cheerleaders, manly sports set the stage for violence against women. When we begin to understand how male coaches and players speak and think about women and masculinity, it ceases to be surprising that college football and basketball players gang-rape women in numbers equaled only by fraternity brothers.[2] Or that male basketball and football players are reported to police for sexual assault 38 percent more often than their male college peers.[3] Or that football and basketball players are more likely to engage in sexually aggressive behaviors (including everything from whistling and unwanted touching to attempted rape) than their peers, including those who play other sports.[4]

"It's just a game," former commissioner Fay Vincent used to say about baseball. But baseball and other manly sports are more than games. They constitute a culture—the dominant culture in America today. Manly sports comprise a world where men are in charge and women are irrelevant at best. Where assaults that would be illegal off the field become an accepted, even celebrated part of "play" and replay. Where big men wearing tight pants embrace each other, openly loving men and male power. Where "girls" flash their underwear.

Sports offer a pre-civil rights world where white men, as owners, coaches, and umpires, still rule. Within a sports arena, a man can express racist, sexist, and homophobic attitudes not tolerated in many other parts of society. The public denigration of women (and minority men) has become such a mainstay of the American sporting experience that when *Sports Illustrated* took an "unscientific" poll of fans in 1988, "everyone who had ever been a spectator of any kind had, at one time or another, experienced the bellowing of obscenities, racial or religious epithets [and] abusive sexual remarks to women in the vicinity."[5]

* * *

Most women, by contrast, don't really "have" a team. They don't ask little girls, Who's your team? Women don't indoctrinate girls into a world of statistics and heroes and athletic history. Few women crave violent entertainment. "In a boxing match, women tend to identify with the loser," says writer Joyce Carol Oates, author of *On Boxing* as well as several dozen other books.[6]

Women often ignore women's sports, not taking seriously their daughters' or even their own athletic passions, not noticing the link between physical strength and personal power, or between female team bonding and female political clout. Without thinking about it, many women attend high school football games but never drop by to see how the girls' basketball team is faring.

Feminists have tried to reduce sexual violence in all its forms: child sexual abuse, sexual harassment at work, battering and rape by husbands and "lovers," rape by strangers, and the glorification of rape through pornography. Women have tried to empower women through jobs, education, health care, politics, and therapy. For the most part, women haven't paid attention to sports. Women tend to ignore the sports section of the newspaper and to avoid living rooms and bars and college dormitories where men gather ritually, as if to worship the televised game.

Women—and fair-minded men—need to pay attention. We live in a country in which the manly sports culture is so pervasive we may fail to recognize the symbolic messages we all receive about men, women, love, sex, and power. We need to take sports seriously—not the scores or the statistics, but the process. Not to focus on who wins, but on who's losing. Who loses when a community spends millions of dollars in tax revenue to construct a new stadium and only men get to play in it, and only men get to work there?

Who loses when football and baseball so dominate the public discourse that they eclipse all mention of female volleyball players, gymnasts, basketball players, swimmers?

Who loses when coaches teach boys that the worst possible insult is to be called "pussy" or "cunt"?

Who loses when rape jokes comprise an accepted part of the game?

Sport is a women's issue because on playing fields, male athletes learn to talk about and think about women and women's bodies with contempt. It's a women's issue because male athletes have disproportionately high rates of sexual assaults on women—including female athletes. It's a women's issue because the media itself cheers for men's sports and rarely covers women's, thereby reinforcing the notion that men are naturally more athletic. It's a women's issue because of the veiled threat, this homage paid to bulky, brutal bodies. And it's a women's issue because female sport participation empowers women, thereby inexorably changing everything.

NOTES

1. Susan Birrell, "The Woman Athlete: Fact or Fiction?" Paper presented at the National Girls and Women in Sport Symposium, Slippery Rock State University, Slippery Rock, Pennsylvania (February 6–9, 1992).
2. Lester Munson, "Against Their Will." *The National Sports Daily* (August 17, 1990), p. 30.
3. Rich Hofman, "Rape and the College Athlete: Part One." *Philadelphia Daily News* (March 17, 1986), p. 104.
4. Mary P. Koss and John A. Gaines, "The Prediction of Sexual Aggression by Alcohol Use, Athletic Participation, and Fraternity Affiliation." *Journal of Interpersonal Violence* 8 (March 1993), pp. 94–108.
5. W. O. Johnson, "Sports and Studs." *Sports Illustrated* (August 8, 1988), p. 70; cited in Myriam Miedzian, *Boys Will Be Boys: Breaking the Link Between Masculinity and Violence* (New York: Doubleday, 1991), p. 188.
6. Joyce Carol Oates, guest, "The Derek McGinty Show." WAMU (Washington, D.C., August 6, 1993).

4. *Sport in Society: An Inspiration or an Opiate?*

JAY J. COAKLEY

People in American society generally see sport in a very positive way. Not only is sport assumed to provide a training ground for the development of desirable character traits and good citizens, but it is also believed to reaffirm a commitment to societal values emphasizing competition, success, and playing by the rules.

Does sport really do all these things? Is it as beneficial and healthy as people believe? These questions have generated considerable disagreement among sport sociologists. It seems that most of us in the sociology of sport are quick to agree that sport is a microcosm of society—that it mirrors the values, structure, and dynamics of the society in which it exists (Eitzen and Sage, 1978). However, we often disagree when it comes to explaining the consequences or the functions of sport in society. This disagreement grows out of the fact that sport sociologists have different theoretical conceptions of how society works. Therefore, they differ on their ideas about how sport functions within society. A description of the two major theoretical approaches used in sociology of sport will illustrate what I mean.

THE FUNCTIONALIST APPROACH

Sport Is an Inspiration

The majority of sport sociologists assume that society is most accurately conceptualized in terms of a *systems model.* They see society as an organized system of interrelated parts. The system is held together and operates because (1) its individual members generally endorse the same basic values and (2) the major parts in the system (such as the family, education, the economy, government, religion, and sport) all fit together in mutually supportive and constructive ways. In sociology, this theoretical approach is called *functionalism.*

SOURCE: "Sport in Society: An Inspiration or an Opiate?" by Jay J. Coakley. From *Sport in Society: Issues and Controversies,* 2nd ed., by Jay J. Coakley. Copyright © 1982 by C. V. Mosby. Reprinted by permission.

When the functionalists describe and analyze how a society, community, school, or any other system works, they are primarily concerned with how the parts of that system are related to the operation of the system as a whole. For example, if American society is the system being studied, a person using a functionalist approach would be concerned with how the American family, the economy, government, education, religion, and sport are all related to the smooth operation of the society as a whole. The analysis would focus on the ways in which each of these subparts of society helps to keep the larger system going.

The functionalists also assume that a social system will continue to operate smoothly only if the four following things happen:

1. The members of the system must learn the values and the norms (i.e., the general rules or guidelines for behavior) that will lead them to want to do what has to be done to keep the system in operation. This process of shaping the feelings, thoughts, and actions of individuals usually creates some frustration and tension. Therefore, there must also be some channels through which people can let off steam in harmless ways.
2. The system must contain a variety of social mechanisms that bring people together and serve as catalysts for building the social relationships needed for coordinated action. Without a certain degree of cohesion, solidarity, and social integration, coordinated action would be impossible and the social system would stop functioning smoothly.
3. The members of the system must have the opportunity to learn what their goals should be within the system and the socially approved ways of achieving those goals.
4. The social system must be able to adjust to the demands and challenges of the external environment. It must have ways of handling and coping with changes in the social and physical environments so that it can continue to operate with a minimal amount of interference and disruption.

According to those using a functionalist approach, these four "system needs" are the basic minimum requirements for the smooth operation of any social system whether it be a society, community, club, large corporation, or neighborhood convenience store (Parsons and Smelser, 1965). These four basic system requirements are referred to as:

1. The need for pattern maintenance and tension management
2. The need for integration
3. The need for goal attainment
4. The need for adaptation

When you start with a functionalist conception of how society works, the answer to the question of what sport does for a society or community is likely to emphasize the ways in which sport satisfies the four basic needs of the social system. A brief review of how sport is related to each of these needs is a good way to summarize this approach.

PATTERN MAINTENANCE AND TENSION MANAGEMENT

The functionalists generally conclude that sport provides learning experiences that reinforce and extend the learning occurring in other settings. In other words, sport serves as a backup or a secondary institution for primary social institutions such as the family, school, and church. Through sport people learn the general ways of thinking, feeling, and acting that make them contributing members of society. They become socialized so that they fit into the mainstream of American life and therefore reaffirm the stability and continued operation of our society (Schafer, 1976).[1]

The pattern maintenance function of sport applies to spectators as well as those who are active participants. Sport is structured so that those who watch or play learn the importance of rules, hard work, efficient organization, and a well-defined authority structure. For example, sociologist Gunther Luschen (1967) shows how sport helps to generate the high levels of achievement motivation necessary to sustain the commitment to work required in industrialized countries. Along similar lines, Kleiber and Kelly (1980) have reviewed a number of studies concluding that participation in competitive games helps children learn how to handle adult roles in general and competitive relationships in particular. In fact, some recent discussions of sex roles have suggested that women may be at a disadvantage in business settings partly because they have not been involved in competitive sports to the same degree as their male counterparts (Hennig and Jardim, 1977; Lever, 1978).

Sport has also been thought to serve tension management functions in society by providing both spectators and participants with an outlet for aggressive energy (Vanderzwaag, 1972; Proctor and Eckard, 1976; Marsh, 1978). This idea prompted two widely respected sociologists, Hans Gerth and C. Wright Mills (1954), to suggest the following: "Many mass audience situations, with their 'vicarious' enjoyments, serve psychologically the unintended function of channeling and releasing otherwise unplacable emotions. Thus, great volumes of aggression are 'cathartically' released by crowds of spectators cheering their favorite stars of sport—and jeering the umpire." The idea that sport may serve tension management functions is complex and controversial.

INTEGRATION

A functionalist approach also emphasizes how sport serves to bring people together and provide them with feelings of group unity, a sense of social identification, and a source of personal identity. In short, a functionalist explains how sport creates and reaffirms the linkages between people so that cooperative action is possible. Luschen (1967) outlines how this occurs in the following: "Since sport is also structured along such societal subsystems as different classes, males, urban areas, schools, and communities, it functions for integration. This is obvious also in spectator sport, where the whole country or community identifies with its representatives in a contest. Thus, sport functions as a means of integration, not only for the actual participants, but also for the represented members of such a system."

Sport has been seen to serve integration functions in countries other than the United States also. For example, others have discussed how sport contributes to unity and solidarity in Switzerland (Albonico, 1967), France (Bouet, 1969), Germany (Brockman, 1969), China (Chu and Segrave, 1979), the Soviet Union (Riordan, 1977), and Brazil (Lever, 1980).

Andrzej Wohl (1970), a sport sociologist from Poland, has argued that competitive sport could not exist if it recognized "local, nation or racial barriers or differences of world outlook." He points out that sport is so widely used to serve integration functions that it "is no secret for anybody any more."

GOAL ATTAINMENT

Someone using a functionalist approach is likely to see sport as legitimizing and reinforcing the primary goals of the system as well as the means to be used to achieve those goals. In the United States, for example, sport is organized so that successful outcomes are heavily emphasized, and success is generally defined in terms of scores and win-loss records. Just as in the rest of society, the proper way to achieve success in sport is through a combination of competition, hard work, planning, and good organization. Therefore, the sport experience not only serves to legitimize the way things are done in other sectors of society but also it prepares people for participation in those sectors.

In other countries, different aspects of the sport experience are emphasized so that it serves as a supportive model for their goal priorities and the proper means to achieve goals. Capitalist countries are more likely to emphasize output and competition in sport while socialist countries will be more likely to emphasize cooperation and the development of a spirit of collectivism (Morton, 1963). Sport seems to be amazingly flexible in this respect; it has been shaped and defined in a variety of ways to serve goal attainment functions in many different social systems. This point has been developed and explained by Edwards (1973): "Most sports have few, if any, intrinsic and invariably social or political qualities . . . and those qualities which such activities do possess are sufficiently 'liquid' to fit comfortably within many diverse and even conflicting value and cultural traditions."

ADAPTATION

In preindustrial societies it is easy to see how sport serves a system's need for adaptation. Since survival in such societies depends on the development and use of physical skills, participation in games and sport activities is directly related to coping with the surrounding environment (Luschen, 1967). Dunlap (1951) makes this case in her study of the Samoans. Additionally, she found that the "factors of physical strength and endurance which were essential for success in their games were also essential for success in their wars."

In industrial societies, it is more difficult to see how sport satisfies the adaptation needs of the social system. However, in two articles on the functions of sport, Wohl (1970, 1979) has suggested that it is in this area that sport makes its most important contributions. He points out that in any society with technologically advanced transportation and communications systems, sport becomes the only sphere of activities in which physical skills are developed and perfected. Through sport it is possible to measure and extend the range of human motor skills and to adapt them to the environments we have created. Without sport it would be difficult to maintain a population's physical well-being at the levels necessary to keep an industrial society operating efficiently. Sport is so crucial in this regard that Wohl (1979) calls for the use of all the sport sciences to plan and control its development. In this way the contributions of sport to satisfying adaptation needs could be maximized.

In concluding our review of the functionalist approach to sport it should be pointed out that social scientists are not the only ones who use such an approach in explaining the relationship between sport and society. Most people view society and the role of sport in terms very similar to those used by the functionalists. They look for the ways in which sport contributes to the communities in which they live. They see sport providing valuable lessons for their children and opportunities for themselves to release the tensions generated by a job or other life events. Sport gives then something to talk about with strangers as well as friends and it provides occasions for outings and get-togethers. Many people believe that sport can serve as a model of the goals we should strive for and the means we should use in trying to achieve those goals. Finally, sport is viewed as a healthy activity for individuals as well as the entire country; it can extend life and keep us physically prepared to defend our country in case of war.

These beliefs about sport have led to policy decisions on Little League programs, the funding of high school and college athletics, the support of professional teams and the Olympic movement, the development of physical education programs in schools, and the use of sport activities in military academies to prepare young men and women to be "combat ready." The widespread acceptance and the pervasive influence of the functionalist approach make it necessary for us to be aware of its weaknesses.

Limitations of the Functionalist Approach

Using a functionalist approach to answer the question of how sport is related to society can provide us with valuable insights, but it is not without its problems. Such an approach tends to emphasize the positive aspects of sport. This is because those using it often assume that if some part or component of a social system has existed for a long time, it is likely to be contributing to the system in a favorable way; if it were not, it would have been eliminated or gradually faded out of existence on its own. Since sport has been around for some time and is an increasingly significant component of our social system, most functionalists conclude that it *does* make positive contributions to society. This conclusion leads them to ignore or underemphasize the negative aspects of sport. After all, it is also possible that sport could distort values and behavioral guidelines (norms). Sport could destroy motivation, create frustration and tensions, and disrupt social integration. It could impede goal attainment and interfere with methods of coming to terms with the external social and physical environment by diverting a group's attention away from crucial personal and social issues.

Another problem with the functionalist approach is that it is based on the assumption that the needs of the individual parts of a social system overlap with the needs of the system as a whole. The possibility of internal differences or basic conflicts of interests within a social system is inconsistent with the assumption that any system is held together by a combination of common values and an interrelated, mutually supportive set of parts. If the needs of the total system were in serious conflict with the needs of the individual parts, the validity of the functionalist approach would be called into question.

This is one of the major weaknesses of functionalism. Although we may agree that many people in our society hold similar values, can we also argue that the structure of American society serves the needs of everyone equally? It would be naive to assume that is does. In fact, it may even frustrate the needs of certain groups and individuals and generate conflict. To conclude that sport exists because it satisfies the needs of the total system overlooks the possibility that sport may benefit some segments of the population more than others. Furthermore, if the interests of some groups within the system are met at the expense of others, the consequences of sport could be described as positive only if you were viewing them from the perspective of those privileged groups. Unfortunately, a functionalist approach often leads to underemphasizing differences of interests as well as the possibility of exploitation and coercion within the social system. It also leads to ignoring the role of sport in generating conflict and maintaining a structure in which at least some relationships are based on exploitation and coercion.

In sociology the theoretical approach that calls attention to these unpleasant characteristics of social systems and how sport is related to them is called conflict theory.

CONFLICT THEORY

Sport Is an Opiate

Conflict theory is not as popular as functionalism. It does fit with what most people think about how society is organized and how it operates. Instead of viewing society as a relatively stable system of interrelated parts held together by common values and consensus, conflict theorists view it as an ever-changing set of relationships characterized by inherent differences of interests and held together by force, coercion, and subtle manipulation. They are concerned with the distribution and use of power rather than with common values and integration. Their analysis of society focuses on processes of change rather than on what is required for a social system to continue operating smoothly.

Most beginning students in the sociology of sport are not very receptive to the use of conflict theory in explaining the relationship between sport and society. They say that it is too negativistic and critical of our way of life and the institution of sport. They prefer the functionalist approach because it fits closely with what they have always believed and because it has implications that do not threaten the structure of either society or sport. My response is that although functionalism is useful, it can often lead us to look at the world unrealistically and ignore a dimension of the relationship between sport and society that should be considered. Neither American society nor sport is without problems. Awareness and understanding of these problems require critical thought, and conflict theory is a valuable stimulus for such thought.

Conflict theory is based primarily on an updated revision of the ideas of Karl Marx. Those who use it generally focus their attention on capitalist countries such as the United States, but it has also been used to describe and understand any social system in which individuals are perceived as not having significant control over their own lives. According to many conflict theorists this includes capitalist systems along with fascist or military/police regimes and socialist systems controlled by centralized, bureaucratic governments (Brohm, 1978).

In order to understand how conflict theorists view the role of sport in society, we will start with a simplified description of capitalism and how contemporary organized sport fits into its structure. Any capitalist system requires the development of a highly efficient work process through which an increasing number of consumer goods can be mass produced. Industrial bureaucracies have been created to meet this need. This means that in the interest of efficiency and financial profit, workers end up performing highly specialized and alienating jobs. These jobs are generally in the production, marketing and sales, or service departments of large organizations where the workers themselves have little control over what they do and experience little or no excitement or satisfaction in their day-to-day work lives. This situation creates a need for escape and for tension-excitement in their nonwork lives. Within capitalist systems, people are subtly manipulated to seek the satisfaction they need through consumerism and mass entertainment spectacles. Sport in such societies has emerged as a major form of entertainment spectacle as well as a primary context for the consumption of material goods. Additionally, the structure of sport is so much like the structure of work organizations and capitalist society as a whole that it serves to stabilize the system and promote the interests of people who are in positions of power.

Conflict theorists see sport as a distorted form of physical exercise that has been shaped by the needs of a capitalist system of production. A specific example of how sport has developed in this manner has been outlined by Goodman (1979) in an analysis of the history of playground and street life in one of New York City's working-class neighborhoods. Goodman shows how the spontaneous, free-flowing play activities of children in New York were literally banned from the streets in order to force participation in organized playground programs. The original goals of the playgrounds are best described through the words of one of the influential playground supervisors early in this century (Chase, 1909): "We want a play factory; we want it to run at top speed on schedule time, with the best machinery and skilled operatives. We want to turn out the maximum product of happiness." Thus the organized activities and sport programs became a means for training the children of immigrants to fit into a world of work founded on time schedules, the stopwatch, and production-conscious supervisors.

For the parents of these children the playground and recreation center programs had a different goal. It was clearly explained in the following section of a 1910 New York City Department of Education report (cited in Goodman, 1979): "The great problem confronting the recreation center principal and teachers is the filling of the leisure time of the working men and women with a combination of recreation and athletic activities which will help make their lives more tolerable." As Goodman points out, the purpose of the centers was to provide controlled leisure activities to take the people's minds off the exploitation and poor working conditions experienced in their jobs. The supervised activities were meant to pacify the workers so that they could tolerate those conditions and continue contributing to the growth of the economy. When they needed to be replaced, the organized playground activities would have prepared their children to take their roles.

Other conflict theorists have not limited their focus to a local community setting. They have talked in more general terms about the relationship between sport and society. Their discussions emphasize four major aspects of the role of sport. These include:

1. How sport generates and intensifies alienation
2. How sport is used by the state and the economically powerful as a tool for coercion and social control.

3. How sport promotes commercialism and materialism
4. How sport encourages nationalism, militarism, and sexism

The following sections summarize the discussions of the conflict theorists on each of these four topics.

ALIENATION

According to the conflict theorists sport serves to alienate people from their own bodies. Sport focuses attention on time and output rather than on the individual. Standardized rules and rigid structure destroy the spontaneity, freedom, and inventiveness characteristic in play. Jean-Marie Brohm (1978), a French sport sociologist, explains how sport affects the connection between athletes and their bodies: "[In sport the body is] experienced as an object, an instrument, a technical means to an end, a reified factor of output and productivity, in short, as a machine with the job of producing maximum work and energy." In other words, sport creates a setting in which the body is no longer experienced as a source of self-fulfillment and pleasure in itself. Pleasure and fulfillment depend on *what is done* with the body. Satisfaction is experienced only if the contest is won, if a record is set or a personal goal achieved, and if the body performs the way if has been trained to perform. When this happens sport becomes a "prison of measured time" and alienates athletes from their own bodies (Brohm, 1978).

Mumford (1934) extends the idea of alienation even further. In a classic analysis of contemporary civilization he describes the sport stadium as an "industrial establishment producing running, jumping or football playing machines." Building on this notion conflict theorists argue that commercialized sport (any sport in which profits are sought) reduces athletes to material commodities (Hoch, 1972). Thus the body becomes a tool not only for the setting of records but also for generating financial profits for nonparticipants—from team owners and tournament sponsors to concession operators and parking lot owners. The athletes may also benefit, but their rewards require them to forfeit the control of their bodies and become "gladiators" performing for the benefit of others.

Conflict theorists have pointed to the use of drugs and computer technology in sport as support for their analysis of how sport affects the definition of an athlete's body (Brohm, 1978). When the body is seen as an instrument for setting records and the improvement of times is defined as the measure of human progress, then the use of drugs, even harmful drugs, will be seen as a valuable aid in the quest for achievement. Computer technology used to analyze and improve the body's productive capacity further separates the physical act of sport participation from the subjective experience of the athlete. Just as on the assembly line, efficiency comes to be the major concern in sport and the worker (athlete) loses control over the means of production (the body).

COERCION AND SOCIAL CONTROL

Goodman's (1979) study of the working-class neighborhood in New York City led him to conclude that sport in that city was used as a means of making the lives of shop workers more tolerable. Other conflict theorists expand this notion and describe sport as an opiate interfering with an awareness of social problems and subverting collective attempts to solve those problems. According to Hoch (1972), sport perpetuates problems by providing people with either "(1) a temporary high . . . which takes their minds off problem[s] for a while but does nothing to deal with [them]; or (2) a distorted frame of reference or identification which encourages them to look for salvation through patently false channels."

Hoch's description of the personal and social impact of sport is similar to Marx's description of religion in society. To Marx, religion focuses attention on the supernatural, provides people with a psychological lift, and emphasizes improvement through changing the self rather than changing the social order. Religion destroys awareness of material reality and promotes the maintenance of the status quo by giving priority to the goal of spiritual salvation. Marx further concluded that organized religion can be exploited by people in positions of power in society. If the majority of individuals in a society believe that enduring pain, denying pleasure, and accepting their status in this life gains them spiritual salvation, those in power can be reasonably sure that those under their control will be hard working and docile. If those in power go so far as to manifest their own commitment to religion, their hold over the people can be strengthened even further. Such a manifestation would, after all, show that they had something in common with the masses.

Conflict theorists make the case that in an advanced capitalist society where people are not likely to look to the supernatural for answers and explanations, religion may be supplemented by other activities with similar narcotic effects. Hoch points out that these contemporary "opiates" include "sport spectacles, whiskey, and repressively sublimated sex." These combined with other opiates such as nationalism, racism, and sexism distort people's perspectives and encourage self-defeating behavior. Among these, sport stands out as an especially powerful opiate. Unlike the others, sport spectatorship is often accompanied by an extremely intense identification with players, teams, and the values perceived to be the basis for success in athletics. According to Hoch, this identification brings sport further into the lives of the spectators and captures their attention on a long-term basis. When the game ends, fan involvement does not cease, but carries on between games and into the off season. This means that workers think about and discuss the fate of their teams rather than the futility of their own lives. Thus they are less likely to become actively involved in political or revolutionary organizations. Petryszak (1978), in a historical analysis of sport, makes the case that the "ultimate consequence of . . . spectator sports in society is the reduction of the population to a position of complete passivity."

Beyond occupying people's time and distracting their attention and energy, sport helps maintain the position of those in power in other ways. Conflict theorists note that the major contact sports, such as football, hockey, and boxing, promote a justification for the use of "official" violence by those in authority positions. In other words, sport shapes our values in ways that lock us into a social system based on coercion and the exploitive use of power. The more we witness violent sports, the more we are apt to condone the use of official violence in other settings—even when it is directed against us.

Sport also serves the interests of those in power by generating the belief that success can be achieved only through hard work and that hard work always leads to success. Such a belief encourages people to look up to those who are successful as being paragons of virtue and to look down on the failures as being lazy and no good. For example, when teams win consistently, their success is attributed to hard work and discipline; when they lose consistently, losing often is blamed on a lack of hustle and poor attitude. Losses lead the fans to call for new players and coaches—not a restructuring of the game or its rules. Hoch (1972) points out that this way of looking at things blinds people to a consideration of the problems inherent in the social and economic structure and engenders the notion that success depends only on attitude and personal effort. It also leads to the belief that failure is to be blamed on the individual alone and is to be accepted as an indication of personal inadequacies and of a need to work harder in the future.

Conflict theories see sport as a tool for controlling people and maintaining the status quo. It is structured to promote specific political ideas and to regiment and organize the lives of young people so that they will become productive workers. For adults, the role of spectator reinforces a passive orientation toward life so that they will remain observers rather than the shapers of their own experience (Aronowitz, 1973).

COMMERCIALISM AND MATERIALISM

The conflict theorists emphasize that sport is promoted as a product to be consumed and that it creates a basis for capitalist expansion. For example, increasing numbers of individuals and families are joining athletic clubs where they pay to participate and pay for the lessons teaching them how to participate correctly and efficiently. Creating and satisfying these expanding interests have given rise to an entire new industry. Summer sport resorts, winter sport resorts, and local athletic clubs are all part of this profit-generating industry.

Furthermore, sporting goods manufacturers have found that effective advertising can lead more and more equipment to be defined as absolutely necessary for successful and healthy involvement. Potential consumers have been convinced that if they want to impress other people with their knowledge about the sport experience, they have to buy and show off only top-of-the-line equipment. It has come to the point where participants can prove themselves in sport through their ability to consume as well as their ability to master physical skills. Thus sport has been used to lead people to deal with one another in terms of material images rather than in terms of the human quality of experience.

Sport not only creates direct profits but also is used as an advertising medium (Brohm, 1978). Sport spectacles serve as important settings for selling cars, tires, beer, soft drinks, and insurance. The tendency for people to personally identify with athletes is also used to sell other products. The role of athlete, unlike most adult occupational roles, is highly visible, prestigious, and relatively easy to emulate. Therefore, the attachment to sport heroes serves as the basis for the creation of an interest in sport along with a general "need" for consumer goods.

This process affects young people as well as adults. Children are lured into the spectator role and the role of consumer by trading cards, Dallas Cowboy pajamas, Yankee baseball caps, NBA basketball shoes, and a multitude of other products that ultimately create adulthood desires to become season ticket purchasers. Participation in highly specialized sport programs leads children to conclude that the proper equipment is always necessary for a good time and that being a good runner, tennis player, and soccer player depends on owning three different pairs of the best shoes on the market.

NATIONALISM, MILITARISM, AND SEXISM

Conflict theorists point out that sport is used by most countries as the showplace for displaying their national symbols and military strength. In many developing countries, national sport programs are administered by the defense department; in industrialized countries sport is symbolically linked with warfare and strong militaristic orientations. The conflict theorists claim that the collective excitement generated by sport participation and mass spectator events can be converted into unquestioning allegiance to political beliefs and an irrational willingness to defend those beliefs. Nationalistic feelings are fed by an emphasis on demonstrating superiority over other countries and other political systems. Furthermore, sport provides a model of confrontation, which polarizes groups of people and stresses the necessity of being militarily prepared.

Finally, the conflict theorists argue that sport divides the sexes and perpetuates distorted definitions of masculinity and femininity. The organization of contemporary sport not only relegates women to a secondary, supportive role, but also leads people to define masculinity in term of physical strength and emotional insensitivity. In fact, the model of the successful male is epitomized by the brute strength and the controlled emotions of the athlete. Sport further reinforces sexism by focusing attention on performance differences in selected physical activities. People then use those differences to argue that male superiority is grounded in nature and that the sexes should continue to be separated. This separation obscures the characteristics men and women have in common and locks members of both sexes into restrictive roles.

Conflict theorists see much of contemporary sport as a source of alienation and a tool of exploitation and control serving the needs of economic and political systems rather than the needs of human beings. They generally argue that it is impossible for sport to provide humanizing experiences when the society in which it exists is not humane and creative (Hoch, 1972).

Limitations of the Conflict Theory Approach

Like the functionalist approach, conflict theory has some weaknesses. The conflict theorists make good use of history, but they tend to overemphasize the role of capitalism in shaping all aspects of social reality since the Industrial Revolution. Capitalism has been a significant force, but other factors must be taken into account in explaining what has happened during the last two centuries.

The emergence and growth of modern sport is a good case in point. Sport has been strongly influenced by capitalism, but the emergence of contemporary sport can be explained in terms of factors that existed prior to the Industrial Revolution. Guttmann (1978) has argued that modern sport is a product of a scientific approach to the world rather than of the needs of capitalist economic systems. This scientific approach to the world grew out of seventeenth-century discoveries in mathematics and is characterized by a commitment to quantification, measurement, and experimentation. According to Guttmann this scientific world-view has given rise to contemporary sport. This is the reason why sport is also popular in noncapitalist countries including China, Cuba, Czechoslovakia, and the Soviet Union.

In their analysis of sport, many conflict theorists are too quick to conclude that sport inevitably creates alienation and serves as an "opiate of the masses." They tend to ignore the testimonials of athletes who claim that sport participation, even in a capitalist society, can be a personally creative, expressive, and liberating experience (Slusher, 1967; Spino, 1971; Bannister, 1980; Csikszentmihalyi, 1975; Sadler, 1977). This possibility, of course, is inconsistent with the idea that the athlete's body automatically becomes a tool of production controlled and used for the sake of political and economic goals.

The argument that sport is an opiate also has some weaknesses. It is probably true that athletes and fans are more likely than other people to have attitudes supportive of the status quo. However, it is not known if their involvement in sport caused these attitudes of if the attitudes existed prior to their involvement and caused them to be attracted to sport. It may be that sport attracts people who are already committed to the status quo. If this is the case, it is difficult to argue that sport provides an escape from reality for those who might otherwise be critical of the social order. Research suggests that the most alienated and the most dissatisfied people in society are the least likely to show an interest in sport. In fact, interest and involvement are greatest among those who are the most economically successful (Sillitoe, 1969; Edwards, 1973; Anderson and Stone, 1979).

Another weakness of conflict theory is that it often overemphasizes the extent to which sport is controlled by those in positions of power in society. The people who control the media, sport facilities, and sport teams do have much to say about the conditions under which top level sport events are experienced and viewed by players and spectators alike. However, it is difficult to argue that all sport involvement is a result of the promotional efforts of capitalists or government bureaucrats. This is especially true when attention is shifted from professional level sport to sport at the local recreational level. Active sport participation generally occurs at levels where the interests of the participants themselves can be used as the basis for creating and developing programs.

Furthermore, certain sports have characteristics making them difficult to control by those who are not participants. Surfing is a good case in point; it does not lend itself to scheduling or television coverage, equipment needs are not extensive, and it does not generate much long-term spectator interest among those who have never been surfers. Therefore, the development of surfing and other similar sports has not been subject to heavy influence from outsiders whose main concerns are generating profits and creating sport spectacles.

SUMMARY AND CONCLUSION: WHO IS RIGHT?

Now that we have looked at the relationship between sport and society (see Table 4-1 for a review) from two different perspectives, which explanation is most correct? Is sport an inspiration or an opiate? I have found that the way people answer this question depends on what they think about the society in which sport exists. For example, those who are generally uncritical of American society will tend to agree with the functionalist approach when they look at sport in the United States. Those who are critical of American society will side with the conflict theorists. However, when the country in question is East Germany or China rather than the United States, some people may shift perspective. Those who do not agree with the way of life in East Germany or China will quickly become conflict theorists in their discussions of sport in these countries; those supportive of socialist systems will tend to become functionalists. It can be confusing to say that sport is an inspiration in one country and an opiate in another.

In order to eliminate some of the confusion on this issue, we need detailed research on how the structure of physical activities is related to the

TABLE 4-1 Functionalism and Conflict Theory: A Summary of Their Assumptions about the Social Order and Their Explanations of the Relationship between Sport and Society

Functionalist Approach	*Conflict Theory*
Assumptions about the Social Order	
Social order based on consensus, common values, and interrelated subsystems	Social order based on coercion, exploitation, and subtle manipulation of individuals
Major Concerns in the Study of Society	
What are the essential parts in structure of social system?	How is power distributed and used in society?
How do social systems continue to operate smoothly?	How do societies change and what can be done to promote change?
Major Concerns in the Study of Sport	
How does sport contribute to basic social system needs such as pattern maintenance and tension management, integration, goal attainment, and adaptation?	How does sport create personal alienation? How is sport used to control thoughts and behavior of people, and maintain economic and political systems serving interests of those in power?
Major Conclusions about the Sport-Society Relationship	
Sport is valuable secondary social institution benefiting society as well as individual members of society	Sport is distorted form of physical exercise shaped by needs of autocratic or production-conscious societies
Sport is basically a *source of inspiration* on personal and social level	Sport lacks creative and expressive elements of play; *it is an opiate*
Goals of Sport Sociology	
To discover ways in which sport's contribution to stability and maintenance of social order can be maximized at all levels	To promote development of humane and creative social order so that sport can be source of expression, creative experiences, and physical well-being
Major Weaknesses	
Assumes that existence and popularity of sport prove that it is serving positive functions	Assumes that structures and consequences of sport are totally determined by needs of political and economic order
Ignores possibility of internal differences and basic conflicts of interest within social systems and therefore assumes that sport serves needs of all system parts and individuals equally	Ignores factors other than capitalism in analyzing emergence and development of contemporary sport Focuses too much attention on top-level spectator sport and overemphasizes extent to which all sport involvement is controlled and structured by power elite

subjective experiences of participants (players and spectators). We also need to know how those experiences are related to attitudes and behavior patterns. We can assume that under certain circumstances, the consequences of sport will be constructive, and under other circumstances they will be destructive. Our task is to be able to clearly describe the circumstances under which these different consequences occur and to explain why they occur the way they do. This means that studies cannot be limited to specific countries or to specific groups of people. We need cross-cultural and comparative research focusing on all dimensions of the phenomenon of sport.

In developing research and exploring these issues we need to be aware of the ideas of both the functionalists and the conflict theorists. Each of their explanations of the relationship between sport and society alerts us to questions that must be asked and hypotheses that must be tested. Unless these and other theoretical perspectives are used our understanding of sport will be needlessly restricted.

Unfortunately, research will never be able to show us what the relationship between sport and society *should* be. It only alerts us to the possibilities and provides us with a starting point for shaping what it will be in the future.

NOTE

1. Although the focus in this [selection] is the United States, the pattern maintenance function of sport has been described in other countries, including the Soviet Union (Morton, 1963; Riordan, 1977), East Germany (Santomier and Ewees, 1979), China (Johnson, 1973; Chu and Segrave, 1979), Finland (Olin, 1979), Australia (Murray, 1979), and Samoa (Dunlap, 1951).

REFERENCES

Albonico, R. 1967. Modern University Sport as a Contribution to Social Integration. *International Review of Sport Sociology* 2:155-162.

Anderson, D., and G. P. Stone. 1979. A Fifteen-Year Analysis of Socio-Economic Strata Differences in the Meaning Given to Sport by Metropolitans. In M. L. Krotee, ed. *The Dimensions of Sport Sociology*. Leisure Press, West Point, N.Y.

Aronowitz, S. 1973. *False Promises*. McGraw-Hill, New York.

Bannister, F. T. 1980. Search for "White Hopes" Threatens Black Athletes. *Ebony* 34(4): 130-134.

Brockmann, D. 1969. Sport as an Integrating Factor in the Countryside. *International Review of Sport Sociology* 4:151-170.

Brohm, J-M. 1978. *Sport: A Prison of Measured Time*. Ink Links, London.

Bouet, M. 1969. Integrational Functions of Sport in the Light of Research Based on Questionnaires. *International Review of Sport Sociology* 4:129-134.

Chase, J. H. 1909. How a Director Feels. *Playground* 3(4):13.

Chu, D. B., and J. O. Segrave. 1979. Physical Culture in the People's Republic of China. *Journal of Sport Behavior* 2(3):119-135.

Csikszentmihalyi, M. 1975. *Beyond Boredom and Anxiety*. Jossey-Bass, San Francisco.

Dunlap, H. L. 1951. Games, Sports, Dancing, and Other Vigorous Recreational Activities and Their Function in Samoan Culture. *Research Quarterly* 22(3): 298-311.

Edwards, H. 1973. *Sociology of Sport.* Dorsey Press, Homewood, IL.

Eitzen, D. S., and G. H. Sage. 1978. *Sociology of American Sport.* Wm. C. Brown, Dubuque, IA.

Gerth, H., and C. W. Mills. 1953. *Character and Social Structure.* Harcourt Brace Jovanovich, New York.

Goodman, C. 1979. *Choosing Sides.* Schocken, New York.

Guttmann, A. 1978. *From Ritual to Record: The Nature of Modern Sports.* Columbia University Press, New York.

Hennig, M., and A. Jardim. 1977. *The Managerial Woman.* Anchor, New York.

Hoch, P. 1972. *Rip Off the Big Game.* Doubleday, New York.

Johnson, W. O. 1973. Faces on a New China Scroll. *Sports Illustrated* 39(14):42-67.

Kleiber, D. A., and J. R. Kelly. 1980. Leisure, Socialization and the Life Cycle. In S. Iso-Aloha, ed. *Social Psychological Perspectives on Leisure and Recreation.* Charles C. Thomas, Springfield, IL.

Lever, J. 1978. Sex Differences in the Complexity of Children's Play. *American Sociological Review* 43(4):471-483

Lever, J. 1980. Multiple Methods of Data Collection: A Note on Divergence. Unpublished manuscript.

Luschen, G. 1967. The Interdependence of Sport and Culture. *International Review of Sport Sociology* 2:127-139.

Marsh, P. 1978. Aggro: *The Illusion of Violence.* J. M. Dent, London.

Morton, H. W. 1963. *Soviet Sport.* Collier, New York.

Mumford, L. 1934. *Technics and Civilization.* Harcourt Brace Jovanovich, New York.

Murray, L. 1979. Some Ideological Qualities of Australian Sport. Australian Journal of Health, Physical Education and Recreation 73:7-10.

Olin, K. 1979. Sport, Social Development and Community Decision-Making. *International Review of Sport Sociology* 14(3-4):117-132.

Parsons, T., and N. J. Smelser. 1965. *Economy and Society.* The Free Press, New York.

Petryszak, N. 1978. Spectator Sports as an Aspect of Popular Culture—An Historical View. *Journal of Sport Behavior* 1(1):14-27.

Proctor, R. C., and W. M. Echard. 1976. "Toot-Toot" or Spectator Sports: Psychological and Therapeutic Implications. *American Journal of Sports Medicine* 4(2):78-83.

Riordan, J. 1977. *Sport in Soviet Society.* Cambridge University Press, New York.

Sadler, W. A. 1977. Alienated Youth and Creative Sports Experience. *Journal of the Philosophy of Sport* 4(Fall):83-95.

Santomier, J., and K. Ewees. 1979. Sport, Political Socialization and the German Democratic Republic. In M. L. Krotee, ed. *The Dimensions of Sport Sociology.* Leisure Press, West Point, N.Y.

Schafer, W. E. 1976. Sport and Youth Counterculture: Contrasting Socialization Themes. In D. M. Landers, ed. *Social Problems in Athletics.* University of Illinois Press, Urbana.

Sillitoe, K. 1969. *Planning for Leisure.* University of Keele, London.

Slusher, H. S. 1967. *Man, Sport and Existence.* Lea & Febiger, Philadelphia.

Spino, M. 1971. *Running as a Spiritual Experience.* In J. Scott, The Athletic Revolution. The Free Press, New York.

Vanderzwaag, H. J. 1972. *Toward a Philosophy of Sport.* Addison-Wesley, Reading, MA.

Wohl, A. 1970. Competitive Sport and Its Social Functions. *International Review of Sport Sociology* 5:117-124.

Wohl, A. 1979. Sport and Social Development. *International Review of Sport Sociology* 14(3-4):5-18.

■ FOR FURTHER STUDY

Eitzen, D. Stanley, and George H. Sage, *Sociology of North American Sport,* 5th ed. (Dubuque, Iowa: Brown and Benchmark, 1993).

Frey, James H., and D. Stanley Eitzen, "Sport and Society," *Annual Review of Sociology* 17 (1991):503-522.

"Functionalism Theory and Sport: Annotated Bibliography," *Sociology of Sport Journal* 8 (September 1991):299-305.

Gruneau, Richard, and David Whitson, *Hockey Night in Canada: Sport, Identities and Cultural Politics* (Toronto: Garamond Press, 1994).

Guttmann, Allen, *Sports Spectators* (New York: Columbia University Press, 1986).

Guttmann, Allen, *A Whole New Ball Game: An Interpretation of American Sports* (Chapel Hill: University of North Carolina Press, 1988).

Harris, Janet C., "Suited Up and Stripped Down: Perspectives for Sociocultural Sport Studies," *Sociology of Sport Journal* 6 (December 1989):335-347.

Harris, Janet C., *Athletes and the American Hero Dilemma* (Champaign, Illinois: Human Kinetics, 1994).

Hoch, Paul, *Rip Off the Big Game: The Exploitation of Sports by the Power Elite* (Garden City, New York: Doubleday Anchor, 1972).

Lever, Janet, *Soccer Madness* (Chicago: University of Chicago Press, 1983).

Nixon, Howard L., II, "Sport Sociology that Matters: Imperatives and Challenges for the 1990s," *Sociology of Sport Journal* 8 (September 1991):281-294.

Roberts, Randy, and James S. Olson, *Winning Is the Only Thing: Sports in America Since 1945* (Baltimore: Johns Hopkins University Press, 1989).

Sage, George H., *Power and Ideology in American Sport: A Critical Perspective* (Champaign, Illinois: Human Kinetics, 1990).

Young, T. R. (ed.), "Critical Perspectives on Sport," *Arena Review* 8 (November 1984).

Part Two

Sport and Socialization: Organized Sports

The involvement of young people in adult-supervised sport is characteristic of contemporary American society. Today, millions of boys and girls are involved in organized baseball, football, hockey, basketball, and soccer leagues. Others are involved in swimming, skating, golf, tennis, and gymnastics at a highly competitive level. School-sponsored sports begin about the seventh grade and are highly organized, win-oriented activities.

Why do so many parents in so many communities strongly support organized sports programs for youth? Primarily because most people believe that sports participation has positive benefits for those involved. The following quotation from *Time* summarizes this assumption.

> Sport has always been one of the primary means of civilizing the human animal, of inculcating the character traits a society desires. Wellington in his famous aphorism insisted that the Battle of Waterloo had been won on the playing fields of Eton. The lessons learned on the playing field are among the most basic: the setting of goals and joining with others to achieve them; an understanding of and respect for rules; the persistence to hone ability into skill, prowess into perfection. In games, children learn that success is possible and that failure can be overcome. Championships may be won; when lost, wait until next year. In practicing such skills as fielding a grounder and hitting a tennis ball, young athletes develop work patterns and attitudes that carry over into college, the marketplace and all of life.[1]

However, parents often ignore the negative side of sports participation, a position that is summarized by Charles Banham:

> It [the conventional argument that sport builds character] is not sound because it assumes that everyone will benefit from sport in the complacently prescribed

manner. A minority do so benefit. A few have the temperament that responds healthily to all the demands. These are the only ones able to develop an attractively active character. Sport can put fresh air in the mind, if it's the right mind; it can give muscle to the personality, if it's the right personality. But for the rest, it encourages selfishness, envy, conceit, hostility, and bad temper. Far from ventilating the mind, it stifles it. Good sportsmanship may be a product of sport, but so is bad sportsmanship.[2]

The problem is that sports produce positive and negative outcomes. This dualistic quality of sport is summarized by Terry Orlick:

> For every positive psychological or social outcome in sports, there are possible negative outcomes. For example, sports can offer a child group membership or group exclusion, acceptance or rejection, positive feedback or negative feedback, a sense of accomplishment or a sense of failure, evidence of self-worth or a lack of evidence of self-worth. Likewise, sports can develop cooperation and a concern for others, but they can also develop intense rivalry and a complete lack of concern for others.[3]

The first selection in this part, by sociologist Jay J. Coakley, describes the organized youth sports of today and compares them with the spontaneous games more characteristic of youth in previous generations. The second selection is an excerpt from H. G. Bissinger's book about football at Permian High School in Odessa, Texas. It demonstrates, forcefully, how football takes precedence over education in one high school.

The third selection, by D. Stanley Eitzen, examines the typical authority structure of athletic teams. He notes an interesting and important contradiction: Sports teams are undemocratic, resembling more what we did not like about Soviet-style societies than the democratic forms we claim to favor. This anomaly raises serious questions for sport in democracies.

The final selection, by sociologist Timothy Jon Curry, reports the findings from an ethnographic study of the men's locker room. What do young men learn in the locker room? What is promoted? What is denigrated? Curry found that the locker room is a place where young men "do gender." Heterosexuality, bravado, physical aggression, and affirmation of the traditional male role are valued and enhanced through the male bonding in locker rooms. Commonly, conversations in locker rooms involve sexual boasting, talk about women as sex objects, homophobic talk, and aggressive and hostile talk toward women. Thus, the peer culture of the locker room tends to channel behaviors and attitudes in ways that destroy human relationships and promote aggression toward "others." Curry concludes: "It is my view that sexist locker room talk is likely to have a cumulative negative effect on young men because it reinforces the notions of masculine privilege and hegemony, making that world view seem normal and typical. Moreover, it does so in a particularly pernicious fashion."

NOTES

1. "Comes the Revolution: Joining the Game at Last, Women Are Transforming American Athletics," *Time* (June 26, 1978): 55.
2. Charles Banham, "Man at Play," *Contemporary Review* 207 (August 1965): 62.
3. T. D. Orlick, "The Sports Environment: A Capacity to Enhance—A Capacity to Destroy," paper presented at the Canadian Symposium of Psycho-Motor Learning and Sports Psychology (1974), p. 2.

5. *Play Group versus Organized Competitive Team: A Comparison*

JAY J. COAKLEY

One way to begin to grasp the nature and extent of the impact of participation in sport is to try to understand the sport group as a context for the behavior and the relationships of youngsters. In a 1968 symposium on the sociology of sport, Gunther Luschen from the University of Illinois delivered a paper entitled "Small Group Research and the Group in Sport." While discussing the variety of different group contexts in which sport activities occur, he contrasted the spontaneously formed casual play group with the organized competitive team. He was primarily interested in the social organization and the amount of structural differentiation existing in sport groups in general, but some of his ideas give us a basis for comparing the characteristics of the spontaneous play group and the organized competitive Little League team in terms of their implications for youngsters. In general, any group engaging in competitive physical activity can be described in terms of the extent and complexity of its formal organization. Simply put, we can employ a continuum along which such groups could be located depending on how formally organized they are. Figure 5-1 illustrates this idea.

The spontaneous play group is an example of a context for competitive physical activities in which formal organization is absent. Its polar opposite is the sponsored competitive team in an organized league. It follows that the amount of formal organization has implications for the actions of group members, for their relationships with one another, and for the nature of their experiences. Table 5-1 outlines the characteristics of the two groups that would most closely approximate the polar extremes on the continuum.

Before going any further, I should point out that the two descriptions in Table 5-1 represent "ideal type" groups. In other words, the respective sets of characteristics represent hypothetical concepts that emphasize each group's most identifiable and important elements. Ideal types are necessarily extreme or exaggerated examples of the phenomenon under investigation and as such are to be used for purposes of comparison rather than as depictions of reality. Our concern here is to look at an actual group in which youngsters participate and to compare the actual group with the ideal types

SOURCE: "Play Group versus Organized Competitive Team: A Comparison" by Jay J. Coakley. From *Sport in Society: Issues and Controversies* by Jay J. Coakley. Copyright © 1978 by C. V. Mosby. Reprinted by permission.

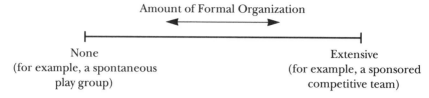

Amount of Formal Organization

None
(for example, a spontaneous
play group)

Extensive
(for example, a sponsored
competitive team)

FIGURE 5-1   A Formal Organization Continuum for Groups in Competitive Physical Activities

TABLE 5-1   Comparison of Two Groups

The Spontaneous Play Group: No Formal Organization	*The Sponsored Competitive Team: High Formal Organization*
Action is an outgrowth of the interpersonal relationships and of the decision-making processes of participating members.	Action is an outgrowth of a predesignated system of role relationships and of the role-learning abilities of group members.
Rewards are primarily intrinsic and are a function of the experience and the extent of the interpersonal skills of the group members.	Rewards are primarily extrinsic and are a function of the combined technical skills of group members.
Meanings attached to actions and situations are emergent and are subject to changes over time.	Meanings are predominantly predefined and are relatively static from one situation to the next.
Group integration is based on the process of exchange between group members.	Group integration is based on an awareness of and conformity to a formalized set of norms.
Norms governing action are emergent, and interpretation is variable.	Norms are highly formalized and specific, with variability resulting from official judgments.
Social control is internally generated among members and is dependent on commitment.	Social control is administered by an external agent and is dependent on obedience.
Sanctions are informal and are directly related to the maintenance of action in the situation.	Sanctions are formal and are related to the preservation of values as well as order.
Individual freedom is high, with variability a function of the group's status structure.	Individual freedom is limited to the flexibility tolerated within role expectations.
Group is generally characterized by structural instability.	Group is generally characterized by structural stability.

in order to make an assessment of what the real group might be like as a context for experience. Of course, the real group will not be an exact replica of either of the ideal types, but will more or less resemble one or the other.

GETTING THE GAME STARTED

The characteristics of each group suggest that the differences between the spontaneous play group and the organized competitive team would be quite apparent as soon as initial contact between the participants occurs. In the spontaneous play group, we might expect that the majority of time would be spent on dealing with organizational problems such as establishing goals, defining means to those goals, and developing expectations of both a general and a specific nature for each of the participants. Being a member of a *completely* spontaneous play group would probably be similar to being involved in the initial organizational meeting of a group of unacquainted college freshmen who are supposed to come up with a class project. Both would involve a combination of some fun, a good deal of confusion, much talking, and little action. For the context of the organized competitive team, we might imagine a supervisor (coach) blowing a whistle that brings a group of preselected youngsters of similar ages and abilities running to fall into a routine formation to await an already known command. This would resemble a "brave new world" of sport where there would be some action, a good deal of listening to instructions, much routinization, and little fun. Fortunately, most group contexts for youngsters' sport participation fall somewhere between these two extremes. The trick is, of course, to find which points on the continuum would have a maximization of both fun and action along with the other characteristics seen as most beneficial to the young participants' development.

From my observations of youngsters in backyards, gyms, parks, and playgrounds, I have concluded that, for the most part, they are quite efficient in organizing their sport activities. The primary organizational details are often partially worked out by physical setting, available equipment, and time of the year, all of which influence the choice of activity and the form the activity will take. To the extent that the participants know one another and have played with each other before, there will be a minimum amount of time devoted to formation of norms—rules from previous games can be used. But despite the ability of most youngsters to get a competitive physical activity going, there seems to be a tendency for adults to become impatient with some of the "childish" disagreements of the young participants. Adults often become impatient because they do not understand the youngsters' "distortions" of the games—games the adults know are supposed to be played another way. Adults who want to teach youngsters to play the game the *right way* and to help young players avoid disagreements and discussions in order to build up more action time seem to be everywhere. These adults see a very clear need for organization, that is, establishing regular practice times, scheduling contests, and giving positive rewards and encouragement to those whose performances are seen as deserving. Although their motives may be commendable, these adults usually fail to consider all of the differences between the informally organized group and the formally organized team.

Most importantly, the game in the park is in the control of the youngsters themselves, whereas the organized competitive team is supervised and controlled by adults. In the play group, getting the game under way depends on the group members being able to communicate well enough to make organizational decisions and to evoke enough cooperation so that a sufficient amount of the group's behavior is conducive to the achievement of the goals of the game, however they have been defined. In this situation, interpersonal skills are crucial, and youngsters will probably be quick to realize that playing the game depends on being able to develop and maintain positive relationships or, at least, learning to cope with interpersonal problems in a way that will permit cooperative action. This constitutes a valuable set of experiences that become less available to participants as the amount of the group's formal organization increases. It is a rare adult coach who allows youngsters to make many decisions on how the game should be organized and played. In fact, most decisions have been made for the coach; the availability of the practice field has been decided, the roles defined, the rules made, the sanctions outlined, the team colors picked, the games scheduled, etc. Occasionally the players are allowed to vote on their team name, but that happens only if the team is new and does not already have one. In all, *the emphasis in the organized setting is on the development of sport skills, not on the development of interpersonal skills.*

PLAY OF THE GAME

Differences between the two groups do not disappear once the game begins. For the spontaneous play group, the game experience is likely to be defined as an end in itself, whereas for the organized team, the game is a means to an end. In the play group, the game is unlikely to have implications beyond the setting in which it occurs, and the participants are primarily concerned with managing the situation so that *action* can be preserved for as long as possible. To this end, it is quite common for the participating youngsters to develop sets of norms accompanied by rather complex sets of qualifications and to establish handicaps for certain participants. These tactics serve to compensate for skill differences and to ensure that the game proceeds with scores close enough so that excitement and satisfaction can be maximized for as many of the players as possible. For example, if one of the pitchers in an informal baseball game were bigger or stronger than the rest of the youngsters, he/she would be required to pitch the ball with "an arch on it" to minimize the ball's speed and to allow all the batters a chance to hit it. Exceptionally good batters might be required to bat left-handed (if they were right-handed) to minimize the chances of hitting a home run every time they came to bat. A youngster having a hard time hitting the ball might be given more than three strikes, and the pitcher might make a special effort to "put the ball over the plate" so that the batter would have a good chance of hitting the ball rather than striking out. Since a strikeout is a relatively unexciting event in a game where the primary goal is the involvement of all players, one of the most frequently made comments directed to the pitcher by his/her teammates in the field is "C'mon, let 'em hit it!"

Similar examples of norm qualifications and handicap systems can be found in other sport groups characterized by a low degree of formal organization. Sometimes these little adaptations can be very clever, and, of course, some participants have to be warned if they seem to be taking unfair advantage of them. This may occur in cases where a young player tends to call time-outs whenever the opposition has his team at a disadvantage or when someone begins to overuse an interference or a "do-over" call to nullify a mistake or a failure to make a play. Although the system of qualifications and handicaps may serve to allow the participants to have another chance when they make mistakes and to avoid the embarrassment associated with a relative lack of skills, the major function of such systems seems to be to equalize not only the players, but also the teams competing against one another. Through such techniques, scores will remain close enough that neither team will give up and destroy the game by quitting. In a sense, the players make an attempt to control the competition so that the fun of all will be safeguarded. Adults do the same thing when given the chance. None of us enjoys being overwhelmed by an opponent or overcoming an opponent so weak that we never had to make an effort.

For the formally organized competitive team, however, the play of the game may be considerably different. The goal of victory or the promotion of the team's place in the league standings replaces the goal of maximizing individual participant satisfaction. The meanings and rewards attached to the game are largely a function of how the experience is related to a desired outcome—either victory or "a good show." Players may even be told that a good personal performance is almost always nullified by a team defeat and that to feel satisfied with yourself without a team victory is selfish (as they say in the locker room, "There is no 'u' in team" or "Defeat is worse than death because you have to live with defeat").

Since victories are a consequence of the combined skills of the team members, such skills are to be practiced and improved and then utilized in ways that maximize the chances for team success. Granting the other team a handicap is quite rare unless any chance for victory is out of their grasp. If this is the case, the weaker players may be substituted in the lineup of the stronger team *unless*, of course, a one-sided score will serve the purpose of increasing the team's prestige or intimidating future opponents.

Also, if one player's skill level far exceeds that of the other participants, that player will often be used where he can be most effective. In the Little League game, it is frequently the bigger youngster with the strongest arm who is made the pitcher. This may help to ensure a team's chances for victory, but it also serves to nearly eliminate the rest of the team's chances for making fielding plays and for being involved in the defensive play of the game. In a 6-inning game, the fact that a large number of the 18 total outs for the opponents come as strikeouts means that a number of fielders may never have a chance to even touch the ball while they are out in the field. A similar thing happens in football. The youth-league team often puts its biggest and strongest players in the backfield rather than in the line. The game then consists of giving those youngsters the ball on nearly every play. For the smaller players on the defensive team, the primary task may be getting out of the way of the runner to avoid being stepped on. Thus on the organized team, intimidation may become a part of playing strategy. Unfortunately, intimidation increases apprehension and inhibits some of the action in the game as well as the involvement of some of the players. Generally, it seems that on the organized team the tendency to employ the skills of the players to win games takes precedence over devising handicaps to ensure fun and widespread participation.

One way to become aware of some of the differences between the informal play group and the formally organized competitive team is to ask the participants in each group the scores of their games. In the formally organized setting, the scores are often one-sided with members of the winning team even boasting about how they won their last football game 77 to 6, their last baseball game 23 to 1, or their last soccer game 14 to 0. Such scores lead me to question the amount of fun had by the players. In the case of the losers, it would be rare to find players who would be able to maintain an interest in a game when they are so completely beaten. If the winners say they enjoyed themselves, the lesson they may be learning through such an experience should be seriously questioned. It may be that the major lesson is if your opponents happen to be weak, take advantage of that weakness so totally that they will never be able to make a comeback. Such experiences, instead of instilling positive relationships and a sincere interest in sport activities, are apt to encourage distorted assessments of self-worth and to turn youngsters off to activities that, in modified forms, could provide them with years of enjoyment.

In addition to the differences in how the game is organized and how the action is initiated, there are also differences in how action for the two groups is maintained. In the informally organized group, the members are held together through the operation of some elementary processes of exchange that, in a sense, serve as the basis for the participants obtaining what they think they deserve out of the experience (Polgar, 1976). When the range of abilities is great, the older, bigger, more talented participants have to compromise some of their abilities so that the younger, smaller, and less talented will have a chance to gain the rewards necessary to continue playing. The play of the game depends on maintaining a necessary level of commitment among all participants. This commitment then serves as a basis for social control during the action. Although there are some exceptions, those in the group with the highest combined skill and social prestige levels act as leaders and serve as models of normal behavior. For these individuals to deviate from the norms in any consistent manner would most likely earn them the reputation of being cheaters or bad sports. In fact, consistent deviation from the group norms by any of the participants is likely to be defined by the others as disruptive, and the violator will be reminded of his/her infraction through some type of warning or through a threat of future exclusion from group activities. When sanctions are employed in the informal play group, they usually serve an instrumental function—they bring behavior in line so that the game can continue. Sanctions are usually not intended to reinforce status distinctions, to preserve an established social structure, or to safeguard values and principles. Interestingly, self-enforcement of norms in the play group is usually quite effective. Deviation is not totally eliminated, but it is kept within the limits necessary to preserve action in the game. The emphasis is not so much on keeping norms sacred, but on making sure that the norms serve to maintain the goal of action. In fact, norms may change or be reinterpreted for specific individuals or in specific situations so that the level of action in the play activities can be maximized. The importance of maintaining a certain level of action is demonstrated by the informal sanctions directed at a participant who might always be insisting on too rigid an enforcement of norms. This is the person who continually cries "foul" or who always spots a penalty. To be persistent in such a hard-nosed approach to norm enforcement will probably earn the player the nonendearing reputation of being a baby, a crier, or a complainer.

In the informally organized play group, the most disruptive kind of deviant is the one who does not care about the game. It is interesting that the group will usually tolerate any number of different performance styles, forms, and individual innovations as long as they do not destroy action. Batting left-handed when one is right-handed is okay if the batter is at least likely to hit the ball, thus keeping the action going. Throwing behind-the-back passes and trying a crazy shot in basketball or running an unplanned pass pattern in football are all considered part of the game in the play group *if action is not destroyed.* Joking around will frequently be tolerated and sometimes even encouraged *if action can continue.* But if such behavior moves beyond the level of seriousness required to maintain satisfying action for all the participants, commitment decreases, and the group is likely to dissolve. In line with this, usually those participants with the highest amount of skill are allowed the greatest amount of freedom to play "as the spirit moves them." Although such behavior may seem to indicate a lack of seriousness to the outsider, the skill of the player is developed enough to avoid a "disruptive" amount of mistakes. At the same time, such freedom gives high-ability participants a means through which their interest level can be maintained. Similar free-wheeling behavior by a low-ability participant would be viewed with disfavor, since the behavior would frequently bring the action level below what would be defined as acceptable by the rest of the group.

In contrast to the play group, the maintenance of action on the formally organized team depends on an initial commitment to playing as a part of the team. This commitment then serves as a basis for learning and conforming to a preestablished set of norms.[1] The norms apply equally to everyone, and control is administered through the coach–supervisor. Regardless of how priorities are set with respect to goals, goal achievement rests primarily on obedience to the coach's directives rather than on the generation of personal interests based on mutually satisfying social exchange processes. Within the structure of the organized competitive team, deviation from the norms is defined as serious not only when it disrupts action, but also when it *could* have been disruptive or when it somehow challenges the organized structure through which action occurs. Thus sanctions take on a value-supportive function as well as an instrumental function. This is demonstrated by the coaches who constantly worry about their own authority, that is, whether they command the respect of their players.

In the interest of developing technical skills, the norms for the formally organized competitive team restrict not only the range of a player's action, but also the form of such actions. Unique batting, throwing, running, shooting, or kicking styles must be abandoned in the face of what the coach considers to be correct form. Joking around on the part of any team member is usually not tolerated regardless of the player's abilities, and the demonstration of skills is usually limited to the fundamentals of the game.

If commitment cannot be maintained under these circumstances, players are often not allowed to quit. They may be told by the coach that "We all have to take our bumps to be part of a team" or "Quitters never win and winners never quit." Parents may also point out that "Once you join a team, it is your duty to stick it out for the whole season" or "We paid our money for you to play the whole season; don't waste what we've given you." With this kind of feedback, even a total absence of personal commitment to the sport activity may not lead to withdrawal from participation. What keeps youngsters going is a commitment to personal honor and integrity or obedience to a few significant people in their lives.

WHEN THE GAME IS OVER: MEANING AND CONSEQUENCES

The implications of the game after completion are different for the members of the informal play group than they are for the members of the formally organized competitive team. For the latter, the game goes on record as a win or a loss. If the score was close, both winners and losers may initially qualify the outcome in terms of that closeness.[2] But, as other games are played, all losses and wins are grouped respectively regardless of the closeness of scores. In the informal play group, the score of a game may be discussed while walking home; however, it is usually forgotten quickly and considered insignificant in light of the actions of individual players. Any feelings of elation that accompany victory or of let-down that accompany defeat are shortlived in the play group—you always begin again on the next day, in the next game, or with the next activity. For the organized competitive team, such feelings are less transitory and are often renewed at some future date when there is a chance to avenge a previous loss or to show that a past victory was not just a fluke. Related to this is the fact that the organized team is usually geared to winning, with the coaches and players always reminding themselves, in the Norman Vincent Peale tradition, that "We can win . . . if we only play like we can." This may lead to defining victories as the expected outcomes of games and losses as those outcomes that occur when you do not perform as you are able. When this happens, the elation and satisfaction associated with winning can be buried by the determination to win the next one, the next one, and so on. Losses, however, are not so quickly put away. They tend to follow you as a reminder of past failures to accomplish what you could have if you had executed your collective skills properly. The element of fun in such a setting is of only minor importance and may be eliminated by the seriousness and determination associated with the activity.

The final difference between the two groups is related to the stability of each. The informal play group is characteristically unstable, whereas the opposite is true of the organized team. If minimal levels of commitment cannot be maintained among some members of the play group, the group may simply dissolve. Dissolution may also result from outside forces. For example, since parents are not involved in the organization of the play group, they may not go out of their way to plan for their youngster's participation by delaying or arranging family activities around the time of the group's existence. When a parent calls a youngster home, the entire group may be in serious jeopardy. Other problems that contribute to instability are being told that you cannot play in the street, that someone's yard is off limits, that park space is inaccessible, or that necessary equipment is broken or unavailable. These problems usually do not exist for the organized team. Consent by parents almost guarantees the presence of a player at a scheduled practice or game, space and equipment are reserved in advance, and substitute players are available when something happens to a regular team member. Because the team is built around a structure of roles rather than a series of interacting persons, players can be replaced without serious disruption, and the action can continue.

NOTES

1. In some cases, "commitment" may not be totally voluntary on the part of the player. Parents may sign up a son or daughter without the youngster's full consent or may, along with peers, subtly coerce the youngster to play.
2. Such qualifications are, of course, used for different effects. Winners use them to show that their challengers were able or that victory came under pressure. Losers use them to show how close they came to victory.

6. *High School Football and Academics*

H. G. BISSINGER

I

If school was boring, Don Billingsley nevertheless did his best to get through it. When the food science teacher made the fatal mistake of asking the class if it knew the meaning of the word *condiment*, Don immediately answered with "lambskin, sheepskin." All joking aside, Don was becoming something of a food science scholar. He had scored a superb 99 on the fill-in-the-blank worksheet on cakes and frostings, not to mention a 96 on his poultry worksheet. The "preparation and service" worksheet was coming a little more slowly; he had gotten only a 60, but there seemed little doubt that Don would eventually get a handle on it. And, of course, when the occasion arose to write out a menu for a black-tie dinner party in Odessa, he would know exactly what to do.

In English, where one of the blackboard panels had a list of questions about *Macbeth* and another a reminder to bring a flashlight to the pep rally, Don had uncovered one of the great secrets of the class with the discovery that if he angled his chair in a certain way behind the other students, the teacher could not see him fall asleep. "Do you like to sleep? This is where I sleep," he said just before he entered the classroom.

A worksheet was due that day deciphering the meaning of some lines from *Macbeth*, and Don was handed a copy of the homework by someone else so he could copy down the answers. The class time was supposed to be spent doing a little crossword puzzle on the play, but Don didn't do much of it and it didn't seem to matter. The instructor for her part believed that the text the students used, *Adventures in English Literature*, which contained selected works by Shakespeare, Edmund Spenser, and Daniel Defoe among others, was too hard for them. She said also that they absolutely hated any assignment in which they had to interpret what they had read. If they had to think about anything, make critical judgments and deliberations, the cause was hopeless. The best they could be expected to do was regurgitate.

SOURCE: "High School Football and Academics" by H. G. Bissinger. From *Friday Night Lights* (pp. 134–148). Copyright © 1980 by H. G. Bissinger. Reprinted by permission of Addison-Wesley Publishing, Inc.

In sociology, Don generously passed around his bag of cookies. He and the other students watched eagerly as accounts of one gruesome murder after another passed over the tiny VCR screen, accompanied by the hushed melodrama of Geraldo Rivera. The teacher gave no instruction the entire period, except to applaud the actions of a man who, in broad daylight at an airport, killed a manacled criminal suspect accused of molesting the man's son.

Don, of course, was a football player, which gave him special status among his peers regardless of how he performed in class. In the hierarchy of the school, where girls and partying and clothes and fancy cars were as important as academics, being a football player opened doors that other students could only dream of. All other achievements seemed to pale in the face of it.

Eddie Driscoll, a wonderfully articulate student ranked number two in the senior class, loved to read and debate and throw out ideas. He stood out in class like a sore thumb. There were some who admired him and others who considered him a pompous windbag. Despite all his academic accomplishments, Eddie himself often wondered what it would be like to sit in those two rows at the front of the pep rally each Friday in a brotherhood as supremely elite as Skull and Bones at Yale or the Porcellian Club at Harvard. Such musings didn't make him resentful of the football players; he liked them. He just felt a little envious. No matter how many books he read, no matter how exquisite his arguments in government class about gun control or the Sandinistas or the death penalty, he never got the latest scoop on who was having the weekend parties. Only the football players were privy to that sacred knowledge.

"The football identity is so glorious," he said. "I always wondered what it would have been like if I had been a football player. I think it would be great to be in the limelight and be part of the team, have a geisha girl bring me candy three times a day."

Roqui Pearce, who had graduated from Permian in 1988 and was going out with starting defensive cornerback Coddi Dean, said there was definitely a mystique in the school about dating a Permian football player. "Everybody's into football. Football is *the* sport. I wouldn't say it's an honor or anything but it's looked up to: 'Wow, you're going out with a football player, a Permian football player.'"

Roqui had been chosen a Pepette her senior year. Lots were drawn to see which player each Pepette would be assigned to for the season. Some of the players were obnoxious and egotistical, but Roqui didn't really mind as long as it was a football player she got and not one of the student trainers. "Nobody wants a trainer. You want a football player."

She had ended up being assigned to Coddi, who was then a junior. At the Watermelon Feed that year, she hadn't worn his number on her jersey, which angered him. But they hit it off well. "I liked him, plus I wanted to be a real good Pepette. I didn't want him to think I was a bad Pepette. I wanted to be a good Pepette." She brought Coddi an ice cream cake in the shape of a football field from Baskin-Robbins. She baked him cakes and brownies. She got him a black trash can and filled it with popcorn balls. She gave him a towel and pillowcase decorated with the insignia of Mojo and Texas. After several months they went on a date and then started going out steadily.

From time to time the role of the Pepette became controversial. A stinging editorial in the school newspaper, the *Permian Press*, applauded a new rule prohibiting Pepettes from placing candy in players' lockers every Friday. "Though losing a tradition, Pepettes have gained much respect," said the editorial. "No longer will a member be the personal Geisha girl of a player. Instead, she can focus more on the organization's original purpose, boosting morale. And in so doing she will carry the image of professionalism she deserves for her work bolstering the famous Mojo spirit." But the Pepettes still spent time baking players cookies and making them signs. Since they could no longer put goodies in the lockers of the players, they just handed the stuff to them instead or dropped it off at their houses.

Their role was symptomatic of the role all girls played at Permian. "You hate to admit it in this day and time, but a lot of girls are conditioned towards liberal arts courses rather than engineering and science," said Callie Tave, who found herself perpetually buried under a blizzard of forms and recommendation requests since she was the only college counselor for the seven-hundred-member senior class.

The attitude that girls at Permian seemed to have about themselves was reflected during an economics class one day when Dorothy Fowler, a spirited and marvelous teacher, tried to wake students up to the realities of the world in West Texas where the days of the fat-paying blue-collar job were over.

"Think about your jobs. Where do you want to be in five years?" asked Fowler of a female student.

"Rich," the student replied.

"How are you going to achieve that?"

"Marry someone."

On the SAT exam, boys who took the test during 1988-89 at Permian had a combined average score of 915 (433 verbal, 482 mathematical), 19 points below the national average for boys. Girls had a combined score of 840 (404 verbal, 436 mathematical), 75 points below their male counterparts at Permian and 35 points below the national average for girls. Of the 132 girls who took the test during the 1988-89 school year, there wasn't one who got above a 650 in either the math or verbal portion of the exam.

"It's very revered to be a Pepette or a cheerleader," said Julie Gardner, who had come to Odessa from a small college town in Montana as a sophomore. "It's the closest they can get to being a football player." Gardner found the transition to Permian enormously difficult. She was utterly unprepared for her first pep rally, for all those fanatical cheers, all those arms pumping so frantically up and down, and she found the girls cliquey and obsessed with appearance. At first she dressed up like everyone else, but then she began to reject it. And because she was intelligent (she graduated from Permian in 1986 and went on to become an honors English major at Swarthmore College), she also felt ostracized.

"It was very important to have a boyfriend and look a certain way. You couldn't be too smart. You had to act silly or they put you in a category right away. It was the end of your social life if you were an intelligent girl." The pressure to conform was so intense, said Gardner, that she knew girls who privately were quite intelligent and articulate, but were afraid to show it publicly because of the effect it would have on their social lives.

Her father, H. Warren Gardner, vice president of the University of Texas of the Permian Basin, a branch of the University of Texas system located in Odessa, believed the disparities in performance between boys and girls were a result of the social hierarchy of the school. Gardner said it was clear to him that girls had to "dumb down" at Permian or else run the risk of being excluded from dating and parties because the boys considered them too smart. "It's not appropriate [for a girl] to be intelligent," he concluded. "It's not popular to be bright."

And being a Pepette, despite the restriction making candy off-limits to the locker room, still carried status. "I hate football players, especially at Permian," said senior Shauna Moody. "They're the most egotistical . . . they think they're God's gift." But for a girl at Permian, the only thing worse than being a Pepette was not being one. Or as Moody explained her own reasoning for having joined, "Well, *everybody's* a Pepette."

Cheerleading had a special cachet for girls at Permian as well. Just as the football players walked down the school halls in their game jerseys on Fridays, so did the cheerleaders in their uniforms. There were five girls on the cheerleading squad, all of them white, and they had enormous visibility.

The most popular of them was Bridgitte Vandeventer, who had always wanted to be a cheerleader. "Everyone knew who Permian was and who Mojo was, and I thought it would be neat to be a Permian cheerleader," said Bridgitte, who had lived with her grandparents since she was eight.

The most wonderful moment of her life, she said, was being crowned Homecoming Queen, and she had vivid memories of it–changing from her cheerleading uniform into a black velvet dress, wearing a fantastic spread of mums adorned with black and white streamers and trinkets in the shape of little footballs that one of the players had given her, dutifully waiting in line with the other finalists at halftime and then hearing her name called, holding the hand of her best friend as she walked around the oval of the stadium with tears in her eyes, receiving four dozen red roses afterward from admirers. Because of her status at school and her friendliness, she had no lack of them.

For a while she went out with Brian Chavez, and it was hard not to feel proud when she saw him on the football field. "It was neat to say, that's my boyfriend out there, that's who I'm dating. The time Brian scored a touchdown, I was never so excited. . . ."

Brian was Hispanic, but that didn't make her uncomfortable. "My grandmother says, 'whites are for whites, Hispanics are for Hispanics, blacks are for blacks.' I don't think blacks are for whites, whites for blacks. I think Hispanics are fine because they're as close to whites as you can get."

She had many ambitions for her life. She wanted to go into the medical field. She wanted to be Miss Universe. She wanted to open a dance studio. She wanted to be famous. She wanted to write a book about her life.

But for the immediate future, her plans included going to the junior college in town, Odessa College. A main reason she was going there was her failure to take the college boards, a requirement for admission at most four-year schools. Bridgitte said she had been advised by a teacher at Permian not to take the SAT exam until after the football season because of her myriad duties as a cheerleader. But she didn't seem upset about it, and one thing was obvious—her popularity at school was unrivaled. Not only was she crowned Homecoming Queen, she was also voted Miss PHS by her classmates. Clearly she was a role model.

"I just want to be known," said Bridgitte in summing up her hopes in life. "I want everybody to know me, but not in a bad way. My dream is to be known, to be successful, and to help people. I love to help people."

"I look forward to getting out on my own and tryin' the world. They say it's a real rat race and I hope to win it."

With his dark, pouty looks, it was hard not to think of Don Billingsley as a movie star when he walked down the halls of Permian, gently fending off female admirers in his black football jersey, except for those two or three or four or five who seemed to have a certain special something. The way he talked to them, with his head ducked low and the words coming out in a sweet, playful cadence, suggested a certain self-recognition of his aura. Sophomore girls fantasized over having him in the same class so they could catch a glimpse of his buttocks in a tight-fitting pair of jeans. He received inquiries about his availability for stripteases. The characterization used by girl after girl to describe him was the same, said with the wistfulness of irrepressible infatuation: "He's so fine!"

Aware of his image as the best-looking guy at Permian and fortunate enough not to have school interfere with the responsibilities that came with such a title, much of his day was spent flirting either silently with his eyes or with his benign naughtiness in the classroom. He might not be learning anything, but school was a blast and everywhere he looked he was fending off girls—the one who sat behind him in government and wanted a relationship (Don had to explain to her gently but firmly that he didn't "do" relationships), the one who sat behind him in food science (he went out with her for a while but it wasn't what he was looking for), the one who came up to him in the hallway.

Then there was the girl who had been dubbed the "book bitch." So desperate was she to ingratiate herself with the football players that she bought one of them a brand-new backpack and then offered him fifty dollars to sleep with her. When that didn't work, she offered to bring the books of several of them to class. Dutifully, she waited in the hallway, whereupon Don and some others loaded her down with books so she could trudge off to class with them with a slightly chagrined smile on her face, as if she knew that what she was doing was the price you paid for trying to gain the acceptance of the football players when you had blemishes on your face and didn't look like Farrah Fawcett.

Don was clearly not motivated to be a scholar. His class rank at Permian going into his senior year was the second lowest of any senior on the football team, 480 out of 720. He reveled in playing the Sean Penn role in his own version of *Fast Times at Ridgemont High*, but beneath all that was a witty, personable kid. During the fall he was voted Mr. PHS, an honor that delighted his classmates and stunned the hell out of his teachers and coaches. The nondemanding, lethargic nature of the classes he was in made it difficult to fault his attitude about school. Left to his own devices, he did what any high school senior in America would do: he took advantage of it.

Asked what the purpose of school was at Permian, Don had a simple answer. "Socializing," he said candidly. "That's all senior year is good for." That, and playing football. If there was any angst about school, it was over the number of girls who desired to spend at least some part of their lives with him. They were everywhere. Girls in short leather skirts. Girls in expensive designer jeans. Girls who spent the last five minutes of class carefully applying rouge and lipstick to their faces because the teacher had run out of things to say. The perplexity of it all gnawed at him a great deal more than the meaning of *Macbeth*. Or as he put it in a line probably not inspired by Shakespeare's play, "There's so much skin around, it's hard to pick out one."

There were other football players who had light schedules. One of his teammates, Jerrod McDougal, had taken senior English the previous summer so that he wouldn't have to grapple with it during the football season. There was something wonderfully soulful about Jerrod. He was unusually sensitive and spoke with pained and poignant sorrow about the confusion of growing up in a world, in an America, that seemed so utterly different from the one that had spawned the self-made success of his father. His class rank was in the top third, but because of football Jerrod wanted as little challenge as possible his senior year. With English out of the way, he was taking government and the electives of sociology, computer math, photography, and food science.

"That's why I took all my hard courses my sophomore and junior year, so I wouldn't have to worry about any of that stuff," he said one afternoon after food science, where Billingsley and he had just spent sixty minutes on a worksheet containing 165 fill-in-the-blanks on the uses of a microwave. "Maybe that's a bad deal. I don't know."

Permian's best and brightest, those ranked in the top ten, reported few demands made of them in the classroom as well. Eddie Driscoll, who would end up attending Oberlin College, said he had never been pushed at Permian and generally had half an hour's worth of homework a night. Scott Crutchfield, another gifted student ranked in the top ten who would end up going to Duke, said he had two to three hours of homework a week. "I think I'd probably learn more if I had to do more work. As it is, I still learn a lot, I guess. In general, I don't do a lot."

II

In computer science, Brian Chavez wore faded blue jeans and black Reeboks. The number 85 jersey around his expansive chest nicely matched his earring with the numeral 85 embossed in gold. He had a fleshy face in need of a shave and his hair looked a little like that of a main character in *Eraserhead,* high and square on top like an elevated putting surface. It came as no surprise that he held the Permian record for the bench press with 345 pounds.

The way he looked, five eleven and 215 pounds, the way he loved to hit on a football field, the way the words came so slowly out of his mouth sometimes as if he had a two-by-four stuck in there somewhere, it was hard to think he had any chance of making it past high school unless he got a football scholarship somewhere.

He fit every stereotype of the dumb jock, all of which went to show how absolutely meaningless stereotypes can be. He was a remarkable kid from a remarkable family, inspired by his father, whose own upbringing in the poverty of El Paso couldn't have been more different.

Ranked number one in his class at Permian, he moved effortlessly between the world of the football and the academic elite. On the field he was a demon, with a streak of nastiness that every coach loved to see in a football player. Off the field he was quiet, serene, and smart as a whip, his passivity neatly hiding an astounding determination to succeed. "He's two different people," Winchell [the team quarterback] said of him. "He's got a split personality when he puts on that helmet."

From computer science he made his way to honors calculus, where a black balloon from the Friday pep rally floated casually from his knapsack. On the way there he was handed a note by Bridgitte that read, "Have fun at lunch and I either will see you before lunch or after lunch. Okay! Smile! Love you!" In calculus class he casually scribbled his answers in a white notebook, an exercise that seemed as mentally strenuous to him as trying to see whether he still remembered the alphabet. While others strained and fretted he just seemed to glide, and inevitably several classmates gathered around him to watch him produce the right answer. After calculus it was off to honors physics and then honors English and then honors chemistry. These courses came easily to him as well. Part of that had to do with what was asked of him—with the exception of English, he said he had almost no homework.

If he wasn't a typical brain filled with anguish and neurosis, he wasn't a typical Permian football player either. He was lucky, but he always knew in the back of his mind that if he failed in football it didn't really matter anyway.

He had become as indoctrinated into the cult of football in Odessa as anyone. After all, it was something he had lived, eaten, and breathed since seventh grade. But as he headed into his senior year he also realized that he wanted something more. No matter how glorious and exciting the season was, he also knew it would come to an end.

In his own private way, he found far more inspiration in the classroom than he did on the football field. And nowhere did he seem more determined than in English class, under the spell of a special teacher named LaRue Moore.

She saw in him a metamorphosis his senior year, a fascination with vocabulary and literature and trying to write essays with perception and clarity. He was striving for something she hadn't quite seen before, and when he told her he was interested in going to Harvard she joyously encouraged him as much as she could and agreed to read his application essays.

It was simply part of her style. Whenever she could, she tried to show students the bountiful world that existed past the corporate limits of Odessa and how they should not be intimidated by it but eager and confident to become a part of it. On five different occasions, she and her husband, Jim, the former principal of Ector High School before it closed, had taken students to Europe to let them see other cultures, other lands. What she aspired to as a teacher was embodied by a written description she prepared of her senior honors English class for a group of observers:

> I work not only for the gathering and assimilation of knowledge, but also to teach the fact that one can be brilliant without being arrogant, that great intellectual capacity brings great responsibility, that the quest for knowledge should never supplant the joy of learning, that one with great capacities must learn to be tolerant and appreciate those with lesser or different absolutes, and that these students can compete with any students at any university anyplace in the world.

A teacher such as LaRue Moore should have been considered a treasure in any town. Her salary, commensurate with her ability and skill and twenty years' teaching experience, should have been $50,000 a year. Her department, of which she was the chairman, should have gotten anything it wanted. She herself should have been given every possible encouragement to continue what she was doing. But none of that was the case, of course.

After all, she was just the head of the English department, a job that in the scheme of natural selection at Permian ranked well behind football coach and band director, among others.

As Moore put it, "The Bible says, where your treasure is, that's where your heart is also." She maintained that the school district budgeted more for medical supplies like athletic tape for athletic programs at Permian than it did for teaching materials for the English department, which covered everything except for required textbooks. Aware of how silly that sounded, she challenged the visitor to look it up.

She was right. The cost for boys' medical supplies at Permian was $6,750. The cost for teaching materials for the English department was $5,040, which Moore said included supplies, maintenance of the copying machine, and any extra books besides the required texts that she thought it might be important for her students to read. The cost of getting rushed film prints of the Permian football games to the coaches, $6,400, was higher as well, not to mention the $20,000 it cost to charter the jet for the Marshall game. (During the 1988 season, roughly $70,000 was spent for chartered jets.)

When it came to the budget, Moore did have reason to rejoice this particular year. The English department had gotten its first computer. It was used by all twenty-five teachers to keep grade records and also to create a test bank of the various exams they gave to students.

The varsity football program, which had already had a computer, got a new one, an Apple IIGS, to provide even more exhaustive analyses of Permian's offensive and defensive plays as well as to keep parents up to date on the progress of the off-season weight-training program. At the end of the year the computer would be used to help compile a rather remarkable eighty-two-page document containing a detailed examination of each of the team's 747 defensive plays. Among other things, the document would reveal that Permian used sixty-six different defensive formations during the year, and that 25.69 percent of the snaps against it were from the middle hash, 67.74 percent of which were runs and 32.26 percent of which were passes.

Moore's salary, with twenty years' experience and a master's degree, was $32,000. By comparison, she noted, the salary of Gary Gaines, who served as both football coach and athletic director for Permian but did not teach any classes, was $48,000. In addition, he got the free use of a new Taurus sedan each year.

Moore didn't object to what the football program had, nor did she object to Gaines's salary. She knew he put in an enormous number of hours during the football season and that he was under constant pressure to produce a superb football team. If he didn't, he would be fired. She had grown up in West Texas, and it was obvious to her that high school football could galvanize a community and help keep it together. All she wanted was enough emphasis placed on teaching English so that she didn't have to go around pleading with the principal, or someone else, or spend hundreds of dollars out of her own pocket, to buy works of literature she thought would enlighten her students.

"I don't mind that it's emphasized," she said of football. "I just wish our perspective was turned a little bit. I just wish we could emphasize other things. The thing is, I don't think we should have to go to the booster club to get books. I don't think we should have to beg everyone in town for materials."

But that was the reality, and it seemed unlikely to change. The value of high school football was deeply entrenched. It was the way the community had chosen to express itself. The value of high school English was not entrenched. It did not pack the stands with twenty thousand people on a Friday night; it did not evoke any particular feelings of pride one way or another. No one dreamed of being able to write a superb critical analysis of Joyce's *Finnegans Wake* from the age of four on.

LaRue Moore knew that. So did Dorothy Fowler, who fumed to a visitor one day, "This community doesn't want academic excellence. It wants a gladiatorial spectacle on a Friday night." As she made that comment a history class that met a few yards down the hall did not have a teacher. The instructor was an assistant football coach. He was one of the best teachers in the school, dedicated and lively, but because of the legitimate pressures of preparing for a crucial game, he did not have time to go to class. That wasn't to say, however, that the class did not receive a lesson. They learned about American history that day by watching *Butch Cassidy and the Sundance Kid* on video.

7. Sports and Ideological Contradictions

D. STANLEY EITZEN

The past two years have been remarkable. We have witnessed a major turning point in history—the demise of communism. It took more than 40 years and $11 trillion to "win" the Cold War, but it happened. We have characterized this as capitalism defeating communism; freedom winning over authoritarian control; democracy overcoming a system ruled by an elite.

This claim of victory for the American "way of life" over the "evil empire" is ironic because American institutions—in families, in corporations, in churches, in government, in the military, and in schools—are not especially democratic. In short, there is a fundamental contradiction in what we claim to be and what we are.

The antidemocratic nature of schools is especially interesting because these are the places where the values and traditions of society are formally cherished, nourished, and inculcated into each succeeding generation. If schools are undemocratic, then their products will be authoritarian as well.

This essay addresses the most undemocratic part of schools—team sports. In effect, I argue that there is a more fundamental problem in sport than the frequent scandals we hear so much about. My seemingly outrageous proposition is that team sports as they are practiced in the high schools and colleges of the United States have a remarkable resemblance to the way communism was practiced in the Soviet Union and its satellites. In short, the values that we have learned to associate with the Soviets and to hate are actually found in our own social system. This effort is in the tradition of the method of immanent critique of the critical theorists. In Robert Antonio's words: "Immanent critique is a means of detecting the societal contradictions which offer the most determinate possibilities for emancipatory social change" (1981, p. 330).

To justify my claim that there is a contradiction between American values and actual behavior, I will list the most common social constructions of the Soviet regime that we found abhorrent. In each case I will show the striking parallels with school team sports, and consequently our own internal

SOURCE: "Sports and Ideological Contradictions: Learning from the Cultural Framing of Soviet Values" by D. Stanley Eitzen. From *Journal of Sport and Social Issues* 16, pp. 144–149. Copyright © 1992 by Sage Publications. Reprinted by permission of Sage Publications, Inc.

contradictions. While I use team sports in the school context as the point of comparison and contradiction, we should recognize that the parallels with the Soviet system could be made with other American institutions as well (see, for example, Chomsky, 1991; Parenti, 1988; Slater, 1991).

THE END JUSTIFIES THE MEANS

The Soviet Union was, as cast by the West, unprincipled. It would do anything to achieve the goal of spreading communism. However, this notion of doing whatever it takes to win is also common in our sport. The rules are often broken by coaches, alumni, and others to secure the services of athletes. Coaches may sometimes exploit the athletic skills of their players while not helping them to move toward graduation. Athletes may be taught to cheat (e.g., how to hold an opponent without being caught by an official), or they may be encouraged to intimidate their opponents with overly aggressive hitting and verbal taunts. Also, athletes may be encouraged to take performance-enhancing drugs or they may be given pain killers so that they might continue playing even when it is not best for their long-range health.

LEVELING OF ECONOMIC DIFFERENCES

One object of communism was to reduce economic inequality among people. This view is antithetical to capitalism, where economic advantages are seen as the primary means to motivate individuals to achieve. In so-called amateur sport, however, all college athletes on scholarship receive identical benefits—tuition, books, food, and lodging, as decreed by the National Collegiate Athletic Association (NCAA).

Despite the avowed goal of a "classless" society, we noted how the leaders of the Communist Party benefiting greatly from their lofty positions was a contradiction. We emphasized that they had luxuries, cars, homes, and incomes many times greater than those of the masses. But this is what occurs in U.S. sport. College athletes in the revenue-producing sports raise millions for their schools, conferences, and the NCAA, yet they receive subsistence wages. Athletes cannot even hold a job during the school year by NCAA fiat. When a football team plays in a bowl game, the players practice an extra month and receive nothing. Their coaches, on the other hand, receive bonuses for the team's success. Similarly, the school may spend over $1 million transporting the band, the team, administrators, and their spouses to the bowl game, yet the parents of the athletes must attend at their own expense. Most egregious, high-profile coaches make as much as $800,000 from salaries, shoe contracts, summer camps, radio, and television, while the athletes they depend on for their success receive minimum wages.

INVASION OF PRIVACY

Another contradiction between our values and our actions involves the violation of privacy rights. We frowned on the KGB and other organizations in the Soviet Union for their clandestine observance of citizens for "deviant" behaviors. We were appalled to hear that even members of their sport teams were enlisted to spy on their teammates. This type of behavior is intolerable in a free society, yet we allow it in our own sport (also the police may have wiretaps with court orders and the FBI and CIA use electronic surveillance with or without court orders). College athletes, not their coaches, are subject to mandatory drug testing. Personnel from the athletic department watch athletes in athletic dorms either in person or on closed circuit television for "deviant" behaviors. There are bed checks. Sometimes there are "spies" who watch and report on behaviors of athletes in local bars and other places of amusement.

NO FREEDOM OF CHOICE

In the former Soviet Union, freedoms were limited. Travel outside the country was refused to many. Religious freedom was denied. People were shifted by the authorities from job to job as needed. On collective farms, the workers were told what to do, what to plant, when to harvest, and so on. In U.S. sport, decisions are made for the athletes. They may be red-shirted (i.e., held from play for a year so they will be more mature) without consent. They may have little or no choice in what position they will play. They may be told to gain or lose weight with penalties for noncompliance. Off-season practices are typically mandatory. And most interesting, college athletes can leave a school to play for another only if they do not play for a year (two years if the coach does not release them).

BUREAUCRATIC AUTHORITARIANISM

A basic flaw in the Soviet system was centralization of authority. This organizational tool, while seemingly rational, had the opposite effect because rules were inflexible, creativity was stifled, and initiative unrewarded. College sport is controlled by a single organization, the NCAA, which has problems with flexibility, authoritarianism, an emphasis on television revenues, and punishments that hurt players more than coaches and institutions.

We criticized the Soviet Union for being run from the top down; for party leaders who made binding decisions without guidance from citizens. Coaches, with very few exceptions, are autocratic. They impose their will on team rules, discipline, personnel decisions, and strategy. Team captains look to the sidelines for guidance on whether to accept a penalty or not.

Quarterbacks receive orders on what play to call. The operant principle is that coaches lead and players follow.

Similarly, we characterized freedom of expression in art, literature, and in the universities as being stifled in the Soviet Union. Still, in American sport, obedience to authority allows coaches to demand dress codes. Mandatory study halls are common. Some coaches insist that their athletes avoid political protest. Sometimes athletes are steered away from courses taught by "radical" professors.

LACK OF INDIVIDUALISM

The Soviet citizens were framed as submerging their individual needs to the goals of the society. Similarly, athletes in team sports are expected to submerge self to team. Thus, when college players consider leaving a team early to become professionals, they are considered traitors to the school for elevating their needs above that of the team and institution.

LACK OF HUMAN RIGHTS

We cast the Soviet Union as particularly flawed because it had no equivalent to our Bill of Rights. We used their lack of free speech and press, and their lack of the rights to assemble and to have a fair trial in our ideological assault against their system. But we tolerate a similar situation for American athletes. If athletes challenge the athletic power structure, they will lose their scholarships and eligibility. Athletes who have a grievance are on their own. They have no union, no arbitration board, and rarely do they have representation on campus athletic committees.

OPPRESSION, BRUTALITY, AND TERROR

U.S. government officials often framed instances of brutality and terror in the Soviet Union as attempts by the powerful to command loyalty and obedience in an "evil empire." But coaches of athletic teams in the U.S. commonly degrade their athletes without being criticized. Often, athletes are the objects of coaches' obscenities; they are belittled; and they are sometimes hit by their coaches. When returning from a road game coaches may punish their players by having the bus driver let them off several miles from the school. Another tactic is to schedule practices at inconvenient times such as 2 A.M. or on holidays. John Feinstein (1986) observed that Coach Bob Knight of Indiana University, when angry with the performance of his players, would dismiss his players from practice without telling them when to report for the next practice or team meeting. Under this circumstance the players had to remain in their rooms to await the word from the coach. These acts of control are similar to those used by the military to train recruits. As Philip Slater has commented:

> Exposure to random punishment, stress, fatigue, personal degradation and abuse, irrational authority, and constant assertions of one's worthlessness as a human being—all tried-and-true techniques of "reeducation" used by totalitarian regimes—are in most cases effective in creating and maintaining an obedient killing machine (1991, pp. 47-48).

These boot camp tactics are also common among coaches. The question: Are such behaviors appropriate in an educational setting that purports to train citizens for a democracy?

CONCLUDING REMARKS

These parallels between what our society interpreted as an authoritarian and oppressive Soviet regime and the way team sports in American schools are organized point to a glaring contradiction between the official ideology of the United States and actual practice. If we truly believe in democracy, then we must democratize our institutions, including sport.

Democracy is learned through practice. Young people do not learn democracy when their leaders are tyrants. They do not learn democracy when they are spied on, demeaned, and degraded by authorities. They do not learn democracy when their lives are regimented from above. They do not learn the qualities of democratic citizenship from verbal and physical punishments imposed arbitrarily. Nor do they learn democracy when they are denied fundamental human freedoms. In short, if young people are to believe in democracy, they must live in a democracy.

We in the West were excited when *perestroika* (restructuring) and *glasnost* (openness) were instituted in the Soviet Union. These initial steps were taken to bring democracy to that country. Can we do the same for sport in our own society?

I am not naive about team sports. Members must strive for excellence. They must pull together to succeed. They must sacrifice to improve. They must strive for excellence as individuals and as a team. There must be leadership and teaching, but must these necessary requirements for success be imposed in an authoritarian way or is there a better way?

STARTING POINTS FOR CHANGE

An important starting point is to hire humanistic coaches who are democratic, open, and just. Second, make coaches part of the faculty so they are part of the educational enterprise rather than separate from it. Third, there must be mechanisms to insure players' rights such as a campus ombudsman, or a committee separate from the athletic department with student representation. And, fourth, the goal of the coaches and their schools must be to build autonomous, self-reliant, self-disciplined individuals. This goal can be achieved in sport by having athletes share in the decision-making in areas such as team rules, discipline, starting line-ups, strategy, play-calling, and game plans (for an example, see Amdur, 1971). Of course, leadership by the coaches is essential, but players can be involved and groomed to accept more and more responsibility as they move up in class rank and experience. Jay Coakley has provided one way to restructure sport along these lines:

> Why should adult coaches make all the decisions on student sport teams? Ideally, the goal should be to prepare the team to be self-coached. In fact, leagues should require that for the last two or three games of the season, coaches sit in the stands and watch while the players take the responsibility for coaching (1990, p. 346).

Leaders in school sports have two choices. They can continue on the same path, which espouses democracy but practices tyranny. This is the easy solution because, while hypocritical, it is accepted by almost everyone— school administrators, coaches, community members, influential friends of the schools, parents, and even players. The tougher choice is to organize sport so that there is a close fit between the democratic ideals we cherish and the way we organize sport. If we choose the former, then our athletes may suffer the ills we attributed to the former Soviet strategy, becoming an intimidated mass who are afraid to speak their minds, do what they are told, and are denied their basic freedoms. The second choice affirms our twin values of democracy and freedom.

Is such a fundamental change possible? A few years ago who dared to imagine that the Soviet Union and its empire would be broken up without a war? And, who believed that these peoples would turn to the values of the West? If those momentous changes are possible, then it might also be possible to change team sports in schools to make them congruent, rather than contradictory, to our own ideals. Since sport reflects society, it cannot achieve democracy without simultaneous and parallel changes in the other institutions of society.

REFERENCES

Amdur, N. (1971). *The fifth down: Democracy and the football revolution.* New York: Delta.

Antonio, R. J. (1981). Immanent critique as the core of critical theory: Its origins and developments in Hegel, Marx and contemporary thought. *British Journal of Sociology, 32,* 330-345.

Chomsky, N. (1991). *Deterring democracy.* London: Verso.

Coakley, J. J. (1990). *Sport in society: Issues and controversies* (4th ed.). St. Louis: Times Mirror/Mosby.

Feinstein, J. (1986). *A season on the brink: A year with Bob Knight of the Indiana Hoosiers.* New York: Macmillan.

Parenti, M. (1988). *Democracy for the few* (5th ed.). New York: St. Martin's Press.

Slater, P. (1991). *A dream deferred: America's discontent and the search for a new democratic ideal.* Boston: Beacon Press.

8. *Fraternal Bonding in the Locker Room*

TIMOTHY JON CURRY

The men's locker room is enshrined in sports mythology as a bastion of privilege and a center of fraternal bonding. The stereotyped view of the locker room is that it is a retreat from the outside world where athletes quietly prepare themselves for competition, noisily celebrate an important victory, or silently suffer a defeat. Given the symbolic importance of this sports shrine, it is surprising that there have been so few actual studies of the dynamics of male bonding in locker rooms. The purpose of this study was to explore a new approach to this aspect of fraternal bonding, by collecting locker room talk fragments and interpreting them from a profeminist perspective. Profeminism in this context meant adapting a feminist perspective to men's experience in sport, giving special attention to sexist and homophobic remarks that reveal important assumptions about masculinity, male dominance, and fraternal bonding.

Although seldom defined explicitly, the fraternal bond is usually considered to be a force, link, or affectionate tie that unites men. It is characterized in the literature by low levels of disclosure and intimacy. Sherrod (1987), for example, suggests that men associate different meanings with friendships than women do, and that men tend to derive friendships from doing things together while women are able to maintain friendships through disclosures. This view implies that men need a reason to become close to one another and are uncomfortable about sharing their feelings.

Some of the activities around which men bond are negative toward women and others who are perceived as outsiders to the fraternal group. For example, Lyman (1987) describes how members of a fraternity bond through sexist joking relationships, and Fine (1987) notes the development of sexist, racist, and homophobic attitudes and jokes even among preadolescent Little Leaguers. Sanday (1990) examines gang rape as a by-product of male bonding in fraternities, and she argues that the homophobic and homosocial environments of such all-male groups make for a conducive environment for aggression toward women.

SOURCE: "Fraternal Bonding in the Locker Room: A Profeminist Analysis of Talk about Competition and Women" by Timothy Jon Curry. From *Sociology of Sport* 8(2), pp. 119–135. Copyright © 1991 by Human Kinetics Publishers, Inc. Reprinted by permission.

Sport is an arena well suited for the enactment and perpetuation of the male bond (Messner, 1987). It affords separation and identity building as individual athletes seek status through making the team and winning games (Dunning, 1986), and it also provides group activity essential for male bonding (Sherrod, 1987) while not requiring much in the way of intimate disclosures (Sabo & Panepinto, 1990). Feminist scholars have pointed out that the status enhancement available to men through sports is not as available to women, and thus sport serves to legitimate men's domination of women and their control of public life (Bryson, 1987; Farr, 1988). In addition, since most sports are rule bound either by tradition or by explicit formal codes, involvement in sports is part of the typical right-and-rules orientation of boys' socialization in the United States (Gilligan, 1982).

For young men, sport is also an ideal place to "do gender"—display masculinity in a socially approved fashion (West & Zimmerman, 1987). In fact the male bond is apparently strengthened by an effective display of traditional masculinity and threatened by what is not considered part of standard hegemonic masculinity. For example, as Messner (1989, p. 192) relates, a gay football player who was aggressive and hostile on the field felt "compelled to go along with a lot of locker room garbage because I wanted that image [of attachment to more traditional male traits]—and I know a lot of others who did too . . . I know a lot of football players who very quietly and secretly like to paint, or play piano. And they do it quietly, because this to them is threatening if it's known by others." Since men's bonding is based on shared activity rather than on the self-disclosures (Sherrod, 1987), it is unlikely that teammates will probe deeply beneath these surface presentations.

Deconstructing such performances, however, is one way of understanding "the interactional scaffolding of social structure and the social control process that sustains it" in displays of masculinity central to fraternal bonding (West & Zimmerman, 1987, p. 147). Pronger (1990, pp. 192-213) has provided one such deconstruction of doing gender in the locker room from the perspective of a homosexual. He notes the irony involved in maintaining the public façade of heterosexuality while privately experiencing a different reality.

Two other studies of locker rooms emphasized the cohesive side of male bonding through sports, but neither of these studies was concerned specifically with gender displays or with what male athletes say about women (Snyder, 1972; Zurcher, 1982). The recent uproar over the sexual harassment of a woman reporter in the locker room of the NFL's New England Patriots, described by Heymann (1990), suggests that this work is a timely and important undertaking.

PROCEDURES

This study of locker room talk follows Snyder (1972), who collected samples of written messages and slogans affixed to locker room walls. However, since the messages gathered by Snyder were originally selected by coaches and were meant to serve as normative prescriptions that would contribute to winning games, they mostly revealed an idealistic, public side of locker room culture. From reading these slogans one would get the impression that men's sports teams are characterized by harmony, consensus, and "esoteric in-group traditions" (Snyder, 1972, p. 99).

The approach taken here focuses on the spoken aspects of locker room culture—the jokes and put-downs typically involved in fraternal bonding (Fine, 1987; Lyman, 1987). Although this side of locker room culture is ephemeral, situational, and generally not meant for display outside of the all-male peer groups, it is important in understanding how sport contributes to male bonding, status attainment, and hegemonic displays of masculinity.

The Talk Fragments

The talk fragments were gathered in locker rooms from athletes on two teams participating in contact sports at a large midwestern university with a "big time" sports program. The first team was approached at the beginning of its season for permission to do a field study. Permission was granted and assurances were made that anonymity would be maintained for athletes and coaches. I observed the team as a nonparticipant sport sociologist, both at practices and during competition, for well over a month before the first talk fragments were collected. The talk fragments were gathered over a 2-month period and the locker room was visited frequently to gather field notes. Note gathering in the locker room was terminated upon saturation; however, the team's progress was followed and field observations continued until the end of the season.

Intensive interviews were conducted with some of the athletes and coaches during all 9 months of the research. These interviews concerned not only locker room interaction but also the sport background and life histories of the respondents. Additionally, after the talk fragments were gathered, five of the athletes enrolled in my class on sport sociology and wrote term papers on their experiences in sport. These written documents, along with the interviews and observations made outside the locker room, provided a rich variety of materials for the contextual analysis and interpretation of the conversations held inside the locker room. They also lent insight into how the athletes themselves defined locker room talk.

The talk fragments were collected in plain view of the athletes, who had become accustomed to the presence of a researcher taking notes. Fragments of talk were written down as they occurred and were reconstructed later. Such obvious note taking may have influenced what was said, or more likely what was not said. To minimize the obtrusiveness of the research, eye contact was avoided while taking notes. A comparison between the types of conversations that occurred during note taking versus when note taking was not done yielded few differences. Even so, more talk fragments were gathered from a second locker room as a way of both increasing the validity of the study and protecting the anonymity of the athletes and coaches from the first locker room.

The Second Locker Room

Field notes concerning talk from a second locker room were gathered by a senior who had enjoyed a successful career as a letterman. His presence in the locker room as a participant observer was not obtrusive, and the other student-athletes reacted to him as a peer. He gathered talk fragments over a 3-month period while his team was undergoing conditioning and selection procedures similar in intensity to that of the original team. He met with me every week and described his perceptions of interaction in the locker room. His collection of talk fragments was included as part of a written autobiographical account of his experience in sport while at college. These research procedures were modeled after Zurcher's (1983) study of hashers in a sorority house and Shaw's (1972) autobiographical account of his experience in sport.

One additional point needs to be stressed here: Unlike anecdotal accounts of locker room behavior or studies based on the recollections of former athletes, these conversations were systematically gathered live and in context over a relatively brief period of time. Consequently the stories and jokes may not be as extreme as those remembered by athletes who reflect upon their entire career in sport (e.g., Messner, 1987; Pronger, 1990), or as dramatic as the episode of sexual harassment that took place in the locker room of the New England Patriots (Heymann, 1990).

The strength of this study lies in situating the conversations within the context of the competitive environment of elite collegiate sport rather than capturing the drama of a single moment or the recollections of particularly memorable occasions. In other words, no one study, including this one, can hope to cover the entire gambit of locker room culture and various distinctive idiocultures of different teams (Fine, 1987). A variety of studies that use different methods and incorporate different perspectives are needed for that endeavor.

Profeminist Perspective

Messner (1990) has recently argued that a profeminist perspective is needed to overcome male bias in research in the sociology of sport. For decades, Messner claims, male researchers have been prone to writing about sport from a masculine standpoint and have neglected gender issues. He further states that since men have exclusive access to much of the social world of sport, they also have the primary responsibility of providing a more balanced interpretation of that world by paying special attention to gender oppression. He maintains that such balance is best achieved at this point by adopting a value-centered feminist perspective rather than a supposedly value-free but androcentric perspective.

Adopting a feminist standpoint requires assuming that "feminist visions of an egalitarian society are desirable" (Messner, 1990, p. 149). Ultimately, research guided by such an assumption will contribute to a deeper understanding of the costs and the privileges of masculinity and may help build a more just and egalitarian world. Messner does not offer explicit guidelines as to how an androcentric researcher might begin to undertake such a shift in perspectives, however, although he does refer to a number of exemplary studies.

As a method of consciously adopting a profeminist perspective in this research, a review of feminist literature on sports and socialization was undertaken, feminist colleagues were consulted on early drafts of the manuscript, and a research assistant trained in feminist theory was employed to help with the interpretation of talk fragments. She shared her ideas and observations regarding the talk fragments, written documents, and field notes with me and suggested some additional references and sources that proved useful.

The talk fragments were selected and arranged to provide a sense of the different themes, ideas, and attitudes encountered. In focusing on the talk fragments themselves, two categories emerged (through a grounded theory approach) as especially important for situating and interpreting locker room behavior from a profeminist perspective: (a) the dynamics of competition, status attainment, and bonding among male athletes, and (b) the dynamics of defending one's masculinity through homophobic talk and talk about women as objects. A numbering system for each talk fragment (Athlete 1, 2, Sam, etc.) is used below to keep track of the different speakers. Names have been changed and the numbering system starts over for each talk fragment.

COMPETITION, STATUS ATTAINMENT, AND BONDING

Locker room talk is mostly about the common interests that derive from the shared identity of male student-athlete. Underlying these interactions is an ever-present sense of competition, both for status and position on the team itself and between the team and its opponents. While sport provides an activity to bond around, one's position on the team is never totally secure. An injury or poor performance may raise doubts about one's ability and lead to one's replacement. Such basic insecurities do not promote positive social relationships in the locker room, and they help explain some of the harshness of the talk that the athletes directed toward each other and toward women.

For example, competition can have a subtle influence on the relationships athletes have with others on the team and cause them to be quite tentative, as illustrated by the following statements obtained from two interviews:

> One of the smaller guys on the team was my best friend . . . maybe I just like having a little power over [him] . . . It doesn't matter if the guy is your best friend, you've got to beat him, or else you are sitting there watching. Nobody wants to watch.

> That's one of my favorite things about the sport, I enjoy the camaraderie. [Who are your friends?] Usually it's just the starters . . . you unite behind each other a lot. The other guys don't share the competition with you like the starters do.

The competition can extend beyond sport itself into other domains. It is not unusual for athletes to have as their closest friends men who are not on the team, which helps them maintain some defensive ego boundaries between themselves and the team. It also provides a relief from the constant competition, as one athlete indicates:

> [My] better friends aren't on the team. Probably because we are not always competing. With my [athlete] friends, we are always competing . . . like who gets the best girls, who gets the best grades . . . Seems like [we] are competitive about everything, and it's nice to have some friends that don't care . . . you can just relax.

Competition, Emotional Control, and Bonding

A variety of studies have indicated that male athletes are likely to incorporate competitive motivation as part of their sport identity (e.g., Curry & Weiss, 1989). As competition and status attainment become important for the male athlete in establishing his identity, noninstrumental emotion becomes less useful, perhaps even harmful to his presentation of a conventionally gendered self (Sherrod, 1987). In addition, by defining themselves in terms of what is not feminine, men may come to view emotional displays with disdain or even fear (Herek, 1987). However, control over emotions in sport is made difficult by the passions created by an intense desire to win. One athlete described his feelings of being consumed by competition while in high school and his need to control the emotions:

> My junior year, I had become so obsessed with winning the district . . . I was so overcome that I lost control a week before the tournament. I was kicking and screaming and crying on the sofa . . . since then I have never been the same. True, now I work harder than that year but now when I start to get consumed [with something] I get fearful and reevaluate its importance.

As part of learning to control emotions, the athletes have learned to avoid public expressions of emotional caring or concern for one another even as they bond, because such remarks are defined as weak or feminine.

For example, the remarks of the following athlete illustrate how this type of socialization can occur through sport. This athlete's father was very determined that his son would do well in sports, so much so that he forced the boy to practice daily and became very angry with the boy's mistakes. To understand his father's behavior, the boy went to his mother:

> I would come up from the cellar and be upset with myself, and I would talk to my mother and say, "Why does he yell so much?" and she would say, "He only does it because he loves you."

While the father emphasized adherence to rules and discipline, the boy had to depend on his mother to connect him to his father's love. Distancing from each other emotionally is of course dysfunctional for the relationships among male athletes and leads to an impoverishment of relationships (Messner, 1987).

Maintaining a "safe" distance from one another also influences what is said and what is not said in front of others about topics of mutual concern, such as grades and women. Failure to address such common problems openly means that they must be dealt with indirectly or by denial. For example, the deriding of academic work by male athletes has been noted by other investigators (Adler & Adler, 1991) and is not typical of female athletes (Meyer, 1990). The reason may be that when athletes make comments that might be construed as asking for help or encouragement, their behavior is considered nonmasculine. They are thus subject to ridicule, as illustrated in the following two talk fragments:

Fragment 1
Athlete 1: [spoken to the athlete who has a locker near him, but loud enough to be heard by others] What did you get on your test?
Athlete 2: 13 [pause], that's two D+'s this week. That's a student-athlete for you. [sighs, then laughs quietly]
Athlete 1: That's nothing to laugh about.
Athlete 2: [contritely] I mean an athlete-student, but things are looking up for me. I'm going to do better this week. How did you do on that test?
Athlete 1: Got a 92.
Athlete 3: Yeah, who did you cheat off of? [group laughter]

Fragment 2
Athlete 1: [to coach, shouted across room] I'm doing real bad in class.
Coach: Congratulations!
Athlete 1: [serious tone, but joking] Will you call the professor up and tell him to give me an A?
Coach: [obviously sarcastically] Sure thing, would tonight at 9 be all right?

Competition and a Sense of Self

Considering the time-consuming nature of big-time college sports, it is not surprising that they become the central focus of athletes' lives. Approximately

30 hours a week were spent in practice, and often the athletes were too tired after a hard practice to do much else than sleep.

Fragment 3
Athlete 1: [collapses on bench] Shit, I'm going to bed right now, and maybe I'll make my 9 o'clock class tomorrow.
Athlete 2: 40 minutes straight! I thought he'd never stop the drills.
Athlete 1: Left you gasping for air at the end, didn't it?
Athlete 2: You mean gasping for energy.

Sports and competition become the greater part of the athlete's world. Through his strivings to excel, to be a part of the team and yet stand out on his own, he develops a conception of who he is. Thus the athlete's sense of self can be seen as being grounded in competition, with few alternative sources of self-gratification (Adler & Adler, 1991). The rewards for such diligence are a heightened sense of self-esteem. When one athlete was asked what he would miss most if he were to leave sports, he declared, "the competition . . . the attitude I feel about being [on the team]. It makes me feel special. You're doing something that a lot of people can't do, and wish they could do." In other words, his knowledge of his "self" includes status-enhancing presumptions about character building through sport.

This attitude is not atypical. For example, another man claimed, "I can always tell a [refers to athletes in same sport he plays]. They give off cues—good attitude, they are sure of themselves, bold, not insecure." This sense of specialness and status presumption cements the male bond and may temporarily cut across social class and racial differences. Later in life the experiences and good memories associated with fellowship obtained through sport may further sociability and dominance bonding (Farr, 1988). For the elite college athlete, however, this heightened self-esteem is obtained at some costs to other activities. Often academic studies and social or romantic involvements get defined as peripheral to the self and are referred to with contempt in the locker room, as illustrated in the next fragment:

Most everyone has vacated the locker room for the showers. Sam and a few of his friends are left behind. Sam is redshirting (saving a year's eligibility by not participating on the team except for practices) and will not be traveling with the team. What he is going to do instead is the subject of several jokes once all the coaches have left the locker room:

Fragment 4
Athlete 1: What are you going to do, Sam, go to the game?
Sam: I can't, I sold my ticket. [laughs] I'm going to the library so I can study. [cynically] Maybe I'll take my radio so I can listen to the game. [pause] I hate my classes.
Athlete 1: Oh, come on, that's not the right attitude.
Sam: And I hope to get laid a few times too.
Athlete 1: Hey come on, that's not a nice way to talk.
Sam: How else are you supposed to talk in a locker room?

Sam's comment also leads us directly to the question of peer group influence on presentation of a gendered self. A general rule of male peer groups is that you can say and do some things with your peers that would be inappropriate almost anywhere else. For male athletes this rule translates into an injunction to be insulting and antisocial on occasion (Fine, 1987; Lyman, 1987). You are almost expected to speak sarcastically and offensively in the locker room, as Sam indicates above. Thus, hostile talk about women is blended with jokes and put-downs about classes and each other. In short, while sport leads to self-enhancement, the peer culture of male athletics also fosters antisocial talk, much of which is directed toward the athletes themselves.

Rigidities of the Bond

Competition in sports, then, links men together in a status-enhancing activity in which aggression is valued (Dunning, 1986). The bond between male athletes is usually felt to be a strong one, yet it is set aside rather easily. The reason for this is that the bond is rigid, with sharply defined boundaries. For example, when speaking about what it is that bonds athletes to their sport and other athletes, a coach remarks,

> They know they are staying in shape, they are part of something. Some of them stay with it because they don't want to be known as quitters. There's no in-between. You're a [team member or not a team member]. The worst guy on the team is still well thought of if he's out there every day going through it. There's no sympathy in that room. No sympathy if you quit. You might die but you're not going to quit.

This rigid definition of who is or is not a team member reflects Gilligan's (1982) concept of a rights/rules moral system for males, which emphasizes individuality, instrumental relations, achievement, and control. In short the male athlete is either on the team or not. There is no grey area: It is clearly a black or white situation. If one follows the "rules," then he has the "right" to participate in bonding. If one does not follow the rules (i.e., quits), he ceases to exist in a bonding capacity. However, as Coakley (1990) has observed, following the rules to their extremes can lead to "positive" deviance, including a refusal to quit in spite of injury. Athlete 1 below endured a number of small and severe injuries, but throughout his ordeal refused to consider leaving the team.

Fragment 5
Athlete 1: My shin still hurts, can't get it to stop.
Athlete 2: Well, that's it then—time to quit.
Athlete 1: Not me, I'm not a quitter.
Athlete 2: Oh, come on, I can see through that. You'll quit if you have to.
Athlete 1: No way.

Even though injured, an athlete is still a member of the team if he attends practice, even if only to watch the others work out. However, his bond with the others suffers if he cannot participate fully in the sport. Sympathy is felt for such athletes, in that their fate is recognized and understood. As one athlete empathized during an interview, "I feel for the guys who are hurt who are usually starters . . . [They] feel lonely about it, feel like they want to be back out there, feel like they want to prove something."

Perhaps what these athletes need to prove is that they are still a part of the activity around which the bonds are centered. As Sherrod (1987) suggests, the meanings associated with friendship for men are grounded in activities, giving them a reason to bond. Past success or status as a team member is not enough to fully sustain the bond; bonding requires constant maintenance. With boundaries so rigid, the athletes must constantly establish and reestablish their status as members involved in the bond by the only way they know how: through competition.

Rigid definitions of performance requirements in sport combine to form an either/or situation for the athlete and his ability to bond with teammates. If he stays within these boundaries, he is accepted and the bond remains intact. If he fails, he is rejected and the bond is severed. One athlete sums up this position with the following comments: "You lose a lot of respect for guys like that. Seems like anybody who's quit, they just get pushed aside. Like [name deleted], when he used to be [on the team] he hung around with us, and now that he's not, he ain't around anymore." Thus an athlete may find his relations severed with someone he has known for half his life, through participation in sport in junior high and high school, simply because the other person has left the team.

TALK ABOUT WOMEN

Competitive pressures and insecurities surrounding the male bond influence talk about women. As discussed above, competition provides an activity bond to other men that is rewarding, even though the atmosphere of competition surrounding big-time sports generates anxiety and other strong emotions that the athletes seek to control or channel. Competition for positions or status on the team also curtails or conditions friendships, and peer group culture is compatible with antisocial talk and behavior, some of which is directed at the athletes themselves.

The fraternal bond is threatened by inadequate role performance, quitting the team, or not living up to the demands of masculinity. Consequently, fear of weakening the fraternal bond greatly affects how athletes "do gender" in the locker room and influences the comments they make about women. In this regard, locker room talk may again be characterized both by what is said and what is not said. Conversations that affirm a traditional masculine identity dominate, and these include talk about women as objects, homophobic talk, and talk that is very aggressive and hostile toward women—essentially talk that promotes rape culture.

Woman as Person, Woman as Object

Two additional distinctions now need to be made in categorizing locker room talk about women. One category concerns women as real people, persons with whom the athletes have ongoing social relationships. This category of locker room talk is seldom about sexual acquisition; most often it is about personal concerns athletes might wish to share with their best friend on the team. Because the athletes do not want their comments to be overheard by others who might react with ridicule, this type of talk usually occurs in hushed tones, as described in the following fragment. Talk about women as objects, on the other hand, often refers to sexual conquests. This type of talk is not hushed. Its purpose seems mainly to enhance the athletes' image of themselves to others as practicing heterosexuals.

Fragment 6
Athlete 1 to 2: I've got to talk to you about [whispers name. They go over to an empty corner of the locker room and whisper. They continue to whisper until the coaches arrive. The athletes at the other end of the locker room make comments:]
Athlete 3: Yeah, tell us what she's got.
Athlete 4: Boy, you're in trouble now.
Assistant coach: You'll have to leave our part of the room. This is where the real men are.

The peer culture of the locker room generally does not support much talk about women as persons. Norms of masculinity discourage talking seriously about social relations, so these types of conversations are infrequent (Fine, 1987; Sabo & Panepinto, 1990). Inevitably, personal revelations will quickly be followed by male athletic posturing, jokes, and put-downs, as in the talk fragment above. While the jokes may be amusing, they do little to enhance personal growth and instead make a real sharing of intimacies quite difficult. The ridicule that follows these interactions also serves to establish the boundaries of gender-appropriate behavior. This ridicule tells the athlete that he is getting too close to femaleness, because he is taking relatedness seriously. "Real men" do not do that. Perhaps just taking the view of women as persons is enough to evoke suspicion in the locker room.

To avoid this suspicion, the athlete may choose to present his attitude toward women in a different way, one that enhances his identity as a "real man." The resulting women-as-objects stories are told with braggadocio or in a teasing manner; they are stage performances usually requiring an audience of more than one, and may be told to no one in particular:

Fragment 7

I was taking a shower with my girlfriend when her parents came home. I never got dressed so fast in my life.

These types of stories elicit knowing smiles or guffaws from the audience, and it is difficult to tell whether or not they are true. In any event the actual truth of such a story is probably less important than the function it serves in buttressing the athlete's claim as a practicing heterosexual.

Fragment 8
Athlete 1: How was your Thanksgiving?
Athlete 2: Fine, went home.
Athlete 1: I bet you spent the time hitting high schools!
Athlete 2: Naw, only had to go back to [one place] to find out who was available.

Women's identities as people are of no consequence in these displays. The fact that women are viewed as objects is also evident in the tendency of men to dissect woman's bodies into parts, which are then discussed separately from the whole person. Athlete 1 in Fragment 9 below is describing a part of a woman's body as if it existed separately from the woman, as if it was in the training room and the woman was not:

Fragment 9
Athlete 1: I just saw the biggest set of Ta-Tas in the training room!
Athlete 2: How big were they?
Athlete 1: Bigger than my mouth.

This perspective toward women highlights the fact that the use of women's bodies is more important than knowing them as people. Perhaps this attitude is also based in the athlete's focus on maintaining control, whether physically through athletic performance or mentally through strict adherence to rules and discipline. Since the male athlete's ideas about control center around physical strength and mental discipline, they stand in sharp contrast to ideas about females, who are generally thought of as physically weak and emotional. Following the implications of these ideas a bit further, women as persons are emotional and cannot be easily controlled; women as objects, however, have no volition and can be more easily controlled.

Doing Gender through Homophobic Talk

From Herek's (1987) notion that through socialization boys learn to be masculine by avoiding that which is feminine or homosexual, it follows that in the locker room an athlete may be singled out if his demeanor is identified as unmasculine in any way. The reasoning may be seen as follows: (a) "real men" are defined by what they are *not* (women and homosexuals);

(b) it is useful to maintain a separation from femaleness or gayness so as not to be identified as such; (c) expression of dislike for femaleness or homosexuality demonstrates to oneself and others that one is separate from it and therefore must be masculine. For example, when an athlete's purple designer underwear is discovered, a teammate asks, "and did you get earrings for Christmas?" When he protests, this reply, directed to all of the athletes in the room is offered: "Guess I hit a . . . nerve. I won't begin on the footsies today, maybe tomorrow."

This example illustrates that every aspect of the athlete's appearance runs the risk of gender assessment. That which is under suspicion of being at odds with traditional definitions of masculinity threatens the bond and will be questioned. Connell (1990, pp. 88-89) provides further graphic example of gender assessment among athletes. He describes the life of a determinedly heterosexual Australian Iron-Man competitor, whose first coital experience at 17 was both arranged and witnessed by his surf-club friends, and who felt he had to "put on a good show for the boys." Presumably, his performance allowed him and his friends to reaffirm to themselves and others that their sexual preferences remained within the boundaries of the bond.

Not only is being homosexual forbidden, but tolerance of homosexuality is theoretically off limits as well. The sanctions associated with this type of boundary maintenance manifest themselves in jokes and story telling about homosexuals.

Fragment 10
Athlete 1: When I was at [high school] we all lined up to watch the other guys come in. Fred pretended to be interested in one of them and said, "I like that one" [he gestures with a limp wrist]. . . . We were all so fucking embarrassed, nobody would give him a ride home. It was the funniest thing!
Athlete 2: Yeah, once we all stopped in at [a local bar] and Tom got up to dance with one of the fags, actually took his hand and started to dance! Boy was the fag surprised. [group laughter]

Making fun of homosexuals by mimicking stereotyped gay gender displays brings laughter in the locker room partly because it helps distance the athletes from being categorized as gay themselves. Such hegemonic gender displays also take more aggressive forms. Perhaps male athletes are especially defensive because of the physical closeness and nudity in the locker room and the contact between males in sport itself. This latter idea is evident in the following remarks of a coach:

We do so much touching that some people think we're queer. In 37 years I've never for sure met a queer [athlete]. At [a certain college] we had a [teammate] that some of the fellows thought was queer. I said "pound on him, beat on him, see what happens." He quit after 3 days. He never approached anyone anyway.

Locker Room Talk Promotes Rape Culture

Maintaining the appearance of a conventional heterosexual male identity, then, is of the utmost importance to the athlete who wants to remain bonded to his teammates. Also, as discussed previously, the perception of women as objects instead of persons encourages expressions of disdain or even hatred toward them on the part of the male athletes. Thus, the striving to do gender appropriately within the constraints of the fraternal bond involves talk that manages to put down women while also ridiculing or teasing each other, as the following fragments indicate:

Fragment 11
Assistant Coach 1: [announcement] Shame to miss the big [football] game, but you have to travel this week to keep you out of trouble. Keep you from getting laid too many times this weekend. Here are the itineraries for the trip. They include a picture of Frank's girlfriend. [Picture is of an obese woman surrounded by children. Frank is one of the best athletes on the team.]
Assistant Coach 2: Yeah, when she sits around the house, she really sits around the house.
Assistant Coach 3: She's so ugly that her mother took her everywhere so she wouldn't have to kiss her good-bye. [group laughter]

Jibes and put-downs about one's girlfriend or lack of sexual success are typified by this exchange. Part of the idealized heterosexual male identity consists of "success" with women, and to challenge that success by poking fun at the athlete's girlfriend is an obvious way to insult him. These jibes were directed at one of the best athletes on the team, whose girlfriend was not in town. It is important to note that these insults were delivered by the assistant coaches, who are making use of their masculine identity as a common bond they share with the student-athletes. By ridiculing one of the better athletes, they are not threatening any of the more vulnerable team members and at the same time they are removing some of the social distance between themselves and the students. After receiving such an insult, the athlete has to think of a comeback to top it or lose this round of insulting. Fine (1987) also noted such escalation of insults in his study of the Little League. This attitude is recognized and understood by other athletes:

Fragment 12
You guys harass around here real good. If you knew my mother's name, you would bring her into it too.

Thus a negative view of women prevails in the locker room and serves to facilitate the bond between athletes and their coaches. At times the competition involved with these exchanges does not involve insults directed at one another. The athletes compete instead to see who can express the most negative attitudes toward women, as illustrated by the final comments from a discussion of different types of women:

Fragment 13
Let me tell you about those [names an ethnic minority] women. They look good until they are 20, then they start pushing out the pups. By the time they're 40, they weigh 400 pounds.

This negative orientation is fed by other, related attitudes about women, such as those that concern women's sports, as indicated by the following remarks made by a coach: "[Our sport] has been taking a beating in lots of colleges. It's because of the emphasis on women's sports. Too bad, because [our sport] is cheaper. Could make money . . . " (he continues with comments about women's sports not paying their way).

At their extreme, these attitudes promote aggression toward women and create an environment supportive for rape culture (Beneke, 1982; Sanday, 1990). A fairly mild form of this aggression is suggested in the following talk fragment, in which two athletes are talking about Jerry, an athlete who is a frequent butt of their jokes. Jerry has just left the locker room and this conversation occurs when he is out of hearing distance:

Fragment 14
Athlete 1: Hey Pete, did you know Jerry is a sexual dynamo?
Pete: Why do you say that?
Athlete 1: He said he was with two different girls in the same day and both girls were begging, and I emphasize begging, for him to stop. He said he banged each of them so hard that they begged for him to stop.
Pete: I think he's becoming retarded.
Athlete 1: Do you believe he said this to me?
Pete: Well, what did you do?
Athlete 1: I laughed in his face.
Pete: What did he do?
Athlete 1: Nothing, he just kept telling me about this; it was hilarious.

The preceding fragment can be seen as describing rape in that the women involved with the athlete "begged for him to stop," and in this case the athletes choose to use the story to put down Jerry and thus negate his claim to sexual dynamism. The rape reference is more obvious in the following fragment. To set the scene, the team was visited by high school athletes and their parents; the athletes were being recruited by the coaches. The mother of one recruit drew attention from a group of athletes because she was extremely attractive. This conversation occurs in the locker room just after she left with her son:

Fragment 15
Athlete 1: She's too young to be his mother!
Athlete 2: Man, I'd hurt her if I got ahold of her.

Athlete 3: I'd tear her up.
Athlete 4: I'd break her hips. [all laugh]
Athlete 3: Yeah, she was hot!

Thus locker room talk about women, though serving a function for the bonding of men, also promotes harmful attitudes and creates an environment supportive of sexual assault and rape. Competition among teammates, the emphasis upon women as objects, sexual conquest as enviable achievement, peer group encouragement of antisocial comments and behavior, and anxiety about proving one's heterosexuality—all of these ideas are combined in the preceding fragment to promote a selfish, hostile, and aggressive approach to sexual encounters with women.

CONCLUSIONS

Sex and aggression are familiar themes in men's talk, and it is no surprise to find them of paramount importance in the locker room. Fine's (1987) work with preadolescent Little League baseball players indicated that the conversations of 9- to 12-year-old boys reflected similar concerns. What comes through less clearly in the conversations is the fulfillment that men find in such talk. It is an affirmation of one's masculine identity to be able to hold one's own in conversations about women, to top someone else's joke, or to share a story that one's peers find interesting. In this way the athlete's identity as a man worthy of bonding with is maintained.

College athletes often speak of the rewards of team membership as being an important reason for participating in a sport, and one of the rewards is the give and take of the peer culture in the locker room. The combination of revelation and braggadocio requires a shifting interpretation between fantasy and reality, and the ready willingness to insult means that a false interpretation may subject one to ridicule.

There are no definitive studies that document the effects of participating in locker room culture. On the one hand, behavior in locker rooms is both ephemeral and situational and probably does not reflect the actual values of all the participants. From this perspective, the locker room is just a place to change clothing and to shower, and one should not make too much of what goes on there. In discussing locker room interaction with some of the athletes involved, I found that most distanced themselves from it and denied its importance to them, particularly with respect to devaluing academic work. In some cases locker room talk even served as a negative reference for athletes, who quietly went about their business and avoided involvement. However, it is important to note that no one ever publicly challenged the dominant sexism and homophobia of the locker room. Whatever oppositional thoughts there may have been were muttered quietly or remained private.

On the other hand, there is evidence that years of participating in such a culture desensitizes athletes to women's and gay rights and supports male supremacy rather than egalitarian relationships with women. For instance, Connell's (1990) life history of an Iron-Man indicated that this incredibly fit young man was unable to tolerate a "girl" who stood up for her own interests, and so had a series of girlfriends who were compliant with his needs and schedule. Moreover, Connell observes that this attitude is typical among the other male supremacists who constitute the Australian surfing subculture.

Another illustration is provided by the recent harassment of Lisa Olson in the locker room of the New England Patriots. This episode also supports the idea that locker room talk promotes aggressive antifemale behavior. The details of this case involved grown men parading nude around the seated reporter as she was conducting an interview. Some of the men "modeled themselves" before her, one "adjusted" his genitals and shook his hips in an exaggerated fashion, and one naked player stood arm's length from her and said "Here's what you want. Do you want to take a bite out of this?"—all to the accompaniment of bantering and derisive laughter (Heymann, 1990, p. 9A). No one tried to stop the humiliating activity, nor did management intervene or sincerely apologize until forced to by the NFL Commissioner. In fact, the initial reaction of the team's owner was to support the players. The owner, Victor ("I liked it so much, I bought the company"—Remington) Kiam, was heard to say, "What a classic bitch. No wonder none of the players like her." However, his concern for the sales of his women's shaving products resulted in the following damage control campaign:

He took out full-page ads in three major U.S. newspapers to protest his inno-cence, offered testimonials from three people who denied he said anything derogatory about Olson, and blamed the Patriots front office personnel for not telling him of the Olson locker room incident sooner. (Norris, 1991, p. 23)

Finally, Sanday (1990, p. 193) concludes her study of gang rape by fra-ternity members by indicating that "Sexism is an unavoidable byproduct of a cultural fascination with the virile, sexually powerful hero who dominates everyone, male and female alike." If this is true, then sexism in locker rooms is best understood as part of a larger cultural pattern that supports male supremacy.

It is my view that sexist locker room talk is likely to have a cumulative negative effect on young men because it reinforces the notions of masculine privilege and hegemony, making that world view seem normal and typical. Moreover, it does so in a particularly pernicious fashion. By linking ideas about masculinity with negative attitudes toward women, locker room cul-ture creates a no-win situation for the athlete who wishes to be masculine and who wants to have successful, loving, nurturing relationships with women: "real men" are not nurturant. Similarly, locker room talk provides no encouragement for the "real man" who seeks egalitarian relationships. As Pronger (1990) notes, the myth of masculinity prevalent in the locker room cannot be maintained in the face of equitable relations between men and women or in the acceptance of homosexuality.

Finally, by linking ideas about status attainment with male bonding and masculinity, locker room culture makes it more difficult for young men to realize that women also desire success and status attainment through hard work and self-discipline. In other words, through participating in sport young men are taught that discipline and effort are needed for success and that one's acceptance depends on successful performance. But since these lessons are usually learned in all-male groups, they do not generalize easily to women and may create barriers to men's acceptance of women in the workplace.

REFERENCES

Adler, P.A., & Adler, P. (1991). *Backboards & blackboards: College athletes and role engulf-ment.* New York: Columbia University Press.

Beneke, T. (1982). *Men on rape.* New York: St. Martin's Press.

Bryson, L. (1987). Sport and the maintenance of masculine hegemony. *Women's Studies International Forum*, **10**, 349-360.

Coakley, J.J. (1990). *Sport in society: Issues and controversies.* St. Louis: Mosby.

Connell, R.W. (1990). An Iron Man: The body and some contradictions of hege-monic masculinity. In M.A. Messner & D.F. Sabo (Eds.), *Sport, men, and the gender order* (pp. 83-95). Champaign, IL: Human Kinetics.

Curry, T.J., & Weiss, O. (1989). Sport identity and motivation for sport participation: A comparison between American college athletes and Austrian student sport club members. *Sociology of Sport Journal*, **6**, 257-268.

Dunning, E. (1986). Social bonding and violence in sport. In N. Elias & E. Dunning (Eds.), *Quest for excitement: Sport and leisure in the civilizing process* (pp. 224-244). Oxford: Basil Blackwell.

Farr, K.A. (1988). Dominance bonding through the good old boys sociability group. *Sex Roles*, **18**, 259-277.

Fine, G.A. (1987). *With the boys: Little League baseball and preadolescent culture.* Chicago: University of Chicago Press.

Gilligan, C. (1982). *In a different voice: Psychological theory and woman's development.* Cambridge, MA: Harvard University Press.

Herek, G.M. (1987). On heterosexual masculinity: Some psychical consequences of the social construction of gender and sexuality. In M.S. Kimmel (Ed.), *Changing men: New directions in research on men and masculinity* (pp. 68-82). Beverly Hills: Sage.

Heymann, P.B. (1990, Nov. 28). Report describes what happened in locker room. *USA Today*, pp. 9A, 7C.

Lyman, P. (1987). The fraternal bond as a joking relationship: A case study of the role of sexist jokes in male group bonding. In M.S. Kimmel (Ed.), *Changing men: New directions in research on men and masculinity* (pp. 148-163). Beverly Hills: Sage.

Messner, M.A. (1987). The meaning of success: The athletic experience and the development of male identity. In H. Brod (Ed.), *The making of masculinities: The new men's studies* (pp. 193-209). Boston: Allen & Unwin.

Messner, M.A. (1989). Gay athletes and the gay games: An interview with Tom Waddell. In M.S. Kimmel & M.A. Messner (Eds.), *Men's lives* (pp. 190-193). New York: Macmillan.

Messner, M.A. (1990). Men studying masculinity: Some epistemological issues in sport sociology. *Sociology of Sport Journal, 7*, 136-153.

Meyer, B.B. (1990). From idealism to actualization: The academic performance of female college athletes. *Sociology of Sport Journal, 7*, 44-57.

Norris, M. (1991, Feb. 2). Mr. nice guy. *T.V. Guide,* pp. 22-29.

Pronger, B. (1990). *The arena of masculinity: Sport, homosexuality, and the meaning of sex.* New York: St. Martin's Press.

Sabo, D.F., & Panepinto, J. (1990). Football ritual and the social reproduction of masculinity. In M.A. Messner & D.F. Sabo (Eds.), *Sport, men, and the gender order* (pp. 115-126). Champaign, IL: Human Kinetics.

Sanday, P.R. (1990). *Fraternity gang rapes: Sex, brotherhood, and privilege on campus.* New York: New York University Press.

Shaw, G. (1972). *Meat on the hoof.* New York: St. Martin's Press.

Sherrod, D. (1987). The bonds of men: Problems and possibilities in close male relationships. In H. Brod (Ed.), *The making of masculinities: The new men's studies* (pp. 213-239). Boston: Allen & Unwin.

Snyder, E.E. (1972). Athletic dressing room slogans as folklore: A means of socialization. *International Review of Sport Sociology, 7*, 89-100.

West, C., & Zimmerman, D.H. (1987). Doing gender. *Gender & Society, 1*, 125-149.

Zurcher, L.A. (1982). The staging of emotion: A dramaturgical analysis. *Symbolic Interaction, 5*, 1-19.

Zurcher, L.A. (1983). Dealing with an unacceptable role: Hashers in a sorority house. In L.A. Zurcher (Ed.), *Social roles: Conformity, conflict, and creativity* (pp. 77-89). Beverly Hills: Sage.

■ FOR FURTHER STUDY

Fine, Gary Alan, *With the Boys: Little League Baseball and Preadolescent Culture* (Chicago: University of Chicago Press, 1987).

Fejgin, Naomi. "Participation in High School Competitive Sports: A Subversion of School Mission or Contribution to Academic Goals?" *Sociology of Sport Journal* 11 (September 1994): 211-220.

Foley, Douglas E., *Learning Capitalist Culture: Deep in the Heart of Tejas* (Philadelphia: University of Pennsylvania Press, 1990).

Frey, Darcy, *The Last Shot: City Streets, Basketball Dreams* (Boston: Houghton Mifflin, 1994).

Miracle, Andrew, and C. Roger Rees, *Lessons of the Locker Room: The Myth of School Sports* (Amherst, New York: Prometheus Books, 1994).

Morris, G. D., and James J. Stiehl, *Changing Kids' Games* (Champaign, Illinois: Human Kinetics, 1989).

Nixon, Howard L., II, "Rethinking Socialization and Sport." *Journal of Sport and Social Issues* 14 (Spring 1990): 33-47.

Sage, George H. "Sports Participation as a Builder of Character?" *The World and I* 3 (October 1988): 629-641.

Part Three

Sport and Socialization: The Mass Media

The mass media have a tremendous impact on sports. First, the popularity of sport is due in large measure to the enormous attention it receives from the mass media. Second, television has infused huge sums of money into sport, affecting franchise moves and salaries. Third, television (and the money it offers) has changed the way sports are played (for example, the scheduling of games, the interruption of the flow of games for commercial breaks, the shift from match play to medal play in tournament golf, and rule changes such as liberalizing offensive holding in football to increase scoring and, therefore, viewer interest). Fourth, television has affected college sports by making recruiting more national than regional and by focusing the nation's attention (and heaping television's money) on the games by a relatively few schools. Thus, television has exacerbated the gap between the "haves" and the "have nots." Moreover, since television money goes to the successful, it has heightened the pressure to win and, for some, the necessity to cheat in order to win.

Another consequence of the media—the effect on perceptions—is the focus of this section. The media direct attention toward certain acts and away from others. While the media appear to simply report what is happening, or what has just happened, during a sporting event, they actually provide a constructed view by what they choose to cover, their focus, and the narrative themes they pursue.[1] As Alan and John Clarke have said:

> It selects *between* sports for those which make "good television," and it selects *within* a particular event, it highlights particular aspects for the viewers. This selective highlighting is not "natural" or inevitable—it is based on certain criteria, certain media assumptions about what is "good television." But the media do

not only select, they also provide us with definitions of what has been selected. They interpret events for us, provide us with frameworks of meaning in which to make sense of the event. To put it simply, television does not merely consist of pictures, but also involves a commentary on the pictures—a commentary which explains to us what we are seeing.... These selections are socially constructed—they involve decisions about what to reveal to the viewers. The presentation of sport through the media involves an active process of re-presentation: what we see is not the event, but the event transformed into something else—a media event.[2]

The two selections in this section focus on this theme. The first, by Michael A. Messner, Margaret Carlisle Duncan, and Kerry Jensen, documents how live, play-by-play (therefore, unscripted) television commentators talk differently about women and men athletes. They find that although contemporary commentators are less overtly sexist than their predecessors, their language nevertheless tends to mark women's sports and women athletes as "other," infantilizes women athletes, and frames their accomplishments negatively or ambivalently.

The second selection, by Dan C. Hilliard, shows that sport itself and the media portrayal of sport are ideological—that is, supportive of conservative values. Moreover, television is antisociological because it focuses on the personal rather than the social and it avoids serious analysis of social problems or political issues.

NOTES

1. D. Stanley Eitzen and George H. Sage, *Sociology of North American Sport*, 5th ed. (Dubuque, Iowa: Wm. C. Brown, 1993), chap. 9.
2. Alan Clarke and John Clarke, "Highlights and Action Replays—Ideology, Sport and the Media," in *Sport, Culture, and Ideology*, Jennifer Hargreaves, ed. (Boston: Routledge & Kegan Paul, 1982), pp. 69, 71.

9. Separating the Men from the Girls: The Gendered Language of Televised Sports

MICHAEL A. MESSNER, MARGARET CARLISLE DUNCAN, AND KERRY JENSEN

INTRODUCTION

Feminist scholars have argued that in the twentieth century, the institution of sport has provided men with a homosocial sphere of life through which they have bolstered a sagging ideology of male superiority.[1] Through the exclusion of women, and the association of males with physical competence, strength, power, and even violence, sport has provided a basis through which men have sought to reconstitute an otherwise challenged masculine hegemony (Bryson, 1987; Hall, 1988; Kidd, 1987; Messner, 1988; Theberge, 1981; Whitson, 1990).

But starting with the 1972 passage of Title IX in the U.S., athletic participation of school-age girls increased dramatically. In 1971, only 294,015 girls participated in high school sports, compared with 3,666,917 boys. By the 1989-90 academic year, there were 1,858,659 girls participating in high school sports, compared with 3,398,192 boys.[2] Increased numerical participation in sports by girls and women has been accompanied by changing attitudes as well. A nationwide survey found large majorities of parents and children agreeing that "sports are no longer for boys only" (Wilson & Women's Sports Foundation, 1988). With increases in opportunities for female athletes, including expanded youth programs, better and earlier coaching, and increases in scholarships for college women athletes, some dramatic improvements in female athletic performance have resulted. In fact, the "muscle gap"—the degree of difference between male and female athletic performance in measurable sports like swimming and track and field—has closed considerably in the past fifteen years (Crittenden, 1979; Dyer, 1983; Kidd, 1990). In short, the dramatic increase in female athleticism has begun to challenge the assumption that sport is and should be a "male world." Organized sports, though still dominated by men at nearly all

SOURCE: "Separating the Men from the Girls: The Gendered Language of Televised Sports" by Michael A. Messner, Margaret Carlisle Duncan, and Kerry Jensen. From *Gender and Society* 7, pp. 121–137. Copyright © 1992 by Sage Publications. Reprinted by permission of Sage Publications, Inc.

levels, has in the past two decades become a "contested terrain" of gender relations (Birrell, 1987/1988; Messner, 1988).

Much of the continued salience of sport as an institutional site for the construction and legitimation of masculine power lies in its role as mass-mediated spectacle (Clarke & Clarke, 1982; Hargreaves, 1986; Willis, 1982). There *has* been a boom in female athletic participation, but the sports media has been very slow to reflect it. Bryant's (1980) two-year content analysis of two newspapers revealed that only 4.4% of total column inches devoted to sports focussed on women's sports. Graydon (1983) observed that in the early 1980's, over 90% of sports reporting covered men's sports. Rintala and Birrell's (1984) analysis of *Young Athlete* magazine, and Duncan and Sayaovong's (1990) examination of *Sports Illustrated for Kids* magazine revealed that visual images of male athletes in these magazines tend to out-number those of female athletes by a roughly two-to-one ratio. Moreover, text and visual images tend to frame female and male athletes "as funda-mentally and essentially different," and thus to support stereotypical notions of natural differences between the sexes (Duncan & Sayaovong, 1990: 91). In a part of our study (not dealt with in this paper), we examined four major metropolitan daily newspapers and found that over a three-month period in 1990, 81% of all sports column inches were devoted exclusively to men's sports, 3.5% covered women's sports, and 15.5% covered both men's and women's sports, or gender-neutral topics. We also examined six weeks of a leading television newscast, and found that 92% of sports news time was devoted exclusively to men's sports, 5% covered women's sports, and 3% covered gender-neutral topics. This sort of ignoring or underreporting of existing women's events contributes to the continuation of what Gerbner (1978) called "the symbolic annihilation" of women's sports.

Despite the paucity of coverage of women's sports by the media, there are some recent signs of increased coverage, especially on cable television (Eastman & Meyer, 1989). If there is indeed a "window of opportunity" for increased coverage of women's sports on television, the question of *how* women's and men's sports are covered becomes crucial. To date, very few analyses of the quality of live, televised, play-by-play coverage of women's sports have been conducted. Studies of the 1970's and 1980's revealed that women athletes (when they were reported on television at all) were likely to be overtly trivialized, infantilized, and sexualized (Boutilier & San Giovanni, 1983; Duncan, 1990; Dyer, 1987; Felshin, 1974). Even excellent perfor-mances by women athletes were likely to be framed "ambivalently" by sports commentators (Duncan & Hasbrook, 1988).

We were interested in comparing how live, play-by-play television sports commentators talk about women's sports and women athletes with how they talk about men's sports and men athletes. We constructed our research design, in part, from the now-vast feminist literature on gender and lan-guage. In short, this literature demonstrates that the ways men and women talk—and the ways we are talked about—are deeply gendered. For instance, a woman secretary would likely use the formal "Mr.," along with the last name, when speaking to her male boss, while he would probably feel free to refer to her by her first name. This kind of language convention tends to (often subtly) mark gender difference (and, in the above example, social class difference as well) in ways that support and reinforce the power and privilege of "dominants" over "subordinates." The micropolitical realm of face-to-face interaction and language both reflects and constructs the micropolitical realm of unequal power relations between groups (Henley, 1977, 1987; Lakoff, 1975; Miller & Swift, 1977; Thorne, Kramarae & Henley, 1985; Schultz, 1975; Spender, 1980).

DESCRIPTION OF RESEARCH

Our aim was to utilize feminist insights on gendered language to examine the ways that television commentators talk about women's and men's sports. We chose to examine two sports where televised coverage of women's and men's contests could be compared: basketball and tennis. For a number of years, women's tennis has been highly visible on television, but women's college basketball is only recently beginning to be televised (albeit mostly on cable T.V., and often on late-night tape delay). We reasoned that a comparison of the more "established" televised sport of tennis with the relative "newcomer" of women's basketball might be revealing.

Live televised coverage of the 1989 women's and men's NCAA final four basketball tournaments were compared and analyzed. (It should be noted that we chose the "final four," rather than regular-season games, because there are so few women's regular season games actually broadcast on television.) This amounted to three women's games and three men's games, including introductions/lead-ins and halftime shows. We also examined the four final days of televised coverage of the 1989 U.S. Open tennis tournament. Televised coverage consisted of four men's singles matches (two quarterfinals, one semifinal, and the final), three women's single matches (two semis and the final), one men's doubles match (the final), two women's doubles matches (a semi and the final), and one mixed-doubles match (the final).

Three general questions guided our analysis: First, do commentators overtly trivialize and/or sexualize women's sports and individual women athletes in the ways that previous analysts have identified? Second, do sports commentators speak about women's and men's athletic contests differently? In particular, to what extent (if any) are women's and men's events verbally "gender marked" (e.g., "the *women's* national championship")? Third, do commentators speak of individual women and men athletes differently? For instance, are women athletes referred to as "girls" or as "women"? Are men athletes referred to as "boys" or as "men"?

First, we recorded the basketball games and tennis matches on video-tape, and conducted a pilot study of the tapes. The pilot study had two outcomes: First the research design was fine-tuned. In particular, a pre-liminary list of specific qualitative and quantitative questions was con-structed. Next, we developed standardized ways of analyzing the verbal commentary. Then, the research assistant viewed all of the tapes and com-piled a detailed record of her observations. Next, all of the tapes were independently viewed and analyzed by one of the investigators, who then added her written analysis to that of the research assistant. Finally, the data was compiled and analyzed by the two investigators, using both sets of written descriptions of the tapes, and by viewing portions of the tapes once again.

Our data revealed very little of the overtly sexist commentary that has been observed in past research. Women's sports and women athletes were not overtly trivialized in tennis or in basketball commentary. And though camera angles at times may have subtly framed women athletes (especially in tennis) as sexual objects in ways that were not symmetrical with the ways men were framed, the verbal commentary did not frame women in this way. However, we did find two categories in the verbal commentary: (1) Gender marking; (2) A "hierarchy of naming" by gender, and to a certain extent by race.

WOMEN MARKED AS OTHER

In women's basketball, gender was constantly marked, both verbally and through the use of graphics. We were continually reminded that we were watch-ing the "*Women's* final four," the "NCAA *Women's* National Championship Game," that these were "some of the best *women's* college basketball teams," that coach Pat Summit "is a legend in *women's* basketball," that "this NCAA *women's* semifinal is brought to you by . . . ." Gender was also marked through the use of graphics in the women's games which CBS broadcasted, but not in the ESPN game. The CBS logo marked the women's championship game: "NCAA Women's National Championship," as did their graphics above game scores. ESPN's graphic did not mark gender: "NCAA Semifinal." As Table 9-1 indicates, over the course of the three women's games, there were 28 instances of graphic, and 49 cases of verbal gender marking, for a total of 77 instances of gender marking. This meant that gender was being marked an average of 25.6 times per women's game.

During the women's games, when commentators were discussing the next day's men's games, the men's games were sometimes gender-marked (e.g., "the *men's* championship game will be played tomorrow"). But during the men's basketball games, we observed no instances of gender marking, either verbal or graphic. Men's games were always referred to as universal,

TABLE 9-1   Gender Marking
in Basketball (three women's
games, three men's games)

	Women	Men
Verbal	49	0
Graphic	28	0
Total	77 (25.6)	0

both verbally and in on-screen graphic logos (e.g., "The NCAA National Championship Game," "The Final Four," etc.).

Women's and men's tennis matches were verbally gender-marked in a roughly equitable manner (e.g., "Men's doubles finals," "Women's singles semifinals," etc.). Verbal descriptions of athletes, though, revealed a tendency to gender-mark women, not men. For instance, in the mixed doubles match, the commentators stated several times that Rick Leach is "one of the best doubles players in the world," while Robyn White was referred to as one of "the most animated girls on the circuit." An instance of graphic gender marking in tennis which we found notable was the tendency by CBS to display a pink on-screen graphic for the women's matches, and a blue on-screen graphic for the men's matches.

How might we interpret these observations? Stanley (1977) suggests that although *asymmetrical* gender marking tends to mark women as "other," *symmetrical* gender marking is not necessarily oppressive. In fact, she argues that the move toward a totally gender-neutral language may serve to further render women invisible. This would probably be the case if the language of sports reporting and commentary became gender neutral. In fact, in certain cases (in the daily television program, for instance) gender marking is probably necessary to clarify what the viewer will be tuning in to watch. We observed this sort of gender marking in tennis, where women's and men's matches (though not always women and men *athletes*) were verbally gender-marked in a roughly symmetrical manner. The rough symmetry of gender marking in tennis might be explained by the fact that the women's and men's tennis tournaments were being played in the same venue, with coverage often cutting back and forth to women's, men's, and mixed-doubles matches. In this context, symmetrical gender marking probably provides a necessary sense of clarity for the viewers, though the pink (for women) and blue (for men) graphic on-screen logos tended to mark gender in a manner which reinforced conventional gender stereotypes.

By contrast, the women's and men's basketball games were played in different cities, on different nights. And our data revealed a dramatic asymmetry in the commentary: Women's games were verbally and graphically gender-marked an average of 25.6 times per game, while men's games were never gender-marked. We did not include gender-marked team names (e.g., "Lady Techsters, Lady Tigers, Lady Volunteers") in these tabulations because we reasoned that team names are the responsibility of their respective universities, not the networks or commentators. Nevertheless, gender-marked team names have recently been criticized as "contributing to the maintenance of dominance within college athletics by defining women athletes and women's athletic programs as second class and trivial" (Eitzen & Baca Zinn, 1989: 362). In several colleges and universities in recent years, faculty and students have attempted to change gender-marked women's team names (Eitzen & Baca Zinn, 1990). In the three women's basketball games which we examine, team names were gender-marked 53 times graphically, 49 times verbally (a total of 102 times). As Table 9-2 reveals, when we add these numbers to our original tabulations, we see that the combination of on-screen graphics, verbal commentary, and team names and logos amounted to a constant barrage of gender marking in the women's games: gender was marked in some fashion an average of 59.7 times per women's game. By contrast, the men's games were always simply referred to as "the national championship games," etc. As a result, the men's games and tournament were presented as the norm, the universal, while the women's were continually marked as the other, derivative (and by implication, inferior) to the men's.

A GENDERED HIERARCHY OF NAMING

There were stark contrasts between how men athletes and women athletes were referred to by commentators. This was true both in tennis and in basketball. First, and as we had expected, women were commonly referred to as "girls," as "young ladies," and as "women." (Often the naming of women athletes was ambivalent. For instance, Steffi Graf was referred to as "the wonder girl of women's tennis.") By contrast, the male athletes, *never* referred to as "boys," were referred to as "men," "young men," or "young fellas." Second, when athletes were named, commentators used the first name only of the women far more commonly than for the men. This difference was most stark in tennis commentary, as revealed in Table 9-3.

In basketball, the degree of difference in the use of first names of women and men players was not as dramatic, but the pattern was similar. In the three women's basketball games, we counted 31 incidents of women athletes being

TABLE 9-2 Gender Marking in Basketball (three women's games, three men's games, including gender-marked team names)

	Women	Men
Verbal	98	0
Graphic	81	0
Total	179 (59.7)	0

TABLE 9-3   First and Last Name Use in Tennis Commentary
(totals [percentages], by sex)

	First Only	Last Only	First and Last
Women	304 (52.7)	166 (28.8)	107 (18.5)
Men	44 (7.8)	395 (69.8)	127 (22.4)

referred to by their first name only. This occurred 19 times in the men's games.

How do we interpret these differences in how commentators talk about male and female athletes? After these research findings were released at a national press conference, Diana Nyad, one of the USA Network tennis commentators, stated that the difference in first and last name use in women's and men's tennis commentary is not due to "sexism," but is simply a result of the fact that the women tennis players are more likely to be "teen-aged girls," while the men players are likely to be older (Herbert, 1990). This was an interesting response, given that in the tennis matches we examined in our study, the range of ages for the male players was 19–29, with mean age 22.8, and the range of ages for female players was 19–32, with the mean age 24.0. In the NCAA basketball tournaments, all of the female and male players were college students, and roughly the same age. Clearly, actual age differences do not explain commentators' tendency to refer to women athletes as "girls," "young ladies," and by first name only.

Research has demonstrated that "dominants" (either by social class, age, occupational position, race, or gender) are more commonly referred to by their last names (often prefaced by titles such as "Mr."). "Dominants" generally have license to refer to "subordinates" (younger people, employees, lower class people, ethnic minorities, women, etc.) by their first names (Henley, 1977; McConnell-Ginet, 1978; Rubin, 1981; Wolfson & Manes, 1980). The practice of referring more "formally" to dominants, and more "informally" (or "endearingly") to subordinates linguistically grants the former adult status, while marking the latter in an infantilizing way. And research suggests that these linguistic differences both reflect and (re)construct inequality. For instance, Brannon (1978) had 462 college students read a story describing a female's application for a high-level executive position, in which she was referred to either as a "girl" or as a "woman." Students' ratings of personality traits described the "woman" as more tough, brilliant, mature, and dignified, more qualified to be hired, and more deserving of a higher salary than the "girl." Similarly, the term "lady" tends to "evoke a standard of propriety, correct behavior, and elegance" (Miller & Swift, 1977), and "carries overtones recalling the age of chivalry, implying that women are helpless and cannot do things for themselves," all of which are characteristics which are "decidedly unathletic" (Eitzen & Baca Zinn, 1990: 5-6). It can be concluded that tennis commentators' tendency to call women athletes "girls" and "young ladies," and their utilization of the first name only of women athletes (52.7% of the time) far more commonly than men athletes (7.8% of the time) reflects the lower status of women athletes. Moreover, it is reasonable to speculate that this language is likely to be received by viewers in such a way that it reinforces any already-existing negative attitudes or ambivalences about women's sports and women athletes.

We can speculate as to why the contrast in gendered patterns of naming was not as stark in basketball as it was in tennis. Perhaps since female tennis players have traditionally been stereotyped in more conventionally "feminine" ways than other female athletes, there is more of a (probably unconscious) tendency for commentators to view them (and talk about them) in an infantilizing manner. Moreover, women tennis players are often participating in the same venue as the men (and in the case of mixed doubles, in the very same *matches* with the men), and perhaps this contributes to an unconscious tendency to verbally separate them from the men by naming them differently. By contrast, female basketball players are participating in a traditionally defined "male" sport that requires a good deal of physically aggressive body-contact. Perhaps as a result, commentators are less likely to (again, probably unconsciously) view them and talk about them using conventionally "feminine" and infantilizing language. And since the women's basketball games are being constantly and thoroughly gender-marked, both graphically and verbally, there is little chance that their games will be confused with those of the men. There may therefore be less of an unconscious tendency on the part of commentators to verbally differentiate them from the men in terms of how they are named.

In addition to the tendency to linguistically infantilize women, while granting men athletes adult status, the quality of commentators' verbal attributions of strength and weakness, success and failure, for women's and men's events also tended to differ. In basketball, verbal attributions of strength to women were often stated in ambivalent language which undermined or neutralized the words conveying power and strength: "big girl," "she's tiny, she's small, but so effective under the boards," "her little jump hook," etc. A difference in descriptions of basketball coaches was also noted. Joe Ciampi (male) "yells" at his team, while Pat Summit (female) was described twice in the Auburn vs. Tennessee game as "screaming" off the bench. Men coaches were not described as "screaming," a term which often implies lack of control, powerlessness, even hysteria.

In tennis, "confidence" was very frequently used to describe strength for women, but not so often for men. We speculated that confidence is considered a "given" for men, but an attribute for which women players must constantly strive. Even very strong descriptors, for women, were often framed ambivalently: "That young lady Graf is relentless," or sexualized: "Sabatini has put together this first set with such naked aggression." And whereas for women, spectacular shots were sometimes referred to as "lucky," for the men, there were constant references to the imposition of their wills on the games (and on opponents). In men's doubles, for example, "You can feel McEnroe imposing his will all over this court. I mean not just with Woodford but Flach and Seguso. He's just giving them messages by the way he's standing at the net, the way he kind of swaggers between points."

There was little ambivalence in the descriptions of men: There are "big" guys with "big" forehands, who play "big games." There was a constant suggestion of male power and agency in the commentary. Even descriptions of men's weaknesses were commonly framed in a language of agency: "He created his own error . . . . " Discussion of men's "nervousness" was often qualified to make it sound like strength and heroism. For instance, early in the Becker/Krickstein match, the two commentators had this exchange: "They're both pretty nervous, and that's pretty normal." "Something would be wrong if they weren't." "It means you care." "Like Marines going into Iwo Jima saying they weren't nervous, something's a little fishy."

In both basketball and tennis, there were also qualitative differences in the ways that success and failure were discussed for women and men athletes. In fact, two formulae for success appeared to exist, one for men, the other for women. Men appeared to succeed through a combination of talent, instinct, intelligence, size, strength, quickness, hard work, and risk-taking. Women also appeared to succeed through talent, enterprise, hard work, and intelligence. But commonly cited along with these attributes were emotion, luck, togetherness, and family. Women were also more likely to be framed as failures due to some combination of nervousness, lack of confidence, lack of being "comfortable," lack of aggression, and lack of stamina. Men were far less often framed as failures—men appeared to miss shots and lose matches not so much because of their own individual shortcomings (nervousness, losing control, etc.), but because of the power, strength, and intelligence of their (male) *opponents*. This framing of failure suggests that it is the thoughts and actions of the male victor that win games, rather than suggesting that the loser's lack of intelligence or ability is responsible for losing games. Men were framed as active agents in control of their destinies, women as reactive objects.

A HIERARCHY OF NAMING BY GENDER AND RACE

It was not simply women athletes who were linguistically infantilized and framed ambivalently. Our research suggests that black male basketball players shared some of this infantilization. Previous research revealed racial bias in televised commentary in men's sports. For instance, Rainville & McCormick (1977) found that white players received more praise and less criticism from football commentators than comparable black players. And Jackson (1989) reported that white male football and basketball players were much more likely to be credited with "intelligence and hard work," while the successes of their black male counterparts were more likely to be attributed to "natural athleticism." Our examination of basketball commentary occurred in the wake of widespread public discussion of Jackson's (1989) research. We observed what appeared to be a conscious effort on the part of commentators to cite both physical ability *and* intelligence when discussing successful black and white male and female players. However, this often appeared to be an afterthought. For instance, a commentator would note of a star white player that "He has so much court intelligence . . . **AND** so much natural ability!" And a typical comment about a black star player was "What a great athlete . . . **AND** he really plays the game intelligently!"

Though it appeared that television commentators were consciously attempting to do away with the "hard work/intelligence" (white) vs. "natural athlete" (black) dichotomy, we did find an indication of racial difference in naming of male basketball players. In the three men's basketball games, in each of the cases in which men were referred to by their first names only, the commentators were referring to men of color (e.g., Rumeal [Robinson], Ramon [Ramos]). Though there were several "star" white male basketball players (e.g., Danny Ferry and Andrew Gaze) in these games, they were *never* referred to by their first names only.

These findings suggest that T.V. sports commentators are (again, probably unconsciously) utilizing a "hierarchy of naming": At the top of the linguistic hierarchy sit the always last-named white "men," followed by (sometimes) first-named black "men," followed by (frequently) first-named "girls" and "young ladies." We found no racial differences in the ways that women athletes were named. We speculate that (at least within televised sports commentary) gender is the dominant defining feature of women athletes' shared subordinate status. By contrast, sports commentary tends to weave a taken-for-granted superordinate, adult masculine status around male athletes. Yet in the case of male athletes of color, the commentary tends to (subtly and partially) undermine their superordinate masculine status. This suggests, following the theory of gender stratification developed by Connell (1987) and applied to sport by Messner (1989), Messner & Sabo (1990) and Kidd (1987), that sports media reinforce the overall tendency of sport to be an institution which simultaneously (1) constructs and legitimizes men's overall power and privilege over women; and (2) constructs and legitimizes heterosexual, white, middle class men's power and privilege over subordinated and marginalized groups of men.

CONCLUSION

An individual who watches an athletic event constructs and derives various meanings from the activity. These meanings result from a process of interaction between the meanings that are built into the game itself (the formal rules and structure, as well as the history and accumulated mythology of the game) and the values, ideologies, and presuppositions that the viewer brings to the activity of watching. But viewing an athletic contest on television is not the same as watching a contest "live." Televised sport is an event which is mediated by the "framing" of the contest by commentators and technical people (Clarke & Clarke, 1982; Duncan & Brummett, 1987; Gitlin, 1982; Gruneau, 1989; Jhally, 1989; Morse, 1983; Wenner, 1989). Thus, any meanings that a television viewer constructs from the contest are likely to be profoundly affected by the framing of the contest (Altheide & Snow, 1979; Antin, 1982; Conrad, 1982; Duncan & Hasbrook, 1988; Fiske & Hartley, 1978; Innis, 1951; McLuhan, 1964; Morse, 1983).

Televised sports are live and largely unscripted, but the language which commentators use to frame the events tends to conform to certain linguistic conventions which are themselves a result of "a complex articulation of technical, organizational, economic, cultural, political, and social factors" (Jhally, 1989: 84). And as Gruneau (1989) has argued, though commentators are often aware of themselves as "storytellers," they are not necessarily aware of the political and ideological ramifications of the linguistic conventions to which they—apparently unconsciously—conform.

Language is never neutral. An analysis of language reveals imbedded social meanings, including overt and covert social biases, stereotypes, and inequities. There is an extensive body of literature which documents how language both reflects and reinforces gender inequalities (Baron, 1986; Henley, 1977, 1987; Lakoff, 1975; Miller & Swift, 1977, 1980; Schultz, 1975; Spender, 1980; Thorne, Kramarae & Henley, 1985; Van Den Bergh, 1987). In a recent study of the gendered language of sport, sociologists D. Stanley Eitzen and Maxine Baca Zinn (1989: 364) argue that

> [Gendered] language places women and men within a system of differentiation and stratification. Language suggests how women and men are to be evaluated. Language embodies negative and positive value stances and valuations related to how certain groups within society are appraised. Language in general is filled with biases about women and men. Specific linguistic conventions are sexist when they isolate or stereotype some aspect of an individual's nature or the nature of a group of individuals based on their sex.

The media—and sports media in particular—tend to reflect the social conventions of gender-biased language. In so doing, they reinforce the biased meanings built into language, and thus contribute to the re-construction of social inequities.

Newspaper editors and television programmers often argue that they are simply "giving the public what it wants." Programming decisions are clearly circumscribed by market realities, and research does indicate that with few exceptions, men's athletic events draw more spectators than women's. But one question that arises concerns the reciprocal effect of, on the one hand, public attitudes, values, and tastes, and on the other hand, the quantity and quality of coverage of certain kinds of athletic events. What comes first: public "disinterest" in televised women's athletics, or lack of quality coverage? Perhaps a more timely question now that women's sports are getting at least incrementally more coverage is: How do the ways that women and men's sports are covered on television affect the "interest" of the public in these events?

Our research on women's and men's tennis and basketball coverage indicated that commentators today are less likely than their predecessors to overtly sexualize or trivialize women athletes. However, the language used by commentators tends to mark women's sports and women athletes as "other," infantilize women athletes, and frame their accomplishments negatively or ambivalently. Our research also suggests that black male athletes share in some of the linguistic infantilization that is commonly used to describe women athletes. As a result, the language of sports commentary tends to (often subtly) reconstruct gender and racial hierarchies.

Though subtle bias is no less dangerous than overt sexism, the decline of overtly sexist language suggests that some commentators are becoming more committed to presenting women's athletics fairly. For instance, women's basketball commentator Steve Physioc re-named "man-to-man defense" as "player-to-player" defense. This is an example of a conscious decision to replace an androcentric language with language which is not gendered. Though Physioc did not do this consistently, the fact that he did it at all was an indication of his awareness of the gender biases built into the conventional language of sports. Critics might argue that changing language subverts the history or the "purity" of the game. But in fact, terminology used to describe sports is constantly changing. For instance, in basketball, the part of the court nearest the basket that used to be called "the key" through the 1950's was re-named "the lane" in the 1960's, and is more recently referred to as "the paint" or "the block." These changes have come about as a result of changes in the rules of the game, changes in the sizes and styles of players, and general changes in social values and mores. But language does not simply change as a "reflection" of social reality. Language also helps to construct social reality (Shute, 1981; Van Den Bergh, 1987). Thus the choice to use non-sexist language is a choice to linguistically affirm the right of women athletes to fair and equal treatment.

Viewed in this context, Physioc's use of "player-to-player defense" can be viewed as a linguistic recognition that something significant has happened to basketball: It is no longer simply a men's game. There are women players out there, and the language used to report their games should reflect and endorse this fact.

NOTES

1. This research is based on a larger study of gender and sports media which was commissioned by the Amateur Athletic Foundation of Los Angeles. The authors gratefully acknowledge the assistance of Wayne Wilson of the AAF, and of Barrie Thorne, who commented on an earlier version of this paper.
2. These statistics are compiled yearly by the National Federation of State High School Associations in Kansas City, MO. The 1989-90 statistics were received via a phone interview with the NFSHSA. For discussion of the implications of this continuing trend of increasing high school athletic participation by girls, see D. Sabo (1988) "Title IX and Athletics: Sex Equity in Schools," in *Updating School Board Policies* 19 (10), November.

REFERENCES

Altheide, D. L., & Snow, R. P. (1979) *Media Logic.* Beverly Hills, CA: Sage.

Antin, D. (1982) "Video: The Distinctive Features of the Medium," pp. 455-477 in H. Newcomb (Ed.). *Television: The Critical View* (3rd ed.). New York: Oxford University Press.

Baron, D. (1986) *Grammar and Gender.* New Haven: Yale University Press.

Birrell, S. (1987-1988) "The Woman Athlete's College Experience: Knowns and Unknowns," *Journal of Sport & Social Issues* 11: 82-96.

Boutilier, M. A., & San Giovanni, L. (1983) *The Sporting Woman.* Champaign, IL: Human Kinetics.

Brannon, R. (1978) "The Consequences of Sexist Language." Paper presented at the American Psychological Association Meetings, Toronto.

Bryant, J. (1980) "A Two-year Investigation of the Female in Sport as Reported in the Paper Media," *Arena Review* 4: 32-44.

Bryson, L. (1987) "Sport and the Maintenance of Masculine Hegemony," *Women's Studies International Forum* 10: 349-360.

Clarke, A., & Clarke, J. (1982) "Highlights and Action Replays: Ideology, Sport, and the Media," pp. 62-87 in J. Hargreaves (Ed.). *Sport, Culture, and Ideology.* London: Routledge & Kegan-Paul.

Connell, R. W. (1987) *Gender and Power.* Stanford, CA: Stanford University Press.

Conrad, P. (1982) *Television: The Medium and Its Manners.* Boston: Routledge & Kegan-Paul.

Crittenden, A. (1979) "Closing the Muscle Gap," pp. 5-10 in S. Twin, (Ed.). *Out of the Bleachers: Writings on Women and Sport.* Old Westbury, NY: The Feminist Press.

Duncan, M. C. (1990) "Sports Photographs and Sexual Differences: Images of Women and Men in the 1984 and 1988 Olympic Games," *Sociology of Sport Journal* 7: 22-43.

Duncan, M. C., & Brummet, B. (1987) "The Mediation of Spectator Sport," *Research Quarterly for Exercise and Sport* 58: 168-177.

Duncan, M. C., & Hasbrook, C. A. (1988) "Denial of Power in Televised Women's Sports," *Sociology of Sport Journal* 5: 1-21.

Duncan, M. C., & Sayaovong, A. (1990) "Photographic Images and Gender in *Sports Illustrated for Kids,*" *Play & Culture* 3: 91-116.

Dyer, G. (1987) "Women and Television: An Overview," pp. 6-16 in H. Baeher & G. Dyer (Eds.) *Boxed In: Women and Television.* New York: Pandora Press.

Dyer, K. (1983) *Challenging the Men: The Social Biology of Female Sport Achievement.* St. Lucia: University of Queensland.

Eastman, S. T., & Meyer, T. P. (1989) "Sports Programming: Scheduling, Costs, and Competition," pp. 97-119 in L. A. Wenner (Ed.). *Media, Sports, & Society.* Newbury Park, CA: Sage Publications.

Eitzen, D. S., & Baca Zinn, M. (1989) "The De-athleticization of Women: The Naming and Gender Marking of Collegiate Sport Teams," *Sociology of Sport Journal* 6: 362-370.

Eitzen, D. S., & Baca Zinn, M. (1990) "Language and Gender Stratification: The Naming of Collegiate Athletic Teams." Paper presented at the meetings of the International Sociological Association, Madrid, Spain (July 9-13).

Felshin, J. (1974) "The Social View," pp. 179-279 in E. W. Gerber, J. Felshin, P. Berlin, & W. Wyrick (Eds.). *The American Woman in Sport.* Reading, MA: Addison-Wesley.

Fiske, J., & Hartley, J. (1978) *Reading Television.* New York: Methuen.

Gitlin, T. (1982) "Prime Time Ideology: The Hegemonic Process in Television Entertainment," pp. 426-454 in H. Newcomb (Ed.). *Television: The Critical View* (3rd ed.). New York: Oxford University Press.

Graydon, M. (1983) "But It's More than a Game: It's an Institution," *Feminist Review* 13: 5-16.

Gruneau, R. (1989) "Making Spectacle: A Case Study in Television Sports Production," pp. 134-154 in L. A. Wenner (Ed.). *Media, Sports, & Society.* Newbury Park, CA: Sage Publications.

Hall, M. A. (1988) "The Discourse on Gender and Sport: From Femininity to Feminism," *Sociology of Sport Journal* 5: 330-340.

Hargreaves, J. (1986) "Where's the Virtue? Where's the Grace? A Discussion of the Social Production of Gender Through Sport," *Theory, Culture and Society* 3: 109-121.

Henley, N. M. (1977) *Body Politics: Power, Sex and Nonverbal Communication.* Englewood Cliffs, NJ: Prentice Hall.

Henley, N. M. (1987) "This New Species that Seeks New Language: On Sexism in Language and Language Change," pp. 3-27 in J. Penfield (Ed.). *Women and Language in Transition.* Albany: State University of New York Press.

Herbert, S. (1990) "Study Charges Sexism in Women's Sports Coverage," *Los Angeles Times,* Thursday, August 30, 1990, p. F-2.

Innis, H. A. (1951) *The Bias of Communication.* Toronto: University of Toronto Press.

Jackson, D. Z. (1989) "Sports Broadcasting: Calling the Plays in Black and White," *The Boston Globe* (Sunday, January 22).

Jhally, S. (1989) "Cultural Studies and the Sports/Media Complex," pp. 70-93 in L. A. Wenner (Ed.). *Media, Sports, & Society.* Newbury Park, CA: Sage Publications.

Kidd, B. (1987) "Sports and Masculinity," in M. Kaufman (Ed.). *Beyond Patriarchy: Essays by Men on Pleasure, Power, and Change.* Toronto and New York: Oxford University Press.

Kidd, B. (1990) "The Men's Cultural Centre: Sports and the Dynamic of Women's Oppression/Men's Repression," pp. 31-44 in M. A. Messner & D. F. Sabo (Eds.). *Sport, Men and the Gender Order: Critical Feminist Perspectives.* Champaign, IL: Human Kinetics.

Lakoff, R. (1975) *Language and Woman's Place.* New York: Harper & Row.

McConnell-Ginet, S. (1978) "Address Forms in Sexual Politics," pp. 23-35 in D. Butturff & E. L. Epstein (Eds.). *Women's Language and Style.* Akron, OH: L & S Books.

McLuhan, M. (1964) *Understanding Media: The Extensions of Man.* New York: Signet Books.

Messner, M. A. (1988) "Sports and Male Domination: The Female Athlete as Contested Ideological Terrain," *Sociology of Sport Journal* 5: 197-211.

Messner, M. A. (1989) "Masculinities and Athletic Careers," *Gender & Society* 3: 71-88.

Messner, M. A., & Sabo, D. F. (1990) "Toward a Critical Feminist Reappraisal of Sport, Men and the Gender Order," pp. 1-16 in M. A. Messner & D. F. Sabo (Eds.). *Sport, Men and the Gender Order: Critical Feminist Perspectives.* Champaign, IL: Human Kinetics.

Miller, C. & Swift, K. (1977) *Words and Women: New Language in New Times.* Garden City, NY: Doubleday/Anchor.

Miller, C., & Swift, K. (1980) *The Handbook of Nonsexist Writing.* New York: Lippincott & Crowell.

Morse, M. (1983) "Sport on Television: Replay and Display," pp. 44-66 in E. A. Kaplan (Ed.). *Regarding Television.* Los Angeles: American Film Institute/University Publications of America.

Rainville, R. E., & McCormick, E. (1977) "Extent of Covert Prejudice in Pro Football Announcers' Speech," *Journalism Quarterly* 54: 20-26.

Rintala, J., & Birrell, S. (1984) "Fair Treatment for the Active Female: A Content Analysis of *Young Athlete* Magazine," *Sociology of Sport Journal* 3: 195-203.

Rubin, R. (1981) "Ideal Traits and Terms of Address for Male and Female College Professors." *Journal of Personality and Social Psychology* 41: 966-974.

Sabo, D. (1988) "Title IX and Athletics: Sex Equity in Schools," *Updating School Board Policies* 19 (10), November.

Schultz, M. (1975) "The Semantic Derogation of Women," pp. 64-75 in B. Thorne & N. Henley (Eds.) *Language and Sex: Difference and Dominance.* Rowley, MA: Newbury House.

Shute, S. (1981) "Sexist Language and Sexism," pp. 23-33 in M. Vetterling-Braggin (Ed.). *Sexist Language: A Modern Philosophical Analysis.* Totowa, NJ: Littlefield, Adams.

Spender, D. (1980) *Man Made Language.* London: Routledge & Kegan-Paul.

Stanley, J. P. (1977) "Gender Marking in American English: Usage and Reference," pp. 43-74 in A. P. Nilsen et al. (Eds.). *Sexism and Language.* Urbana, IL: National Council of Teachers of English.

Theberge, N. (1981) "A Critique of Critiques: Radical and Feminist Writings on Sport." *Social Forces* 60: 387-394.

Theberge, N., & Cronk, A. (1987) "Work Routines in Newspaper Sports Departments and the Coverage of Women's Sports," *Sociology of Sport Journal* 3: 195-203.

Thorne, B., Kramarae, C., & Henley, N. (1985) "Language, Gender and Society: Opening a Second Decade of Research," pp. 7-24 in B. Thorne & N. Henley (Eds.). *Language, Gender and Society.* Rowley, MA: Newbury House.

Van Den Bergh, N. (1987) "Renaming: Vehicle for Empowerment," pp. 130-136 in J. Penfield (Ed.). *Women and Language in Transition.* Albany: State University of New York Press.

Wenner, L. A. (1989) "Media, Sports and Society: The Research Agenda," pp. 13-48 in L. A. Wenner (Ed.). *Media, Sports and Society.* Newbury Park, CA: Sage Publications.

Whitson, D. (1990) "Sport in the Social Construction of Masculinity," pp. 19-30 in M. A. Messner & D. F. Sabo (Eds.). *Sport, Men and The Gender Order: Critical Feminist Perspectives.* Champaign, IL: Human Kinetics.

Willis, P. (1982) "Women in Sport in Ideology," pp. 117-135 in J. Hargreaves (Ed.). *Sport, Culture, and Ideology.* London: Routledge & Kegan-Paul.

Wilson Sporting Goods Co. & the Women's Sports Foundation (1988) "The Wilson Report: Moms, Dads, Daughters and Sports." (June).

Wolfson, N., & J. Manes (1980) "Don't 'Dear' Me!" pp. 79-92 in S. McConnell-Ginet, R. Borker, & N. Furman (Eds.). *Women and Language in Literature and Society.* New York: Praeger.

10. Televised Sport and the (Anti)Sociological Imagination

DAN C. HILLIARD

I recently began my undergraduate course in sociology of sport by outlining the cultural studies paradigm and showing how I thought it could be used to understand sport as a prime purveyor of ideology. After class a student came forward to ask me to clarify some points I had made in the lecture. After I answered her questions, she said, "I've been involved in sports all my life, but I've never looked at sport that way before." Her experience is, I think, typical. Sage (1990) states,

> Although sport practices embody specific and identifiable purposes, values, and meanings, they are typically viewed by both participants and spectators as ahistorical and apolitical in nature. This is true largely because most of our written and broadcast information does not confront people with questions about the larger social issues and political and economic consequences of modern sport and physical activity. Instead, we are fed a diet of traditional slogans, cliches, and ritualized trivia about sport. These may all be very comforting but they do not come to grips with reality. (p. 11)

In his 1959 landmark essay, C. Wright Mills urged the adoption of a "sociological imagination," which articulated the connection between "personal troubles" and "public issues." If Mills's pleading is the basis for a critical sociology, then the "sport-media complex" (Jhally, 1989) is profoundly antisociological.

In the past decade, a great deal of attention has been paid to the ideological work of sport in general and mediated sport in particular. Commercialized, professionalized, rationalized, mediated sport has been found to reproduce all sorts of hegemonic values. What may have been overlooked is that this fundamentally antisociological perspective provides a foundation for the ideological work of mediated sport by foreclosing the possibility of any significant criticism of the status quo.

Clearly, the powerful of the SportsWorld (Lipsyte, 1975) benefit from an uncritical rendering of sport by the mass media. Without invoking conspiracy theories or notions of a monolithic cultural elite, Gruneau (1989) has

SOURCE: "Televised Sport and (Anti)Sociological Imagination" by Dan C. Hilliard. From *Journal of Sport and Social Issues* 18, pp. 88–99. Copyright © 1994 by Sage Publications. Reprinted by permission of Sage Publications, Inc.

noted an "elective affinity" between the interests of athletes, sports promoters, sponsors, and television sports production personnel that leads producers of television sports programming to frame their coverage in conventional ways. In addition to preexisting values, sports television work routines are also likely to be involved. In a related context, Theberge and Cronk (1986) have demonstrated that the work routines of newspaper sportswriters affect the coverage given to women athletes.

My purpose here is to explore more fully the sources of the antisociological bias in television programming in general and televised sport in particular. I intend to do so by looking at three aspects of the literature on television: television's "media logic," televised sport as news, and televised sport as entertainment. I shall then apply points gleaned from this literature to NBC's coverage of the 1992 Summer Olympic Games.

TELEVISION'S MEDIA LOGIC

Duncan and Brummett (1987) identify four dimensions of television's "media logic": narrative, intimacy, commodification, and rigid time segmentation. They claim that each is present in the various sports television programs they analyzed. I would argue that the presence of each encourages a focus on "personal troubles" rather than "public issues" within the world of sport.

By *narrative* Duncan and Brummet (1987) mean that television tells a story, usually in a predictable fashion using stock plots and characters. Gruneau (1989), in his observational study of a Canadian television sports production, discovered how directors and reporters constructed a story line for the telecast. Of course, the athletic contest itself provides a basis for narrative, but if the drama in insufficient, television commentators move the story along by "the deliberate invention of moments" (Sorkin, 1986, pp. 180-181). Duncan and Brummett (1987) indicate that conflict or opposition is often a part of the narrative, and of course, in televised sport, conflict between opposing teams is the basis for drama. But conflict does not necessarily reveal social issues. Hallin (1986) notes, "A great deal of television's conflict is good-against-evil conflict, evil being located outside the mainstream of society" (p. 33). Fiske (1987) argues that narrative is essentially conservative in positing a disruption, solution, and restoration of equilibrium, and that it does its ideological work by identifying the sources of disruption and restoration. This would seem particularly true of the world of sport, where the disruption is ordinarily the "artificial" conflict between competing teams which is resolved by the "best team winning."

Intimacy refers both to the visual closeness of the television viewer to the subject matter and to the development of an emotional attachment between actor and viewer. The former is certainly present in televised sport, but it is the latter that is critical in producing an antisociological frame for televised sport. The development of audience identification with characters is a principal means by which viewers' attention to the narrative is maintained. As Gitlin (1985) says, "Whether in sports, entertainment, documentaries, or news, the networks believe that what glues the audience to the tube is this personal feeling for the characters" (p. 187). Sports telecasts create audience identification with athletes through human interest features which become the basis for the story line of the telecast and by on-the-sport interviews with winners. Gruneau (1989) found that Canadian sport television producers did background research on the athletes they were to cover; this research resulted in "hero notes" that were integrated into the telecast. This focus on the individual athlete diverts attention away from any social or collective issues. Fiske (1987) states, "Individualism diverts attention away from any questioning of the social system, for individual 'solutions' to social problems are always possible" (p. 153).

Commodification refers both to the close tie between programming and commercial time and to the use of the language of commodification in the description of sports events (Duncan & Brummett, 1987). In sports telecasts, as in all of television, there is an attempt to produce a seamless relation of programming to commercials, so that viewers will not be tempted to "zap" the commercials with their remote controls. Miller (1986) argues that this is accomplished by a process of "mutual approximation" in which programs and commercials become more and more alike. Certainly, the concerns of advertisers loom large in television programming. Gitlin (1985) quotes the advertising executive's adage "Television programs are the meat in a commercial sandwich" (p. 92). More analytically, Miller (1988) argues that the purpose of television programming is not only to attract an audience that can be sold to advertisers but also to put that audience in a buying mood. It seems obvious that programming that raises serious questions about social justice or that dwells on patterns of exploitation or inequality in society would risk taking the audience out of the buying mood.

Rigid time segmentation refers to the way in which program segments, commercials, and entire programs are organized into short, rigid blocks of time (Duncan & Brummett, 1987). Although sports programming may be somewhat more flexible than other types of programming in this regard, it is still rigidly segmented, as the failure of constant action sports like soccer and the necessity of "television timeouts" in football and basketball attest. Rigid time segmentation contributes to a focus on events and people rather than conditions and analysis by virtue of limiting the time that may be devoted to any particular topic. A typical "sound bite" is about 10 seconds, in which time one may convey an emotion or an attitude but not an argument. Most news segments are about 1.5 minutes; the longest are rarely longer than 3 minutes. In my experience with NBC's telecast of the 1992 Summer Olympics, event coverage segments rarely lasted more than 8 minutes, features rarely more than 3 minutes, and on-the-spot interviews rarely 1 minute. Such short segments militate against more than a mention of underlying social conditions or issues.

TELEVISED SPORT AS NEWS AND ENTERTAINMENT

Televised sport contains elements of both the news and entertainment genres (Critcher, 1987). Perhaps the distinction is irrelevant; as Hallin (1986) points out, television news has taken on many of the features of entertainment. However, the point is that, whether one thinks of televised sport as being similar to news or similar to entertainment programming, there are tendencies that work against any significant analysis of social issues.

To the extent that televised sport attempts to present real events in real time, it follows some of the conventions of television news programs. Although this may be more true of the NFL Game of the Week, which is broadcast live, than of the 1992 Summer Olympics, which was broadcast to North American audiences taped and heavily edited, all sports programming relies on an aura of realism to keep its audience. Gitlin (1980) summarizes the assumptions of television news personnel about their work as follows:

> Several assumptions about news value serve, for the most part, to secure (the hegemonic) boundary: that news involves the novel event, not the underlying, enduring condition; the person, not the group; the visible conflict, not the deep consensus; the fact that "advances the story," not the one that explains or enlarges it. (p. 263)

Thus the canons of television news work to focus the viewer's attention on personal troubles rather than public issues. Hargreaves (1986) identifies a similar set of "media sport news values" that guides production work and tends to support dominant ideology.

Several of the major characteristics of television entertainment programming have been discussed above in reference to narrative and intimacy. However, two additional characteristics of television programming emerge from the literature that seem to apply directly to sports programming. The first has to do with the protagonists represented in television drama (and sport is surely represented as drama on television). Protagonists are heroic figures, fighting against stiff odds and ultimately prevailing over the various obstacles they encounter. Gitlin (1987) notes that throughout television "the major characters are winners" (p. 255). Gitlin (1986) sharpens this notion about protagonists as winners by referring to such action series as the A-Team and Miami Vice. In shows such as these, the protagonists are individuals or teams of rugged individualists waging war against faceless evil and the interference of meddling bureaucrats. Televised sport frequently develops the story of an athlete on the quest for excellence, overcoming seemingly insurmountable obstacles along the way. This is a story line that television viewers are well prepared to accept.

The second characteristic of television as entertainment is more a matter of style. Television is discussed as the postmodern medium *par excellence* (Miller, 1986), "the ultimate recombinant form" (Gitlin, 1985, p. 80) juxtaposing discordant images in a collage of visuals that levels images and their attendant meanings. This style becomes evident in sports coverage such as the Olympics telecasts, with coverage jumping from venue to venue, from studio to event, from event coverage to commercial to studio interview. Such a style discourages the viewer from making any meaningful connections among the stream of images; each is simply to be enjoyed for its own sake.

In summary, the literature on television as a medium suggests a number of ways in which television programming—whether entertainment, news, or sport—discourages the development of a "sociological imagination." Television deals with controversy and conflict by focusing on the personal and anecdotal rather than on social patterns. Thus television can, for example, be highly critical of individual business persons without being critical of capitalism (Gitlin, 1980). Television discourages its audience from critical social analysis.

REFLECTIONS ON NBC'S COVERAGE OF THE 1992 SUMMER OLYMPICS

Without attempting any systematic empirical analysis, I wish to illustrate the previous discussion of the antisociological bias of television by reference to NBC's coverage of the 1992 Summer Olympics from Barcelona. I have organized my remarks into two categories: the first dealing with the structure of the two weeks of coverage and the second dealing with the handling of controversy as part of that coverage.

The structure of the telecast is interesting in that the two weeks of coverage, consisting of over 150 hours of air time, is much more extensive than the typical sports telecast. Coverage was divided into several segments each day. Weekday coverage consisted of a morning show, a prime-time show, and a late night show. Weekend coverage featured extended coverage during the middle of the day, usually from 11 a.m. until 5 p.m., followed by a 1-hour news break and then prime-time evening coverage.

It became clear to me that the different portions of sports coverage mimicked their nonsport counterpart; that is, the morning coverage mimicked *Today*, prime-time coverage attempted to emulate nighttime drama, and the late night coverage tried to adopt many of the features of late night television more generally. The morning show was hosted by veteran sportscaster Dick Enberg and *Today* host Katie Couric; it incorporated many studio interviews, inserted brief reports on world news, and took regular breaks for local news and weather to provide a format with which regular morning viewers would be familiar. Prime-time coverage developed major athletic story lines that might be expected to draw a general audience as well as committed sports fans, such as the women's gymnastics competition between the U.S. and Unified teams and men's basketball featuring Michael Jordan, Charles Barkley, and other members of the "Dream Team." These story lines were developed with ample use of human interest features. The late night coverage was billed as "Club Barcelona" and integrated celebrity interviews, features on Barcelona nightlife, and music videos into its sports coverage to create a program that fans of Jay Leno, David Letterman, and Arsenio Hall would be comfortable with.

It is also clear to me that the narrative and intimacy themes discussed by Duncan and Brummett (1987), and more particularly the disruption, solution, restoration type of narrative discussed by Fiske (1987), were the principal organizing features of the coverage. Time after time, the audience was presented with stories of athletes overcoming difficulty in their pursuit of Olympic gold. Pablo Morales's swimming comeback was called the most compelling story of the games so far. Canadian rower Silken Laumann's return to competition only 6 weeks after a devastating injury was an incredible story of courage and fortitude. Mike Barrowman set a swimming world record after he dedicated these Olympics to his father's memory. Boxer Oscar de la Hoya was moved to tears in the studio when he saw for the first time the feature detailing his dedication of his quest for gold to his deceased mother. Trent Dimas's gold medal on the high bar, after injuries and financial difficulties almost forced him out of gymnastics, was called "the single biggest gold medal surprise of these Olympic games." Distance runner Mirsada Buric from Bosnia-Hercegovina trained amid sniper fire and was held captive by Serbian troops for 13 days; Katie Couric dubbed her "a true Olympian" for reaching the competition in Barcelona. Even the region of Cataluna and the city of Barcelona were fit into this overarching story line, overcoming the oppression of Franco's regime in order to modernize and play host to the Olympics.

Given the almost limitless amount of material that would fit this story line, it is not surprising that analytical or investigative pieces were rare during the two weeks of coverage. Indeed, controversy hardly raised its ugly head in Barcelona. During the entire two weeks of coverage, only four stories involving controversy emerged. Three of these had to do with scoring, judging, and administration of events. These were the U.S. men's volleyball team's loss to Japan as a result of an official protest, the judging of the boxing competition, and the results of the men's 10 kilometer run. In each case, coverage carried over several days and focused on "the fact that advances the story" (Gitlin, 1980) rather than on analysis or explanation.

The volleyball controversy developed when match officials gave U.S. player Bob Samuelson a second yellow card with Japan leading 15-14 in the fifth game of the match. This should have resulted in an automatic point being awarded to the Japanese team, which would also have given them the game and the match. Officials failed to award the penalty point, Japan protested after the match, their protest was upheld, and an apparent American victory was negated. Early coverage focused on the competence of the officials and asked how the officials could have overlooked the fact that a second yellow card had been awarded and whether it was proper to award a yellow card at such a critical juncture in the match. Later, it was reported that one of the match officials had been dismissed. After all members of the U.S. team shaved their heads in support of the bald Samuelson, NBC turned the shaving into a story in its own right; indeed, the new story line became "U.S., men undefeated since shaving their heads." The coverage was superficial and repetitive and focused attention on the competence and judgment of individuals rather than on the rules themselves.

The scoring of the boxing competition developed as a story after U.S. team captain Eric Griffin, an overwhelming favorite for the gold medal in his weight class, lost a close decision in a pre-medal round. Following the bout, detailed explanations of the computerized judging system, which required three ringside judges to register a blow within 3 seconds of one another for the blow to "score," were given. Commentators went over slow-motion tapes of the bout and pointed out blows that should have "scored" but did not. Later, the scorecards of the individual judges were analyzed, and all three scored the fight in favor of Griffin. An official protest was filed, but the original scoring was upheld. Griffin's "surrogate father" was interviewed and declared the international amateur boxing administrators "a bunch of gutless old men." Thereafter, the scoring of boxing became the story line of the boxing coverage. Virtually every bout was discussed in terms of the scoring system. Some remarks seemed to implicate the system as a whole (for example, Dick Enberg remarked that Eric Griffin had been defeated by a computer), whereas the boxing analysts consistently argued that it was the incompetence of individual judges and referees that was at fault. Expert commentator Al Bernstein stated, "The refereeing in this tournament has been worse than atrocious," and later added, "Forget the system. It's the judges."

The third controversial ruling involved the men's 10,000 meter run, where Moroccan Khalid Skah pulled away from a Kenyan runner late in the race. The Kenyan delegation protested on the basis that another Moroccan runner who had been lapped interfered in the race. The Kenyan protest was initially upheld but was later overturned by the IAAF, the governing body of track and field. Skah received his gold medal to the jeers of the crowd. Because no U.S. athlete was involved, coverage of this controversy was less extensive. Expert distance running commentator Craig Masbach argued that the IAAF ruling was just, as Skah would have won without the interference of his countryman.

Another controversy involved U.S. sprinter Gwen Torrence's allegation that several finalists in the women's 100 meter sprint had used illegal performance-enhancing drugs. Torrence was interviewed on several occasions and explained that her statement was based on "personal suspicions" rather than specific knowledge. In interviews with other track and field stars, such as Florence Griffith Joyner and Carl Lewis, the issue of drugs was raised, but the athletes argued that better drug testing had reduced levels of illegal drug use in the sport. In the absence of hard evidence or specific allegations, the reporting centered more on the judgment Torrence used in making her remarks than on the substance of her "suspicions."

In summary, the controversies covered were either explained away as being noncontroversial after all, as in the Khalid Skah case, or as being the result of individual misjudgment or incompetence. Coverage of controversy does not result in a focus on social or political issues.

Equally revealing of the antisociological bias of television coverage is a look at the potentially controversial stories that were not covered in depth. There were frequent references to serious injury of competitors in the coverage of gymnastics but always in the form of background information on athletes. These remarks were made in passing and were never the basis for serious discussion. Whereas a public issues approach would have treated the rate of injuries as an issue, the personal troubles approach fit within existing narrative forms by treating injury as just another obstacle to be overcome. Similarly, coverage of the 3-day equestrian cross-country event included visuals of horses hung up on immovable rock walls, exhausted at the end of competition, and even being hauled away in ambulances. The course was so difficult that it was criticized by both animal rights activists and many experienced equestrians. But rather than raise serious questions about the safety of the event, the television commentators reassured their audience that every precaution was being taken to care for the horses.

Yet another issue that might have resulted in more systematic investigation was that of drug use. A Chinese woman volleyball player, a woman marathoner representing the Unified team, and U.S. hammer thrower Jud Logan were disqualified after they failed postevent drug tests. These events were briefly reported, but no details were ever provided. When U.S. shotputters Mike Stulce and Jim Doehring won gold and silver medals, respectively, no mention was made of the fact that each had previously been suspended by the IAAF for steroid use. Other than Gwen Torrence's stated "suspicions," the only attention given to drug use involved rumors concerning steroid use by the Chinese women swimmers. Bob Costas referred to the Chinese women as "uncommonly masculine" and reported in a studio segment that rumors were rife during the swim competition about their use of drugs; however, no U.S. coaches or athletes were willing to make allegations on camera. Costas's studio discussion pointed out that former East German coaches were now involved with the Chinese swim program and were suspected of having introduced illegal drugs into their training program. Late night cohost Jim Lampley later picked up this same theme, making remarks that made the distinction between individual athletes who chose to use drugs versus athletic training systems, such as those of the Chinese and East Germans, who exploited unknowing young girls for the purposes of national glory.

This last example illustrates a major exception to the television rule of emphasizing the personal over the public: Communist states are represented in stereotypical fashion as monolithic systems exploiting their citizens. Eitzen (1992) has recently demonstrated the "framing of cultural values," which stereotypically juxtaposes negative traits of the Soviet system with positive ones of our own. By July 1992, the Soviet Union was no more, and Soviet hegemony was no longer newsworthy. Whereas CBS's coverage of the 1992 Winter Olympics had focused considerable attention of the demise of the Soviet Union, NBC's coverage of the summer games treated it as ancient history. However, the remaining communist states of China and Cuba were the focus of attention, as was the East German sports program of the earlier era.

A feature on the Chinese diving program used negative wording and implied exploitation as it discussed the process whereby the Chinese identify and develop talent. A feature on Cuban boxer Felix Savon referred to Cuba as "archaic" and as "the land time forgot." Savon was portrayed as "the last great soldier of the revolution"; at one point, he was pictured in front of a billboard that read "Marxismo, Leninismo, o Muerte." Savon was portrayed to American audiences as the fool who would devote himself to a system doomed to failure. Another feature dealt with Cuban boxing coaches who have left Cuba to coach around the world. After the feature ended, Jim Lampley in the studio editorialized, "Better they should send coaches to Ireland than guns and soldiers to Mozambique." The point is that a double standard is in operation. Television uncovers the sport-ideology connection in its coverage of the communist states, just as it obscures the same connection in coverage of American athletes.

A final example illustrates several of the points made here. By far the most extensive feature of the entire two weeks of coverage was a retrospective on the terrorist actions at the 1972 Munich Olympics in which 12 Israeli athletes were murdered. Some 45 minutes of taped narrative, interrupted by a commercial break, recounted the events that unfolded in Munich. A studio introduction asserted that part of the reason for the decision to air the feature was that "new information" had recently become available. Once coverage began, the only "new" information was that "recently released secret German documents indicate that the [Black September commandos] picked up weapons from the East Germans" after they entered the Olympic compound. Using 1972 footage as well as interviews with German authorities and the surviving Israeli athletes, the events of the tragic day were recounted. It was described as "a tragedy of errors," and Israelis criticized the decisions made by German authorities. The next day, Anouk Spitzer, the daughter of one of the Israeli athletes killed in the attack, was interviewed in the studio and stated, "The Germans made so many mistakes." The reading of the events offered by this coverage was that individuals in positions of authority in West Germany made questionable decisions that cost the lives of the Israeli athletes. The audience was left to ask not "What social forces contributed to such an extreme act?" but "What could have been done differently to save innocent lives?" At the same time, the communist bogeyman was implicated.

CONCLUSION

The literature on television as a medium suggests that television, whether news or entertainment, has reason to focus on the personal rather than on the social and to avoid serious analysis of social problems or political issues. My review of NBC'S coverage of the 1992 Summer Olympics shows this to be the case for sports coverage as well. This should not be surprising. Newspaper and magazine sports coverage rarely delves too deeply into the real workings of the SportsWorld (Lipsyte, 1975), and the print medium is much more disposed to in-depth analysis than is television (Postman, 1985). Because television is so much a part of the way most people experience sport, recognition of the antisociological bias in televised sport may be a first step in developing greater public awareness of the ideological work embedded in sports programming.

REFERENCES

Critcher, C. (1987). Media spectacles: Sport and mass communication. In A. Cashadan (Ed.), *Studies in communication*. Oxford: Blackwell.

Duncan, M. C., & Brummett, B. (1987). The mediation of spectator sport. *Research Quarterly, 58,* 168-177.

Eitzen, D.S. (1992). Sports and ideological contradictions: Learning from the cultural framing of Soviet values. *Journal of Sport & Social Issues, 16* (2), 144-149.

Fiske, J. (1987). *Television culture*. New York: Methuen.

Gitlin, T. (1980). *The whole world is watching*. Berkeley: University of California Press.

Gitlin, T. (1985). *Inside prime time*. New York: Pantheon.

Gitlin, T. (1986). We build excitement. In T. Gitlin Ed.), *Watching television* (pp. 136-161). New York: Pantheon.

Gitlin, T. (1987). Television's screens: Hegemony in transition. In D. Lazare (Ed.), *American media and mass culture* (pp. 240-265). Berkeley: University of California Press.

Gruneau, R. (1989). Making spectacle: A case study in television sports production. In L. Wenner (Ed.), *Media, sports & society* (pp. 134-154). Newbury Park, CA: Sage.

Hallin, D. (1986). We keep America on top of the world. In T. Gitlin (Ed.), *Watching television* (pp. 9-41). New York: Pantheon.

Hargreaves, J. (1986). *Sport, power and culture.* New York: St. Martin's.

Jhally, S. (1989). Cultural studies and the sports/media complex. In L. Wenner (Ed.), *Media, sports & society* (pp. 70-93). Newbury Park, CA: Sage.

Lipsyte, R. (1975). *SportsWorld.* New York: Quadrangle.

Miller, M. C. (1986). Deride and conquer. In T. Gitlin (Ed.), *Watching television* (pp. 183-228). New York: Pantheon.

Miller, M. C. (1988). *Boxed in: The culture of TV.* Evanston, IL: Northwestern University Press.

Postman, N. (1985). *Amusing ourselves to death.* New York: Viking.

Sage, G. (1990). *Power and ideology in American sport.* Champaign, IL: Human Kinetics.

Sorkin, M. (1986). Faking it. In T. Gitlin (Ed.), *Watching television* (pp. 162-182). New York: Pantheon.

Theberge, N., & Cronk, A. (1986). Work routines in newspaper sports departments and the coverage of women's sports. *Sociology of Sport Journal, 3,* 195-203.

■ FOR FURTHER STUDY

Duncan, Margaret Carlisle, "The Politics of Women's Body Images and Practices: Foucault, the Panopticon, and *Shape* Magazine," *Journal of Sport & Social Issues* 18 (February 1994):48-65.

Ducan, Margaret Carlisle, and Barry Brummett, "The Mediation of Spectator Sport," *Research Quarterly for Exercise and Sport* 58 (1987):168-177.

"Gender and the Media: Annotated Bibliography," *Sociology of Sport Journal* 7 (December 1990):412-421.

Higgs, Catriona T., and Karen H. Weiller, "Gender Bias and the 1992 Summer Olympic Games: An Analysis of Television Coverage," *Journal of Sport & Social Issues* 18 (August 1994):234-246.

Shifflett, Bethany, and Rhonda Revelle, "Gender Equity in Sports Media Coverage: A Review of the *NCAA News,*" *Journal of Sport & Social Issues* 18 (May 1994):144-150.

Wenner, Lawrence A. (ed.), *Media, Sports & Society,* (Newbury Park, California:Sage, 1989).

Wenner, Lawrence A, "The Dream Team, Communicative Dirt, and the Marketing of Synergy: USA Basketball and Cross-Merchandising in Television Commercials," *Journal of Sport & Social Issues* 18 (February 1994):27-47.

Part Four

Sport and Socialization: Symbols

A symbol is anything that carries a particular meaning recognized by members of a culture. A wink, a raised finger (which one is important), a green light, a double stripe on the highway, and a handshake are all symbols with meaning for people in the United States. Part of the socialization process for children or other newcomers to a culture is the learning of symbols. While some symbols are relatively unimportant, others—such as the Constitution, the U.S. flag, or a cross—have great importance to certain segments of the population. Some of the symbols found in sport are very important.

The three selections in this section consider three symbols. The first, by Douglas Lederman, describes the use of the confederate flag and the singing of the Southern anthem, "Dixie," in conjunction with sports at the University of Mississippi. These symbols represent pride by whites in their heritage. For others, especially African Americans, these are symbols of centuries of racial oppression. Should these symbols be used by a school that is supposed to represent all of the citizens of Mississippi?

The second selection, by Ward Churchill, highlights another battle over symbols. Here the issue is the use of Native American names, mascots, and ceremonial acts by athletic teams. There are teams such as the Scalpers and the Savages, as well as the Indians with mascots dressed in warpaint and fans doing the "tomahawk chop." Many Native Americans object to these common practices because they demean Native American heritage and encourage negative stereotypes. Churchill argues that it is crucial for the American public to think about the implications of watching "a gaggle of face-painted and war-bonneted buffoons doing the 'Tomahawk Chop' at a baseball or football game."

The third essay, by D. Stanley Eitzen and Maxine Baca Zinn, looks at sexist naming of women's athletic teams. They found in a study of all four-year colleges and universities in the United States that over half had sexist names, logos, or mascots. This use of demeaning symbols for women's teams has several negative functions for women: through their use women are trivialized, made invisible, and deathleticized.

11. *Old Times Not Forgotten: A Battle over Symbols*

DOUGLAS LEDERMAN

As the ball carrier sprints across the goal line for a touchdown, thousands of University of Mississippi students erupt in cheers.

They thrust their arms to the sky, many holding flags aloft, as the band breaks into a stirring song. Backs are slapped, high fives exchanged. It is one of those magical moments that bring classmates together and unify a community.

But not one of the university's 700 black undergraduates is seated among the thousands in the students' section. Most blacks say they don't feel at home there, in part because the flags the students are waving are those of the Confederacy, and the song is the Southern anthem, "Dixie."

Much has changed here since 1962, when the university and the state gained national notoriety for resisting James Meredith's attempts to enroll as the institution's first black student. Blacks are now integrated into most aspects of daily life on the campus.

But the progress is obscured, and even undermined, by an enduring battle over the university's continued use of its Old South symbols, official and informal. The debate ignited again last spring when three black members of the band refused to play "Dixie," saying the song should not be performed at university-sponsored events because it offends black students.

Most white students and alumni insist—no, more than that, they practically swear—that there is nothing racist in their use of the symbols. Whatever link the flag and song might once have had with slavery and the South's segregationist past, they argue, has been supplanted in their hearts and minds by an association with the university they love. Waving the flag and cheering the playing of "Dixie" evince Southern heritage, they say, not bigotry.

'THEY'RE OUR FRIENDS'

"They just represent Ole Miss to us," says Lettye Williams, a retired school-teacher who picnicked with her husband and fellow alumni before a football game last month. "We do not see these as racist symbols. Just because you're proud to be a Southerner doesn't mean you don't like blacks. They're our friends. We work with them. We live with them."

Black students don't believe that everyone who waves the Confederate battle flag or claps along to "Dixie" is racist. But history, most of them agree, has forever tainted the flag and the song, making them inappropriate symbols for an institution that is supposed to represent all of Mississippi's citizens. The flag and "Dixie" were adopted by the university only in the late 1940's, embraced defiantly by students opposed to integration. Mississippians who violently protested Mr. Meredith's admission also rallied around the flag and "Dixie," facts not easily forgotten by many blacks here.

They, along with many faculty members, believe Mississippi must cast off the vestiges of its Old South past if it is to thrive in the New South. Symbols, they argue, should unite, not divide, especially at a public institution in a state with a black population of 35 per cent.

"No matter how much things have changed, African Americans will always remember why all of this was brought here—to keep us out," says Jesse Holland, a black senior who edits the *Daily Mississippian*, the student newspaper.

Many critics of "Dixie" want the university's chancellor, R. Gerald Turner, to stop or at least discourage the band from playing the song, just as the university officially dissociated itself from the Confederate flag a decade ago.

Many white alumni and students vow to fight such a move, and some alums say they will halt their financial support if Mississippi abandons "Dixie." Some professors also complain that banning the song by fiat would be a form of censorship.

Mr. Turner has been grappling with this issue on and off since he got here in 1983, and has won praise from many quarters for his efforts to improve race relations. The chancellor is under pressure from all sides, but is asking for patience. Mississippi, he believes, must at some point formally review the appropriateness of all its symbols, but he says the time is not yet right for such a study.

When that discussion does take place, Mr. Turner and others say, it will focus on a broader question raised by the dispute over Dixie: Is it possible for an institution to shed its Confederate roots, yet remain fervently, profoundly Southern?

The university is not alone in facing that dilemma. Georgia, for instance, is bitterly divided over whether to strip the Confederate battle flag from its state banner. And just this month, the University of Alabama stirred protests when it adopted an Old South theme for its football homecoming. But few institutions have been identified so closely with the Old South legacy, good and bad, as this one.

"If this university isn't Southern," Mr. Turner says, "it's not anything."

CULTIVATING AN IMAGE

That's true partly because of its location and history. The main administration building was a hospital for Civil War soldiers, over 700 of whom are buried in a graveyard here. And the university and Oxford have been home to Southern writers who have shaped the country's perceptions of the region, from William Faulkner to Eudora Welty.

The university has also cultivated that image, carving out a niche among other public universities in the region as a bastion of the Old South. It has done that largely through its use of symbols, which extend well beyond the flag and "Dixie," which is neither fight song nor alma mater, but a popular, unofficial theme song.

The sports teams are called the Rebels, and the mascot is Colonel Reb, a caricature of an Old South plantation owner. Even the university's nickname, Ole Miss, has antebellum origins. It isn't short for Old Mississippi, as most people think, but rather is what some slaves called the wives of their owners.

The institution's image attracts students who yearn as much for its conservative, traditional nature as for the beauty of its campus and the quality of its education. But Mississippi has had trouble distancing itself from the negative aspects of what the Old South stood for, despite its advances.

'THERE IS A NEW ORDER HERE'

Signs of those advances are plentiful. This summer Mr. Turner hired the university's first black vice-chancellor; its basketball coach also is black. This year's group of 701 black undergraduates (8 per cent of the 10,369 total) is its largest in history, and two white fraternities became integrated last year for the first time.

"You see white and black students together here today in ways that never before were possible," says William Ferris, director of the university's Center for the Study of Southern Culture. "That gives you hope. There is a new order here."

That's not so obvious on Saturdays during football season.

Ten hours before an evening home game, alumni and students begin filling the tree-lined expanse known as "the Grove" with picnic tables and tents. For the rest of the day, they eat, reminisce, and get fired up for the game. The people are friendly, the atmosphere inviting.

THE OLD OLE MISS

But Confederate flags hang from trees and serve as centerpieces amid the fried chicken and iced tea on many a picnic table. And just as at the game, blacks are virtually invisible in the Grove—except when the football squad, half of whose players are black, parades through the crowd en route to the stadium.

This is the *old* Ole Miss, the one that was in its prime when the university first embraced its Confederate trappings.

The university's teams became known as "the Rebels" in 1936, but Confederate flags and "Dixie" did not become an exalted part of the football ritual until 1948, when dozens of Mississippi students took part in the "Dixiecrat" political convention, which was dedicated to the fight against desegregation.

"The song and the Confederate battle flag were adopted by the all-white university specifically as a gesture of white supremacy," says Warren Steel, a music professor whose arguments helped persuade the Faculty Senate last spring to discourage the playing of "Dixie" at campus events. "People can honestly say, 'I don't think about bigotry,' but the history is there."

Tim Jones didn't know that history when he joined Mississippi's band. But after learning the origins of the university's affiliation with "Dixie" and its other symbols, he decided he could no longer play the song in good conscience.

TIME FOR PROTEST

So at a basketball game last spring, as the band took up "Dixie," Mr. Jones put down his drum, got to his feet, and crossed his arms in front of his chest.

"There's a line in the song that says, 'Old times there are not forgotten,'" says Mr. Jones, a senior. "When you talk about old times in the South, the only thing my people think about is slavery."

Mr. Jones's protest, which was backed by the Black Student Union, came 10 years after the last major flare-up over the symbols. In 1983, a black cheerleader refused to carry the Rebel flag and the alumni association discouraged its use. Saying the flag's meaning had changed because it had been appropriated by groups like the Ku Klux Klan, the university abandoned it as an official symbol.

Mississippi stopped distributing flags before games and selling them in the bookstore, and dropped the symbol from all its T-shirts and other items. The university also introduced the "Battle M" flag, a blue M with white stars on a red background, hoping it would replace the Confederate in its fans' hearts.

That hasn't happened. Although use of the Confederate banner waned in the mid-1980's, Rebel flags now vastly outnumber the "Battle M" at football games. If anything, the dispute over the university's symbols seems to make many whites more, not less, inclined to cling to the past.

"If it wasn't so controversial, we probably wouldn't want to wave them," says John Kennedy, a junior. "I can understand how they feel, but we feel kind of abused. If they take 'Dixie" away, I think race relations will get worse."

'AN ESCAPE' FROM DISCUSSION

The widening gap between the two sides is evidenced by T-shirts. On the front of one is the "X" popularized by the movie *Malcolm X,* under the words "You wear yours . . ." On the back is the Confederate flag, framed by the words "We'll wear ours."

"The controversy tends to polarize people and worsen race relations, and it is an escape from discussing real issues in race relations," says Mr. Steel, the music professor. "That's why I wish we would just resolve this now."

Mr. Turner says the issue will be decided not by the advocates on either side but by the "middle ground," which he says has not yet formed a consensus. The chancellor admits that people may be uneasy about the continuing debate, but he says it is necessary. Meanwhile, Mr. Turner is formulating what he calls a "framework" for the coming debate about how the university should present itself in the future.

"It is difficult to communicate how much things have changed here when you have symbols that are Confederate, not Southern," says Mr. Turner. "Somehow we need to ferret out things that are Southern from those that are Confederate."

UPDATING TRADITION

Charles Reagan Wilson, a professor of history and Southern studies, argues that for Southern tradition to survive, it must be "extended," or updated, to take recent history into account. The trick for the university, he argues, is to remain relevant to all Mississippians, black and white, without losing its distinctive character.

One alternative, he says, is to mix symbols of the confederacy with those of the civil-rights movement, reflecting Mississippi's "complex, tortured history by focusing on the two events that most shaped the South."

Another option, he says, is to give new meaning to traditional symbols. Keep using the Confederate flag, Mr. Wilson says, but redefine it: "Make a new flag that shows a white and a black hand grasping the Confederate flag," for instance. As for "Dixie," he and others say, the band's repertoire already includes a compromise: "From Dixie With Love," which meshes "Dixie" with "The Battle Hymn of the Republic," and "All My Trials," an old spiritual, reflecting all of the factors at work in the Civil War.

A third possibility, Mr. Wilson says, is to focus on Southern cultural symbols that are "anchored in the past but are not Confederate." A flag featuring a magnolia tree, for example, could be a "good common symbol of the South and of Mississippi."

Whether any of those solutions would appease either side of the debate is another question.

The problem, says Charles W. Eagles, a history professor who specializes in race relations and the civil-rights movement, is that the campus houses two very different institutions: the University of Mississippi and Ole Miss.

Every time Mr. Eagles walks through the student union, he is irked by a quotation from an alumnus that adorns a wall. It says: "The University is respected, but Ole Miss is loved. The University gives a diploma and regretfully terminates tenure, but one never graduates from Ole Miss."

CAPTURING THE PLACE

"That captures this place. For some of us—those who believe in the University of Mississippi—the symbols prevent the university from being everything it can be. Others—those that are faithful to Ole Miss—think that if you took the symbols away, there wouldn't be anything there.

"The symbols are seen as a real burden for the University of Mississippi. But they're the backbone of Ole Miss."

12. *Crimes against Humanity*

WARD CHURCHILL

During the past couple of seasons, there has been an increasing wave of controversy regarding the names of professional sports teams like the Atlanta "Braves," Cleveland "Indians," Washington "Redskins," and Kansas City "Chiefs." The issue extends to the names of college teams like Florida State University "Seminoles," University of Illinois "Fighting Illini," and so on, right on down to high school outfits like the Lamar (Colorado) "Savages." Also involved have been team adoption of "mascots," replete with feathers, buckskins, beads, spears, and "warpaint" (some fans have opted to adorn themselves in the same fashion), and nifty little "pep" gestures like the "Indian Chant" and "Tomahawk Chop."

A substantial number of American Indians have protested that use of native names, images, and symbols as sports team mascots and the like is, by definition, a virulently racist practice. Given the historical relationship between Indians and non-Indians during what has been called the "Conquest of America," American Indian Movement leader (and American Indian Anti-Defamation Council founder) Russell Means has compared the practice to contemporary Germans naming their soccer teams the "Jews," "Hebrews," and "Yids," while adorning their uniforms with grotesque caricatures of Jewish faces taken from the Nazis' anti-Semitic propaganda of the 1930s. Numerous demonstrations have occurred in conjunction with games—most notably during the November 15, 1992 match-up between the Chiefs and Redskins in Kansas City—by angry Indians and their supporters.

In response, a number of players—especially African Americans and other minority athletes—have been trotted out by professional team owners like Ted Turner, as well as university and public school officials, to announce that they mean not to insult but to honor native people. They have been joined by the television networks and most major newspapers, all of which have editorialized that Indian discomfort with the situation is "no big deal," insisting that the whole thing is just "good, clean fun." The country needs more such fun, they've argued, and "a few disgruntled Native Americans" have no right to undermine the nation's enjoyment of its leisure time by complaining. This is especially the case, some have argued, "in hard times

SOURCE: "Crimes against Humanity" by Ward Churchill. From *Z Magazine* 6, pp. 43–47. Copyright © 1993 by the Institute for Social and Cultural Communication.

like these." It has even been contended that Indian outrage at being systematically degraded—rather than the degradation itself—creates "a serious
barrier to the sort of intergroup communication so necessary in a multicul-
tural society such as ours."

Okay, let's communicate. We are frankly dubious that those advancing
such positions really believe their own rhetoric, but, just for the sake of argument, let's accept the premise that they are sincere. If what they say is true,
then isn't it time we spread such "inoffensiveness" and "good cheer" around
among *all* groups so that *everybody* can participate *equally* in fostering the
round of national laughs they call for? Sure it is—the country can't have too
much fun or "intergroup involvement"—so the more, the merrier. Simple
consistency demands that anyone who thinks the Tomahawk Chop is a swell
pastime must be just as hearty in their endorsement of the following ideas,
which—by the logic used to defend the defamation of American Indians—
should help us all really start yukking it up.

First, as a counterpart to the Redskins, we need an NFL team called
"Niggers" to honor Afro-Americans. Halftime festivities for fans might include a
simulated stewing of the opposing coach in a large pot while players and cheerleaders dance around it, garbed in leopard skins and wearing fake bones in
their noses. This concept obviously goes along with the kind of gaiety attending
the Chop, but also with the actions of the Kansas City Chiefs, whose team
members—prominently including black team members—lately appeared on a
poster looking "fierce" and "savage" by way of wearing Indian regalia. Just a bit
of harmless "morale boosting," says the Chiefs' front office. You bet.

So that the newly formed Niggers sports club won't end up too out of
sync while expressing the "spirit" and "identity" of Afro-Americans in the
above fashion, a baseball franchise—let's call this one the "Sambos"—should
be formed. How about a basketball team called the "Spearchuckers"? A
hockey team called the "Jungle Bunnies"? Maybe the "essence" of these
teams could be depicted by images of tiny black faces adorned with huge
pairs of lips. The players could appear on TV every week or so gnawing on
chicken legs and spitting watermelon seeds at one another. Catchy, eh? Well,
there's "nothing to be upset about," according to those who love wearing
"war bonnets" to the Super Bowl or having "Chief Illiniwek" dance around
the sports arenas of Urbana, Illinois.

And why stop there? There are plenty of other groups to include.
"Hispanics"? They can be "represented" by the Galveston "Greasers" and San
Diego "Spics," at least until the Wisconsin "Wetbacks" and Baltimore
"Beaners" get off the ground. Asian Americans? How about the "Slopes,"
"Dinks," "Gooks," and "Zipperheads"? Owners of the latter teams might get
their logo ideas from editorial page cartoons printed in the nation's newspapers during World War II: slant-eyes, buck teeth, big glasses, but nothing
racially insulting or derogatory, according to the editors and artists involved
at the time. Indeed, this Second World War–vintage stuff can be seen as just

another barrel of laughs, at least by what current editors say are their "local standards" concerning American Indians.

Let's see. Who's been left out? Teams like the Kansas City "Kikes," Hanover "Honkies," San Leandro "Shylocks," Daytona "Dagos," and Pittsburgh "Polacks" will fill a certain social void among white folk. Have a religious belief? Let's all go for the gusto and gear up the Milwaukee "Mackerel Snappers" and Hollywood "Holy Rollers." The Fighting Irish of Notre Dame can be rechristened the "Drunken Irish" or "Papist Pigs." Issues of gender and sexual preference can be addressed through creation of teams like the St. Louis "Sluts," Boston "Bimbos," Detroit "Dykes," and the Fresno "Fags." How about the Gainesville "Gimps" and Richmond "Retards," so the physically and mentally impaired won't be excluded from our fun and games?

Now, don't go getting "overly sensitive" out there. None of this is demeaning or insulting, at least not when it's being done to Indians. Just ask the folks who are doing it, or their apologists like Andy Rooney in the national media. They'll tell you—as in fact they *have* been telling you—that there's been no harm done, regardless of what their victims think, feel, or say. The situation is exactly the same as when those with precisely the same mentality used to insist that Stepin Fetchit was okay, or Rochester on the Jack Benny Show, or Amos and Andy, Charlie Chan, the Frito Bandito, or any of the other cutesy symbols making up the lexicon of American racism. Have we communicated yet?

Let's get just a little bit real here. The notion of "fun" embodied in rituals like the Tomahawk Chop must be understood for what it is. There's not a single non-Indian example used above which can be considered socially acceptable in even the most marginal sense. The reasons are obvious enough. So why is it different where American Indians are concerned? One can only conclude that, in contrast to the other groups at issue, Indians are (falsely) perceived as being too few, and therefore too weak, to defend themselves effectively against racist and otherwise offensive behavior.

Fortunately, there are some glimmers of hope. A few teams and their fans have gotten the message and have responded appropriately. Stanford University, which opted to drop the name "Indians" from Stanford, has experienced no resulting drop-off in attendance. Meanwhile, the local newspaper in Portland, Oregon recently decided its long-standing editorial policy prohibiting use of racial epithets should include derogatory team names. The Redskins, for instance, are now referred to as "the Washington team," and will continue to be described in this way until the franchise adopts an inoffensive moniker (newspaper sales in Portland have suffered no decline as a result).

Such examples are to be applauded and encouraged. They stand as figurative beacons in the night, proving beyond all doubt that it is quite possible to indulge in the pleasure of athletics without accepting blatant racism into the bargain.

NUREMBERG PRECEDENTS

On October 16, 1946, a man named Julius Streicher mounted the steps of a gallows. Moments later he was dead, the sentence of an international tribunal composed of representatives of the United States, France, Great Britain, and the Soviet Union having been imposed. Streicher's body was then cremated and—so horrendous were his crimes thought to have been—his ashes dumped into an unspecified German river so that "no one should ever know a particular place to go for reasons of mourning his memory."

Julius Streicher had been convicted at Nuremberg, Germany of what were termed "Crimes Against Humanity." The lead prosecutor in his case—Justice Robert Jackson of the United States Supreme Court—had not argued that the defendant had killed anyone, nor that he had personally committed any especially violent act. Nor was it contended that Streicher had held any particularly important position in the German government during the period in which the so-called Third Reich had exterminated some 6,000,000 Jews, as well as several million Gypsies, Poles, Slavs, homosexuals, and other untermenschen (subhumans).

The sole offense for which the accused was ordered put to death was in having served as publisher/editor of a Bavarian tabloid entitled *Der Sturmer* during the early-to-mid 1930s, years before the Nazi genocide actually began. In this capacity, he had penned a long series of virulently anti-Semitic editorials and "news" stories, usually accompanied by cartoons and other images graphically depicting Jews in extraordinarily derogatory fashion. This, the prosecution asserted, had done much to "dehumanize" the targets of his distortion in the mind of the German public. In turn, such dehumanization had made it possible—or at least easier—for average Germans to later indulge in the outright liquidation of Jewish "vermin." The tribunal agreed, holding that Streicher was therefore complicit in genocide and deserving of death by hanging.

During his remarks to the Nuremberg tribunal, Justice Jackson observed that, in implementing its sentences, the participating powers were morally and legally binding themselves to adhere forever after to the same standards of conduct that were being applied to Streicher and the other Nazi leaders. In the alternative, he said, the victorious allies would have committed "pure murder" at Nuremberg—no different in substance from that carried out by those they presumed to judge—rather than establishing the "permanent benchmark for justice" which was intended.

Yet in the United States of Robert Jackson, the indigenous American Indian population had already been reduced, in a process which is ongoing to this day, from perhaps 12.5 million in the year 1500 to fewer than 250,000 by the beginning of the 20th century. This was accomplished, according to official sources, "largely through the cruelty of [Euro-American] settlers," and an informal but clear governmental policy which had made it an articulated goal to "exterminate these red vermin," or at least whole segments of them.

Bounties had been placed on the scalps of Indians—any Indians—in places as diverse as Georgia, Kentucky, Texas, the Dakotas, Oregon, and California, and had been maintained until resident Indian populations were decimated or disappeared altogether. Entire peoples such as the Cherokee had been reduced to half their size through a policy of forced removal from their homelands east of the Mississippi River to what were then considered less preferable areas in the West.

Others, such as the Navajo, suffered the same fate while under military guard for years on end. The United States Army had also perpetrated a long series of wholesale massacres of Indians at places like Horseshoe Bend, Bear River, Sand Creek, the Washita River, the Marias River, Camp Robinson, and Wounded Knee.

Through it all, hundreds of popular novels—each competing with the next to make Indians appear more grotesque, menacing, and inhuman— were sold in the tens of millions of copies in the U.S. Plainly, the Euro-American public was being conditioned to see Indians in such a way as to allow their eradication to continue. And continue it did until the Manifest Destiny of the U.S.—a direct precursor to what Hitler would subsequently call Lebensraumpolitik (the politics of living space)—was consummated.

By 1900, the national project of "clearing" Native Americans from their land and replacing them with "superior" Anglo-American settlers was complete; the indigenous population had been reduced by as much as 98 percent while approximately 97.5 percent of their original territory had "passed" to the invaders. The survivors had been concentrated, out of sight and mind of the public, on scattered "reservations," all of them under the self-assigned "plenary" (full) power of the federal government. There was, of course, no Nuremberg-style tribunal passing judgment on those who had fostered such circumstances in North America. No U.S. official or private citizen was ever imprisoned—never mind hanged—for implementing or propagandizing what had been done. Nor had the process of genocide afflicting Indians been completed. Instead, it merely changed form.

Between the 1880s and the 1980s, nearly half of all Native American children were coercively transferred from their own families, communities, and cultures to those of the conquering society. This was done through compulsory attendance at remote boarding schools, often hundreds of miles from their homes, where native children were kept for years on end while being systematically "deculturated" (indoctrinated to think and act in the manner of Euro-Americans rather than as Indians). It was also accomplished through a pervasive foster home and adoption program—including "blind" adoptions, where children would be permanently denied information as to who they were/are and where they'd come from—placing native youths in non-Indian homes.

The express purpose of all this was to facilitate a U.S. governmental policy to bring about the "assimilation" (dissolution) of indigenous societies. In other words, Indian cultures as such were to be caused to disappear. Such policy objectives are directly contrary to the United Nations 1948 Convention on Punishment and Prevention of the Crime of Genocide, an element of international law arising from the Nuremberg proceedings. The forced "transfer of the children" of a targeted "racial, ethnical, or religious group" is explicitly prohibited as a genocidal activity under the Convention's second article.

Article II of the Genocide Convention also expressly prohibits involuntary sterilization as a means of "preventing births among" a targeted population. Yet, in 1975, it was conceded by the U.S. government that its Indian Health Service (IHS), then a subpart of the Bureau of Indian Affairs (BIA), was even then conducting a secret program of involuntary sterilization that had affected approximately 40 percent of all Indian women. The program was allegedly discontinued, and the IHS was transferred to the Public Health Service, but no one was punished. In 1990, it came out that the IHS was inoculating Inuit children in Alaska with Hepatitis-B vaccine. The vaccine had already been banned by the World Health Organization as having a demonstrated correlation with the HIV-syndrome, which is itself correlated to AIDS. As this is written, a "field test" of Hepatitis-A vaccine, also HIV-correlated, is being conducted on Indian reservations in the northern plains region.

The Genocide Convention makes it a "crime against humanity" to create conditions leading to the destruction of an identifiable human group, as such. Yet the BIA has utilized the government's plenary prerogatives to negotiate mineral leases "on behalf of" Indian peoples paying a fraction of standard royalty rates. The result has been "super profits" for a number of preferred U.S. corporations. Meanwhile, Indians, whose reservations ironically turned out to be in some of the most mineral-rich areas of North America, which makes us the nominally wealthiest segment of the continent's population, live in dire poverty.

By the government's own data in the mid-1980s, Indians received the lowest annual and lifetime per capita incomes of any aggregate population group in the United States. Concomitantly, we suffer the highest rate of infant mortality, death by exposure and malnutrition, disease, and the like. Under such circumstances, alcoholism and other escapist forms of substance abuse are endemic in the Indian community, a situation which leads both to a general physical debilitation of the population and a catastrophic accident rate. Teen suicide among Indians is several times the national average.

The average life expectancy of a reservation-based Native American man is barely 45 years; women can expect to live less than three years longer.

Such itemizations could be continued at great length, including matters like the radioactive contamination of large portions of contemporary Indian country, the forced relocation of traditional Navajos, and so on. But the point should be made: Genocide, as defined in international law, is a continuing fact of day-to-day life (and death) for North America's native peoples. Yet there has been—and is—only the barest flicker of public concern about, or even consciousness of, this reality. Absent any serious expression of public outrage, no one is punished and the process continues.

A salient reason for public acquiescence before the ongoing holocaust in Native North America has been a continuation of the popular legacy, often through more effective media. Since 1925, Hollywood has released more than 2,000 films, many of them rerun frequently on television, portraying Indians as strange, perverted, ridiculous, and often dangerous things of the past. Moreover, we are habitually presented to mass audiences one-dimensionally, devoid of recognizable human motivations and emotions; Indians thus serve as props, little more. We have thus been thoroughly and systematically dehumanized.

Nor is this the extent of it. Everywhere, we are used as logos, as mascots, as jokes: "Big Chief" writing tablets, "Red Man" chewing tobacco, "Winnebago" campers, "Navajo" and "Cherokee" and "Pontiac" and "Cadillac" pickups and automobiles. There are the Cleveland "Indians," the Kansas City "Chiefs," the Atlanta "Braves," and the Washington "Redskins" professional sports teams— not to mention those in thousands of colleges, high schools, and elementary schools across the country—each with their own degrading caricatures and parodies of Indians and/or things Indian. Pop fiction continues in the same vein, including an unending stream of New Age manuals purporting to expose the inner works of indigenous spirituality in everything from pseudo-philosophical to do-it-yourself styles. Blond yuppies from Beverly Hills amble about the country claiming to be reincarnated 17th-century Cheyenne Ushamans ready to perform previously secret ceremonies.

In effect, a concerted, sustained, and in some ways accelerating effort has gone into making Indians unreal. It is thus of obvious importance that the American public begin to think about the implications of such things the next time they witness a gaggle of face-painted and war-bonneted buffoons doing the "Tomahawk Chop" at a baseball or football game. It is necessary that they think about the implications of the grade-school teacher adorning their child in turkey feathers to commemorate Thanksgiving. Think about the significance of John Wayne or Charlton Heston killing a dozen "savages" with a single bullet the next time a western comes on TV. Think about why Land-o-Lakes finds it appropriate to market its butter with the stereotyped image of an "Indian princess" on the wrapper. Think about what it means when non-Indian academics profess—as they often do—to "know more about Indians than Indians do themselves." Think about the significance of charlatans like Carlos Castaneda and Jamake Highwater and Mary Summer Rain and Lynn Andrews churning out "Indian" bestsellers, one after the other, while Indians typically can't get into print.

Think about the real situation of American Indians. Think about Julius Streicher. Remember Justice Jackson's admonition. Understand that the treatment of Indians in American popular culture is not "cute" or "amusing" or just "good, clean fun."

Know that it causes real pain and real suffering to real people. Know that it threatens our very survival. And know that this is just as much a crime against humanity as anything the Nazis ever did. It is likely that the indigenous people of the United States will never demand that those guilty of such criminal activity be punished for their deeds. But the least we have the right to expect—indeed, to demand—is that such practices finally be brought to a halt.

13. The De-Athleticization of Women: The Naming and Gender Marking of Collegiate Sport Teams

D. STANLEY EITZEN AND MAXINE BACA ZINN

Sport is an institution with enormous symbolic significance that contributes to and perpetuates male dominance in society (Hall, 1984, 1985). This occurs through processes that exclude women completely, or if they do manage to participate, processes that effectively minimize their achievements. Bryson (1987) has argued that sport reproduces patriarchal relations through four minimalizing processes: definition, direct control, ignoring, and trivialization. This paper examines several of these processes but focuses especially on how the trivialization of women occurs through the sexist naming practices of athletic teams.

THE PROBLEM

American colleges and universities typically have adopted nicknames, songs, colors, emblems, and mascots as identifying and unifying symbols. This practice of using symbols to achieve solidarity and community is a common group practice, as Durkheim showed in his analysis of primitive religions (Durkheim, 1947). Durkheim noted that people in a locality believed they were related to some totem, which was usually an animal but occasionally natural objects as well. All members of a common group were identified by their shared symbol, which they displayed by the emblem of their totem. This identification with an animal, bird, or other object is common in institutions of higher learning where students, former students, faculty members, and others who identify with the local academic community display similar colors, wave banners, wear special clothing and jewelry, and chant or sing together. These behaviors usually center around athletic contests. Janet Lever (1983, p. 12) connects these activities with totemism:

SOURCE: "The De-Athleticization of Women: The Naming and Gender Marking of Collegiate Sport Teams" by D. Stanley Eitzen and Maxine Baca Zinn. From *Sociology of Sport Journal* 65(4), pp. 362–370. Copyright © 1989 by Human Kinetics Publishers, Inc. Reprinted by permission.

Team worship, like animal worship, makes all participants intensely aware of their own group membership. By accepting that a particular team represents them symbolically, people enjoy ritual kinship based on a common bond. Their emblem, be it an insignia or a lapel pin or a scarf with team colors, distinguishes fellow fans from both strangers and enemies.

A school nickname is much more than a tag or a label. It conveys, symbolically as Durkheim posits, the characteristics and attributes that define the institution. In an important way, the school's symbols represent the institution's self-concept. Schools may have names that signify the school's ethnic heritage (e.g., the Bethany College Swedes), state history (University of Oklahoma Sooners), mission (U.S. Military Academy at West Point Cadets), religion (Oklahoma Baptist College Prophets), or founder (Whittier College Poets). Most schools, though, use symbols of aggression and ferocity (e.g., birds such as Hawks, animals such as Bulldogs, human categories such as Pirates, and even the otherworldly such as Devils) (see Fuller & Manning, 1987).

While school names tend to evoke strong emotions of solidarity among followers, there is also a potential dark side. The names chosen by some schools are demeaning or derogatory to some groups. In the past two decades or so, Native American activists have raised serious objections to the use of Indians as school names or mascots because their use typically distorts Native American traditions and reinforces negative stereotypes about them by depicting them as savages, scalpers, and the like. A few colleges (e.g., Stanford and Dartmouth) have taken these objections seriously and deleted Indian names and mascots. Most schools using some form of reference to Indians, however, have chosen to continue that practice despite the objections of Native Americans. In fact, Indian or some derivative is a popular name for athletic teams. Of the 1,251 four-year schools reported by Franks (1982), some 21 used Indian, 13 were Warriors, 7 were Chiefs, 6 were Redmen, 5 were Braves, 2 were Redskins, and individual schools were Nanooks, Chippewas, Hurons, Seminoles, Choctaws, Mohawks, Sioux, Utes, Aztecs, Savages, Tribe, and Raiders. Ironically though, Native Americans is the only racial/ethnic category used by schools where they are *not* a significant part of the student body or heritage of the school. Yet the members of schools and their constituencies insist on retaining their Native American names because these are part of their collective identities. This allegiance to their school symbol is more important, apparently, than an insensitivity to the negative consequences evoked from the appropriation and depiction of Native Americans.

The purpose of this paper is to explore another area of potential concern by an oppressed group—women—over the names given their teams. The naming of women's teams raises parallel questions to the issues raised by Native Americans. Are the names given to university and college women's sport teams fair to women in general and women athletes in particular, or do they belittle them, diminish them, and reinforce negative images of women and their secondary status?

THEORETICAL BACKGROUND: LANGUAGE AND GENDER

Gender differentiation in language has been extensively documented and analyzed. An expanding body of literature reveals that language reflects and helps maintain the secondary status of women by defining them and their place (Henley, 1987, p. 3). This is because "every language reflects the prejudices of the society in which it evolved" (Miller & Swift, 1980, p. 3). Language places women and men within a system of differentiation and stratification. Language suggests how women and men are to be evaluated. Language embodies negative and positive value stances and valuations related to how certain groups within society are appraised (Van Den Bergh, 1987, p. 132). Language in general is filled with biases about women and men. Specific linguistic conventions are sexist when they isolate or stereotype some aspect of an individual's nature or the nature of a group of individuals based on their sex.

Many studies have pointed to the varied ways in which language acts in the defining, deprecation, and exclusion of women in areas of the social structure (Thorne, Kramarae, & Henley, 1985, p. 3). Our intent is to add to the literature by showing how the linguistic marking systems adopted by many college and university teams promote male supremacy and female subordination.

Names are symbols of identity as well as being essential for the construction of reality. Objects, events, and feelings must be named in order to make sense of the world. But naming is not a neutral process. Naming is an application of principles already in use, an extension of existing rules (Spender, 1980, p. 163). Patriarchy has shaped words, names, and labels for women and men, their personality traits, expressions of emotion, behaviors, and occupations. Names are badges of femininity and masculinity, hence of inferiority and superiority. Richardson (1981, p. 46) has summarized the subconscious rules governing the name preference in middle-class America:

> Male names tend to be short, hard-hitting, and explosive (e.g., Bret, Lance, Mark, Craig, Bruce, etc.). Even when the given name is multisyllabic (e.g., Benjamin, Joshua, William, Thomas), the nickname tends to imply hardness and energy (e.g., Ben, Josh, Bill, Tom, etc.). Female names, on the other hand, are longer, more melodic, and softer (e.g., Deborah, Caroline, Jessica, Christina) and easily succumb to the diminutive "ie" ending form (e.g., Debbie, Carrie, Jessie, Christie). And although feminization of male names (e.g., Fredricka, Roberta, Alexandra) is not uncommon, the inverse rarely occurs.

While naming is an important manifestation of gender differentiation, little research exists on naming conventions other than those associated with gender and given names. Only one study (Fuller & Manning, 1987) examines the naming practices of college sport teams, but it focuses narrowly on the sexism emanating from the violence commonly attributed to these symbols. Because of their emphasis Fuller and Manning considered only three sexist naming practices. The study presented here builds on the insights of Fuller and Manning by looking at eight sexist naming categories. The goal is to show that the naming traditions of sports teams can unwittingly promote the ideology of male superiority and sexual difference.

Our argument is that the names of many women's and men's athletic teams reinforce a basic element of social structure—that of gender division. Team names reflect this division as well as the asymmetry that is associated with it. Even after women's advances in sport since the implementation of Title IX, widespread naming practices continue to mark female athletes as unusual, aberrant, or invisible.

DATA AND METHODS

The data source on the names and mascots of sports teams at 4-year colleges and universities was Franks (1982). This book provides the required information plus a history of how the names were selected for 1,251 schools. Since our research focused on comparing the names for men's and women's teams, those schools limited to one sex were not considered. Also, schools now defunct were omitted from the present analysis. This was determined by eliminating those schools not listed in the latest edition of *American Universities and Colleges* (American Council of Education, 1987). Thus the number of schools in the present study was 1,185.

The decision on whether a school had sexist names for its teams was based on whether the team names violated the rules of gender neutrality. A review of the literature on language and gender revealed a number of gender-linked practices that diminish and trivialize women (Henley, 1987; Lakoff, 1975; Miller & Swift, 1980; Schulz, 1975; Spender, 1980).

1. Physical markers: One common naming practice emphasizes the physical appearance of women ("belle"). As Miller and Swift (1980, p. 87) argue, this practice is sexist because the "emphasis on the physical characteristics of women is offensive in contexts where men are described in terms of achievement."
2. Girl or gal: The use of "girl" or "gal" stresses the presumed immaturity and irresponsibility of women. "Just as *boy* can be blatantly offensive to minority men, so *girl* can have comparable patronizing and demeaning implications for women" (Miller & Swift, 1980, p. 71).

3. Feminine suffixes: This is a popular form of gender differentiation found in the names of athletic, social, and women's groups. The practice not only marks women but it denotes a feminine derivative by establishing a "female negative trivial category" (Miller & Swift, 1977, p. 58). The devaluation is accomplished by tagging words with feminine suffixes such as "ette" or "esse."

4. Lady: This label has several meanings that demean women athletes. Often "lady" is used to indicate women in roles thought to be unusual, if not unfortunate (Baron, 1986, p. 114). Lady is used to "evoke a standard of propriety, correct behavior, and elegance" (Miller & Swift, 1977, p. 72), characteristics decidedly unathletic. Similarly, lady carries overtones recalling the age of chivalry. "This makes the term seem polite at first, but we must also remember that these implications are perilous: they suggest that a 'lady' is helpless, and cannot do things for herself" (Lakoff, 1975, p. 25).

5. Male as a false generic: This practice assumes that the masculine in language, word, or name choice is the norm while the feminine is ignored altogether. Miller and Swift (1980, p. 9) define this procedure as, "Terms used of a class or group that are not applicable to all members." The use of "mankind" to encompass both sexes has its parallel among athletic teams where both men's and women's teams are the Rams, Stags, or Steers. Dale Spender (1980, p. 3) has called this treatment of the masculine as the norm as "one of the most pervasive and pernicious rules that has been encoded."

6. Male name with a female modifier: This practice applies the feminine to a name that usually denotes a male. This gives females lower status because it indicates inferior quality (Baron, 1986, p. 112). Examples among sports teams are the Lady Friars, Lady Rams, and Lady Gamecocks. Using such oxymorons "reflects role conflict and contributes to the lack of acceptance of women's sport" (Fuller & Manning, 1987, p. 64).

7. Double gender marking: This occurs when the name for the women's team is a diminutive of the men's team name and adding "belle" or "lady" or other feminine modifier. For example, the men's teams at Mississippi College are known as the Choctaws, while the women's teams are designated as the Lady Chocs. At the University of Kentucky the men's teams are the Wildcats and the women's teams are the Lady Kats. By compounding the feminine, the practice intensifies women's secondary status. Double gender marking occurs "perhaps to underline the inappropriateness or rarity of the feminine noun or to emphasize its negativity" (Baron, 1986, p. 115).

8. Male/female paired polarity: Women's and men's teams can be assigned names that represent a female/male opposition. When this occurs, the names for the men's teams always are positive in that they embody competitive and other traits associated with sport while the names for

women's teams are lighthearted or cute. The essence of sports is competition in which physical skills largely determine outcomes. Successful athletes are believed to embody such traits as courage, bravura, boldness, self-confidence, and aggression. When the names given men's teams imply these traits but the names for women's teams suggest that women are playful and cuddly, then women are trivialized and de-athleticized. Some egregious examples of this practice are, Fighting Scots/Scotties, Blue Hawks/Blue Chicks, Bears/Teddy Bears, and Wildcats/Wildkittens.

Although these eight categories make meaningful distinctions, they are not mutually exclusive. The problem arises with teams using the term lady. They might be coded under "lady" (Lady Threshers), or "male name with a female modifier" (Lady Rams), or "double gender marking" (Lady Kats). Since team names of all three types could be subsumed under the "lady" category, we opted to separate those with lady that could be included in another category. In other words, the category "lady" includes only those teams that could not be placed in either of the other two categories.

FINDINGS

The extent and type of symbolic derogation of women's teams were examined in several ways. We found, first, that of the 1,185 four-year schools in the sample, 451 (38.1%) had sexist names for their athletic teams. Examining only team logos (903 schools, or 76% of the sample, provided these data), 45.1% were sexist. For those schools with complete information on both names and logos, 493 of the 903 (54.6%) were sexist on one or both. We found that many schools have contradictory symbols, perhaps having a gender-neutral name for both male and female teams (Bears, Tigers) but then having a logo for both teams that was clearly having stereotypical and therefore unathletic characteristics. The important finding here is that when team names and logos are considered, more than half of the colleges and universities trivialize women's teams and women athletes.

The data on names were analyzed by the mode of discrimination, using the naming practices elaborated in the previous section (see Table 13-1). This analysis reveals, first, that over half the cases (55.1%) fall into the category of using a male name as a false generic. This usage contributes to the invisibility of women's teams. The next popular type of sexism in naming is the use of "lady" (25.2%) in Table 13-1, but actually 30.8% since some of the teams using lady are classified in what we considered more meaningful categories—see second footnote under Table 13-1). This popular usage clearly de-athleticizes women by implying their fragility, elegance, and propriety. This is also the consequence of the use of the feminine suffix (6.4%).

TABLE 13-1 Naming Practices That De-Athleticize Women's Teams

Naming Practices	N	%	Examples
Physical markers	2	0.4	Belles, Rambelles
Girl or Gal[a]	1	0.2	Green Gals
Feminine suffix	29	6.4	Tigerettes, Duchesses
Lady[b]	114	25.3	Lady Jets, Lady Eagles
Male as false generic	248	55.0	Cowboys, Hokies, Tomcats
Male name with female modifier	21	4.7	Lady Rams, Lady Centaurs, Lady Dons
Double gender marking	10	2.2	Choctaws/Lady Chocs, Jaguars/Lady Jags
Male-/Female-paired polarity	26	5.8	Panthers/Pink Panthers, Bears/Teddy Bears
Totals	451	100.0	

[a]Several female teams were designated as Cowgirls, but they were not included if the male teams were Cowboys. We assumed this difference to be nonsexist.
[b]Actually 139 of the 451 schools (30.8%) used Lady, but we placed 25 of them in other, more meaningful categories.

Another 5.8% of the schools with sexist naming patterns use the male/female paired polarity where male teams have names with clear referents to stereotypically masculine traits while the names for women's teams denote presumed feminine traits that are clearly unathletic. The other important category was the use of a male name with a female modifier (4.7%). This naming practice clearly implies that men are more important than women; men are represented by nouns whereas women are represented by adjectives. Few schools use the other linguistic categories (physical markers, girl or gal, and double gender marking).

The next question addressed was whether the institutions that diminished women through team naming were clustered among certain types of schools or in a particular geographical region. We thought perhaps that religious schools might be more likely to employ traditional notions about women than public schools or private secular schools (see Table 13-2). The data show that while religious colleges and universities are slightly more likely to have sexist naming practices than public or independent schools, the differences were not statistically significant.

We also controlled for region of the country, assuming that southern schools might be less likely than schools in other regions of the United States to be progressive about gender matters (see Table 13-3). The data show that the differences between schools in the South and the non South are indeed statistically different, with Southern schools more likely to use sexist names for their athletic teams. Table 13-4 analyzes these data by type of discrimination. Three interesting and statistically significant differences are found. Southern schools are much more likely than non Southern schools to incorporate feminine

TABLE 13-2   Prevalence of Sexist Team Names by Type of School

Naming Practice	PUBLIC[a]		INDEPENDENT		RELIGIOUS	
	N	%	N	%	N	%
Nonsexist	289	64.7	135	63.4	310	59.0
Sexist	158	35.3	78	36.6	215	41.0
Totals	447	100.0	213	100.0	525	100.0

$\chi^2 = 3.45$, $df = 2$, not significant.

[a]The determination of public, independent, or religious was provided in the description of each school in American Council of Education (1987).

TABLE 13-3   Prevalence of Sexist Team Names by Region

Naming Practice	NON SOUTH		SOUTH[a]	
	N	%	N	%
Nonsexist	500	65.4	264	34.6
Sexist	264	34.6	187	44.4
Totals	764	100.0	451	100.0

$\chi^2 = 10.79$, corrected for continuity $df = 1$, $p < .001$.

[a]Included in the South are schools from Missouri, Arkansas, Virginia, West Virginia, Mississippi, Maryland, Texas, Oklahoma, Louisiana, Alabama, Georgia, Kentucky, Tennessee, North Carolina, South Carolina, Florida, and the District of Columbia.

TABLE 13-4   Naming Practices That De-Athleticize Women's Teams by Region

Naming Practices	NON SOUTH		SOUTH		Level of Significance
	N	%	N	%	
Physical markers	0	0.0	2	100.0	n.s.
Girl or Gal	0	0.0	1	100.0	n.s.
Feminine suffix	10	34.4	19	65.6	$p < .025$
Lady	47	41.2	67	58.8	$p < .001$
Male as false generic	173	70.0	75	30.0	$p < .001$
Male name with female modifier	14	66.7	7	33.3	n.s.
Double gender marking	5	50.0	5	50.0	n.s.
Male-/Female-paired polarity	15	58.0	11	42.0	n.s.
Totals	264	58.5	187	41.0	

suffixes and use lady in their naming of female teams. Both of these naming practices emphasize traditional notions of femininity. The other difference in this table is in the opposite direction—non Southern schools are more likely to use male names as a false generic than are Southern schools. This naming practice ignores women's teams. Southern schools on the other hand, with their disproportionate use of feminine suffixes and lady, call attention to their women's teams but emphasize their femininity rather than their athleticism.

DISCUSSION

This research has shown that approximately three eighths of American colleges and universities employ sexist names and over half have sexist names and/or logos for their athletic teams. This means that the identity symbols for athletic teams contribute to the maintenance of male dominance within college athletics. As Polk (1974) has noted in an article on the sources of male power, since men have shaped society's institutions they tend to fit the value structure of such institutions. Nowhere is this more apparent than in sport. Since the traditional masculine gender role matches most athletic qualities better than the traditional feminine gender role, the images and symbols are male. Women do not fit in this scheme. They are "others" even when they do participate. Their team names and logos tend to perpetuate and strengthen the image of female inferiority by making them either invisible or trivial or consistently nonathletic.

Institutional sexism is deeply entrenched in college sports. The mere changing of sexist names and logos to nonsexist ones will not alter this structural inequality, but it is nevertheless important. As institutional barriers to women's participation in athletics are removed, negative linguistic and symbolic imagery must be replaced with names and images that reflect the new visions of women and men in their expanding and changing roles.

In the past decade the right of women to rename or relabel themselves and their experiences has become a tool of empowerment. For feminists, changing labels to reflect the collective redefinition of what it means to be female has been one way to gain power. As Van Den Bergh (1987) explains, renaming can create changes for the powerless group as well as promoting change in social organization. Renaming gives women a sense of control of their own identity and raises consciousness within their group and that of those in power. Because language is intimately intertwined with the distribution of power in society, the principle of renaming can be an important way of changing reality.

Since language has a large impact on people's values and their conceptions of women's and men's rightful place in the social order, the pervasive acceptance of gender marking in the names of collegiate athletic teams is not a trivial matter. Athletes, whether women or men, need names that convey their self-confidence, their strength, their worth, and their power.

REFERENCES

American Council of Education. (1987). *American universities and colleges* (14th ed.). New York: Walter de Gruyter.

Baron, D. (1986). *Grammar and gender.* New Haven: Yale University Press.

Bryson, L. (1987). Sport and the maintenance of masculine hegemony. *Women's Studies International Forum,* **10,** 349-360.

Durkheim, E. (1947). *The elementary forms of religious life* (J. W. Sivain, Trans.). New York: Free Press.

Franks, R. (1982). *What's in a nickname? Exploring the jungle of college athletic mascots.* Amarillo, TX: Ray Franks Publ.

Fuller, J. R., & Manning, E. A. (1987). Violence and sexism in college mascots and symbols: A typology. *Free Inquiry in Creative Sociology,* **15,** 61-64.

Hall, M. A. (1984). Feminist prospects for the sociology of sport. *Arena Review,* **8,** 1-9.

Hall, M. A. (1985). Knowledge and gender: Epistemological questions in the social analysis of sport. *Sociology of Sport Journal,* 25-42.

Henley, N. M. (1987). This new species that seeks a new language: On sexism in language and language change. In J. Penfield (Ed.), *Women and language in transition* (pp. 3-27). Albany: State University of New York Press.

Lakoff, R. (1975). *Language and woman's place.* New York: Harper & Row.

Lever, J. (1983). *Soccer madness.* Chicago: University of Chicago Press.

Miller, C., & Swift, K. (1977). *Words and women: New language in new times.* Garden City, NY: Doubleday/Anchor.

Miller, C., & Swift, K. (1980). *The handbook of nonsexist writing.* New York: Lippincott & Crowell.

Polk, B. B. (1974). Male power and the women's movement. *Journal of Applied Behavioral Sciences,* **10**(3), 415-431.

Richardson, L. W. (1981). *The dynamics of sex and gender* (2nd ed.). Boston: Houghton Mifflin.

Schulz, M. (1975). The semantic derogation of women. In B. Thorne & N. Henley (Eds.), *Language and sex: Difference and dominance* (pp. 64-75). Rowley, MA: Newbury House.

Spender, D. (1980). *Man made language.* London: Routledge & Kegan Paul.

Thorne, B., Kramarae, C., & Henley, N. (1985). Language, gender, and society: Opening a second decade of research. In B. Thorne & N. Henley (Eds.), *Language, gender, and society* (pp. 7-24). Rowley, MA: Newbury House.

Van Den Bergh, N. (1987). Renaming: Vehicle for empowerment. In J. Penfield (Ed.), *Women and language and transition* (pp. 130-136). Albany: State University of New York Press.

■ FOR FURTHER STUDY

Banks, Dennis J., "Tribal Names and Sports Mascots," *Journal of Sport & Social Issues* 17 (April 1993):5-8.

Davis, Laurel R., "Protest Against the Use of Native American Mascots: A Challenge to Traditional American Identity," *Journal of Sport & Social Issues* 17 (April 1993):9-22.

Duncan, Margaret Carlisle, "Representation and the Gun That Points Backwards," *Journal of Sport & Social Issues* 17 (April 1993):42-46.

Edelson, Paula, "Just Whistlin' Dixie," *Z Magazine* 4 (November 1991):72-73.

Eitzen, D. Stanley, and Maxine Baca Zinn, "The Sexist Naming of College Athletic Teams and Resistance to Change," *Journal of Sport & Social Issues* 17 (April 1993):34-41.

Fuller, J. R., and E. A. Manning, "Violence and Sexism in College Mascots and Symbols: A Typology," *Free Inquiry in Creative Sociology* 15 (1987):54-61.

Malec, Michael A., "Patriotic Symbols in Intercollegiate Sports During the Gulf War," *Sociology of Sport Journal* 10 (March 1993):98-106.

Peweewardy, C. D., "Native American Mascots and Imagery: The Struggle of Unlearning Indian Stereotypes," *Journal of Navajo Education* 9 (1991):19-23.

Part Five

Problems of Excess: Sport and Violence

Of the many questions concerning violence in sport, one takes precedence: Why are violent sports so popular in some societies and less so in others? Is it because aggressive activities have a cathartic effect, releasing pent-up hostility in a socially healthy way? Thus, they are needed in those societies where tensions are high. Research shows again and again, however, that aggression actually produces more aggression. In the first selection, anthropologist Richard Grey Sipes provides evidence for a related explanation—that violent societies have violent sports. There is ample evidence that America is a violent society (for example, the history of slavery; the forcible taking of land from Native Americans; vigilante law in the West; a foreign policy of Manifest Destiny; our contemporary crime rates, which tend to be about ten times greater than those found in Great Britain, France, Sweden, and Japan; our high imprisonment rate; and the popularity of violence in literature, movies, and television). Similarly, violent sports are popular in American society.

Violence is inherent to many sports. Athletes hit, tackle, block, and collide as they engage in various sports. Even some non-contact sports such as basketball have become very "physical." In these sports settings some violence is "normative" while other aggressive acts go beyond the acceptable. The second selection, by sociologist Michael Smith, helps us to sort out the differences by providing a typology of sports violence.

The third selection is by Rick Telander, a sports journalist and a former football player from Northwestern. Telander describes the essence of football—violence.

14. Sports as a Control for Aggression

RICHARD GREY SIPES

From as early as our first recorded thoughts of man, we have been attempting to control what we call aggression. We haven't tried to eliminate it, but rather to have it manifest how, when, and where we wish it and to have it absent in all other situations. Most of the time, on a day-to-day basis, we succeed, but we become quite concerned when our control fails and results in muggings, fist-fights, child abuse, riots, police brutality, or a war not to our benefit.

Can we significantly improve the precision of our control of aggression? I do not think so. My opinion is based on research results [1,2,3] indicating that, with massive effort, we could raise or lower the *general* aggressiveness of a society and its members, but that we cannot control manifestations of aggression much more precisely than we presently do.

Sport has been seen as an activity that can be used to at least influence the manifestation of aggression on the social and individual levels. It is true that sport is theoretically and practically more controllable by social institutions, up to and including the governmental level, than virtually any other widespread activity. How we would use our control of sports, though, depends on which of two opposing models of human behavior we use in our thinking.

TWO MODELS OF BEHAVIOR

According to what I have called the *Drive Discharge Model* of human behavior, there is a certain level of aggression in every individual and in every society. The aggression is like a liquid substance generated by an innate drive or by interaction with the environment. Although its level may vary somewhat from time to time, and from one society to another and one person to another, it generally is higher than desired, and must be discharged along acceptable paths. This is the model with which most psychiatric and psychological writers work, and it is the one most commonly used by the layman.

SOURCE: "Sports as a Control for Aggression" by Richard Grey Sipes. From *The Humanistic and Mental Health Aspects of Sports, Exercise and Recreation* by Timothy T. Craig (ed.), pp. 46–49. Copyright © 1976 by the American Medical Association.

154

According to this model, we can decrease unwanted manifestations of violence and other aggressive behavior by encouraging its manifestations in innocuous behavior. Simplistically, we can reduce the frequency of fistfights by increasing the frequency of attendance at boxing matches, and decrease the likelihood of war by increasing combative sports.

The alternative model, which I label the *Culture Pattern Model,* assumes something quite different about human behavior. It stresses the fact that we learn our individual patterns of behavior, and that our culture supplies us with these patterns. It sees individuals and entire societies as fundamentally consistent in most of their behavior patterns, with similar generalized modes manifesting themselves in divergent arenas of action. According to this model, we can decrease unwanted violence and other aggressive behavior by reducing the aggressive component of culture patterns wherever this component is found. Simplistically, we would reduce the frequency of fistfights if we eliminated the sport of boxing, and could reduce the likelihood of war by not engaging in combative sports.

The "treatments" indicated by these two models, then, are mutually exclusive—indeed opposite.

But both models, if we stop here, are only unsubstantiated speculations . . . informed opinions. They must survive rigid, controlled tests if they are to pass to the category of substantiated theories, and they must be in this category before we are justified in acting on them.

TESTING THE MODELS

Both models have been tested through hypotheses logically derived from them. The *Drive Discharge Model* predicts that as the incidence of one form of aggression goes up, the incidence of other forms will go down. We should find a lower incidence of combative sports in societies that are more warlike, and within any given society a lower incidence during periods of increased military activity. So with other forms of aggressive behavior. More warlike societies should have a lower need for—and consequently have a lesser occurrence of—such venting behavior as the practice of malevolent magic, harsh punishment of deviants, or body mutilation. More peaceful societies, on the other hand, denied the release of aggression in the form of warfare, should show a higher occurrence of these aggressive outlets. More generally, we could predict that the more any one or more of these aggressive channels are used, the less the remainder are likely to be needed by the society.

The *Culture Pattern Model,* on the other hand, predicts that the above channels, including warfare, are likely to vary directly. That is, a society low in one is most likely going to be low in all and a society high in one probably will be high in all, since the same general orientation or cultural motif will govern these and many other behaviors of, and within, the society.

METHODOLOGY

I subjected these hypotheses to test, using the cross-cultural correlation method. This method has been accepted and employed by anthropologists, sociologists, psychiatrists, and psychologists to test numerous hypotheses.[4] It has been brought to a high level of confidence and rigor in recent years.[5]

A cross-cultural correlation study utilizes a representative sample of societies from the universe of human societies. Within this sample it tests for Variable A relative to Variable B. If A and B tend systematically to occur or otherwise vary together (correlation studies are statistical—not mechanical—in orientation and admit of disconformity), it is assumed that there is some functional relationship, direct or indirect, between A and B. A biological parallel is the correlation between the presence (or absence) of certain parasitic protozoans in the bloodstream of humans and the periodic manifestation (or absence) of symptoms we term malaria. The correlation is not unity, but it is strong enough to suggest an important functional, perhaps causal, connection between the two phenomena.

THE TEST AND RESULTS

I randomly selected ten warlike and ten peaceful societies throughout the world and ethnographically coded them for the presence or absence of combative type sports.[1] A combative type sport was defined as one involving the acquisition of disputed territory, generally symbolized by the placing of an object in a guarded location (a hockey puck in the cage, a basketball through the ring, or a football at the opponent's end of the field), the subduing of an opponent (as in some—but not all—forms of wrestling), or patently combat situations (fencing, dodging thrown spears, karate). If a society had even one combative sport, it was coded as having combative sports. Of the ten warlike societies, nine had combative sports and one did not. Of the ten peaceful societies, only two had combative sports and eight lacked them. This indicates that warlikeness and combative sports tend to occur together. The *phi* value of this distribution is 0.7035. The Fisher Exact Test shows that the probability of getting this, or a rarer distribution of cases in the same direction, by chance alone is less than 0.0028, or about three in a thousand tries. The test supports the *Culture Pattern Model* and vitiates the *Drive Discharge Model*.

To verify my cross-cultural results, I conducted a temporal-variation study in the United States. The level of military activity was measured by the percent of the adult male population in the United States Armed Forces each year between 1920 and 1970. This spanned three periods of active combat. I used two relatively combative sports: hunting (a participation sport) and attendance at football games (spectator activity). I also used two relatively noncombative sports: race-track betting (participant) and attendance at baseball games (spectator). Yearly measures of activity in these sports were correlated with yearly level of military activity. Technical reasons led me to divide the data into two periods: pre-1946 and post-1946. Of the eight resulting correlation tests, six showed a non-significant—often insignificant—relationship between sports and military activity, of which five were direct. The only significant *inverse* relationship was between military activity and betting in the period following 1946. This was balanced by an equally significant *direct* relationship between military activity and betting in the pre-1946 period. This also is the least sport-like of the four sports used, according to common interpretations. Moreover, if graphed, it becomes evident that the eight-fold increase in betting between 1942 (in the midst of World War II) and 1970 probably was due to increasing affluence, and may have nothing to do with the fact that the percent of males in the military shrank from twenty-five to five in the same period. (During the actual World War II and Korean periods of conflict, there was a strong rise in betting, providing a direct correlation between betting and warfare for that specific time span.)

The *Drive Discharge Model* predicts a negative dischronic relationship between sports and war, whereas the *Cultural Pattern Model* predicts a positive *or no* dischronic relationship over this length of time. The case study test results, therefore, confirm the results of the synchronic cross-cultural study and tend to support the *Cultural Pattern Model* at the expense of the *Drive Discharge Model.*

AN ETHNOSCIENTIFIC STUDY OF SPORTS AND CONFLICT

Professor Kendall Blanchard has conducted a comparative ethnoscientific linguistic analysis and emic conflict-model study of "perceived conflict"—fights, wars, aggressive displays, and sports—in the contemporary Choctaw Indian and "Anglo" societies. (This approach studies, in depth, the terms, grammar, values, and logic used by the members of a culture themselves, to arrive at the *meaning* of behavior in the cultural context.[6]) Through personal correspondence he informs me that his unpublished results[7] support my findings that sports, especially combative team sports, do not serve as functional alternatives to other forms of aggression, such as warfare. Sports and war would appear to be components of a broader cultural pattern.

MALEVOLENT MAGIC, MUTILATION, AND PUNISHMENT

I anticipated the objection that the choice and test of merely two alternative channels of aggression discharge might not give a valid or sufficiently complete picture of the situation. This prompted me to later test three other activities, using the same sample societies and the cross-cultural method.[3] I selected the practice of malevolent magic as a way in which an individual could secretively aggress upon a fellow community member. Cosmetic/status mutilation was chosen because it has been claimed to represent a turning-inward of aggression against one's self (although this claim certainly can be disputed). The punishment of deviants was used because it represents aggression of society against the individual.

Three indicator variables were used to measure malevolent magic: (1) how important such magic looms in the minds of most members of the society (importance), (2) roughly what proportion of misfortunes are attributed to it (scope), and (3) the amount of harm it can produce (intensity).

Body mutilation was broken down into tattooing, scarification, piercing, shape molding, and amputation. The *measure of mutilation* was the sum of measures of (1) how many different types of mutilation were practiced for cosmetic reasons, by what proportion of the population, and by either male or female or both; and (2) the occasions at which mutilation was used to mark changes in the social status or role (adulthood, marriage, widow[er]-hood) of the individual, male or female or both, and the proportional incidence of such mutilation.

Punishment of deviants was measured as the sum of coding values for the severity of usual punishment for (1) murder, (2) major theft, and (3) forbidden sexual intercourse.

Each of the above three theoretical (indirectly measured) variables, and their indicator (directly measured) variables, was tested against the warlikeness of the societies, and the results of the correlation tests are shown in Table 14-1. (Results of the earlier combative-sports test also are shown for comparison and completeness.) A nonwar summarized aggression value for each society also was computed from all four theoretical variable scores (sports, magic, mutilation, and punishment) and tested against warlikeness, with the result of that test also shown. Note that all directly-measured indicator variables show a positive correlation with warlikeness. The more warlike societies are those likely to have higher "aggressiveness" in each of these variables. The results are somewhat more impressive when we look at the theoretical variables—the correlations tend to be more significant. The overall aggressive measure is singularly impressive, with the probability of finding that correlation by chance alone being about five in ten thousand.

These results emphatically support the *Culture Pattern Model* and invalidate the *Drive Discharge Model*. The functional relationship between various aggression-containing activities is one of mutual support, not one of alternative discharge paths.

TABLE 14-1 Warlikeness versus Other Traits

	Phi^*	$CumP^{**}$
Malevolent Magic	0.6710	0.0070
Importance	0.4725	0.1002
Scope	0.5164	0.0593
Intensity	0.7135	0.0038
Punishment	0.6250	0.0305
Murder	0.4910	0.0835
Theft	0.5006	0.1186
Sex	0.5774	0.0468
Body Mutilation	0.4000	0.0900
Cosmetic	0.2041	0.3257
Male	0.2182	0.3142
Female	0.2182	0.3142
Status	0.2000	0.3258
Male	0.1005	0.5000
Female	0.1155	0.5000
Sports	0.7035	0.0028
Combined	0.8000	0.0005

*Phi is a statistical measure of strength of association between two dichotomized variables. The higher the value, the stronger the association.

**$CumP$, computed with Fisher's Exact Probability Test, represents the probability of getting the observed distribution, or one more rare, in the direction predicted by chance alone. The lower the value, the more significant the association.

DISCUSSION

Sports and war (and other "aggressive" forms of behavior) obviously do not, as often claimed, act as alternative channels for the discharge of accumulable aggressive tensions.

The *Cultural Pattern Model* seems better able to predict and explain human behavior. It says that each society and its culture (and perhaps each individual?) is characterized by one or more motifs or themes. The consistency typical of any culture leads us to expect to find similar attitudes, orientations, and behaviors manifesting themselves in different activities. If indifference to suffering, zero-sum games, bravery, aggressiveness, or other generalized characteristics are found strongly present in one activity, they most likely will be found throughout the culture rather than be limited to that one activity.

COMMENT

The hope would seem dim of using sports to influence warfare, or any of the other forms of undesirable aggressive behavior. Aggression by society, or by components thereof, or as manifested in the individuals who make up society, is an integral part of the total cultural configuration. To significantly attenuate one form of aggression would require us to simultaneously attenuate most or all forms; that is, to overhaul our entire culture.

Modification of behavior—individual or social—is difficult at best. If we wish to take on this task, though, my research would indicate that aggressive behavior is best reduced by eliminating combative or conflict-type sports. Attempting to siphon off aggressive tension by promulgating the observation of or participation in aggressive sports is more than a futile effort; to the degree that it had any effect at all, it most likely would raise the level of aggression in other social and individual behavior patterns.

NOTES

1. Sipes, R. G.: War, sports and aggression: an empirical test of two rival theories. *American Anthropology* 75 (1):64-86, 1973.
2. Sipes, R. G.: War, combative sports and aggression: A preliminary causal model of cultural patterning, in Nettleship, M. A. (ed): *War: Its Causes and Correlates*. The Hague, Mouton Press, 1975.
3. Sipes, R. G., Robertson, B. A.: Malevolent magic, mutilation, punishment, and aggression. Read before the American Anthropological Association, San Francisco, 1975.
4. Naroll, R.: What have we learned from cross-cultural surveys? *American Anthropology* 72:1227-1288, 1970.
5. Sipes, R. G.: Rating hologeistic method. *Behavior Science Notes* 7:157-198, 1972.
6. Tyler, S. A.: *Cognitive Anthropology*. New York, Holt, Rinehart, and Winston, 1969.
7. Blanchard, K.: Team sports and violence: An anthropological perspective. Read before the Association for the Anthropological Study of Play, Detroit, 1975.

15. A Typology of Sports Violence

MICHAEL D. SMITH

No rules or practice of any game whatever can make that lawful which is unlawful by the law of the land; and the law of the land says that you shall not do that which is likely to cause the death of another. For instance, no persons can by agreement go out to fight with deadly weapons, doing by agreement what the law says shall not be done, and thus shelter themselves from the consequences of their acts. Therefore, in one way you need not concern yourself with the rules of football. (Hechter, 1977:444)

These were Lord Justice Bramwell's instructions to the jury in an 1878 British court case, *Regina* v. *Bradshaw*. A soccer player was accused of manslaughter after he charged and collided with an opposing player, who subsequently died, in a game played under Football Association rules. The defendant was acquitted, but the judge's pronouncement has been cited of late in North America by those who wish to make the point that sports should not be exempt from the laws that govern our behavior elsewhere.

Seventeen years later, in 1895, Robert Fitzsimmons engaged in a public boxing exhibition with his sparring mate, Riordan, in Syracuse, New York. Riordan was knocked unconscious by a punch to the head and died five hours later. Fitzsimmons was indicted for manslaughter. The judge directed the jury as follows:

If the rules of the game and the practices of the game are reasonable, are consented to by all engaged, are not likely to induce serious injury, or to end life, if then, as a result of the game, an accident happens, it is excusable homicide . . . (Hechter, 1977:443)

Fitzsimmons was acquitted. What is noteworthy about this case is that the rules and practices of the game were taken into account in determining criminal liability, a precedent directly contrary to that established in *Regina* v. *Bradshaw*. It is the Fitzsimmons ruling that has more or less held ever since.

The fact is, sports violence has never been viewed as "real" violence. The courts, except for isolated flurries of activity, have traditionally been reluctant to touch even the most outrageous incidents of sports-related bloodletting; legal experts still flounder in their attempts to determine what constitutes

SOURCE: "A Typology of Sport Violence" by Michael D. Smith. From *Violence and Sport* by Michael D. Smith, pp. 8–14. Copyright © 1983 by author. Reprinted by permission.
It is a violation of the law to reproduce this selection by any means whatsoever without the written permission of the copyright holder.

violence in sports. The great majority of violence-doers and their victims, the players, even though rule-violating assaults often bring their careers to a premature close, have always accepted much of what could be called violence as "part of the game." Large segments of the public, despite the recent emergence of sports violence as a full-blown "social problem," continue to give standing ovations to performers for acts that in other contexts would be instantly condemned as criminal. An examination of sports violence that fails to consider these perspectives "does violence," as it were, to what most people, not to mention those involved with criminal justice systems, regard as violence.

Following is an attempt to answer the question: what is sports violence? I shall go about this task by constructing a typology. A typology is a device for categorizing a phenomenon into at least two types on each of one or more dimensions. In the present case, sports violence will be divided into four types, ranging roughly from greater to lesser, on a scale of *legitimacy,* as shown in Table 15-1. I shall take into account the viewpoints of the law, the players, and the public in so doing. This exercise is confined to acts performed by players during the game, or in its immediate context.

BRUTAL BODY CONTACT

This category of sports violence comprises all significant (i.e., high magnitude) body contact performed within the official rules of a given sport: tackles, blocks, body checks, collisions, legal blows of all kinds. Such contact is inherent in sports such as boxing, wrestling, ice hockey, rugby, lacrosse, football, and to lesser degrees in soccer, basketball, water polo, team handball, and the like. It is taken for granted that when one participates in these activities one automatically accepts the inevitability of contact, also the probability of minor bodily injury, and the possibility of serious injury. In legal terms

TABLE 15-1   A Sports Violence Typology

Relatively Legitimate	
Brutal body contact	*Borderline violence*
Conforms to the official rules of the sport, hence legal in effect under the law of the land; more or less accepted.	Violates the official rules of the sport and the law of the land, but widely accepted.
Relatively Illegitimate	
Quasi-criminal violence	*Criminal violence*
Violates the official rules of the sport, the law of the land, and to a significant degree informal player norms; more or less not accepted.	Violates the official rules of the sport, the law of the land, and players' informal norms; not accepted.

players are said to "consent" to receive such blows (*volenti non fit injuria*—to one who consents no injury is done). On the other hand, no player consents to be injured intentionally. Suppose a blitzing linebacker levels a quarterback with a ferocious but legal tackle; the quarterback is severely injured; a civil court case ensues. Theoretically, the law suggests, if it can be shown that the linebacker foresaw that his blow would severely injure the quarterback, hence *intended* to injure him, the linebacker is culpable. The probability of such a legal outcome, however, is close to zero. In effect, any blow administered within the formal rules of a sport is legal under the law of the land (Lambert, 1978).

Legal body contact is nevertheless of interest as violence when it develops (or as some might prefer, degenerates) into "brutality." A rising toll of injuries and deaths, followed by public expressions of alarm, then demands for reform, typically signal this condition. An "intrinsically brutal" sport like boxing always hovers not far from this point; for this reason, boxing is almost everywhere regulated by the state, albeit often inadequately. When body contact assumes an importance out of proportion to that required to play the game—when inflicting pain and punishing opponents are systematized as strategy, and viciousness and ferocity are publicly glorified—a stage of brutality can be said to have been reached. Such practices may strain the formal rules of sports, but they do not necessarily violate those rules.

Sports brutality is not a new phenomenon. The history of football, to take probably the best example, is in part a chronicle of intermittent waves of brutality, public censure, and reform. In 1893 indignation against alleged viciousness in American college football, smoldering for some time, erupted across the country. A campaign led by the magazines *Saturday Evening Post* and *The Nation* caused several institutions to drop the game, including Harvard, one of the first schools to play it on a regular intercollegiate basis. Parke Davis [1911:98], then the University of Wisconsin coach and later a historian of the game, wrote that the reports of brutish play were somewhat exaggerated. Among the most hysterical must have been that appearing in a German publication, *Münchener Nachrichten*. This report, quoted by Davis, described the Harvard-Yale game of 1893 as "awful butchery," seven participants reportedly being carried in "dying condition" off the field with broken backs, broken legs, and lost eyes.) A popular vaudeville ditty of the day is revealing (Betts, 1974: 244):

> Just bring along the ambulance,
> And call the Red Cross nurse,
> Then ring the undertaker up,
> And make him bring a hearse;
> Have all the surgeons ready there,
> For they'll have work today,
> Oh, can't you see the football teams
> Are lining up to play.

Antifootball sentiment swept the United States again in 1905. In a report somewhat more measured than the one above, a Chicago newspaper published a compilation for the 1905 season showing 18 players dead, 11 from high schools and 3 from colleges, and 159 more or less serious injuries. President Roosevelt called representatives of Yale, Harvard, and Princeton to the White House and threatened to ban the game unless its brutality was eliminated. Stormed Teddy "Rough Rider" Roosevelt, "Brutality and foul play should receive the same summary punishment given to a man who cheats at cards" (Stagg, 1927:253). Rule changes resulted, including the outlawing of the notorious V formation, and the furor abated.

Roughing up and intimidating opponents as a legal tactic, however, seems to have gained new life of late. Football is still in the vanguard. Consider the "hook," a sort of on-field mugging, whereby a defensive back in the course of making a tackle flexes his biceps and tries to catch the receiver's head in the joint between the forearm and upper arm. Professional player Jack Tatum (Tatum and Kushner, 1979:18), who likes to think that his hits "border on felonious assault," fondly recalls a well-executed hook (the tactic was outlawed soon after):

> I just timed my hit. When I felt I could zero in on Riley's head at the same time the ball arrived in his hands, I moved. . . . Because of the momentum built up by the angles and speed of both Riley and myself, it was the best hit of my career. I heard Riley scream on impact and felt his body go limp.

The casualty rates, the ultimate result of this type of play, are not insignificant. The rate in the National Football League is said to be 100 percent—at least one serious injury per player per season (Underwood, 1979). About 318,000 football injuries annually require hospital emergency room treatment in the United States (Philo and Stine, 1977). In the Canadian Football League, according to a survey conducted by the *Toronto Star* (November 25, 1981), 462 man-games were lost in the 1981 season owing to injury (down slightly from the year before). Observers seem to agree that the high injury rates at all levels of the game are attributable in significant measure to the way football is taught and played: brutishly.

BORDERLINE VIOLENCE

In this category are assaults that, though prohibited by the official rules of a given sport, occur routinely and are more or less accepted by all concerned. To wit: the hockey fist-fight, the late hit in football, the high tackle in soccer, the baseball knock-down pitch, basketball "body language," the sometimes vicious elbowing and bumping that takes place in track and road races. Such practices occasionally produce serious injuries, but these are usually dismissed as unfortunate accidents. Borderline violence is essentially the province of referees, umpires, and other immediate game officials, higher league officials and law enforcement authorities seldom becoming involved. Sanctions never exceed suspension from the game being played, and perhaps a fine.

Borderline violence is nonetheless illegal under civil law, as the U.S. *Restatement of Torts* makes clear (Rains, 1980:800):

> Taking part in a game manifests a willingness to submit to such bodily contacts or restrictions of liberty as are permitted by its rules or usages. Participating in such a game does not manifest consent to contacts which are prohibited by rules or usages of the game if such rules or usages are designed to protect the participants and not merely to secure the better playing of the game as a test of skill. This is true although the player knows that those with or against whom he is playing are habitual violators of such rules.

Thus a football lineman who goes offside and injures his opposite number with a legal block has broken a rule designed to "secure the better playing of the game" and is not legally liable under civil law for his action. But a defensive back who hits a ball carrier just after the whistle has blown has broken a safety rule, a rule designed "to protect the participants," and *is* liable on grounds of negligence or recklessness. Playing football does not, in the eyes of the law, include "consenting" to be the recipient of a late hit. Yet the law almost never intervenes in such cases, for reasons that will begin to emerge shortly.

Borderline violence is tolerated and justified on a number of grounds, most of which boil down to some version of the "part of the game" argument. Take hockey fisticuffs. A National Hockey League player, one of sixty interviewed in 1976-1977 by the author (see Smith, 1979), provides this familiar (non) explanation:

> I don't think that there's anything wrong with guys getting excited in a game and squaring off and throwing a few punches. That's just part of the game. It always has been. And you know if you tried to eliminate it, you wouldn't have hockey any more. You look at hockey from the time it was begun, guys get excited and just fight, and it's always been like that.

Naturally because fist-fighting is considered legitimate it is not defined by its practitioners as "violence." Also nobody gets hurt in a punch-up, players insist. (This is not precisely true. Of 217 "minor injuries" suffered by players on a Southern Professional Hockey League team over a three-year period in the mid-1970s, most involved the hand or forearm [fractures, sprains, lacerations, etc.] and were usually incurred during fights [Rovere et al., 1978:62].) To the majority of professional players interviewed by the author the periodic public fuss over hockey fighting is simply a product of the rantings of publicity-hungry politicians:

I think it's really blown out of proportion. A lot of these politicians trying to get somewhere are just trying to crack down on fighting to get their name in the paper. Most of the guys that say things like that don't know anything about hockey, and they're trying to talk about violence, and they don't even know what they're talking about. I don't think a punch in the head is going to hurt you, unless it's, you know, a sick thing where a guy pummels a guy into the ice and things like that.

There are, of course, more elaborate folk theories in circulation. Apologists are prone to claim, for example, that hockey fisticuffs are safety valves for aggressive impulses (usually described as "frustration") that inevitably accumulate due to the speed, the contact, the very nature of the game. Because these aggressive urges must be vented, the argument goes, if not one way then another, prohibiting fist-fighting would result in an increase in the more vicious and dangerous illegal use of the stick. In the words of John Ziegler, President of the NHL (*Toronto Star*, December 13, 1977:C2): "I do not find it unacceptable in a game where frustration is constant, for men to drop their sticks and gloves and take swings at each other. I think that kind of outlet is important for players in our games."

The logic is shaky. Would Ziegler argue that the pugnacious Philadelphia Flyers, NHL penalty leaders nine years in a row, get more penalties than other teams because they get more frustrated? Or that the Flyers are somehow compelled to respond to frustration with aggression, whereas other teams are not? Hockey may well have its frustrating moments (what sport does not?), but as researchers have repeatedly shown, human beings may or may not respond to frustration with aggression. Like most human behavior, responses to frustration are shaped by culture and learning. "Frustration" seems more an excuse for, than a cause of, violence in hockey.

Belief in the inevitability of hockey violence generally is so entrenched, that a judge in the famous Ted Green–Wayne Maki assault trials (stemming from a stick-swinging duel during a 1969 game in Ottawa that nearly ended Green's life) concluded that the game "can't be played without what normally are called assaults." Both players were acquitted, needless to say (*New York Times*, September 4, 1979:31).

As for public opinion, polls have revealed that substantial minorities find the hockey fist-fight more or less acceptable. Just months after the Green–Maki episode, almost 40 percent of the respondents in a Canada-wide survey sponsored by *Maclean's* magazine said they "liked to see fighting at a hockey game"; among males the figure was 46 percent (Marshall, 1970). In a 1972 *Canadian Magazine* reader survey (over 30,000 questionnaires were returned), 32 percent of all respondents and 38 percent of the male respondents thought NHL players should *not* be given automatic game penalties for fighting (Grescoe, 1972). In the United States a state-wide survey of

Minnesota residents conducted by Mid-Continent Surveys of Minneapolis, shortly after the 1975 assault trial in Minnesota of Boston hockey player David Forbes, found that 61 percent of Minnesotans thought punishment for fighting in professional sports should be left to the leagues. Twenty-six percent preferred court punishment, and 5 percent preferred both (Hallowell and Meshbesher, 1977). More recently, 26 percent of over 31,000 Ontario residents surveyed in 1979 responded "No" to the general question, "Do you feel there is too much violence in professional hockey?" (McPherson and Davidson, 1980).

QUASI-CRIMINAL VIOLENCE

Quasi-criminal violence is that which violates not only the formal rules of a given sport (and the law of the land), but to a significant degree the informal norms of player conduct. It usually results, or could have resulted, in serious injury, which is what brings it to the attention of top league officials and generates public outrage in some quarters. This in turn puts pressure on legal authorities to become involved. League-imposed penalties for quasi-criminal violence usually go beyond the contest in question and range from suspensions from several games to lifetime bans, depending on the sport; each league seems to decide how much and what types of violence it will tolerate. Increasingly, civil legal proceedings follow, though perhaps less often than thought; up to 1978 only about ten civil suits involving personal injury in the National Football League took place; in the National Basketball Association, there were perhaps two (Horrow, 1980). Criminal proceedings, rare in the past, are occurring more frequently, but convictions remain few and far between. In 1976 the Attorney General of Ontario, after several public warnings, ordered a crackdown on violence in amateur and professional sports in the province. According to an internal memorandum provided by the Director of Regional Crown Attorneys, sixty-eight assault charges were laid in less than a year (sixty-seven in hockey, one in lacrosse), but only ten convictions were obtained, although sixteen cases were still pending at the time of the memorandum. Apparently all the convictions, and almost all the charges, were against amateur athletes. . . .

Still, a small number of episodes of quasi-criminal violence in professional sports have resulted in litigation, and it is these cases that have generated the greatest publicity. Several civil disputes have received continent-wide attention. One of the first in sport's modern era took place in baseball during a 1965 game between the San Francisco Giants and the Los Angeles Dodgers. Giant batter Juan Marichal felled Dodger catcher John Roseboro with his bat following an acrimonious verbal exchange. Roseboro sustained considerable injury; Marichal was fined $1,750 by the League and suspended for eight games. Roseboro filed a $110,000 civil suit for damages against Marichal and the San Francisco club; it was reportedly settled out of court for $7,500 (Kuhlman, 1975).

A decade and a half later, in 1979, Houston Rockets basketball player Rudy Tomjanovich was awarded the whopping sum of $3.25 million in a civil suit for injuries received as a result of a single, devastating punch thrown by Kermit Washington of the Los Angeles Lakers during a 1977 game, a blow described by a Laker assistant coach as "the hardest punch in the history of mankind." Tomjanovich suffered a fractured jaw, nose, and skull, severe lacerations, a cerebral concussion, and was not surprisingly out for the season. The League Commissioner suspended Washington for sixty days and fined him $10,000. The jury, in making an award of more than half a million dollars above what Tomjanovich's attorneys had demanded, found that Washington had acted "intentionally," "maliciously," and "with reckless disregard for the safety of others." The Lakers as an organization were deemed negligent because they "failed to adequately train and supervise Washington," even though they were aware that "he had a tendency for violence while playing basketball" (nine fights in four years, according to the plaintiff's attorneys). The Lakers paid (Horrow, 1981; Rains, 1980).

A similar case is one that began in 1975, *Hackbart* v. *Cincinnati Bengals Inc.* This litigation arose out of an incident in a National Football League game in 1973 in which the plaintiff, Dale Hackbart of the Denver Broncos, was given an illegal forearm blow on the back of the head by an opposing player, Charles Clark of the Cincinnati Bengals, in a "malicious and wanton" manner five seconds after the play had been whistled dead. The referees did not see the action, and no penalty was called. Hackbart returned to the sidelines, but later discovered he had suffered a career-ending spinal fracture. The district court ruled that Hackbart had taken an implied risk by playing a violent game and that "anything" happening to him "between the sidelines" was part of that risk. The case was dismissed. But an appeals court reversed this decision, stating that although Clark may not have specifically intended to injure, he had engaged in "reckless misconduct"; the accountability of his employer (the Cincinnati Bengals) could therefore now be legally considered (Gulotta, 1980; Rains, 1980). New proceedings have apparently been scheduled. The way now seems clear for a professional sports team, as an employer, to be held accountable under civil law for the actions of the players, its employees. (An alternative approach, the Sports Violence Arbitration Act of 1983, is now before the U.S. Congress. This act would force each major professional sports league to establish an arbitration board with the power to discipline players for using "excessively violent conduct" and to make their teams financially liable for injuries suffered by the victims.)

In none of the above cases were criminal charges laid. Why this near immunity to criminal prosecution and conviction? First, most players seem reluctant to bring charges against another athlete. Based on a mail survey of

1,400 major-league basketball, football, and hockey players (no response rate is given), Horrow (1980) concludes that professional athletes, in particular, tend to believe that player disputes are best settled privately and personally on the field of play; that team management does not appreciate "trouble-makers" who go "outside the family" (i.e., the league) for justice, and contract difficulties or worse probably await such individuals; that the sheer disrup-tiveness of litigation can ruin careers, and so on. Bolstering these beliefs is the apparent willingness of most players to dismiss virtually any during-the-match assault short of using a gun or a knife as part of the game.

From the point of view of the law, says Horrow, based on information obtained from twenty United States county prosecutors in whose jurisdiction most of the country's major professional teams operate, many officials are reluctant to prosecute sports violence because they believe that they have more important things to do, like prosecuting "real" criminals; that the leagues themselves can more efficiently and effectively control player misbe-havior; that civil law proceedings are better suited than criminal for dealing with an injured player's grievances; that most lawyers do not have the exper-tise to handle sports violence cases; and that it is almost impossible to get a guilty verdict anyway.

There are two other more subtle, nonlegal reasons for the hands-off pol-icy of criminal justice officials. One is the "community subgroup rationale." As explained by Kuhlman (1975), this is the tacit recognition by law enforce-ment authorities that certain illegal activities by members of some social groups ought more or less to be tolerated because they are widespread within the group and because group members look upon them as less seri-ous than does society in general. Moreover, it would be unfair to single out and punish an individual member when almost everyone else in the group behaves similarly. In other words, the illegal conduct is rendered less crimi-nal because everybody does it. This rationale sometimes arises in connection with the issue of differential law enforcement for minority groups. In some tough police jurisdictions, for instance, police rarely make an arrest for felo-nious assault involving family members and neighbors, even though such assaults are frequent. Police in these areas tend to define domestic violence as a mere "disturbance," whereas officers in other jurisdictions are more inclined to define it as genuine violence. It seems that certain assaultive practices in sports are looked upon with the same benevolent tolerance. At the very least, the severity of the penalties for violence provided by the law is widely regarded within the legal community, as well as the sports community, as out of proportion to the seriousness of the illegal acts.

The "continuing relationship rationale" applies in assault cases where offender and victim have an ongoing relationship. Legal authorities may wish to avoid straining the relationship further by prosecuting one or both parties. Husbands and wives may wish to continue living together; neighbors may have to; athletes typically compete against each other at regular intervals (Kuhlman,

1975). Criminal prosecution in sport could exacerbate already-present hostility to the point where league harmony is seriously threatened. The 1976 prosecutions on various assault charges of four Philadelphia Flyers hockey players, arising out of a game in Toronto, caused considerable strain between the Philadelphia and Toronto Maple Leafs hockey clubs, and even a public squabble between the Philadelphia District Attorney and the Ontario Attorney General (*Toronto Star,* April 22, 1976). The assumption underlying this rationale is that society has an interest in maintaining such social relationships, that professional sport in this instance serves some socially useful purpose.

Finally there is the premise of "legal individualism"—the notion that the individual is *wholly* responsible for his or her own criminal acts—which has resulted in a virtual immunity to criminal charges of sports organizations in cases where an individual member of the organization has been indicted for assault. The leading case is *State* v. *Forbes,* apparently the only criminal prosecution ever of a professional athlete in the United States.

On January 4, 1975, during an NHL game in Bloomington, Minnesota, an altercation occurred between David Forbes of the Boston Bruins and Henry Boucha of the Minnesota North Stars. Both players were sent to the penalty box, where Forbes repeatedly threatened Boucha verbally. As they left the box at the expiration of the penalties—Boucha first and Forbes seconds later—Forbes skated up behind Boucha and struck him with the butt end of his stick just above the right eye. Boucha fell to the ice stunned and bleeding (with a badly damaged eye, it turned out). Forbes jumped on him, punched him on the back of the head, then grabbing him by the hair, proceeded to pound his head into the ice. Eventually another Minnesota player separated the two. The President of the NHL suspended Forbes for two games, but shortly afterward a Minnesota grand jury charged him with the crime of aggravated assault by use of a dangerous weapon. Forbes pleaded not guilty. The jury, after a week and a half of testimony and eighteen hours of deliberation, was unable to reach a unanimous verdict. The court declared a mistrial, and the case was dismissed (Flakne and Caplan, 1977).

Described in law journals as a "landmark" case because it focused so much legal and public attention on the issue of violence in sports, *State* v. *Forbes* also raised the important and still unanswered question of legal individualism as it applies to the occupational use of violence; namely, who should be held responsible in such cases, the individual or the group? Should not only Forbes, but the Boston Bruins and even the League, have been on trial? Was Forbes merely doing his job, his duty, as a good hockey soldier? The defense counsel tried to ask these questions during the trial, to instruct the jury to consider, for example, the "context" in which the assault took place, but the judge demurred, insisting the indictment applied only to Forbes, the individual (Hallowell and Meshbesher, 1977).

The public, too, is divided on legal individualism, if an opinion poll conducted shortly after Forbes' trial, and regarding accountability in the trial of

Lieutenant Calley of My Lai massacre notoriety, is any indicator. As reported by Hallowell and Meshbesher (1977), 58 percent of the respondents in this survey disapproved of criminal sanctions being applied to an individual acting in a legitimate role and following what that individual believed to be "at least implicit orders." Are orders to perform acts of violence implicit in professional hockey? The question should be: how explicit are such orders?

As for legally raising (let alone demonstrating) criminal liability on the part of an employer in sports violence disputes, Kuhlman (1975) suggests that although problems of proof are substantial (the burden of proof on the prosecution in a criminal trial is heavier than in a civil trial), the most promising route is probably via the statutes on conspiracy; that is, the prosecution should attempt to prove that the organization and the individual conspired to commit an assault. Owners, coaches, and teammates—all members of the "system"—are thus potentially implicated; sociological reality becomes legal fact.

By way of a footnote to *State* v. *Forbes,* the author was engaged in 1980 by the Detroit law firm of Dykema, Gossett, Spencer, Goodnow, and Trigg as a consultant and "expert witness" in a civil suit being brought by Boucha against the Boston Bruins and NHL. (After several only partly successful eye operations, Boucha's career had ground to a halt.) The charge was, in effect, "creating an unsafe work environment." The case was settled out of court for an undisclosed amount two days before before the trial was to begin in Detroit.

CRIMINAL VIOLENCE

This category consists of violence so serious and obviously outside the boundaries of what could be considered part of the game that it is handled from the outset by the law. Death is often involved, as in the 1973 Paul Smithers case, which received world-wide publicity. Smithers, a seventeen-year-old black hockey player, was convicted of manslaughter after killing an opposing player in a fight in a Toronto arena parking lot following a game (Runfola, 1974). Almost always such incidents, though closely tied to game events, take place prior to or after the contest itself. (One suspects that if Smithers' attack had occurred during the game he would have received a five-minute or match penalty, and the victim's death would have been dismissed as an "unfortunate accident.") On the extreme fringe of this category are assaults and homicides only incidentally taking place in a sports setting.

An extended, first-hand account of another hockey incident provides an illustration of a typical episode of criminal violence in sports, while at the same time conveying something about a social milieu that encourages such misbehavior. This assault took place in a Toronto arena after the final game of a Midget playoff series that had been marred by bad behavior in the stands and on the ice, including physical and verbal attacks on opposing players by the assailant in question. The victim was the coach of the winning team. He had been ejected from the game for making a rude gesture at the referee and was standing against the boards some distance from his team's bench when the assault took place. He also happened to be a student at York University. Three days after the incident he came to my office seeking some advice, his face barely recognizable. He left promising to lay an assault charge, which he had not yet done, and to write down in detail his version of what happened. He did both. (The offending player was later convicted of assault.)

REFERENCES

Betts, J. R. (1974). *America's Sporting Heritage: 1850-1950.* Reading, MA: Addison-Wesley.

Davis, P. H. (1911). *Football: The American Intercollegiate Game.* New York: Charles Scribner.

Flakne, G. W., and A. H. Caplan (1977). "Sports violence and the prosecution." *Trial* 13:33-35.

Grescoe, P. (1972). "We asked you six questions." *Canadian Magazine,* January 29:2-4.

Gulotta, S. J. (1980). "Torts in sports—deterring violence in professional athletics." *Fordham Law Review* 48:764-93.

Hallowell, L. (1978). "Violent work and the criminal law: An historical study of professional ice hockey." In J. A. Inciardi and A. E. Pottieger, eds., *Violent Crime: Historical and Contemporary Issues.* Beverly Hills: Sage.

Hallowell, L., and R. I. Meshbesher (1977). "Sports violence and the criminal law." *Trial* 13:27-32.

Hechter, W. (1977). "The criminal law and violence in sports." *The Criminal Law Quarterly* 19:425-53.

Horrow, R. B. (1980). *Sports Violence: The Interaction between Private Law-Making and the Criminal Law.* Arlington, VA: Carollton Press.

Horrow, R. B. (1981). "The legal perspective: Interaction between private lawmaking and the civil and criminal law." *Journal of Sport & Social Issues* 5:9-18.

Kuhlman, W. (1975). "Violence in professional sports." *Wisconsin Law Review* 3:771-90.

Lambert, D. J. (1978). "Tort law and participant sports: The line between vigor and violence." *Journal of Contemporary Law* 4:211-17.

Marshall, D. (1970). "We're more violent than we think." *Maclean's,* August: 14-17.

McPherson, B. D., and L. Davidson (1980). *Minor Hockey in Ontario: Toward a Positive Learning Environment for Children in the 1980s.* Toronto: Ontario Government Bookstore.

Philo, H. M., and G. Stine (1977). "The liability path to safer helmets." *Trial* 12:38-42.

Rains, J. (1980). "Sports violence: A matter of societal concern." *Notre Dame Lawyer* 55:796-813.

Rovere, G. D., G. Gristina, and J. Nicastro (1978). "Medical problems of a professional hockey team: A three season experience." *The Physician and Sports Medicine* 6:59-63.

Runfola, R. T. (1974). "He is a hockey player, seventeen, black and convicted of manslaughter." *New York Times,* October 17:2-3.

Smith, M. D. (1979). "Towards an explanation of hockey violence." *Canadian Journal of Sociology* 4:105-24.

Stagg, A. A. (1927). *Touchdown!* New York: Longmans, Green.

Tatum, J., with B. Kushner (1979). *They Call Me Assassin.* New York: Everest House.

Underwood, J. (1979). *The Death of an American Game: The Crisis in Football.* Boston: Little, Brown.

16. *Football and Violence*

RICK TELANDER

The one part of football that separates it from all other sports is tackling. Tackling is the primitive, essential element that both thrills and terrifies the game's participants and viewers. I know the Chicago Bears' Mike Singletary fairly well, and I wrote a feature on him before Chicago played in Super Bowl XX in 1986. Singletary, several times the NFL's Defensive Player of the Year, began describing some of his helmet-busting, guided-missile tackles in a near-rapturous tone that sprang from his Zen-like immersion in the chaos of the game. One brutal hit on running back Eric Dickerson stuck out in his mind.

"I don't feel pain from a hit like that," he said. "What I feel is joy. Joy for the tackle. Joy for myself. Joy for the other man. You understand me; I understand you. It's football, it's middle-linebacking. It's just . . . good for everybody."

The clarity and reward for a hit like that are deeply rooted in the dark essence of the game. But the type of tackling we see now—"I try to visualize my head all the way through the man," says Singletary, "my whole body through him"—is relatively new and different from the way tackling was done in the past, and the main reason is the advent a couple of decades ago of the hard-shell, air- and water-filled helmet with the increasingly large and protective face mask. Modern-day helmets allow face-first tackles, burying "your nose on his numbers" as the coaches say, so that the helmet is now less a protective device than a weapon, a rock-hard spear point that is almost always the first part of a defensive player's uniform to touch the ballcarrier. Don Cooper, the team physician at Oklahoma State, calls the helmet "the damnedest, meanest tool on the face of the earth." And if you've ever been hit by one, with someone else's head inside it, moving at a high rate of speed, you know what the doctor means.

I was reading former Oakland Raider and Buffalo Bills wide receiver Bob Chandler's book, *Violent Sundays,* a few years ago when I came to a part that grabbed my attention. I remembered covering Chandler when he played for Southern Cal and our teams met in the Coliseum in Los Angeles. "My junior year, we played Northwestern in our opening game," he wrote. "I went down to catch a low ball, and the halfback speared me in my lower back. I wasn't sure what was damaged, but I couldn't feel my right leg, which scared the hell out of me. I hobbled off the field. Later, back at my apartment, I was in such agony that by the middle of the night my roommate Gerry Mullins literally had to pick me up, carry me to his car, and take me to the hospital. After a battery of X rays, [Coach] John McKay came in and said matter-of-factly, 'Looks like you broke your back.'"

Chandler said he was hit by a "halfback," which meant it had to have been either Jack Dustin or I who had done the damage, since we were the two cornerbacks who played for Northwestern that night. I remembered Chandler as a shifty, glue-fingered little white guy, but my biggest concern that game had been trying to stay with 6′3″, lightning-bolt split end Sam Dickerson. I didn't remember hitting anybody particularly hard or making much of an impact on the game in any way, but the fact was, I might have broken an opponent's back with my helmet and not even realized I had done so. I asked Dustin, who is now a physician, if he remembered hitting Chandler in the back. He said he couldn't recall.

I finally ran into Chandler himself in the press box at an NFL game. Chandler was working as a sportscaster for a TV station in L.A., and he looked about the same as I remembered him from college. I asked him if it could have been I who had broken his back years ago, if he remembered the player's number. He said he didn't remember the number, but for some reason, he didn't think I was the man. Why, he couldn't say. Probably, it was because I just looked too harmless standing there with my notebook in my back pocket and press ID hanging from a shirt button. Still, the incident haunts me. The thought that any player could do such damage to an opponent with his helmet and not even know it is an indictment of some fundamental part of the game.

A friend of mine, sportswriter Don Pierson, who covers the NFL for the *Chicago Tribune,* recently loaned me a notebook of his from his undergrad days at Ohio State. The notebook is from a credited course Pierson took in 1966 called The Coaching of Football, taught by one Woodrow Wilson Hayes, and open to all students at the university. The maintaining of a notebook was the main work for the course, and at the back of Pierson's notebook is written in red ink: "'A' Excellent! W.W.H." The reason Pierson wanted me to take a look at the notes was to see the section on tackling. Hayes called in his right-hand man to class that day, defensive coordinator Lou McCullough, and let him explain the proper way to stick an opponent. McCullough, who would later become the athletic director at Iowa State, had a Southern drawl, Pierson informed me, and I needed to keep that in mind as I read the text. Herewith:

> We don't like to see a kid making a tackle like he is trying to hug the man down. We want to give him cancer of the breast by knocking his titty off. We want to knock his anus up through his *haid.*

That's verbatim, and I still howl every time I read it. But I think you can see why the helmet now comes with a product liability sticker on it, one that must remain on the helmet during play, as if players might stop to casually peruse the warning during lulls in the action. The label reads, "Do not use this Helmet to butt, ram or spear an opposing player. This is in violation of the football rules and such use can result in severe head or neck injuries, paralysis or death to you and possible injury to your opponent. No helmet can prevent all head or neck injuries a player might receive while participating in football."

In other words, the way coaches teach their players to tackle, face-first, may be damaging to their health. But that's how the game is played—if such a harmless word as "play" can be applied to this increasingly violent spectacle.

Worse, some players feel invincible once they strap on their headgear, at least partly because the helmets themselves make the players feel like Kralite-hulled gladiators. Back in November 1987, I read something in the newspaper that haunted me as I went about covering college football. A boy named Doug Mansfield, a 5'10", 165-pound senior noseguard at Humboldt High School in Tennessee, had run headfirst into a brick wall in frustration after a loss to Lexington High and was now paralyzed from the neck down. The wire service report stated that moments after the game ended, the youth had run in full football gear directly into the wall outside the dressing room. The blow broke his neck and severed his spinal cord and left him in critical condition. "The doctors said there is nothing we can do, that he won't ever get any better," his mother, Susan Mansfield, was quoted as saying. "We're just praying and waiting it out."

I thought about the incident so much as the months went by, wondered what it was that had forced such a horrible fate on the football player, that a year and a half after the accident I decided to track down young Mansfield himself. I heard from Billy Reed, an *SI* writer in Kentucky, that Mansfield had been an "A" student and apparently had been offered an academic scholarship to Mississippi State or some other large southern school before the tragedy.

I spoke with Jim Potee, the principal and athletic director at Humboldt High. "I was within twenty-five to thirty yards of him when it happened," said Potee. "He was going up the hill where the dressing room is, and he had his helmet in his hand. He put it on, buckled both chin straps, lowered his head, and ran straight into the wall. That was the last time he moved."

The only question I could ask was, why?

"He was frustrated. It was the first round of the state playoffs, and we had the game won but gave it away when we had a touchdown called back and then fumbled to let them score. We lost, fourteen to thirteen. He had nothing to do with the loss, but he was a fierce competitor. What he had, he gave you. He was a great person, too—a fine student and a great artist. We still use some of his paintings in our yearbook."

I asked the principal if he thought the boy had been trying to hurt himself.

"Oh, no, it was not intentional," Potee answered. "He had no concept of the danger. It was like if you would kick a car tire or hit a door with your fist in anger. In that uniform and helmet you think you're protected against all elements."

I remembered the old football cliché that tells players that with enough heart and guts a kid can run right through a brick wall. Coaches love to expound on that. I wondered if that myth had played a role in Doug Mansfield's tragedy.

I asked Potee how the boy was doing now, if there was any hope for recovery.

"Oh," said the man. "You didn't know. He's dead. He died at the spinal injury center in Atlanta three months after the game."

Pete Gent once wrote, "Psychotic episodes are a daily occurrence in a business where the operative phrase is, 'Stick you head in there.'" And he is right. The use of the head—the thinking center, the housing (scientists and philosophers now suspect, for the soul), the very thing that contains that which separates us from beasts—as the primary weapon in football tends to warp logic and reward people on the fringes of sanity. It's not enough to say that the sport rewards aggressiveness. The best players often are those who are the most reckless with their own well-being, the most willing to do crazy, dangerous things with their own bodies and, consequently, to other people's bodies. "Nobody will know what I'm talking about unless they strap on a helmet and run forty yards downfield and hit a guy who doesn't see you coming," says Phoenix Cardinals special-teams player Ron Wolfley on the joys of football. "Now that's comedy to me." Is anybody laughing?

I think about the profile I had to do for *SI* on Detroit Lions linebacker Jimmy Williams two years ago. Williams can be almost rabid on the field, fighting and swearing like a man possessed, though off the field he is quiet and retiring, a Sunday school teacher at a Baptist church in Pontiac, Michigan, among other things. Of course, such Jekyll and Hyde behavior is pretty normal for high-level football players. But I asked Williams specifically if he liked hurting people on the field. "If it's between getting an interception and putting a hit on the receiver," he said, "I'll always hit the receiver. I like to hit a man and hear that . . . "

He smiled warily, afraid that maybe he had revealed too much.

Hear what, I asked.

"Hear that little . . . "

Yes?

He though a moment. His smile grew. "That little moan."

When Auburn linebacker Aundray Bruce, the first player taken in the 1988 NFL draft, was in college, he sometimes worked himself into such a frenzy of malevolence at the line of scrimmage that tears would stream down his face. There has been at least one study done that shows that in certain adolescent boys the line between aggression or violence and sexual stimulation is so thin that young football players have been known to achieve orgasm from the excitement of the game. The craziness of the sport sometimes affects players' ability to think rationally about their own safety. Last season Bears safety Shaun Gayle fractured the seventh vertebra in his neck when his helmet collided with teammate Singletary's hip during a tackle in a game against Detroit. Singletary had to come out of the game because of the collision, but Gayle stayed in, even though his neck was broken and his hands were numb. He dropped a ball he should have intercepted because he couldn't grip with his fingers, and still he remained in the game. He made another hit, on Lions fullback Garry James, and promptly lost feeling in his right arm. Still, he stayed in the game. Later, after he had been diagnosed and put on injured reserve for the rest of the season, he started working out at a health club I sometimes visit. I ran into him at the club and asked him how in the world he could have taken his own potential paralysis so lightly.

He laughed. Gayle is a bright man; he has a degree from Ohio State in recreation education and is one of the most well-spoken NFL players I have ever interviewed. But he just chuckled with the question.

"I didn't think it was that serious," he said.

Later I would read in the paper that Gayle was eagerly awaiting the 1989 season now that his neck was healed. "I will wear a built-in neck brace with my shoulder pads," he said. "It will allow me movement so I can see the ball but not much movement forwards or backwards. It should be interesting. I'll become a human missile."

I remember visiting Ohio State during the summer of 1987 to talk to all-American linebacker Chris Spielman about the coming season. Spielman, I knew, had been called "the most intense player I've ever coached" by then–head coach Earle Bruce. His father, Sonny Spielman, a high school football coach, recalled that when Chris was five years old he had tackled his own grandmother. "A perfect-form tackle," Dad said. "He broke her nose. He wiped her out on the spot. That's when I knew I had a maniac on my hands."

So I wanted to sit for a few minutes and just observe this athlete who against Iowa the previous year had broken his helmet, tossed it aside since there wasn't time to fix it, and dived into a pile headfirst. He sat in a coach's office at St. John's Hall and simply twitched. He was like a bug on a needle. I asked him what his style of play was and he said, "Controlled insanity." He added that what's important "is not how you play the game, it's whether you win or lose." He looked at the floor, avoided eye contact, bounced his knees. Playing Michigan, he said, was like freedom versus communism. "Football is almost a life or death situation for me," he said. Later, Chicago Bears quarterback Mike Tomczak, a teammate of Spielman's at Ohio State, would tell me that before each season Spielman would rent a room in a Cincinnati flophouse and simply lie on a bed for a day or two, staring at a bare light bulb hanging from the ceiling, getting his mind right for football.

I asked Spielman now if maybe things might not be a little easier for him if he weren't so totally focused on this violent game. He looked up.

"Easier for me, or the people around me?" he asked with an edge in his voice. "I have blinders on. I'm in a tunnel, a train is coming, and I don't see anything but the light approaching. That's how I want it."

A few years ago I was at the University of Pittsburgh to write about the Pitt team's response to the untimely death of sophomore linebacker Todd Becker. Becker was a special-teams demon, a 6'2", 214-pound live wire with a tattoo on his left calf of a grinning Sylvester the Cat hanging Tweety Bird by the neck and whose favorite pastime, according to the Pitt press guide, was lifting weights. The young man had climbed out a third-story window at a dorm toga party to avoid detection by campus police who had raided the party, and when he tried to jump to the pavement thirty-five feet below, he spun in midair, hit his head on the cement, and died instantly. Becker was drunk at the time, but he also didn't think he could be hurt by the fall. "He had no fear," said head coach Foge Fazio. "I'm sure he thought, 'This is easy for me. I can do this.'" Becker's father, Al, a long-distance trucker, said, "He was such a good football player. He was a killer."

But that same aggressiveness that delighted every coach Becker ever had got him into a lot of problems off the field. The reason Becker was jumping was that he had already been banned from the Pitt dorms for causing disturbances there and he didn't want to jeopardize his football career by getting caught again. In the course of researching my story, I spent some time with Pitt athletic director Ed Bozik, a former Air Force colonel, and during one interview he grew philosophical about the tragedy.

"Football training is very much analogous to military training," he said. "In both cases young men are trained to do things they instinctively would not do. This has to condition your psyche, but the question is, can you convert that training and use its positive elements in normal life? In the military we have what we call 'war lovers,' the ones who can't turn it off. But everyone is constantly trained to act like gentlemen when not in a battle situation."

"Basically, I believe in the Aristotelian philosophy of striking a median, a balance. Any characteristic taken to an extreme becomes a vice. After all, getting into trouble, doing stupid things—that's not really the province of football players. It's traditional for *young people* to get into trouble."

This is true, but when football players get into trouble, they just seem to do it a little harder, to take things a little further than other kids do, and this may be because the sport attracts, trains, conditions, and develops men who are predisposed to wildness and encourages them to push themselves beyond their limits. Perhaps Todd Becker would have done something equally stupid and self-destructive if he'd never heard of football. But were it not for football, he certainly wouldn't have been so praised and prized for these self-destructive tendencies, and he wouldn't have been so doggedly sought out by universities, by institutions of learning, eager to reward him for the qualities that led to his death: recklessness, fearlessness, aggressiveness.

Syndicated columnist Stephen Chapman has suggested getting rid of hard-shell helmets and imposing weight limits on players to lessen the violence of the game and the resulting injuries and unhealthy behavior such violence causes. But the helmets have been around for too long to downgrade, and ironically, they do prevent many of the head injuries that players in the olden days sometimes died from. And limiting the size of players would not be particularly effective in reducing violence, either, since speed is at least as devastating as weight in collisions. And in truth, many of the smaller players are the meanest players anyway. Safety Jack Tatum weighed just over 200 pounds when he paralyzed wide receiver Darryl Stingley with a vicious blow. And Detroit cornerback James Hunter weighed only 195 pounds when he nailed the Vikings' Ahmad Rashad and broke his back in 1982, ending Rashad's final season prematurely. Ironically, Hunter hit another Minnesota receiver in almost the same fashion later in the game and injured his own neck so severely from the blow that he himself was forced to retire.

I tried to get hold of Hunter after the '82 season to see what he thought about ending two careers in one game, but he wouldn't take my calls. I caught up with Rashad a year or so later in Miami, where he was preparing to work a Dolphins game as a TV reporter, and asked him what he felt about the incident.

"It was the weirdest pain I've ever had," he said. "I couldn't feel my legs for about five minutes. I was just like paralyzed. I told the trainer, 'When you get this helmet and these pads off me, I'll never play this game again.'"

What did he think of Hunter's blow to his back?

"I never thought it was too violent," Rashad answered. "I just got a good shot is all."

And there is the twisted truth that injuries are not only a part of the game, but a welcome part. One of the very reasons players play the game is to have the chance to give and receive injuries. You think I'm kidding? I remember lying in bed after a college game with my own ankle throbbing, my shoulder aching, and feeling very . . . comfortable . . . about it all. The pain signified something. It wasn't the gratuitous pain of a disease or chronic illness, but a friendly, masculine reminder of my accomplishments as a player, and subliminally, as a man, in a dangerous sport.

"It's that instant when . . . artistry is threatened by violence and the outcome is in doubt, that epitomizes the game's attraction," wrote Oregon State English professor Mike Oriard in an essay on football violence in the *New York Times* a few years ago. "Injuries are not aberrations in football, or even a regrettable byproduct. They are essential to the game." He then added that any efforts to make the game safer must grapple first with the "ideological underpinning" of the game itself, since "it's not possible to have the (desired) danger without the injuries to confirm that the danger is real." Oriard had been a captain of the Notre Dame football team and had played four seasons with the Kansas City Chiefs in the early seventies. He was a center, and I remembered him from my brief stay with the Chiefs in 1971 as being a tall, quiet, observant man who did not seem to fit in with the rowdier, veteran Chiefs. If I had known the thinking going on in his brain, I might have made it a point to get to know him a little better before Hank Stram unceremoniously booted me out of pro football.

Pain itself is a funny bird. In an article on the matter in the June 11, 1984, edition of *Time,* pain researcher Dr. Ronald Dubner of the National Institutes of Health stated that "pain is a complex experience that involves emotions, previous experiences with pain, and what the pain means to us at any given time." "In short," concluded the article's author, "the borderline between the physiology and psychology of pain is a blurry one." Thus it is that, to a football player, pain can be something akin to rapture. I am reminded here of the saints of the Middle Ages, who likewise often got off on the self-inflicted pain that brought them closer to their God. One who stands out in particular was Henry Suso, a fourteenth-century saint who carved religious symbols in his chest with a stylus, wore a hair shirt, a heavy iron chain, and a tight-fitting hair undergarment with 150 nails imbedded in the straps, the points directed inward. Suso wore this gear at night, too, and when he picked at the outfit in his sleep, he had leather gloves made, fitted over with brass tacks, so that he could not enjoy the pleasure of touching himself. Suso mutilated himself to such an extent that according to historian Richard Kieckhefer, writing in *Unquiet Souls: Fourteenth-Century Saints and Their Religious Milieu,* "suffering became for Suso almost an end in itself, or more precisely, a token of divine favor, such that an absence of suffering was for him the greatest cause of suffering."

I can compare that nut to former Chiefs all-pro middle linebacker and center E. J. Holub, who, when I wrote about him for *Esquire* in 1980, was believed to have had more knee operations, twelve, than any other athlete in the world, with more cuttings scheduled for the future. Holub, a cowboy from West Texas, had undergone seventeen operations in all, including two on his hands, two on his elbows, and one on a hamstring, yet missed only eleven games in his eleven-year pro career. At forty-two, he walked like a man twice his age. Forget running. Holub destroyed his knees partly by coming back from the initial surgeries way too soon, once tearing off a cast almost three months before it was due to be removed. He would drain his knee joints himself, using a 16-gauge needle or sometimes a plain old razor. For a year with the Chiefs he wore a sanitary napkin on one knee to absorb the liquid that seeped out constantly.

"People are always asking me if it was worth it, the operations and all," he said to me cheerily. "Yep, it sure was, I tell 'em. I enjoyed the hell out of football."

There are many other players like Holub in the game, at all levels. Trust me. Tommy Chaikin told me one night about how he and some of his

South Carolina teammates started drinking in his home while he was an undergrad and ended up carving each other's arms with a butcher knife in the kitchen, just for the hell of it, just to show pain was no big deal. They got a little carried away, stabbing one of the players pretty hard in the forearm. They went to bed after that, leaving the knife and blood on the table, forgetting that it might not be the pleasantest of sights for Tommy's parents in the morning. I found myself laughing, thinking back on some of my own lunacies in college. Looking back, I'm not particularly proud of that response.

Last fall I received a letter from a *Sports Illustrated* reader, and after reading it, I wrote back to its author, G. Bruce Mills of Lexington, North Carolina, asking him if I could print the letter in a book on college football that I was considering writing. Mills wrote back that he would be flattered to have his letter printed. Here it is:

Dear Mr. Telander:

After reading your story about Tommy Chaikin, I'm left asking a question to which I can't provide the answer: "What is it about football that drives participants to total disregard for their well-being in the quest for success?" Perhaps it's peer acceptance, or just a way to impress the girls. At my son's high school practice today I watched a player who was last in sprints (gasping for breath), struggled through drills, was hammered in the scrimmage, was the object of his teammates' ridicule, and will never get any better or make any contribution to his team. He's not alone, for practically every team at every level of amateur football has a player like him. Why do they do it? Why do the Tommy Chaikins of today risk their lives with drugs to achieve success in football?

They're really no different from players of days gone by. I, like you, played college football in the late sixties and early seventies. As an all-conference player at Duke University, I wasn't aware of this "edge" called steroids. But I, too, had an abusive addiction, which was playing with pain. At one time or another every player has been asked to "suck it up," and doing anything less is unacceptable. Nobody wants to be told "you can't cut it." I'll skip the details, but let it suffice to say that I've had four operations on my left knee, one on my right knee, two on my right ankle with the third scheduled in for January. I must visit the chiropractor regularly for back pains, I walk club-footed and struggle with inclines and rough terrain. I haven't been able to do anything resembling a jog or a run in four years, and my athletic sons are growing up without the benefit of playing backyard ball with their father.

The scariest thing, Rick, is that knowing what I've gone through and will continue to endure . . . **I'D DO IT ALL OVER AGAIN!** What is this mystical hold that football has over me and thousands like me?

I don't think anybody knows.

■ FOR FURTHER STUDY

Buford, Bill, *Among the Thugs* (New York: W. W. Norton, 1992).

Dunning, Eric, "Sociological Reflections on Sport, Violence and Civilization," *International Review for the Sociology of Sport* 25(1990):65-82.

Friend, Tom, "Blood Sport," *Sport* (December 1992):28-36.

Messner, Michael A., "When Bodies Are Weapons: Masculinity and Violence in Sport," *International Review for the Sociology of Sport* 25(1990):203-219.

Miedzian, Myriam, *Boys Will Be Boys: Breaking the Link Between Masculinity and Violence* (New York: Doubleday, 1991).

Smith, Michael D., *Violence and Sport* (Toronto: Butterworths, 1983).

Weisman, Jacob, "Pro Football—The Maiming Game," *The Nation* (January 27, 1992):84-87.

Young, Kevin, "Violence in the Workplace of Professional Sport from Victimological and Cultural Studies Perspectives," *International Review for the Sociology of Sport* 26(1991):3-14.

Young, Kevin, "Violence, Risk, and Liability in Male Sports Culture," *Sociology of Sport Journal* 10(December 1993):373-396.

Part Six

Sport and Deviance

Sport and *deviance* would appear on the surface to be antithetical terms. After all, sports contests are bound by rules, school athletes must meet rigid grade and behavior standards in order to compete, and there is a constant monitoring of athletes' behavior because they are public figures. Moreover, sport is assumed by many to promote those character traits deemed desirable by most in society: fair play, sportsmanship, obedience to authority, hard work, and commitment to excellence.

The selections in this part show, to the contrary, that deviance is not only prevalent in sport but that the structure of sport in American society actually promotes deviance. Players and coaches sometimes cheat to gain an advantage over an opponent. As we saw in Part Five, some players engage in criminal violence on the playing field. Some players use performance-enhancing drugs. Some players are sexually promiscuous, as the tragic example of Magic Johnson illustrates. Not only did he contract HIV from his sexual escapades, but he, in turn, may have infected many of his sexual partners with the fatal virus.

The first selection, by D. Stanley Eitzen, provides an overview of deviance by looking at the dark side of competition in society as well as sport. This is an important consideration because the value Americans place on competition is at the heart of much deviance.

The second essay, by sociologist James H. Frey, looks at gambling on sports, especially the policy issues surrounding legalized sports gambling. Gambling on sport, of course, has many ramifications for deviant behavior.

Next, sociologists John R. Fuller and Marc J. La Fountain focus on a major problem in sport—drug use by athletes. Just like other members of their age cohort, they may take recreational drugs. Many of them also take what might be called "vocational" drugs—that is, drugs taken to enhance sport performance. This type of drug usage represents a health danger as well as a profound ethical problem in the sports world.

The final selection, by journalist Jill Neimark, summarizes what is known about the serious problem of gang rape by athletes. This essay is related to others in this volume, especially Nelson's "We Don't Like Football, Do We?" and Curry's "Fraternal Bonding in the Locker Room."

17. *The Dark Side of Competition*

D. STANLEY EITZEN

Some believe that competition is the behavioral equivalent of gravity, a natural and inevitable force. A student in one of my classes once remarked that he was very competitive but that no one had ever taught him to be that way. His argument was that competition is part of the DNA of the animal and human worlds, with the best surviving. This is the credo of the Social Darwinists—that is, as people vie for a prize, honor, advantage, space, sex, or whatever, excellence is rewarded and progress is achieved. In the process, the best minds and the best bodies win and rise to the top while the less able lose and sink to the bottom. This logic has been used to justify social inequality with the able seen as deserving of their rewards and the failures deserving of their lesser fate. This school of thought was prevalent in the United States around the turn of the century and remnants are found today, in the White House and Congress, sometimes in editorials, always among racists, and even occasionally by academicians.

My argument is that if competition is "natural" among the human species, so, too, is cooperation. Stated more strongly, I argue that cooperation is more critical to human progress and to get the things we want than competition. A sports team composed of competitive individuals without teamwork is, by definition, relatively ineffective. The most notable human accomplishments, such as the building of railroads or cathedrals, the forming of a constitution, the damming of mighty rivers, and the overturning of tyranny by a Gandhi or a Martin Luther King, Jr., are monuments to cooperative behavior.

My goal in this presentation is to analyze competition, this most central value of American society, focusing on its negative consequences. I'll conclude by presenting some alternatives.

THE PERVASIVENESS OF COMPETITION

Recall my student who said that "no one ever taught him to be competitive." Well, I believe that he was so immersed in a competitive environment that he could not see it, just like a fish doesn't understand water because it does not know anything different. Let me elaborate.

SOURCE: "The Dark Side of Competition in American Society" by D. Stanley Eitzen. From *Vital Speeches of the Day* 56, pp. 184–187. Copyright © 1990 by the author.

Parents instill competition in their children at a young age. There is evidence that first-borns tend to be more bowlegged than later-borns. I do not know the explanation for this but one possibility is that parents are so interested in showing off the prowess of their parenting *and* their progeny that they force their first child to walk earlier than they should. Having proven their point, parents are less demanding of later-borns, at least with early walking. At a more blatant level, some parents enter their children in "diaper derbies" (crawling races for those under one year), beauty contests, baton twirling contests, and the like. Others enroll their preschoolers in music lessons, ballet lessons, swimming lessons, and other efforts to give their children a head start in the competitive world.

At the elementary school level, there are spelling contests, selection of soloists or actors on the basis of tryouts, ability grouping based on test performance, and so on. Outside of school, there are community-sponsored competitions for the very young, such as in Florida where boys age five play tackle football for a three-and-one-half month season. Adults have organized triathlons (where the contestants participate in a three-part race involving swimming, bicycling, and running) for children as young as seven. The Cub Scouts have one event that epitomizes the American emphasis on competition—the Pinewood Derby. Each scout is given a block of wood and some wheels, from which they are to create a model racing car. Each scout (and his father, no doubt) works at making the fastest car. At the big event, of course, there is only one winner, with the rest of the pack losers. Such an event is very American.

During the junior high and senior high school years, youth are exposed even more to competition. At school, there is grading on the curve, trying out for athletic teams, cheerleader, debate, acting roles, competing for valedictorian, acceptance in top colleges, and intense competition for first chair for each instrument in band and orchestra. Outside of school there are community-based sports, including age-group swimming, elite music groups, beauty and talent contests, 4-H judging, and other forms of competition. An egregious example is the "punt, pass, and kick" contest sponsored by Ford Motor Company. In this contest, winners are selected at the local level and proceed through the various state and regional tournaments until a winner is found for each age category. In one year, there were 1,112,702 entrants in this contest and only six eventual winners. An interesting question is why an organization such as Ford would sponsor an event with six winners and 1,112,696 losers. This, too, is very American.

At the adult level, life is often a zero-sum situation where one wins at the expense of others. The business world in a capitalist society, of course, is highly competitive (except among the large corporations where parallel pricing, shared monopolies, and government subsidies reduce competition substantially). At work, employees compete for limited promotions and salary raises. At my university, for example, each academic department ranks its members from "best" to "worst" and the yearly raises are divided accordingly. One year the philosophy department refused to participate in this exercise, arguing that its members were uniformly excellent. The dean insisted that the faculty must be ranked or else no monies would be allocated to the department. Once again, this type of motivational scheme is very American.

Even during leisure, many, if not most Americans engage in competitions, involving all manner of sports, participation in fantasy sports leagues, tryouts for community plays, music groups, gambling, art contests, county fair competitions for best quilt or pickles, and such competitions as the "Pillsbury Bakeoff," and "Mrs. USA." Finally, competition even intrudes into our most intimate of relationships. In families, there are sibling rivalries, parent-child competition, and even efforts by spouses (or lovers) to outdo the other. Eric Berne, the transactional analyst, wrote of the various "games people play" in relationships. One of those "games" employed even among lovers, he called, if you'll excuse his language, "Now, I've got you, you son of a bitch." Isn't it curious, that people in love would find themselves engaged in behaviors that elevate themselves by diminishing their partners.

THE POSITIVE CONSEQUENCES OF COMPETITION

I'm sure that we are quite familiar with the arguments supporting competition, so I will merely list them. The two most common reasons given for competition are that it is a strong motivator and it pushes everyone to strive for excellence. These qualities have led American society to greater societal achievements in productivity than found in less competitive societies. This emphasis on competition and its justification of inequality, of course, fit nicely with capitalism.

THE NEGATIVE CONSEQUENCES OF COMPETITION

I am going to overlook the more obvious negative consequences of a highly competitive society such as war, the arms race, and imperialism. Similarly, I will not consider here the negative behaviors of corporations in a highly competitive environment such as fraud, misleading advertising, cheating, and the like. These are very important, and I have written a book about these political and economic misadventures. Rather, I will focus here on the more subtle negative results of competition, ones that we might be more likely to miss.

One negative impact of the emphasis on competition is that it is unhealthy for individuals. In 1988 over $1 billion was spent in the United States for one drug—Zantac—which combats ulcers. Surely a major source of ulcers is the stress we face daily in our competitive environments. Similarly, those of us who are "Type A" are competitive, combative, impatient, overscheduled, teethgrinders. "Type B" people, in contrast, are relaxed, without a sense of urgency, and tolerant. They say the equivalent of "que pasa" a lot. With no expertise on this, I can only speculate that while the boundaries of temperament are encoded genetically, a competitive environment brings out the worst in Type A persons, which heightens their tendency for high blood pressure, stroke, and heart disease. These same people living in a less driven culture likely would live longer.

Another problem with competition is that, by definition, people are sorted into a very few "winners" and many "losers." What is the effect on a youngster's self-esteem when he or she is "cut" from the basketball team or when she or he rarely gets to play in games? What is the level of motivation for a junior high school student who is twenty-third chair flute in the school band? Will she or he strive ever more to achieve in music or give up?

When competition supersedes other values, it may be dysfunctional for the participants and even society. Several years ago, an experiment was made comparing ten-year-olds in the United States and Mexico. This experiment involved a marble-pull game. The investigator told pairs of children that they could obtain prizes by playing the game. The object of the game was for each player to pull a string that manipulated a marble holder so that the marble would drop into a goal at their end of the table. However, if both children pulled on their strings at the same time, the marble holder would break apart and neither child could win a prize. The children soon figured out that they could engage in a tug-of-war where no one would win or they could cooperate and take turns winning prizes. The Anglo-American children tended to choose the former route, which meant no one won, while the Mexican children opted for the latter, where they shared prizes. Now which response was the more rational? My interpretation is that the American youth were possessed with an irrational competitive spirit that was dysfunctional. Let me give another illustration of how competition can have irrational consequences, this time looking at medical students. Norman Cousins, an especially keen observer of American life, has criticized the process whereby students are selected for and graduate from medical school. He says:

> [Since admission to medical schools is so competitive, grades have become] the most tangible measure on which the school can base its admission decisions. Grades may be an indication of ability to learn, but when they make students fiercely competitive, the end product is not necessarily good scholarship but more often a sharpening of academic predatory skills. . . . It is important to ask whether we really want to foster a barracuda psychology for young people who will have to carry the responsibility for maintaining the health and well-being of the American people. Do we really want them to be trained in an atmosphere that sharpens their teeth even more than it develops their minds?

When winning is the primary standard for evaluation, several negative outcomes result. Let me enumerate these, using sport for examples. First, in a competitive society there is a tendency to evaluate people by their accomplishments rather than their character, personality, and other human qualities. When "winning is everything," then losers are considered just that. One successful university basketball coach once counseled prospective coaches that if they wanted to be winners, then they should associate only with winners. Is this an appropriate guiding principle for conducting our lives?

Second, when winning is paramount, schools and communities organize sports for the already gifted. This elitist approach means that the few will be given the best equipment, the best coaching, and prime time reserved for their participation, while the less able will be denied participation altogether or given very little attention. If sports participation is a useful activity, then it should be for the many, not the few, in my view.

A third problem with the emphasis on winning is that parents may push their children beyond the normal to succeed. Two examples make this point. Is it appropriate behavior for parents to hire a swimming coach for their twenty-two-month-old daughter, one who has the girl swim one-fourth of a mile three times a week, switching to one-half a mile three times a week when she turned two? This happened for a California youngster in 1980. The parents' goal is for this youngster to be an Olympic champion in 1992. In 1972 the national record for one-year-olds in the mile run was established by Steve Parsons of Normal, Illinois (the time was 24:16.6). Are these instances of child abuse or what?

A fourth problem with the primacy of winning is that coaches may push their charges too hard. Coaches may be physically or emotionally abusive. They may limit their players' civil rights. And, they may play their injured athletes by using pain killers without regard for their long-term physical well-being.

Fifth, when the desire to win is so great, the "end may justify the means." Coaches and players may use illegal tactics. Athletes may use performance-enhancing drugs such as steroids and amphetamines to achieve a "competitive edge" or more subtly, but nonetheless unethical, using such means as blood doping or getting pregnant to get positive hormonal changes, and then having an abortion. Both of these practices occur among endurance athletes. As we all know, big-time college coaches in their zeal to win have been found guilty of exploiting athletes, falsifying transcripts, providing illegal payments, hiring surrogate test takers, paying athletes for nonexistent summer jobs, and illegally using government Pell grants and work study monies for athletes. So much, I would argue, for the myth that "sport builds character."

Sixth, when winning is all important, there may be a tendency to crush the opposition. This was the case when Riverside Poly High School girls basketball team played Norte Vista several years ago. Riverside won by a score of

179–15 with one player, Cheryl Miller, scoring a California record of 105 points. Was the Riverside coach ethical? I think not. Moreover, what were the consequences of his actions on his team and on the players and community of Norte Vista? Will the Norte Vista girls be motivated to improve their performance or will this humiliating experience crush their spirit?

Seventh, many people in a competitive society have difficulty with coming in second. In 1986, Kathy Ormsby, an excellent student and an All-American distance runner at North Carolina State, veered off the track during a race, ran away from the stadium and jumped off a bridge, suffering, as a result, a life-long paralysis. I can only speculate on her motives. I suspect that losing was so abjectly appalling to her that she could fathom no alternative but to end her life. This is an extreme example but it illustrates the intolerance some of us have for losers, even those who came close to winning. Let me illustrate this point with two examples. The Denver Broncos have made it to the Super Bowl three times but they have lost that big game each time. In the minds of the Bronco players, fans, as well as others across the United States, the Broncos were losers in each of those years even though they were second out of twenty-eight teams, which, if you think about it, is not too shabby an accomplishment. My other illustration involves a football team, composed of fifth-graders, in Florida. They were undefeated going into the state finals but lost there in a close game. At a banquet following that season each player on this team was given a plaque on which was inscribed a quote from Vince Lombardi:

> There is no room for second place. I have finished second twice at Green Bay and I never want to finish second again. There is a second place bowl game but it is a game for losers played by losers. It is and always has been an American zeal to be first in anything we do and to win and to win and to win.

In other words, the parents and coaches of these boys wanted them to never be satisfied with being second. Second is losing. The only acceptable placement is first.

Finally, when "winning is the only thing" the joy in participation is lost. I have observed that organized sports from youth programs to the professional level is mostly devoid of playfulness. When the object is to win, then the primacy of the activity is lost. In this vein, America's premier cross country skier, Bill Koch, has said:

> If 100 people enter a race that means there have to be 99 losers. The worst thing that you can teach children is that so many of them will be losers. Because then they won't even try. It's the striving, the attempt, the fight, that's the important thing.

In other words, it's the process that is primary, not the outcome. White water rafters and mountain climbers understand this. So, too, do players in a pickup touch football game. Why can't the rest of us figure out this fundamental truth?

ALTERNATIVES

I am not naive enough to think that we can eliminate competition in American society. We will not become like the Hopi or the Zuni. Competition is built into the fabric of our society. I must admit, too, that I like competition, I thrive on it. But the problems inherent in competition bother me. I would like to find alternatives that would eliminate or at least diminish some of these problems. Let me provide a few possibilities for you to consider as you form families, become active in communities, and establish yourself in occupations.

Can we improve our competitive environment? I suggest that we shift from a competitive reward structure to an individualistic reward structure. The former is what we have—a system that rewards participants in relation to their competitors, such as grading on a curve or crowning a single winner. An individualistic reward structure, on the other hand, rewards individuals as they measure up to some absolute standard. The striving for excellence is still there but the number of winners is limitless. Grading according to a percentage is one example. Karate provides an excellent example as competitors strive to master different levels of achievement as symbolized by different colored belts. In my department in a research university, faculty members receive annual merit raises based mostly on the number of articles and books they publish annually. This system rewards the most prolific individual the most. Why can't we have a reward system based on a standard, which says that everyone who publishes at least one article a year in a refereed journal is judged as "excellent"? Those who publish one article every other year would be classified as "very good," and rewarded accordingly. Such a plan would encourage everyone in the department to be active scholars. The current system, in contrast, discourages some because they will never be labeled "excellent" and rewarded for that achievement. I believe that the department and individual faculty members suffer from our current practice.

The number of winners can also be maximized by rewarding different skills. Suppose, for example, that we engage in a two-mile race. Who might the winner be? In our society, the winner would be established by whoever is the fastest. But Gandhi said that "there is more to life than increasing its speed." Why not reward those who come closest to predicting their finishing time? Or, how about rewarding form, with judges evaluating the stride, arm swing, posture, and pelvic tilt of the runners? How about rewarding everyone who established a personal best? Why not have a number of categories with winners determined for each?

What about removing sports competition from schools. Schools in many European countries, for example, do not have sports. There are sports clubs in the community but the schools stay out of it, leaving the school day for education and not for the defeat of enemies on Friday evenings. This would free the facilities and equipment for maximum use by the students, not just the elite.

Let me conclude with a special example from the Special Olympics. A friend of mine observed a 200 meter race among three evenly matched 12-year-olds at a Special Olympics event in Colorado Springs. About twenty-five yards from the finish line, one of the contestants fell. The other two runners stopped and helped their competitor to his feet, brushed him off, and jogged together hand in hand to the finish line, ending the race in a three-way tie. The actions of these three, especially the two who did not fall, are unAmerican. Perhaps because they were retarded, they did not understand the importance of winning in our society. To them, the welfare of their opponent was primary. Can we learn this lesson from the retarded? My message is that the successful life involves the pursuit of excellence, a fundamental respect for others, even one's competitors, and enjoyment in the process. Competition as structured in our society with its emphasis on the outcome undermines these goals. I enjoin you to be thoughtful about the role of competition in your life and how it might be restructured to maximize humane goals.

18. *Gambling on Sport: Policy Issues*

JAMES H. FREY

INTRODUCTION

Battle lines are being formed in the war over the extended legalization of gambling on the outcome of professional and amateur sports events. On the one hand, caught up in a wave of economic recession, states are looking to legalize sports betting in hopes of raising revenues for various public service programs. On the other hand, Congress, professional sports leagues, college regulatory agencies, and the horse racing industry are working to prohibit gambling on sports, citing the links of betting to organized crime, the potential for "fixing" outcomes, and the negative impact betting will have on the perceived integrity of events. This conflict is being waged at a time when the country's tolerance for gambling is higher than ever and when several forms of gambling, including casino gaming, have been recently legalized. Sports betting remains the one form of gambling that is yet untapped by the legalization movement, except for the state of Nevada and forms of sport lotteries found in Oregon and Montana. Resolution of the conflict over sports betting will ultimately come with what is perceived to be the policy that is most consistent with protecting the public interest. At issue is the ratio of the social costs of gambling to its economic benefits. It is this controversy that has been the basis of contention for all efforts to legalize gambling; sports betting is no different. The issues of the policy debate are reviewed below, but the decision to legalize will be made in favor of economic, commercial interests and not consistent with social, moral, or religious positions. That public policy issues have been decided in this manner is made easier by the fact that Americans feel rather ambivalent about activity that was once viewed as morally suspect (Rosecrance, 1988; Dombrink and Thompson, 1990; Abt, Smith, and Christiansen, 1985). Gambling no longer carries the social and moral stigma it once did.

SOURCE: "Gambling on Sport: Policy Issues" by James H. Frey. From *Journal of Gambling Studies* 8, pp. 351–360. Copyright © 1992 by Human Sciences Press, Inc. Reprinted by permission.

LEGALIZATION: THE KEY PUBLIC POLICY ISSUE

Stimulating the movement to legalization is the knowledge that there is a very high demand for gambling in general and sports wagering in particular. Nearly two-thirds of Americans participate in some form of gambling each year. Studies also show that nearly a quarter of adult Americans bet on sports events each year (Frey, 1985). Most of the money is bet via illegal venues or among friends by white middle-class males for the purposes of excitement, recreation, and camaraderie, not to make a profit (Commission, 1976; Filby and Harvey, 1989). Contrary to what might be expected, those with higher incomes are more likely to be involved in sports wagering than those with lower incomes. This means that a considerable amount of discretionary income is available for betting, a fact not lost on state revenue watchers. Thus, any tax on wagering would not seem to be regressive, contrary to other typical (i.e., lottery) state-operated gambling ventures.

The major argument on behalf of legalization is economic. That is, states feel that based on the interest in sports betting and the high rate of illegal wagering, taxes generated by legal and controlled wagering would reap considerable income for the state. At this point in time, thirteen states, including New York, Nebraska, Pennsylvania, Massachusetts, and Louisiana, have gone on record favoring some form of legalized wagering on sports. On the surface, the dollars bet on sport seem vast (e.g., $50 million bet legally on the 1992 Super Bowl and nearly one billion illegally), but closer analysis reveals that sport betting operations produce small profit margins and are very risky for the operator.

In 1980 thirty legal sports betting outlets in Nevada won $7.7 million on a total wager of $359.7 million for a gross win of 1.9 percent. In 1990 seventy-five outlets won $48.3 million on a total wagered of nearly $1.5 billion and a win percentage of 2.92. During this time period, revenue and total wagered increased over 530 percent. A significant reason for the increase in the wagering handle was the reduction of the federal tax to 0.25 percent and the establishment of sports books as a standard part of the profile of casino/hotels. Currently, legal sports books absorb this cost, making the legal sports betting market somewhat more competitive with the illegal version. At the same time, illegal wagering on sports events, the most prominent form of illegal gambling, grew 91 percent from revenue of $918 million in 1982 to $1.246 billion in 1989. In 1989, the last year calculations of illegal wagering were made, a total of $29.5 billion was bet illegally. This produced a win percentage of 4.5 (Christiansen, 1991:27 & 34). These figures represent just a small percentage of the total of $246 billion wagered on all forms of gambling in 1990. With a win percentage of 2–3 percent available for taxable income, states will not realize much revenue. More money could be raised by adding a small percent to existing sales or income taxes without having to establish an additional regulatory bureaucracy. In fact, sports betting represents less than 1 percent of the gambling market share and contributed just 0.38–1.62 percent of casino win in 1990 for Nevada (Gaming Control Board, 1990). At a 6 percent tax rate on a gross win of $48 million in 1990, this resulted in only $2.9 million for Nevada's treasury. Oregon found that their Sports Action pool cards produced a peak bet of $440 thousand in the eighth week and declined on the average the remainder of the 1990 season. It was not a lucrative operation (Christiansen, 1990). Sports betting has the smallest retention percentage of any form of commercial gambling. It produces the lowest net tax revenue for states of any game (Suits, 1979). It also gives the bettor the greatest chance of winning and, conversely, the operator the greatest chance of losing. Thus, if the operator does not set the line properly on a particular game, a considerable loss could result.[1] Bettors are very sophisticated today; they have access to information that equals or exceeds that of the bookmaker. Over 700 sports services exist to provide information; and media outlets are willing partners with gambling interests as they include gambling related information as a regular feature of programs and columns (Frey and Rose, 1987). The demise of Canadian Select Baseball and the Delaware football lottery came as a result of the lack of expertise in running a profitable sports betting operation. If a state wants to implement a sports betting operation, it has to be prepared both to take a loss and to justify the use of state tax dollars to pay off losses (Frey, 1985). This is particularly true if states permit head-to-head wagering (e.g., one team versus another with an established point spread), rather than sports pools or lotteries. Gambling revenue can be very unpredictable and tax dollars can be costly to collect. According to one analyst, it costs 1.5 cents to collect a regular tax dollar and 37 cents to collect a gambling dollar (Rose, 1986:11). Given the already meager tax revenue possible from sports wagering, the costs of collection make sports betting more dismal as a source of state revenue. Any state that operates a sports betting system will want a guaranteed profit, and that is something a sports bookmaker cannot provide.

The second major argument for legalization is the curtailment of illegal gambling and any organized crime activity associated with gambling. According to Rose, "No serious student of gambling today believes that legalized gambling hurts organized crime. A legal game almost never attracts players from the illegal game" (1986:9). The legal game is rarely competitive with the illegal version. Illegal bookmakers can provide credit and telephone wagering; they can provide confidentiality, take bets over $10,000 without disclosure to the Internal Revenue Service, and they can offer a better price because the illegal bookmaker does not have the same costs as the states (Rosecrance, 1988; Commission, 1976; Abt, Smith, and Christiansen, 1985). To raise money, the state must operate a game with a high take-out rate, but this will mean that the illegal game will be more attractive to bettors. A game that matches price and payout schedules of the illegal game will impact that game but it will not generate revenue. This makes sports betting a poor candidate for legalization because it cannot help the state meet either goal (Frey, 1985). As I have stated elsewhere:

> It must be kept in mind that all commercial gambling has a built-in operator edge or advantage. This house advantage must provide a sufficient operator return to cover the costs of the game, including insurance, loan amortization, payroll, and of course profit. The edge also must be large enough to cover gambling taxes. Thus the legal industry needs a higher edge than what is required by the illegal enterprise. This will be a problem as long as the states view gaming as a revenue source. Finally, the taxes extracted from legal commercial gambling must (1) be sufficient to cover any costs associated with supervising, operating, or controlling the gaming enterprise; (2) provide enough dollars to cover losses to tax revenue from similar legal games (such as OTB versus on-track), and (3) generate enough monies to have an impact on the social maladies that were used to promote the implementation of the legal game in the first place. Lotteries, casinos, and some forms of parimutuel betting may satisfy these revenue needs, but sports betting, particularly if the state is the operator, will not. If states adopted a parimutuel system of sports betting, as some have suggested, the states' takeout percentage would be guaranteed, but the game would not be competitive with its illegal counterparts (Frey, 1985:207).

The state is caught in a paradox. On the one hand, it sees the revenue possibilities of gaming taxes and the political advantages of implementing a "voluntary" tax. On the other hand, state revenue demands raise the price of gambling, making the illegal version more attractive. In reality, state-run gambling stimulates illegal gambling rather than eliminating it (Abt, Smith, and Christiansen, 1985).

The control of illegal gambling by means of sanction or legalization has had almost no impact on organized crime. State efforts to control gambling have been ineffective (Dombrink and Thompson, 1990). Gambling enforcement has been of low priority to all branches of law enforcement and their pattern of enforcement has been guided by the principles of de facto decriminalization. In fact, the direct connection of organized crime to sports betting has been questioned in significant research (Reuter and Rubenstein, 1982; Reuter, 1984; Reuter, 1983; D'Angelo, 1983), which suggests that the mob does not control sports betting and that it will not be impacted by legalization. There is a separate connection between illegal gambling and organized crime, except where it is necessary to mediate disputes between gamblers (Reuter, 1983).

The government also places itself in a precarious position by legalizing gambling because it may appear to be hypocritical. There are several questions to be asked in this light. First, should the state be involved in regulating victimless crimes to protect the public from itself; second, can a state condone one form of gambling and prohibit others; third, by permitting gambling does the government play to the public's weakness, thereby taking advantage of the very people they are to protect; and fourth, should the government be promoting an otherwise "immoral activity"? The latter is particularly a problem if the government is still viewed as a moral leader (Frey, 1985).

Anti-gambling forces point out the disadvantages of legalizing gambling from an economic standpoint, but they also point out that the increased availability of gambling can result in increased addiction, reduced worker productivity, negatively impacted youth, and exploited citizenry. However, with respect to sports wagering, the concern has been with the possibility of the integrity of the sporting event being degraded or compromised by virtue of the increased possibility of the outcome being manipulated in such a way that the uncertainty of that outcome is somehow reduced. In other words, the game has been "fixed."

This sentiment has been the rationale behind the introduction of S.474, The Professional and Amateur Sports Protection Act by Senators DeConcini, Bradley, and others in the 1991 Congress. This act calls for the prohibition of wagering on sports events in any state except where it is currently legal (i.e., Nevada, Oregon, Delaware, Montana). New Jersey has one year to evaluate the prospect of legal wagering before its exemption is withdrawn. Most of the arguments directed at this bill's defeat come from state governments considering the legalization of sports betting. They assert that it should be a state, not federal, decision to restrict gaming. This has also been the position of the North American Association of State and Provincial Lotteries, which sees the legislation in terms of state sovereignty, but which also foresees financial opportunity for their local operations if sports wagering can be legalized. Since most legal operations would probably have a pool or lottery, rather than head-to-head format, the existing lottery operators would be logical candidates for running the sports betting counterparts.

Detractors of the bill believe the federal government should continue its operating policy of leaving gaming regulation and control to the states. The federal government has made episodic efforts to enforce Section 1084 of the U.S. Code, which prohibits taking of bets and supplying of information across state lines, but if it was really serious about gambling enforcement, then just about every newspaper, television channel, radio station, and sport information service could be found guilty of violating this law (Frey and Rose, 1987). Before S.474, Congress just wasn't interested in gaming enforcement except to resolve Indian gaming issues. It is more likely that the impetus for S.474 has come from the professional sports leagues, which appeal to tenets of morality and integrity, and the horse racing industry, which is concerned about the diversion of money from the race track to the sports book. The following statements from testimony given by league officials (quoted in *USA Today*) provide a clear indication of their position:

Fay Vincent, Major League Baseball: It would be tragic if the importance of batting averages and baseball cards were overshadowed by betting odds and lottery
tickets.

Paul Tagliabue, National Football League: Sports gambling threatens the
integrity of and public confidence in team sports. Youth look up to athletes
(but) our players cannot be expected to function as healthy role models for
youth if they are made to function as participants in gambling enterprises.

Gary Bettman, National Basketball Association: Betting doesn't enhance our
game. Betting changes the rooting interest. If there was wide-spread legal gambling, we'd be less popular because the environment of the game would change.
Players will come under suspicion (Staff writer, 1991, page 2C).

The statement of Pete Rozelle, former commissioner of the National
Football League, before a 1976 Congressional inquiry into professional
sports best summarizes the view of the professional leagues:

Professional football depends for its survival on the public's perception of the
integrity of the games, owners, and players. . . . The pressure on players and club
and league personnel from increased numbers of people seeking inside information would quickly become intolerable. . . . Legal sports betting would seriously erode public confidence in the games. It would create a generation of
cynical fans, obsessed with point spreads and parimutuel tickets and constantly
suspicious of the motives of players and workers (U.S. House of Representatives,
1977:137).

Professional sports leagues resist legalization because they feel gambling
will increase the likelihood that the betting line or point spread will replace
the win/loss outcome as the focus. They fear that the outcome of an event
will not be the natural result of the struggle of opponents, but that it will be
contrived action consistent with a betting line (Frey, 1985). Professional
leagues already fight an image problem with drug scandals, commercial
exploitation of cities and fans, racial inequities among players and administrative personnel, as well as a few gambling scandals involving high-profile
players such as Pete Rose and Lenny Dykstra. Even though there is little evidence that professional games have been fixed in the past, the leagues are
very concerned that no impropriety be even suggested.

While the leagues' position on gambling is admirable, it is also hypocritical. League enforcement personnel work very closely with the legal betting
operations to monitor betting patterns; leagues provide injury information
and other personnel data readily; leagues know that gambling helps to create an interest in their product and may even put many fans into the stands.
Despite protestations, the universal existence of illegal betting has not
apparently hurt the professional, or for that matter, the college ranks, in
terms of popularity or gate receipts. Legal bookmakers also find the stand of
professional sports leagues to be ironic since both have a vested interest in

the integrity of the game. Any of these bookmakers will assert that the scandals of the past have emanated from illegal, not legal, operations. Publicly the leagues take a prohibitive stance, but operationally they coordinate and sometimes depend on gambling interests.

Professional and amateur sports leagues also resist legalization because they fear the intrusion of government into their private enterprise (Frey, 1985). They see the possibility of the licensing and certification of owners, background investigation of key personnel, mandatory drug testing, and the official certification of outcomes as natural extensions of legalization. Owners and league commissioners, professional and amateur, see their teams and leagues as private property that should be relatively free of state control. However, the states could feel these teams are public entities requiring state supervision because of the investment states make in the form of tax breaks, facility rental subsidies, sweetheart vendor contracts (e.g., teams get 100 percent of vendor revenue), and reduced fees. This is not, however, a big issue in the wagering debate. The leagues also resent the apparent copyright infringement by gambling interests in the use of team names and logos in the promotion of wagering information and behavior. Perhaps, if the gambling operators paid a rights or users fee to the owners, they would be more interested in further legalization. In addition, some owners may fear legalization because it will stimulate investigation into their direct and indirect ties to the gambling industry (Moldea, 1989). The leagues, along with the media, and with some support from the horse racing industry and current legal bookmakers (who would have their monopoly even further entrenched) form a powerful lobby to resist further legalization even though several federal commissions recommended legalization. This will make it extremely likely that S.474 or similar legislation prohibiting sports wagering will be enacted in the future. [Editor's Note: S.474 became law effective October 28, 1992.]

CONCLUSION

It is unlikely that the legalization of sports betting will be expanded despite the expressed interest of many states. Legalized sports betting will not yield the revenues projected unless players are asked to spend more to win less. If this does take place, the illegal version will continue to flourish. The revenue projections will be further compromised by the cost states will endure in regulation, collection, and control. The state will be placed in a precarious position of having to potentially draw from other sources of state funds should the betting operation take a substantial loss. Finally, a general mandate permitting legalization will find public resistance because sport is still viewed as a virtuous activity that provides a setting for the articulation of the values Americans hold most dear. These values could be undermined by the apparent governmental approval of a direct and intimate association of sport with what is a socially acceptable activity but still somewhat morally disapproved—gambling. The public would rather acknowledge the behavioral association of sport and gambling, which has a long history, rather than intertwine the two ideologically.

Still, legalization may remain attractive to states facing a fiscal crisis. They may decide that the public interest is better served if the state is able to provide all of the public services required and needed. If this means playing to the vices of the citizenry, then it will be done.

NOTE

1. The theory behind the line or point spread is to "split the action," that is, to have the same amount of money bet on both sides. A faulty line will usually produce a great deal of action on one side. This forces the bookmakers to adjust the line to generate more betting on the other team, thus "balancing" the book. The bookmaker's profit comes from the "vigorish" or the price/commission received for handling the bet. Bettors in Nevada, for example, will have to bet eleven dollars to win ten. For states to make any money on sports betting they may have to price a wager such that the bettor will have to bet twelve or thirteen dollars to win ten. Point spreads create the perception of equal opportunity to win by the transformation of mismatches into competitive contests.

REFERENCES

Abt, V., Smith, J. F., & Christiansen, E. M. (1985). *The business of risk: Commercial gambling in mainstream America.* Lawrence, KA: University of Kansas Press.

Christiansen, E. M. (1990). Sports betting in the United States. Paper presented at the meetings of the Horse Tracks of America, Boca Raton, Florida.

Christiansen, E. M. (1991). Gaming operators win record $25.9 billion in '90. *Gaming and Wagering Business, 12,* 26–34, 38.

Commission on the Review of the National Policy Toward Gambling (1976). *Gambling in America: Final report of the Commission on the Review of the National Policy Toward Gambling.* Washington, D.C.: Government Printing Office.

D'Angelo, R. (1983). *The social organization of sports gambling: A study in conventionality and deviance.* Ph.D. dissertation. Bryn Mawr University.

Dombrink, J. & Thompson, W. N. (1990). *The last resort: Success and failure in campaigns for casinos.* Reno, NV: University of Nevada Press.

Filby, M. & Harvey, L. (1989). Recreational betting: Individual betting profiles. *Leisure Studies, 8,* 219–227.

Frey, J. H. (1985). Gambling, sport, and public policy. In A. T. Johnson & J. H. Frey (Eds.), *Government and sport: The public policy issues* (pp. 189–218). Totowa, NJ: Rowman and Allenheld.

Frey, J. H. & Rose, I. N. (1987). The role of sports information services in the world of sports betting. *Arena Review, 11,* 44–51.

Gaming Control Board (1990). *Nevada gaming abstract.* Carson City, NV: State of Nevada.

Moldea, D. E. (1989). *How organized crime influences professional football.* New York: William Morrow and Company.

Reuter, P. (1983). *Disorganized crime.* Cambridge, MA: The MIT Press.

Reuter, P. (1984). Police regulation of illegal gambling: Frustrations of symbolic enforcement. *Annals, 474,* 36–47.

Reuter, P. & Rubenstein, J. (1982). *Illegal gambling in New York: A case study in the operation, structure, and regulation of an illegal market.* Washington, D.C.: Government Printing Office.

Rose, I. N. (1986). *Gambling and the law.* Hollywood, CA: Gambling Times Inc.

Rosecrance, J. (1988). *Gambling without guilt: The legitimation of an American pastime.* Pacific Grove, CA: Brooks/Cole Publishing Company.

Staff writer (1991). League officials favor regulation of sport betting. *USA Today,* June 25, page 2C.

Suits, D. B. (1979). Economic background for gambling policy. *Journal of Social Issues, 35,* 43–61.

United States House of Representatives (1977). Inquiry into professional sports. Select Committee on Professional Sport. 95th Congress, 1st session.

19. *Performance-Enhancing Drugs in Sport*

JOHN R. FULLER AND MARC J. LA FOUNTAIN

The growing concern in the United States about drug abuse among young people is mobilizing teachers, parents, law enforcement officers, and youth-serving professionals in an effort to educate, treat, and prevent the recreational use of drugs. Laudable as their efforts are, they can have only a minimal effect without some major rethinking about which substances should be sanctioned, the approaches (criminal or medical) that should be used to discourage drug use, and the level of threat from drug use that can offset violation of civil rights which some popular remedies (i.e., drug testing) may imply. A logical, coherent drug policy to deal with recreational drugs has yet to emerge despite the universal concern of those who deal with the problems of youth. In the spirit of broadening the examination of drugs in our society, this article looks at another form of drug abuse that is frequently overlooked. Young athletes are using anabolic steroids and a substance called human growth hormone to increase the size and strength of their bodies. Because this form of drug use is potentially more harmful to the body of a young person than almost any of the popular recreational drugs, it deserves greater attention.

The purposes of this paper are (1) to discuss the seriousness and prevalence of the use of performance-enhancing drugs, and (2) to report the results of a series of interviews with steroids users to determine their rationales for drug use.

PERFORMANCE-ENHANCING DRUGS: THE HEALTH PROBLEMS

In the summer between his junior and senior years in high school, Bob (not his real name), an all-city, 205-lb. linebacker, works out with weights at a local gym amid a number of older football players, bodybuilders, and competitive weight lifters. When he returns to school in the fall, his coach is delighted to see the changes in Bob. Not only is he now 235 lbs. of lean muscle, but he

SOURCE: "Performance-Enhancing Drugs in Sport: A Different Form of Drug Abuse" by John R. Fuller and Marc J. La Fountain. From *Adolescence* 22, pp. 969–976. Copyright © 1987 by Libra Publishers. Reprinted with permission.

also has gained an intense attitude and killer instinct which are sure to make him all-state and possibly an all-American. The transformation in Bob's body and demeanor makes the coach marvel at the advances in body shaping available to almost every young athlete. If the coach had looked more closely, he would not have been so delighted at some of the other changes that occurred in Bob: He is in a constant state of anxiety; he cannot concentrate on his studies; he is constantly arguing with his parents; and he is having problems with his girlfriend—jealousy, pressuring for sex, and much to her surprise, beating her up when he gets frustrated.

Bob's unusual behavior should be a sign to parents, coaches, and teachers that he may have a serious drug problem. In addition to his aggressive attitude, he is suffering damage to his heart, liver, reproductive system, and stomach as a result of taking performance-enhancing anabolic steroids. The medical case against the use of anabolic steroids, human growth hormones, and ergogenic aids in sport is clear (Brubaker, 1985; Stone & Lipner, 1980; Goldman, 1984; Taylor, 1982, 1985a, 1985b; Todd, 1984). The real question is why anyone who has heard about the harmful effects of these drugs would expose himself to heart attacks, sterility, ulcers, and liver tumors, not to mention psychological and emotional instabilities. Perhaps the current "win at all costs" mentality costs too much.

INTERVIEW THE MESOMORPHS: WHY THEY USE STEROIDS

In an effort to understand the rationale and motivation of those who use performance-enhancing drugs we interviewed 50 athletes who admitted to steroid use. With the help of some key informants we were introduced to several steroid-using weight lifters, football players, wrestlers, and bodybuilders. These athletes ranged in age from 15 to 40 years, with an average age of 19. Since this is considered a self-selected sample, any claims of generalization are offered with qualifications. No systematic differences between the high school and college-level athletes were found and the type of sport did not seem to play a major role in the decision to use steroids.

We were interested in how these athletes rationalized engagement in three types of deviant behavior: (1) taking unfair advantage in sport (using performance-enhancing drugs is prohibited by all sport-sanctioning bodies), (2) breaking the law (with the exception of one athlete who had received a doctor's prescription for his steroids, all the athletes interviewed received their drugs through black market purchase), and (3) exposing the body to health risks (these athletes were all aware of the risks). They were asked quite directly why they used the drugs, how they had learned about them, and the values they associated with this form of drug use.

In order to understand human behavior, the meanings people attach to their own behavior must be considered (Mills, 1940). Researchers interested in deviant behavior have examined how a justificatory vocabulary has been developed to explain involvement in homicide (Luckenbill, 1977), rape (Scully & Marolla, 1984), child molestation (McCaghy, 1968), and gang violence in prisons (Jacobs, 1977). In order to analyze the motivations of steroid-using athletes, Sykes and Matza's (1957) "techniques of neutralization" were used as the basis for the interviews. These are the techniques juvenile delinquents use to rationalize responsibility for their crimes. Sykes and Matza labeled the techniques as denial of victim, denial of injury, condemnation of condemners, and appeal to higher loyalties.

DENIAL OF VICTIM

Athletes who use steroids do not believe they are causing harm to anyone. They view their drug use as a "victimless crime"—one that should not be the concern of other people. Those interviewed felt that the serious athlete is required to use steroids if he wants to be competitive nationally and internationally. Most of them said that if the athletes against whom they competed did not use drugs, they would consider not using steroids themselves. One recurrent theme in the rationalization of steroid use is finger-pointing at the Eastern-block nations. Steroid use was justified as an act of patriotism, and as paying the price necessary to be competitive:

> We should be allowed to take them because all those other countries take them. Those guys from East Germany, Bulgaria, and Russia all use steroids. The women too. If we don't take them you can kiss off ever winning an Olympic medal for America.

> You have no choice if you want to compete in the big-time. Everyone does from other countries so we should also. If you want to dance you have to pay the fiddler. I wish they would outlaw them but at most meets all of them are juiced up so you have to be too.

The consistent paranoia that other athletes use steroids seems to be pervasive in the weight-lifting and football subcultures. When athletes look around the gym and see steroid use among their peers, they are quick to attribute drug use to all athletes who achieve a high degree of success. It is clear that this is not the case since some of the best athletes have demonstrated that they are drug-free (Todd, 1984).

DENIAL OF INJURY

The athletes interviewed were not very concerned with the potential health problems that are linked to steroid use. In discounting the health risks they displayed a remarkable lack of knowledge about the effect on their bodies. Many had little interest in sorting out the conflicting evidence on the health risks and seemed to view their bodies as simply a tool or machine that could be manipulated for results. They picked up their attitudes toward steroid use and the techniques for administering them from the more experienced athletes at the gyms where they worked out. These served as "gym gurus" who advised athletes as to the type of drug to use, how often to use it, and which drugs could be used in combination—called "stacking" in the weight lifters' argot. The athletes do not see steroid use as being injurious to their health, employing a variety of rationalizations to discount the potential risks:

> Every drug has side effects. Did you ever read the printed matter that comes with Tylenol? There is a long list of side effects. Steroids have less side effects than other drugs.

> You can abuse anything. Even aspirin. I don't think there is any proven test that says steroids really do hurt you. I know you hear a lot of talk but I know of nothing conclusive. A lot of us who use them are walking around but none of us have any health problems. Some may develop health problems because we do it on a hit or miss basis, not like the Russians who have it down to a science. We have these local gym gurus who make money off these guys and sell them too much, but even then I don't see any harmful effects.

> I use small doses. I don't use that much. I only know of about three people who have had trouble. One guy almost died. He was really good and had a chance to go to the L.A. Olympics but he took too much. If I ever have trouble I'll come off it.

> I see so many bodybuilders who take ungodly amounts and they never have problems. Only one guy got messed up and that's because he went off his cycle.

> The one I was on they give to people recovering from surgery, so how bad can that be for your body. It's not like they are poison or anything bad like that. It's like medicine. They help you grow. Besides I only take two a day so I don't feel I take enough to harm myself.

Few of the athletes considered the aggressive behavior associated with steroids as cause for concern. The emotional and psychological mood changes that result from taking hormonal drugs are dismissed as unimportant. They do not consider their behavior toward parents and girlfriends as injurious. It should be noted, however, that the girlfriends of a few of these athletes sought us out to complain about aggressive behavior and implored us to convince the athletes to quit using the drugs.

None of the athletes we talked to had done any reading or research on the potential health risks of steroid use. Most of their information was derived from muscle magazines or from peers at the gym.

CONDEMNATION OF CONDEMNERS

Another way steroid-using athletes deflect responsibility for their deviant behavior is by condemning the condemners, i.e., they question the knowledge, motives, and integrity of their critics.

> The people who do those studies are not athletes and don't really know what's going on. Those studies are not valid because they lasted only a couple of weeks and were done on rats. American studies are not sophisticated and I don't believe them because so many athletes say it works and that proves the studies false.

> People just don't understand what it means to be an athlete. Why don't they raise hell when they see all the knee operations done on football players. Sports eat up the body for those who reach the top and all those loudmouth purists don't blink an eye especially where big money is involved. Rules should not be made and enforced by people who don't know what they are talking about.

APPEAL TO HIGHER LOYALTIES

The athletes commonly spoke of what can be described as an appeal to higher loyalties—a vague, loosely defined "code of commitment" to sport. The dominant normative system is not repudiated by the appeal of higher loyalties technique of neutralization, but rather is violated with reluctance and with the justification that other norms are more pressing. The patchwork of rules and regulations which are inconsistently enforced are viewed as impediments—not guidelines for the practice of sport. Warnings about health risks, appeals to the ideals of fair play, and the threat of arrest are all dismissed as secondary to the code of commitment as expressed by these athletes. Steroid use is equated with having a dedicated attitude. For many of the athletes, steroid use was the only feature of their sport-related behavior that suggested sacrifice.

> I think you should take care of your body. I have not always taken care of mine but I do now. I get a lot of fun and enjoyment from powerlifting. It gives me a chance to achieve for myself and I do all I can to make my body stronger. I don't use drugs or drink or smoke and if my coach says steroids will make me stronger I will use them.

> I enjoy being with athletes more than with other people. I have changed my social life since we got into weightlifting. I don't like negative-thinking people, and being on steroids makes me feel very positive. I live fast. I had one hour of sleep last night, and I'm still going strong. If your mind is thinking positive you can do anything you want.

> I use them because they give me the White Moment (defined as a mystical, ecstatic feeling). If you have never experienced the high, then you don't know what

I'm talking about. I load up on roids and take a hit of speed and I'm on top of the world.

The appeal to higher loyalties rationale had an additional aspect worth noting. According to the reports of almost all the athletes interviewed, the chemical reaction resulted in an intensification of the sex drive. Several reported having personal problems with girlfriends during steroid cycles. One bodybuilder said he took only oral steroids because of threats of abandonment by his girlfriend. The increased sex drive results from the increase in excitability, aggressive behavior, and irritability. Thus, this side effect of taking hormonal drugs is not surprising. However, the athletes' perception and consequent lauding of the aphrodisiac effects of the drugs is disturbing. If these drugs become more widely used as a result of the perceived sexual effect, we may see even greater abuse.

DISCUSSION

The interviews revealed several problems. First, from the ease with which our sample was collected, and from the comments of the athletes, it appears that performance-enhancing steroid use is widespread. Thought at one time to be the province of only the world-class athlete, we are now seeing the less serious and younger athlete consuming steroids as casually as he would select a new pair of running shoes. There is an absence of expert medical supervision and rigorous experimental design necessary to evaluate steroid use; instead, athletes at all levels in several sports, some of them quite young (17-21), are self-administering massive doses of different types of steroids.

A second problem is the loss of credibility of the medical and coaching professions. The athletes dismissed local doctors and coaches as naive and ignorant about the technology and pharmacology of contemporary sport, acquiring information from popular magazines and local gym gurus/pushers. It appears that athletes of the 1980s are no more likely to heed the warnings about the dangers of steroid use than youths of the 1960s were to heed the warnings about marijuana.

The haphazard self-administration of steroids and the repudiation of traditional experts (coaches and doctors) have led athletes to adopt a new line of justifications for the way in which they participate in their sport. The vocabulary of motives adopted by the athletes closely resembles the techniques of neutralization noted by Sykes and Matza (1957) to explain deviant behavior of juvenile delinquents.

The modes of rationalization used by these athletes have important implications. On one level, the potential deleterious effects on health are sufficient cause for concern. The athletes interviewed did not appear to have adequate knowledge to be self-administering these drugs. On another level, the effects of drugs on the way we participate in sports are important considerations. Sports require a certain amount of cooperation to ensure fair play and even competition. To the extent that performance-enhancing steroids provide an advantage, the time may come (the interviewees claimed it is already here) when it must be used in order to be competitive. Escalation of the sacrifice involved in sports participation is clearly getting out of hand, and if drug use becomes more popular, inevitably the socialization process will expand to include adolescents.

At yet another level, a serious question of policy arises as to whether youths who use steroids are in fact deviants or criminals. This paper has tried to display the mindsets of young athletes and their relationship to the institutions of society, i.e., education, sports, medicine, media, and government. This has been done by focusing on the symbolic and actual language of steroid users (techniques of neutralization). What happens in the lives of the athletes is intimately connected with, and reflective of, the order of society. In order to alter the actions of youths, administrators, coaches, and families must reflect on society's values and institutions as they relate to the current philosophy of games and winning that is generating this form of drug abuse.

REFERENCES

Brubaker, B. (1985, Jan. 21). A pipeline full of drugs. *Sports Illustrated,* pp. 18-21.

Goldman, B. (1984). *Death in the locker room: Steroids and sports.* South Bend, IN: Icarus Press.

Jacobs, J. B. (1977). *Stateville: The penitentiary in mass society.* Chicago: University of Chicago Press.

Luckenbill, D. (1977). Criminal homicide as a situated transaction. *Social Problems,* 25(2), 176-187.

McCaghy, C. (1968). Drinking and deviance disavowed: The case of child molesters. *Social Problems,* 16(1), 43-49.

Mills, C. W. (1940). Situated actions and vocabularies of motive. *American Sociological Review,* 33(1), 46-62.

Scully, D., & Marolla, J. (1984). Convicted rapists' vocabulary of motive: Excuses and justifications. *Social Problems,* 31(5), 530-544.

Stone, R., & Lipner, H. (1980, summer). The use of anabolic steroids in athletics. *Journal of Drug Issues,* 10(3), 351-360.

Sykes, G.M., & Matza, D. (1957). Techniques of neutralization. *American Sociological Review,* 22(6), 644-670.

Taylor, W. N. (1982). *Anabolic steroids and the athlete.* Jefferson, NC: McFarland & Company.

Taylor, W. N. (1985a). *Hormonal manipulation: A new era of monstrous athletes.* Jefferson, NC: McFarland & Company.

Taylor, W. N. (1985b). Super athletes made to order. *Psychology Today,* 19(5), 63-66.

Todd, T. (1984, Oct. 15). The use of human growth hormone poses a grave dilemma for sport. *Sports Illustrated,* pp. 10-18.

20. *Out of Bounds: The Truth about Athletes and Rape*

JILL NEIMARK

Meg Davis was gang-raped in the spring of her freshman year by seven members of the university's football team—guys she used to hang out with at fraternity parties. "I knew the guys I 'buddied' with sometimes had group sex, and that they even hid in a closet and took pictures of the event," she says now, "but I never thought it would happen to me." She was sexually assaulted for nearly three hours. She blacked out as she was being sodomized, and came to later with a quarterback's penis in her mouth. When she tried to push him off, he shouted, "Hey, what are you doing? I haven't come yet!" Back at the dorm that night, she says, "I took shower after shower. I stayed in until there was no hot water left. I felt so dirty. Even so, I didn't call what happened to me rape. These were guys I knew. It wasn't until I went to a woman's center in town that someone explained I'd been gang-raped."

Men have been raping in gangs for centuries, from Russian soldiers in Germany and American soldiers in My Lai, to the infamous gang of boys "wilding" in New York's Central Park two years ago. When we think of group rape, it is exactly those packs of men who come to mind. But these days a disproportionate number of gang rapes are being committed by men whom we look to as our heroes, whom we laud and look up to for their grace and power and seeming nobility: young male athletes.

Psychologist Chris O'Sullivan, Ph.D., of Bucknell University in Lewisburg, Pennsylvania, studied 26 alleged gang rapes that were documented between 1980 and 1990, and found that fraternity groups committed the highest number, followed by athletic teams. In addition, she found that "the athletes who do this are usually on a star team, not just any old team. It was the football team at Oklahoma, the basketball team at Minnesota, the lacrosse team at St. John's." It seems to be our most privileged athletes—the ones, by the way, most sought after by women—who are often involved in gang rape.

From June 1989 to June 1990, at least 15 alleged gang rapes involving about 50 athletes were reported. Among the most publicized cases: At Berkeley, a freshman claimed she was raped and sodomized in a dark stairwell, among shards of a shattered light bulb, and then dragged by her

SOURCE: "Out of Bounds: The Truth about Athletes and Rape" by Jill Neimark. From *Mademoiselle* (May 1991), pp. 196–199. Copyright © 1991 by Jill Neimark. Reprinted by permission.
It is a violation of the law to reproduce this selection by any means whatsoever without the written permission of the copyright holder.

assaulter—a member of the football team—to his room, where three team-mates joined him. In Glen Ridge, New Jersey, four high-school athletes—all of them former football teammates—have been charged with wielding a small baseball bat and a broomstick to rape a 17-year-old slightly retarded girl. In Washington, D.C., a 17-year-old girl maintained, four members of the Washington Capitals hockey team assaulted her after the team was eliminated at the Stanley Cup play-offs (but none were indicted by a grand jury); and at St. John's University in New York, five members of the lacrosse team (plus one member of the rifle club) were accused of raping a student.

In spite of surging publicity about the phenomenon, athletes accused of rape usually escape with little more than a reprimand. Virtually every athlete accused of participating in a gang rape insists that it was not rape: He says the victim wanted group sex. *She asked for it.* Juries and judges seem to agree, for charges are often dropped. Pressing charges is crucial for rape victim's recovery. "A guy gets suspended for half a season and then he's back," notes Ed Gondolf, Ed.D., a sociologist at the Indiana University of Pennsylvania and author of *Man Against Woman: What Every Woman Should Know About Violent Men* (Tab Books, 1989). In the occasional gang-rape cases that proceed to prosecution, notes Claire Walsh, Ph.D., director of Campus and Community Consultation, an organization in St. Augustine, Florida, that specializes in presenting rape-prevention workshops across the country, "convictions are very difficult and rare."

"This act is so heinous," explains Dr. Walsh, "that we don't want to admit we have this kind of brutality in our culture. We don't want to believe our athletes are capable of this. So we immediately rename it, call it group sex, and perform a character assassination on the victim. It's her fault—no matter what the circumstances." What professionals involved in studying gang rape are beginning to understand is that there seems to be something very specific about the gloriously physical, sometimes brutal camaraderie of team sports that can set the stage for a brutal act.

One clue to the trigger for such an act may lie in the dynamics of the team experience itself: You don't find gang rape among tennis players or swimmers or those who participate in other solo sports. According to Bernice Sandler, Ph.D., director of the Project on the Status and Education of Women at the Association of American Colleges, it is athletes on football, basketball, and hockey teams who are most prone to group rape. Athletes who work and play together—hours each day, for months and years—become profoundly bonded. I remember my first, and only, outsider's taste of this bond: I was the sole woman attending a stag party for former rowers on the Yale crew team. I was to play waitress. The men wore nothing but loin-cloths. They were told to gulp down as many shots of whiskey as they could when they walked in the door. Then they slathered one another with mud and beer and spent much of the evening wrestling with a kind of wild, erotic joy. These guys never once talked about women. I went home shaken but, I admit, also envious. I knew I would never experience that raw, physical aban-don with my own sex.

One rape victim recalls a similar experience. The group of athletes and fraternity brothers who later raped her, she said, used to dance a tribal dance in a darkened room, finally collapsing on one another in a heap. The "cir-cle" dance, as it was called, was ecstatic and violent. "They'd be jumping up and pounding the ceiling and singing a song that began, 'When I'm old and turning gray, I'll only gang-bang once a day.'"

Most psychologists believe that powerful male bonding is the essence of gang rape—that, in fact, the men are raping for one another. Peggy R. Sanday, Ph.D., University of Pennsylvania anthropologist and author of *Fraternity Gang Rape* (NYU Press, 1990), explains: "They get a high off doing it with their 'brothers.'" The male bonding in these groups is so powerful and seductive that, says Dr. Walsh, "one man leads and the others follow because they cannot break the male bonds." Those men present who don't rape often watch—sometimes even videotaping the event. And, explains Gail Abarbanel, L.C.S.W., director of the Rape Treatment Center at Santa Monica Hospital in California, "There has never been a single case, in all the gang rapes we've seen, where one man tried to stop it." Even the voyeur with a stab of guilt never reports his friends. "That's the crux of the group rape," explains Abarbanel. "It's more important to be part of the group than to be the person who does what's right."

But there is more to team-gang rape than male bonding. These athletes see the world in a special way—a way that actually legitimizes rape. They develop a powerful subculture founded on aggression, privilege, and the scapegoating of women. Friendship is expressed through hostile teasing one player calls "busting." And, according to Dr. O'Sullivan, "Sports fosters this supermasculine attitude where you connect aggression with sexuality. These men see themselves as more sexual because they're more aggressive. I talked to one pro-basketball player who says that for years he raped women and didn't know it. Sex was only satisfying if it was a conquest."

According to Dr. Gondolf, who was also a football player, "For some ath-letes, there's an aggression, a competition, that's heightened in team sports. You come off the field and your adrenaline is still flowing, you're still revved up, and some of these guys may expect to take what they want by force, just like they do on the field." Dr. Gondolf says that he recalls certain moments from his time as a player, "where the whole team was moving as one, where we become part of a collective whole, rather than individuals."

Within that collective whole, according to experts and some athletes themselves, one way the men can demonstrate their power is by scapegoat-ing women. "There was a lot of classic machismo talk," recalls Tommy*, now 24, who played on the football team at Lafayette College in Pennsylvania. "The talk was very sexist, even threatening. I recall some guys sharing that they were really drunk as a big excuse for having sex with a girl everyone thought was a dog. The guy would say, 'I had my beer goggles on.' He'd act like he was embarrassed, but the fact was he did have sex, so it was a bragging kind of confession."

The pressure to score is powerful. Months after one gang rape had taken place, one of the men who had participated in it was still uneasily lamenting his impotence that night. Dr. Gondolf recalls how some men tended to talk about scoring on and off the field as if they were the same thing: "Abuse of women became the norm—not necessarily out of meanness, but because we saw the person as an opponent, an object to be maneuvered. Because the camaraderie among us was so important, we never questioned or challenged one another when these things came up. I remember hearing about forced sex, group sex, naked showers with women, and the tendency was to shrug your shoulders or chuckle. The locker-room subculture fed on itself."

And when the adrenaline rush of the field does get translated to a sexual assault, Dr. Gondolf theorizes, "a high definitely takes over during the rape, and it has a neutralizing effect. There is enough momentum present that it negates any guilt, fear, or doubt. The man thinks to himself, 'Oh, we're just having a good time, nobody's gonna get hurt.' It's the same rationalization men use when they beat or abuse their wives: 'She had it coming, she asked for it, she didn't get hurt that bad, I was drunk, it wasn't my fault.'"

What is perhaps most difficult to comprehend about gang rape is that the men involved *don't* feel guilty; they don't see this act of group violence as rape. Mary Koss, Ph.D., a University of Arizona psychologist, studied over 6,000 students at 32 universities and found that 1 of 12 college males admits to acts legally defined as rape or attempted rape, and yet only 1 out 100 admits they have raped or attempted rape. "Of the one hundred thirty-one men who had committed what we would legally define as rape," says Dr. Koss, "eighty-four percent argued that what they did was definitely not rape."

In many of the team-gang-rape cases around the country, the athletes involved readily, almost eagerly, admitted they'd had sex with the victim. In fact, they seemed to offer up their confessions as juicy tidbits. One witness in a case against members of the Kentucky State football team, in which all the men were found not guilty, testified that guys had lined up in the hall holding their crotches and saying, "Me next." And in an Oklahoma case, a player testified that he saw three former teammates—who were also subsequently acquitted—take turns having sex with a screaming girl, saying, "If we have to, we're going to take some from her." In many of the cases the athletes described how they viewed their victim as different from other women: cheap, a slut, a whore. Many quoted the old cliché, "When she says no, she really means yes." Usually they'd heard she was "easy"—sometimes because a teammate had already slept with her. At Kentucky, a teammate testified that he'd had oral sex with the victim three days before the alleged rape. "Any woman who would do that would do anything," he'd said. In fact, according to Dr. O'Sullivan, "Some of these guys are really sweet. They can be very nice to other women in their lives. But once a woman is in this category, it's almost as if she isn't a human being. All their beliefs say it's okay to abuse her."

I found the same disturbing paradox when I interviewed athletes. When confronted with the abstract idea of rape, these men use words like "shattering, disgusting, immoral." (Jay*, 25, a former football player at the University of Rochester, said, "I'll tell you something, I'd never even dream of doing anything like that, it makes me sick to my stomach.") But if they personally know of a case involving their teammates, they're curiously lenient and forgiving. A former starting quarterback at Lafayette College recalled rumors of a gang rape by his teammates on campus. "From what I understand she came on to one of the guys. Not that this justifies it, but she did like one of the guys who allegedly raped her, and she was willing to come up to the room with him." Even when I interviewed an old friend of mine formerly on an Ivy League track team, he mentioned offhandedly that some members of his team had shared a girl with a baseball team in Alabama, which "offered" her to the visitors. My friend never questioned whether it might have been rape: He assumed the girl was willing.

One possible reason for the astounding lack of guilt among athletes who rape is the special privilege accorded a star athlete—and the constant female adoration he attracts. "The 'hotshot syndrome' is inevitably part of team sports," says Dr. Gondolf. "If you're an athlete in college, you're given scholarships, a nice dorm, doctors, trainers, a lot of support and attention and cheerleaders who ogle you. That sense of privilege influences you, and some guys may then think, 'I deserve something for this, I can take women, the rules don't apply to me.' They feel they're above the law."

"I used to have girls call me up" says former quarterback Jay, "and say, 'I go to football games and watch you, I look at your picture in the program, I'm writing a paper on you.' It happened all the time. You get this attitude where you can do anything you want and nobody is ever going to say anything to you."

Coaches and universities contribute to the athlete's unique sense of entitlement. As Dr. Walsh notes, "When we're talking about athletic teams and gang rape, we see how, time after time, the entire community comes to the support of the team. Athletes are very important in the fabric of a campus or town. They keep alumni interested, and produce money for the community."

Says one outraged father of a 17-year-old rape victim, "The college threatened her. They told her if she went to the police her name would be in the paper, and her grandparents, who lived in a neighboring town, would see it. She went to the assistant dean, who never told the dean. He simply made an investigation himself, and wrote her a few months later saying the investigation had led nowhere and he was going to close the matter. The police chief even bragged to me that he'd worked hard to cover it up. As for the boys who raped her, they admitted having sex, but said she was a slut—she'd asked for it. It didn't matter that she'd gone on less than a dozen dates in her life."

Coaches also do their best to help their "boys" slip through the adverse publicity unpunished. Perhaps that's not too surprising, since the coaches themselves are often former players. "Twenty years ago someone could have talked to *me* about all this stuff," confessed Ray Tellier, former football coach and facilitator of campus discussions on rape at the University of Rochester. And three years ago, Bobby Knight, basketball coach at Indiana University, created an uproar by telling broadcaster Connie Chung: "I think that if rape is inevitable, relax and enjoy it."

The attitude of juries is often similarly lenient: Sergeant Danny Conway, a detective in Frankfort, Kentucky, who prosecuted the gang-rape case at Kentucky State University, recalls his fury when the five players prosecuted for rape were set free. "We charged five men on the football team—although there must have been more, because there were semen samples that didn't belong to any of the five. All of them said she was a willing participant, because she had snuck into the dorm with one of them. And all of them were dismissed. These guys made sport of it. In the trial they were giving one another high-fives and holding their fists up in the air and saying, 'First I got her, then he got her,' and they were smiling at one another in open court. The jury didn't seem fazed at all. Their decision tore me to pieces. It never seemed to faze them that this was a young lady whose life was probably ruined."

In the past few years those entrenched attitudes have finally, slowly, begun to be challenged. "At least now we recognize how often gang rape occurs," notes Dr. Walsh. Many universities and fraternities have begun education programs about rape, and Santa Monica's Rape Treatment Center offers an educational video that is being distributed across the country, starring Susan Dey and Corbin Bernsen of *L.A. Law.* At Syracuse University in New York, where last year six rapes were reported in the first five weeks of the school year, activists have formed a group called SCARED (Students Concerned About Rape Education). And New York recently passed a law that requires freshman rape orientation for schools receiving state funds.

New studies are showing that there is no such thing as a typical rape victim. Many women who are raped in college are virgins, according to Mary Koss's study—and the vast majority (75 to 91 percent) of rape victims cannot be differentiated from nonvictims in terms of risk factors like personality or circumstance. Women are often raped in the "honeymoon" period, however: those first few months of school when they're learning to negotiate their new world. And drinking is almost always involved; in fact, states Dr. Walsh, "alcohol is used deliberately to impair the woman." At parties, punch is massively spiked with liquor—to the point where some rape victims complain that they had only two drinks before they passed out drunk. One victim at San Diego State University recalls asking for a nonalcoholic beverage. Instead she was brought punch spiked with Everclear, a 95-percent-alcohol drink that is illegal in California.

But if outside observers have difficulty finding common attributes among victims of team rape, it seems clear that the men themselves have an unspoken code that divides women into classes—the nice-girl girlfriend and the party-girl rape victim. The scary part is that the cues are so hidden most women are completely unaware of them—and the rules may be different among different teams, different campuses, different locker rooms. Athletes will sometimes let drop a few clues: Usually a woman is more vulnerable if she's had sex with one of the group before; if she's buxom, wears tight clothes and lots of makeup; if she's from a college that has a certain reputation. One fraternity actually stuck colored dots on women's hands as they came to a party, color-coded to indicate how "easy" each woman was. It's that kind of hidden code that has more and more colleges warning young women to stay away altogether from the fraternity and house parties where athletes and their buddies gather—just as one must avoid dark alleys at night. Dr. Gondolf explains: "Athletes are so tangled up in their glory and their privilege, and they get such big benefits for it. We need women to prompt them to check up on one another." But that is only half the answer.

In the case of gang rape, almost all college women are so devastated they drop out of school. "These are overwhelming rapes, and the trauma is profound," explains Abarbanel. "A lot of these women are freshmen who are just beginning to test their independence. They have hopes and dreams about college and achievement, meeting new people, a career, a future. After gang rape, everything that college means is lost to them. They're afraid to be alone, afraid of a recurrence. And since these are often men they know, the sense of betrayal is very profound."

In some cases, says Dr. Sanday, a woman may have subconsciously been courting danger. She knows she should avoid certain parties, be careful about her drinking, come and leave with friends. But she's looking for power, on male territory. "We all, at certain times in our life, test ourselves. It's like going into the inner city on a dare. These women are using the men that way. They want to court and conquer danger. And legally and morally, they have a right to go and have sex with whomever they want, without being gang-raped."

One of the most important ways to prevent rape may be to understand what the word means. Many men and women don't know that the law *requires* that a woman give consent to sexual intercourse. If she's so inebriated that she can't say yes, or so frightened that she won't say no, the act is rape.

But just knowing that distinction is not quite enough; the seeds of team-gang rape are buried deep, even subconsciously, in the athletic culture. Dr. O'Sullivan tells of an incident outside the courtroom of the Kentucky State football-team trial. According to her, "We were all standing by the candy machine, and some guy mentioned that it was broken. And Big Will, a huge man who had charmed everybody, and who was testifying in behalf of his dormmate, said, I'll make it work. Everybody always does what I want.' And everybody laughed. I couldn't believe it. This is exactly the kind of attitude that can lead to the rape." The perception that force is "okay," that it is masculine and admirable, is really where gang rape begins—and where the fight against it will have to start.

NOTE

* Names have been changed.

■ FOR FURTHER STUDY

Eitzen, D. Stanley, "Ethical Dilemmas in Sport," *Journal of Sport & Social Issues* 12:1 (1988):17-30.

"Ethics and Morality in Sport: Annotated Bibliography," *Sociology of Sport Journal* 6 (1989):84-91.

Kane, Mary Jo, and Lisa J. Disch, "Sexual Violence and Reproduction of Male Power in the Locker Room: The 'Lisa Olson Incident,'" *Sociology of Sport Journal* 10 (December 1993):331-352.

Lueschen, Guenther, "Doping in Sport: The Social Structure of a Deviant Subculture," *Sport Science Review* 2 (1993):92-106.

Melnick, Merrill, "Male Athletes and Sexual Assault," *Journal of Physical Education, Recreation, and Dance* 63 (May/June 1992):32-35.

Messner, Michael A., and William S. Solomon, "Outside the Frame: Newspaper Coverage of the Sugar Ray Leonard Wife Abuse Story," *Sociology of Sport Journal* 10 (June 1993):119-134.

National Strength and Conditioning Association, "Anabolic-Androgenic Steroid Use by Athletes," position statement. *National Strength and Conditioning Association Journal* 15 (March/April 1993):9.

Nelson, Mariah Burton, "Bad Sports," *The New York Times* (June 22, 1994):21.

Rozin, Skip, "Steroids and Sports: What Price Glory?" *Business Week* (October 17, 1994):176.

Scheinin, Richard, *Field of Screams: The Dark Underside of America's National Pastime* (New York: W. W. Norton, 1994).

Simon, Robert L., *Fair Play: Sport, Values & Society* (Boulder, Colorado: Westview Press, 1991).

Part Seven

Problems of Excess: Big-Time College Sport

Interschool sports are found in almost all American schools and at all levels. There are many reasons for this universality. Sports unite all segments of a school and the community or neighborhood they represent. School sports remind constituents of the school, which may lead to monetary and other forms of support. School administrators can use sport as a useful tool for social control. But the most important reason for the universality of school sports is the widespread belief that the educational goals are accomplished through sport. There is much merit to this view; sports do contribute to physical fitness, to learning the value of hard work and perseverance, and to being goal-oriented. There is some evidence that sports participation leads to better grades, higher academic aspirations, and positive self-concept.

However, there also is a negative side to school sports. They are elitist, since only the gifted participate. Sports often overshadow academic endeavors (e.g., athletes are disproportionately rewarded and schools devote too much time and money to athletics that could be diverted to academic activities). Where winning is paramount—and where is this not the case?—the pressure becomes intense. This pressure has several negative consequences, the most important of which is that participants are prevented from fully enjoying sport. The pressure is too great for many youngsters. The game is work. It is a business.

The pressure to win also contributes to abuse by coaches, poor sportsmanship, dislike of opponents, intolerance of losers, and cheating. Most significant, although not usually considered so, is that while sport is a success-oriented activity, it is fraught with failure (losing teams, bench warmers, would-be participants cut from teams, the humiliation of letting down your teammates and school, and so on). For every ego enhanced by sport, how many have been bruised?

While this description fits all types of schools, big-time college sports deserve special attention, for they have unique problems. Athletes in these settings are athletes first and students second; thus they are robbed of a first-class education. They are robbed by the tremendous demands on their time and energy. This problem is further enhanced by athletes being segregated from the student body (in special classes, housed in athletic dorms); thus they are deprived of a variety of influences that college normally facilitates.

Another problem of college sports is that they tend to be ultraelitist. The money and facilities go disproportionately to the *male* athletes in the revenue-producing sports rather than to intramurals, minor sports, and club sports.

The greatest scandal involving college sports is the illegal and immoral behavior of overzealous coaches, school authorities, and alumni in recruiting athletes. In the quest to bring the best athletes to a school, players have been given monetary inducements, sexual favors, forged transcripts, and surrogates to take their entrance exams. In addition to the illegality of these acts, two fundamental problems exist with these recruiting violations: (1) Such behaviors have no place in an educational setting, yet they are done by some educators and condoned by others, and (2) these illicit practices by so-called respected authorities transmit two major lessons—that greed is the ultimate value and that the act of winning supersedes how one wins.

Finally, the win-at-any-cost ethic that prevails in many of America's institutions of higher learning puts undue pressure on coaches. They must win to keep their jobs. Hence, some drive their athletes too hard or too brutally. Some demand total control over their players on and off the field. Some use illegal tactics to gain advantage (not only in recruiting but also in breaking the rules regarding the allowed number of practices, ineligible players, and unfair techniques). But coaches are not the problem. They represent a symptom of the process by which school sports are big business and where winning is the only avenue to achieve success.

The articles in Part Seven reflect on these problems and offer some solutions. The first article, by Indiana University English professor and former sportswriter Murray Sperber, demythologizes college sport. In doing so he shows, among other things, how the athletic establishment is *not* part of the educational mission of academic institutions. The second selection, by sociologists Peter and Patricia Adler, reports their first-hand observations of unprepared college athletes grappling with the demands of academics. The Adlers found that the athletes responded to this mismatch by emphasizing sport all the more, leading to a relatively high rate of failed academics among the athletes.

The final essay, by D. Stanley Eitzen, looks at racism in college sports. This is especially important because African Americans are the most likely category among the athletes to be exploited—to play for their schools but not graduate. Eitzen provides twenty-two specific proposals to eliminate racism in college sports.

21. *Myths about College Sports*

MURRAY SPERBER

> In interviews with UK [University of Kentucky] students, fac-
> ulty members and administrators, a picture of two UKs
> emerges. One is a top-of-the-line $14-million-a-year athletic
> program, run largely by and for off-campus supporters; the
> other is a chronically underfinanced, "fair-to-middlin" aca-
> demic institution that seems to languish in the shadow of the
> "Big Blue" [athletic] monolith.
>
> Item in the *Louisville Courier-Journal*

A great number of myths shield college sports from casual scrutiny and burden any discussion of the subject. The following refutations of the most common myths should introduce the reader to the reality of contemporary
sports. . . .

*Myth: College sports are part of the educational mission of American colleges and
universities.*

Reality: The main purpose of college sports is commercial entertainment.
Within most universities with big-time intercollegiate programs, the athletic
department operates as a separate business and has almost no connection to
the educational departments and functions of the school—even the research
into and teaching of sports is done by the physical education department.

The reason elite athletes are in universities has nothing to do with the
educational missions of their schools. Athletes are the only group of students
recruited for entertainment—not academic—purposes, and they are the
only students who go through school on grants based not on educational
aptitude, but on their talent and potential as commercial entertainers.

If colleges searched for and gave scholarships to up-and-coming rock
stars so that they could entertain the university community and earn money
for their schools through concerts and tours, educational authorities and

SOURCE: "Myths about College Sports" by Murray Sperber. From *College Sport Inc: The Athletic
Department vs. the University* by Murray Sperber, pp. 1–11. Copyright © 1990 by Murray Sperber.
Reprinted by permission of Henry Holt and Company, Inc.

the public would call this "a perversion of academic values." Yet every year, American institutions of higher education hand out over a hundred thousand full or partial athletic scholarships, worth at least $500 million, for reasons similar to the hypothetical grants to rock performers.

Myth: The alumni support—in fact, demand—that their alma maters have large and successful college sports programs.

Reality: Studies indicate that most alumni—people who were students at a particular school—contribute to the academic units of their colleges and universities and that only 1 to 2 percent of them donate to athletic programs. In fact, alumni often withhold contributions from their alma maters when the athletic teams are too successful or are involved in sports scandals: they are embarrassed by their schools' becoming "jock factories" and/or are angered by the bad publicity from scandals, and they believe that their college degrees are being devalued.

Other research indicates that the major donors to athletic programs actually are boosters—people who never attended the school, who give money only to the athletic department and in proportion to its teams' success on the field or court, and who refuse to contribute to the institution's academic programs.

Myth: College sport is incredibly profitable, earning huge sums of money for American colleges and universities.

Reality: One of the best-kept secrets about intercollegiate athletics—well guarded because athletic departments are extremely reluctant to open their financial books—is that most college sports programs lose money. If profit and loss is defined according to ordinary business practices, of the 802 members of the NCAA (National Collegiate Athletic Association), the 493 of the NAIA (National Association of Intercollegiate Athletes), and the 1,050 non-affiliated junior colleges, only 10 to 20 athletic programs make a consistent albeit small profit, and in any given year another 20 to 30 break even or do better. The rest—over 2,300 institutions—lose anywhere from a few dollars to millions annually.

Because athletic departments are allowed to engage in "creative accounting," covering many of their expenses with money from their schools' general operating funds and other university sources, it is difficult to ascertain the full extent of their losses. One expert, Don Canham, longtime athletic director at the University of Michigan, estimated that "about 99 percent of the schools in this country don't balance their budgets in athletics." Canham balanced his, but the year after he retired (1988–89), Michigan's athletic program was, according to an NCAA official, "$2.5 million in the red."

Myth: The NCAA Division I men's basketball tournament makes millions of dollars for American colleges and universities.

Reality: Of the total revenue from the tournament, the NCAA keeps at least half or more for itself; for example, of the millions received from the 1987 tourney, the association distributed only 44 percent directly to the schools involved.

The new NCAA contract with CBS Sports will increase tournament revenue but, rather than share the pot o' gold, the NCAA plans to exclude a large number of schools from reaching it. According to Tom Hansen, commissioner of the Pac-10, the NCAA may soon drop as many as 50 schools from Division I basketball, including four or five conferences. In addition, if past performance is any indication, the richer pot will increase lottery fever among the remaining 240 Division I basketball programs, with coaches engaging in "checkbook recruiting" and sparing no cost to build winning teams.

In the 1990s, Final Four squads will win the lottery (probably the perennial powers will triumph most often), the 60 other teams invited to the tournament will break even on their basketball program expenses, and the hundreds of also-rans will either pay large sums of money to purchase losing lottery tickets or be shut out entirely.

Myth: Schools receive millions of dollars when their teams play in football bowl games.

Reality: Often the numbers given in newspaper articles are for the "projected payout," whereas the actual payout can be much lower. Moreover, most participating schools must split their bowl revenue with other members of their conferences. As a result, when the headline announces that a Pac-10 team received $1 million for a bowl appearance, that school kept only $100,000 because of the conference's ten-way split.

In addition, athletic departments like to turn bowl and tournament trips into all-expenses-paid junkets for hundreds of people, including their employees and friends. Their travel, hotel, and entertainment costs often eat up the actual bowl or tourney payouts and transform post-season play into a deficit item!

Myth: The money earned from college sports helps other parts of the university.

Reality: Because athletic department expenses usually exceed revenues, any money earned by college sports teams stays in the athletic department. Moreover, athletic departments admit that they have no intention of sharing their revenue; an NCAA survey reported that fewer than 1 percent of all athletic programs defined their "fiscal objective" as earning money "to support nonathletic activities of the institution."

Rather than financially help the university, most athletic programs siphon money from it: for example, the enormous maintenance costs of stadiums and other facilities—used exclusively for athletic program events and by their elite athletes—are often placed in the "Building-and-Grounds" line in the university-wide budget, and the multimillion-dollar debt servicing on these facilities is frequently paid by regular students in the form of mandatory "Fees."

To cover athletic program losses, schools must divert money from their budgets and other financial resources. Thus funds that could go to academic programs, student scholarships, faculty and staff salaries disappear into the athletic department deficit.

Myth: College coaches deserve their high annual incomes because they generate huge profits for their athletic programs.

Reality: A few years ago, the athletic director at the University of South Carolina commented: "For someone to make $250,000 in the business world, he'd have to generate $60 million to $70 million in sales. When coaches say they're worth it, they don't know what's going on out there."

John Wooden, the most successful men's basketball coach in NCAA history, was never paid more than $25,000 a year by UCLA. Today, only a few coaches generate as much revenue for their schools as Wooden did for his, and the vast majority direct programs that lose money for their institutions. Nevertheless, the annual incomes of at least one hundred NCAA Division I men's basketball coaches, and seventy-five Division I-A football coaches, approach or top $100,000, and many program heads in the "nonrevenue sports" (so termed because they always lose money) like soccer, baseball, track, and swimming earn over $75,000 a year.

Myth: College coaches deserve their high annual incomes because they are the key to producing winning teams and are irreplaceable.

Reality: Sonny Smith, a longtime Division I men's basketball coach, commented, "It's a make-it-while-you-can thing. . . . If I quit tomorrow, there'd be three hundred names in the ring." Except for a handful of truly outstanding and innovative coaches, most of the others are interchangeable and can be replaced by any number of the "three hundred names in the ring." When Bill Frieder, making over $400,000 a year, quit the University of Michigan on the eve of the 1989 NCAA men's basketball tournament, an unheralded assistant, earning a fraction of Frieder's income, was given the top job. Under Steve Fisher, Michigan swept through the tourney and won the national championship.

Myth: Hired to be fired—that's the fate of most college coaches.

Reality: Firings are not the reason most college coaches change jobs. Coaches leave schools for a variety of reasons, most often to take better-paying positions, to quit jobs that are not working out, or to keep one step ahead of the NCAA sheriff. Only in a minority of cases are they asked to leave.

An analysis of the major coaching appointments listed weekly in the *Chronicle of Higher Education* over the last decade reveals the following typical sequence: the head man at Bigtime Sports U. quits in midcontract to go to the pros or to become an AD; the coach at Southern Jock State leaves his school to take the more lucrative package at Bigtime U.; the coach at Western Boondock sees a chance to move up and grabs the job at Southern; finally, if Western cannot hire another head coach, it offers its smaller package to an assistant at a major program or, in desperation, promotes one of its own assistants. When this Coach in Motion Play ends, at least three head coaches, as well as innumerable assistants, have changed jobs—not one of them fired by a college or university.

Myth: College athletic programs provide a wonderful opportunity for black coaches.

Reality: White athletic directors and program heads keep college coaching lily white by hiring their duplicates. In a 1987 study of the racial backgrounds of head coaches in football, basketball, baseball, and men's track at 278 Division I schools, only 4.2 percent were black. However, the real surprise was the percentage of black assistant coaches—3.1, lower than the percentage of black head coaches. On the other hand, another study of big-time programs found that over 50 percent of the football players and 70 percent of the men's basketball players, as well as a high percentage of baseball and track athletes, were black. Since 1987, the percentage of black head and assistant coaches in college sports has not changed significantly.

Myth: College athletic programs provide a wonderful opportunity for women coaches.

Reality: Women coaches, unlike blacks, once had a strong position in college sports. However, in the 1970s and early 1980s, male athletic directors and program heads took over women's college sports as well as the jobs of female ADs and many coaches. The most comprehensive study of this phenomenon shows that in the early 1970s, 90 percent of the athletic directors of women's college sports programs were female, whereas by 1988, the percentage had dropped to 16. In the same time span, the percentage of female coaches of women's sports teams went from the mid-90s to 48.

Paralleling the male takeover of individual jobs was the NCAA's cynical demolition of the main women's college sport group, the AIAW (Association of Intercollegiate Athletics for Women), and the NCAA's subsequent control of women's athletic programs.

Myth: Talented athletes, like other high school graduates, should enroll in higher education.

Reality: Only about 30 percent of American high school students go on to four-year colleges and universities; one subsection of these students, with little interest in and preparation for higher education, is nevertheless required to attend university—aspiring professional athletes in football and men's basketball.

An anomaly of American history—that intercollegiate football and basketball began before the professional versions of those games and excluded viable minor leagues in those sports—has created a situation that is unknown and unthinkable in other countries: *To become a major-league player in a number of sports, an athlete must pass through an institution of higher learning.* And to compound the problem, American schools now take on the training of young athletes in sports, particularly baseball and hockey, for which there *are* excellent minor professional leagues, as well as Olympic sport athletes for which there is a strong club system.

Myth: College athletes are amateurs and their athletic scholarships do not constitute professional payment for playing sports.

Reality: A school gives an athlete a "full ride" grant worth $5,000 to $20,000 a year in exchange for the athlete's services in a commercial entertainment venture, namely, playing on one of the school's sports teams. If the athlete fails to keep his or her part of the agreement and quits the team, the institution withdraws the financial package—even if the athlete continues in school as a regular student. Moreover, once the athlete's playing eligibility ends, the grant is usually terminated.

At one time in NCAA history, athletic scholarships were for four years and, once awarded, could not be revoked. In 1973, under pressure from coaches who wanted greater control over their players and the ability to "fire" them for poor athletic performances, the NCAA instituted one-year scholarships, renewed annually at the athletic department's discretion.

Under their current terms, athletic scholarships appear indistinguishable from what the IRS calls "barter payment for services rendered," thus making college athletes professional wage earners. In addition, a number of courts have found that the one-year grants constitute an employer-employee relationship between a school and an athlete.

Myth: College sports provide an excellent opportunity for black youngsters to get out of the ghetto and to contribute to American society.

Reality: Research by Harry Edwards, professor of sociology at the University of California, Berkeley, indicates that many athletic programs treat black athletes as "gladiators," bringing them to campus only to play sports, not for an education. The low graduation rate of black college athletes supports Edwards' thesis.

Most schools with major athletic programs, as well as many with smaller ones, recruit black athletes much more intensively and systematically than they do regular black students. Moreover, some schools fund their "black gladiators" by diverting money from scholarship sources, such as opportunity grants, earmarked for academically motivated minority students. Thus, not only do the "black gladiators" fail to receive college educations, but many black high school graduates—whose academic potential is far greater than the athletes'—are deprived of the chance of entering university.

Myth: For college athletes, the opportunity for a university education is as important as playing intercollegiate sports.

Reality: Formal and informal studies indicate that most college athletes in big-time programs hope to play their sport at the professional or Olympic level, and they regard college as their path to the pros or the national team. That very few of these athletes ever achieve their dream is irrelevant to its power over them and its role in shaping their college careers, especially their willingness to devote as many as sixty hours a week to their sports and their inability to sustain a serious course of studies. Jim Walden, head football coach at Iowa State University, says that in his sport, "Not more than 20 percent of the football players go to college for an education. And that may be a high figure."

Myth: Athletes, like Bill Bradley and Tom McMillen, who were outstanding in sports and in the classroom prove that college sports works.

Reality: In any large sample of people in any endeavor, there are always a few at the end of the bell curve. In fact, the widespread notice taken of Bradley's and McMillen's success in both sports and academics suggests that intercollegiate athletics is a system that works for only a few. No one bothers to name all of the outstanding Americans who were once top college students but not athletes, because they are not unusual; higher education is supposed to produce them.

From their first day of college, however, athletes face a conundrum—how to be a "student-athlete"—that few can solve. Their only response is to erase one of the terms and to highlight the other: neglect a meaningful education and pursue sports full-time, or, in a few cases, drop out of intercollegiate athletics and seriously go to school.

Most big-time athletic programs try to finesse this problem by sheltering their athletes in special "hideaway curricula" and having them major in eligibility (the NCAA has minimal rules for "good academic standing" and playing eligibility). But time spent in a school's Division of Ridiculous Studies does not constitute a real college education. For the vast majority of athletic scholarship holders, the current system does not work; it also corrupts the host institutions and makes faculty, regular students, and the public cynical about the entire academic enterprise.

Myth: The high graduation rates of athletes announced each year by the NCAA and the College Football Association are accurate.

Reality: These rates are manipulated by the NCAA and CFA to produce the appearance of athletes doing well academically. Instead of basing the percentage of athlete-graduates at a school on the total number who began in an athletic program as freshmen, the NCAA and CFA do not count all those who transferred or who dropped out of school in "good academic standing." Because leaving in "bad academic standing"—i.e., flunking out—usually takes a grade point average *below D*, the NCAA and CFA exclude large numbers of academically marginal athletes from their pools, among them those who drop out after using up their college eligibility but have a D or better average. Not counting transfers has a similar statistical effect: many transfers do not graduate from their next institution, but their absence from the original pools raises the graduation rates.

Some schools even base their rates on only their senior class of athletes: such common pronouncements as "Of our senior student-athletes in football, 90 percent graduated this June" can mean "We based our rates on those ten football players who made it to the senior class—out of the thirty who started in our program as freshmen." Not surprisingly, after this numerical sleight of hand, the NCAA and CFA graduation rates reflect their propaganda, not reality.

Myth: The NCAA represents the will of its member colleges and universities and it tries to keep intercollegiate athletics in line with their educational objectives.

Reality: The NCAA functions mainly as a trade association for college coaches and athletic directors, implementing their wishes regardless of whether these are in the best interests of the member schools. Real power in the association resides in the forty-four-person Executive Council and the twelve-member Executive Committee; for many years, a large majority of Executive Council and Executive Committee members have been athletic directors. These two groups control NCAA legislation, choose future council and committee members, and supervise the executive director of the association, currently Dick Schultz, a former coach and AD.

Myth: NCAA athletic programs sponsor teams in many sports, including Olympic events, because they want to give those sports a chance to grow.

Reality: Most athletic directors and program heads are empire builders. Through their control of the NCAA, they have instituted key legislation that ensures expansion—even though costly athletic department growth is not in the financial or academic interest of most of their schools.

The NCAA requires a minimum number of teams for participation in its various divisions, for example, for Division I-A, thirteen teams (men's and women's) in seven sports. If an institution fails to meet the requirement, the NCAA drops it to "unclassified membership," bars all of its teams from NCAA play, and penalizes it in various other ways.

The NCAA's rationale for the sports and team minimums is that schools should have "well-balanced athletic programs." In practice, these regulations serve the college sports establishment's self-interest: ADs and coaches want their programs to be as large as possible, and to employ as many administrators, assistant coaches, and athletes as possible. The NCAA, by locking athletic departments into a high number of sports and teams, deprives member institutions of a large degree of autonomy over their athletic budgets.

Myth: The NCAA can correct the problems in college sports.

Reality: The athletic directors and coaches who control the NCAA deny the existence of any significant problems in college sports. For them, the present system works well—after all, it provides them with extremely comfortable livings—and they see no need to repair it, except for some minor tinkerings.

Bo Schembechler, when head football coach at the University of Michigan, speaking for his fellow coaches and most ADs, once shouted at an audience of reform-minded college presidents, "*We are not the enemy.*" Bo was wrong. But he was true to the NCAA's self-serving denials of any responsibility for the current problems.

The bottom line on meaningful NCAA reform is clear: the NCAA cannot solve the systemic problems in college sports because the coaches and ADs who control it are a central source of those problems. Moreover, the association will fight any attempts at real reform, even if—as is probable in the 1990s—College Sports Inc. begins to destroy the academic and fiscal integrity of some member institutions.

22. *From Idealism to Pragmatic Detachment: The Academic Performance of College Athletes*

PETER ADLER AND PATRICIA A. ADLER

In recent years, the relationship between the athletic participation and academic performance of college athletes has become a topic of scholarly concern. The sociological literature in this area, however, has been inconsistent in its findings. Some studies have cited a weak positive relationship, claiming that although most college athletes had poor academic records in high school, they have higher GPAs, lower attrition rates, and a greater likelihood of graduating than nonathletes because they receive extra tutoring, more attention, and special "breaks" (Hanks and Eckland, 1976; Henschen and Fry, 1984; Michener, 1976; Shapiro, 1984). But most studies of college athletes have found a negative relationship between athletic participation and academic performance. These studies conclude that athletes are unprepared for and uninterested in academics, that they come to college to advance their athletic careers rather than their academic careers; therefore, they have lower GPAs, higher attrition rates, and lower chances of graduating than other students (Cross, 1973; Edwards, 1984; Harrison, 1976; Nyquist, 1979; Purdy, Eitzen, and Hufnagel, 1982; Sack and Thiel, 1979; Spivey and Jones, 1975; Webb, 1968).

Our research, which also finds a negative relationship, extends previous studies in several ways. First, we show that although most college athletes ultimately become disillusioned with and detached from academics, many begin their college careers idealistically, caring about academics and intending to graduate. Second, we show that the structure of college athletics fosters the academic deindividuation of athletes. We trace the stages through which athletes progress as they become socialized to their position in the university environment and learn its structural characteristics. We describe how their academic goals and behavior become increasingly influenced by their athletic involvement. The initial academic aspirations of freshman athletes are considerably varied, but these various individual ideals gradually

SOURCE: "From Idealism to Pragmatic Detachment: The Academic Performance of College Athletes" by Peter Adler and Patricia A. Adler. From *Sociology of Education* 58, pp. 241–250. Copyright © 1985 by the American Sociological Association. Reprinted by permission.

give way under the force of the structural conditions athletes encounter. Thus, by the time athletes complete their eligibility requirements, their academic attitudes and goals closely resemble each other's. This process, which reduces individual differences between athletes, is accompanied by collective academic detachment and diminished academic performance. Third, using a longitudinal analysis of process and change, made possible by our method of data collection, we show the influence of interconnecting factors on athletes' progression through college. This is the first systematic participant-observation study of college athletics. Such an in-depth, ethnographic investigation of this area (suggested by Coakley, 1982; Fine, 1979; Loy, McPherson, and Kenyon, 1978; Purdy, Eitzen, and Hufnagel, 1982) is useful for two reasons: (1) it enables us to determine whether athletic participation hinders or enhances academic performance, and (2) it reveals the factors and processes that produce this relationship.

We begin by discussing the setting in which this study was conducted and our involvement with members of the scene. We then examine the athletes' academic attitudes, goals, and involvement in their first months on campus. Next, we analyze their involvement in three spheres of university life—athletic, social, and classroom—and the impact of this involvement on their academic attitudes and performance. Last, we discuss the series of pragmatic adjustments they forge, which reflect the gradual erosion of their earlier academic goals and idealism. We conclude by offering a structural analysis of athletes' experiences within the university, which shows how and why they become progressively alienated and detached from academics. We suggest several educational and athletic policies that might help to ameliorate this situation.

METHODS AND SETTING

The Research

Over a four-year period (1980–1984), we conducted a participant-observation study of a major college basketball team. We used team field research strategies (Douglas, 1976) and differentiated, multiperspectival roles to enhance our data gathering and analysis. I (first author) was initially granted access to the team because the coaches became interested in our earlier works on the sociology of sport (Adler and Adler, 1978; Adler, 1981). After reading these and talking with me, they perceived me as an expert who could provide valuable counsel on interpersonal, organizational, and academic matters. Although college and professional sports settings are generally characterized by secrecy and an extreme sensitivity to the insider-outsider distinction (see Jonassohn, Turowetz, and Gruneau, 1981), I gradually gained the trust of significant gatekeepers, particularly the head coach, and was granted the status and privileges of an assistant coach. As the "team sociologist," my primary duty was to informally counsel players on social, academic, and personal matters and help them make the adjustment to college life and athletics. This role allowed me to become especially close to the athletes, who came to me with their problems, worries, or disgruntlements. Becoming an active member (Adler and Adler, 1987) and interacting with other members on a daily basis was also the only way I could penetrate the inner sanctum and achieve the type of rapport and trust necessary for the study.[1]

The second author assumed the outsider role, "debriefing" me when I returned from the setting, looking for sociological patterns in the data, and ensuring that I retained a sociological perspective on my involvement. She helped me conduct a series of intensive, taped interviews with 7 of the coaches and with the 38 basketball players who passed through the program during the four years.[2] She also helped construct the final analysis and written reports.

The Setting

The research was conducted at a medium-size (6,000 students) private university (hereafter referred to as "the University") in the mid-south-central portion of the United States. Most of the students were white, suburban, and middle class. The University, which was striving to become one of the finer private universities in the region, had fairly rigorous academic standards. The athletic department, as a whole, had a very successful recent history: The women's golf team was ranked in the top three nationally, the football team had won their conference in each of the previous four seasons, and the basketball team was ranked in the top forty of Division I NCAA schools and in the top twenty for most of two seasons. They had played in postseason tournaments every year, and in four complete seasons they had won approximately four times as many games as they had lost. Players were generally recruited from the surrounding region. Most of them came from the lower and middle classes, and 70 percent of them were black. In general, the basketball program represented what Coakley (1982) and Frey (1982) have termed big-time college athletics. Although it could not compare to the upper echelon of established basketball dynasties or to the really large athletic programs that wield enormous recruiting and operating budgets, its recent success has compensated for its small size and lack of historical tradition. The University's basketball program could best be described as up-and-coming. Because the basketball team (along with other teams in the athletic department) was ranked nationally and sent graduating members into the professional leagues, the entire athletic milieu was imbued with a sense of seriousness and purpose.

ACADEMIC EXPECTATIONS

Contrary to the recent negative thought, noted earlier, most of the athletes we observed entered the University feeling idealistic about their impending academic experience and optimistic about their likelihood of graduating. Their idealistic orientation and aspirations derived from several sources. First, they had received numerous cultural messages that a college education would enhance their ability to be successful in our society (cf. Semyonov and Yuchtman-Yaar, 1981). These messages were reinforced by their families, their most outspoken significant others. One sophomore described his family's involvement in his academic career: "When my mom calls she always asks me, first, 'How you feelin',' second, 'How you doin' in school?' She won't even let me talk 'bout basketball 'til she hear I'm doin' okay in school. She always be thinkin' 'bout my future and wantin' me to get that degree." College coaches also reinforced these messages. During recruitment, the coaches stressed the positive aspects of a college education and the importance of graduating (cf. Cross, 1973). The athletes accepted the rhetoric of these sports personnel (what Tannenbaum and Noah [1959] called "sportuguese"), but they never really considered what a higher education entailed. Thus, a third factor fostering their optimism about academics was their naïve assumption that after attending college for four years they would automatically get a degree. They never anticipated the amount or kind of academic work they would have to do to earn that degree. Many of them had not taken a sequence of college preparatory courses in high school.[3] Thus, their optimism was based largely on their "successful" academic careers in high school ("I graduated high school, didn't I?") and on their belief that as college athletes they would be academically pampered ("I heard you can get breaks on grades because you're an athlete"). Arriving freshmen commonly held the following set of prior expectations about their future academic performance: (1) they would go to classes and do the work (more broadly conceived as "putting the time in"); (2) they would graduate and get a degree; and (3) there would be no problem.

Of the entering athletes we observed, 47 percent ($n = 18$) requested placement in preprofessional majors in the colleges of business, engineering, or arts and sciences, indicating their initially high academic aspirations and expectations. One sophomore gave the rationale behind his choice of a major: "You come in, you want to make money. How do you make money? You go into business. How do you go into business? You major in business, and you end up having to take these business courses, and you really don't think about it. It sounds okay." Despite warnings from coaches and older teammates that it would be difficult to complete this coursework and play ball, they felt they could easily handle the demands.

Another group of freshmen, who had no specific career aspirations beyond playing professional basketball (45 percent, $n = 17$), were enrolled by their coaches in more "manageable," athletic-related majors such as physical education or recreation.[4] However, most of these individuals believed that they too would get a degree. Though they had no clear academic goals, they figured that they would somehow make it through satisfactorily. Only a small number of individuals in our sample (8 percent, $n = 3$) entered college with no aspirations of getting a degree. Either these individuals were such highly touted high school players that they entered college expecting to turn professional before their athletic eligibility expired, or they were uninterested in academics but had no other plans. Their main concern, then, was to remain eligible to play ball. But they never seriously considered the possibility that they would be barred from competition because of low grades.

In their first few months on campus, athletes' early idealism was strengthened. During these summer months, the coaches repeatedly stressed the importance of "getting that piece of paper." Once the school year began, freshman athletes attended required study halls nightly, were told how to get tutors, and were constantly reminded by the coach to go to class. One freshman, interviewed during the preseason, indicated his acceptance of the coaches' rhetoric: "If I can use my basketball ability to open up the door to get an education, hopefully I can use my degree to open up the door to get a good job. . . . I think that's really important to Coach, too, 'cause in practice he always be mentioning how important the degree is an' everything."

Although these athletes unquestionably cared more about their athletic and social lives than their academic performance, getting through school, at least in the abstract, was still important to them. For most, this period of early idealism lasted until the end of their freshman year. After this time, their naïve, early idealism gradually became replaced by disappointment and growing cynicism as they realized how difficult it was to keep up with their schoolwork. They encountered unexpected problems in the articulation of the athletic, social, and academic spheres of the University.

ATHLETIC EXPERIENCES

A major difference athletes encountered in moving from high school to college lay in the size of the athletic sphere. In high school, athletics was primary to their self-identities; but in college, it played an even more central role in their lives. It dominated all facets of their existence, including their academic involvement and performance.

A primary change in their athletic involvement was rooted in the *professionalization* of the sport. Upon entering college, freshman athletes immediately noticed its commercialization (cf. Coakley, 1982; Eitzen, 1979; Hoch, 1972; Sack, 1977; Underwood, 1980). They were no longer playing for enjoyment. This was big business ("there's a lotta money ridin' on us"). As a result, basketball changed from a recreation to an occupation (cf. Ingham, 1975). The occupational dimensions of the sport and their desire to perform well intensified the pressure to win (cf. Odenkirk, 1981; Underwood, 1980). A senior described this emphasis on winning: "In college the coaches be a lot more concerned on winning and the money comin' in. If they don't win, they may get the boot, and so they pass that pressure on to us athletes. I go to bed every night and I be thinkin' 'bout basketball. That's what college athletics do to you. It take over you mind."

Professionalization also brought with it the fame and glamour of media attention. During the season, athletes were regularly in the newspaper and on television and were greeted as celebrities whenever they ventured off campus. Overall, then, the professionalization of college athletics drew athletes' focus to this arena and riveted it there.

Playing on the basketball team also demanded a larger share of athletes' *time* in college than it had in high school. In addition to the three hours of practice daily ("two-a-days" on weekends during the preseason), players were expected to watch films of other teams, to be available for team meetings, to return to their dorm rooms by curfew, and to leave the campus for two to five days at a time for road trips.[5] They also had to spend a certain amount of their time with athletically related others: the media, fans, and boosters (rich businesspersons who contributed money and wanted to feel close to the program). This involvement often conflicted with potential academic time: Afternoon practice conflicted with the required courses or labs in certain majors, games and road trips conflicted with the time athletes needed for exams and term papers, and booster functions cut into their discretionary time. By the end of their first year, most athletes acknowledged that their athletic-related activities affected their academic performance. As one senior explained: "We got to go two-a-days, get up as early as the average student, go to school, then go to practice for three hours like nothing you have ever strained. . . . It's brutal 'cause you be so tired. Fatigue is what makes a lot of those guys say 'Chuck it, I'm goin' to sleep.' You don't feel like sittin' there an' readin' a book, an' you not goin' comprehend that much anyway 'cause you so tired." Fatigue (cf. Edwards, 1984) and restricted time for studying caused many athletes to give up and cease caring about their academic work. Thus, rather than use the little free time they had to catch up on their studies, they usually chose to spend it socializing or just sleeping.

Athletes' academic performance was also affected by *coaches' intervention* in their academic lives. Assistant coaches handled academic matters for the athletes, declaring their majors, registering them for courses, adjusting their schedules, and periodically contacting their professors (to monitor their progress). Athletes, therefore, were largely uninvolved in academic decision-making and did not interact directly with professors, academic counselors, or academic administrators. As a result, they failed to develop the knowledge, initiative, or, in many cases, the interest to handle these academic matters themselves. As one sophomore stated, "The day before class you go up to the office and they hand you a card that got your schedule all filled out on it. You don't say nothin' or think nothin' 'bout it, you just go. And it kinda make you feel like you not involved in it, 'cause you don't have nothin' to do with it. Like it's they's job, not yours."

Because the coaches managed these administrative matters, the athletes developed a false sense of security, a feeling that someone was looking out for them academically and would make sure that they were given another chance, a feeling that they could foul up and not have to pay the consequences. They believed that their coaches dominated their professors and the administrators, that they would be "taken care of" academically, and that they need not involve themselves in this arena. This also led them to distance themselves from their academics and to diminish their effort.

Having formed this belief, many athletes were surprised to discover, usually sometime during their sophomore or junior year, that this overseeing and management extended to administrative areas only. Coaches placed them in their courses, but they could not guarantee them special breaks. Athletes then realized, often too late, that they were responsible for attending classes and completing their assignments on their own and that they had to do the same work that other students did to pass their courses. Many athletes were shepherded through high school; therefore, they were ill-equipped to assume responsibilities in college and often failed to fulfill them.

Finally, the athletes received greater *reinforcement* for athletic performance than for academic performance. No one closely monitored their academic behavior, but they were carefully watched at games, practices, booster functions, and on road trips. The celebrity and social status they derived from the media, boosters, and fans brought them immediate gratification, which the academic realm, with its emphasis on future rewards, could not offer.

With a few exceptions, athletes' experiences within the academic realm brought neither close contact nor positive reinforcement. Like many other college students, athletes generally found their professors aloof and uninterested. One freshman gave his impressions of college professors:

> At my high school back home, the teachers would make sure everyone done the reading before we went on to the next subject. The teachers really cared if the students got behind, so sometimes they would teach individually. But here, by the next time the class meets, they ask if anyone has any questions, and if no one says anything, then most of them would give a pop quiz. I cannot really say the teachers care here, because if you get behind it's your problem, not theirs.

Given the paucity of contact with the faculty, the lack of reinforcement within the academic realm, and the omnipresence of the coaches, media, fans, and boosters, who provided both positive and negative feedback on daily athletic performance, it became easier for athletes to turn away from academics and concentrate their efforts on sport.

SOCIAL EXPERIENCES

The athletes' social experiences also affected their academic performance. Their social lives at the University were dominated by their relationships with other athletes. They had initially expected to derive both friendship and status recognition from a wide variety of students, both athletes and nonathletes, as they had in high school (cf. Coleman, 1961; Cusick, 1973; Eitzen, 1975; Rehberg and Schafer, 1968; Spady, 1970). But instead of being socially integrated, they found themselves isolated (cf. Antonelli, 1970). They were isolated geographically because they were housed in the athletes' dorm in a remote part of campus. They were cut off temporally by the demands of their practices, games, study halls, and booster functions. They were isolated culturally by their racial and socioeconomic differences from the rest of the student body. They were isolated physically by their size and build, which many students, especially women, found intimidating. A freshman described his feelings of social alienation:

> This school is nothing like I thought it would be when I left home. The social life is very different and I have to adjust to it. A main problem for me are the white people. Where I grew up, all my friends were black, so I really don't know how to act toward whites. Here, when I speak to some of them, they just give me a fake smile. I really can't understand the people here because this is college and everyone should have a good time socially.

Since they had few opportunities to interact with nonathletes, they formed extremely strong social bonds among themselves. Housed together in a dorm reserved almost exclusively for male athletes (primarily football and basketball players), they were bonded together into a reference group and peer subculture. Relations within this group were especially cohesive because they lived, played, and traveled together.

Within the dorm, athletes exchanged information about various individuals and how to handle certain situations. This helped them form common attitudes and beliefs about their athletic, social, and academic experiences. The peer subculture thus provided them with a set of norms and values that guided their interpretations and behavior within these three realms.

One of the most predominant influences of the peer subculture was its anti-intellectual and anti-academic character (cf. Coleman, 1960; Sack, 1977). Typically, dorm conversation centered on the athletic or social dimensions of the athletes' lives; little reference was made to academic, cultural, or intellectual pursuits (cf. Meggysey, 1971; Shaw, 1972). As one junior remarked, "If a athlete was living in the dorm with just ordinary people, what do you think they'll be talkin' about? Ordinary things. But you got all athletes here. What are they goin' be talkin' about? It won't be Reaganomics, believe me. It'll definitely be *Sports Illustrated*." Separating athletes from other students thus made their athletic reality dominant and distanced them from any academic inclinations they may have had. The same athlete continued:

> The two images are set apart because one side of us is, "My momma send me to school to be an engineer, and in order to be an engineer I gots to go to class every day and study hard," and the other side is "I come to school to play basketball. I didn't come to school to study that hard." So to keep those two images apart, to keep you thinking basketball night and day, they puts you in with all these other jocks dreamin' in they dream worlds.

The athletes' peer subculture also subverted academic orientations by discouraging them from exerting effort in academics. In fact, individuals who displayed too much interest, effort, or success in academics were often ridiculed, as one player described: "When most of the other guys are making D's and F's, if I work hard and get a B on a test, if I go back to the dorm and they all see I got a B, then they goin' snap on [make fun of] me. So most of the guys, they don't try. They all act like it's a big joke." Like the Chicano subculture Horowitz (1983) observed, the athletes' peer subculture valued education in the abstract, yet the commitments valued by the athletes' subculture conflicted with the commitments necessary to make that value carry over into practical reality. Their peers thus provided them with excuses and justifications that legitimated their poor academic performance and neutralized the importance of this realm in their self-identities.

CLASSROOM EXPERIENCES

Athletes' attitudes toward academics and their effort and performance were also affected by the difficulties and disillusionments they encountered in the classroom. Athletes believed that many professors labeled them as jocks because they looked different from most of the other students, they were surrounded in their classes by other athletes, and they were identified by coaches early in the semester to the professors as athletes. They perceived, then, that professors treated them differently from the general student body. On the one hand, because of the widely held subcultural lore that as college athletes they would have special privileges and because of the important and visible role they played at the University, they commonly thought that professors would accord them greater tolerance—i.e., extra tutoring sessions, relaxed deadlines, relaxed academic standards (cf. Raney, Knapp, and Small,

1983). This perception was fostered by their placement, especially in their freshman year, in courses taught by sympathetic faculty members who tried to give them extra attention or assistance. Because of these placements, athletes often began college thinking that academics would not be a major concern. On the other hand, athletes also encountered a number of less sympathetic professors who they thought stereotyped them as dumb jocks or cocky athletes. In these cases they "rejected the rejectors" (Sykes and Matza, 1957), using persecution as a rationale for disengaging from academics. One player discussed his experiences with professors:

> Some are goin' help you, if they can, and you can always tell who they are 'cause you got a bunch o' athletes in your class. Some try to make it harder on you. They're out to get you 'cause they feel like you living like a king and it shouldn't be that way. With those jerks, it don't matter how hard you try. They gonna flunk you just 'cause you a athlete.

This differential treatment served to reinforce their perceptions that they were athletes more than students. Therefore, when they returned to their dorm rooms at night, exhausted and sore from practicing, it became easier for them to rationalize, procrastinate, and "fritter" (Bernstein, 1978) their time away instead of studying.

Athletes also became uninterested in academics because of the *content* of their classes. Many individuals placed in physical education or recreation courses, even those who were fairly uninterested in academics from the beginning, felt that their courses lacked academic or practical merit and were either comical, demeaning, or both. One sophomore articulated the commonly held view: "How could I get into this stuff? They got me takin' nutrition, mental retardation, square dancing, and camp counseling. I thought I was goin' learn something here. It's a bunch o' b.s."

When athletes enrolled in more advanced or demanding courses to fulfill their requirements, they often found themselves unequipped for the type of work expected. Because of their inadequate academic backgrounds, poor study habits, tight schedules, peer distractions, and waning motivation, the athletes often became frustrated and bored. Their anticipated positive feedback from academics was replaced by a series of disappointments from low grades and failed classes. One player described how his failures made him feel inadequate and uncertain: "When I first came here I thought I'd be goin' to class all the time and I'd study and that be it. But I sure didn't think it meant studyin' all the time. Back in high school you just be memorizin' things, but that's not what they want here. Back in high school I thought I be a pretty good student, but now I don't know."

Athletes' experiences in the classroom were thus very different from their preconceptions. The work was harder and they were not taken care of to the extent they had imagined. Because of the intense competition in the athletic arena, they became obsessed with success (Harris and Eitzen, 1978). Their frequent academic failures (or, at best, mediocre grades) led to their embarrassment and despair, which caused them to engage in role-distancing (Ball, 1976) and to abandon some of the self-investment they had made in their academic performance. To be safe, it was better not to try than to try and not succeed. As we noted earlier, this posture was reinforced by their peer subculture.

ACADEMIC ADJUSTMENTS

As college athletes progressed through school, they changed their perspectives and priorities, re-evaluating the feasibility of their original optimistic, albeit casually formed, academic goals. This caused them to effect a series of *pragmatic adjustments* in their academic attitudes, efforts, and goals.

First, whenever possible, athletes externalized the blame for their academic failures. Failures, for instance, were not caused by their own inadequacies or lack of effort but by boring professors, stupid courses, exhaustion, the coaches' demands, or injury. This allowed them to accept the frequent signs of failure more easily and served as an important neutralizing mechanism for their competitiveness.

More importantly, athletes re-examined their academic goals. Because of their initially optimistic expectations, some athletes had declared majors based on career choices that sounded good to them or their parents (e.g., doctor, teacher, engineer, or businessman). About one-fourth of the individuals who began in preprofessional majors stayed in these majors all the way through college and graduated.[6] Nevertheless, these individuals generally expended less effort and had less success than they had initially anticipated. Though they graduated in their original major, their academic performance was largely characterized by an attitude of getting by; in most cases, they achieved only the minimum GPA and took the minimum number of hours required for eligibility. One junior described how his attitude toward academics had changed during his years at college: "If I was a student like most other students I could do well, but when you play the calibre of ball we do, you just can't be an above-average student. What I strive for now is just to be an average student. My best GPA was 2.75. You just don't find the time to do all the reading."

More commonly, athletes in preprofessional majors found that a more concrete adjustment was necessary. The remaining three quarters of this group dropped out of preprofessional programs and enrolled in more manageable majors. This shift indicated that they had abandoned both their academic idealism and their earlier career goals. Nevertheless, they still maintained the goal of graduating, regardless of the major. As one player commented, "Look at George [a former player]. He was a rec major, but now he's got a great job in sales, working for some booster. It don't matter what you major in as long as you keep your nose clean and get that piece of paper."

Athletes who began their college careers with lower academic aspirations, majoring in physical education or recreation, made corresponding adjustments. Approximately one-fifth of these athletes held onto their initial goal and graduated in one of these fields. But like the preprofessional majors, they did not perform as well as they had planned. The other four-fifths realized, usually relatively late, that their chances of graduating from college were slight. This genuinely distressed them, because getting a degree had become both a hope and an expectation. They shifted their orientation, then, toward maintaining their athletic eligibility. A junior's remarks illustrate how this shift affected his attitude toward academics:

> I used to done thought I was goin' to school, but now I know it's not for real. . . .
> I don't have no academic goals no more. A player a coach is counting on, that's all he think about is ball. That's what he signed to do. So what you gotta do is show up, show your smilin' face, try as hard as you can. Don't just lay over in the room. That's all the coach can ask. Or else you may not find yourself playing next year.

By their senior year, when they had completed their final eligibility requirements, many members of this last group entirely abandoned their concern with their academic performance.[7] As one senior put it, "I just be waitin', man. I be waitin' for my shot at the NBA. I be thinking about that all the time. Once the season is over, I be splittin'. I don't see no reason to go to classes no more."

As a result of their experiences at the University, athletes grew increasingly cynical about and uninterested in academics. They accepted their marginal status and lowered their academic interest, effort, and goals. They progressively detached themselves from caring about or identifying themselves with this sphere.

DISCUSSION

We have just described how college athletes progress from an early phase of idealism about their impending academic experiences to an eventual state of pragmatic detachment. The initial differences among the athletes in academic aptitudes, skills, and expectations eventually erode, causing even motivated freshmen to slip into a pattern of diminished interest and effort. The universality of this transformation (albeit with variations) suggests that there is something endemic to universities with big-time athletic programs that significantly affects athletes' orientations and behavior. An overview of the structural characteristics and embedded processes athletes encounter can help explain how and why their behavior changes.

First, athletes are overwhelmed by the demands and intensity of the athletic realm, which absorbs their concentration and commitment. They react by willingly entering the vortex of media celebrity and fantasies about future professional athletic careers. Second, athletes find themselves socially isolated from other students because of their geographic and temporal separation and their physical and cultural differences. In this way, athletes resemble Simmel's strangers—i.e., individuals who are full-fledged members of the group yet at the same time are outside of the group (cited in Wolff, 1950:402–408). By being part of, but not like, the larger student body, athletes experience the tension between nearness and distance. This heightens their sensitivity to their strangeness and focuses their attention on those elements they do not share with other students. As a result, the internal cohesion of their peer subculture becomes strengthened and their self-identities become more firmly anchored within it. Finally, for many athletes, the gap between their academic abilities and the university's expectations brings failure, frustration, and alienation. The peer subculture exacerbates the situation by devaluing academic involvement and neutralizing academic failure. Athletes respond by gradually withdrawing from their commitment to academics.

These structural factors are ultimately much stronger predictors of athletes' academic success than any of their initial individual characteristics. Their early academic involvement varies according to their goals, intelligence, talents, parents' attitudes, and other individual attributes, but the common structure of their experiences erodes many of these distinctions. Some athletes excel in all areas of college, and their success is well-publicized (cf. Looney, 1984). But most college athletes become disillusioned with academics by the time their athletic eligibility expires. This combination of structural factors influencing athletes' behavior, admittedly an extreme example, could also explain the academic careers of other students. Students who are distracted by an outside interest (i.e., a job or an avocation), who belong to a peer group that de-emphasizes the value of academics (i.e., a fraternity), and who become frustrated in the academic realm are likely to be academically unsuccessful in college.

The transformation athletes undergo corresponds to Goffman's (1959) conception of occupational role progression, in which the attitudes of persons socialized to a new social status (here, college athlete) evolve from belief to disbelief. This process begins with the learning and internalization of charter values. For college athletes, this occurs during the final year of high school and the freshman year of college, when they form moderately high aspirations and expectations about their academic futures. A period of desocialization then ensues, in which athletes progressively realize the structural constraints framing their situation. They become unable to accommodate the myriad, often conflicting, expectations and demands confronting them. As a result, they make choices and establish priorities that compromise their early idealism. Expediency thus supplants a concern for academics (Ingham and Smith, 1974), leading them to engage in role-distancing and to forge pragmatic adaptations that undermine their academic performance.

This in-depth investigation confirms the findings and interpretations of those studies positing a negative relationship between athletic participation and academic performance at universities with big-time athletic programs. We extend these analyses by showing that college athletes' academic performance is multifaceted and is determined less by demographic characteristics and high school experiences than by the structure of their college experiences. Athletes progress through a pattern of experiences, which first raises their hopes and then diminishes their opportunities for attaining the professed goals of the educational system.

Given the revenue that athletic programs generate, it may be unrealistic to expect this structure to change dramatically. However, there are several policy implications that can be derived from this research. First, athletes should be sheltered, as much as possible, from the enticing whirlwind of celebrity. This can best be accomplished by reinstituting the ban on freshman eligibility. Second, athletic dorms should be abolished and athletes should be better integrated into the larger university culture. In these ways we can begin to transform college athletes from strangers into neighbors. Third, athletes should be provided with more academic role models and advisors. The current arrangement, in which athletic personnel masquerade as academic advisors, functions counterproductively to the academic goals of the university. Only after these changes are made can college athletes begin to meet the goals of the educational system.

NOTES

1. For a more detailed discussion of the methodological issues involved in this research, see Adler (1984).
2. Some individuals were interviewed several times, at various stages of their socialization process.
3. Several sociological studies have noted that the admission standards for athletes are lower than those for the general student body, leading to the admission of academically marginal, ill-prepared students (Edwards, 1984; Purdy, Eitzen, and Hufnagel, 1982; Sack, 1977; Shapiro, 1984; Spady, 1970).
4. This figure includes a small number of athletes who decided, usually during their sophomore or junior year, not to play professionally but to go into an athletically related occupation such as coaching.
5. Edwards (1984:7) has estimated that during the season, basketball players spend fifty hours a week preparing for, participating in, recovering from, and traveling to games.
6. These figures represent rough estimates based on the number of individuals who graduated, the number of individuals who used up their eligibility, and projections for individuals still in the program. They are intended to be suggestive rather than exact.
7. Ironically, however, even the marginal players never abandoned their dreams of making it in the NBA.

REFERENCES

Adler, P., *Momentum: A Theory of Social Action.* Beverly Hills, CA: Sage, 1981.

Adler, P., "The sociologist as celebrity: The role of the media in field research." *Qualitative Sociology* (1984) 7:310-26.

Adler, P. and P. A. Adler, "The role of momentum in sport." *Urban Life* (1978) 7:153-76.

Adler, P. A. and P. Adler, *Joining the Crowd: Membership Roles in Field Research.* Beverly Hills, CA: Sage, 1987.

Antonelli, F., "Psychological problems of top-level athletes." *International Journal of Sport Psychology* (1970) 1:34-39.

Ball, D., "Failure in sport." *American Sociological Review* (1976) 41:726-39.

Bernstein, S., "Getting it done: Notes on student fritters." Pp. 17-23 in J. Lofland (ed.), *Interaction in Everyday Life.* Beverly Hills, CA: Sage, 1978.

Coakley, J. J., *Sport in Society,* 2nd ed. St. Louis: Mosby, 1982.

Coleman, J. S., "Adolescent subculture and academic achievement." *American Journal of Sociology* (1960) 65:337-47.

Coleman, J. S., *The Adolescent Society.* New York: Free Press, 1961.

Cross, H. M., "The college athlete and the institution." *Law and Contemporary Problems* (1973) 38:151-71.

Cusick, P. A., *Inside High School.* New York: Holt, Rinehart and Winston, 1973.

Douglas, J. D., *Investigative Social Research.* Beverly Hills, CA: Sage, 1976.

Edwards, H., "The collegiate arms race: Origins and implications of the 'Rule 48' controversy." *Journal of Sport and Social Issues* (1984) 8:4-22.

Eitzen, D. S., "Athletics in the status system of male adolescents: A replication of Coleman's 'The Adolescent Society'." *Adolescence* (1975) 10:268-76.

Eitzen, D. S., "Sport and deviance." Pp. 73-89 in D. S. Eitzen (ed.), *Sport in Contemporary Society.* New York: St. Martin's, 1979.

Fine, G. A., "Preadolescent socialization through organized athletics: The construction of moral meanings in little league baseball." Pp. 79-105 in M. Krotee (ed.), *Dimensions of Sport Sociology.* Corning, NY: Leisure Press, 1979.

Frey, J. H., "Boosterism, scarce resources and institutional control: The future of American intercollegiate athletics." *International Review of Sport Sociology* (1982) 17:53-70.

Goffman, E., *The Presentation of Self in Everyday Life.* Garden City, NY: Anchor Doubleday, 1959.

Hanks, M. P. and B. K. Eckland, "Athletics and social participation in the educational attainment process." *Sociology of Education* (1976) 49:271-94.

Harris, D. S. and D. S. Eitzen, "The consequences of failure in sport." *Urban Life* (1978) 7:177-88.

Harrison, J. H., "Intercollegiate football participation and academic achievement." Paper presented at the Annual Meeting of the Southwestern Sociological Association, Dallas, 1976.

Henschen, K. P. and D. Fry, "An archival study of the relationship of intercollegiate athletic participation and graduation." *Sociology of Sport Journal* (1984) 1:52-56.

Hoch, P., *Rip Off the Big Game.* New York: Doubleday, 1972.

Horowitz, R., *Honor and the American Dream.* New Brunswick, NJ: Rutgers University Press, 1983.

Ingham, A. G., "Occupational subcultures in the work world of sport." Pp. 337-89 in D. W. Ball and J. W. Loy (eds.), *Sport and Social Order: Contributions to the Sociology of Sport.* Reading, MA: Addison-Wesley, 1975.

Ingham, A. G. and M. D. Smith, "The social implications of the interaction between spectators and athletes." Pp. 189-224 in J. Wilmore (ed.), *Exercise and Sport Science Reviews,* Vol. 2. New York: Academic Press, 1974.

Jonassohn, K., A. Turowetz, and R. Gruneau, "Research methods in the sociology of sport." *Qualitative Sociology* (1981) 4:179-97.

Looney, D. S., "He came out picture perfect." *Sports Illustrated* (1984) 60, 22:44-50.

Loy, J. W., B. D. McPherson, and G. Kenyon, *Sport and Social Systems*. Reading, MA: Addison-Wesley, 1978.

Meggysey, D., *Out of Their League*. Berkeley, CA: Ramparts, 1971.

Michener, J. A., *Sports in America*. New York: Random House, 1976.

Nyquist, E. B., "Wine, women, and money: College athletics today and tomorrow." *Educational Review* (1979) 60:376-93.

Odenkirk, J. E., "Intercollegiate athletics: Big business or sport?" *Academe* (1981) 67:62-66.

Purdy, D. A., D. S. Eitzen, and R. Hufnagel, "Are athletes also students? The educational attainment of college athletes." *Social Problems* (1982) 29:439-48.

Raney, J., T. Knapp, and M. Small, "Pass one for the gipper: Student athletes and university coursework." *Arena Review* (1983) 7:53-59.

Rehberg, R. A. and W. E. Schafer, "Participation in interscholastic athletics and college expectations." *American Journal of Sociology* (1968) 73:732-40.

Sack, A. L., "Big time college football. Whose free ride?" *Quest* (1977) 27:87-97.

Sack, A. L. and R. Thiel, "College football and social mobility: A case study of Notre Dame football players." *Sociology of Education* (1979) 52:60-66.

Semyonov, M. and E. Yuchtman-Yaar, "Professional sports as an alternative channel of social mobility." *Sociological Inquiry* (1981) 1:47-53.

Shapiro, B., "Intercollegiate athletic participation and academic achievement: A case study of Michigan State University student-athletes." *Sociology of Sport Journal* (1984) 1:46-51.

Shaw, G., *Meat on the Hoof*. New York: St. Martin's, 1972.

Spady, W. G., "Lament for the letterman: Effects of peer status and extra-curricular activities on goals and achievements." *American Journal of Sociology* (1970) 75:680-702.

Spivey, D. and T. A. Jones, "Intercollegiate athletic servitude: A case study of the black Illinois student-athletes, 1931-1967." *Social Science Quarterly* (1975) 55:939-47.

Sykes, G. M. and D. Matza, "Techniques of neutralization." *American Sociological Review* (1957) 22:664-70.

Tannenbaum, P. M. and J. E. Noah, "Sportuguese: A study of sports page communication." *Journalism Quarterly* (1959) 36:163-70.

Underwood, J., "The writing is on the wall." *Sports Illustrated* (1980) 52, 21:36-71.

Webb, H., "Social backgrounds of college athletes." Paper presented at the Annual Meeting of the American Alliance for Health, Physical Education, and Recreation, St. Louis, 1968.

Wolff, K. H. (ed. and trans.), *The Sociology of Georg Simmel*. New York: Free Press, 1950.

23. *Racism in College Sports: Prospects for the Year 2000*

D. STANLEY EITZEN

INTRODUCTION

The United States has never lived up to its promise of social justice for all. Social justice for African-Americans has also fallen short, way short, in the college sports world. This is especially ironic because (a) sport is one arena where achievement, not ascribed status, should be the fundamental criterion for participation and reward; and (b) colleges and universities claim to hold progressive ideals, leading by example and by persuasive argument, one would hope, to accomplish a climate of positive race relations in higher education and in society.

THE CONTEMPORARY CONTEXT FOR AFRICAN-AMERICANS IN BIG-TIME COLLEGE SPORTS

The Societal Context

The evidence is clear and consistent that African-Americans are disadvantaged in the United States (information for this section is taken from Rainie, 1991; Eitzen & Baca Zinn, 1991, pp. 286–296). A few examples make this point:

- The median wealth for African-American families is one tenth that of white families.
- The unemployment rate for African-Americans is twice that for whites.
- Overall, African-Americans earn an average of just 59 cents for every dollar earned by whites. This is explained in part by the lower educational level of African-Americans, but when controlling for education, whites still make more. For example, well-educated young African-Americans earn only about 85% of what their white counterparts earn.

SOURCE: "Racism in College Sports: Prospects for the Year 2000" by D. Stanley Eitzen. From *Racism in College Athletics: The African-American Athlete's Experience* by D. D. Brooks and R. C. Althouse (eds.), pp. 269–285. Copyright © 1993 by Fitness Information Technology. Reprinted by permission.

- African-Americans experience discrimination in jobs (getting them, keeping them, and advancing within them).
- Thirty percent of African-Americans live in racial isolation in segregated neighborhoods. Housing is where researchers find the most persistent open discrimination.
- About one-third of African-Americans attend public schools that are "intensely segregated," that is, 90% or more black.
- About one-third of African-Americans live below the government's official poverty line. From two to three million poor African-Americans are locked in an underclass of extreme deprivation.

Although some African-Americans are economically successful, many are not. The accrued disadvantages stemming from discrimination lead to poorer life chances for most. For example:

- Whites live about ten years longer than do African-Americans; black babies are nearly twice as likely as white babies to die within the first year; 22% of the African-American population is without health insurance compared to 14% of the white population.
- One out of four black men between ages 20 and 29 is under the jurisdiction of the criminal justice system (in prison, on parole, or on probation), which is higher than the proportion of African-American men this age in college.
- Sixty-one percent of African-American children are born out of wedlock (up from 23.6% in 1965). This is a consequence, according to William J. Wilson (1987), of wage discrimination and joblessness. That is, black fathers who are employed are more likely to marry than are those who are unemployed. Similarly, men with higher incomes are more likely to be married than are men with lower incomes.
- Urban, poor, African-American neighborhoods are often saturated with crime, drugs, and dysfunctional schools.

The societal context is characterized by growing racial polarization. Race relations are growing hotter rather than cooler. Racially motivated attacks on individuals and organizations have increased in the past decade. The membership of the Ku Klux Klan and other white supremacist groups is on the rise. Racial tensions are often caused by deteriorating economic conditions—lack of jobs, housing, and other resources—that lead to minority scapegoating on the part of whites. They are also fueled by the new patterns of immigration that are changing the racial composition of society.

Bigotry is not confined to white working-class or poor settings. Racist acts are becoming widespread on college campuses (Williams, 1992). Instances at MIT; University of Michigan; University of California–Berkeley; and on other campuses reveal an extensive problem of intolerance in settings where tolerance is essential to the pursuit of knowledge.

Contemporary racial division has been exacerbated by reactionary government policies. Conservative economic strategies during the Reagan and Bush years accelerated the economic decline of racial minorities. These strategies involved severe cutbacks in social programs as well as the appointment of judges to the federal courts and the Supreme Court who favored the dismantling of civil rights legislation, especially affirmative action and other protections against discrimination for minorities.

Big-Time College Sport

Many economically, socially, and educationally disadvantaged African-American males are recruited from this environment to play football and basketball in big-time university athletic programs. These programs are big-business operations (the following is taken from Eitzen & Sage, 1993, ch. 6). Some have budgets exceeding $20 million (the average for an athletic program in the 106 football schools in Division IA is $12.5 million). In 1990 the schools in the bowl games divided $57 million. The annual incomes for some of the coaches (from salaries, bonuses, perks, endorsements, shoe contracts, and television and radio programs) approach $1 million. The NCAA's 1990–91 budget was $160.6 million. CBS agreed to pay the NCAA $1 billion over seven years ($143 million annually) for the television rights to the NCAA men's basketball tournament. Syracuse has a basketball arena that seats 50,000, which it sells out. The University of Florida rents skyboxes at its football games for $30,000 a year, with a minimum five-year lease. Each year, supporters of university athletic programs donate about $400 million.

These examples show that big-time college sport is a large-scale commercial entertainment enterprise. The success of programs at individual schools (and of coaches) depends on winning, interesting the media, and attracting spectators. This requires getting the best athletes and extracting the most from them. In many cases, this search for talent has led to abuses, such as illegal recruiting practices, alteration of transcripts, physical and psychological abuse of athletes, and exploitation of athletes (for a summary, see Sperber, 1990). William F. Reed (1990) of *Sports Illustrated* has characterized college basketball (and the description fits football as well) in these harsh, but accurate, terms:

> Every fan knows that underneath its shiny veneer of color, fun and excitement, college basketball is a sewer full of rats. Lift the manhole cover on the street of gold, and the odor will knock you down. Look at this season [1990]: The programs at North Carolina State, Florida, Illinois, Missouri, and Nevada–Las

Vegas—to cite only the most prominent examples—are up to their backboards in scandal.

> The misdeeds allegedly committed by college basketball programs today are the same stuff that has plagued the game for decades—buying players, cheating in academics, shaving points, etc. And the NCAA is powerless to stop it. Make a statement by coming down hard on a Kentucky or a Maryland, and what happens? Nothing, really. The filth merely oozes from another crack (p. 66).

These programs want winners, and if the past serves as a guide, we have not cared how they won. As John Underwood (1981) has characterized the situation:

> We've told them that it doesn't matter how clean they keep their programs. It doesn't matter what percentage of their athletes graduate or take a useful place in society. It doesn't even matter how well the coaches teach their sports. All that matters are the flashing scoreboard lights (p. 81).

Young men are recruited into this setting. Some athletes are recruited even though their high school records and test scores show they have little hope of educational success in college. At Tulane University, for example, in 1985 entering freshmen had average SAT scores of 1132, whereas the scores for athletes in football and men's basketball averaged 648 (Select Committee, 1986, p. 5), which was 52 points *below* the requirement of 700 later instituted by the NCAA in Proposition 48.

In the words of syndicated columnist George Will (1986):

> The worst scandal does not involve cash or convertibles. It involves slipping academically unqualified young men in the back doors of academic institutions, insulating them from academic expectations, wringing them dry of their athletic-commercial usefulness, then slinging them out the back door even less suited to society than they were when they entered. They are less suited because they spent four years acquiring the idea that they are exempt from normal standards (p. 84).

Some athletes, perhaps, are not in college for an education, viewing college, rather, only as a necessary avenue to the professional sport level (an unrealistic goal to all but very few). Those who want an education find that they have signed a contract that makes them an employee (not in the eyes of the NCAA, but an employee nonetheless), and the demands of sport come first. Achieving an education is incidental to the overriding objective of big-time sports (there are exceptions such as Notre Dame and Duke, but as exceptions they prove the rule). Since a primary concern of some coaches is the eligibility of their athletes, rather than the education of their athletes, the athletes are enrolled in phantom courses (correspondence or residence courses that give credit for no work or attendance) or in easy courses with professors sympathetic to the athletic department.

The research by Peter and Patricia Adler (1985; 1991) shows how the athletic experience actually tends to extinguish educational goals of the athletes. Adler and Adler found that most athletes entered the university feeling idealistic about their impending academic performance; that is, they were optimistic about graduating, and they considered ambitious majors. This idealism lasted until about the end of the first year, when it was replaced by disappointment and a growing cynicism as the athletes realized how difficult keeping up with their schoolwork would be. The athletic role came to dominate all facets of their existence. Coaches made huge demands on the time and commitment of their athletes. The athletes received greater positive reinforcement from their athletic performance than from their academic performance. They were isolated increasingly from the student body. They were segregated in an athletic dormitory. They were isolated culturally by their racial and socioeconomic differences from the rest of the students. They were even isolated from other students by their physical size, which some found intimidating. They interacted primarily with other athletes, and these peers tended to demean academics. In their first year they were given courses with sympathetic professors, but this changed as athletes moved through the university curriculum. The academic expectations escalated, and the athletes were unprepared. The resulting academic failure or, at best, mediocre academic performance led to embarrassment and despair. The typical response, according to the Adlers, was role distancing: "To be safe, it was better not to try than to try and not succeed" (1985, p. 247). This attitude, and the resulting behaviors, were reinforced by the peer subculture.

The noneducation and miseducation of college athletes is especially acute for African-Americans. Every study that has compared black athletes to their white counterparts has found black athletes less prepared for college and more likely to fulfill this prophecy in college: African-American athletes tend to enter college as marginal students and to leave the same way. Harry Edwards (1984) has argued that the black "dumb jock" is a social creation: "'Dumb jocks' are not born; they are systematically created" (p. 8).

This social construction results from several factors. First, black student-athletes must contend with two negative labels: the dumb athlete caricature and the dumb black stereotype. This double negative tends to result in a self-fulfilling prophecy as teachers, fellow students, and the athletes themselves assume low academic performance. Moreover, many African-Americans are ill-prepared for college because of their socioeconomic background, inadequate schools, and the special treatment often given athletic stars in junior high school and high school. This special treatment continues in college with professors who inflate grades, surrogate test takers, and coaches who intercede for student-athletes with the police when necessary. Thus, there is "little wonder that so many black scholarship student-athletes manage to go through four years of college enrollment virtually unscathed by education" (Edwards, 1984, p. 9).

African-Americans (athletes or not) on mostly white campuses typically constitute only 4 or 5% of the student body. Thus, they are frequently alienated by the actual or perceived racism they experience and by their social isolation.

A major unintended consequence of this situation in which black athletes find themselves is that their individual adaptations—denigrating education, opting for easy courses and majors, not making progress toward a degree, emphasizing the athlete role, and eventually dropping out of education without a degree—reinforce the vary racial stereotypes an integrated education is meant to negate. Thus, unwittingly, the universities with big-time programs that recruit marginal students and do not educate them offer "proof" for the argument that African-Americans are genetically inferior to whites in intellectual potential.

In sum, African-Americans are disadvantaged in the United States. To use a sports metaphor, for them the playing field is not level: To succeed, they must advance *uphill*. For a few African-American males, a way to advance is through athletic accomplishment, which will, at a minimum, provide a college education. The college scholarship, however, is no guarantee of a college education. Only about 20% of African-American males who play in big-time college programs graduate. Some of these young men are responsible for not graduating. They may have sought the easy way that did not lead to graduation. However, many of the 80% of African-American athletes who do not graduate have been victims. They have been exploited by universities that used their athletic skills for economic gain but did not help to develop the intellectual skills of these students in their employ.

ANTICIPATING THE YEAR 2000

Societal Trends Affecting Race Relations in the 1990s

There are three major trends that will shape race relations in the near future. The first is the dramatic change in the racial composition of the United States. From 1980 to 1990 while the white population grew by 6%, the number of African-Americans grew by 13.2%, Hispanics by 53%, and Asians by 107.8% (the proportions for the racial minorities are actually understated because approximately 5 million people—mostly poor and racial minorities—were missed in the 1990 Census) (Barringer, 1991). From 1990 to 2000 the racial composition of the United States will become more racially diverse—from 20% nonwhite in 1990 to nearly one-third in 2000. The growing racial minority presence will add tensions in society. The growth will occur mostly in urban areas, straining already exhausted budgets. The urban, minority underclass will continue to grow. In cities and regions experiencing economic hard times, the presence of growing racial minorities will be a source of turmoil between whites and the minorities and among the minorities themselves, as individuals compete for a shrinking number of jobs.

The tensions among these groups increase when there is a perception that the economy is not expanding to include oneself and one's group. This leads to the second important trend: The unequal distribution of wealth (and income) in society is becoming even more disparate. From 1977 to 1988 average incomes in 1991 dollars rose 122% after taxes for the top 1% of households (the top 20% rose by 34%) but fell 10% for the bottom fifth, and 3% for the second-poorest fifth (Rich, 1991). The gaps between both the rich and poor and the rich and the middle class are wider now than at any time since World War II (Sklar, 1991). Ironically, the resentment fostered by this situation is not aimed at the benefactors—the rich—but toward the poor, who are viewed, typically, as wanting government entitlements for doing nothing. These feelings lead to combustible race relations because racial minorities are disproportionately in the poor category.

The third trend that does not augur well for race relations in the near future is the transformation of the economy. There are four interrelated forces that are fundamentally changing the economy: new technologies based on microelectronics, globalization, capital flight, and the shift from manufacturing to services (Eitzen & Baca Zinn, 1989). As a result, the nature of work is shifting, and this has had, and will continue to have, devastating effects on minority communities across the United States. The employment status of minorities has fallen (employment rates, occupational standing, and wage rates), especially in areas of industrial decline. In effect, African-Americans have fewer job opportunities, and what is available for minority skilled and semiskilled workers tends to have lower pay and fewer, if any, benefits compared to manufacturing jobs. Again, this increases racial acrimony as whites and blacks, affected by automation and competition from overseas, compete for fewer and fewer good jobs.

Trend in Universities and Athletics Affecting Race Relations

One disturbing trend is that fewer African-Americans are attending colleges and universities. This is the result of three factors: even higher tuition rates (increasing 6 to 12% a year), combined with the lower federal contributions to scholarships (a legacy of the Reagan administration), and the relatively low economic status of African-American families. Rising tuition also squeezes middle-class families (white and black), making college more difficult for their children to obtain. The result may be student bodies composed more and more of the children of the elite, with the shrinking number of blacks on campus more isolated than ever.

There are two countervailing trends on college campuses regarding race relations. On the one hand, there appears to be a growing commitment on the part of many university administrators and boards of regents toward greater racial diversity in student bodies and faculties. Thus, there is extra effort to recruit minority students (not just athletes) and minority faculty members. At the same time, there is a backlash on the part of some within and outside the academic communities against what they consider racial favoritism (in scholarships and hiring), racial enclaves (e.g., "African-American Studies," "Asian Studies") and what they see as the erosion of Western values through the adding of multiculturalism to the curriculum. Both of these efforts have heightened, and will continue to heighten, racial tensions on college campuses.

A potentially favorable trend in universities is the changing of the professorate. During the 1990s about one-third of professors (overwhelmingly white and male) will be retiring, a trend that will accelerate after 2000. These powerful individuals (senior full professors, for the most part) will be replaced by much younger and more diverse (in terms of race, gender, and world-view) assistant professors.

On the athletic side, there seems to be no pause in the quest by universities with big-time programs for success on the field and for profit from sport. When Richard Lapchick, Director of the Center for the Study of Sport in Society, was asked the cause of the illness in college athletics, he replied:

> Beyond any question in my mind, the root of the problem is money. Only thirty or forty athletic departments in the country make a profit. But the rainbow that is out there is so extraordinary . . . what that thirty or forty *do* make . . . that the others want to chase it (cited in Marchese, 1990, p. 2).

A second trend is that the NCAA has begun, tentatively, to consider efforts to reform the wrongs in college sport. Throughout its history the NCAA has been relatively powerless to control the scandals of big-time intercollegiate sport or to run sport in congruence with the goals of higher education. The fundamental reason for this was that athletic directors at the member schools cast the votes for their schools, meaning that the rules were determined by the athletic establishment rather than by the academic establishment. This began to change in 1984 when a commission of university presidents was formed by the NCAA to help in the reform and redirection of intercollegiate athletics.

The Presidents' Commission had little impact on the rules of the NCAA until the 1991 convention. At that time, the major agenda items were the commission's; members of the commission lobbied actively for their proposals, and a number of presidents (about 100 more than usual) attended to cast votes for their institutions. Many observers felt that the passage of their reform package signaled a turning point. That's the good news. The bad news is that the proposals of the commission did *not* address many of the key issues. Instead, they concentrated on cost containment. Scholarships were reduced by 10% (reducing the number of athletes on scholarship by 1,500 nationwide), and coaching staffs were reduced (limiting, by the way, the number of jobs for black coaches). To their credit, rules were passed by the NCAA members, to help student-athletes: (a) All Division I schools must make counseling and tutoring services available to all recruited athletes; (b) all athletic dormitories are to be eliminated by August 1996; and (c) in-season practice time must be limited to a maximum of 4 hours a day and 20 hours a week. Although these rule changes were in the right direction, that is, in the direction of bringing the "student" back into the student-athlete role, they were mild and timid moves at best. The convention did not address the issue of freshman eligibility. It did not confront the scheduling of games at odd times for the convenience of television but at the expense of athletes' missing class time. A proposal was defeated that would have required Division I schools to graduate 50% of their scholarship athletes. A proposal to require athletes to post minimum gradepoint averages each year was also defeated. Thus, it appears that although the presidents seem to be taking more of a role in the NCAA, the resulting rule changes have been cosmetic, not really addressing the ills of big-time college sports. Clearly, the commercial nature of sport, and the problems related to this, have not been questioned by the presidents.

Reforming College Sport to Eliminate Racism

Contemporary trends in society suggest that racism will intensify in the near term. Big-time college sport will occur in that environment, adding to the racism as it exploits African-American athletes for profit, often discarding them without an education. When this occurs, the stereotype that African-Americans have physical but not intellectual gifts is reinforced. This section addresses what ought to be done by the NCAA, the schools, the coaches, and the athletes to correct this situation. I will not attempt to address how big-time sport itself should be reformed (for suggestions to reform the system see Eitzen & Sage, 1993, ch. 6, and Lapchick & Slaughter, 1989, sec. 4). The discussion is limited specifically to racism and the general issues regarding exploitation and miseducation of African-American athletes in big-time programs. Although the following recommendations are made specifically for African-American athletes, they often apply to all college athletes (I am indebted to Lapchick & Slaughter, 1989, for many of these recommendations).

Problem: African-American athletes are sometimes ill-prepared for college academics.

1. Athletes should not be admitted into college unless there is evidence of their potential to graduate. In short, if the academic potential of recruits is doubtful, then they should not be recruited. If the recruits have potential, they must be provided with the academic assistance (tutors and remedial courses) to get them to their appropriate academic level quickly.
2. The demands of Proposition 48 should be strengthened. At current levels, the limits are so low that recruits can be admitted with SAT scores 300–400 points below the student average. This places them at high risk educationally.
3. Middle schools and high schools must prepare their potentially college-bound athletes for college.
4. Athletes at all educational levels, as well as their parents, and leaders from their communities must be counseled to realize that (a) a college education is the most significant step they can take for success in American society; and (b) odds of a professional career in sport are very long and even if attained, that career will last but a few years.

Problem: African-American athletes often come from economically disadvantaged backgrounds.

5. Athletes must be provided with a monthly stipend ($300 or so) for incidentals, clothing, and entertainment. This will provide some justice by paying the athletes a portion of the money they generate for their universities. Moreover, it will permit students from poor families a chance to fit in with their more privileged classmates.
6. Athletes must be provided two trips home during each school year. Moreover, the parents of athletes should be provided with two trips to the university each year. These actions will accomplish three goals: (a) provide the athletes with a form of financial aid that they have earned; (b) promote better ties between the athletes and their communities; and (c) promote family bonding.

Problem: African-American athletes who are admitted have low graduation rates.

7. Freshman must be ineligible for athletic competition so that they can concentrate on the adjustment to the social and intellectual demands of college.
8. The institution must provide adequate study time, counseling, and tutoring. The object of these aids is not eligibility for sports participation but satisfactory progress toward a degree.
9. The time demands of sport on the athletes in-season and off-season must be reasonable. Thus (a) practice time must be limited; (b) the number of games in a season must be limited; and (c) the number of

class days missed because of sport must be limited. The NCAA has begun to place some restrictions on excessive time demands.

10. The athlete's academic progress must be closely monitored by the school's (not just the athletic department's) academic advisors.

11. Athletes must retain their scholarships, including housing, meals, and books, for up to two years, if needed, after their athletic eligibility is completed. This recognizes the necessity of at least five years for graduation in most cases. At present, many schools eliminate educational assistance to athletes who have used up their eligibility, which makes it especially difficult for the economically disadvantaged to continue.

12. Coaches should be evaluated in part by the graduation rate of their athletes. This form of institutional control of coaches will, of course, increase the efforts of coaches to recruit athletes with academic potential and for them to see that those whom they do recruit make progress towards a degree.

Problem: African-American athletes are isolated in athletic ghettos, and there is often racial segregation within them.

13. Athletic dormitories and separate eating facilities for athletes must be eliminated. (Athletic dormitories will be eliminated by NCAA action, by 1996.)

14. Athletes should be encouraged to become involved in social, organizational, and academic activities within the school context. At a minimum, this means that coaches should not impose restrictions on the nonathletic campus activities of their athletes, which is often the case.

15. Housing arrangements, meals, and road trip accommodations must be integrated. This can easily be accomplished through random assignments.

16. Positional segregation by race (stacking) must be eliminated. Racial stacking promotes racial stereotypes (e.g., whites are "naturally" more intelligent and better leaders whereas blacks are "naturally" more gifted physically). Moreover, it tends to make competition for starting positions intraracial. This is a difficult proposal to implement because the procedures are often subtle. However, at a minimum coaches should declare their acceptance of open competition for each position, and the results of this competition should be monitored by the administration.

Problem: There are not enough African-Americans in leadership positions in athletic departments.

17. African-Americans must be considered seriously for positions of athletic director and head coach. As this is written, only two Division I football schools have an African-American as athletic director. Moreover, not one of these schools has an African-American head football coach.

18. African-Americans must be considered seriously for positions of assistant athletic director, trainer, and sports information director, positions where they are rarely found.
19. Black assistant coaches must be given more responsibilities beyond the typical ones of recruiting black athletes and serving as a liaison between the black athletes and the white coaches.

Problem: Some coaches are racist and dehumanizing.

20. Players must have a mechanism by which they can report the racist and dehumanizing acts of coaches and others in the athletic department to the administration without fear of reprisal.
21. The university and athletic department administration must take strong and immediate action to eliminate discriminatory and dehumanizing practices.

Problem: Racial stereotypes are sometimes promoted unwittingly by the members of the athletic department.

22. Athletic department personnel must be educated about the subtleties of racism, including the negative use of language. In particular, the sports information director must be sensitized to the negative and sometimes subtle ways that minorities are often portrayed in press guides and press releases, and in the media.

There are three fundamental requirements if these recommendations are to be implemented. First, the NCAA must expand its recent reforms, focusing on the explicit goal of promoting educational and humane values in college athletics. All other goals, including making money, are secondary to meeting the educational needs of student-athletes. Put another way, the operating principle must be that the health and education of student-athletes are infinitely more important than television ratings, corporate sponsorships, and profits. If the NCAA does not prove capable of this, and there is reason to suspect that it is not (see Sperber, 1991), then the member universities through their presidents must form an organization that will.

Second, university presidents must make a commitment to their athletes as students. They must take responsibility for the educational and moral integrity of their institutions. They must establish mechanisms to monitor their athletic programs, devise rules to insure compliance with educational goals, and budget the necessary monies to implement them.

Finally, money must be raised by the NCAA and distributed to the schools equitably to fund the expensive items in these recommendations. This is not as difficult as it seems. Richard Lapchick has proposed an "Academic Superfund" that would tap the various profit centers in sport:

One of my suggestions was that for every player who makes it to the pros, the NBA and NFL would donate the equivalent of a full four-year scholarship to the Superfund. The money would then be used for those players who don't make it to the pros, to continue their educations in a fifth or sixth year.

Given that 50 players a year enter the NBA and 150 the NFL, and given an average of $10,000 a year for tuition costs, the total comes to about $8 million a year. That sounds like a lot of money, but consider that the telesports are worth $1.675 billion a year.

I also proposed a one percent federal tax on ticket sales for all sporting events. Even on a $30 ticket, the tax would cost only 30 cents; yet, that 1% would raise $33 million a year, because we sell $3.3 billion in tickets.

I've also written to NCAA Executive Director Dick Schultz, suggesting that 10 percent of the increase in the NCAA's television revenues . . . just of the $83 million *increase* . . . go into the Superfund. That's another $8.3 million.

The total amount in this new Superfund would be something like $50 million a year (Lapchick, cited in Marchese, 1990, p. 4).

To conclude, despite the impediments to achieve social justice in college sport, the situation can be improved mightily. We know what's wrong. That's the easy part. We must acknowledge the problems and demand that sport be cleaned up. The NCAA has allowed social injustice to occur and is now only beginning to reform. But these efforts, so far, are weak. That organization or one like it must oversee university sport to insure that educational values prevail. The administrators at each university along with faculties, students, and the public must insist on the same. At present, these groups demand excellence on the fields and in the arenas. This type of tunnel vision is at the heart of the problem because it has led to abuses, compromises, and hypocritical behaviors that are contrary to educational goals. Most important, it has allowed athletes, most often African-American athletes, to be used by these schools for their athletic skills and then discarded without diplomas. This is not only embarrassing but also immoral. Since educational institutions exist to serve their students, it is obvious that big-time college sport must be restructured to focus on the educational outcomes of athletes. To do otherwise makes a mockery of the educational mission of universities.

SUMMARY

African-American athletes in big-time college athletic programs are part of two contexts, both of which disadvantage them. The first context is the interracial climate of U.S. society. On every dimension related to health, housing, work, income/wealth, and education, African-Americans when compared to whites are disadvantaged. Conservative economic strategies have cut back social programs that might help reduce the problems of the disadvantaged.

Moreover, racial tensions are increasing. Bigotry, even on college campuses, is real. This situation will not ease in the near term as politicians focus on the needs of the middle class, the economy remains weak, and racial/ethnic minorities increase their proportion of the population.

African-American athletes recruited to big-time college programs are also part of a corporate/entertainment world. They are hired (for room, board, books, and tuition) to perform on the athletic fields and in the arenas to generate monies, media interest, and public relations for universities. They are recruited for their athletic talents but not necessarily for their intellectual abilities. Since African-American athletes come disproportionately from economically, socially, and educationally disadvantaged backgrounds, the situation is loaded against them. From the perspective of many coaches and athletic administrations, these young men are athletes first and only incidentally students. As a result, many of these athletes who are marginal students retain their athletic eligibility by being "taken care of" through phantom courses, "friendly" professors, surrogate test takers, and the like. This means, of course, that many African-Americans will not graduate, even though they have played for four years. In effect, they have been used by the universities.

The NCAA has begun to take tentative steps to reform the wrongs in college sport. But these weak steps are not enough. The universities through the NCAA (or other organization) need to be bold in their initiatives. As they consider reforms to eliminate racism, the following broad changes are essential: (a) Athletes admitted to universities must be prepared for college-level academics. (b) Athletes should receive fair compensation for their work, which will especially help athletes from economically disadvantaged backgrounds. (c) Athletes must be provided with whatever it takes for them to achieve educational goals. (d) Racial/ethnic minorities must be integrated into all athletic and university activities. (e) The staff of athletic departments must be integrated at all levels. (f) Athletic departments must be monitored carefully to determine that procedures are fair and nonracist, and to ensure that educational goals have the first priority.

REFERENCES

Adler, P., & Adler, P. A. (1985). From idealism to pragmatic detachment: The academic performance of college athletes. *Sociology of Education, 58,* 241-250.

Adler, P. A., & Adler, P. (1991). *Backboards and blackboards: College athletes and role engulfment.* New York: Columbia University Press.

Barringer, F. (1991, March 11). Census shows profound change in racial makeup of the nation. *New York Times,* pp. A1, A12.

Edwards, H. (1984). The black "dumb jock": An American sports tragedy." *The College Review Board, 131,* 8-11.

Eitzen, D. S., & Baca Zinn, M. (1989). *The reshaping of America: Social consequences of the changing economy.* Englewood Cliffs, NJ: Prentice-Hall.

Eitzen, D. S., & Baca Zinn, M. (1991). *In conflict and order: Understanding society* (5th ed.). Boston: Allyn and Bacon.

Eitzen, D. S., & Sage, G. H. (1993). *Sociology of North American sport* (5th ed.). Dubuque, IA: Wm. C. Brown.

Lapchick, R. E., & Slaughter, J. B. (1989). *The rules of the game: Ethics in college sport.* New York: Macmillan.

Marchese, T. (1990). After the cheers: Is higher education serving its student-athletes? An interview with Richard E. Lapchick. *AAHE Bulletin, 42,* 1-10.

Rainie, H. (1991, July 22). Black & white. *U.S. News & World Report,* pp. 18-21.

Reed, W. F. (1990, March 26). Absolutely incredible! *Sports Illustrated,* p. 66.

Rich, S. (1991). Rich got richer, poor got poorer during the 1980s. *The Washington Post,* reported in the Fort Collins *Coloradoan* (July 24), A4.

Select Committee on Intercollegiate Athletics. (1986, March). Report. Tulane University.

Sklar, H. (1991). The truly greedy III. *Zeta Magazine, 4,* 10-12.

Sperber, M. (1990). *College sports, inc.* New York: Henry Holt.

Sperber, M. (1991). Why the NCAA can't reform college athletics. *Academe, 77,* 13-20.

Underwood, J. (1981, February 23). A game plan for America. *Sports Illustrated,* p. 81.

Will, G. (1986, September 15). Our schools for scandal. *Newsweek,* p. 84.

Williams, M. L. (1992, January 1). Racial and ethnic relations in American higher education. *Vital Speeches of the Day, 58,* 174-177.

Wilson, W. J. (1987). *The truly disadvantaged.* Chicago: University of Chicago Press.

■ FOR FURTHER STUDY

Adler, Patricia A., and Peter Adler, *Backboards & Blackboards: College Athletics and Role Engulfment* (New York: Columbia University Press, 1991).

American Association for Higher Education, "Ethics and Intercollegiate Sport," *AAHE Bulletin* 42 (February 1990).

Brooks, Dana D., and Ronald C. Althouse (eds.), *Racism in College Athletics: The African-American Athlete's Experience* (Morgantown, West Virginia: Fitness Information Technology, Inc., 1993).

Fleisher, Arthur, Brian Goff, and Robert Tollison, *The National Collegiate Athletic Association: A Study in Cartel Behavior* (Chicago: University of Chicago Press, 1993).

Frey, Darcy, *The Last Shot* (Boston: Houghton Mifflin, 1994).

Frey, James H., "Hitting the Wall: Breaking the Corporate Hold on College Sport," paper presented at the annual meeting of the North American Society for the Sociology of Sport, Savannah, Georgia (November 1994).

McMillen, Tom, *Out of Bounds: How the American Sports Establishment Is Being Driven by Greed and Hypocrisy—And What Needs to Be Done about It* (New York: Simon & Schuster, 1992).

Sack, Allen L., "The Underground Economy of College Football," *Sociology of Sport Journal* 8 (March 1991):1-15.

Siegel, Donald, "Higher Education and the Plight of the Black Male Athlete," *Journal of Sport & Social Issues* 18 (August 1994): 207-223.

Sperber, Murray, "Flagrant Foul: How Professors Let Jocks Push Them Around," *Lingua Franca* 4 (November/December 1993):1, 26-31.

Thelin, John R., *Games Colleges Play: Scandal and Reform in Intercollegiate Athletics* (Baltimore: Johns Hopkins University Press, 1994).

Wolff, Alexander, and Armen Keteyian, *Raw Recruits: The High Stakes Game Colleges Play to Get Their Basketball Stars—and What It Costs to Win* (New York: Picket Books, 1990).

Yaeger, Don, and Douglas S. Looney, *Under the Tarnished Dome: How Notre Dame Betrayed Its Ideals for Football Glory* (New York: Simon & Schuster, 1993).

Part Eight

Problems of Excess: Sport and Money

A dilemma that characterizes professional sport and much of what is called amateur sport in the United States has been described by Roger Kahn: "Sport is too much a game to be a business and too much a business to be a game."[1] The evidence indicating a strong relationship between sport and money is overwhelming. Consider the following examples:

Item: Notre Dame has a $38 million contract to televise its football games. The sale of Notre Dame merchandise brings the school $1 million a year, and an appearance in a bowl game raises another $3 to $6 million.

Item: An estimated $2.5 billion a year in college merchandise is sold under license, generating about $100 million to the schools in royalties. The University of Michigan receives the most income from this source—$5.8 million in 1994, up from $725,000 in 1989.[2]

Item: In 1994 CBS agreed to pay the NCAA $1.725 billion ($215.6 million a year) for the rights to the men's basketball tournament through 2002.

Item: Mike Krzyzewski, basketball coach at Duke University, signed a fifteen-year shoe endorsement contract for a $1 million bonus plus $375,000 a year.

Item: In 1994 the top endorsement earnings by professional athletes were $31 million for Michael Jordan, $13.5 million for Shaquille O'Neal, and $12 million each for Arnold Palmer and Jack Nicklaus. The top endorsement money for a woman was $6 million for Chris Evert.

Item: In 1994 the *median* player salary in major league baseball was $410,000; the *average* salary was $1.2 million, more than sixty times the yearly earnings of U.S. nonmanagement private-sector employees.[3]

Item: Total revenue from major league baseball increased from $521 million in 1983 to almost $2 billion in 1993.

Item: "Nine years after Norman Braman bought the Philadelphia Eagles for $65 million, he sold the franchise [in 1994] for $185 million."[4] Similarly, the Baltimore Orioles were purchased for $12 million in 1979, sold for $70 million in 1989, and sold again in 1993 for $173 million.

Item: An estimated 21 percent of ticket sales income for the major professional sports comes from the leasing of luxury suites to individuals and corporations (for $800 to $15,000 a game).

Item: Gross retail sales during 1993 for NBA merchandise were $2.85 billion. NFL and major league baseball sales were $3 billion each, and sales for the NHL were $1 billion.

Item: In 1994 United Airlines signed a twenty-year deal, paying $17.5 million to have its name on the new arena of the Chicago Bulls and Chicago Blackhawks. Similarly, Coors Brewing Company paid $30 million to have the stadium of the Colorado Rockies named "Coors Field."

Although these examples are diverse, there is a common thread—money. Money is often the motivator of athletes. Players and owners give their primary allegiance to money rather than to the sport or to the fans. Modern sport, whether professional, big-time college, or Olympic, is "corporate sport." The original purpose of sport—pleasure in the activity—has been lost in the process. Sport has become work. Sport has become the product of publicity agents using superhype methods. Money has superseded the content as the ultimate goal. Illicit tactics are commonplace. In short, U.S. sport is a microcosm of the values of American society. Roger Angell has said of baseball what is applicable to all forms of corporate sport:

> Professional sports now form a noisy and substantial, if irrelevant and distracting, part of the world, and it seems as if baseball games taken entirely—off the field as well as on it, in the courts and in the front offices as well as down on the diamonds—may now tell us more about ourselves than they ever did before.[5]

The selections in Part Eight illustrate the problems and issues involving the impact of money on professional sports. The first, by George H. Sage, examines the contradiction that while the public subsidizes professional teams and sports facilities, the public has little or no power over professional team owners. The second selection is a 1992 statement by Senator Howard

Metzenbaum arguing for the repeal of baseball's antitrust immunity. His bill was defeated that year and again in 1994. The final selection addresses the baseball strike of 1994 (professional hockey also went on strike that year). This statement by Michael Zielinski argues that the issues in the baseball strike transcend sports, since they represent efforts by management to set wages and conditions of employment in a union-free workplace. Once again, we see that sport is a microcosm of the larger society.

NOTES

1. Roger Kahn, quoted in CBS Reports, "The Baseball Business," television documentary, narrated by Bill Moyers (1977).
2. Dana Rubin, "You've Seen the Game. Now Buy the Underwear," *New York Times* (September 11, 1994): F5.
3. Andrew Zimbalist, "Field of Schemes," *New Republic* (August 15, 1994): 11.
4. Jack McCallum, "Blame the Bosses," *Sports Illustrated* (October 10, 1994): 32.
5. Roger Angell, "The Sporting Scene: In the Counting House," *New Yorker* (May 10, 1976): 107.

24. *Public Policy in the Public Interest: Pro Franchises and Sports Facilities That Are Really "Yours"*

GEORGE H. SAGE

Denver Nuggets public address announcer: "And now ladies and gentlemen, please welcome *YOUR* Denver Nuggets."

Seattle Mariners public address announcer: "And now the starting lineup for *YOUR* Seattle Mariners."

Buffalo Bills public address announcer: "Ladies and gentlemen, now taking the field *YOUR* Buffalo Bills."

Professional sports live in the charmed circle of the imagination, and their advertising and media hype sell civic identity and community ownership through slogans like *"Your* Denver Nuggets." Further, team owners go to great lengths to conceal the reality of ownership from the public. Jerry Jones, owner of the Dallas Cowboys, said: "I don't feel I own the Dallas Cowboys. . . . All I . . . do is use my talents to husband the Cowboys for our fans" (Caulk, 1989, p. 17S). The owner of the Denver Broncos, Pat Bowlen, often claims that it is the citizens and fans of Denver and Colorado who are the real owners of the Broncos.

The reality is that a pro sports franchise is no more "yours" than is IBM, Texaco, or Wal-Mart, despite the wishfulness that makes the claim. With only one exception, these franchises are privately owned, profit-driven corporations that have never really belonged to fans and local citizens. But those who shape the images for pro sports are aware of the public's willingness to believe the discourse of collective community ownership, and the pro sports industry has benefited greatly from that myth.

In spite of the fact that most major cities in North America are in a state of financial crisis, over the past three decades millions of taxpayer dollars in these cities have been spent to attract and retain pro sports franchises. While free market capital accumulation theory is the rhetorical discourse of pro franchise owners, there are no more persistent and successful applicants for

SOURCE: "Public Policy in the Public Interest: Pro Franchises and Sports Facilities That Are Really 'Yours'" by George H. Sage. Originally presented as a paper at the North American Society for the Sociology of Sport Conference, Savannah, Georgia, 1994. Reprinted by permission of George H. Sage.

public assistance than the owners of professional sports franchises. As Cleveland Browns owner, Art Modell, acknowledged, "We are . . . fat cat Republicans that sit around the league meetings and vote socialist" (Scorecard, 1994, p. 14). Economists Jim Quirk and Rod Fort (1992) say that cities and states provide an *annual* subsidy to pro sports franchises of some $500 million. The major subsidy has been in the form of publicly funded arenas and stadiums (see Bartimole, 1994, and Sage, 1990, 1993, for recent examples).

An obvious question is, why would the public subsidize sports franchises which are privately owned by millionaires and billionaires (Steinbreder, 1993)? There are several reasons for such action. Like other cultural industries, there are both economic and popular cultural dimensions to pro sports. Business and political interests, folklore, and the public's sentiment about imagined community must be considered in any attempt to understand pro sports' continuing success in obtaining public assistance (Anderson, 1991; Schiller, 1989).

THE PROFESSIONAL TEAM SPORT MONOPOLY

Undoubtedly, the most powerful factor behind the professional team sport industry's success in obtaining public subsidies is its unique legal status. The number of cities, states, and regions with professional team sport franchises has always been limited because major league baseball (MLB) is a legally sanctioned monopoly through an antitrust exemption granted to it (Hoffman, 1989; Ross, 1989; Scully, 1984; Steadman, 1984). As Corliss (1992) has noted, MLB owners are members "of a most exclusive club—a monopoly, thanks to the U.S. Supreme Court, which in 1922 ruled baseball exempt from antitrust legislation and the demands of the open market" (p. 52). Although other pro sports leagues do not enjoy baseball's antitrust immunity, they too have received a variety of protections by the courts and Congress that have enabled owners to monopolize their industry and allowed pro sport leagues to operate as cartels. This has enabled owners to engage in collusion, price and wage fixing, and various restraints of trade (e.g., leaguewide negotiation of TV contracts), thus maximizing their profits. It has also protected each franchise within a league from competition because the number of franchises is controlled by the team owners; no franchise is allowed to locate in a given territory without approval of the owners (Jennings, 1990; Lowenfish, 1991; Zimbalist, 1992).[1]

The consequences of sport league franchise control are nicely illustrated by the case of baseball. In 1901 there were sixteen major league baseball teams, eight in the American League and eight in the National League, and the population of the United States was 76 million. From 1901 until 1961—sixty years—no expansion occurred, while the U.S. population more than doubled (to 179 million). In the 1960s and 1970s the American League added six teams and the National League added four. No franchises were added in the 1980s, but two were added in 1991.

Using 1901 as a standard, and assuming that the United States is capable of developing the same proportion of major league–caliber baseball players today, there ought to be fifty-three major league teams rather than the current twenty-eight. And that does not take into account the fact that African Americans were totally excluded from MLB in 1901; thus, with African Americans now playing, a case could be made for more than fifty-three teams (Zimbalist, 1992).

The other professional team sports leagues have followed a similar pattern of controlled expansion.

Demand for pro sport teams exceeds supply, but pro sports' unique status has left many cities without franchises and has created enormous barriers for cities wanting a franchise. Until Colorado was awarded a MLB franchise in 1991, the entire Rocky Mountain time zone was without a MLB team (Hoffman, 1989). For the two new MLB expansion franchises awarded in 1991, the owners set a $95 million price tag on each, which was $88 million more than the last expansion go-round in 1977. And they decided that new franchise owners would not receive national television revenues during the first two years, which in effect raised the expansion fee to $106 million, considering the TV revenues each new team would have to forgo (Clarke, 1990a; Gorman & Calhoun, 1994; Ozanian & Taub, 1992). Finally, the owners set specific stadium requirements for the new franchises. For Denver, this meant the city and potential franchise owners would be forced to build a new baseball stadium—no new baseball stadium, no chance of acquiring a franchise. Following are some examples of how its monopoly status enables pro sports to dictate terms to cities seeking a franchise. As political scientist Charles Euchner (1993) noted, "Teams manipulate cities by selling them against each other in a scramble for the limited number of major league teams. While the cities fight each other, the teams sit back and wait for the best conditions and terms" (p. 179).

Stadiums and Arenas for Professional Sports

Control over the number of franchises under conditions of intense demand for them gives professional sports franchise owners powerful leverage in persuading municipalities to build stadiums and arenas at public expense. Before 1960 most of the facilities used by professional team sports were privately owned. Over the past three decades, the trend among owners has turned away from private ownership of stadiums and arenas and toward demands that public money be used to build new facilities. Since 1960 cities and states have invested approximately $3 billion in sports facilities used by professional teams (Quirk & Fort, 1992). Indeed, since 1960 all of the new stadiums—with the exception of Dodger Stadium, Joe Robbie Stadium, the

Rangers' Arlington Stadium, and Foxboro Stadium—have been constructed with public money. Most arenas built in the past thirty years are publicly owned as well. Today about 80 percent of all professional teams sports facilities have been publicly financed.

The reason that few owners own the facilities in which their teams play is that when the local government owns them, the owners are relieved of the burden of property taxes, insurance, and maintenance costs, not to mention construction. Owners pay rent on the facilities, of course, but this usually covers only a fraction of overall operating expenses.

Another reason for team owners not owning their facilities is that it makes it much easier for them to move franchises to other cities, should they become unhappy with existing arrangements. Since 1960 there have been over fifty franchise or playing site relocations in the four major league team sports, attesting to the mobility inherent in not being burdened by ownership of a facility and to the leagues' power to accomplish what they consider beneficial to the business of professional sports (Freedman, 1987). In the 1980s three NFL owners actually made such a move—the Oakland Raiders to Los Angeles, the Baltimore Colts to Indianapolis, and the St. Louis Cardinals to Phoenix—and the incidence of owner "extortion" is increasing. Indeed, during the past twenty years, virtually every major professional franchise at one time has threatened to move if local or state officials did not meet demands for a new facility or provide other benefits (Euchner, 1993). This movement of franchises vividly reveals the lie in the "your team" rhetoric advanced by pro teams public relations.

POWERFUL INTERESTS PROMOTE THE ACQUISITION OF FRANCHISES AND THE BUILDING OF FACILITIES

Support for seeking and securing professional sport franchises and the construction of stadiums and arenas at public expense usually comes from coalitions of urban elites: local politicians; businesses, especially restaurants and hotels; developers; construction firms; local mass media; and, of course, the pro sport industry. Collectively, they have small numbers, but enormous clout and the vision to coordinate and press their demands on the community. It is they who create local interest in and a vivid symbolism of collective community on behalf of franchises and facilities (Sage, 1993). Faced with pressures from such powerful and well-organized individuals and groups, local voters, city councils, and state legislatures frequently accede to the urgings for franchises and facilities (Baade & Dye, 1988; Zimbalist, 1992).

Urban elites and professional sport team owners seek to rationalize public subsidies in terms of economic development, arguing that communities profit by increased revenues, business, and taxes; thus an economic renaissance is created by a major league sports franchise. In support of arenas and stadiums, they usually point to various intangible benefits, such as neighborhood redevelopment and enhanced civic identity and pride. These claims are largely based on wishful thinking because they have never been well documented in any city. In fact, most economic analyses have concluded that new franchises and new facilities largely shift expenditures and economic resources instead of generating new activity, despite any economic multiplier effects. They show that the prime beneficiaries are a small group of wealthy individuals, and those most likely to bear the costs are low-income citizens. They show that the employment arising directly from new franchises and new sports arenas and stadiums are relatively low-paying service-sector jobs. A study by economist Dean Baim (1994) of fourteen cities with publicly funded stadiums found no direct gains to most cities as a result of municipal stadium investments. Neighborhood redevelopment has not been successfully carried out in cities where stadiums and arenas have been built by public funds (Baade & Dye, 1988; Grisi & Reichert, 1988; Lipsitz, 1984; Okner, 1974; Rosentraub & Nunn, 1978; Zimbalist, 1992).

A key role in every new franchise and facility promotion is played by the media, for they are the conduits for urban elites' public relations efforts on behalf of pro sports. The media are often unabashed boosters and cheerleaders for a local sports franchise or for an affirmative vote for a proposed sports facility. Opposition usually receives little coverage in the local media, while supporting views receive lavish coverage. This is not surprising because the media are one of the biggest beneficiaries of urban development. Newspapers, radio, and local television gain increased subscribers, listeners, and viewers with urban development and the population increases that typically accompany it. Moreover, new businesses buy advertising, a major source of revenue for the media.

During the 1990 referendum on a publicly funded stadium for a new MLB franchise in Denver, the *Rocky Mountain News,* the largest regional newspaper, virtually ran a campaign in support of the proposed stadium. Then, on the first morning after the vote on the baseball stadium (August 15), William Fletcher, chairman of the board of the *Rocky Mountain News,* revealed that the *News* "has been involved in a series of preliminary discussions" about becoming an owner of the franchise (Clarke, 1990b, p. 87). He disclosed that "he has had discussions with baseball interests" about becoming an owner of a Denver major league franchise. "We're interested in becoming a part of it," he said (Staff, 1990, p. 92). In addition to the usual economic benefits a newspaper expects to gain from a pro sports franchise, the *Rocky Mountain News* planned on becoming part of the ownership, while not disclosing any of this to its readers before the vote on the stadium.

FIGHTING BACK: RESISTANCE AND AGENCY

Why are citizens not more active in questioning and resisting public subsidies to pro sport owners? Lawrence Rothstein's (1986) concept of faces of power helps illuminate how attitudes and beliefs in cities are shaped in such a way as to convince the public that they must agree to subsidize pro sport franchises and new facilities if they expect to land and keep a major league sports franchise.[2] First, there is a public and institutional form of power held by local decision makers, especially in initiating proposals on behalf of the community that are the focus of public attention and debate. In the promotion and support for franchises and facilities one sees an example of Rothstein's first face of power in the influence of politicians, businesses, and mass media in support of such initiatives. They are often able to prevail in public decision making through artful legitimating descriptions and definitions of the situation, which are then dutifully reported by the local media. Thus, organized power dominates the decision-making process, while the unorganized voices of citizens tend to be marginalized and rendered impotent.

A second form of power can be found by focusing on "which people and issues are left out of public decision making. Power in this respect means the barriers and roadblocks that preclude or make difficult participation of some individuals and groups and the appearance of some issues" (Rothstein, 1986, p. 4). To the extent that urban elites are able to create barriers to the public airing of initiatives, and are able to set the agenda and suppress or obstruct the full exposure of certain issues and grievances without public scrutiny, those individuals or groups have the power to restrict full public debate of the issues and the gathering and consideration of evidence that might be useful to citizens attempting to fully understand the implications of proposed initiatives. The consequence of this form of power is that citizens are largely silenced and excluded from the process; thus, urban elite biases are fortified "against the raising of certain issues and the participation of certain groups" (Rothstein, 1986, pp. 8–9; see also Bachrach & Baratz, 1970).

A third dimension of power is rooted in the first two. Because of the operation of the first two forms of power, citizen groups often come to "accept their powerlessness and the illegitimacy or inexpressibility of their grievances. They accept as natural and unchallengeable the practices and rationales that guarantee" their compliance, despite vague rumblings of discontent with the status quo (Rothstein, 1986, p. 9).

These three forms of power provide a framework for understanding how major league sports, working through local politicians, business groups, and the media, are able to obtain public funding for new franchises and facilities with very little opposition from the taxpayers whose money actually pays for pro sports. With no political machinery to shape a collectively determined position, with no organized coalitions to defend and guide them, and faced with the combination of overt and covert power, taxpayers often accept as unchallengeable the practices and rationales provided by pro sports and urban elites, despite sporadic and unorganized expressions of dissatisfaction.

In spite of the obstacles to opposing the professional sports industry, it would be a grave mistake to believe there has been no resistance. Citizens are not simply passive recipients of culture, duped by owners, businesses, politicians, and the media. Wherever there is power—especially the abuse of it—there arises resistance to it, and the existence of opposition plays an active constitutive part in every social process (Scott, 1985, 1990). There is a long history of opposition and resistance to the owners' monopoly power, which has come from both citizens and professional athletes.

Perhaps the most obvious resistance to owners' hegemony has come from the various players' unions that exist in all professional sport leagues. Despite the fact that professional players' unions have been rudimentary and inadequate, and that they have aroused the unbridled wrath of the owners, they have nevertheless successfully challenged those who own and control the pro sport industry, and they have won a series of stunning victories through the court system.[3] In addition, they have generally been successful when they have had to strike to obtain direct concessions from the owners. So resistance by the players to the monopoly power of owners has been persistent and successful in a number of ways (Gorman & Calhoun, 1994). Most important, successes by the players' unions serve as examples to citizens that owner hegemony can be challenged and defeated.

Although the fragmented citizenry typically "do not have the time, resources, or common purpose to make a [significant] impact on city policy" with regard to pro sports (Euchner, 1993, p. 59), citizens/taxpayers have successfully resisted. Over the past decade several citizen groups have blocked the proposed construction of pro sports facilities with public money. For example, referenda have failed in New Jersey (1987); Phoenix (1989); Cuyahoga County, Ohio (1984); Addison, Illinois (1986); San Jose twice (1990 and 1992); Miami three times (1988); and San Francisco three times (1987, 1989, and 1992). In 1987 a vote on a new stadium complex for Baltimore, which polls showed voters would likely reject, was stopped by a state constitutional technicality (Euchner, 1993).

Alternative Models to the Sport Cartel

The cartel model of the current professional team sports industry is a model that has been socially constructed and as such is capable of being changed; indeed, it is a model that desperately needs changing in the interests of citizens, especially sports fans, who would like to have professional sports teams in their own communities. Economist Roger Noll (1992) argues that the major problem in pro sports is the "lack of competition among teams and leagues for fans, as manifested most clearly by the gap between the number of teams and the number of viable franchise locations" (p. 369).

An obvious step in the creation of an alternative to the present model would be the abolishment of the antitrust exemption to MLB and the removal of similar protection in the other professional sports leagues. This would not only create possibilities for additional franchises in baseball, but it would make more feasible the development of more franchises, even entire leagues, in the other professional team sports. Congress and the courts have broken up monopoly formations before. The breakup of AT&T is a recent example. The result has been the creation and development of the "Baby Bells," Sprint, MCI, and other telephone corporations. Just as telephone consumers have been the beneficiaries of this action, a breakup of the pro sports leagues monopoly, and the creation of a market competition model, would be beneficial for cities and sports fans. As a spokesman for the Consumer Federation of America told a congressional committee looking into the validity of MLB's exemption from the antitrust laws, "Our nation's pro-competition laws are good enough for everyone else. . . . we believe they should be good enough for major league baseball" (Kimmelman, 1992, p. 418).

Private sport team ownership so overwhelmingly dominates professional sports that few people have ever considered that there might be alternative ownership models. For the few who have considered alternatives, there is little understanding of what they might be. Certainly, one that might be considered is a not-for-profit municipalization model of franchise ownership; after all, it already exists and has existed successfully for over seventy years— the Green Bay Packers.[4]

One way municipal ownership of a professional team franchise can work is to have fans within a municipality set up a sports authority and issue public stock. The sports authority could then negotiate with the team's owners to purchase the franchise, using the capital raised from the stock drive as a down payment. The authority could then float general obligation bonds to fund the rest of the purchase price, or it might sell special revenue bonds, using a tax on tickets as a revenue stream to guarantee long-term payments. Management could be delegated, so that the franchise could run on a day-to-day basis like any other franchise (Goodman, 1988).

Another potential means for municipalities to own pro sports franchises is through the laws of eminent domain, which enable municipalities and states to acquire private property forcibly to facilitate projects for public benefit, so long as the owner is compensated for the value of the property. Indeed, this strategy has been tried three times in recent years—by a Massachusetts legislator who introduced legislation to seize the Boston Red Sox during the first prolonged baseball strike, by the city of Oakland when the Raiders moved to Los Angeles, and by Baltimore when the Colts fled to Indianapolis (Katz, 1994; Euchner, 1993). Although all three efforts ultimately failed, legal scholars have said that such actions by municipalities can be won, if properly pursued.

There is even the possibility that a franchise might be given to a city by a philanthropic owner. Don't laugh—that is exactly what happened in 1990 when the owner of the San Diego Padres, Joan Kroc, offered to give the Padres to the city of San Diego, along with a $100 million trust fund to finance the continued operation of the ball club (Goodman, 1990). The city government wanted to go through with it, but it was torpedoed by the MLB owners ("Kroc Wanted to Give . . .," 1990).[5] Their actions reaffirmed that pro sports corporations are entertainment businesses and, like all private corporations, they exist to pursue their own profit maximization, not the collective aspirations of a community (Greider, 1993).

The current pro team sports franchise model is not the only model that can be conceived. There is nothing to prevent a national municipalization of professional team sports. Any city in the country that wishes to have a symphony orchestra can have one, any city wishing to have a zoo can have one; and hundreds of American cities have municipally funded cultural activities such as these. So assuming that professional sports entertainment contributes something to the culture of a city, a nationwide system of professional team sports might be organized in which any city wishing to be a part of that system could develop a team and seek entry into the organization of leagues composing that system. Granted, such public expenditures for sport entertainment would have to be considered in light of pressing social services needs—health, education, housing, food, and so on. Still, publicly owned pro sport teams might be profitable, or at least not be a financial drain on public funds.

CONCLUDING REMARKS

There are alternative models to the current professional team sports ownership system. The antitrust exemption, which has been the foundation of professional team sports monopoly power, can be removed from MLB. Municipal or public ownership, or even a municipally controlled league organization, might be a popular new form of owning and organizing professional team sports. Under such models, pro sport teams would then really become "yours."

NOTES

1. Major league baseball's antitrust exemption has been under attack in the courts and in Congress for over seventy years, but it has remained intact.
2. Rothstein has synthesized the seminal insights of Bachrach and Baratz (1962, 1970), who conceptualized what they called "the two faces of power," and Lukes (1974), who articulated a "three-dimensional" view of power.
3. For example, members of the National Football League Players Association are getting $30 million in back pay for unfair labor practices committed by team owners during the 1987 players' strike.

4. The Boston Celtics of the NBA are a publicly traded firm, but private ownership still controls the franchise.
5. Neither baseball nor football permits community ownership. The NFL requires that one person have operating control over the team. But in *Sullivan* v. *NFL* (1993) Massachusetts federal district court jury concluded that the NFL illegally restrained trade when it imposed a rule that prohibits public ownership of NFL teams. Green Bay's public ownership is permitted under a grandfather clause written during the league's formative years.

REFERENCES

Anderson, B. (1991). *Imagined Communities: Reflections on the Origin and Spread of Nationalism*. New York: Verso.

Baade, R. A., & R. F. Dye (1988). "Sports stadiums and area development: A critical view," *Economic Development Quarterly 2*, 265–275.

Bachrach, P., & M. S. Baratz (1970). *Power and Poverty: Theory and Practice*. New York: Oxford University Press.

Baim, D. (1994). *The Sports Stadium as a Municipal Investment*. Westport, Connecticut: Greenwood Press.

Bartimole, R. (1994, June). "'If you build it, we will stay,'" *The Progressive 58*, 28–31.

Caulk, S. (1989, June 18). "The villain," *Rocky Mountain News*, pp. 1S, 16S-17S.

Clarke, N. (1990a, August 2). "NL expansion price pegged at $95 million," *Rocky Mountain News*, pp. 73, 84.

Clarke, N. (1990b, August 15). "Ownership groups ready to emerge," *Rocky Mountain News*, p. 87.

Corliss, R. (1992, August 24). "Build it, and they might come," *Time* 50–52.

Euchner, C. C. (1993). *Playing the Field: Why Sports Teams Move and Cities Fight to Keep Them*. Baltimore: Johns Hopkins University Press.

Freedman, W. (1987). *Professional Sports and Antitrust*. New York: Quorum Books.

Goodman, M. (1988). "The home team," *Z Magazine 1* (1), 62–65.

Goodman, M. (1990, November). "Why not nonprofit sports?" *Z Magazine 3*, 88–90.

Gorman, J., & K. Calhoun (1994). *The Name of the Game: The Business of Sports*. New York: Wiley.

Greider, W. (1993). *Who Will Tell the People: The Betrayal of American Democracy*. New York: Simon & Schuster.

Grisi, A. J., & J. D. Reichert (1988, April 4). "Municipalities try to win sports arena trophies," *Standard & Poor's Creditweek*, pp. 18–19.

Hoffman, D. (1989). *Sportsbiz: An Irreverent Look at Big Business in Pro Sports*. Champaign, Illinois: Leisure Press.

Jennings, K. (1990). *Balls and Strikes: The Money Game in Professional Baseball*. New York: Praeger.

Johnson, A. (1993). *Minor League Baseball and Local Economic Development*. Champaign: University of Illinois Press.

Katz, B. (1994, September 26). "Seize every team!" *The Nation 259*, 297.

Kimmelman, G. (1992). Testimony. Subcommittee on Antitrust, Monopolies and Business Rights of the Committee on the Judiciary, United States Senate, 102nd Congress, second session. (1993) *The Validity of Major League Baseball's Exemption from the Antitrust Laws* (serial no. J-102-90). Washington, D.C.: U.S. Government Printing Office.

"Kroc wanted to give Padres to San Diego," *Rocky Mountain News*, p. 6S.

Lipsitz, G. (1984). "Sports stadia and urban development: A tale of three cities." *Journal of Sport & Social Issues 8*(2), 1–18.

Lowenfish, L. (1991). *The Imperfect Diamond: The Story of Baseball's Reserve System and the Men Who Fought to Change It*, rev. ed. New York: Stein and Day.

Lukes, S. (1974). *Power: A Radical View*. London: Macmillan.

Noll, R. G. (1992). Testimony. Subcommittee on Antitrust, Monopolies and Business Rights of the Committee on the Judiciary, United States Senate, 102nd Congress, second session. (1993) *The Validity of Major League Baseball's Exemption from the Antitrust Laws* (serial no. J–102-90). Washington, D.C.: U.S. Government Printing Office.

Okner, B.A. (1974). "Subsidies of stadiums and arenas." In R. G. Noll (ed.), *Government and the Sports Business* (pp. 325–347). Washington, D.C.: Brookings Institution.

Ozanian, M. K., & S. Taub (1992, July 7). "Big leagues, bad business," *Financial World 161*, 34–51.

Quirk, J., & R. D. Fort (1992). *Pay Dirt: The Business of Professional Team Sports*. Princeton, New Jersey: Princeton University Press.

Rosentraub, M. S., & S. R. Nunn (1978). "Suburban city investment in professional sports," *American Behavioral Scientist 21*, 393–414.

Ross, S. F. (1989). "Monopoly sport leagues," *Minnesota Law Review 73*, 643–761.

Rothstein, L. E. (1986). *Plant Closings: Power, Politics, and Workers*. Dover, Massachusetts: Auburn House.

Sage, G. H. (1990). *Power and Ideology in American Sport: A Critical Perspective*. Champaign, Illinois: Human Kinetics.

Sage, G. H. (1993). Stealing Home: Political, economic, and media power and a publicly funded baseball stadium in Denver," *Journal of Sport & Social Issues 17*, 110–124.

Schiller, H. I. (1989). *Culture Inc.: The Corporate Takeover of Public Expression*. New York: Oxford University Press.

Scorecard (1994, October 31). *Sports Illustrated 81*, 11–12, 14.

Scott, J. C. (1985). *Weapons of the Weak: Everyday Forms of Peasant Resistance*. New Haven, Connecticut: Yale University Press.

Scott, J. C. (1990). *Domination and Arts of Resistance*. New Haven, Connecticut: Yale University Press.

Scully, G. W. (1984). Testimony. *Antitrust policy and professional sports*. Oversight hearings, Subcommittee on Monopolies and Commercial Law, Committee on the Judiciary, House of Representatives. Washington, D.C.: U.S. Government Printing Office.

Staff (1990, August 15). "News considers ownership share," *Rocky Mountain News*, p. 92.

Steadman, R. M. (1984). "Professional baseball and the antitrust laws: An arbitrated impasse?" Master's thesis, California State University, Hayward.

Steinbreder, J. (1993, September 13). "The owners," *Sports Illustrated 79*, 64–86.

Sullivan, N. J. (1992). *The Diamond Revolution: The Prospects for Baseball after the Collapse of Its Ruling Class*. New York: St. Martin's Press.

Zimbalist, A. (1992). *Baseball and Billions*. New York: Basic Books.

25. *Baseball's Antitrust Immunity Should Be Repealed*

HOWARD METZENBAUM

This morning, the Antitrust Subcommittee holds an oversight hearing on the validity of major league baseball's exemption from the antitrust laws. All of us recognize that today's hearing does not involve one of the critical problems facing the new President and the new Congress, but there is, nevertheless, intense interest in this subject among the public, the press, and my colleagues.

The reason for this interest is simple. Baseball has been a special part of American life for over a century. It provides millions of fans with a well-deserved break from the rigors of everyday life. Americans from all walks of life and from all parts of the country have grown up with this game. It has been a bridge of tradition and nostalgia that connects the past with the present and parents with their children.

But while the game of baseball remains a simple pleasure, the business of baseball has become complicated and, at times, cutthroat. As a consequence, there has been a certain element of disenchantment as to the fans. Major league baseball is not just a sport. It is also a billion-dollar big business, and it is a big business which enjoys unique treatment under the law.

A LEGALIZED CARTEL

Unlike any other big business in America, major league baseball is a legally sanctioned, unregulated cartel. The Supreme Court conferred that extraordinary privilege upon baseball 70 years ago when it granted major league baseball a complete exemption from the antitrust laws. Justice Holmes reasoned that the antitrust laws did not apply because baseball could not be considered interstate commerce. Although the soundness of this ruling has often been questioned even by the Court itself, it has never been overturned. Instead, the Court has tossed the ball to Congress, which is why we are here today.

SOURCE: "Baseball's Antitrust Immunity Should Be Repealed" by Howard Metzenbaum. Opening statement by Senator Howard Metzenbaum, chairman of the Subcommittee on Antitrust, Monopolies, and Business Rights, Committee on the Judiciary (December 10, 1992). It is a violation of the law to reproduce this selection by any means whatsoever without the written permission of the copyright holder.

While Congress did not create baseball's blanket antitrust immunity, we do have the authority to remove it. Many in this body now believe that it is time to repeal the exemption. The burden is on major league baseball to demonstrate that the exemption is in the public interest.

Baseball's antitrust exemption is a privilege that the baseball owners may be abusing. I am particularly concerned that their ouster of [former major league baseball commissioner] Fay Vincent . . . and their plans to weaken the commissioner's powers invites more abuse of that privilege. Fay Vincent understood that the antitrust exemption placed a special obligation on the commissioner to govern the sport in a manner that protected the public interest. Vincent had independent authority to put the interests of the fans and the interests of the sport of baseball ahead of the business interests of the team owners. That is no longer the case.

Jerry Reinsdorf, the owner of the Chicago White Sox, and one of the key participants in Vincent's ouster, has stated that the job of the next baseball commissioner will be to "run the business for the owners, not the players or the umpires or the fans.". . .

It appears that the owners don't want a strong and independent commissioner who can act in the best interests of the sport or act as a potential check against abuse of their monopoly power. Instead, they want a commissioner who will function as the cruise director for their cartel. If decisions about the direction and future of major league baseball are going to be dictated by the business interests of team owners, then the owners should be required to play by the same antitrust rules that apply to any other business.

Even if the owners give the next commissioner a fig leaf of authority, Vincent's ouster sends a clear signal that he or she should not cross them. It also raises questions about whether baseball can respond credibly and effectively to allegations of misconduct by an owner or league official. . . .

There are other issues that need to be explored aside from the question of the commissioner's authority. The other three major professional sports—football, basketball, and hockey—function quite well without the blanket exemption from the antitrust laws enjoyed by baseball. Why should baseball be treated differently?

A number of commentators assert that baseball uses its privileged status to maintain an artificial scarcity of franchises. The recent tug of war between Tampa Bay [St. Petersburg] and San Francisco is a perfect illustration. It is clear that the number of cities which can support baseball franchises greatly exceeds the number of franchises established by the owners.

A scarcity of franchises inflates the resale value of existing teams and increases each owner's share of baseball's national broadcasting revenue, the total of which is about $380 million annually. It also enables owners to squeeze concessions and subsidies from their home cities by threatening relocation to another city. Many cities badly in need of revenues for schools, hospitals, their police and fire forces, and other vital projects have been forced to obtain public funding of elaborate new stadiums or risk having their team move to another city. This blackmail game is unseemly and a disservice to the fans.

The baseball owners trumpet their commitment to franchise stability even though they routinely threaten to abandon their home city whenever it suits them financially, and the owners reportedly have refused to permit municipal ownership of teams, which is probably the most effective way to protect fans from franchise relocations. When Joan Kroc tried to give the Padres to the city of San Diego, baseball's barons said no.

For decades, the owners also used their antitrust exemption to suppress players' salaries and stifle player mobility through the use of the reserve clause. As it now stands, the reserve clause can bind a player to a single team for 6 years. Players have gained a limited amount of movement through the collective bargaining process, but the reopening of the labor agreement means that the players will once again have to bargain for some semblance of a free market. Moreover, minor league players, who constitute the vast majority of professional ballplayers, still labor under conditions reminiscent of indentured servitude.

HURTING THE FANS

Baseball's special treatment under the antitrust laws also has helped to inflate the value of its TV contracts. The baseball owners have agreed among themselves to impose territorial restrictions on the broadcasting of games by local TV stations. These restrictions can facilitate the movement of games to pay TV and hurt fans who can't afford or don't have access to cable.

The sport of baseball is a national treasure, and both Congress and the team owners must be careful not to take actions that would hurt the game and alienate fans. But if the antitrust exemption does provide some benefit to the fans and the game, the owners are going to have to prove it. If the public does not benefit, then the exemption should be restricted or repealed.

26. *The Baseball Strike: A View from the Left*

MICHAEL ZIELINSKI

Sports fans of the left unite. You have nothing to lose but next year's baseball season. Confronted by a host of troubles—from the rise of Oliver North to U.S. military interventions in Haiti and the Middle East—why should the left concern itself with a delay of games in the narrow world of professional sports?

If the players prevail in baseball's labor showdown, the beneficiaries will be fewer than a thousand privileged athletes. The issues at stake, however, transcend sports. The dynamics which disrupted this year's baseball season are being played out across the U.S. economy. Baseball's owners are attempting to assert once and for all management's power to set wages and conditions of employment in a union-free workplace.

Baseball is run by an ownership notable for "gross individual and collective mismanagement, their fierce factional fights, their cynical disregard for decency and honor, their deliberate alienation of press and public, and their tyrannical treatment of their players."

These sentiments could be lifted from yesterday's newspapers, voiced by leaders of the baseball players' union or by a member of Congress seeking to end the baseball business's antitrust exemption. Instead, they appeared in an editorial written for the sports press in 1900.

The roots of baseball's labor troubles stretch to the beginnings of the professional game in the last quarter of the 19th century. At the same time, baseball's current strike reveals a great deal about the state of labor relations in the last years of the 20th century. Most media coverage of the strike depicts the conflict as a tug of war between spoiled millionaire players and arrogant millionaire owners. What's missing from this picture is any sense that the owners are engaged in the true national pastime of American business: union busting.

In an era when permanent replacement workers, contract employees, and give-backs define dealings between workers and bosses, baseball players have created what is arguably the country's strongest union. The Major

League Baseball Players' Association has survived lockouts and won strikes, forcing baseball's owners to cave in during 7 labor disputes in the last 20 years.

The players' biggest victory was free agency, the right to bargain with a team of their choosing after a set number of years in the league. For the preceding century players were virtually indentured servants, bound to a single team for life through baseball's reserve clause.

The current conflict was sparked by the owners' attempt to force a salary cap on the players. Incapable of sharing revenue among themselves, the owners want to redistribute the players' wealth to smaller-market teams. The owners have advanced a number of unconvincing rationales as to why this is necessary. The owners claim that a salary cap is the only way to ensure that poorer teams aren't perpetually outbid for players, allowing the richer teams to dominate. Yet during the first 15 years of free agency 20 of the then 26 teams won division titles, demonstrating the competitive balance of the game. The owners also initially insisted that nearly three-quarters of the teams were losing money under the current financial system. Challenged to produce numbers to back up these claims, the owners backtracked, acknowledging that the majority of teams are profitable.

WORKERS CALLED OUT

Management's unwillingness to bargain in good faith indicates that their ultimate objective is not to reach a settlement, but to destroy the union. Nor are baseball's owners alone. The National Hockey League has adopted a similar strategy, going so far as to reject a no-strike pledge from the players' union so management could proceed with a lockout. Even in the National Basketball Association, widely regarded as a model of enlightened cooperation between players and owners, there were rumors of a lockout if players didn't accept modifications in their bargaining rights.

After two decades of steadily rising players' salaries, the owners are striking back. This new militancy by owners is indicative of the changing nature of sports business and reflects trends in the larger corporate world. Increasingly, major corporations linked to the entertainment industry are buying into sports. Disney, Blockbuster Video, and ITT all obtained franchises in recent years. These corporate giants bring experience battling unions to their new field and are prepared to force on the players the same discipline they demand from labor in their more work-a-day ventures.

Ownership hopes to restructure baseball business similar to the changes turning other industries inside out. A salary cap would lead to a two-tier wage system in baseball. Superstars would still receive top dollar for their services, but veteran players of more average skill would be compelled to take pay cuts or be out of the lineup. Eventually, teams would consist of younger players earning the minimum wage, veterans willing to settle for lower wages, and one or two highly paid stars able to attract fans.

Capital's attempt to force wages downward is a universal trend from the maquila to the locker room. Downsizing is the order of the day as businesses release longtime employees and strip their workforce to a small core of skilled workers surrounded by part-time and contract employees. Ironically, these anti-worker developments may make corporations more vulnerable to pressure from unions. Corporate cutbacks have hit at middle management as well as the rank and file. This makes companies even more dependent on what remains of the skilled work force to run their plants and assembly lines.

The battle being waged by the Major League Baseball Players' Association may herald a revival of craft unionism where workers with unique skills can organize to win concessions. The successful assertion of workers' rights in baseball will not better conditions in sweatshops, but it would strengthen a trend which is pushing certain sectors of the labor movement to reclaim the strike as a strategic weapon. The Communications Workers of America and the United Auto Workers have led successful strikes recently, further demonstrating the growing clout of skilled workers.

Labor's principal task remains organizing the new "contingent" workforce made up largely of women and people of color, with a growing percentage of recent immigrants, competing for low-wage, low-skill dead-end jobs. Even so, victories by the highly skilled sector of the labor movement cannot help but limit corporate power and increase the possibilities for resistance on other fronts.

LIES, DAMN LIES, AND STATISTICS

Much of the press coverage surrounding the strike has helped to weaken any identification union members and working people might feel with players campaigning against management.

The media's depiction of the baseball strike as a grudge match among millionaires is far from accurate. While baseball players are well compensated, a minority approach millionaire status. Virtually every press story has featured the misleading "fact" that the average player salary is $1.2 million. A handful of highly paid stars skew the average upwards. A more meaningful measure of a players' economic worth is the median salary (half make more, half less), which is pegged at $410,000. This pay scale makes for an affluent life, but does not begin to match the rewards of ownership.

The vast majority of professional baseball players undergo an extensive apprenticeship in the minor leagues, where salaries dip below $1,000 a month in most cases. Seven out of every eight professional ballplayers are currently under minor league contracts. Furthermore, the minority of players who make it to the major leagues enjoy brief careers which average less than five years.

The current strike is largely about protecting the rights of the next generation of ballplayers. Most of baseball's top performers have guaranteed contracts that will make them immune to a salary cap in the near future. The owners have offered to phase in a cap over several years, meaning that a majority of active players will be retired before the impact of capped salaries can be felt. While much of the media and many fans berate the players for their selfishness, the strike actually involves a good deal of self-sacrifice to defend what the union has won and guarantee the same rights for younger players who have not yet made it to the big leagues.

The players, of course, may not be what John Lennon had in mind when he sang "a working class hero is something to be." With a minimum wage of $109,000 for their seasonal employment, baseball players are not in the same league as farm workers. Some players earn more in a single season than as much as half the U.S. workforce will take home in a lifetime. The players union has shown no interest in trying to organize among baseball's underclass, the minor leaguers, nor has the union used its high visibility to promote issues of concern to the larger labor movement like universal health care.

Still, the press has consistently relied on partial data and misleading figures to help wipe out any sympathy the players may have received from working people. At least one commentator, Gerald Early, suggests that the hostility that many white fans have expressed towards the players is fueled by racism. While whites have a virtual monopoly on management posts in baseball, many of the game's most talented and best-paid stars are African Americans. By almost exclusively focusing on the perks enjoyed by ballplayers, the press has given the owners a free ride, overlooking the huge profits reaped in recent years through TV contracts and the rental of corporate luxury boxes.

Jim Bouton, former pitcher for the Yankees and author of the clubhouse expose *Ball Four*, summed it up best: "While the players don't deserve all that money, the owners don't deserve it even more."

It's not just the players who are being squeezed by sports magnates. Cities which host professional sports teams are victimized by owners demanding publicly financed stadiums, tax breaks, and increased cuts on parking and concession revenues from municipally owned arenas.

Sports, like the auto and steel industries, has become "delocalized," no longer dependent on a particular community, but ready to pounce on the most profitable deal whether it means moving a steel plant to South Korea or a football team to Indianapolis, as happened to the Baltimore Colts in 1984.

Just as corporations use the threat of relocation to extract tax breaks and favorable labor policies, sports teams strong-arm cities into surrendering a grab bag of goodies to retain or attract a franchise. These include publicly financed stadium renovations which produce luxury boxes for corporate ticket holders, guaranteed ticket sales, and even control over the construction of public roads and transportation systems.

Cities in decline are especially vulnerable to the manipulations of sports moguls. Hosting major league sports is seen as a quick fix to urban disrepair, holding out the promise of revitalization. Contrary to the claims of stadium boosters, economic studies show that cities usually spend more than they gain by courting sports teams.

The owners' ability to wring concessions from local governments rests on the most basic economic premise: where demand exceeds supply the supplier sets the price. In the case of baseball these manipulations are facilitated by its unique status as a two-billion-dollar-a-year business which enjoys an antitrust exemption courtesy of a 1922 Supreme Court decision.

The owners keep a tight grip on expansion, driving up the cost of the product. In 1990, baseball stopped former Padres owner Joan Kroc from giving the team to the city of San Diego, citing the bad precedent that community control would set.

The owners' decision to cancel the season and the World Series has produced renewed questioning of their antitrust exemption. Congressional committees are beginning to reconsider baseball's special status as an officially approved monopoly. Leading the trust busters is outgoing Senator Howard Metzenbaum (D-OH) and Representative Jack Brooks (D-TX).

These efforts may be stymied by the shrewd decision of baseball's owners to make Senate Majority Leader George Mitchell a top candidate to become the next commissioner of baseball. This move has already yielded dividends. Soon after Mitchell indicated interest in the job, the Senate put the antitrust issue on hold. Some of Mitchell's closest allies, including liberal icon Ted Kennedy, cast crucial votes in favor of the baseball owners, blocking Metzenbaum's attempts to move the bill from the Judiciary Committee to the Senate floor.

PLAYERS IN A LEAGUE OF THEIR OWN

Never at a loss for schemes to make a quick buck, owners are floating the idea of operating a scab league next season. Under this scenario teams would stock their spring training camps with minor leaguers hungry for a place in the big leagues, while trying to entice major leaguers to break with the union and begin collecting fat paychecks once again. If they succeed, the owners will be the undisputed lords of baseball.

The players may counter by forming a league of their own, reasoning that they are the source of all baseball's wealth. There is historical precedent for such a move. In 1890, the hired help revolted from the National League and established the Players' League. This experimental enterprise shared profits among the players and their financial backers, giving players equal voice and vote on all decisions affecting business operations as well as the game on the field. The radical notion of the workers running the show was unacceptable to the robber barons who ran 19th-century baseball, and the upstart league was crushed after a year. The time may now be ripe for baseball to go back to the past for its future.

Even if the players do take the dramatic step of forming a league run by its employees, no one would make the claim that baseball players are on the cutting edge of social activism in America. All the same, the left should not be indifferent to the final outcome of the strike.

Progressives need to break out of the cultural isolation which prevents us from engaging the attention of larger sectors of our society. Sports is a place to start. By and large the left ignores sports, condemns it as a violent manifestation of patriarchal power, or reduces it to a bread-and-circus extravaganza which can only distract people from the real work of political activism. There's much truth in all of the above.

At the same time, sports does offer a version of community to our increasingly fragmented society (predominantly—but far from exclusively—the male portion). It may not be much in terms of egalitarianism, but where else besides the ballpark do brokers and burger flippers regularly come together in a society increasingly segregated by race and class.

Sports provides what sociologists call a "contrived community" which at its best unites people. Unlike television or the movies, which rely on an ethic of individualized consumption, sports by their very nature bring large numbers of people together in a common endeavor.

Baseball is a vital part of America's popular culture. Developments on the diamond do have an impact on society. The struggle of Jackie Robinson, and other, less-celebrated African Americans, served as a bellwether in beginning to dismantle segregation in the 1950s. Tens of millions of people are passionate about baseball. They realize, on some level, that corporate greed is destroying something they love. The left needs to communicate with—not lecture—the nation's sports fans, initiating a dialogue on the destructive power which corporations wield over our lives.

■ **FOR FURTHER STUDY**

Angell, Roger, "Hardball," *The New Yorker* (October 17, 1994): 65–68, 72–76.

Bartimole, Roldo, "'If You Build It, We Will Stay.' Baseball Holds a City Hostage," *The Progressive* 58 (June 1994): 28–31.

Eitzen, D. Stanley, "The Sociology of Amateur Sport: An Overview," *International Review for the Sociology of Sport* 24 (1989): 95–104.

Euchner, Charles C., *Playing the Field: Why Sports Teams Move and Cities Fight to Move Them* (Baltimore: Johns Hopkins University Press, 1993).

Goodman, Matthew, "Behind the Ball," *Z Magazine* 4 (January 1991): 86–87.

Gorman, Jerry, and Kirk Calhoun, *The Name of the Game: The Business of Sports* (New York: Wiley, 1994).

Katz, Donald, 1994. *Just Do It: The Nike Spirit in the Corporate World* (New York: Random House, 1994).

Lipsyte, Robert, "The Dying Game: Why Major League Baseball Has Gotten Too Big for Its Own Jockstrap," *Esquire* (April 1993): 101–105.

Lowenfish, Lee, *The Imperfect Diamond: A History of Baseball's Labor Wars* (New York: Da Capo Press, 1991).

McMillen, Tom, *Out of Bounds: How the American Sports Establishment Is Being Driven by Greed and Hypocrisy—and What Needs to Be Done About It* (New York: Simon & Schuster, 1992).

Miller, Marvin, *A Whole Different Ball Game: The Sport and Business of Baseball* (New York: Birch Lane, 1991).

Quirk, James, and Rodney D. Fort, *Pay Dirt: The Business of Professional Team Sports* (Princeton, New Jersey: Princeton University Press, 1992).

Sage, George H., "Stealing Home: Political, Economic, and Media Power and a Publicly Funded Baseball Stadium in Denver," *Journal of Sport & Social Issues* 17 (August 1993): 110–124.

Sands, Jack, and Peter Gammons, *Coming Apart at the Seams: How Baseball Owners, Players, and Television Executives Have Led Our National Pastime to the Brink of Disaster* (New York: Macmillan, 1993).

Simpson, Vyv, and Andrew Jennings, *Dishonored Games: Corruption, Money, and Greed at the Olympics* (New York: S.P.I. Books, 1992).

Simpson, Vyv, and Andrew Jennings, *The Lords of the Rings: Power, Money and Drugs in the Modern Olympics* (London: Simon & Schuster Ltd., 1992).

Strasser, J. B., and Laurie Becklund, *Swoosh: The Unauthorized Story of Nike and the Men Who Played There* (New York: Harcourt Brace Jovanovich, 1991).

Part Nine

Structured Inequality: Sport and Race / Ethnicity

By definition, a minority group is one that (1) is relatively powerless compared with the majority group, (2) possesses traits that make it different from others, (3) is systematically condemned by negative stereotyped beliefs, and (4) is singled out for differential and unfair treatment (that is, discrimination). Race (a socially defined category on the basis of a presumed genetic heritage resulting in distinguishing social characteristics) and ethnicity (the condition of being culturally distinct on the basis of race, religion, or national origin) are two traditional bases for minority group status and the resulting social inequality. Sociologists of sport are interested in the question: Is sport an area of social life where performance counts and race or ethnicity is irrelevant? The three selections in this section examine four racial or ethnic minorities—Native Americans, Asian Americans, Latinos, and African Americans to answer this question.

The first selection, by journalist Kevin Simpson, seeks an answer to the dilemma posed by the typical behaviors of excellent Native American athletes from reservations: Why do so many who are given scholarships either refuse them or return quickly to the reservation? These responses do not make sense to Anglos because the reservation has high unemployment, a life of dependency, and disproportionate alcohol abuse. Simpson points to these young men being "pulled" by the familiar, by the strong bonds of family, and by their unique culture. They are also "pushed" back to the reservation by social isolation, discrimination, poor high school preparation for college, and little hope for a return on their investment in a college education.

The second selection, by Mark A. Grey, reports the findings from ethnographic research in Garden City, Kansas. This city is undergoing significant demographic change. The students in Garden City High School are one-third minority (Latinos, Southeast Asians, and African Americans), with a sizable number of these minority students being recent immigrants. Grey's study describes the degree to which sport aids or hinders the assimilation of minority students.

The final selection, by Richard E. Lapchick and Jeffrey R. Benedict of the Center for the Study of Sport in Society, provides the most recent data on the extent of racial discrimination in professional sports.

27. *Sporting Dreams Die on the "Rez"*

KEVIN SIMPSON

Last season, basketball fans followed Willie White everywhere through the unforgiving South Dakota winter. Mesmerized by smooth moves and spectacular dunks, they watched the most celebrated product of the state's hoop-crazy Indian tribes secure his status as local legend by leading his high school to an undefeated season and state championship.

They would mob him after games in an almost frightening scene of mass adulation, press scraps of paper toward him and beg for an autograph, preferably scribbled beneath some short personal message. White would oblige by scrawling short, illegible phrases before signing. He made certain they were illegible for fear someone would discover that the best prep basketball player in South Dakota could barely read or write.

As the resident basketball hero on the impoverished Pine Ridge Reservation, where there was precious little to cheer about before the state title rekindled embers of Indian pride, White was allowed to slip undisturbed through the reservation school system until, by his senior year, he could read at only the sixth-grade level. Ironically, the same hero status moved him to admit his problem and seek help. The constant humiliation at the hands of autograph-seekers proved more than he could take.

"I had to face up to it," says White, a soft-spoken 6-foot-4 Sioux who looks almost scholarly behind his wire-rimmed glasses. "I couldn't go on forever like that. In school I didn't study. I cheated on every test they gave me. I couldn't read good enough to answer the questions."

After some intense individual help with his reading and writing, this fall White enrolled at Huron (S.D.) College, where he intends to continue his basketball career and take remedial reading courses. If he manages to play four years and complete his degree, he'll be the first schoolboy athlete from Pine Ridge to do so.

Other than his close friends, nobody thinks he stands a chance. Indians usually don't.

Every year, all over the western U.S., promising native American athletes excel in high school sports only to abandon dreams of college, return

SOURCE: "Sporting Dreams Die on the 'Rez'" by Kevin Simpson. From *The Denver Post*, September 6, 1987, pp. 1C, 19C. Copyright © 1987 *The Denver Post*. Reprinted by permission.

to economically depressed reservations, and survive on their per capita checks, welfare-like payments from the tribal government, or the good will of more fortunate relatives. They waste away quietly, victims of alcohol, victims of inadequate education, victims of boredom, victims of poverty, but nearly always victims of their own ambivalence, caught between a burning desire to leave the reservation and an irresistible instinct to stay.

"We've had two or three kids get scholarships in the eight years I've been here," says Roland Bradford, athletic director and basketball coach at Red Cloud High School, just a few miles down the highway from Pine Ridge. "None have lasted. It's kind of a fantasy thing. In high school they talk about going to college, but it's not a reality. They have no goals set. They start out, things get tough and they come home."

At 6-foot-7 and 280 pounds, Red Cloud's Dave Brings Plenty inspired enough comparisons to the Refrigerator to lure a photographer from *People* magazine out to the reservation. He went to Dakota Wesleyan to pursue his football career, but returned home after suffering a mild concussion in practice. He never played a game. Brings Plenty says he might enroll at a different school sometime in the future, but his plans are vague. For now, he's content to hang out on the reservation and work as a security guard at a bingo parlor.

Some of the athlete-dropouts have squandered mind-boggling potential. Jeff Turning Heart, a long-distance legend on South Dakota's Cheyenne River Reservation, enrolled at Black Hills State College in Spearfish, S.D., on a Bureau of Indian Affairs grant in 1980 amid great expectations. He left eight days later.

In 1982, he wound up at Adams State College in Alamosa. Longtime Adams State coach Joe Vigil, the U.S. men's distance coach for the 1988 Olympics, says that as a freshman Turning Heart was far more physically gifted than even Pat Porter, the Adams State graduate who now ranks as the premier U.S. runner at 10,000 meters. Both Porter and Vigil figured Turning Heart was on a course to win the national cross country title—until he left school, supposedly to tend to his gravely ill father in North Dakota. He promised to return in a few days. The story was bogus and Turning Heart never went back.

At Black Hills State, where in 19 years as athletic director and track coach, David Little has seen only one Indian track athlete graduate, Turning Heart wasn't the first world-class, native American runner to jilt him. Myron Young Dog, a distance man from Pine Ridge who once won 22 straight cross country races in high school, came to Black Hills after dropping out of Ellendale (N.D.) Junior College in 1969. Although he was academically ineligible for varsity sports and hadn't trained, Young Dog stepped onto the track during a physical conditioning class and ran two miles in 9:30 "like it was a Sunday jog," according to Little. Three weeks later he entered a 15-km road race and ran away from all the collegiate competition.

It was a tantalizing glimpse of talent ultimately wasted. Little still rates Young Dog as one of the top 10 athletes ever to come out of South Dakota, but in the spring of 1970 he returned to the reservation, never to run competitively again.

It doesn't take many heartbreaks before the college coaches catch on to the risky business of recruiting off the reservations. Although Indian athletes often are immensely talented and given financial backing from the tribe and the BIA—a budgetary boon to small schools short on scholarship funds— they suffer from a widespread reputation as high-risk recruits who probably won't stick around for more than a few weeks.

That's part of the reason so many schools backed off Willie White—that and his reading deficiency. Huron College coach Fred Paulsen, who made White his first in-state recruit in four years, thought the youngster's potential made him worth the risk.

"I hate to stereotype," says Paulsen, "but is he the typical Indian? If Willie comes and doesn't make it, nobody will be surprised. My concern is that he'll go home for the weekend and say he'll be back on Monday. Which Monday?"

Talented Indians are diverted from their academic and athletic career courses for many reasons, but often they are sucked back to subsistence-level life on the reservation by the vacuum created by inadequate education and readily available escapes like drugs and alcohol.

Ted Little Moon, an all-state basketball player for Pine Ridge High School in 1984 and '85, still dominates the asphalt slab outside the school. At 6-foot-6, he roams from baseline to baseline jamming in rebounds, swatting away opponents' shots and threading blind passes to teammates beneath the basket. He is unmistakable small-college talent.

But Little Moon missed his first opportunity to play ball in college when he failed to graduate from high school. By the following August, though, he had passed his high school equivalency exam and committed to attend Huron College. But when the basketball coach showed up at his house to pick him up and drive him to school, Little Moon said he couldn't go because he had gotten his girlfriend pregnant and had to take care of a newborn son.

He played independent basketball, a large-scale Indian intramural network, until last fall, when he planned to enroll at Haskell Junior College, an all-Indian school in Lawrence, Kan. He and some friends drank heavily the night before he was to take the bus to Kansas. Little Moon was a passenger in a friend's car when they ran a stop sign and hit another vehicle. He spent four days in jail, missed his bus and missed out on enrolling at Haskell.

Now he talks of going back to school, of playing basketball again, but there's ambivalence in his voice. He has become accustomed to cashing his bi-weekly per capita check for $28.50, drinking beer, and growing his own marijuana at a secret location on the reservation. He distributes it free to his friends.

"I guess I'm scared to get away," Little Moon admits. "But also I'm afraid I'll be stuck here and be another statistic. You grow old fast here. If I get away, I have a chance. But I'm used to what I'm doing now. Here, your mom takes care of you, the BIA takes care of you. You wait for your $28.50 and then party. It's something to look forward to."

"I started drinking as a freshman in high school, smoking dope as a sophomore. I used to get high before practice, after practice. I still do it, on the average, maybe every other day. After I play, I smoke some. It makes you forget what you're doing on the reservation."

At home, alcohol offers whatever false comfort family ties cannot. Then it kills. Two years ago, Red Cloud's Bradford tallied all the alcohol-related deaths he had known personally and came up with some sobering statistics. In 13 years of teaching, 18 of his former students have died in alcohol-related tragedies. Aside from students, he has known an incredible 61 people under the age of 22 who have lost their lives in one way or another to the bottle.

Many died along a two-mile stretch of Highway 407 that connects Pine Ridge with Whiteclay, Neb., a depressing cluster of bars and liquor stores that do a land-office business. Three years ago, South Dakota's highway department began erecting metal markers at the site of each alcohol-related fatality. Locals say that if they'd started 10 years ago, the signs would form an unbroken chain along the road. They'd have run out of signs before they ran out of death.

Among Indians nationwide, four of the top 10 causes of death are alcohol-related: accidents, suicides, [cirrhosis] of the liver, and homicide. Alcohol mortality is nearly five times higher among Indians, at 30 per 100,000 population, than for all other races. According to Dr. Eva Smith of the Indian Health Service in Washington, D.C., between 80 and 90 percent of all Indian accidents, suicides, and homicides are alcohol-related.

Fred Beauvais, a research scientist at Colorado State University, points out that Indians not only start using drugs and alcohol earlier than the general population, but the rate of use also tends to be higher. According to a 1987 study of 2,400 subjects in eight western tribes Beauvais conducted with funding from the National Institute on Drug Abuse, 50 percent of Indian high school seniors were classified as "at risk" of serious harm because of drug and alcohol use. An amazing 43 percent are at risk by the seventh grade. The figure for seniors probably is too low, Beauvais explains, because by 12th grade many Indian students already have dropped out.

He attributes these phenomena not to racial or cultural idiosyncrasies, but socio-economic conditions on the reservations.

"Once it becomes socially ingrained, it's a vicious cycle," Beauvais says. "The kids see the adults doing it and they see no alternatives. It's a real trap. For some Indian kids to choose not to drink means to deny their Indianness. That can be a powerful factor."

Even those athletes who excel in the classroom are not necessarily immune to the magnetic pull of alcohol. Beau LeBeau, a 4.0 student at Red Cloud High who has started for the varsity basketball team since he was in eighth grade, recognizes the dangers but speaks of them as if they are elements quite out of his control. He estimates that 90 percent of his friends abuse alcohol.

"I'm going to the best academic school on the reservation," he says. "I should get a good education if I don't turn to drugs and alcohol in the next few years and ruin it for myself. In my room before I go to sleep I think, 'Is this how I'm going to spend the rest of my life? On the reservation?' I hope not."

For all the roadside signs that stand as chilling monuments to death around Pine Ridge, the drinking continues, a false and addictive cure for boredom and futility.

"If they win they want to celebrate," offers Bryan Brewer, athletic director at Pine Ridge High School. "If they lose, that's another excuse to drink. People who didn't make it want to drag the good athletes down with them."

Consequently, the road to a college athletic career sometimes ends before it even begins.

"I'm not opposed to recruiting the Indian athlete," offers Black Hills State athletic director Little. "I'm selective about who I recruit, though. I don't have the answer to the problem and don't know I totally understand the situation. I do know that what's going on now is not working."

Something definitely isn't working in Towoac (pronounced TOI-ahk), in southwestern Colorado, where Indian athletes don't even wait until after high school to see their careers disintegrate. There, on the Ute Mountain Reservation, a multitude of Indian athletes compete and excel up to eighth grade and then quit rather than pursue sports at Montezuma-Cortez High, a mixed-race school 17 miles north of the reservation in the town of Cortez.

They drop out at the varsity level sometimes for academic reasons but often because of racial tension—or what they feel is bias on the part of white coaches. Pressed for particulars, current and former athletes make only vague accusations of negative attitudes and rarely cite specific instances. But how much of the discrimination is real and how much imagined is academic. The perception of discrimination remains, passed down among the athletes almost as an oral tradition.

For instance, today's athletes hear stories like those told by former Cortez High athlete Hanley Frost, who in the mid-1970s felt the wrath of the school administration when he was a sophomore on the basketball team and insisted on wearing his hair long, braided in traditional Indian style. He played four games with it tucked into his jersey but then was told school policy demanded that he cut it off. Eventually, he quit the team and began experimenting with drugs and alcohol.

Frost: "Really, it was the towns-people who didn't enjoy having a long-haired Indian on the team. There were a lot of people out there who would rather see their kids in a position on the team an Indian kid has."

"There's something about Towoac that just doesn't sit right," adds reservation athletic director Doug Call, a Mormon who came to the Ute Mountain Reservation from Brigham Young University. "I don't know if people are afraid or what, but there's a stigma if you live out here."

Those Indians who do participate in sports at the high school level tend to live in Cortez, not on the reservation. An invisible wall of distrust seems to surround Towoac, where most of the young athletes play what is known on reservations as "independent ball," a loosely organized kind of intramural basketball.

"They feel they're not getting a fair chance, I know they do," says Gary Gellatly, the Cortez High School athletic director who once served as recreation director on the reservation. "And I'm sure they have been discriminated against, directly or indirectly. It's tough to get them to compete. Yet you go out there on any weekend and watch those independent tournaments you'll see kids playing basketball that you've never seen before. But I'm afraid if we start an overt effort to get them to participate you crowd them into a tighter corner. In a sense, not participating because they think they might be discriminated against is a cop-out, but it's been perpetuated by circumstances. Somewhere, something happened that wasn't good."

After massive turnover in the school's coaching staff, some new hires have expressed a desire to see more Indians become involved in the school's sports programs. Bill Moore, the new head football coach, heard the rumors that Indian kids wouldn't even try out for the squad and mailed tryout invitations to much of the student body including as many Indian boys as he could find addresses for. Even so, the turnout hasn't been markedly different from previous years.

"The solution," says varsity basketball coach Gordon Shepherd, "is that something has to give. Cultural groups that remain within themselves don't succeed. For Indians to succeed in white society terms, they have to give up some cultural ethnicity."

Ethnic idiosyncrasies present a whole range of problems—from students' inclination or ability to perform in the classroom to conflicts such as the one currently under way at Jemez Pueblo, a small reservation north of Albuquerque, N.M. There, in a hotbed of mountain running, a cross country coach at a mixed-race school has struggled with athletes who reject modern training techniques for the less formal but highly traditional ways of their ancestors.

On some reservations, Indian student-athletes are merely ill-prepared to cope with the stringent academic demands of college. According to BIA statistics, the average Indian high school senior reads at the ninth-grade level.

Of the 20 percent of high school seniors who go on to attempt college, 40 percent drop out.

And with some reservations approaching economic welfare states, students considering college confront a serious question about the value of an education: Why spend four years pursuing a college degree only to return to a reservation that has few or no private sector jobs?

Indians often find themselves without any real ethnic support system in college and become homesick for reservation life and the exceptionally strong bonds of an extended family in which aunts, uncles, and grandparents often live under the same roof. In some tribal cultures, 18- or 19-year-olds still are considered mere children and haven't been pressed to formulate long-term goals. It's no coincidence, says an education administrator for the Arapahoe tribe on the central Wyoming's Wind River Reservation, that most successful Indian students are in their mid- to late 20s—when, incidentally, athletic eligibility has gone by the board.

Even the basic incentive of athletics tends to evaporate in a more intense competitive climate far removed from the reservation.

Myron "The Magician" Chavez, a four-time all-state guard from Wyoming Indian High School on the Wind River Reservation, enrolled at Sheridan (Wyo.) College last fall but left school during pre-season workouts when he was asked to redshirt. He felt he had failed because he didn't step immediately into a starting position. Jeff Brown, who preceded Chavez at WIHS, had a scholarship offer from the University of Kansas in 1982 but turned it down because he feared he would fail—academically if not athletically.

Dave Archambault, a Sioux who started the athletic program at United Tribes Junior College in Bismarck, N.D., has found the fear of failure to be a familiar theme among talented Indian athletes. On the reservations, he points out, athletes become heroes, modern extensions of the old warrior society that disappeared after defeat at the hands of the white man.

"They're kicking butt on the reservation," Archambault explains, "and then all of the sudden they're working out with juniors and seniors in college and getting their butts kicked. They're not held in that high regard and esteem. But they can go back to the reservation any time and get it."

They recapture their high school glory through independent ball, the intramural network among reservations that quenches an insatiable thirst for basketball competition among all age groups. There are tournaments nearly every weekend and an all-Indian national tournament each spring, where the best teams often recruit talent from a wide area by offering modest incentives like cash and expenses. At most levels, though, independent ball resembles extremely organized pickup basketball.

For most Indian athletes, it represents the outer limits of achievement, caught though it is in a void between the reservation and the outside world. It's in that limbo—socially as well as athletically—that most Indians play out their careers.

"There's no way to return to the old way, spiritually and economically," observes Billy Mills, the 1964 Olympic gold medalist at 10,000 meters who grew up on the Pine Ridge Reservation. "It's like walking death—no goals, no commitment, no accomplishment. If you go too far into society, there's a fear of losing your Indian-ness. There's a spiritual factor that comes into play. To become part of white society you give up half your soul. Society wants us to walk in one world with one spirit. But we have to walk in two worlds with one spirit."

28. *Sport and Immigrant, Minority, and Anglo Relations in Garden City (Kansas) High School*

MARK A. GREY

Football is like life. . . . If you don't play to win, why keep score?

Assistant football coach, Garden City High School

Despite anthropological evidence to the contrary, the notion that the United States is a melting pot persists. Schools are often viewed as important agencies for the assimilation of immigrants and minorities. As an integral part of high school life in America, sports are often assumed to have an essential role in the assimilation process. However, many researchers (e.g., Allison & Lueschen, 1979; Blanchard, 1974, Cochran, 1976) have refuted this notion, challenging both the assertion that assimilation is necessarily normal, and inevitable, and previous assumptions that established sports in dominant society are accepted by minority groups in toto.

In terms of whether groups must necessarily adopt dominant game forms in toto, the Navajo have been observed to adapt the game of basketball to reflect aspects of their culture that differ from those of the core society (Allison, 1982; Allison & Lueschen, 1979). Similar observations have been made regarding adaptations of basketball among Utes (Blanchard, 1974) and African-Americans (Cochran, 1976).

Others have indicated how sports that are popular among immigrant and minority groups are emphasized in efforts to maintain an ethnic identity separate from dominant American culture. Pooley (1976), for example, has demonstrated how the structure and function of ethnic soccer clubs in Milwaukee inhibited the structural assimilation of their members into dominant American society.

SOURCE: "Sport and Immigrant, Minority and Anglo Relations in Garden City (Kansas) High School" by Mark A. Grey. From *Sociology of Sport Journal* 9(3), pp. 255–270. Copyright © 1992 by Human Kinetics Publishers, Inc. Reprinted by permission.

In terms of assimilation and acculturation, Allison (1979, p. 50) has challenged what she refers to as the "assimilation–acculturation paradigm," which assumes that "differing recipient ethnic groups will eventually adopt the values and hence behavioral repertoires of a host or donor culture." This paradigm in sport research assumes that

> the degree to which assimilation has occurred can be measured by identifying the degree to which a recipient culture rejects its own play and game forms and adopts those of the donor culture. Thus, it is often implied in the literature that a group is less assimilated if it clings to its own forms of activity or displays any ethnic expression in the indigenous American sport forms which are adopted. (Allison, 1979, p. 51)

In this sense, sport has "been frequently assumed to be an active agent which can help accelerate the process" (p. 53) of assimilation and acculturation. As a part of the popular melting pot ideology, sport has also been considered "an homogenizing agent wherein ethnicity is inactive. . . . [It] is a vehicle through which minority members can learn the value orientations of the dominant culture" (Allison, 1979, p. 53).

While social scientists can no longer assume that sports necessarily have an assimilationist role, we must also examine how emphasis upon established American sports in schools can actually work to marginalize immigrant and other minority students in both the school and community. Sports and their associated rituals often form the most important point of contact between the high school and community, and this is certainly the case in the present study of Garden City, Kansas, High School. This study is concerned with how participation or nonparticipation in these activities is often used by established residents to determine the commitment of immigrant and other minority students to assimilate into mainstream American life. Recognizing this emphasis on established sports and their importance as vehicles for assimilation, I demonstrate how they exacerbate a hierarchy of student social status along which immigrant and many established-resident minority students have been given a marginal status within the school.

Equally important is how a general nonacceptance of sports that are popular among immigrant students (primarily soccer) in Garden City High School helps to establish, *and* exists as an indication of, their lower status.

GARDEN CITY HIGH SCHOOL

This research was conducted as part of a 2-year study of ethnic relations in Garden City, Kansas.[1] A team of five anthropologists and one geographer undertook this research in the entire Garden City community to determine the degree and nature of social and economic change in Garden City after the opening of the world's largest beef-packing plant by IBP, Inc., in

December 1980. The new plant brought a rapid influx of immigrant minority peoples from Latin America and Southeast Asia (Stull et al., 1990).

This paper is based upon ethnographic research undertaken in Garden City High School during the academic year 1988–89. The research involved over 700 hours of observation, much of it as a participant observer, and 50 audiotaped formal interviews.

Garden City is located in southwestern Kansas. Its present population is approximately 25,000, which represents an increase of nearly 36% since the establishment of the IBP beef-packing plant in 1980. The influx of new residents dramatically increased enrollments in local schools. Throughout the 1980s some 1,976 new students were enrolled, representing a 43% increase. The demand for new school space was met with the construction of three new elementary schools.

Many of the new students were immigrants. Although the number of these students has remained relatively stable through the decade, the origins of these students began to shift during the latter part of the decade. In 1989 Hispanic enrollments grew from 25% of total enrollments to 29%. The percentage of Southeast Asians enrolled in the school district fell slightly, from 6% in 1987 to 5% in 1989 (Hope, 1989; Unified School District 457, 1987).

Garden City High School (GCHS), the community's only high school, also experienced rapid growth in its enrollment through the decade. The 1988–89 academic year started with an enrollment of 1,111. Approximately one-third of the school's enrollment is composed of minorities, including both established-resident and immigrant Hispanic (21.4%), new-arrival Southeast Asians (7.8%), and some African-Americans (1.4%). Like the Garden City community, the school is characterized by a high degree of mobility among its populations, both Anglo and minority. Nearly one-third of GCHS students were not enrolled for the entire school year of 1988–89, and of these students, the average duration of enrollment was approximately 4½ months.

Because GCHS is the community's only high school, the community tends to identify with the school and in particular its athletic programs, although this community support is shared to some extent with the Garden City Community College. Varsity and junior varsity sports at GCHS include volleyball, basketball, swimming, cross-country, and track and field for girls, and football, cross-country, basketball, wrestling, baseball, and track and field for boys. Athletics form the most direct and important context for contact between the community at large and the school, and it is in terms of athletics that the community forms its primary expectations for the school and its students. Not only do many Garden Citians hope for a winning football team in particular, but with the hiring of a new coaching staff before the 1988–89 school year and a dramatic increase in the financial resources of the team, many people actually came to expect a winning football team. (Prior to the 1988 season, the GCHS football team had not had a winning season in 14 years.)

Sport and Student Relations

Athletics and other extracurricular activities such as clubs, music, and plays were promoted by the school administration because of a fundamental conviction that involvement in activities plays a significant role in the establishment of student identity with the school, and that this identity maintains student interest in school and deters them from dropping out.

While the number of students involved in extracurricular activities at Garden City High did rise during the 1988–89 school year, there are two important aspects of this trend in terms of ethnic relations in the school. First, increased participation in school activities and athletics was found among those students who are less likely to drop out of school in the first place, namely the majority of middle- and upper-middle class Anglo students and male Hispanic students of well-established, generally higher socioeconomic status. There was no appreciable increase in participation on the football team in 1988 from the lower-socioeconomic-status Hispanic students, the group with the highest tendency to drop out.

Second, activities and athletics designed to meet the interest of immigrant Southeast Asian students actually declined during the 1988–89 school year. A Southeast Asian club had been established, but both of the previous sponsors of the club—discouraged by a lack of institutional support for both the club and the English as a Second Language (ESL) program—had to be persuaded to continue their involvement by a persistent school administrator and a leader of a community refugee assistance center. The Southeast Asian club did make an effort to participate in mainstream school activities, for example, by entering the annual homecoming parade float competition, in which the club was awarded third place. The relative success of the club was short-lived, however. One sponsor resigned, and the remaining sponsor of the club, an Anglo ESL teacher, submitted her resignation in the early spring of 1989 because of a perceived lack of support.

The number of immigrant Hispanic and Southeast Asian students who participated in so-called established school sports programs was minimal (Grey, 1990). This limited immigrant participation in extracurricular activities has been noted by others. Becker (1990), for example, cited a New England high school physical education instructor who "lamented the fact that Portuguese boys don't ever try out for any sports, not even soccer. 'They don't want to do anything'" (p. 50). Gibson (1988), in her study of Punjabi immigrants in a California high school, also noted reactions to the lack of immigrant participation in extracurricular activities:

School administrators were troubled by the Punjabi students' reluctance to get involved. Extracurricular activities were considered integral to the life of the school and overall education of students . . . In high school where heavy involvement in extracurricular activities was the norm for [local residents], Punjabis were conspicuous for their absence. (Gibson, 1988, p. 162)

The question remains, however, why such emphasis is placed on these activities and why the immigrant students' failure to participate is regarded so negatively. The answers appear to involve sports, particularly football, and their role in the reaffirmation of core American life values.

In one sense the importance of sport in Garden City may be a reaction to the many social and economic changes experienced in the community since 1980, and in particular the dramatically changing nature of local demographic patterns. However, it seems unlikely that sports have taken on any particular new meaning since the early part of the decade. Several members of the high school and surrounding community pointed out that sports are very conservative rituals in the sense that established-resident Anglos and some Hispanics are the primary supporters of these activities. It appears they wish to see the reproduction of the same performances and interpretations that comprised the activities when *they* were participating. Many Garden Citians have held football season tickets for as long as 20 years, frequently retaining the same seat in the school's stadium.

The suggestion that these rituals have become reemphasized because of an influx of new immigrant and minority populations loses further support when it is acknowledged that a Hispanic community has been in Garden City since the turn of the century. Members of this community have participated in sports activities for decades. Indeed, established-resident Hispanic participation in sports and related activities form an important link between the Anglo and Hispanic communities.

Increased emphasis on sports in reaction to change is found, however indirectly, in one aspect of the game itself, namely that one team will win and the other will lose. Raphael, in his work concerning rites of passage for American males, points out that

By diverting complex questions of right and wrong into more comprehensible questions of winning and losing, sports can even supply us with a simplified sense of moral purpose. This simplification offers an antidote to some of the ambiguities of our pluralistic culture, where questions of meaning are hard to answer and precise definition of rank is often difficult to achieve. (1988, p. 134)

Certainly Raphael's notion of sport as a simplifier of moral questions gains support in the Garden City High School context and was directly supported by the head football coach while addressing the first school pep rally of 1988 in the school gymnasium. With the aid of a loudspeaker, he encouraged the 1,100 students and faculty present to make the trip to the nearby town where the season's first football game was to be played. After stating how proud he was of the team and its players, and how hard they had all worked, he closed by saying, "Let's go down there and show them that what we believe in is right and proper."

That Friday evening, over 700 GCHS students and Garden City citizens made the 1-hour drive to attend the game and indeed demonstrate that their values are the same as (or perhaps even better than) those held by the rival community. Garden City won the game, beating the team from the smaller school for the first time in several years. This victory and a subsequent winning record for the year provided one assistant coach with a more comfortable opportunity to later tell me, "The American dream, you know, is to win."

Raphael's notion of sports as an antidote to the "ambiguities of our pluralistic culture" also seems appropriate in this case. Since a large proportion of the local population are immigrant minorities, ambiguities may be observed in the dual role held by immigrants in the community. On the one hand these immigrant peoples, many of whom do not speak English, are recognized as a necessary part of economic growth. Most Garden Citians realize that the local beef-packing industry cannot fill its employment quotas with local labor and that in order for these plants to continue operation, labor from other parts of the United States, or indirectly from other nations, must be recruited. Certainly the local economy, and therefore many local residents, benefit from their presence.

On the other hand, the presence of immigrant minorities is uncomfortable for some residents. Their interaction with immigrants is often limited (Stull et al., 1990). This ambiguity toward the presence of immigrant peoples drives home for many Anglo (and some Hispanic) Garden City natives the reality of life in an increasingly pluralistic society. Sports provide one forum for these people to resolve the ambiguities associated with this reality.

Autumns of Renewal

Another explanation for the importance of sport, and in particular football, is found in its perceived contribution to the success of the school year. In this sense, football, as the first major sport of the school year, becomes a catalyst of success for the rest of the school year. This aspect of football was explained by the head football coach:

> Football happens to fall at the time of year when it's one of the first things, so it kind of takes on a level of importance that maybe it wouldn't if it were in the spring or in the summer or something like that for school. But there is a definite difference just in the atmosphere and the way kids perceive each other and teachers. And people, again, people can say that's not true and they can be upset at the thought of that, but the fact is that it makes a difference in just the general outlook that everybody has just towards being here and working together and

everything. . . . the plain truth is, you know, whatever takes place at the beginning of the year that is successful, there is a good different feeling among the kids.

The head coach's perceptions were echoed by one of his assistants:

I've been in three schools now and [in] all three schools, the school year starts off with football and it goes about as good as what the football season goes. If you have a good football season, then usually you have a pretty good school year.

Many community members believed that success on the football field would help to lower the school's dropout rate, which had been on of the five highest in the state for several years. One Garden City citizen predicted at the beginning of the 1988–89 school year that student attendance would rise if the football team continued to win. When questioned about why this should be, he replied, "because it will mean the kids will be more likely to be part of something they have pride in. Who wants to be part of a loser?"[2]

Since coaches, administrators, student athletes, and community members believe that as goes football, so goes the school year, football does not have to be justified in and of itself. Nor is it necessary to be concerned about its emphasis vis-à-vis academic programs. After a long hot summer, and with the anticipation of a new school year, the football season ushers in an autumn of renewal and the resultant possibility of a successful school year.

Community Participation

Varsity sports and their surrounding rituals are often rather complex affairs with many different forms of participation with varying levels of perceived importance. The players themselves, and their coaches, are the central focus. Cheerleaders work to maintain the interest and enthusiasm of the crowd, particularly the students, and in a sense act as intermediaries (both physically and psychologically) between the crowd and the team on the field. Entertainment per se, and a temporary relief from the intensity and emotion of the game, is provided by the marching band, particularly at halftime. Like the players and cheerleaders, the importance and central place of the band members is indicated by the provision of special, and costly, uniforms.

Spectators are far more marginal in status, and the activity is open to all because no talent is required. However, without spectators from both the community and the student body, there would be no one for whom to perform. The efforts of the team, band, and cheerleaders are in effect legitimized by those who observe and approve of the performers' work. But the majority of those who do observe the game and its associated activities are adults from the surrounding community, not the students who supposedly will benefit from the school year promised by a successful football season.

Foley (1990) noted the involvement of parents in a booster club that played a central role in the ritual complex of high school football in one Texas town. Prominent citizens "who want to maintain their social position, promote their interests through booster clubs" (1990, p. 125). The booster club provided parents and other citizens an opportunity to reproduce their class privileges in the community. Burnett also noted the active involvement of adults in school activities:

> Without the participation of adults and community members as spectators, these events would have gradually disappeared from the calendar of events. . . . The adult was spectator to the performance, learning about success or failure of the young. Much of this learning was from peers, but it was then tested against the positive or negative response of adults as spectators. The adults in the community, through their interest in local high school athletics and other entertainment events, ultimately influenced and affected the value system of the students in the school—not a one-to-one, adult-to-young relationship, but through a complex network of influence. (Burnett, 1969, pp. 8-9)

Through their support of school sports rituals, adults help form and perpetuate a value system for students. Their expectations for participation in these activities are an integral part of their value systems that are passed along to the young members of the community.

While football can be justified as a catalyst for a successful school year by community members, it does not explain how sport creates a link between the community and the school. The following excerpt from an interview with the head football coach illustrates one answer to this question:

> Q: What is the role of sports, football as an example, in relations between the school and community?
> A: Well, one of the biggest functions that I see is that it gives a common bond or a common tie to everybody from this area whether you're an athlete or not or whether you are a student or not . . . it gives everybody something to kind of unite behind and basically the type of thing that says basically "this is ours. It's all of ours." One of the problems over the last several years and the reason that I'm here, is that the success [of the football team] had been so limited that the community was missing that link, that bond that gave them something to feel good about. And you know it makes a difference. A lot of people would be insulted if you mentioned that to them, that it does make a difference. But whether they like it or not, athletics at the high school level in a town particularly as isolated as Garden City is it is a kind of unifying factor. It does bring people together and even though they may not all be at the ball game, they are all at least aware that those things are happening and that we did well or we didn't do well.

This common bond created by rallying around football and other established American sports is also said to be available to all regardless of "whether you've lived here forever or you've just come in to town or whatever," as the head coach suggested. New Anglo and American Hispanic students and their parents readily fit into this scheme, and they bring with them knowledge of the game and appropriate forms of participation. For these people, the coach's remarks are correct; it doesn't matter whether they have "lived here forever" or "just come in to town." For immigrant students, however, the remark takes on a different meaning. Certainly immigrant and other minority students are welcome to join. Since they usually do not choose to participate, they are open to criticism and to a perception that they are not interested in learning to become a part of established school life, or in a more general sense, to become active members of American society on "American" terms.[3]

The head football coach recognized the different cultural background of immigrant students, but did not suggest that other alternatives be opened to them:

> Athletics, you know, we don't, unfortunately we don't get a whole lot of Oriental-type kids involved. We get quite a few Spanish, some black, although we don't have very many black kids here in Garden City, but we keep making the attempt to involve those kids. They just haven't grown up in a culture where that's an important part of their life and they probably don't feel like they are included in that, but if we could ever try to break the ice and get two or three in it, I think athletically they would have a lot of talent and they would probably do well and it might open the door for others.

Sport and Assimilation

Prior to the 1988–89 school year many immigrant students were interested and involved in a school soccer club. During the year of the study, interest among immigrant students remained high and conversations could be heard among immigrant students in the halls during the first few days of the school year in anticipation of playing with the team. However, during the 1988–89 school year there was no interest in sponsoring the club among the 70 full-time teachers at the school. The teacher who had sponsored and who was the driving force behind the club in previous years had left for the year to be an exchange teacher in Europe, and no other faculty member was willing to become involved.

The school principal, who publicly advocated student activities, showed little interest in finding a sponsor for the soccer club (Grey, 1990, p. 423). There is even some evidence to suggest that he actively worked against its regeneration because it would create a distraction from the excitement of the anticipated new football program. His views were no doubt colored by his own experience as a football player in high school and at a major university. In addition, his son was a key player on the team.

With the demise of the school soccer club in 1988, the one school activity that involved many Southeast Asian and Mexican students outside the classroom was eliminated. Even if the soccer club was allowed to continue, it would have done so as a "nonestablished" sport (as deemed by a member of the Board of Education) and certainly one not readily recognized by the larger community or the majority of the student body.

In this sense, the soccer club did not provide an acceptable form of activity and therefore could not reinforce what the community held as established or "American." When asked about the soccer club, the football coach responded,

It wasn't really a school soccer team. The ESL group had a lot of kids that wanted to play and they incorporated that as part of their class, and I think they did play a couple of scrimmages with folks around.

Q: What happened? Why didn't it regenerate?

A: I guess the sponsors didn't really encourage it this year. One of the big things, which was a good thing last year, that got it going . . . was the deal that while you are there at soccer practice or in the game, everybody has to speak English, regardless of what country you're from. . . . Well that turned out to be a positive thing for the kids in that they had to practice using expressions and so on that maybe they normally wouldn't.

Although the existence of a soccer club was a form of accommodation to the unique cultural backgrounds of immigrant students, according to the football coach, the most positive aspect of the club was that students were required to speak English during practice and games. This institutional adjustment was not recognized or valued as a modification for the unique cultural interests of immigrant students, but because of its *acculturative and assimilationist* function.

Two examples of related phenomena provide further evidence of this point. I watched the first game of the football season in 1988 standing next to a respected Garden City businessman and prominent member of the high school sports booster club. Some time after I briefly explained my research, he pointed out that there were no Southeast Asians on the football team. I concurred. He then added, however, that "there are a lot of Hispanic kids on the team." And I agreed with him again. He then said, with reference to the minority students on the team, "I guess that's the way they earn their stripes." And, indeed, he was correct. The marginal status of many Hispanic students was only overcome when the student "made the team" and showed skill in a particular sport. Not only did the Hispanic student who excelled at sports raise his relative status in the school and become a member of the so-called jocks or preppies subgroups, but his status in the community increased as well.

Throughout the entire 1988–89 school year, only three immigrant students participated on any school sports teams: one Laotian girl played on the sophomore volleyball team, and two boys, one Mexican and the other Vietnamese, joined the junior varsity wrestling team. These immigrant students earned their stripes in a sense, but did so on very low-profile teams.

Established-resident Hispanic students were active in low-profile sports, particularly junior varsity wrestling, and they too could earn their stripes in this manner. However, most did not gain the prominence associated with standing out on major varsity teams.

That immigrant students must gain respect on "American" terms is also illustrated in the case of an exceptional Laotian (male) volleyball player. An established form of gender role reversal—much like "Powder-Puff" football for girls (cf. Foley, 1990, pp. 118-119)—is "Twinkle Toes" volleyball for boys at Garden City High. During this annual fall event, male members of the junior and senior classes form teams to play volleyball and be coached by members of the girls' varsity volleyball team. Two Southeast Asian boys were involved, one on each of the junior and senior class teams. One of the boys on the junior team was a Laotian with remarkable talent. There were rumors that he had played professionally in Thailand before coming to the United States. His ability impressed a number of people observing the game, including the school principal, who made a point of discussing the boy's talent with me and how it was "too bad" that the school didn't have a boys' volleyball team. "It would be a good way to get these kids into the mainstream," he said.

After our brief conversation about the Laotian boy's athletic abilities, the principal left and spoke with the football coach, who was himself impressed by the boy's athletic ability. Others suggested that the coach should try to recruit the boy to play football. Within days the boy was the subject of an article with photographs in the local newspaper, raising the boy to near, albeit temporary, celebrity status. "Since the beginning of the year when _____ caught [the] volleyball coach's eye, word of the mysterious boy from Laos has spread through the halls of Garden High. He's 'that kid' who can hurl his 5-foot-8, 135 pound frame 37 inches into the air and shoot it like a cannon back over the 8-foot net" (Unruh, 1988).

"That kid," as he was referred to in the newspaper, was spotted for his athletic ability first, but ultimately for the contribution he could make to sports. It is very unlikely, for example, that the school principal or football coach would have given the boy a second thought, barring a serious discipline problem, unless he had demonstrated the ability to assist in important mainstream activities: to help a school team win.

The football coach later remarked, "There is one follow that really excels as a volleyball player, one of the Laotian kids. I can't remember his name." "He's gone now," I replied, "he went to Florida." "Well," said the coach, "I hope something develops for him because he is an incredible athlete. He had big-time talent in that area and maybe something will develop for him."

One Hispanic student echoed concerns that athletes received preferential status:

> [The] jock is trying to do something for the school, you know, I mean he's doing it for the school. (You know he's not. He's doing it so he can play or do whatever, you know, participate in sports) . . . he's going to make our school a better place and make it more known and what's that Mexican doing? He ain't doing that. His grades are probably bad and stuff like that. So he's not doing anything to make it up. He's just going to make it [the school] look bad so [the principal] don't want to talk to him.
>
> Q: So what should he do about the Mexican?
>
> A: I mean you should at least make an effort to talk to them and stuff like that. The only time you see Mr. _____ talk to them, someone like the Mexicans or one of these kinds of people, is because the person is getting in trouble or . . . you know.
>
> Q: Really?
>
> A: That's a lot of Mexicans' fault too but, you know, he doesn't do nothing to help them out. At least, if you were to talk to them, you know. It's like, teachers too, teachers do the same thing. . . . If you saw the same situation. If you saw a jock and then you saw someone else, a Mexican, you know, the teacher is going to talk to the jock before [the Mexican] because they are more interested in school and stuff like that. They're smarter and stuff like that.

SPORT AND DEMOCRATIZATION

Implied and explicit in most arguments for the maintenance of interscholastic sports programs in schools is that these programs promote the democratization of the student body. This notion was presented as early as 1961 by Coleman, who concluded, "it does seem clear . . . that athletics introduces an important democratizing factor in the status system for boys in high school by undercutting social background as a basis for status" (Coleman, 1961, p. 39). His statement would no doubt be broadened in the contemporary context to include girls and their participation in athletics.

Ostensibly, Coleman's argument seems pertinent, and certainly some of the evidence presented here appears to support his notion: For some members of lower-status, established-resident minorities in Garden City High School and the community, athletics provide an opportunity to escape the relative marginal status of their social backgrounds (Grey, 1989a). This is particularly the case for Hispanic boys in the school, a number of whom enjoy celebrity status for their contributions to varsity sports. They escape the marginal status given to their peers from similar socioeconomic backgrounds who are more often referred to as at-risk.

Support of Coleman's notion, however, must be qualified. First, the number of GCHS students who benefit from this "undercutting [of] social background as a basis for status" is limited. Minority students who receive recognition for successful contributions to popular sports represent only a handful of their minority cohort. They become members of another, higher status group in the school social hierarchy and their contact with former peers in lower status groups, at least in school, diminishes. Hispanic students who make this adjustment in their social standing are often referred to as "white Hispanics" by Anglo teachers and others at GCHS, and they can often be seen lined up with Anglo athletes along the so-called jock wall at a busy junction in the halls between classes.

That sports are able to democratize relations in high schools may be challenged in another way. While a relatively limited number of students benefit from this democratizing process, by extension, many others retain marginal status as a consequence of the limited and narrowly defined means by which one can gain status in the school. Emphasis upon participation in sports as a means to achieve status not only contributes to the relatively isolated status of those minorities who do not participate, but also to the creation of an elite which further stretches the spectrum of possible relations among different groups in the school. Knight (1974) elaborated on this theme:

> What becomes important within the allowable limits of the school experience is a form of school status, defined by successful participation in academic work, athletics, music, and other extra-curricular activities. . . . Thus not only are students selected and encouraged into particular flows of school experience through bureaucratic procedures, rules and rituals, but this process defines school success. (p. 113)

In this sense, rituals and other functions of the school act as gatekeepers to school success, and to "the social and economic reward systems of the outside community" (Knight, 1974, p. 113).

Jocks and preppies form the dominant cliques, and their status vis-à-vis nonathlete minorities and immigrants was described by one student:

> They get away with a lot more. They do! . . . I don't know. Like, if you saw a real preppie person walking down the hall in the middle of class and Mr. _____ was out and he saw a Mexican or Vietnamese walking down the hall or head banger or anybody, he ain't going to stop the preppie person. I mean the real smart person, you know, because he ain't going to say, "well where's your pass." He ain't going to ask them that. Their grades are all right so it don't matter if they're ditching anyway.
> Q: So are all these things obvious to you?
> A: I think they are. I think they are real obvious to me. I notice it every day.

That interscholastic athletic programs are elitist and tend to isolate their student participants from the mainstream was made particularly clear at Garden City High School during a brief conversation with two members of the football team while standing in the lunch line. One of the boys wore a

"Hog Pride" T-shirt, only worn, I was told, by linemen of the football team. I inquired as to the availability of the shirts to others, noting the shirt's interesting and colorful design. After the boys replied that only football players could own them, I stated that it was "too bad" that I or anyone else could not have one. One boy them replied, "yeah, but then they wouldn't be anything different."

While this notion of the development of an elite within the student body explains to some extent the maintenance of lower status for immigrant and other minority students, it does not explain the rules under which these relations are formed. Formal, public statements of these rules existed in the form of an open letter at the beginning of the sports program during the 1988–89 school year. In this statement, explicit guidelines for how students can "become better citizens" and achieve "tolerance and understanding of others" were directly linked to students' participation in designated sports and other activities. Democracy among the student body can be achieved only under the terms of participation in these programs. When no (or very few) immigrant and few minority students participate in these programs and the associated rituals, they fail to seek to become "better citizens" and achieve "tolerance and understanding of others" under the established and acceptable terms of the institution (Stull et al., 1990).

Not all teachers agreed with the emphasis on sports as a democratizing agent. Although an active fan, one teacher explained his perceptions this way:

> I get real impatient—it's probably the nicest word I can use—with people, coaches, parents, and anybody else that will stand up and tell me about sports programs building character and teaching leadership skills and all this other crap, and I go [to games] and listen to kids bitch and swear and bait their opponents . . . and then I hear people tell me how good this is . . . We talk about participation. The ideal situation is that every kid gets to play, and that is a crock. They don't want every kid to play. The only time they want every kid to play is when you're 30 points ahead. If the game is on the line, everyone . . . want[s] the best team in there so we can win. Everybody cares about winning. We say winning isn't important or we try to say winning is not important. The greater goal is personal growth. But that's not true. Personal growth, leadership, character building, all goes out the window when the games are on.

This teacher echoed the feeling of other teachers and students as well. Clearly, while some value sports in and of themselves, they did not accept the prevailing public notion that sports act as agents of democratization.

Immigrant Reactions

Public reactions of immigrant students to the pressure to participate in mainstream sports are muted due to their relative powerlessness. Although students privately expressed concern that the school soccer club was not regenerated during the 1988–89 school year, they were confused about who was responsible for its demise and were not informed about where or to whom they could express their feelings beyond ESL instructional staff. Advocacy for the establishment of the soccer club (as well as other immigrant concerns) was undertaken by Anglo faculty members who recognized that these students had no power to express their own needs, and because institutional processes for achieving tolerance and understanding of others through established athletics were so narrowly defined (Grey, 1990).

Immigrant students occasionally did express feelings of not being heard. When the senior class met in small groups to suggest ideas for graduation week activities, two Vietnamese boys grew frustrated and left their group to sit in the gymnasium bleachers. One complained that the other students in their group were only interested in "American" activities and that they didn't find these things interesting. They added that there were no activities for them, and both mentioned the lack of a soccer club that year. Some other immigrant students remained with their small groups but did not submit suggestions.

Both of these Vietnamese boys did participate in the "Twinkle Toes" volleyball match. This was an effort on their part to gain status in the school through an exhibition of their abilities in this particular sport. Only this one-time activity offered them any opportunity to gain recognition for their participation in an established activity. As its name implies, however, this particular activity is a parody of its institutionalized (and publicly recognized) counterpart. While varsity and junior varsity volleyball is available for girls, it is not available for boys.

The absence of the soccer club points out that an emphasis on sports per se does not contribute to a marginal status for immigrant students but rather to the emphasis on "established" American sports such as football and basketball and their surrounding activities. In fact, the maintenance of a valid, administratively supported soccer club would have helped to legitimize the presence of immigrants in the school without drawing attention away from established, mainstream sports activities.

Instead, this situation begs the question of why immigrant students actively avoided participation in mainstream sports in the first place. Was this merely a response to their recognition that they held marginal status and that they avoided "trying out" in order to escape the potential additional ridicule associated with not making the team? Or was a soccer club necessary to indicate to them that the school was genuinely interested in accommodating their unique cultural backgrounds, and by extension their athletic interests? I believe the latter explanation to be more accurate. Immigrant and other minority students do play many of the games enjoyed by their mainstream counterparts, at least informally outside of the auspices of the high school. For example, many immigrant students played basketball in pick-up games at local elementary schools on weekends and after school. Many students also admitted an interest in watching sports on television, particularly basketball, and they could name several high-profile professional players as well as recount recent games.

Clearly, the interest in playing common American games was present among immigrant and other minorities. What was lacking was any mechanism to accommodate their athletic interests in the school. On the contrary, by narrowly defining the range of athletic (and related) activities recognized by the school, these students were given few legitimate opportunities to demonstrate their willingness to become integrated members of "American" society on their own terms.

CONCLUSION AND POLICY IMPLICATIONS

To some extent, the differential and lower status given to immigrant and other minority students at Garden City High School is predictable due to their unique cultural backgrounds and, in the case of immigrants, lack of English proficiency. The evidence considered here, however, suggests that the process of isolating and marginalizing immigrant and minority students is exacerbated by an emphasis upon established forms of American athletics and their related rituals.

The terms under which immigrant and other minority students in the school and community can escape from an isolated and marginal status are narrowly defined and directly related to participation in established athletics. While participation in sports is the primary means by which lower-status established-resident Hispanic students achieve increased social standing, much the same may be said for immigrant students. The status of immigrant minorities in the school is complicated further by the use of American sports as a standard by which to judge these students' willingness to assimilate into mainstream American life. Not only are the terms by which an immigrant student can become "American" rather narrowly defined, but their enforcement actually works to create an elite structure in the student body that further heightens the social hierarchy and leaves most minority students even further removed from gaining a higher status in the school environment.

In the case of GCHS, the importance of the soccer club as an indication of the school's willingness to welcome immigrants was pointed out to school district administrators (Grey, 1989b), and suggestions for its reestablishment were formally submitted (Grey, 1989c). Included in this set of suggestions were provisions not only to develop a soccer program with a paid coach but also an intramural volleyball program that would appeal to both female and male immigrants and other students as well.

The reestablishment of a soccer club would provide two important opportunities. First, the club could be the "primary mechanism within the school for the promotion of accord between immigrant Southeast Asian and immigrant Hispanic students" and, to some extent, the club could also promote interaction between immigrants and established residents (Grey, 1989c, p. 6). Second, the soccer club had the

> potential to promote an attachment to the school similar to that found among participants in many of the school's other activities and athletics. It [will] provide a means through which immigrant students in particular can develop an additional dimension of their "identity" with the school. (Grey, 1989c, p. 7)

A soccer club was established the following year with a paid coach/sponsor from one of the middle schools. But because practices were held at a middle school and because transportation was not provided, the level of participation was disappointing. Middle-school students were also permitted to play. It was not, in short, specifically a high school activity, and no doubt many students remained discouraged.

Demands by immigrant and minority students for alternative sports activities must be met in order for schools to demonstrate their willingness to address the needs of all students, not just those chosen few who have a background and can participate in an established sport. This could be a primary indication that the presence of these students in the school is valued, and that their lack of interest and participation in established sports will not influence judgments about their willingness to become "Americans."

NOTES

1. This research was made possible by the Ford Foundation Changing Relations Project. Garden City was one of six sites in the Changing Relations Project and the only rural site. The present research was part of a larger study of ethnic relations in GCHS, one of several "arenas" of research in Garden City. The results of this community-wide research were reported in a special edition of *Urban Anthropology*, Vol. 19(4).
2. A winning football season in 1988 did not reduce the dropout rate in the high school. On the contrary, the percentage of students who dropped out of the school rose to 14%, a 3% increase over the previous year and an 8% increase over the 1986–1987 school year.
3. Despite the fact that many Hispanics and a few Southeast Asians are U.S. citizens, I use the term "American" to denote mainstream American culture.

REFERENCES

Allison, M.T. (1979). On the ethnicity of ethnic minorities in sport. *Quest, 31,* 50-56.
Allison, M.T. (1982). Sport, ethnicity and assimilation. *Quest, 34,* 165-175.
Allison, M.T., & Lueschen, G. (1979). A comparative analysis of Navajo and Anglo basketball systems. *International Review of Sport Sociology, 3-4,* 76-86.
Becker, A. (1990). The role of the school in the maintenance of ethnic group affiliation. *Human Organization, 49,* 48-55.

Blanchard, K. (1974). Basketball and the culture-change process: The Rimrock Navajo case. *Council on Education and Anthropology Quarterly*, **5**(4), 8-13.

Burnett, J.H. (1969). Ceremony, rites and economy in the student system of an American high school. *Human Organization*, **28**, 1-10.

Cochran, R. (1976). Folk elements in a non-folk game: The example of basketball. *Journal of Popular Culture*, **10**, 399-403.

Coleman, J.S. (1961, November). Athletics in high school. *Annals of the American Society of Political and Social Science*, pp. 33-43.

Foley, D.E. (1990). The great American football ritual: Reproducing race, class and gender inequality. *Sociology of Sport Journal*, **7**, 111-135.

Gibson, M.A. (1988). *Accommodation without assimilation: Sikh immigrants in an American high school*. Ithaca: Cornell University Press.

Grey, M.A. (1989a). *Rite, ritual and immigrant-resident relations in Garden City, Kansas, High School*. Paper presented at the annual meeting of the American Anthropological Association, Washington, DC.

Grey, M.A. (1989b). *A summary of research results: Ethnic relations at Garden City High School*. Report to Unified School District No. 457, Garden City, Kansas.

Grey, M.A. (1989c). *Suggestions for program improvement: Garden City High School and English as a Second Language program*. Report to Unified School District No. 457, Garden City, Kansas.

Grey, M.A. (1990). Immigrant students in the heartland: Ethnic relations in Garden City, Kansas, High School. *Urban Anthropology and Studies of Cultural Systems and World Economic Development*, **19**, 409-427.

Hope, D. (1989, Oct. 2). School enrollments still climbing. *Garden City Telegram*.

Knight, T. (1974). Powerlessness and the student role: Structural determinants of school status. *Australian and New Zealand Journal of Sociology*, **10**, 112-117.

Pooley, J.C. (1976). Ethnic soccer clubs in Milwaukee: A study in assimilation. In M. Hart (Ed.), *Sport in the sociocultural process* (2nd ed.) (pp. 475-492). Dubuque, IA: W.C. Brown.

Raphael, R. (1988). *The men from the boys: Rites of passage in male America*. Lincoln: University of Nebraska Press.

Stull, D.D., Benson, J.E., Broadway, M.J., Campa, A.L., Erickson, K.C., and Grey, M.A. (1990). *Changing relations: Newcomers and established residents in Garden City, Kansas* (Report No. 172). Lawrence, KS: University of Kansas, Institute for Public Policy and Business Research.

Unified School District No. 457, Garden City, Kansas. (1987). *Enrollment by school, race and sex*.

Unruh, T. (1988, Oct. 27). Spiking out a future. *Garden City Telegram*.

29. *1994 Racial Report Card*

RICHARD E. LAPCHICK AND JEFFREY R. BENEDICT

In recent years a few high-profile incidents have exposed the underlying prejudices that prevent many minorities from being considered for front-office positions. While the public's attention was focused on the Marge Schott case, groups such as the Rainbow Commission for Equality in Sports and the Coalition of Equality in Sports were insisting that the overwhelming majority of minorities performing on the field was grossly disproportionate to the lack of minority representation in team management. These groups were formed to use public pressure to ensure that steps be taken to reduce barriers for minority advancement. Partly as a result of their efforts, 1994 was a year of notable progress.

Three of the four expansion teams in the NFL and NBA are partly owned by Blacks. Deron Cherry (Jacksonville Jaguars) and Charlotte businessman William Simms (Carolina Panthers) became the only current black owners in the NFL. Isiah Thomas (Toronto Raptors) and Earvin "Magic" Johnson, who purchased nearly 10 percent of the Los Angeles Lakers, became new owners in the NBA.

While many of the personnel positions on the expansion teams have not yet been filled, three of the teams named Blacks to fill the role of general manager: Michael Huyghue, vice president for the Jacksonville Jaguars; Isiah Thomas, vice president in charge of basketball operations for the Toronto Raptors; and Stu Jackson, general manager and vice president of basketball operations for the NBA Vancouver expansion franchise.

In addition to the expansion teams, M.L. Carr (Boston Celtics) was named vice president and chief of basketball operations; John Lucas (Philadelphia 76ers) was named vice president, general manager, and head coach; Bill McKinney (Detroit Pistons) was promoted to vice president of basketball operations; John Wooten (Philadelphia Eagles) was promoted to vice president of player personnel/operations; and Bob Watson (Houston Astros) was named general manager. M.L. Carr, formerly the director of community relations, John Wooten, formerly a talent scout, and Bob Watson, formerly the assistant general manager, were promoted from within their own organizations. Bill McKinney was previously performing the function of a general manager.

SOURCE: "1994 Racial Report Card" by Richard E. Lapchick and Jeffrey R. Benedict. Excerpts from *1994 Racial Report Card*. Copyright © 1994 Center for the Study of Sport in Society. Reprinted by permission.

The tremendous success of Black coaches continues to break the stereotype that Blacks lack the intellectual capabilities required to manage and coach at the highest levels. In 1987 Al Campanis, then vice president of the Los Angeles Dodgers, said, "I truly believe that [Blacks] may not have some of the necessities to be . . . a field manager or perhaps a general manager."[1] The public nature of Mr. Campanis's remarks sparked a flurry of national media attention toward the issue of minority hiring practices in professional sports. Since these remarks were made, a significant number of Blacks have been hired as head coaches and general managers. The result has been a dismantling of false perceptions regarding the ability of Blacks to manage and coach at the highest levels.

During the 1993–94 sports year, a Black was named Coach of the Year in college basketball (Nolan Richardson, Arkansas Razorbacks), in the NBA (Lenny Wilkens, Atlanta Hawks), and in the National League (Dusty Baker, San Francisco Giants). In addition, Cito Gaston became the first Black manager to win consecutive World Series championships, and Nolan Richardson became the second Black coach to lead a team to a national championship in men's college basketball.

Additionally, major league baseball's Equal Opportunity Committee (EOC) published a comprehensive report outlining the initiatives that owners have taken to improve the inclusion of minorities and women throughout baseball. Just prior to the release of this report in June, the National League named Leonard Coleman, Jr., who is Black, as its president. He replaced Bill White as the highest-ranking person of color in any of the three sports.

One of the most significant developments over the past year is baseball's commitment to contract with more minority and female vendors. The EOC reported that every team in the league is committed to doubling the dollar amount of contracts with minority and female vendors within the next year.

In the area of top management, the percentage of minorities employed remains very low. This year's numerous changes in ownership in the three leagues has produced an indication of future gains in top management positions for minorities. Another sign of increased opportunities for minorities is the action taken by new leadership in baseball. Two of the six members on baseball's EOC are new owners, Drayton McLane (Houston Astros) and Peter Magowan (San Francisco Giants). Currently, Houston has the league's only Black general manager, and San Francisco is one of four teams with a Black manager.

A new ownership group in Boston promoted M.L. Carr to be in charge of basketball operations for the Celtics.

As of this writing, there are fourteen head coaches or managers who are Black or Latino in the three leagues. With two head coaching vacancies remaining in the NBA, last year's record high number of fifteen minority coaches throughout the three leagues will likely be intact by the end of the summer.

However, top management positions (chairman of the board, chief executive officer, president, vice president, and general manager) continue to show minimal representation by minorities. National Basketball Association teams have sixteen people of color (10 percent) working in high-level management positions, major league baseball has ten (4 percent), and the NFL has six (five percent).

Administrative positions (areas of business operations, community relations, finance, game operations, marketing, promotions, publications, public relations, and various other areas) continue to be predominantly held by whites. Sixteen percent of such positions are held by minorities in both the NBA and major league baseball, while 12 percent are held in the NFL.

There were no significant changes in minority representation on the field. Blacks now make up 79 percent of the players in the NBA, 65 percent of the players in the NFL, and 18 percent of the players in major league baseball. Latinos also constitute 18 percent of the players in major league baseball.

SPORT IN THE CONTEXT OF SOCIETY

Professional sports continues to offer minorities outstanding opportunities for employment as it is a model industry for hiring people on the basis of their abilities. Furthermore, the sport industry is also unique in that the salaries of minorities are consistent with those of whites.

However, the fact that the majority of NFL and NBA players are Black, in conjunction with the unprecedented visibility of professional athletics through television and advertising, conveys a false impression about opportunities for minorities to achieve wealth through sports. Over 50 percent of high school athletes who are Black believe they will make it in professional sports.[2] Yet the number of jobs available in the field of professional athletics is minuscule in comparison to the minority population in the United States.

While a pro sports career is not a realistic opportunity for most youths today, it remains one of the few areas in American society where individuals from different races and ethnic backgrounds work together and compete against each other with minimal conflict. Reaction to the recent criminal charges filed against O.J. Simpson demonstrate that Blacks and whites across the United States have clashing views regarding race, equality, and justice in America today.

Despite the advancement of civil rights during the 1960s and 1970s, minorities, and particularly Blacks, represent a disproportionate percentage of those living in poverty in America. Currently, there are three times as many poor Blacks as poor whites, and the median income for whites has increased 9 percent, as opposed to just a 1 percent increase for Blacks. Finally, the unemployment rate for Blacks is 11.2 percent as opposed to 5.3 percent for whites.[3]

At the same time, college students who are Black are graduating at a significantly lower rate than white college students. Only 37 percent of Black college students entering Division I universities in 1987 graduated, as opposed to 59 percent of white students during the same period.[4] In addition, the salaries of Blacks with college degrees are 25 percent below those of college graduates who are white. Meanwhile, the number of blacks earning doctorate degrees has declined 9 percent over the past decade. Black men in particular received nearly 20 percent fewer doctorates between 1982 and 1992.[5]

Coinciding with the increase in poverty and the decrease in education has been a rise in victims of violent crime who are Black. Although Blacks account for only 12 percent of the population in the United States, they were the victims of nearly half of the nation's 23,760 homicides in 1992.[6]

THE COMMISSIONERS AND LEAGUE OFFICES

There has been little change in the racial composition of the commissioner's office in each of the three leagues within the past year. Commissioners David Stern and Paul Tagliabue have taken the lead within their respective leagues to expand minority hiring as well as extend the role of their respective leagues in the community. Major league baseball continues to be presided over by Bud Selig, owner of the Milwaukee Brewers. He has also encouraged outreach by major league teams within their own communities. In addition, the Executive Committee has been actively supporting initiatives by the Equal Opportunity Committee, co-chaired by Jerry Reinsdorf and Bill Bartholomay, to double the dollar value of business to minority and female vendors.

Major league baseball has taken a step toward improving minority representation by publishing its most comprehensive report outlining the initiatives of owners designed to afford minorities equal opportunity in hiring. There were significant areas of improvement in the central offices of major league baseball. Twenty-three percent of executives and department heads were minorities in 1993–94. That is the highest percentage ever in baseball. The number of Blacks employed in major league baseball's central offices has nearly doubled since 1989. Similarly, the number of employed Latinos has doubled from six to twelve since 1989. It should be noted that part of the improvement in minority representation is due to the expansion of the central offices over the past five years.

Furthermore, over the past five years MLB central offices have seen a dramatic increase in the number of women employed. In 1989 there were only 48 female employees. Today there are 111, which is over half of the total staff. Major league baseball reports that teams are currently using 501 minority-owned vending businesses and 1,228 female-owned vending businesses. This represents what may be sport's biggest area of improvement on the racial issue.

Gene Washington, who is African American, was recently named Director of Football Development in the NFL league office. In addition, two female attorneys were appointed, Jodi Balsam as attorney in the office of the league counsel and Belinda Lerner as staff labor attorney. Despite these hirings, the league office underwent a reduction in the percentage of minorities employed in management. Of the employees working in management, 18 percent are minorities as opposed to 23 percent in 1993.

Of the three league offices, the NBA is leading the way in minority representation. John Rose, who is Black, was promoted in January 1994 to senior vice president over player relations and administration. He is one of three senior vice presidents in the league office. In addition, there are three vice presidents in the league office who are Black. Nearly 23 percent of all management positions are held by minorities.

In addition, 47 percent of management positions in the NBA league office are held by women—including three vice presidents and fifteen attorneys. This is by far the highest percentage of women working in any league front office. . . .

OWNERSHIP

Isiah Thomas and Earvin Johnson joined Edward and Bettiann Gardner, who are limited partners in the Chicago Bulls franchise, and Julio Iglesias and Amancio Suarez, who are part owners of the Miami Heat, as the only limited partners in the NBA who are from minorities. This marks the first time that players who are Black were given the opportunity to participate in ownership after retirement. Isiah Thomas purchased part of the Toronto Raptors in addition to being named the team's vice president in charge of basketball operations. Earvin Johnson, who purchased nearly 10 percent of the Los Angeles Lakers, is the only new minority limited partner whose access to ownership did not transpire with an expansion team.

In the NFL, Deron Cherry with the Jacksonville Jaguars and William Simms with the Carolina Panthers became the only owners who are Black. Both are part of multimember ownership groups. They join Dr. Norman Francis, a former part owner of the New Orleans Saints, as the only Black owners in the history of the National Football League.

Minoru Arakawa, as partner in the investment group that purchased the Seattle Mariners, became a limited partner in ownership on July 1, 1992. The majority owner, Hiroshi Yamauchi, resides in Japan and is the only majority owner of a pro sports team living outside the United States or Canada.

The Equal Opportunity Committee for major league baseball reports that there are currently six minority owners/limited partners and thirty-one female owners/limited partners. Considering that there are twenty-eight teams in major league baseball, these numbers are significant. Unfortunately, the committee is unable to identify the total number of owners/limited partners in the league. Thus, comparisons that provide perspective cannot be made.

A number of women acquired part ownership of a major league team in the past year through inheritance.[7] Pam Shriver, who is part of the twenty-four member group that purchased the Baltimore Orioles, is one of the few female owners in professional sports who attained limited partner status through a purchase in 1993–94. She is neither a relative of the majority owner nor the member of a family ownership.

Meanwhile, there are seven NBA teams in which women have ownership interest in excess of 5 percent; in all cases, the woman is a relative of the majority owner or a member of the family that owns the team. Marge Schott (Cincinnati Reds) and Georgia Frontiere (Los Angeles Rams) are the only female majority owners/senior partners in the three leagues. The National Basketball Association has no female majority owners or senior partners.

It should be noted that few teams in any of the three leagues are owned entirely by one person. Typically there is a group of investors, ranging from two to upwards of twenty-five, that have part ownership in a franchise. A group of investors owning a team typically designate one individual to function as the chief executive officer of the organization. The chief executive officer, although identified as "the owner," is not necessarily a majority owner or senior partner. . . .

TOP MANAGEMENT

Currently there is no member of a minority acting as chairman of the board, president, or chief executive officer of any team in any league. There are three women who occupy these positions in professional sports. Marge Schott and Georgia Frontiere preside over their respective teams. Susan O'Malley, while not an owner, is the president of the Washington Bullets. In May of 1991, she became the first woman to be hired as the president of an NBA franchise. She is described as the club's top business executive. . . .

While there are no minorities functioning as chairman of the board, president, or CEO, there continues to be an increase in the number of vice presidents who are from minorities. In the past year, Stu Jackson (Vancouver expansion team), Bill McKinney (Detroit Pistons), Earvin Johnson (Los Angeles Lakers), John Lucas (Philadelphia 76ers), Isiah Thomas (Toronto Raptors), M.L. Carr (Boston Celtics), Michael Huyghue (Jacksonville Jaguars), John Wooten (Philadelphia Eagles), and Jorge Costa and John Yee (San Francisco Giants) became team vice presidents. Presently, 12 percent of the vice presidents in the NBA are from minorities compared with 7 percent and 6 percent in the NFL and major league baseball, respectively. . . .

There are currently more minority members who are principally in charge of day-to-day team operations than at any other time in the history of sport. In the past year Bob Watson of the Houston Astros became the first black general manager in major league baseball.[8] Stu Jackson was named general manager and vice president of basketball operations for the Vancouver expansion team. John Lucas of the Philadelphia 76ers was named vice president in charge of basketball operations, general manager, and head coach. Isiah Thomas purchased part ownership in the Toronto Raptors and was named team vice president in charge of basketball operations. M.L. Carr of the Boston Celtics was promoted to chief of basketball operations. Bill McKinney of the Detroit Pistons was promoted to vice president in charge of basketball operations. Finally, Michael Huyghue was hired by the Jacksonville Jaguars to oversee football operations as the club's vice president, and John Wooten was promoted to vice president of player personnel/operations by the Philadelphia Eagles. These additions result in fourteen Blacks or Latinos functioning as principals in charge of day-to-day operations of teams in the three leagues. . . .

COACHING POSITIONS

As indicated in Table 29-1, there has been a decrease in the number of minority coaches since 1992–93, when a significant number of minority members

TABLE 29-1 Head Coaches and Managers

	NBA	NFL	MLB
	1988–89	1988	1989
White	80% (20)	100% (28)	96% (27)
Black	20% (5)	(0)	4% (1)
	1989–90	1989	1990
White	78% (21)	96% (27)	96% (27)
Black	22% (6)	4% (1)	4% (1)
	1990–91	1990	1991
White	78% (21)	96% (27)	93% (26)
Black	22% (6)	4% (1)	7% (2)
	1991–92	1991	1992
White	93% (25)	93% (26)	89% (25)
Black	7% (2)	7% (2)	7% (2)
Latino	(0)	(0)	4% (1)
	1992–93	1992	1993
White	74% (20)	89% (25)	79% (22)
Black	26% (7)	7% (2)	14% (4)
Latino	(0)	4% (1)	7% (2)
	1993–94	1993	1994
White	80% (20)	89% (25)	82% (23)
Black	20% (5)	7% (2)	14% (4)
Latino	(0)	4% (1)	4% (1)

*Figures for the NBA reflect the hiring of John Lucas in Philadelphia, P.J. Carlesimo in Portland, and Butch Beard in New Jersey. At the time of publication, coaching vacancies remained for the San Antonio Spurs and the Los Angeles Clippers.

were named as head coaches or managers. Despite the naming of Butch Beard (New Jersey Nets) as a first-time head coach in the NBA, no gains were made, because Quinn Buckner (Dallas Mavericks) and Fred Carter (Philadelphia 76ers) were fired at the end of the season. Wes Unseld also resigned as head coach of the Washington Bullets. Neither major league baseball nor the NFL saw any of its teams name a new head coach or manager who was a minority member, even though there were eight vacancies filled between the two leagues since June 1993.

As Table 29-2 indicates, there are twenty-three assistant coaches (32 percent) in the NBA who are Black. This is the highest percentage of the three leagues.

The NFL has seventy-five assistant coaches (22 percent) who are minorities, indicating an 8 percent improvement over the past two seasons. Of the fifty-one offensive and defensive coordinators listed, six (12 percent) are Black. This is notable since these positions are considered pipelines to head coaching posts.

After the 1993–94 season ended, the Arizona Cardinals (David Atkins), Los Angeles Rams (Chick Harris), and the New York Jets (Ray Sherman) hired offensive coordinators who are Black. With Sherman Lewis of Green Bay, there

TABLE 29-2 NBA and NFL Assistant Coaches and MLB Coaches

	NBA	NFL	MLB*
	1989–90	1989	
White	78% (51)	80% (197)	
Black	22% (14)	20% (50)	
	1990–91	1990	
White	79% (46)	81% (208)	
Black	21% (12)	19% (50)	
	1991–92	1991	
White	67% (51)	84% (289)	
Black	33% (25)	16% (54)	
	1992–93	1992	1993
White	73% (49)	80% (264)	80% (133)
Black	27% (18)	20% (65)	13% (22)
Latino	(0)	(0)	6% (10)
Other	(0)	(0)	1% (2)
	1993–94	1993	1994
White	68% (48)	76% (217)	78% (126)
Black	32% (23)	23% (65)	14% (22)
Latino	(0)	<1% (2)	8% (13)
Other	(0)	(0)	<1% (1)

*MLB statistics for 1990, 1991, and 1992 were unavailable.

are now four offensive coordinators who are Black. The Washington Redskins replaced Emmitt Thomas as defensive coordinator, leaving only two defensive coordinators who are Black. They are Ray Rhodes in San Francisco and Tony Dungy in Minnesota.

There was a slight increase in the number of coaches who are from minorities in major league baseball. Fourteen percent are Black and 8 percent are Latino.

Table 29-3 summarizes minority hiring for coaching positions.

MEDICAL STAFF

As shown in Table 29-4, 166 of the 173 physicians (96 percent) who work for the teams in the three leagues are white. It should be noted that, in almost all cases, team physicians also have private practices. Since last year, the following physicians from minorities were hired: Dallas Mavericks appointed T.O. Souryal, who is Indian, as senior physician. Dr. J.R. Zamarano, who is Latino, acts as a consulting physician to both the Dallas Mavericks and Dallas Cowboys. Hugo Cuadros is a physician for the Chicago White Sox.

TABLE 29-3   Total Coaches (Heads, Managers, and Assistants)

	NBA	NFL	MLB*
	1989–90	1989	
White	78% (72)	84% (274)	
Black	22% (20)	16% (51)	
	1990–91	1990	
White	78% (67)	85% (285)	
Black	22% (18)	15% (51)	
	1991–92	1991	
White	80% (76)	85% (315)	
Black	20% (19)	15% (56)	
	1992–93	1992	1993
White	73% (69)	81% (289)	80%(155)
Black	27% (25)	19% (67)	13% (26)
Latino	(0)	<1% (1)	6% (12)
Other	(0)	(0)	1% (2)
	1993–94	1993	1994
White	72% (71)	78% (284)	78%(149)
Black	28% (27)	21% (77)	14% (26)
Latino	(0)	1% (3)	7% (14)
Other	(0)	(0)	<1% (1)

*MLB statistics for 1990, 1991, and 1992 were unavailable.

TABLE 29-4   Physicians

	NBA	NFL	MLB
	1993	1993	1993
White	98% (66)	98% (66)	94% (32)
Black	2% (1)	2% (1)	3% (1)
Latino	(0)	(0)	3% (1)
	1994	1994	1994
White	95% (59)	97% (71)	95% (36)
Black	2% (1)	1% (1)	2% (1)
Latino	2% (1)	1% (1)	2% (1)
Other	2% (1)	(0)	(0)

*MLB statistics for 1990, 1991, and 1992 were unavailable.

Each team maintains one doctor as a senior physician or primary doctor. Most teams list a number of other physicians in their media guides, but for the most part these doctors are used as consultants and are not employed by the teams.

Dr. Clarence Shields, Jr., of the Los Angeles Rams remains the only senior club physician who is Black. There are no Black senior physicians in the NBA or in the major league baseball. Other Black doctors listed on the medical staff for a professional team are Dr. Norman Elliot, associate physician for the Atlanta Braves, and Dr. Joe Clift, internist for the Golden State Warriors. Robert Flores, who is Latino, is a consulting physician for the Oakland As. He and Dr. Zamarano (Dallas Cowboys and Mavericks) are the only two Latino physicians working for a team in any of the three leagues.

At the league level, the National Football League office employs Dr. Lawrence Brown, who is Black, as the NFL Advisor for Drugs of Abuse. The NBA retains Dr. Lloyd Bachus, who is Black, as the medical director of its aftercare program. While there are increasing numbers of Blacks and Asian Americans receiving professional degrees in medicine, they have not been able to break into professional sport medical staffs.

Professional sports teams continue to lag behind the national average of minority members who are employed as physicians. According to a Current Population Survey by the Bureau of the Census, 3.2 percent of the physicians in the United States are Black, 4.4 percent are Latino, and 20.7 percent are female.[9] In the three leagues combined, 4 percent of the physicians are from minorities and none are women.

As Table 29-5 indicates, there continues to be great disparity among races in the position of head trainer. Although the Washington Bullets hired Kevin Johnson, who is Black, as their head trainer, five (only 6 percent) of

TABLE 29-5 Head Trainers

	NBA		NFL		MLB	
	1993		1993		1993	
White	92%	(25)	92%	(25)	100%	(23)
Black	4%	(1)	4%	(1)		(0)
Other	4%	(1)	4%	(1)		(0)
	1994		1994		1994	
White	89%	(24)	92%	(26)	100%	(23)
Black	7%	(2)	4%	(1)		(0)
Asian American	4%	(1)		(0)		(0)
Pacific Islander		(0)	4%	(1)		(0)

the seventy-eight trainers in the three leagues are from minorities. In the past year there was no change in the number of minority trainers.

RADIO AND TELEVISION BROADCASTERS

Although public address announcers are employed directly by individual teams, radio and television announcers are almost always employed by the radio and television stations that broadcast the games. In most cases the teams have little or no control over the selection of announcers, nor are the announcers on the teams' payrolls.

Two significant hirings took place in the area of broadcasting and announcing in the past year. The Boston Red Sox replaced legendary Sherm Feller with Leslie Sterling, the first Black female public address announcer in major league baseball. She joins Sherri Davis of the San Francisco Giants as the only female public address announcers. L.A. Williams was hired to broadcast Arizona Cardinals games over the radio in the Navajo language. She was hired in August 1993.

Gene Honda, who is Asian American, is the public address announcer for the Chicago White Sox.

Overall, there were no gains made in this category by minorities. Out of 145 radio and television announcers and public address announcers covering major league baseball, only 6 are Black. There are 18 who are Latino. In the NBA, 15 out of 122 announcers (12 percent) are Black and 9 (7 percent) are Latino. In the NFL, there is only one Black announcer and seven Latino announcers. The seven Latino announcers cover the Dallas Cowboys, Miami Dolphins, and Houston Oilers—all teams with a significant Latino fan base.

These percentages are not a reflection of the percentage of Blacks or Latinos playing on the field in any of the three leagues. This is another revealing fact considering the current trend of hiring announcers who are former players. . . .

REFEREES AND UMPIRES

There are fourteen officials in the NBA who are Black, as well as one who is Latino. Combined, they make up 28 percent of the officials in the league. On the other hand, major league baseball has just three umpires who are Black (5 percent) and two umpires who are Latino (3 percent). Meanwhile, the NFL has 13 officials out of 107 who are Black (12 percent). . . .

MINORITIES PLAYING PROFESSIONAL SPORTS

Professional sport is a rare sector of the economy where minorities play a major role. This is especially true in the NBA and NFL. This past year remained consistent with the trend of increasing numbers of Blacks playing professional basketball and Latinos playing professional baseball.

As Table 29-6 indicates, Blacks represent 77 percent of the players in the NBA, replicating the 2 percent increase that took place in 1993. Meanwhile, there was a 3 percent decrease, from 68 percent to 65 percent, in the number of Blacks playing football. This represents the first decline in the percentage of Black players in the NFL since we have been tracking this data.

The number of Blacks playing major league baseball increased for only the second time in a decade while the number of Latinos continued to rise. In 1994 nearly 200 players (18%) are of Latino descent. This is the highest representation in the history of the league. The number of Latinos playing professional baseball is equal to the number of Blacks who are playing. Combined, they represent 36 percent of the players.

STACKING IN PROFESSIONAL SPORTS

When Charlie Ward was not chosen in the 1994 NFL draft, it marked the first time in the history of the National Football League that the Heisman trophy winner went unselected. He had guided his team to a national championship, produced very good passing statistics, and demonstrated tremendous leadership skills on the nation's most prolific offense for the past four years. The reasons cited for not drafting him ranged from inadequate arm strength to lack of height. In addition, many NFL personnel, including John

TABLE 29-6   Racial Composition of Players

	NBA	NFL	MLB
	1989–90	1989	1990
White	25%	40%	70%
Black	75%	60%	17%
Latino	0%	0%	13%
	1990–91	1990	1991
White	28%	39%	68%
Black	72%	61%	18%
Latino	0%	0%	14%
	1991–92	1991	1992
White	25%	36%	68%
Black	75%	62%	17%
Latino	0%	2%	14%
	1992–93	1992	1993
White	23%	30%	67%
Black	77%	68%	16%
Latino	0%	<1%	16%
Other*	0%	1%	<1%

*There were twenty-two Pacific Islanders playing in the NFL during the 1992 season.

Wooten and Dennis Green, publicly stated that teams were not sure he would sign an NFL contract, in part due to his NBA capabilities. Therefore, teams did not want to jeopardize wasting a draft pick.

Despite the growing number of college quarterbacks who are Black, only seven of the ninety-six quarterbacks who played in the NFL last year were Black. Of those seven, only Randall Cunningham, Warren Moon, and Andre Ware were starters. Further, only four of the league's sixty-eight backup quarterbacks are Black.

The position of quarterback is not the only position in the NFL that is dominated by a particular race. Sociologists have demonstrated that words such as *intelligence, leadership, emotional control, decision making,* and *technique* are associated with positions such as quarterback and center. Furthermore, they have demonstrated the association of descriptive words such as *speed, quick reaction,* and *athleticism* with positions such as wide receiver, running back, cornerback, and safety.

It is worth examining the positions held by Blacks and whites. Ninety-two percent of the running backs are Black, as are 90 percent of the receivers, 80 percent of the safeties, and 168 of the 169 cornerbacks. Meanwhile, whites make up 79 percent of the centers, 64 percent of the offensive guards, and 93 percent of the kickers and punters.

Major league baseball has a similar disproportionate representation of white players in "thinking positions" and Black players in "speed positions." As Table 29-7 indicates, out of 505 pitchers on major league rosters, only 34 are Black. Furthermore, of the ninety catchers in the league, only three are Black. Meanwhile, Blacks, who compose just 18 percent of the overall players in the league, make up over 50 percent of the outfielders. Jerry Reinsdorf, co-chairman of baseball's Equal Opportunity Committee and the owner of the Chicago White Sox, said, "There is no stacking in major league baseball. All the owners are trying to get the best player they can get."

The NBA is the only league where a traditional "thinking position" is now filled overwhelmingly by players who are Black. During the 1993–94 season there were five starting point guards who are white: John Stockton, Mark Price, Bobby Hurley, Vinny Del Negro, and Scott Skiles. The percentage of point guards who are white (18%) is consistent with the overall percentage of guards in the NBA who are white (15%), as shown in Table 29-8.

Although officials from all three leagues continue to insist that there are no racial implications to the absence of Blacks in positions such as quarterback, pitcher and catcher, the "thinking positions" continue to be dominated by white players and the "speed positions" by Black players, as shown in Table 29-9.

TABLE 29-7   MLB Positional Breakdown

	WHITE PLAYERS (%)				BLACK PLAYERS (%)				LATINO PLAYERS (%)			
	1983	1992	1993	1994	1983	1992	1993	1994	1983	1992	1993	1994
P	86	84	82	78	7	5	5	7	7	11	12	15
C	93	87	87	86	0	1	1	3	7	12	12	11
1B	55	57	69	63	38	28	19	29	7	15	11	8
2B	65	60	58	47	21	21	13	21	14	19	26	32
3B	82	76	75	71	5	12	12	13	13	12	12	16
SS	73	52	42	50	11	14	8	8	9	34	50	42
OF	45	36	33	31	46	49	50	51	9	15	17	18

Compiled by Northeastern University's Center for the Study of Sport in Society. Based on 1983, 1992, 1993, and 1994 opening-day rosters as reported in the *New York Times, USA Today*, and team media guides.

TABLE 29-8   NBA Positional Breakdown

	1992–93		1993–94	
	White	*Black*	*White*	*Black*
Guard	17%	83%	15%	85%
Forward	20%	80%	18%	82%
Center	45%	55%	42%	58%
Total	23%	77%	21%	79%

TABLE 29-9   Stacking in the NFL

	WHITE PLAYERS (%)				BLACK PLAYERS (%)			
	1983	1991	1992	1993	1983	1991	1992	1993
Offense								
Quarterback	99	92	94	93	1	8	6	7
Running back	12	8	7	8	88	90	92	92
Wide receiver	23	10	11	10	77	89	88	90
Center	97	89	76	79	3	10	19	18
Guard	77	67	62	64	2	31	35	32
Tight end	52	49	39	39	48	51	59	60
Tackle	68	60	50	51	32	31	46	47
Kicker	98	88	83	94	2	0	7	0
Defense								
Cornerback	8	4	2	1	92	96	98	99
Safety	43	20	12	18	57	80	88	80
Linebacker	53	29	28	27	47	68	71	72
Defensive end	31	28	26	27	69	70	73	71
Defensive tackle	47	44	30	30	53	54	67	63
Nose tackle	n/a	42	35	42	n/a	49	60	58
Punter	0	92	85	91	0	3	10	3

Notes:
65% of all players in NFL are Black.
34% of all players in NFL are White.
1% of all players in NFL are other (Pacific Islander, Latino, and Asian American).

CONCLUSION

Attention to the issue of employment opportunities for Blacks in professional sports is at an all-time high. After a significant increase in the number of Black coaches during the 1992–93 season, there were some notable advances for minorities in the area of top management during the 1993–94 season.

Although the overall number of Blacks in senior positions of team management is still quite low in comparison to the number of Blacks performing on the field, the inroads made in the past two years will greatly enhance future opportunities for other players who are Black and who wish to go into management after retirement.

Women, on the other hand, have few opportunities in the management levels of team front offices. Rarely is a female found in an executive position on any of the teams in the three leagues. On the other hand, the commissioner's offices in all three leagues have recently hired a significant number of female executives.

There are obvious areas in need of improvement in the sports industry, particularly the hiring of qualified women and minorities. With so much attention on hiring former players, it is easy to forget that there are many positions for skilled professionals on each team. Few are filled by minorities or women. The sports industry continues to have little diversity in positions such as physician, attorney or team counsel, accountant, financial officer, and vendor. Again, the advancement of Blacks into key influential positions will likely improve opportunities for other Blacks to be hired in professional positions previously dominated by whites.

One major area of significant gain is baseball's use of minority and female vendors. Currently, all offices and clubs are using minority and female vendors or contractors. The league is committed to doubling the dollar amount of contracts with minority firms within the next year. In addition, the teams have been asked to attain the same goal with regard to female-owned firms.

Our goal in issuing the Report Card is not to get reactions to the grades, but to keep professional sport responding to the fact that sport, which is America's most integrated workplace for players, is not too much better than society in terms of who it hires in front-office and decision-making positions. White males continue to control the management on most teams in spite of enlightened leadership in the league offices of the NBA and the NFL and on baseball's Executive Committee.

NOTES

1. *ABC News Nightline,* April 6, 1987.
2. Lou Harris, *Racism and Violence in American High Schools: Project TEAMWORK Responds.* Boston: Northeastern University's Center for the Study of Sport in Society, 1993.
3. Bureau of Labor Statistics, June 1994.
4. 1993 NCAA Division I Graduation Rates Report.
5. *Chronicle of Higher Education,* September 29, 1993.
6. *USA Today,* October 28, 1993.
7. Among them are Terry Seidler of the Los Angeles Dodgers, who inherited ownership from her father, and Barbara Jacobs of the Cleveland Indians and Mrs. Ewing Kauffman of the Kansas City Royals, who inherited ownership from their husbands.
8. The late Bill Lucas performed the function of a general manager for the Atlanta Braves in 1976. His official title was director of player personnel. Lucas was the first Black to be responsible for player personnel decisions.
9. *Statistical Abstract of the United States 1992,* p. 392.

■ FOR FURTHER STUDY

Ashe, Arthur R. Jr., *A Hard Road to Glory: A History of the African-American Athlete,* 3 vols. (New York: Warner Books, 1988).
Brooks, Dana, and Ronald Althouse (eds.), *Racism in College Athletics: The African-American Experience* (Morgantown, West Virginia: Fitness Information Technology, 1993).

Cattau, Daniel, "Baseball Strikes Out with Black Fans," *Chicago Reporter* 20 (April 1991):1, 6-13.

CSSS Digest (Boston: Northeastern University Center for the Study of Sport and Society, any issue).

Davis, Laurel R., "The Articulation of Difference: White Preoccupation with the Question of Racially Linked Genetic Differences among Athletes," *Sociology of Sport Journal* 7 (June 1990):179-187.

Edelson, Paula, "Baseball's Minority Scam," *Z Magazine* 5 (March 1992):82-83.

Foley, Douglas E., *Learning Capitalist Culture: Deep in the Heart of Tejas* (Philadelphia: University of Pennsylvania Press, 1990).

Loy, John W., Jr., and Joseph F. McElvogue, "Racial Segregation in American Sport," *International Review of Sport Sociology* 5 (1970):5-24.

Messner, Michael A., "White Men Misbehaving: Feminism, Afrocentrism, and the Promise of a Critical Standpoint," *Journal of Sport and Social Issues* 16 (December 1992):136-143.

Ruck, Rob, *Sandlot Seasons: Sport in Black Pittsburgh* (Urbana: University of Illinois Press, 1987).

Smith, Yevonne R., "Women of Color in Society and Sport," *Quest* 44 (August 1992):228-250.

Yetman, Norman R., and Forrest J. Berghorn, "Racial Participation and Integration in Intercollegiate Basketball: A Longitudinal Perspective," *Sociology of Sport Journal* 10 (September 1993):301-314.

Part Ten

Structured Inequality: Sport and Gender

Traditionally, gender role expectations have encouraged girls and women to be passive, gentle, delicate, and submissive. These cultural expectations clashed with those traits often associated with sport, such as assertiveness, competitiveness, physical endurance, ruggedness, and dominance. Thus, young women past puberty were encouraged to bypass sports unless the sport retained the femininity of participants. These "allowable" sports had three characteristics: (1) they were aesthetically pleasing (e.g., ice skating, diving, and gymnastics); (2) they did not involve bodily contact with opponents (e.g., bowling, archery, badminton, volleyball, tennis, golf, swimming, and running); and (3) the action was controlled to protect the athletes from overexertion (e.g., running short races, basketball where the offense and defense did not cross half-court).

In effect, these traditional expectations for the sexes denied women equal access to opportunities, not only to sports participation but also to college and to various occupations. Obviously, girls were discriminated against in schools by woefully inadequate facilities—compare the "girls' gym" with the "boys' gym" in any school—and in the budgets. The consequences of sexual discrimination in sport were that: (1) the femininity of those who defied the cultural expectations was often questioned, giving them marginal status; (2) approximately one-half of the population was denied the benefits of sports participation; (3) young women learned their "proper" societal role (i.e., to be on the sidelines supporting men who do the actual achieving); and (4) women were denied a major source of college scholarships.

Currently, quite rapid changes are occurring. Unquestionably, the greatest change in contemporary sport is the dramatic increase in and general acceptance of sports participation by women. These swift changes have occurred for several related reasons. Most prominent is the societal-wide women's movement that has gained increasing momentum since the mid-1960s. Because of the consciousness raising resulting from the movement and the organized efforts to break down the cultural tyranny of gender roles, court cases were initiated to break down sexual discrimination in a number of areas. In athletics, legal suits were successfully brought against various school districts, universities, and even the Little League.

In 1972 Congress passed Title IX of the Education Amendments Act. The essence of this law, which has had the greatest single impact on the move toward sexual equality in all aspects of schools, is: "No person in the United States shall, on the basis of sex, be excluded from taking part in, be denied the benefits of, or be subjected to discrimination in any educational program or activity receiving federal financial assistance."

Although the passage of Title IX and other pressures have led to massive changes, discrimination continues. The selections in this part show the progress and the difficulties that remain in achieving equality.

The first selection, by sociologist Don Sabo, identifies six myths about American women athletes and demythologizes each with the results from empirical research. The second selection, by physical educator Annelies Knoppers, discusses and evaluates the various explanations for male dominance in the coaching profession. The third selection, by journalist Susanne Levin, answers the question: Among women athletes, who gets big money from sponsors, and why? In answering this question, Levin notes the disadvantages women encounter because their sports are considered relatively unimportant by the media. Also, and most significant, corporate sponsors seek women with good looks and a charming personality, qualities much less important to sponsors when they consider male athletes.

While sport has been limiting to females in so many ways, it presents problems of a different sort to males. Boys and men are expected to be successful in sports. They are expected to develop "masculine" traits from sports. But what are the effects of sports failure on the identities of boys and men? What are the consequences of developing the traits of traditional masculinity in intimate relationships? What happens to the identity of male athletes after they have left sport? These questions and issues are discussed perceptively by sociologist Michael Messner in the final selection.

30. Psychosocial Impacts of Athletic Participation on American Women: Facts and Fables

DON SABO

Patriarchal myths are encoded within American culture and transmitted through art and literature, religion and law, fables and folkways. These myths help to legitimate structured sex inequality in all sectors of society, including sport. Feminist theorists argue that patriarchal myths in American sport are more than mere cultural beliefs or "gender stereotypes." They are historically constructed ideologies that exaggerate and naturalize sex differences and, in effect, sustain men's power and privilege in [relation] to women (Messner and Sabo, in press; Birrell and Cole, 1986; Hargreaves, 1986). These same ideologies have also kept sport researchers from seeing women athletes as they really are as well as what they are capable of becoming.

This paper identifies six beliefs about American women athletes which are grounded more in myth than empirical reality. Each myth is examined in light of current sport research, which includes findings from three recent nationwide surveys which the author helped to design and execute. The first of these latter studies, the *American High School Survey* (AHSS), is a longitudinal analysis of a national, two-state, stratified probability sample of 569 female students. This study is unique because it overcomes a critical defect present in most previous studies of the effects of athletic participation, namely, their reliance on cross-sectional rather than longitudinal analysis and the resulting inability to adequately discuss change (see Melnick, Sabo, & Vanfossen, 1988). The second study, the 1985 *Miller Lite Report on Women in Sports* (MLR), is the first nationwide survey of "active and committed" adult female athletes (Pollock, 1985). A random sample of 7,000 members of the Women's Sports Foundation were surveyed in fall of 1985 and questioned about participation in sports and fitness activities. Finally, *The Wilson Report: Moms, Dads, Daughters and Sports* (TWR) focused on how family factors influence girls' athletic participation (Garfield, 1988). Telephone interviews were conducted with a national random sample of 702 mothers, 302 fathers, and 513 of their daughters aged 7-18.

Whereas the AHSS provides solid methodological grounds for making causal inferences, the data reported in the MLR and TWR are descriptive and interpretations are made with caution.

The goals of this paper are to (1) identify several "myth-conceptions" about women athletes, and (2) scrutinize their merit in light of sport research. The intent is to move sport research and theory away from andro-centric assumptions and their resultant biases (Hall, 1987).

THE MYTH OF FEMALE FRAILTY

The "myth of female frailty" in sport holds that women lack the necessary physical strength and energy to fully participate in athletics. As Lenskyj (1986) amply documents, such beliefs helped justify women's exclusion from sport and fitness activities. The belief in the fragility of female physiology is evident in 19th century medical writings which depict upper-class women as being inherently weak, sickly, hypochondriacal, and intellectually incapable of understanding medical matters and their own bodies. Well-to-do women were considered especially vulnerable to a variety of ailments. Because of their "innate" frailness, many medical scientists reasoned that women's activities had to be limited to the more moderate demands of motherhood and homemaking (Ehrenreich & English, 1979). Likewise, American sociologist W. I. Thomas argued in 1907 that women's peculiar anatomical traits were "very striking evidence of the ineptitude of woman for the expenditure of physiological energy through motor action" (1907).

The most recent evidence of the belief in female frailty issued in May of 1986 when the American College of Obstetricians and Gynecologists (ACOG) issued thirteen pages of "Safety Guidelines for Women." Women were advised to consider 30 minutes of moderate exercise followed by a "day of rest" as a safe limit to avoid injury. These prescriptions were challenged by women's sports advocates and researchers who point out that ACOG's recommendations were not based on rigorously scientific studies of women athletes. In contrast to ACOG's medical prescriptions, studies show that very few physical obstructions stand in the way of women's full participation in sport and fitness activities (Harris, 1973, 1980; Wilmore, 1974; Ryan, 1975; Adrian & Brame, 1977; Hudson, 1978).

ACOG's recommendations also do not reflect the life experiences of active American women athletes who, according to MLS and TWR data, feel their health is bettered by participation. Seventy-four percent of the MLS respondents ranked "improved health" and "stress reduction" as main reasons for engaging in sports activity (Pollock, 1985:17). Fifty-five percent of the TWR parents interviewed cited fitness and health as chief benefits of their daughters' participation in sports (Garfield, 1988:15). Finally, data from both studies show that, while the exercise regimen of many of the female subjects exceeded ACOG's guidelines, there were no negative physiological effects other than a normal incidence of athletic injury.

Rather than "excessive" exercise, socialization for physical passivity and the more sedentary character of many women's roles may in fact be responsible for many of women's health problems. For example, about 43.4% of American women between the ages of 25 and 34 are obese (National Center for Health Statistics, 1983). American children are growing fatter. The National Children and Youth Fitness Study found significant increases in the percentage of body fat in young people since 1960 (U.S. Department of Health and Human Services, 1985). Obesity is a risk factor in the development of hyperlipidemia, hypercholesterolemia, hypertension, and diabetes, which are also cardiac risk factors (Schroeder, 1982). Obesity increases the risk of osteoarthritis, a crippling disease prevalent among elderly women (Bray, 1978; Mayer, 1968). Similarly, osteoporosis afflicts 25% of American women over age 60, a disease which is propitiated by sedentary lifestyles (Veinga, 1984). Moreover, emerging research shows that regular and strenuous exercise curtails or prevents the development of osteoarthritic symptoms (Larson & Shannon, 1985; Yeaker & Martin, 1984; Huddleston et. al., 1980; Nilsson & Westlin, 1971).

In summary, both the increased number and apparent vitality of female athletes debunk the sexist assumptions of many health professionals. Feminist scholars are challenging the purportedly "objective" and "neutral" pronouncements of medical science, especially as regards women's bodies (Lenskyj, 1986; MacPherson, 1985; Hubbard, 1983). Women athletes themselves, the MLS shows, want unbiased information about the effects of participation; 70% selected "Physiology of Women as Athletes" as one of the "most important areas for future research on women in sport" (Pollock, 1985:31). What appears to be needed is a more accurate assessment of women's athletic capabilities and the formation of sound health policy which encourages rather than squelches their physical potentials.

THE MYTH OF PSYCHIC DAMAGE

The "myth of psychic damage" contends that women do not have the necessary psychological assets for athletic competition and, in contrast to men, women do not reap psychological benefit from sport. These notions are partly rooted in psychological theory. Around 1900, the American school of functionalism developed the view that female psychology and behavior are molded by evolution and instincts. Within this biologistic framework, the observable differences between women's and men's physiology, intellectual interests, and cultural achievements were interpreted as evidence of women's inferiority. Women's subordination to men thus found scientific legitimacy (Williams, 1977). These views (and their implicit values) became fused within the development of psychoanalytic theory and psychiatric practice (Effron, 1985; Smith, 1975). Within the framework of psychoanalytic theory, for example, nonconformity to traditional roles and stereotypes was considered pathological. Hence, women's interest and involvement in business, engineering, athletics, or other "masculine" activities were clinically suspect.

What does empirical research say about the psychological impacts of athletic participation on women? Generally, sport researchers have found sport involvement betters rather than worsens psychological health. Prior research suggests that, compared to nonathletes, female athletes are more achievement-motivated, independent, poised, and inner-controlled (Burke, Straub, & Bonney, 1975; Kleiber & Hemmer, 1981). Some studies find that women athletes feel that their sport involvement contributes to their self-confidence, higher energy levels, better health, and a general well-being (Snyder & Kivlin, 1977; Snyder & Spreitzer, 1983). Other research shows women are deriving elevated self-esteem, self-image, and self-actualization from athletic participation (Harris, 1975, 1973; Snyder & Kivlin, 1975; Snyder & Spreitzer, 1976). As regards body image, a widely accepted index of overall psychological health, the 1985 MLR found that 62% of respondents felt much more positively about their bodies now than five years ago, and another 23% felt the same. Also, 41% of the TWR parents believed their daughters derived character benefits from athletic participation.

The AHSS findings, however, indicate that understanding the psychological impacts of athletic participation on women (and men) may be more complex than previously assumed. Earlier studies of both female and male athletes have mainly used convenient samples and cross-sectional data; hence it has been impossible to untangle the effects of selectivity into and out of the sport stream from the socialization that occurs within sport itself. Almost all studies to date, moreover, fail to systematically account for the confounding impacts of race and/or social class on psychological well-being. In contrast, the AHSS yielded no discernible psychological effects which were directly attributable to athletic participation itself (Melnick, Sabo, & Vanfossen, 1988). The researchers initially uncovered several correlations between athletic participation and self-esteem, self-mastery, and body-concept. When controls for socioeconomic status and sophomore participation were introduced, however, these associations disappeared.

There are two interpretations of this outcome. First, since greater numbers of middle-class than working-class girls participate in high school athletic programs, the initial correlations may be picking up class differences rather than differential outcomes of athletic socialization. Secondly, the AHSS focused solely on athletic socialization between the sophomore and senior years. That no psychological effects accruing from athletic participation were found, therefore, might suggest that the impact of sport involvement upon overall personality development for many girls occurs before the sophomore year (Melnick, Sabo, & Vanfossen, 1988). In any event, contrary to patriarchal myth, no evidence of negative psychological outcomes emerged in any study!

THE MYTH OF THE "MACHO" FEMALE ATHLETE

The "myth of the 'macho' female athlete" holds that playing sports makes women think, act, and feel like men. It derives from the cultural assumption that sport is a "man's domain" and being an "athlete" means being "masculine." In this view, athletic participation is believed to exert a "masculinizing" effect on women's gender identities and, in turn, results in "abnormal" personality traits. This view was so well entrenched in American culture in the early 20th century that Dr. Dudley Sargent, a physician and physical educationist, created a stir in 1912 when he wrote in the *Ladies Home Journal* that women and men shared the same athletic potential. Sargent observed that "Many persons honestly believe that athletics are making girls bold, masculine, and overassertive; that they are destroying the beautiful lines and curves of her figure, and are robbing her of that charm and elusiveness that has so long characterized the female sex" (quoted in Twin, 1979:53-54). Today, one often hears the assertion that sports turn women into lesbians, which, according to some sexual stereotypes, means "masculine" women. Is there any empirical basis for these assumptions?

Research shows that athletic participation more probably "androgynizes" rather than "masculinizes" women's identities. Psychological androgyny means that a mixture or balance of feminine and masculine traits reside in the same personality (Bem, 1975). The outcomes of athletic socialization vis-à-vis androgyny are different for males and females (Sabo, 1985). Traditional sport endorses stereotypical gender expectations and idealizes manliness. For boys, sport socialization represents a CONTINUATION of previous gender learning; traditionally masculine expectations often become exaggerated as boys spend more time in the athletic subculture. In contrast, when girls enter the "masculine" world of sport, their experiences are apt to have an androgynizing effect on gender identity development. Athletic involvement for girls is a source of social and psychological counterpoint but, for boys, just another variation on a theme. Theoretically, therefore, gender socialization in sport is often one-sided and narrowing for boys and multifaceted and expansive for girls.

The expansion of women's gender identity in sport does not appear to produce psychological ill effects (Oglesby, 1973; Duquin, 1978). For example, Harris and Jennings (1977, 1978) studied college women athletes and found that those with androgynous identities also scored significantly higher on self-esteem than "masculine," "feminine," or "undifferentiated" individuals. These findings parallel studies of non-athletic subgroups which indicate that, regardless of their sex, androgynous individuals enjoy the highest level of self-esteem when compared with "masculine" (next highest), "feminine" (third highest), and "undifferentiated" (lowest) (Spence, Helmreich, & Stapp, 1974). Finally, data on female athletes and high achievers show they "are more likely than their male counterparts to possess masculine and feminine attributes without suffering any deficit to their femininity" (Harris, 1980:234). In other words, there does not appear to be any trade-off between women's sports involvement and "femininity" or self-esteem.

Sport researchers must recognize that the discussion of female athleticism within the conceptual framework of "androgyny" can be a form of psychological reductionism which actually reinforces patriarchal notions about gender differences. If athletic participation helps females to expand gender identity and behavior beyond narrow patriarchal standards (which include passivity, weakness, heterosexual appeal, etc.), then this means that the dominant cultural standard for femininity, or what Connell (1987) calls "emphasized femininity," is being challenged. Hence, the social construction of alternative definitions of femininity in sport departs from hegemonic views of gender which reflect and reinforce male dominance. So-called "psychological androgyny" in sport, therefore, is more accurately seen as a challenge to the social and political status quo. Indeed, data from the TWR show that most adults now accept sport as an appropriate cultural terrain for girls: 97% of parents were pleased with their daughters' involvement or want them to be more highly involved; 87% of parents believed that sports are just as important for daughters as sons; 85% of daughters felt it is no more important for boys to play sports than it is for girls.

THE MYTH OF THE "FEMALE APOLOGETIC"

A variety of sport researchers have suggested that female athletes tend to espouse a more traditional or conventional view of the women's role in society, in effect, to "apologize" for their participation in a non-traditional and "manly" activity. More recently the usefulness of the "apologetic" concept has fallen into disfavor among researchers, and it is sometimes vehemently denied by feminists who claim women athletes have nothing for which to apologize. Where does the truth lay?

Research on college samples has not demonstrated the existence of the apologetic (Colker & Widom, 1980; Del Ray, 1977; Snyder & Kivlin, 1977; Uguccioni & Ballantine, 1980). The AHSS found no evidence that the "female apologetic" is a pervasive reality among American female high school athletes; female athletes were no more apt to endorse conservative gender expectations than nonathletes. In addition, the MLS found that 94% of the respondents disagreed with the statement "Participation in sports diminishes a woman's femininity." However, at that same time, 57% of the sample agreed with the statement that "In this society, a woman is forced to choose between being an athlete and being feminine." This latter finding may mean that, while women athletes are aware of other people's (especially men's) reservations or hangups about sports and femininity, they themselves are generally self-confident about their participation. Finally, the TWR findings revealed that, while some girls still feel that "boys will make fun of them" for playing sports (22% of the 7-10 year olds), this concern ebbs as they grow older (10% of 11-14 year olds and only 3% of 15-18 year olds).

On one hand, the data may indicate that generally favorable attitudes toward women's sports now exist among American girls and women. Negative attitudes toward female athletic participation were more pervasive and intense in earlier decades. In short, during the last two decades of women's increased participation in American sport, the "masculinizing" taint surrounding women's athletic involvements may have lost its former venom. On the other hand, the very existence of the apologetic in previous decades has never received unambiguous empirical documentation. Hence, the "apologetic" may have been more a figment of the social scientific imagination rather than a fixture in the psyche of women athletes. In any event, there is no evidence for its existence in the 1980s.

THE MYTH OF COED CATASTROPHE

The "myth of coed catastrophe" assumes that athletic competition between or among BOTH sexes is harmful to women, men, and society. Negative assumptions are that physiological disparities between the sexes (size and strength differences) would make females injury prone, that men's masculine self-esteem and women's feminine self-image would be destroyed, that any further erosion of gender differences would lead to individual pathology and social anarchy. In contrast, proponents of cross-sex sport see a potential for positive outcomes: e.g., destructive gender stereotypes would be eroded; greater contact between the sexes would translate into enhanced respect and empathy; girls would learn competitive and team skills which would help them function more effectively in adult occupational settings; boys would learn how to work WITH rather than against women and apply these lessons to other sectors of their lives; many women athletes would gain access to the higher levels of competition they desire. Where does the truth lay?

Chief among myth-conceptions about cross-sex sport is that it is a "totally new" and scarce phenomenon. In fact, many types of cross-sex sport have emerged during the last few decades, e.g., coed volleyball leagues, baseball and softball leagues, racquetball, touch or flag football, floor and ice hockey, and team tennis. Whereas some forms of cross-sex sport pit individual females against males, team sports most often mix males and females on the same team; competitions between all-female and all-male teams are comparatively rare.

Reliable data on the actual extent of coed participation are scarce, but the MLR offers some intriguing descriptive statistics which may serve as a starting point for further theory and research. Table 30-1 shows the percentage of times the respondents participated in the 11 most popular athletic and fitness activities as either single-sex or coed participants. The overall data show that the subjects participate in coed sports about half of the time.

A second myth is that women do not want to participate in cross-sex sport. Emerging evidence only partly disconfirms this notion. On one hand, the desire for coed athletic alternatives is growing in some sectors. The TWR found that most girls (58%) would prefer to play coed sports while only 33% would prefer to play with girls only; no significant differences issued across age subgroups. Among the MLR respondents, 79% indicated that, when playing sports, they "seek out people with the same skill level REGARDLESS OF SEX." On the other hand, however, women's desire for male competitors with similar athletic skills NEED NOT stem from personal preferences as much as from social necessity. The fact is that women's athletic skills have greatly expanded in recent decades. For highly skilled women athletes, it may be easier to find accessible and challenging competition among men than women simply for demographic reasons; i.e., there are more highly skilled male athletes than women athletes within the general population.

Reservations about coed competition were also evident among the MLR respondents. For example, only about half (52%) of the sample were generally WILLING to play with members of the opposite sex, and 69% believed women's sports should be "kept separate from men's." Moreover, 78% felt that "women have something to teach men about humane competition" and 82% felt that "in coed sports men are often threatened by losing to a

TABLE 30-1 Percentage of Single-Sex and Cross-Sex Participation in the Eleven Most Popular Athletic and Fitness Activities among Active, Committed Woman Athletes

	Single-Sex %	Cross-Sex %	Total Number N=
Calisthenics/Aerobics	66	34	987
Jogging/Running	66	34	1010
Softball/Baseball	56	44	874
Walking	55	45	1117
Bicycling	54	46	996
Weightlifting	53	47	821
Basketball	49	51	774
Tennis, Squash	41	59	1076
Swimming	40	60	1025
Volleyball	40	60	854
Dance	25	75	773

Adapted from the 1985 *Miller Lite Report on Women in Sports,* in cooperation with the Women's Sports Foundation.

woman." Finally, though 82% disagreed that sports diminish a woman's PER-SONAL SENSE of her femininity, 57% recognized that women are often forced by social pressures to choose between being athletes and being feminine. In summary, therefore, the issue of whether many women athletes actually prefer or simply settle for coed sport remains blurred. What does seem clear is that, for personal and sociopolitical reasons, they are wading rather than diving headlong into the waters of coed sport.

One final question clouded by patriarchal myth and sadly in need of empirical scrutiny is whether cross-sex participation eroticizes male-female relations. The argument is sometimes made that cross-sex sport would lead to sexual contact, especially where boys and girls are playing contact sports together such as wrestling or basketball. This position conjures up visions of sexually aroused adolescents spending their post-game hours in heated, coital clinches. There are reasons to suspect this kind of thinking. First of all, sex research consistently shows that physical familiarity usually de-eroticizes male-female relations; e.g., coital frequency decreases the longer a couple is married (Kinsey, 1948, 1953; Hunt, 1974). Secondly, the proposition that physical contact automatically leads to sexual arousal assumes that the human sexual response is physiologically or instinctually motivated. This is not so. For humans, sexual behavior is orchestrated by the mind's capacity to internalize cultural meanings rather than some primeval or genetically triggered instinctual program (Davis, 1971). It is culture that establishes what is sexual and what is not; e.g., hand-to-genital petting in a movie theater is sexual and a gynecological examination is not. Thirdly, there is no scientific evidence that SAME-SEX contact in sport results in excessive amounts of homosexual arousal or behavior. It is theoretically inconsistent, therefore, to assert that CROSS-SEX athletic activity would inflame heterosexual passion.

In summary, the "myth of coed catastrophe" reflects and shores up patriarchy's mandate for sex segregation. To propose that men and women enter direct competition with one another violates this structural imperative. Such a proposition also challenges patriarchal beliefs about men's athletic superiority and physical powers and women's athletic inferiority and physical vulnerability. Sport researchers can inject needed empirical clarity into current controversies surrounding cross-sex sport by separating fact from fancy, reason from sentiment, and theory from ideology.

THE MYTH OF IMMOBILITY

Many sport researchers conclude that, for males, athletic participation leads to increased status among peers, greater educational attainment and aspiration, and upward mobility (Curry & Jiobu, 1984; Sack & Theil, 1979; Loy, 1969). In comparison, researchers are less contentious about whether sport involvement favorably impacts on the status and mobility of females. Whereas many researchers lean toward inferring upward mobility for men, they hesitate to do so for women. Are these dispositions based on social fact or patriarchal bias?

To begin with, most of the research on this question has focused on MALES and not FEMALES. This very disparity may reflect underlying and unconscious patriarchal norms which emphasize upward mobility and achievement for men but not women. Secondly, statements about upward mobility and male athletes remain methodologically suspect because most are based on studies using cross-sectional data and convenient samples.

Finally, the few studies of women athletes to date have produced mixed findings. For example, Feltz (1978) discovered that sports involvement ranked low among a variety of status criteria among high school students. She suggests that this is due to the stigma associated with female athletes in the high school subculture. Wells and Picou (1980), in contrast, found that among Louisiana high school females, athletes were more apt to be members of the college-oriented crowd and to hold higher educational aspirations than nonathletes. Finally, the MLR indicates that female athletes themselves endorse the view that sport involvement is related to social mobility for women. Ninety-three percent of the respondents agreed with the statement "if young girls compete successfully on the athletic fields, they will be better able to compete successfully in later life."

The AHSS generated several significant findings which may help dispel some of the current ambiguity. First, athletic participation exerted a modest impact on female athletes' self-reported popularity in the high school. Though socioeconomic status explained most of the variance in popularity, athletic participation exerted an independent effect between the sophomore and senior years. Findings also showed that athletic participation produced a slight but statistically significant effect on educational aspiration; athletes aspired toward greater educational attainment. Finally, athletic participation significantly increased the extent of girls' extracurricular activities; athletes were more involved in school and community activities than non-athletes. Melnick, Sabo, and Vanfossen (1988) infer that athletic participation expands the spectrum of activities which girls consider appropriate for self-expression. They add that, "As the high school career unfolds, the personal lessons learned through athletic socialization may interact with the status gains gleaned from sports activity thereby facilitating social experimentation and involvement within and outside the school social network" (p. 15).

CONCLUSION

This paper has identified six patriarchal myths about women athletes and examined them in light of current research knowledge. Several conclusions can be made.

[1] There is no evidence that women are too physiologically frail for athletic involvement. In fact, data indicate that strenuous exercise is a health asset while women's traditional socialization for physical passivity is a risk factor for several diseases.

[2] Contrary to the "myth of psychic damage," the evidence does not suggest that women are psychologically harmed by athletic participation.

[3] Rather than becoming "masculinized" by athletic participation, girls and women appear to be adopting a wider array of psychological traits and behaviors which goes beyond narrow, patriarchal definitions of femininity.

[4] Findings indicate that American girls and women in the 1980s no longer feel defensive or "apologetic" about their athletic involvement.

[5] Research on psychosocial impacts of coed sport on participants is so sparse at this time that inferences are not warranted. However, many young females prefer coed activities, and active and committed adult athletes frequently engage in coed sports and with no apparent negative social or psychological effects.

[6] The data show that, though participation in sport slightly heightens high school girls' educational aspirations, it significantly expands the extent of their involvement in extracurricular activities. In addition, athletic participation modestly increases girls' perceived status within the high school.

Patriarchal myths may be fading within American culture but they continue to influence perceptions of women athletes. All cultures defend their fictions and, ordinarily, we see only what we assume we know. When new information challenges mythic assumptions, two alternatives emerge: to discard the myths that establish the realities, or to cling unquestionably to the beliefs which emanate from and invigorate the status quo. Both women athletes and sport researchers now find themselves between these two alternatives. Simone de Beauvoir stated, "It is always difficult to describe a myth; it cannot be grasped or encompassed; it haunts the human consciousness without ever appearing before it in fixed form. The myth is so various, so contradictory, that at first its unity is not discerned" (1953).

The patriarchal myths described in this paper are only part of a larger, unified web of beliefs which not only contain and conceal the true abilities and potentials of women athletes, but women in ALL sectors of North American society. Empirical research will hopefully continue to play an important role in sifting fact from fable, and reality from sexist ideology.

REFERENCES

Adrian, M. & Brame, J. (eds.). 1977. National Association of Girls' and Women's Sports. Research Reports, 3. Washington, DC: American Alliance for Health, Physical Education, and Recreation.

Bem, S. 1975. Sex-role adaptability: One consequence of psychological androgyny. *Journal of Personality and Social Psychology,* 31: 634-643.

Birrell, S. & Cole, C. 1986. Resisting the canon: Feminist cultural studies and sport. Paper presented at NASSS meeting, Las Vegas, Oct.

Bray, G. A. (ed.). 1978. Obesity in perspective: Proceedings of the conference. Washington, DC: U.S. Government Printing Office.

Burke, E. J., Straub, W. F. & Bonney, A. R. 1975. Psycho-social parameters in young female long distance runners. *Movement. Actes du 7, Symposium en apopresentissage psycho-moteur et psychologie du sport,* 367-371.

Carpenter, L. J. & Acosta, R. V. 1983. The status of women in intercollegiate athletics. Cited in P. Miller, The organization and regulation of sport. Proceedings of The New Agenda, Nov. 3-6, Washington, DC.

Colker, R. & Widom, C. S. 1980. Correlates of female athletic participation: Masculinity, femininity, self-esteem and attitudes toward women. *Sex Roles,* 6:47-58.

Connell, R. W. 1987. *Gender and power.* Stanford, CA: Stanford University Press.

Curry, T. J. & Jiobu, R. M. 1984. *Sports: A social perspective.* Englewood Cliffs, NJ: Prentice Hall.

Davis, K. 1971. The prostitute: Developing a deviant identity. In J. M. Harris (ed.). *Studies in the sociology of sex.* New York: Appleton-Century-Crofts.

de Beauvoir, S. 1953. *The second sex.* New York: Knopf.

Duquin, M. 1978. Effects of culture on women's experience in sport. *Sport Sociology Bulletin,* 6:20-25.

Effron, A. 1985. The sexual body: An interdisciplinary perspective. *The Journal of Mind and Behavior,* 6: (1 & 2).

Ehrenreich, B. & English, D. 1979. *For her own good.* New York: Anchor Books.

Feltz, D. L. 1978. Athletics in the status system of female adolescents. *Review of Sport & Leisure,* 3:98-108.

Garfield, E. 1988. The Wilson report: Moms, dads, daughters and sport. Copies may be secured by writing Women's Sports Foundation, 342 Madison Avenue, Suite 728, New York, NY 10017.

Hall, M. A. 1987. The gendering of sport, leisure, and physical education. *Women's Studies International Forum,* 10 (4).

Hargreaves, J. A. 1986. Where's the virtue? where's the grace? A discussion of the social production of gender through sport. *Theory, Culture & Society,* 3: 109-121.

Harris, D. V. 1973. *Involvement in sport.* Philadelphia: Lea & Febiger.

Harris, D. V. 1975. Research studies on the female athletes: Psychosocial considerations. *Journal of Physical Education and Recreation,* 46: 32-6.

Harris, D. V. 1980. Femininity and athleticism: Conflict or consonance? Pp. 222-239 in D. Sabo & R. Runfola (eds.). *Jock: Sports & male identity.* Englewood Cliffs, NJ: Prentice Hall.

Harris, D. & Jennings, S. E. 1977. Self-perception of female distance runners, in P. Milvy (ed.). *The marathon: Physiological, medic, epidemiological, and psychological studies.* NY: New York Academy of Sciences.

Harris, D. & Jennings, S. E. 1978. Achievement motivation: There is no fear of success among female athletes. A paper presented at the Fall Conference of the Eastern Association of Physical Education of College Women. Hershey, PA. October.

Hubbard, R. 1983. Social effects of some contemporary myths about women. Pp. 1-8 in M. Lowe & R. Hubbard (eds.). *Woman's nature: Rationalization of inequality.* New York: Pergamon Press.

Huddleston, A. L., Rockwell, D., Kulund, D. N. & Harrison, B. 1980. Bone mass in lifetime tennis athletes. *Journal of the American Medical Association,* 244:1107-1109.

Hudson, J. 1978. Physical parameters used for female exclusion from law enforcement and athletics. In C. A. Oglesby (ed.). *Women and sport: From myth to reality.* Philadelphia: Lea & Febiger.

Hunt, M. H. 1974. *Sexual behavior in the 1970's.* New York: Dell Publishing Company.

Kinsey, A. 1948. *Sexual behavior in the human male.* Philadelphia, PA: Saunders Publishing Company.

———1953. *Sexual behavior in the human female.* Philadelphia, PA: Saunders Publishing Company.

Kleiber, D. A. & Hemmer, J. D. 1981. Sex differences in the relationship of locus of control and recreational sport participation. *Sex Roles,* 7: 801-810.

Larson, K. A. & Shannon, S. C. 1985. Decreasing the incidence of osteoporosis-related injuries through diet and exercise. *Public Health Reports,* 99 (6): 609-613.

Lenskyj, H. 1986. *Out of bounds: Women, sport and sexuality.* Toronto: The Women's Press.

Loy, J. 1969. The study of sport and social mobility. Pp. 112-117 in G.S. Kenyon. *Aspects of contemporary sport psychology.* Chicago: The Athletic Institute.

MacPherson, K. 1985. Osteoporosis and menopause: A feminist analysis of the social construction of a syndrome. *Advances in Nursing Science,* 7 (4): 11-22.

Mayer, J. 1968. *Overweight: Causes, costs, controls.* Englewood Cliffs, NJ: Prentice Hall.

Melnick, M., Sabo, D., & Vanfossen, B. 1988. Developmental effects of athletic participation among high school girls. *Sociology of Sport Journal,* 5 (1): 22-36.

Messner, M. & Sabo, D. (In press.) *Sport, men, and the gender order: Critical feminist perspectives.* Champaign, IL: Human Kinetics.

Nilsson, D. E. & Westlin, N. E. 1971. Bone density in athletics. *Clinical Orthopedics and Related Research,* 77: 179-182.

Oglesby, C. 1973. Athleticism and sex role. A paper presented at The New Agenda Conference, Washington, DC, November 3-6.

Pollock, J. 1985. *The 1985 Miller Lite report on women in sports.* Copies can be obtained from New World Decisions, Ltd., 120 Wood Avenue South, Iselin, NJ 08830.

Ryan, J. 1975. Gynecological considerations. *Journal of Physical Education and Recreation,* 46:40.

Sabo, D. 1985. Sports, patriarchy & male identity. *Arena Review,* 9 (2): 1-30.

Sabo, D. & Runfola, R. (eds.). 1980. *Jock: Sports and male identity.* Englewood Cliffs, NJ: Prentice Hall.

Sack, A. L. & Theil, R. 1979. College football and social mobility: A case study of Notre Dame football players. *Sociology of Education,* 52: 63.

Schroeder, M. A. (ed.). 1982. Symposia on obesity. *The Nursing Clinics of North America,* 17 (2): 189-251.

Smith, Dorothy. 1975. Women and psychiatry. Pp. 1-19 in D. Smith and S. David (eds.). *Women look at psychiatry.* Vancouver: Press Gange Publishers.

Snyder, E. E. & Kivlin, J. E. 1975. Women athletes and aspects of psychological well-being and body image. *Research Quarterly,* 46: 191-199.

Snyder, E. E. & Kivlin, J. E. 1977. Perceptions of the sex role among female athletes and nonathletes. *Adolescence.* 12: 23-29.

Snyder, E. D. & Spreitzer, E. A. 1976. Correlates of sport participation among adolescent girls. *Research Quarterly,* 47: 804-09.

Snyder, E. D. & Spreitzer, E. A. 1983. *Social aspects of sport.* Englewood Cliffs: NJ: Prentice Hall.

Spence, J. T. & Helmreich, R. L. 1978. *Masculinity and femininity: Their psychological dimensions, correlates, and antecedents.* Austin: University of Texas Press.

Thomas, W. I. 1907. *Sex and society.* Chicago: University of Chicago Press.

Twin, S. 1979. *Out of the bleachers: Writings on women and sport.* New York: McGraw-Hill.

Uguccioni, S. M. & Ballantine, R. H. 1980. Comparison of attitudes and sex roles for female athletic participants and nonparticipants. *International Journal of Sport Psychology,* 11: 42-48.

U.S. Department of Health and Human Services. 1985. The national children and youth fitness study. Office of Disease Prevention and Health Promotion, Washington, D.C. 20201. This study is also published in the *Journal of Physical Education, Recreation & Dance,* 56 (1): NCYFS 1-NCYFS 48.

Veinga, K. S. 1984. Osteoporosis: Implications for community health nursing. *Journal of Community Health Nursing,* 1 (4): 227-233.

Wells, R. H. & Picou, J. S. 1980. Interscholastic athletes and socialization for educational achievement. *Journal of Sport Behavior,* 3: 119-128.

Willhelm, S. 1983. *Black in a White America.* Cambridge, MA: Schenkman Publishing Company.

Williams, Juanita H. 1977. *Psychology of women: Behavior in a biosocial context.* New York: W. W. Norton.

Wilmore, J. (ed.). 1974. Research methodology in the sociology of sport. *Exercise and Sport Sciences Review,* 2, New York: Academic Press.

Yeaker, R. A. & Martin, R. B. 1984. Senile osteoporosis: The effects of calcium. *Postgraduate Medicine,* 75 (2): 147-159.

31. Explaining Male Dominance and Sex Segregation in Coaching

ANNELIES KNOPPERS

Coaching, a male-dominated occupation, has been subjected to attempts to increase the number of women: workshops, certification programs, affirmative action, brochures, job postings, recruitment, and so on. Theberge (n.d.) found that the female coaches in her study had benefited from such approaches. Their entry into the coaching ranks had been relatively easy; in fact, many had been asked to apply for the jobs they were currently holding. Yet, in spite of these and other efforts, the proportion of female coaches has declined. In 1978, 58.2% of the coaches of women's college teams were women; in 1988, that percentage was 48.3%, and in 1990 it was 47.3% (Acosta & Carpenter, 1990). There is good reason to believe this revolving-door pattern will continue. Only 12.3% of the women and 50.3% of the men respondents in a study of Division I college coaches indicated that they intended to coach until they were 65 years old (Knoppers, Meyer, Ewing, & Forrest, 1991). If women, who are already underrepresented in coaching, continue to leave at the rate that this percent indicates, then coaching will stay a male-dominated occupation. In addition, although women are still becoming coaches of women's college teams, less than 1% of the coaches of men's teams at the college level are women, a figure that has changed little over the past 5 years (Acosta & Carpenter, 1990). If one combines the total number of coaches in women's and men's programs, it is obvious that coaching is a male-dominated occupation and is becoming increasingly more so.

Some may argue that coaching has been a gender-neutral occupation because women and men both coached within same-sex sport programs prior to the passage of Title IX. Consequently, these changes in the percentage of female coaches could be seen as evidence of men appropriating the coaching of women, a female-dominated job. However, the coaching of women has been, historically, an activity that was assumed to be part of the job of a physical education instructor, for which she received little or no pay. In this article I define coaching as a distinct and paid activity and argue that

SOURCE: "Explaining Male Dominance and Sex Segregation in Coaching: Three Approaches" by Annelies Knoppers. From Quest 44(2), pp. 210–227. Copyright © 1992 by National Association for Physical Education in Higher Education. Reprinted by permission.

only when the coaching of women became such did it become a job and part of the occupation of coaching. I base my discussion on the assumption that coaching as a full-time, paid occupation has existed primarily for men and has been defined by them.

In the past 10 years, sociologists have begun to look at the sex segregation of waged work, including coaching. In this article I review individual, structural, and social relational approaches used to explain sex segregation of waged work as well as the existence of the revolving door for women in these jobs. I apply these approaches to coaching, drawing upon my own research in this area,[1] and draw attention to issues that must be addressed if we wish to diminish male dominance in coaching.

THE INDIVIDUAL APPROACH

Sex role socialization theory and human capital theory both try to explain sex segregation of jobs and occupations in terms of the gendered interests and choices of individuals (for a more detailed explanation of these two individual perspectives, see Epstein, 1988; Knoppers, 1987, 1988). Sex role socialization assumes that we learn gender-appropriate behavior in childhood and adolescence from our families, churches, schools, peers, and the media. We are assumed to have internalized these views by the time we reach adulthood. This internalization then dictates the jobs we choose. Consequently, because girls do not see many female coaches and are not brought up to view coaching as a desirable job for women, they tend not to choose it or even think about entering that area.

In the paid work world, human capital consists of the formal qualifications, such as experience and education, one has for a job (see for example, Becker, 1985). Human capital theory sees wage differences (including those associated with gender) and sex segregation as a result of differences in human capital. Women are assumed to prefer jobs that do not penalize work interruptions, that do not have excessive overtime or travel, and that are flexible in case of emergencies (Epstein, 1988). Sex segregation in waged work is therefore seen as a result of choice in the context of a free market. On the basis of this perspective, it would be assumed that women do not choose jobs such as coaching or refereeing because of the excessive demands these jobs make on time and travel.

Together, the socialization and human capital approaches are called *individual approaches* because they attribute sex segregation of labor to the interests, abilities, and choices of individual women. Individual approaches are quite popular in the athletic world. For example, when athletic administrators were asked to explain the lack of female coaches, they cited lack of qualifications (i.e., human capital) and time demands of the job/family responsibilities as the main reasons (Acosta & Carpenter, 1985). Similarly, the women and men who participated in a study of national Canadian sport organizations agreed that in part, the relatively small number of female coaches, especially at the elite level, was due to the lack of experience and qualifications of women (cited in Theberge, in press). In a study of Division I college coaches (Knoppers, Meyer, Ewing, & Forrest, 1989), we found that human capital accounted for 24% and 12% of the variances in women's and men's salaries, respectively.

Undoubtedly, interests and qualifications do play a role in job selection and in the gendering of wages; consequently, recruitment strategies, internships, workshops, and brochures serve a purpose. There is evidence available, however, to show that individual approaches are inadequate in explaining sex segregation and gendered wages. First, socialization theory seems to suggest that we are fixed by our early childhood experiences and that all those teach us the same ideology and living patterns. The number of female athletes at both the Olympic and college level has increased greatly since 1972 (Coakley, 1990). Because a history of athletic participation seems to be part of the job socialization pattern for coaches (Sage, 1975) and because the number of coaching jobs post–Title IX has also increased (Acosta & Carpenter, 1990), these numbers suggest that the proportion of female coaches should be increasing. Instead, the reverse has occurred. Fishwick (1988) named this paradox "the illusion of equality."

Second, there is little evidence of a causal connection between sex role socialization and sex segregation of jobs in part because changes in technology mean that jobs and their titles change (Marina & Brinton, 1984). For example, 20 years ago, jobs in athletics such as sports information director, sports medicine trainer, sport consultant, and executive/technical director were virtually nonexistent. Yet these jobs are primarily filled by men (Macintosh & Whitson, 1987). Jacobs (1989) has shown that vocational aspirations tend to have short life expectancies and that most people have very fluid career patterns or histories. Consequently, explaining the domination of men in coaching solely by gender-differentiated socialization patterns has its weaknesses.

Third, human capital approaches are also fraught with inadequacies when used to explain a sex-segregated work force. As the previously cited salary data of Division I coaches indicate, human capital may determine a person's salary but does so more for one gender than for the other. Perhaps in our discussions about the shortage of women in male-dominated occupations such as coaching, we have paid too little attention to the human capital of male coaches.

The human capital approach assumes that education plays a large role in determining a person's location in the labor market. In our study of the salaries of Division I coaches (Knoppers, Meyer, Ewing, & Forrest, 1989), we found that the number of years of higher education was a significant predictor of salaries of female coaches. In contrast, the number of years of higher education did not serve as a significant predictor of men's salaries. In addition, a look at cross-gender comparisons of other qualifications explored in our study and in others (Anderson & Gill, 1983; Eitzen & Pratt, 1989; Knoppers, Meyer, Ewing, & Forrest, 1989; Macintosh & Beamish, 1988; Macintosh & Whitson, 1987) revealed that significantly more female than male coaches and administrators have majored in physical education and have competed as varsity athletes. These results show that human capital plays a gender-differentiated role in the occupation of coaching.

The human capital approach also seems to assume that women's absence from the labor market to care for children leads to a deterioration of skill. However, men have temporary absences from their jobs as well. Data from the study of Division I coaches (Knoppers et al., 1991) revealed that significantly more male coaches (35.5%) than female coaches (25.7%) had been temporarily absent from coaching, although on the average, women had been absent a half year longer than men. Women were absent because they had another job, had no job, or were taking care of children. Men were absent because they participated in military service, held political office, had another job, or were on leaves of absence. Interestingly, men's leaves of absence from a job, including coaching, are rarely assumed to lead to a deterioration in their human capital. For which coaching jobs does learning to kill and to conduct warfare enhance one's human capital? In contrast, the caretaking skills acquired while one cares for children, aging parents, or a disabled partner may be skills that are crucial in the athletic workplace. The 49 national and provincial coaches who participated in a study exploring the connections among careers, work, and life seemed to accept the idea that "athletes have a kind of natural right to their coaches' undivided attention" (Theberge, in press). This seems to echo the expectations children have of parents, teachers, and other adults. Also, almost half of both female and male coaches in our study said that dealing with athletes was the source of greatest satisfaction in their coaching (Knoppers et al., 1991). The possession of nurturing skills may therefore be a great asset to coaches. As is obvious, the exclusion of relational skills from the definition of human capital not only devalues those skills but also fails to account for the competencies and qualities developed in nonpaying jobs (Waring, 1980).

Finally, human capital theory confers too much rationality on the marketplace (Epstein, 1988; Peterson, 1989). If women can be hired for less, if the goal of athletic programs is to make a profit (or at least not suffer financial loss), and if the marketplace is based on rational decisions, then one would expect women to be hired instead of men for coaching all non-revenue sports. Such a hiring pattern might make an athletic program more cost effective. Yet this pattern has not occurred, indicating that all decisions made in the marketplace are not based solely on outcome. Similarly, not all women are married and/or have children, so for them, family responsibilities would be less likely to "interfere" with the ability to give time to coaching. Yet female coaches who are childless or single are channeled into coaching women, rarely coach men, and also experience discrimination (Knoppers, Ewing, Forrest, & Meyer, 1989). Consequently, human capital theory fails to explain inconsistencies concerning gender and waged work.

THE STRUCTURAL APPROACH

Dissatisfaction with the aforementioned theories in explaining sex segregation and the gendered wage gap has led researchers to explore other explanations. One such approach focuses on the structure of organizations and occupations. It asks how this structure constrains individual choice and determines work behavior (Epstein, 1988). Gendered wage differences and sex segregation of jobs are seen not so much as a function of the interests, choices, and abilities of women but of position within the structure of an organization. That is, women, as well as people of color, work in positions that are low in the organizational hierarchy. The location of these positions plays a large role in determining both wages and work-related behavior and attitudes (Kanter, 1977).

Kanter (1977), on the basis of the results of her study of a large corporation, argued that three structural determinants (opportunity, power, and proportion) play a large role in determining work behavior and attitudes, including exiting from a job or occupation. People who have little opportunity to advance to other jobs or to be upwardly mobile in the organizational hierarchy tend to exit from the job; those with little access to resources (that is, power) tend to be less satisfied with their jobs than those with a great deal of access to resources. The lower the gender proportion (the number of women to men), the greater the possibility that women are treated as tokens.[2] Kanter's approach suggests that women drop out of male-dominated occupations not necessarily because they are women but because they are in positions of little opportunity, where they have limited access to resources and where there are few of them. Anyone, regardless of gender or race, would show similar work behaviors if they were in these positions. This approach deserves attention because it shifts the focus from women to structure and thus avoids "blaming the victim."

Opportunity

Kanter (1977) suggested that degree of perceived opportunity for mobility and growth impacts work behavior and attitudes. A person perceives opportunity if she or he has many viable career and financial options, has access to a job information network, and receives informal on-the-job training. The smaller the perception of opportunity, the more likely a person will experience dissatisfaction with the job, have lower vocational aspirations, and exit from the job. There is evidence, in addition to what Kanter found in her study, supporting this idea. Gerson (1985), in a study of women who were engaged full-time in either domestic or waged work, found that women's decisions about their place in the waged labor market were strongly influenced by their perceptions of visible opportunities and their experiences (favorable or unfavorable) in waged work. Women who had exited from waged work did so in reaction to blocked opportunities in the workplace.

We (Knoppers et al., 1991) explored how access to positions, opportunities for income, networking for jobs, and frequency of feedback from supervisors were gendered for female and male Division I coaches. Measures of work behavior and attitudes were career aspiration, degree of satisfaction, and likelihood of leaving coaching. The results indicated that opportunities for female coaches were more truncated than those for men. For example, a woman who coaches basketball at the Division I level can only make horizontal moves to other women's basketball coaching positions, and if she wishes to move into an administrative position, her chances of attaining this are less than those of men. In contrast, a man who coaches women's basketball at the Division I level can move to other basketball coaching positions of *both* women's and men's teams and has a greater chance of moving into athletic administration jobs, including that of athletic director. The results of the study also showed that men were significantly more satisfied with their jobs or careers and were less likely to envision leaving coaching than were women. Overall, these results indicated support for opportunity as a structural determinant of gendered work behavior.

Power

Kanter (1977) defined power as having access to and the ability to mobilize resources, support, and supplies. Our study of power, as defined by Kanter, produced mixed results (Knoppers, Meyer, Ewing, Forrest, 1990). Female coaches of nonrevenue sports were most limited in their access to and use of critical resources; male coaches of revenue sports had the greatest degree of access to and use of these resources. Thus, differences in power could possibly be attributed to the type (revenue or nonrevenue) of sport. Yet differences in access to resources were also found between female and male coaches in the same location—that is, between female and male basketball coaches and between female and male nonbasketball coaches. Other research (see Ragin & Sundstrom, 1989, for a summary) has produced similar results and has led to the conclusion that gendered access to critical resources is only partially due to differences in location in the organizational hierarchy.

Proportion

Kanter (1977) also assumed that changing the gender ratio, simply adding more of whomever is in the minority, will help to erase gender segregation. This seems to make sense intuitively and is supported by empirical evidence. An increase in the gender ratio has often paralleled a positive change in the attitude of women who perceived the job to be women-friendly (Izraeli, 1983; Toren & Kraus, 1987). Similarly, Theberge (n.d.) reported general collegiality among female and male coaches even though women were in the minority. We (Knoppers, Meyer, Ewing, & Forrest, in press) tested this hypothesis in terms of frequency of social interactions between female and male Division I college coaches: Women reported more woman-woman interactions under high gender-ratio conditions than under low. We concluded that an increase in gender ratio decreased the isolation of women.

However, an increase in the number of women does not necessarily guarantee that male workers welcome women (Reskin, 1988). Izraeli (1983) found that although an increase in the number of women made the job seem more women-friendly, there was little change in men's acceptance of or relations with women. South, Bonjean, Markham, and Corder (1982) reported a negative correlation between the number of women and interactions of women with men co-workers. Similarly, the results of the Division I study cited previously (Knoppers et al., in press) revealed that men tended to interact with other men with similar frequency regardless of the number of female coaches. Men who worked in athletic departments where there were relatively many female coaches reported a similar number of interactions with women as those who worked with few female coaches. Overall, men interacted more frequently with men than with women, regardless of the number of female coaches in the athletic department.

There is also evidence to show that tokenism is gendered; that is, the situation is different for token women than for token men. For example, 6% of all nurses are men, yet these token men earn on the average 10% more than female nurses. Two percent of construction workers are women, yet these token women earn on the average 25% less than their male counterparts ("Odds and Trends," 1990). Zimmer (1988), in a review of the literature on tokenism, has shown that being a male token in a female-dominated occupation is quite different and often more advantageous than being a female token in a male-dominated profession. Williams (1989), in a study of female marines and male nurses, found that male marines were much less welcoming to women than female nurses were to their male colleagues. As the foregoing makes abundantly clear, changing the gender ratio of a job or workplace may work positively for women with respect to other women but not necessarily with respect to other men.

Inadequacies of the Structural Approach

It is clear, then, that a structural approach can be only partially helpful in explaining sex segregation in coaching and the decline in the number of female coaches. Overall, the research indicates that a structural explanation such as that of Kanter (1977) can be more helpful in explaining women's work behavior than that of men in male-dominated occupations. This is not to say that structural approaches should not be used to bring about change. As Theberge's (1987) research has shown, programs such as affirmative action have helped bring more women into coaching. Sole reliance on a structural approach, however, may mean that other aspects of gender in coaching are overlooked or ignored.

There may be several reasons why a structural approach may be inadequate in explaining male dominance in coaching. First, the athletic workplace is, in itself, loosely structured (Theberge, 1987). Some coaches may be employed full-time or part-time by a university, others by clubs or organizations. The absence of clearly defined job ladders and hiring and firing criteria, as well as variations in sports, prevents a thorough investigation of gendered structures because such structures may be idiosyncratic or may not exist. Formal and informal hierarchies may vary by institution. In some, the athletic director may be the person with the most power; in other institutions, the coaches of men's football and basketball may have a great deal of say in the appointment and retention of an athletic director. Consequently, a structural approach may be inadequate in explaining male dominance and sex segregation in coaching.

THE SOCIAL RELATIONAL APPROACH

An approach that may resolve some of the aforementioned inadequacies views gender as a social relation. Social relations such as those of gender, race, and class are characterized by domination/subordination and by human agency. Domination occurs in the material, ideological, and cultural sense so that what the dominant group thinks or values becomes common sense, that is, dominant or hegemonic. The dominant group has more power; it has the ability to make its meanings or interpretations of social facts "stick." The subordinate group is not passive, however, and challenges this domination as best it can in circumscribed circumstances. The results of two studies of female and male coaches (Hall, cited in Theberge, in press; Knoppers, Ewing, Forrest, & Meyer, 1989) indicated that most female coaches did not see themselves as victims but did report discriminatory practices. Theberge (in press) concluded her study about the careers, work, and domestic life of 49 female coaches by praising female coaches who make it to the top for their resourcefulness and for overcoming so many obstacles.

The following analogy may be helpful in explaining the concept of gender relations. It is as if women and men are engaged in a tug-of-rope game. The struggle is over who gets to define the nature of the game. Many of the men (especially if they are white, middle class, and heterosexual) have special advantages such as cleats, special gloves, and sun visors to help them in the game; in addition, they attempt to control the rules and to ensure that these rules will not disadvantage men. Women devise strategies to pull on the rope within the rules set by the men but often without many special privileges or resources. When the women persist and gain a little distance or manage to get a rule changed, the men counter with a new strategy. As the game goes on, the women counteract with another strategy. This is not to suggest that all involved in the game want to play it; many women and some men would rather play another game, such as jump rope. However, most of the men have invested a great deal in the game and therefore would like to continue it. The tug-of-rope analogy is used to show that in this perspective, the relationship between women and men is seen as being dynamic. It is marked by a struggle over who gets to give dominant meanings to gender, that is, meanings that most people accept. Consequently, gender becomes a verb, so that *we gender.*

Gender relations do not, however, operate in a vacuum. They intersect with other forms of social relations marked by power imbalances. The type of social relations existing in a society varies over time, but currently we also have race, class, sexual, and age relations, all of which intersect in myriad ways. For example, gender relations intersect with class relations, although the manner in which they do so will vary according to the nature of the economic system (see for example, Bray, 1988; Hartmann, 1976; Walby, 1986). Gender relations have given opportunities for power and profit, and these opportunities have led, in part, to the constitution of capitalism.

Obviously, those engaged in the gender tug-of-rope are also engaged in other games. A white heterosexual middle-class woman may be on the subordinate side in the gender game, but in the class, race, and sexuality games she is on the dominant side. She rarely experiences these games or social relations in isolation from each other, making it difficult to tease out which game is being played at any given moment in her life. Messner and Sabo (1990) used the analogy of a wheel to describe how these social relations act as spokes within the construction of social reality. That analogy may be helpful in conceptualizing the distinctness and commonalities of various forms of social relations but fails to capture the complexity of how these social relations are situated within a person. For example, a woman who is the only person of color and one of three female coaches in an athletic department may have difficulty discerning whether some of her experiences should be attributed to racism, to sexism, to both, or to other factors. Similarly, one of her coaching colleagues, a white middle-class woman, may perceive that gender is the basic social relation that provides the central core of her identity. She, however, unknowingly, is also experiencing the privileges of class (she is undoubtedly paid more than secretaries and has more social status than they do) and race.

These intersections of social relations indicate the difficulty of focusing on one, for example, gender, as I am doing. As Messner and Sabo (1990) pointed out, this can be done as long as we do not privilege gender, or any one relation, above other relations and remember its connection to other social relations. In this article I raise questions concerning gendered power in a dynamic sense: Who gets to define what it means to be a coach, whose definition becomes dominant, and what happens when that definition is challenged? As I grapple with these questions, I will try to raise other questions that show how definitions of *coach* encompass other social relations as well.

If men are to stay the dominant group with respect to gender, they have to continually show their difference from women and attribute superiority to that difference. For example, men, especially those who are white, heterosexual, and middle class, have appropriated sport as part of the hegemonic or dominant form of masculinity (Messner, 1988; Theberge, 1985). Because the strongest man is usually stronger than the strongest woman, the way sport is currently practiced gives visible proof of the "natural superiority" of men.

Yet gender relations are not static; their form is always challenged so that what it means to be male or female is continually reconstructed. Sport provides an example of this challenge and subsequent reconstruction. Although men have always claimed sport as theirs, women have always engaged in sport, sometimes on their own terms but at other times on the terms of men. The increase in the number of female athletes has challenged the exclusiveness of this domain so that, in general, sport is no longer a distinctly gendered activity. Male superiority therefore must be reconstructed in other dimensions in the sport world. One such dimension is in leadership or coaching. The interests of many men may now be best served by excluding women from coaching and especially from coaching men's teams. Such exclusion serves to promote the superiority of men and thus reinforce the current nature of gender relations.

Similar appropriation and reconstruction has occurred for waged work. A masculinity existed in the beginning of this century in which men, especially those who were white, heterosexual, and middle-class, collectively appropriated waged work and assigned responsibility for domestic work, including child care, to women (Cockburn, 1985; Cohn, 1985; Connell, 1987). Thus, a division of labor based on gender sustained this version of masculinity. Hegemonic masculinity thus became associated with being the breadwinner (Brittan, 1989).[3]

Middle-class women began to engage in waged work in large numbers in the middle of the 20th century and not only stayed in the work force but continued to increase in number (Epstein, 1988). Their class privilege often meant that they could hardly call their wages supplemental to those of the male breadwinner. If engaging in paid work is a characteristic that helps define a masculinity that is hegemonic, and if women engage in paid work, then the dominant form of masculinity must be reconstructed. Thus, the definition of what it meant to be masculine had to be reconstructed, that is, the tug-of-rope had to be altered so that the dominant group could still be recognized as superior or dominant and would not lose its privileges.

This reconstruction was supported by a division of labor within waged work as well (Connell, 1987). To maintain any gendered division of labor, a society has to define positions and tasks as masculine or feminine and then find ways to enforce those definitions (Jacobs, 1989). Social rules for the allocation of jobs by gender are found in almost all paid employment and in all industrial societies. Let us examine some of the dynamics that ensure that jobs become associated more with one sex than the other and how those definitions are challenged and reconstructed.

Gendered Structure

One assumption associated with the gendering of a job has to do with complexity, which in turn is embedded in meanings given to organizational hierarchies (Reskin & Roos, 1987). Jobs that men do are seen as difficult, important, and more complex than those that women do (Acker, 1989, 1990; Epstein, 1988). The creation of most organizational and occupational hierarchies is based on the assumption that jobs requiring few skills are situated at the bottom and those requiring complex skills are at the top (Acker, 1989, 1990). Facilitating, nurturing, working with girls and women, and managing multiple demands are defined as simple skills because they supposedly can be done by anyone, are believed to be innate especially to women, and thus require relatively little training. In contrast, "real" skills (needed when one works with men) are assumed to need training, which means a greater investment in and by the worker, which then translates into more pay and higher placement in the hierarchy.

Although there is no research available that describes status hierarchies in coaching, I suggest that, generally, coaching women is viewed as being simpler than coaching men because of assumptions about women's lower skill levels and higher relational needs and because one is working with women. Consequently, the job of coaching women will have less prestige and lower wages and can be filled by women. In contrast, if the job of coaching men, especially in the revenue-producing sports, is seen as requiring "real" skills and associations with hegemonic masculinity, then it may be difficult for women to be considered as qualified candidates. The greater complexity of coaching men would then contribute to the higher status of coaches of men's sports.

Yet this definition and resulting hierarchy is beginning to be challenged because a few women do coach men, primarily in individual sports (Knoppers, Ewing, Forrest, & Meyer, 1989). This challenge to gender boundaries may intersect with capitalistic interests. Women may be "allowed" to coach a men's team if the sport is not so closely allied with hegemonic masculinity or with the need to make a profit. Thus we find a few women coaching teams such as men's tennis and swimming and challenging the assumption about who is able to coach men.

Gendered Jobs

Another dynamic in gendering a job is the assumption about who will fill that job. For example, male-dominated jobs are created on the assumption that those who fill them will give priority to waged work over domestic work and will have a backup person taking care of the home, children, and physical and emotional needs. It should come as no surprise that men fit best in those jobs. This has certainly been true of coaching, which has been a two-person single career for men in which their wives were primarily responsible for raising the children, entertaining recruits and coaches, doing the housekeeping, and attending athletic events (Sabock, 1979; Sabock & Jones, 1978). We (Knoppers, Ewing, Forrest, & Meyer, 1989) found that married male coaches were most likely to shoulder relatively fewer domestic work responsibilities than married female coaches.

The assumption that married male coaches will have someone at home to take care of domestic work will be challenged. There are few women left who are not engaged in waged labor. Among the increasing number of middle-class women who enter the labor market are sure to be spouses of coaches. Most of these women will probably do a double shift, that is, engage in both waged and domestic work (Hochschild, 1989). Yet the more decision-making responsibility a woman has in her waged work, the more influence she may have on the division of domestic work (Aytac, 1990). It is possible that the spouses of male coaches will demand that their husbands assume more domestic responsibilities and make them responsible for entertaining recruits and other activities. Male coaches are already realizing that they are missing out on important parts of their children's lives (Sage, 1987). Rules reforming athletics such as the curtailing of recruiting seasons could enable a coach to be home more often. Possibly, the athletic department will assume responsibility for other tasks previously assigned to the spouses of coaches, and gradually the definition of coaching as a two-person single career will change. It is also possible that some responsibilities will be assigned to other women, for example, secretaries and (underpaid) day-care workers. We need to be attentive to these shifting responsibilities in defining the formal and informal tasks assigned to coaches so that in redefining the job we do not simply add to the burdens of other women.

Gendered Activities

Another interrelated dynamic in the gendering of an occupation is the dominant meaning we give to the activity itself (Hearn & Parkin, 1983). Hegemonic masculinity is enhanced through definitions of work that emphasize the job's association with stereotypical characteristics assigned to men in a specific race and class (Jacobs, 1989). Thus, job activities that are associated with men are defined differently than those assigned to women. The results of a recent study illustrate this process.

Leidner (1991) studied two similar jobs, selling fast food and selling insurance, to show how one is constructed as being more appropriate for one sex than the other. The selling of fast food and of insurance requires the employee to be pleasant at all times and to adjust her or his mood to the customer's demands. Such pleasing and submissive actions are usually associated with females; thus it is no wonder that girls and women are hired for the service counters of fast-food establishments. In contrast, insurance people are taught to see that such deference to customers is really calculated, that the salesperson is the one in control, and that nonresponse in the face of abuse is a refusal to let someone else take control. By this reasoning, women are ill-suited for insurance work and well-suited for fast-food service, and the reverse holds for men. One job is thus defined for women and the other for men. The latter, of course, is seen as more complex and important and is assigned higher wages.

We need to explore how similar definitional processes have shaped our understanding of coaching. For example, 46% of both male and female coaches participating in the Division I study (Knoppers et al., 1991) cited dealing with athletes as their greatest source of satisfaction in coaching. If we defined coaching as a job that consisted primarily of nurturing athletes and facilitating their team play, coaching would be primarily associated with women and would be a low-status activity. If coaching is a job where coaches feel that athletes have the right to the undivided attention of the coach (Theberge, in press), then it could be defined as similar to domestic work, where children and male spouses claim the undivided attention of women. Yet that has not been the dominant definition of coaching, regardless of whether one coaches women or men. It is that dominant definition we must see as problematic. Which historical processes have helped create the current definition? How has that definition been challenged? How did the job of coaching become defined so that it is so attractive to men that they overlook relatively low pay, long hours, job insecurity, and lack of family time? One would think that a man whose sexual preference is for males might best understand male athletes, for example. Why is the norm for coaching a white heterosexual man? How does this definition shape job evaluations and hiring and firing criteria? To what extent do coaches of color, gay and lesbian coaches, and physically challenged coaches adopt the dominant definition, and to what extent do they challenge it? How has the coaching of men come to be defined differently than the coaching of women so that men can do both and women can only coach women, if at all? It is these questions we must try to answer, paying attention to what happens when dominant definitions are challenged.

Gendered Workers in the Gendered Workplace

The gendering of waged work stretches beyond gendered structures and jobs to workers and the workplace. Regardless of how people end up in their jobs, they experience the dynamics of gender relations on a daily basis in their work. Each workplace is a microcosm of meanings about gender, and in each workplace a work culture is formed that is often unique to the situation. In the workplace, power (i.e., the ability to make definitions dominant) is constantly negotiated and constructed. Consequently, social relations such as those of race, class, sexuality, age, and gender, which are based on negotiated power, can be used to broker power on the job.

Because compulsory heterosexuality plays a large role in the current nature of white middle-class culture, gendered power in the workplace is often negotiated through sexual behavior. Only recently have researchers begun to pay attention to this dimension (e.g., Gutek, 1989; Hall, Cullen, & Slack, 1989; Hearn & Parkin, 1987; Pringle, 1989). It has been neglected in most discussions pertaining to women in male-dominated occupations, including coaching.

In work settings where men are the majority, the norm of heterosexuality may often determine the nature of gender relations. For example, Pringle (1989), in a study of secretaries, found that the most common mode of interaction between male bosses and female secretaries resembled "institutional heterosexuality," a relationship in which the secretaries functioned as "office wives." Similarly, in athletics, the norm of heterosexuality is so strong that

> the sexual relationship between a male coach and his female athletes is often known and visible, while the sexual preference of competent, assertive, and strong-willed women is the subject of gossip and innuendo. In these organizations, visible heterosexuality, whether positive or negative, is implicitly condoned, while homosexuality or lesbianism, whether real or imagined, is explicitly condemned. (Hall et al., 1989, p. 41).

Because heterosexuality is assumed to be the norm in the workplace, men can safely be seen in the company of other men. Few people are suspicious of the amount of time men spend with other men. Male-dominated activities such as coaching and sport are so congruent with hegemonic masculinity that male athletes and coaches can spend an inordinate amount of time together without questions about sexuality being raised. It is a testimony to the strength of hegemonic masculinity that such bonding can occur without weakening the norm of compulsory heterosexuality. This male homosociality is often problematic for women because male camaraderie is a conduit for talk about jobs, politics, sports, cars, and the pursuit of women (Gutek, 1985). Women, of course, form their own group, as the previously cited research on social interactions indicates. There is, however, a difference between the two groups: access to those with influence and to critical resources (Lipman-Blumen, 1984). For example, men who coach Division I are more likely to rely on informal networks (the old boys network) to find out about a job vacancy; women are more likely to rely on formal job advertisements (Knoppers et al., 1991).

Interactions between women and men may be mediated by sexuality. This sexual behavior is often a currency for reinforcing male power. Feminists have named this type of behavior *sexual harassment*. Currently, sexual harassment involves "sexual behaviors which represent an unwanted and unsought intrusion by men into women's feelings, thoughts, behaviors, space, time, energies and bodies" (Wise & Stanley, 1987, p. 71). Sexual harassment includes a variety of actions, such as frankly looking a person over, giving subtle suggestive looks, making sexual remarks and jokes, invading a person's personal space without permission, grabbing, displaying pinups or sexist cartoons, and so on (Cockburn, 1985; Gutek, 1985).

The popular belief that women want or use sexual behaviors in the workplace to achieve an advantage has often been used as an excuse to limit women's options in waged work. When people discuss women coaching men, the issue of sexual attraction is often raised, but the same does not occur when men coach women (Hall et al., 1989). Pringle (1989) found little evidence to support the stereotype about women's use of sexual behavior to gain advantages in the workplace; however, she discovered that men were more likely than women to say they had used sexual behavior to gain an advantage in the workplace. We tend not to see this because

> men can behave in a blatantly sexual way without it being identified. Playboys and harassers go largely unnoticed because "organizational man," goal oriented, rational, competitive, is not perceived in explicitly sexual terms. It is ironic that women are perceived as using sex to their advantage. They are much less likely to initiate sexual encounters and more likely to be hurt by sex at work. (Pringle, 1989, p. 94)

Thus, for men, being sexual on the job and everywhere, including in sports, is so much a part of the atmosphere that we do not see it. It is possible that men who are accused of sexual harassment or of seducing female players may be convinced that the accusation is unjust because they have no active memory of engaging in this behavior. Such behavior is simply unseen, as are other behaviors that we consider routine or ordinary.

A great deal of research is needed to explore the manner in which sexual harassment is used to negotiate power within athletics before we can have a clear picture of the dynamics of gender relations in the athletic workplace. Hall et al. (1989) have suggested that we begin to examine how sexuality is used to negotiate and construct power in sport organizations.

Challenging, Resisting, and Reconstructing

If many women move into jobs that have been associated with hegemonic masculinity, new meanings have to be given to the definition of what makes men different or superior to women. Yoder (1991) pointed out that a few token women are easily assimilated and, as the novelty of their presence wears off, their work situation may become somewhat more comfortable. Yet when the number of women in a male-dominated occupation becomes substantial, then men begin to resist their entry. Ott (1989) argued that this resistance occurs when the proportion of women is somewhere between 20 and 40%. She suggested that at this point, the increased competition for jobs may be a threat to male workers. Although individual men may support and encourage token women, collectively, men often close ranks in a hostile way when more women appear on the scene.

Not only does the entry of women into an occupation often fail to integrate the social climate in the workplace, it also leads to job reconstruction, resulting in an increase in sex-segregated jobs within that occupation. Stanley (1990) called this the hydra phenomenon: As women enter a male-dominated occupation, it divides into male- and female-dominated jobs. Similarly, in coaching we now have two nonparallel jobs: coaching men and coaching women. A gendered wage gap exists not only between these two jobs but also within them, that is, between female and male basketball coaches and between female and male coaches of nonrevenue sports (Knoppers, Meyer, Ewing, & Forrest, 1989).

Often, then, when women move into jobs that have strong associations with hegemonic masculinity, men exercise agency. They may move to adjacent jobs, set up barriers for women, routinize the skill, subdivide the job, or create new jobs that have higher status (Cockburn, 1985). Teaching and clerical work were historically male-dominated occupations. They have become female-dominated through a process of redefinition, and their social status has declined accordingly. Bielby and Baron (1987) studied the effects of changing gender ratios in 400 firms and reported that when women became a sizable minority in a firm, it became known as a women's firm and its social status decreased. Sorrel (1990) cited statistics showing that every 1% increase in the number of women in an occupation is associated with a wage decline of $42. These declines were not just confined to the entry of women into a male-dominated occupation; the same occurred when people of color entered a white-dominated occupation (Sorrel, 1990).

As I pointed out earlier, there is no gender symmetry in tokenism. Similarly, the decrease in social status and wages tends not to accompany the entry of men into female-dominated jobs. At this point it is difficult to pinpoint causality. Are women and people of color admitted in large numbers to an occupation or firm when its social status and wages are on the decline, or does their presence cause this? I suggest that it is probably a combination of these two, plus possibly other factors.

We can expect strong resistance to women entering the ranks of coaches of men's football and basketball, especially at the college level. As indicated earlier, coaching, especially that of men's basketball and football, is strongly associated with hegemonic masculinity. Theberge (1990) has suggested that "within sport, coaching is a key site for the production of masculinity" (p. 64). If women persist and succeed in becoming a visible presence as coaches in these sports, then it is very possible that the nature of these programs will change. Possibly, reformers of sport will have their way before women enter these jobs and will reduce the emphasis on men's revenue-producing sports. Subsequently, women would be allowed to coach these sports. Or, with more and more male athletes opting to play professional rather than college sport, professional team sports may receive increasing emphasis, and interest will shift gradually from collegiate to professional sport. A decrease in the importance of collegiate men's basketball and football may be accompanied by an influx of women into the coaching ranks.

As the foregoing discussion of the social relations approach indicates, untangling the dynamics of male dominance and sex segregation in coaching is a complex task. It requires us to explore the ways structures, jobs, workers, and the workplace are gendered. In addition, such explorations need to be accompanied by a sensitivity to human agency and the constraints placed upon it.

CONCLUSION

I have tried to make clear that if we are to truly understand coaching as a male-dominated occupation we can no longer focus on the qualifications of women (individual approach) or assume gender neutrality of structures, jobs, workers, or workplaces (structural approach). Instead, we need to use the social relations approach to ask questions that focus on definitions of coaching. Obviously just adding blacks, women, and homosexuals will not necessarily change the definition of coaching. Hall et al. (1989) warned that women should not have to become honorary men in order to be considered good coaches or to be admitted into the elite coaching ranks. We need to explore how the definitions of coach are constructed, challenged, and renegotiated. We also need to ask questions that explore the interconnectedness of several social relations simultaneously: Why is the leadership in sport predominantly white, male, and heterosexual? We need to explore the agency of women as they challenge the norms and cope with sexual harassment. For example, the female coaches interviewed by Theberge (1990) tried to overcome obstacles related to male dominance in coaching by trying to be excellent coaches and by grounding their coaching methods in science. We need more studies to explore these strategies and those used by female coaches to resist sexual harassment. If we want the social groups who are minimally represented in the coaching ranks to enter coaching and not exit through the revolving door, then we obviously have to change the dominant definitions surrounding the occupation of coaching.

NOTES

1. A nationwide study of gender in coaching (for a description of the methodology, see Knoppers, Ewing, Forrest, & Meyer, 1989) used a sample of 947 head coaches of Division I institutions who coached women's or men's baseball/softball, basketball, cross-country/track, golf, gymnastics, swimming/diving, tennis, and volleyball. These sports were selected for their popularity within women's programs so that comparisons could be made across sport and gender with a reasonable sample size. The sample was mostly Caucasian (94%), with 308 women (32.5%) and 639 men (67.5%).
2. When women are in the minority, the ways they differ from the norm (male coaches) may be exaggerated. Female coaches may be seen as representing all women when they have losing records or problem athletes: when they do well, they tend to be seen as exceptions. Also, tokens are often socially isolated.
3. This ideology was so dominant that it was also adopted by members of the working class even though both women and men often engaged in waged work. The concept of the man as the breadwinner was sustained by attributing women's wages to be supplemental to those of their husbands (Rosen, 1987).

REFERENCES

Acker, J. (1989). *Doing comparable worth: Gender, class and pay equity.* Philadelphia: Temple University Press.

Acker, J. (1990). Hierarchies, jobs, bodies: A theory of gendered organizations. *Gender & Society,* **4,** 139-158.

Acosta, R., & Carpenter, L. (1985). Status of women in athletics: Changes and causes. *Journal of Physical Education, Recreation & Dance,* **56**(6), 35-37.

Acosta, R., & Carpenter, L. (1990). *Women in sport: A longitudinal study—Thirteen year update.* Unpublished manuscript, Brooklyn College, New York.

Anderson, D., & Gill, K. (1983). Occupational socialization patterns of men's and women's interscholastic basketball coaches. *Journal of Sport Behavior,* **6,** 105-116.

Aytac, I. (1990). Sharing household tasks in the United States and Sweden: A reassessment of Kohn's theory. *Sociological Spectrum,* **10,** 357-371.

Becker, G. (1985). Human capital, effort and the sexual division of labor. *Journal of Labor Economics,* **3,** 533-558.

Bielby, W., & Baron, J. (1987). Undoing discrimination: Job integration and comparable worth. In C. Bose & G. Spitze (Eds.), *Ingredients for women's employment policy* (pp. 211-232). Albany, NY: State University of New York Press.

Bray, C. (1988). Sport and social change: Socialist feminist theory. *Journal of Physical Education, Recreation & Dance, 59,*(6), 50-53.

Brittan, A. (1989). *Masculinity and power.* New York: Basil Blackwell.

Coakley, J. (1990). *Sport in society: Issues and controversies* (4th ed.). St. Louis: Times Mirror/Mosby.

Cockburn, C. (1985). *Machinery of dominance: Women, men and technical knowhow.* London: Pluto Press.

Cohn, S. (1985). *The process of occupational sex-typing: The feminization of clerical labor in Great Britain.* Philadelphia: Temple University Press.

Connell, R. (1987). *Gender and power: Society, the person and sexual politics.* Stanford, CA: Stanford University Press.

Eitzen, D.S., & Pratt, S.R. (1989). Gender differences in coaching philosophy: The case of female basketball teams. *Research Quarterly for Exercise and Sport, 60,* 152-158.

Epstein, C.F. (1988). *Deceptive distinctions: Sex, gender and the social order.* New Haven, CT: Yale University Press.

Fishwick, L. (1988). *Where have all the coaches gone? Placing the question in context.* Working Papers in Sociology, Department of Sociology, University of Illinois, Urbana.

Gerson, K. (1985). *Hard choices: How women decide about work, career, and motherhood.* Berkeley, CA: University of California Press.

Gutek, B. (1985). *Sex and the workplace.* San Francisco: Jossey-Bass.

Gutek, B. (1989). Sexuality in the workplace: Key issues in social research and organizational practice. In J. Hearn (Ed.), *The sexuality of organizations* (pp. 56-70). London: Sage.

Hall, M.A., Cullen, D., & Slack, T. (1989). Organizational elites recreating themselves: The gender structure of national sport organizations. *Quest, 41,* 28-45.

Hartmann, H. (1976). Capitalism, patriarchy, and job segregation by sex. *Signs: Journal of Women in Culture and Society, 1,* 137-169.

Hearn, J., & Parkin, W. (1983). Gender and organizations: A review and a critique of a neglected area. *Organization Studies, 4,* 219-242.

Hearn, J., & Parkin, W. (1987). *"Sex" at work: The power and paradox of organization sexuality.* New York: St. Martin's Press.

Hochschild, A. (1989) *The second shift: Working parents and the revolution at home.* New York: Viking Press.

Izraeli, D. (1983). Sex effects or structural effects: An empirical test of Kanter's theory of proportions. *Social Forces, 62,* 153-165.

Jacobs, J. (1989). *Revolving doors: Sex segregation and women's careers.* Stanford, CA: Stanford University Press.

Kanter, R.M. (1977). *Men and women of the corporation.* New York: Basic Books.

Knoppers, A. (1987). Gender and the coaching profession. *Quest, 39,* 9-22.

Knoppers, A. (1988). Men working: Coaching as a male-dominated and sex segregated occupation. *Arena Review, 12*(2), 13-18.

Knoppers, A., Ewing, M., Forrest, L., & Meyer, B.B. (1989). *Dimensions of coaching: A question of gender?* Report submitted to the National Collegiate Athletic Association, Mission, KS.

Knoppers, A., Meyer, B.B., Ewing, M., & Forrest, L. (1989). Gender and the salaries of coaches. *Sociology of Sport Journal, 6,* 348-361.

Knoppers, A., Meyer, B.B., Ewing, M., & Forrest, L. (1990). Dimensions of power: A question of sport or gender? *Sociology of Sport Journal, 7,* 369-377.

Knoppers, A., Meyer, B.B., Ewing, M., & Forrest, L. (1991). Opportunity and work behavior in college coaching. *Journal of Sport and Social Issues, 15*(1), 1-20.

Knoppers, A., Meyer, B.B., Ewing, M., & Forrest, L. (in press). Gender ratio and social interaction among college coaches. *Sociology of Sport Journal.*

Leidner, R. (1991). Serving hamburgers and selling insurance: Gender, work, and identity in interactive service jobs. *Gender & Society, 5,* 154-177.

Lipman-Blumen, J. (1984). *Gender roles and power.* Englewood Cliffs, NJ: Prentice-Hall.

Macintosh, D., & Beamish, R. (1988). Socio-economic and demographic characteristics of national sport administrators. *Canadian Journal of Sport Sciences, 13,* 66-72.

Macintosh, D., & Whitson, D. (1987, November). *Equality of opportunity for females: A non- issue in Canadian national sport organizations.* Paper presented at the annual conference of the North American Society for the Sociology of Sport, Edmonton, AB.

Marina, M., & Brinton, M. (1984). Sex typing and occupational socialization. In B. Reskin (Ed.), *Sex segregation in the workplace: Trends, explanations, remedies* (pp. 192-232). Washington, DC: National Academy Press.

Messner, M. (1988). Sport and male domination: The female athlete as contested ideological terrain. *Sociology of Sport Journal, 5,* 197-211.

Messner, M., & Sabo, D. (1990). *Sport, men, and the gender order.* Champaign, IL: Human Kinetics.

Odds and trends (1990, Fall). *Time,* p. 26.

Ott, E. (1989). Effects of male-female ratio at work. *Psychology of Women Quarterly, 13,* 41-57.

Peterson, R. (1989). Firm size, occupational segregation, and the effects of family status on women's wages. *Social Forces, 68,* 397-414.

Pringle, R. (1989). *Secretaries talk: Sexuality, power and work.* New York: Verso Press.

Ragin, R., & Sundstrom, E. (1989). Gender and power in organizations: A longitudinal perspective. *Psychological Bulletin, 105,* 5-88.

Reskin, B. (1988). Bringing the men back in: Sex differentiation and the devaluation of women's work. *Gender & Society, 2,* 58-81.

Reskin, B., & Roos, P. (1987). Status hierarchies and sex segregation. In C. Bose & G. Spitze (Eds.), *Ingredients for women's employment policy* (pp. 3-12). New York: State University of New York Press.

Rosen E. (1987). *Bitter choice: Blue-collar women in and out of work.* Chicago: University of Chicago Press.

Sabock, R. (1979). *The coach* (2nd ed.). Philadelphia: Saunders.

Sabock, R., & Jones, D. (1978). The coaching profession: Its effect on the coach's family. *Coaching Review, 1*(6), 4-13.

Sage, G. (1975). An occupational analysis of the college coach. In D. Ball & J. Loy (Eds.), *Sport and social order* (pp. 391-456). Reading, MA: Addison-Wesley.

Sage, G. (1987). The social world of high school coaches: Multiple role demands and their consequences. *Sociology of Sport Journal, 4,* 213-228.

Sorrel, L. (1990). What women are worth. *Off our backs, 20,* 4, 29.

South, S., Bonjean, C., Markham, W., & Corder, J. (1982). Social structure and intergroup interaction: Men and women of the federal bureaucracy. *American Journal of Sociology, 84,* 160-170.

Stanley, A. (1990). Gender segregation in the workplace: Plus ça change . . . *National Women's Studies Association Journal, 2,* 640-645.

Theberge, N. (1985). Toward a feminist alternative to sport as a male preserve. *Quest, 37,* 193- 202.

Theberge, N. (1987). A preliminary analysis of the careers of women coaches in Canada. In T. Slack & C. Hinings (Eds.), *The organization and administration of sport* (pp. 173-192). London, ON: Sports Dynamics Publishers.

Theberge, N. (1990). Gender, work, and power: The case of women in coaching. *Canadian Journal of Sociology,* **15,** 59-75.

Theberge, N. (n.d.). *Career patterns of women coaches in Canada.* Unpublished manuscript, University of Waterloo, Department of Kinesiology.

Theberge, N. (in press). *Careers, work and domestic life: Women coaches managing the challenge.* Working Paper Series, Program for the Study of Women and Men in Society, University of Southern California, Los Angeles.

Toren, N., & Kraus, B. (1987). The effects of minority size on women's position in academia. *Social Forces,* **65,** 1096-1100.

Walby, S. (1986). *Patriarchy at work: Patriarchal and capitalist relations in employment.* Oxford, England: Polity Press.

Waring, M. (1980). *If women counted: A new feminist economics.* San Francisco: Harper Collins.

Williams, C. (1989). *Gender differences at work: Women and men in nontraditional occupations.* Berkeley, CA: University of California Press.

Wise, S., & Stanley, L. (1987). *Georgie Porgie: Sexual harassment in everyday life.* London: Pandora Press.

Yoder, J. (1991). Rethinking tokenism: Looking beyond numbers. *Gender & Society,* **5,** 178-192.

Zimmer, L. (1988). Tokenism and women in the workplace: The limits of gender-neutral theory. *Social Problems,* **35,** 64-77.

32. The Spoils of Victory: Who Gets Big Money from Sponsors, and Why

SUSANNA LEVIN

There's an incomparable thrill that comes with winning, a moment of pure, electric ecstasy. But emotion doesn't put food on the table. For a competitive athlete, corporate sponsorship and endorsement contracts are the tangible payoff for years of hard training.

In order to feast on the corporate gravy train, a woman must be at the top of her sport and have the right combination of brains, looks, and personality. Then, if she's willing to work at self-promotion, she can make money: Steffi Graf's $6 million worth of deals makes her one of the most highly rewarded athletes in the world. A top golfer such as Nancy Lopez can earn entry into the millionaire's club as well, and top performers in sports from triathlon to diving to rock climbing make upward of $100,000 a year in endorsements.

The overwhelming majority of athletes, of course, are lucky if they get free gear, travel expenses, and entry fees, or—praise the Lord—enough income to train full time. In general, women athletes have a tough time getting backing because their sports lack the visibility that corporations want. Companies are even less likely to spend on women's sports when the economy is bad. "The economy plays a big role and I think 1992 is going to be a tough year for everyone," says Nola Miyasaki, manager of the LPGA division at IMG, a top management firm.

LOVE ME, LOVE MY SPONSOR

The relationship between athletes and corporations is a simple business proposition: A top performer earns the public's respect and admiration. A company tries to buy that respect. "The athlete has created an image that lends credibility to a product," says Murphy Reinschreiber of PCH Sports Marketing in Encinitas, California, manager of Ironman champion Paula Newby-Fraser.

In order for the arrangement to work for the company, however, the athlete has to be liked by potential customers, and that's where the problems start for women athletes. "Women's sports get less visibility," explains Liz Dolan, vice president of corporate communications for Nike. "If you have no visibility, there's nothing for us to buy."

Right off the bat, women athletes are at a disadvantage in all but a few sports. According to a 1990 study by the Amateur Athletic Foundation of Los Angeles, only five percent of TV sports news coverage is devoted to women's sports. That begins to explain why a male basketball or football player can get $15,000 for a speaking engagement or $50,000 to $100,000 for a TV commercial. A top woman—or a man in a nonmajor sport—is lucky to get a fraction of that.

TURNING GOLD INTO MONEY

Every four years, women have an opportunity for a veritable bonanza of visibility, when a handful of Olympians become the toast of the nation. The goldest medals of all, in terms of endorsements, are those that hang from the necks of American women figure skaters and gymnasts. Mary Lou Retton's deals—worth over a million dollars following her 1984 gold medal—are still the high-water mark for any Olympic athlete.

For women and men in nontraditional sports, Olympic gold delivers lower, but still impressive, earning potential. According to Parkes Brittain, vice president, Olympic Division, Advantage International, the Olympics are the great equalizer in terms of payoffs. "Male and female performances generally result in the same types of success in the market," he says. This winter's big pre-Olympic winner was speedskater Bonnie Blair, the only returning American gold medalist at Albertville. Despite the relative obscurity of her sport, Blair's deals with Evian, Oakley, Xerox, Mizuno, Visa, Kraft, and Jeep/Chrysler enabled her to tuck away an estimated $100,000 before ever setting foot on French soil.

SORRY, WRONG SPORT

Although Blair's success is phenomenal, it's a far cry from how much she would have made if she were a figure skater—the big bucks are still in traditionally feminine sports. Athletes in figure skating, tennis, and golf are most likely to boost their incomes with contracts to sell things other than sporting goods—Jennifer Capriati, for example, represents Oil of Olay, and golfer Betsy King has a deal with Dove soap.

"It's a carryover from the time when tennis and skating were the only acceptable sports for women," says Sally Sullivan, a Washington attorney who represents basketball stars Jennifer Azzi and Katy Steding. Getting deals for basketball clients compared with tennis players is like "night and day," says Sullivan. "My basketball clients are some of the most exceptional women I've ever met. They're attractive, warm, and bright, yet we've had a tough time getting them deals," she says. "It's been very frustrating."

Sullivan compares Azzi, who led Stanford to the national championship in 1990, to 16-year-old millionaire Jennifer Capriati. Says Sullivan, "If Jennifer Azzi had been born a tennis player, she'd be making that much, too."

THE RIGHT STUFF?

Although the sport in which an athlete competes largely determines her financial future, individual factors enhance an athlete's "marketability." Performance is 50 percent of the equation, says Reinschreiber; the other 50 percent is a combination of looks, personality, and brains that make a person "a good promotion."

"Companies have gotten a lot more creative in how they use athletes," says Reinschreiber. "Some athletes earn a living as spokespeople, making presentations to retailers and customers." That calls for public speaking ability and people skills, he explains, citing the experience of Paula Newby-Fraser, who earns in excess of $200,000 through contracts with Brooks shoes, Mrs. T's Pierogies, Aerodynamics apparel, and others. "She's done an incredible job with her speaking ability and she pays attention to people," says Reinschreiber. "That all added up for her."

Greg Rorke, president of Danskin, which sponsors 15 women through Team Danskin, says he looks for performance first. "I like a world champion more than anything," says Rorke. If the top two performers in a sport are unavailable, it gets a little more tricky. "I would choose personality, what they call in television the Q factor: personal charm." Rorke cites bodybuilder Carla Dunlap as an example of an athlete with good people skills. "Carla's great at appearances. She's a good spokesperson and she gets great response," he says.

Looks, Rorke says, are not a determining factor. "Does someone have to be in a certain ballpark? Possibly." But Reinschreiber is more direct. "It's real important," he says. "Far too many people don't pay enough attention to presentation. You need to do the best with what you've got."

This is particularly true if you're selling food or cosmetics instead of sports equipment. "Looks are much less important to Nike than they would be to a cosmetics company," says Dolan. And although a sporting goods company is generally looking for the best athlete, the attractive woman "may get endorsements that don't normally go to athletes," she says.

Every now and then, an athlete combines talent with extraordinary looks: Florence Griffith-Joyner wowed the world in 1988, and her post-Olympic endorsements were estimated at several million dollars, uncommonly high for a track athlete. Diver Wendy Williams and miler Suzy Favor are current knockouts in the world of sport. Williams, 1988 Olympic bronze medalist, already has several lucrative deals. "She could have a career as a model, and anytime that happens in sports, for both male and female athletes, it helps your portfolio," says Brittain, who compares Williams to 1984 Olympic gold medalist and all-around hunk Steve Lundquist.

Favor, 1991 national champion in the 1,500 meters, is sponsored by Reebok; her contract is reported to be worth between $50,000 and $100,000, despite the fact that she has yet to win internationally. "She's a great talent," says PattiSue Plumer, the current 5,000-meter national champion, "but if she were just an average-looking woman, she wouldn't receive the same kind of money." Plumer, the number two finisher in the 1,500, adds that it makes good business sense to sponsor the blonde-haired, blue-eyed Favor, because magazines often put her on the cover. "You can call it sexism, or you can call it business," says Plumer.

Before signing Favor early last year, "Reebok didn't have a super star in the women's ranks," says promotions manager Mark Bossardet. Favor's unprecedented four NCAA championships in the same event gave her that status, says Bossardet. "And along with her performance credentials comes her personality and attractiveness."

NO FREE LUNCH

As in any job, time equals money. Sponsorship can buy an athlete time to train, but it can also cost her. The athlete who gets a good deal can quit her job, but now she has to make time for things like photo shoots and public appearances. The demands can be considerable.

World champion rock climber Lynn Hill has been on both sides of the equation. For years, she made her living at everything from working at Carl's Jr. to running a climbing guide business. "I never dreamed I could make money as a climber," recalls Hill. Her big breakthrough came in 1988, when her modest income from winnings and a deal with Chouinard equipment allowed her to quit her job.

In the last couple of years, Hill's stock got higher, which she attributes to a combination of climbing success, image—both hers and the sport's—and publicity surrounding her surviving a terrible fall. Reebok, Hind, Timex, and Dare perfume all came knocking at her door. The financial rewards enabled her to buy a house in France, where she lives, but the commitments took their toll. "If the sponsorship is big, you have to be willing to spend more time," says Hill.

After several months of competing in Europe and traveling around the U.S. for her sponsors, Hill was exhausted. "I really got spread thin. I couldn't do everything for my sponsors and do well in competition," Hill says. "I ended up not entering the last few competitions of the season. It was a mistake, and I learned a lot from that."

Plumer, who thought she was rich when she first made $10,000, has turned down offers that were "too much work for too little money." When her training allows, she makes time for speaking engagements and photo shoots; compensation from her major sponsors, Nike and Oakley, now approaches $100,000 a year.

Plumer readily acknowledges that the financial rewards keep her going. "I don't run just for the money, but I couldn't do it were it not for the money," she says. The world's top-ranked 5,000-meter runner won't hazard a guess at what an Olympic gold medal would be worth to her, but she admits that the potential windfall is a major motivation. "I'm not Mary Lou Retton," says Plumer, "but I have enough of the right things to make me more marketable than a lot of people."

THE CREEPING PROBLEM OF MORALS

In addition to being at the beck and call of a sponsor, the athlete has two other responsibilities. First, she has to perform. "You get hurt, you don't run, your contract can be cut, and you don't get any appearance fees," says Plumer. In addition, the athlete has to avoid what Reinschreiber calls "the creeping problem of morals."

Although performance is definitively determined by the final score or the finish line, morals are judged by a corporate executive's idea of what is socially acceptable. Reinschreiber lists drugs and criminal charges among the major no-nos; Advantage's Phil de Picciotto goes a step further: "An athlete has to be very stable and noncontroversial in order to have the broadest appeal possible."

Few in the business like to discuss it, but sexual behavior—particularly homosexuality—is another creeping moral problem. Athletes such as Billie Jean King and Martina Navratilova have brought the issue into the open in recent years, and Navratilova claims to have lost endorsements because of it.

Figures don't lie. Navratilova, the winningest active player in tennis with 54 Grand Slam titles, has contracts worth about $2 million a year. Graf, with 11 Grand Slam victories, earns three times that amount. Monica Seles, with four Grand Slam wins, makes roughly $3.5 million. Capriati and Gabriela Sabatini, neither of whom has ever been ranked number one in the world, each makes as much or more than Navratilova.

With Navratilova, performance is clearly not the question. Whether the discrepancy is entirely attributable to sexuality, or—as many in the business would have you believe—is also explained by age, looks, or personality, the bottom line is the same. "Ironically, companies want to associate with someone who is honest," notes de Picciotto. "Unfortunately, being honest hasn't helped Martina."

It's not just about homosexuality, either. When Magic Johnson tested HIV positive last fall, Navratilova caused a stir by stating that a woman in Johnson's shoes would be dropped like a hot potato. What is amazing is that anyone found the tennis star's statement shocking. Says Nike's Dolan, "A woman with a reputation for promiscuity would be dropped in a second. [Navratilova] was absolutely right to point out that what happened to Magic is terrible, but a woman wouldn't be treated with the same kid gloves."

FIGHTING FOR CRUMBS

For Navratilova, at least, there is some consolation in the fact that she is a multi-millionaire. Thousands of equally devoted athletes are struggling to get an entry fee paid here, a free case of PowerBars there. For every Wendy Williams, there are a hundred Jennifer Azzis; for every Bonnie Blair, a hundred Shari Rodgers. In 1991, Rodgers was the national criterium champion and a gold medalist at the Pan Am games. She has a shot at the Olympic team, but because she's not a member of the national team, Rodgers must work 20 hours a week as a personal trainer to subsidize her cycling.

It's a common tale, and until more women athletes become household names, sponsorship will be limited. "There are a lot of good athletes and nice people out there," says Reinschreiber. "There are very few good promotions."

33. *The Meaning of Success: The Athletic Experience and the Development of Male Identity*

MICHAEL A. MESSNER

Vince Lombardi supposedly said, "Winning isn't everything; it's the only thing," and I couldn't agree more. There's nothing like being number one.

Joe Montana

The big-name athletes will get considerable financial and social remuneration for their athletic efforts. But what of the others, the 99% who fail? Most will fall short of their dreams of a lucrative professional contract. The great majority of athletes, then, will likely suffer disappointment, underemployment, anxiety, or perhaps even serious mental disorders.

Donald Harris and D. Stanley Eitzen

What is the relationship between participation in organized sports and a young male's developing sense of himself as a success or failure? And what is the consequent impact on his self-image and his ability to engage in intimate relationships with others? Through the late 1960s, it was almost universally accepted that "sports builds character" and that "a winner in sports will be a winner in life." Consequently, some liberal feminists argued that since participation in organized competitive sports has served as a major source of socialization for males' successful participation in the public world, girls and young women should have equal access to sports. Lever, for instance, concluded that if women were ever going to be able to develop the proper competitive values and orientations toward work and success, it was incumbent on them to participate in sports.[1]

In the 1970s and 1980s, these uncritical orientations toward sports have been questioned, and the "sports builds character" formula has been found wanting. Sabo points out that the vast majority of research does *not* support the contention that success in sports translates into "work success" or "happiness" in one's personal life.[2] In fact, a great deal of evidence suggests that the contrary is true. Recent critical analyses of success and failure in sports have usually started from assumptions similar to those of Sennett and Cobb and of Rubin:[3] the disjuncture between the *ideology* of success (the Lombardian Ethic) and the socially structured *reality* that most do not "succeed" brings about widespread feelings of failure, lowered self-images, and problems with interpersonal relationships.[4] The most common argument seems to be that the highly competitive world of sports is an exaggerated reflection of advanced industrial capitalism. Within any hierarchy, one can actually work very hard and achieve a lot, yet still be defined (and perceive oneself) as less than successful. Very few people ever reach the mythical "top," but those who do are made ultravisible through the media.[5] It is tempting to view this system as a "structure of failure" because, given the definition of *success,* the system is virtually rigged to bring about the failure of the vast majority of participants. Furthermore, given the dominant values, the participants are apt to blame themselves for their "failure." Schafer argues that the result of this discontinuity between sports values/ideology and reality is a "widespread conditional self-worth" for young athletes.[6] And as Edwards has pointed out, this problem can be even more acute for black athletes, who are disproportionately channeled into sports, yet have no "social safety net" to fall back on after "failure" in sports.

Both the traditional "sports builds character" and the more recent "sports breeds failures" formulas have a common pitfall: Each employs socialization theory in an often simplistic and mechanistic way. Boys are viewed largely as "blank slates" onto which the sports experience imprints values, appropriate "sex-role scripts," and orientations toward self and world. What is usually not taken into account is the fact that boys (and girls) come to the sports experience with an *already gendered* identity that colors their early motivations and perceptions of the meaning of games and sports. As Gilligan points out, observations of young children's game-playing show that girls bring to the activity a more pragmatic and flexible orientation toward the rules—they are more prone to make exceptions and innovations in the middle of the game in order to make the game more "fair" and maintain relationships with others.[7] Boys tend to have a more firm, even inflexible orientation to the rules of a game—they are less willing to change or alter rules in the middle of the game; to them, the rules are what protects any "fairness." This observation has profound implications for sociological research on sports and gender: The question should not be *simply* "how does sports participation affect boys [or girls]?" but should add "what is it about a developing sense of male identity that *attracts* males to sports in the first place? And how does this socially constructed male identity develop and change as it interacts with the structure and values of the sports world?" In addition to being a social-psychological question, this is also a *historical* question: Since men have not at all times and places related to sports the way they at present do, it is important to explore just what kinds of men exist today. What are their needs, problems, and dreams? How do these men relate to the society they live in? And how do organized sports fit into this picture?

THE "PROBLEM OF MASCULINITY" AND ORGANIZED SPORTS

In the first two decades of this century, men feared that the closing of the frontier, along with changes in the workplace, the family, and the schools, was having a "feminizing" influence on society.[8] One result of the anxiety men felt was the creation of the Boy Scouts of America as a separate sphere of social life where "true manliness" could be instilled in boys *by men*.[9] The rapid rise of organized sports in roughly the same era can be attributed largely to the same phenomenon. As socioeconomic and familial changes continue to erode the traditional bases of male identity and privilege, sports became an increasingly important cultural expression of traditional male values—organized sports became a "primary masculinity-validating experience."[10]

In the post–World War II era, the bureaucratization and rationalization of work, along with the decline of the family wage and women's gradual movement into the labor force, have further undermined the "breadwinner role" as a basis for male identity, thus resulting in a "problem of masculinity" and a "defensive insecurity" among men.[11] As Mills put it, the ethic of success in postwar America "has become less widespread as fact, more confused as image, often dubious as motive, and soured as a way of life. [Yet] there are still compulsions to struggle, to 'amount to something.'"[12]

How have men expressed this need to "amount to something" within a social context that seems to deny them the opportunities to do so? Again, organized sports play an important role. Both on a personal-existential level for athletes and on a symbolic-ideological level for spectators and fans, sports have become one of the "last bastions" of traditional male ideas of success, of male power and superiority over—and separation from—the perceived "feminization" of society. It is likely that the rise of football as "America's number-one game" is largely the result of the comforting *clarity* it provides between the polarities of traditional male power, strength, and violence and the contemporary fears of social feminization.

But these historical explanations for the increased importance of sports, despite their validity, beg some important questions: Why do men fear the (real or imagined) "feminization" of their world? Why do men appear to need a separate male sphere of life? Why do organized sports appear to be such an attractive means of expressing these needs? Are males simply "socialized" to dominate women and to compete with other men for status, or are they seeking (perhaps unconsciously) something more fundamental? Just what is it that men really *want*? To begin to answer these questions, it is necessary to listen to athletes' voices and examine their lives within a social-psychological perspective.

Daniel Levinson's concept of the "individual life structure" is a useful place to begin to construct a gestalt of the life of the athlete.[13] Levinson demonstrates that as males develop and interact with their world, they continue to change throughout their lives. A common theme during developmental periods is the process of individuation, the struggle to separate, to "decide where he stops and where the world begins." "In successive periods of development, as this process goes on, the person forms a clearer boundary between self and world. . . . Greater individuation allows him to be more separate from the world, to be more independent and self-generating. But it also gives him the confidence and understanding to have more intense attachments in the world and to feel more fully a part of it."[14]

This dynamic of separation and attachment provides a valuable social-psychological framework for examining the experiences and problems faced by the athlete as he gropes for and redefines success throughout his life course. In what follows, Levinson's framework is utilized to analyze the lives of 30 former athletes interviewed between 1983 and 1984. Their *interactions* with sports are examined in terms of their initial boyhood attraction to sports; how notions of success in sports connect with a developing sense of male identity; and how self-images, relationships to work and other people, change and develop after the sports career ends.

BOYHOOD: THE PROMISE OF SPORTS

Given how very few athletes actually "make it" through sports, how can the intensity with which millions of boys and young men throw themselves into athletics be explained? Are they simply pushed, socialized, or even *duped* into putting so much emphasis on athletic success? It is important here to examine just what it is that young males hope to get out of the athletic experience. And in terms of *identity*, it is crucial to examine the ways in which the structure and experience of sports activity meet the developmental needs of young males. The story of Willy Rios sheds light on what these needs are. Rios was born in Mexico and moved to the United States at a fairly young age. He never knew his father, and his mother died when he was only 9 years old. Suddenly he felt rootless, and at this time he threw himself into sports, but his initial motivations do not appear to be based upon a need to compete and win. "Actually, what I think sports did for me is it brought me into kind of an instant family. By being on a Little League team, or even just playing with all kinds of different kids in the neighborhood, it brought what I really wanted, which was some kind of closeness."

Similar statements from other men suggest that a fundamental motivational factor behind many young males' sports strivings is a need for connection, "closeness" with others. But why do so many boys see *sports* as an attractive means of establishing connection with others? Chodorow argues that the process of developing a gender identity yields insecurity and ambivalence in males.[15] Males develop "rigid ego boundaries" that ensure separation from others, yet they retain a basic human need for closeness and intimacy with others. The young male, who both seeks and fears attachment with others, thus finds the rulebound structure of games and sports to be a psychologically "safe" place in which he can get (nonintimate) connection with others within a context that maintains clear boundaries, distance, and separation from others. At least for the boy who has some early successes in sports, some of these ambivalent needs can be met, for a time. But there is a catch: For Willy Rios, it was only after he learned that he would get attention (a certain kind of connection) from other people for being a good athlete— indeed, that this attention was *contingent* on his *being good*—that narrow definitions of success, based on performance and winning, became important to him. It was years before he realized that no matter how well he performed, how successful he became, he would not get the closeness that he craved through sports. "It got to be a product in high school. Before, it was just fun, and having acceptance, you know. Yet I had to work for my acceptance in high school that way, just being a jock. So it wasn't fun any more. But it was my self-identity, being a good ballplayer. I was realizing that whatever you excel in, you put out in front of you. Bring it out. Show it. And that's what I did. That was my protection. . . . It was rotten in high school, really."

This conscious striving for successful achievement becomes the primary means through which the young athlete seeks connections with other people. But the irony of the situation, for so many boys and young men like Willy Rios, is that the athletes are seeking to get something from their success in sports that sports cannot deliver—and the *pressure* that they end up putting on themselves to achieve that success ends up stripping them of the ability to receive the one major thing that sports really *does* have to offer: fun.

ADOLESCENCE: YOU'RE ONLY AS GOOD AS YOUR LAST GAME

Adolescence is probably the period of greatest insecurity in the life course, the time when the young male becomes most vulnerable to peer expectation, pressures, and judgments. None of the men interviewed for this study, regardless of their social class or ethnicity, seemed fully able to "turn a deaf ear to the crowd" during their athletic careers. The crowd, which may include immediate family, friends, peers, teammates, as well as the more anonymous fans and media, appears to be a crucially important part of the process of establishing and maintaining the self-images of young athletes. By the time they were in high school, most of the men interviewed for this study had found sports to be a primary means through which to establish a sense of manhood in the world. Especially if they were good athletes, the expectations of the crowd became very powerful and were internalized (and often *magnified*) within the young man's own expectations. As one man stated, by the time he was in high school, "it was *expected* of me to do well in all of my contests—I mean by my coach and my peers, and my family. So I in turn expected to do well, and if I didn't do well, then I'd be very disappointed."

When so much is tied to your performance, the dictum that "you are only as good as your last game" is a powerful judgment. It means that the young man must continually prove, achieve, and then *re*prove, and *re*achieve his status. As a result, many young athletes learn to seek and *need* the appreciation of the crowd to feel that they are worthy human beings. But the internalized values of masculinity along with the insecure nature of the sports world mean that the young man does *not* need the crowd to feel *bad* about himself. In fact, if one is insecure enough, even "success" and the compliments and attention of other people can come to feel hollow and meaningless. For instance, 48-year-old Russ Ellis in his youth shared the basic sense of insecurity common to all young males, and in his case it was probably compounded by his status as a poor black male and an insecure family life. Athletics emerged early in his life as the primary arena in which he and his male peers competed to establish a sense of self in the world. For Ellis, his small physical stature made it difficult to compete successfully in most sports, thus feeding his insecurity—he just never felt as though he belonged with "the big boys." Eventually, though, he became a top middle-distance runner. In high school, however: "Something began to happen there that later plagued me quite a bit. I started doing very well and winning lots of races and by the time the year was over, it was no longer a question for me of *placing*, but *winning*. That attitude really destroyed me ultimately. I would get into the blocks with worries that I wouldn't do well—the regular stomach problems—so I'd often run much less well than my abilities—that is, say, I'd take second or third."

Interestingly, his nervousness, fears, and anxieties did not seem to be visible to "the crowd": "I know in high school, certainly, they saw me as confident and ready to run. No one assumed I could be beaten, which fascinated me, because I had never been good at understanding how I was taken in other people's minds—maybe because I spent so much time inventing myself in their regard in my own mind. I was projecting my fear fantasies on them and taking them for reality."

In 1956 Ellis surprised everyone by taking second place in a world-class field of quarter-milers. But the fact that they ran the fastest time in the world, 46.5, seemed only to "up the ante," to increase the pressures on Ellis, then in college at UCLA.

> Up to that point I had been a nice zippy kid who did good, got into the *Daily Bruin* a lot, and was well-known on campus. But now an event would come up and the papers would say, "Ellis to face so-and-so." So rather than my being *in* the race, I *was* the race, as far as the press was concerned. And that put a lot of pressure on me that I never learned to handle. What I did was to internalize it, and then I'd sit there and fret and lose sleep, and focus more on not winning than on how I was doing. And in general, I didn't do badly—like one year in the NCAA's I took fourth—you know, in the *national finals*. But I was focused on winning. You know, later on, people would say, "Oh wow, you took fourth in the NCAA?—you were *that good?*" Whereas I thought of these things as *failures*, you know?

Finally, Ellis's years of training, hopes, and fears came to a head at the 1956 Olympic trials, where he failed to qualify, finishing fifth. A rival whom he used to defeat routinely won the event in the Melbourne Olympics as Ellis watched on television. "That killed me. Destroyed me. . . . I had the experience many times after that of digging down and finding that there was infinitely more down there than I ever got—I mean, I know that more than I know anything else. Sometimes I would really feel like an eagle, running. Sometimes in practice at UCLA running was just exactly like flying—and if I could have carried that attitude into events, I would have done much better. But instead, I'd worry. Yeah, I'd worry myself sick."

As suggested earlier, young males like Russ Ellis are "set up" for disappointment, or worse, by the disjuncture between the narrow Lombardian definition of success in the sports world and the reality that very few ever actually reach the top. The athlete's sense of identity established through sports is therefore insecure and problematic, *not simply* because of the high probability of "failure," but also because *success* in the sports world involves the development of a personality that *amplifies* many of the most ambivalent and destructive traits of traditional masculinity. Within the hierarchical world of sports, which in many ways mirrors the capitalist economy, one learns that if he is to survive and avoid being pushed off the ever-narrowing pyramid of success, he must develop certain kinds of relationships—to himself, to his body, to other people, and to the sport itself. In short, the successful athlete must develop a highly goal-oriented personality that encourages him to view his body as a tool, a machine, or even a weapon utilized to defeat an objectified opponent. He is likely to have difficulty establishing intimate and lasting friendships with other males because of low self-disclosure, homophobia, and cut-throat competition. And he is likely to view his public image as a "success" as far more basic and fundamental than any of his interpersonal relationships.

For most of the men interviewed, the quest for success was not the grim task it was for Russ Ellis. Most men did seem to get, at least for a time, a sense of identity (and even some happiness) out of their athletic accomplishments. The attention of the crowd, for many, affirmed their existence as males and was thus a clear motivating force. Gary Affonso, now 42 years old and a high school coach, explained that when he was in high school, he had an "intense desire to practice and compete." "I used to practice the high jump by myself for hours at a time—only got up to 5'3"—scissor! [*Laughs.*] But I think part of it was, the track itself was in view of some of the classrooms, and so as I think back now, maybe I did it for the attention, to be seen. In my freshman year, I chipped my two front teeth in a football game, and after that I always had a gold tooth, and I was always self-conscious about that. Plus I had my glasses, you know. I felt a little conspicuous." This simultaneous shyness, self-consciousness, and conspicuousness *along with* the strongly felt need for attention and external validation (attachment) so often characterize athletes' descriptions of themselves in boyhood and adolescence. The crowd, in this context, can act as a distant, and thus nonthreatening, source of attention and validation of self for the insecure male. Russ Ellis's story typifies that what sports seem to *promise* the young male—affirmation of self and connection with others—is likely to be *undermined* by the youth's actual experience in the sports world. The athletic experience also "sets men up" for another serious problem: the end of a career at a very young age.

DISENGAGEMENT TRAUMA: A CRISIS OF MALE IDENTITY

For some, the end of the athletic career approaches gradually like the unwanted houseguest whose eventual arrival is at least *known* and can be planned for, thus limiting the inevitable inconvenience. For others, the athletic career ends with the shocking suddenness of a violent thunderclap that rudely awakens one from a pleasant dream. But whether it comes gradually or suddenly, the end of the playing career represents the termination of what has often become the *central aspect* of a young male's individual life structure, thus initiating change and transition in the life course.

Previous research on the disengagement crises faced by many retiring athletes has focused on the health, occupational, and financial problems frequently faced by retiring professionals.[16] These problems are especially severe for retiring black athletes, who often have inadequate educational backgrounds and few opportunities within the sports world for media or coaching jobs.[17] But even for those retiring athletes who avoid the pitfalls of financial and occupational crises, substance abuse, obesity, and ill health, the end of the playing career usually involves a crisis of identity. This identity crisis is probably most acute for retiring *professional* athletes, whose careers are coming to an end right at an age when most men's careers are beginning to take off. As retired professional football player Marvin Upshaw stated, "You find yourself just scrambled. You don't know which way to go. Your light, as far as you're concerned, has been turned out. You miss the roar of the crowd. Once you've heard it, you can't get away from it. There's an empty feeling—you feel everything you wanted is gone. All of a sudden you wake up and you find yourself 29, 35 years old, you know, and the one thing that has been the major part of your life is gone. It's gone."

High school and college athletes also face serious and often painful adjustment periods when their career ends. Twenty-six-year-old Dave Joki had been a good high school basketball player, and had played a lot of ball in college. When interviewed, he was right in the middle of a confusing crisis of identity, closely related to his recent disengagement from viewing himself as an athlete. "These past few months I've been trying a lot of different things, thinking about different careers, things to do. There's been quite a bit of stumbling—and I think that part of my tenuousness about committing myself to any one thing is I'm not sure I'm gonna get strokes if I go that way. [*Embarrassed, nervous laugh.*] It's scary for me and I stay away from searching for those reasons . . . I guess you could say that I'm stumbling in my relationships too—stumbling in all parts of life. [*Laughs.*] I feel like I'm doing a lot but not knowing what I want."

Surely there is nothing unusual about a man in his mid 20s "stumbling" around and looking for direction in his work and his relationships. That is common for men of his age. But for the former athlete, this stumbling is often more confusing and problematic than for the other men precisely because he has lost the one activity through which he had built his sense of identity, however tenuous it may have been. The "strokes" he received from being a good athlete were his major psychological foundation. The interaction between self and other through which the athlete attempts to solidify his identity is akin to what Cooley called "the looking-glass self." If the athletic activity and the crowd can be viewed as a *mirror* into which the athlete gazes and, in Russ Ellis's words, "invents himself," we can begin to appreciate how devastating it can be when that looking-glass is suddenly and permanently *shattered,* leaving the young man alone, isolated, and disconnected. And since young men often feel comfortable exploring close friendships and intimate relationships only *after* they have established their separate work-related (or sports-related) positional identity, relationships with other people are likely to become more problematic than ever during disengagement.

WORK, LOVE, AND MALE IDENTITY AFTER DISENGAGEMENT

Eventually, the former athlete must face reality: At a relatively young age, he has to start over. In the words of retired major league baseball player Ray

Fosse, "Now I gotta get on with the rest of it." How is "the rest of it" likely to take shape for the athlete after his career as a player is over? How do men who are "out of the limelight" for a few years come to define themselves as men? How do they define and redefine success? How do the values and attitudes they learned through sports affect their lives? How do their relationships with friends and family change over time?

Many retired athletes retain a powerful drive to reestablish the important relationship with the crowd that served as the primary basis for their identity for so long. Many men throw themselves wholeheartedly into a new vocation—or a confusing *series* of vocations—in a sometimes pathetic attempt to recapture the "high" of athletic competition as well as the status of the successful athlete in the community. For instance, 35-year-old Jackie Ridgle is experiencing what Daniel Levinson calls a "surge of masculine strivings" common to men in their mid 30s.[18] Once a professional basketball player, Ridgle seems motivated now by a powerful drive to be seen once again as "somebody" in the eyes of the public. When interviewed, he had recently been hired as an assistant college basketball coach, which made him feel like he again had a chance to "be somebody."

> When I say "successful," that means somebody that the public looks up to just as a basketball player. Yet you don't have to be playing basketball. You can be anybody: You can be a senator or a mayor, or any number of things. That's what I call successful. Success is recognition. Sure, I'm always proud of myself. But there's that little goal there that until people respect you, then—[*Snaps fingers.*] Anybody can say, "Oh, I know I'm the greatest thing in the world," but *people* run the world, and when *they* say you're successful, then you *know* you're successful.

Indeed, men, especially men in early adulthood, usually define themselves primarily in terms of their position in the public world of work. Feminist literature often criticizes this establishment of male identity in terms of work-success as an expression of male privilege and ego satisfaction that comes at the expense of women and children. There is a great deal of truth to the feminist critique: A man's socially defined need to establish himself as "somebody" in the (mostly) male world of work is often accompanied by his frequent physical absence from home and his emotional distance from his family. Thus, while the man is "out there" establishing his "name" in public, the woman is usually home caring for the day-to-day and moment-to-moment needs of her family (regardless of whether or not she also has a job in the paid labor force). Tragically, only in midlife, when the children have already "left the nest" and the woman is often ready to go out into the public world, do some men discover the importance of connection and intimacy.

Yet the interviews indicate that there is not always such a clean and clear "before-after" polarity in the lives of men between work-success and care-intimacy. The "breadwinner ethic" as a male role *has* most definitely contributed to the perpetuation of male privilege and the subordination and economic dependence of women as mothers and housekeepers. But given the reality of the labor market, where women still make only 62 cents to the male dollar, many men feel very responsible for providing the majority of the income and financial security for their families. For instance, 36-year-old Ray Fosse, whose father left his family when he was quite young, has a very strong sense of commitment and responsibility as a provider of income and stability in his own family.

> I'm working an awful lot these days, and trying not to take time away from my family. A lot of times I'm putting the family to sleep, and working late hours and going to bed and getting up early and so forth. I've tried to tell my family this a lot of times: The work that I'm doing now is gonna make it easier in a few years. That's the reason I'm working now, to get that financial security, and I feel like it's coming very soon . . . but, uh, you know, you go a long day and you come home, and it's just not the quality time you'd like to have. And I think when that financial security comes in, then I'm gonna be able to forget about everything.

Jackie Ridgle's words mirror Fosse's. His two jobs and striving to be successful in the public world mean that he has little time to spend with his wife and three children. "I plan to someday. Very seldom do you have enough time to spend with your kids, especially nowadays, so I don't get hung up on that. The wife does sometimes, but as long as I keep a roof over their heads and let 'em know who's who, well, one day they'll respect me. But I can't just get bogged down and take any old job, you know, a filling station job or something. Ah, hell, they'll get more respect, my kids for me, right now, than they would if I was somewhere just a regular worker."

Especially for men who have been highly successful athletes (and never have had to learn to "lose gracefully"), the move from sports to work-career as a means of establishing connection and identity in the world is a "natural" transition. Breadwinning becomes a man's socially learned means of seeking attachment, both with his family and, more abstractly, with "society." What is salient (and sometimes tragic) is that the care that a woman gives her family usually puts her into direct daily contact with her family's physical, psychological, and emotional needs. A man's care is usually expressed more abstractly, often in his absence, as his work removes him from day-to-day, moment-to-moment contact with his family.

A man may want, even *crave*, more direct connection with his family, but that connection, and the *time* it takes to establish and maintain it, may cause him to lose the competitive edge he needs to win in the world of work—and that is the arena in which he feels he will ultimately be judged in terms of his success or failure as a man. But it is not simply a matter of *time* spent away from family which is at issue here. As Dizard's research shows clearly, the more "success oriented" a man is, the more "instrumental" his personality will tend to be, thus increasing the psychological and emotional distance between himself and his family.[19]

CHANGING MEANINGS OF SUCCESS IN MIDLIFE

The intense, sometimes obsessive, early adulthood period of striving for work and career success that we see in the lives of Jackie Ridgle and Ray Fosse often begins to change in midlife, when many men experience what Levinson calls "detribalization." Here, the man "becomes more critical of the tribe—the particular groups, institutions, and traditions that have the greatest significance for him, the social matrix to which he is most attached. He is less dependent upon tribal rewards, more questioning of tribal values. . . . The result of this shift is normally not a marked disengagement from the external world but a greater integration of attachment and separateness."[20]

Detribalization—putting less emphasis on how one is defined by others and becoming more self-motivated and self-generating—is often accompanied by a growing sense of *flawed* or *qualified* success. A man's early adulthood dream of success begins to tarnish, appearing more and more as an illusion. Or, the success that a man *has* achieved begins to appear hollow and meaningless, possibly because it has not delivered the closeness he truly craves. The fading, or the loss, of the dream involves a process of mourning, but, as Levinson points out, it can also be a very liberating process in opening the man up for new experiences, new kinds of relationships, and new dreams.

For instance, Russ Ellis states that a few years ago he experienced a midlife crisis when he came to the realization that "I was never going to be on the cover of *Time*." His wife had a T-shirt made for him with the message *Dare to Be Average* emblazoned on it.

> And it doesn't really *mean* dare to be average—it means dare to take the pressure off yourself, you know? Dare to be a normal person. It gets a funny reaction from people. I think it hits at that place where somehow we all think that we're going to wind up on the cover of *Time* or something, you know? Do you have that? That some day, somewhere, you're gonna be *great*, and everyone will know, everyone will recognize it? Now, I'd rather be great because I'm *good*—and maybe that'll turn into something that's acknowledged, but not at the headline level. I'm not racing so much; I'm concerned that my feet are planted on the ground and that I'm good.
>
> [It sounds like you're running now, as opposed to racing?]
>
> I guess—but running and racing have the same goals. [*Laughs, pauses, then speaks more thoughtfully.*] But maybe you're right—that's a wonderful analogy. Pacing myself. Running is more intelligent—more familiarity with your abilities, your patterns of workouts, who you're running against, the nature of the track, your position, alertness. You have more of an internal clock.

Russ Ellis's midlife detribalization—his transition from a "racer" to a "runner"—has left him more comfortable with himself, with his abilities and limitations. He has also experienced an expansion of his ability to experience intimacy with a woman. He had never been comfortable with the "typical jock attitude" toward sex and women,

> but I generally maintained a performance attitude about sex for a long time, which was not as enjoyable as it became after I learned to be more like what I thought a woman was like. In other words, when I let myself experience my own body, in a delicious and receptive way rather than in a power, overwhelming way. That was wonderful! [*Laughs.*] To experience my body as someone desired and given to. That's one of the better things. I think I only achieved that very profound intimacy that's found between people, really quite extraordinary, quite recently. [*Long pause.*] It's quite something, quite something. And I feel more fully inducted into the human race by knowing about that.

TOWARD A REDEFINITION OF SUCCESS AND MASCULINITY

"A man in America is a failed boy," wrote John Updike in 1960. Indeed, Updike's ex-athlete Rabbit Angstrom's struggles to achieve meaning and identity in midlife reflect a common theme in modern literature. Social scientific research has suggested that the contemporary sense of failure and inadequacy felt by many American males is largely the result of unrealistic and unachievable social definitions of masculinity and success.[21] This research has suggested that there is more to it than that. Contemporary males often feel empty, alienated, isolated, and as failures because the socially learned means through which they seek validation and identity (achievement in the public worlds of sports and work) do not deliver what is actually craved and needed: intimate connection and unity with other human beings. In fact, the lure of sports becomes a sort of trap. For boys who experience early success in sports, the resulting attention they receive becomes a convenient and attractive means of experiencing attachment with other people within a social context that allows the young male to maintain his "firm ego boundaries" and thus his separation from others. But it appears that, more often than not, athletic participation serves only to exacerbate the already problematic, insecure, and ambivalent nature of males' self-images, and thus their ability to establish and maintain close and intimate relationships with other people. Some men, as they reach midlife, eventually achieve a level of individuation—often through a midlife crisis—that leads to a redefinition of success and an expansion of their ability to experience attachment and intimacy.

Men's personal definitions of success often change in midlife, but this research, as well as that done by Farrell and Rosenberg,[22] suggests that only a *portion* of males experience a midlife crisis that results in the man's transcending his instrumental personality in favor of a more affective generativity. The midlife discovery that the achievement game is an unfulfilling rat race can as easily lead to cynical detachment and greater alienation as it can to detribalization and expanded relational capacities. In other words, there is no assurance that Jackie Ridgle, as he ages, will transform himself from a "racer" to a "runner," as Russ Ellis has. Even if he does change in this way, it is likely that he will have missed participating in the formative years of his children's lives.

Thus the fundamental questions facing future examinations of men's lives should focus on building and understanding of just what are the keys to such a shift at midlife? How are individual men's changes, crises, and relationships affected, shaped, and sometimes contradicted by the social, cultural, and political contexts in which they find themselves? And what *social* changes might make it more likely that boys and men might have more balanced personalities and needs at an *early* age?

An analysis of men's lives that simply describes personal changes while taking social structure as a given cannot adequately *ask* these questions. But an analysis that not only describes changes in male identity throughout the life course but also critically examines the socially structured and defined meaning of "masculinity" can and must ask these questions.

If many of the problems faced by all men (not just athletes) today are to be dealt with, class, ethnic, and sexual preference divisions must be confronted. This would necessarily involve the development of a more cooperative and nurturant ethic among men, as well as a more egalitarian and democratically organized economic system. And since the sports world is an important cultural process that serves partly to socialize boys and young men to hierarchical, competitive, and aggressive values, the sporting arena is an important context in which to begin to confront the need for a humanization of men.

Yet, if the analysis presented here is correct, the developing psychology of young boys is predisposed to be attracted to the present structure and values of the sports world, so any attempt *simply* to infuse cooperative and egalitarian values into sports is likely to be an exercise in futility. The need for equality between men and women, in the public realm as well as in the home, is a fundamental prerequisite for the humanization of men, sports, and society. One of the most important changes that men could make would be to become more equally involved in parenting. The development of early bonding between fathers and infants (in addition to that between mothers and infants), along with nonsexist childrearing in the family, schools, and sports would have far-reaching effects on society: Boys and men could grow up more psychologically secure, more able to develop balance between separation and attachment, more able at an earlier age to appreciate intimate relationships with other men without destructive and crippling competition and homophobia. A young male with a more secure and balanced personality might also be able to *enjoy* athletic activities for what they really have to offer: the opportunity to engage in healthy exercise, to push oneself toward excellence, and to bond together with others in a challenging and fun activity.

NOTES

1. J. Lever, "Sex Differences in the Games Children Play," *Social Problems* 23 (1976).
2. D. Sabo, "Sport Patriarchy and Male Identity: New Questions about Men and Sport," *Arena Review* 9, no. 2, 1985.
3. R. Sennett and J. Cobb, *The Hidden Injuries of Class* (New York: Random House, 1973); and L. B. Rubin, *Worlds of Pain: Life in the Working Class Family* (New York: Basic Books, 1976).
4. D. W. Ball, "Failure in Sport,"*American Sociological Review* 41 (1976); J. J. Coakley, *Sports in Society* (St. Louis: Mosby, 1978); D. S. Harris and D. S. Eitzen, "The Consequences of Failure in Sport," *Urban Life* 7 (July 1978): 2; G. B. Leonard, "Winning Isn't Everything: It's Nothing," in *Jock: Sports and Male Identity*, ed. D. Sabo and R. Runfola (Englewood Cliffs, NJ: Prentice Hall, 1980); W. E. Schafer, "Sport and Male Sex Role Socialization," *Sport Sociology Bulletin* 4 (Fall 1975); R. C. Townsend, "The Competitive Male as Loser," in Sabo and Runfola, eds., *Jock;* and T. Tutko and W. Bruns, *Winning Is Everything and Other American Myths* (New York: Macmillan, 1976).
5. In contrast with the importance put on success by millions of boys, the number who "make it" is incredibly small. There are approximately 600 players in major-league baseball, with an average career span of 7 years. Approximately 6-7% of all high school football players ever play in college. Roughly 8% of all draft-eligible college football and basketball athletes are drafted by the pros, and only 2% ever sign a professional contract. The average career for NFL athletes is now 4 years, and for the NBA it is only 3.4 years. Thus the odds of getting anywhere *near* the top are very thin—and if one is talented and lucky enough to get there, his stay will be brief. See H. Edwards, "The Collegiate Athletic Arms Race: Origins and Implications of the 'Rule 48' Controversy," *Journal of Sport and Social Issues* 8, no. 1 (Winter-Spring 1984); Harris and Eitzen, "Consequences of Failure"; and P. Hill and B. Lowe, "The Inevitable Metathesis of the Retiring Athlete," *International Review of Sport Sociology* 9, nos. 3-4 (1978).
6. Schafer, "Sport and Male Sex Role," p. 50.
7. C. Gilligan, *In a Different Voice: Psychological Theory and Women's Development* (Cambridge: Harvard University Press, 1982); J. Piaget, *The Moral Judgment of the Child* (New York: Free Press, 1965); and Lever, "Games Children Play."
8. P. G. Filene, *Him/Her/Self: Sex Roles in Modern America* (New York: Harcourt Brace Jovanovich, 1975).
9. J. Hantover, The Boy Scouts and the Validation of Masculinity," *Journal of Social Issues* 34 (1978): 1.
10. J. L. Dubbert, *A Man's Place: Masculinity in Transition* (Englewood Cliffs, NJ: Prentice Hall, 1979).
11. A. Tolson, *The Limits of Masculinity* (New York: Harper and Row, 1977).
12. C. W. Mills, *White Collar* (London: Oxford University Press, 1951).
13. D. J. Levinson, *The Seasons of a Man's Life* (New York: Ballantine, 1978).
14. Ibid., p. 195.
15. N. Chodorow, *The Reproduction of Mothering* (Berkeley: University of California Press, 1978).
16. Hill and Lowe, "Metathesis of Retiring Athlete," pp. 3-4; and B. D. McPherson, "Former Professional Athletes' Adjustment to Retirement," *Physician and Sports Medicine*, August 1978.
17. Edwards, "Collegiate Athletic Arms Race."
18. Levinson, *Seasons of a Man's Life.*
19. J. E. Dizard, "The Price of Success," in *Social Change and the Family*, ed. J. E. Dizard (Chicago: Community and Family Study Center, University of Chicago, 1968).
20. Levinson, *Seasons of a Man's Life*, p. 242.
21. J. H. Pleck, *The Myth of Masculinity* (Cambridge: MIT Press, 1982); Sennett and Cobb, *The Hidden Injuries of Class;* Rubin, *Worlds of Pain;* and Tolson, *Limits of Masculinity.*
22. M. P. Farrell and S. D. Rosenberg, *Men at Midlife* (Boston: Auburn House, 1981).

■ FOR FURTHER STUDY

Bryson, Lois, "Sport and the Maintenance of Masculine Hegemony," *Women's Studies International Forum* 10 (1987): 349-360.

Creedon, Pamela J. (ed.), *Women, Media, and Sport: Challenging Gender Values* (Thousand Oaks, California: Sage, 1994).

Guttmann, Allen, *Women's Sports: A History* (New York: Columbia University Press, 1991).

Hall, M. Ann, "The Discourse of Gender and Sport: From Femininity to Feminism," *Sociology of Sport Journal* 5 (1988): 330-340.

Klien, Alan, *Little Big Men: Bodybuilding Subculture and Gender Construction* (New York: State University of New York Press, 1993).

Klien, Michael (ed.), "The Macho World of Sport," *International Review for the Sociology of Sport* 25 (1990): entire issue.

Messner, Michael A., "Men Studying Masculinity: Some Epistemological Issues in Sport Sociology," *Sociology of Sport Journal* 7 (June 1990): 136-153.

Messner, Michael A., *Power at Play: Sports and the Problem of Masculinity* (Boston: Beacon Press, 1992).

Messner, Michael A., and Donald F. Sabo (eds.), *Sport, Men, and the Gender Order: Critical Feminist Perspectives* (Champaign, Illinois: Human Kinetics, 1990).

Messner, Michael A., and Donald F. Sabo, *Sex, Violence & Power in Sports: Rethinking Masculinity* (Freedom, California: The Crossing Press, 1994).

Nelson, Mariah Burton, *Are We Winning Yet? How Women Are Changing Sports and Sports Are Changing Women* (New York: Random House, 1991).

Nelson, Mariah Burton, *The Stronger Women Get, the More Men Love Football: Sexism and the American Culture of Sports* (New York: Harcourt Brace, 1994).

Part Eleven

Structured Inequality: Sport and Sexuality

Previous units on structured inequality examined categories of people designated as minorities in society because of their impoverishment, race/ethnicity, or gender. The members of these social categories suffer from powerlessness, negative stereotypes, and discrimination. This unit looks at another type of minority group. Unlike the other three minorities, which are disadvantaged because of economic circumstances or ascribed characteristics, the distinguishing feature of the minority examined in this unit—homosexuality—is the object of discrimination because it is defined by the majority as different and, therefore, deviant. It is important to underscore a crucial point: *Homosexuality is not inherently deviant, but it is defined and labeled as deviant.*[1] Put another way, "Variance from the societal norm of heterosexuality is not a social problem; *the societal response to it is.*"[2]

An estimated 14 million adults in the United States identify themselves as gay or lesbian. Among these are elite athletes: Glenn Burke (major league baseball), David Kopay (professional football), Greg Louganis and Tom Waddell (former Olympians), and Martina Navratilova (tennis). Athletes who publicly acknowledge their homosexuality, however, are rare because of the extent of homophobia among athletes, coaches, fans, and the sports media.

The extent of homophobia in the sports world is staggering: manifestations range from eight-year-old boys who put each other down with taunts of "queer," "faggot," or "sissy" to high-school locker-room boasting (and, often, lying) about sexual conquests of females, and to college athletes bonding together with a little Saturday night "queer-bashing." To be suspected of being gay, and to be unable to prove one's heterosexual status in the sports world, is clearly not acceptable——indeed, it can be downright dangerous.[3]

Women in sport, more than men, endure intense scrutiny about their sexual identities.[4] This is the subject of the first selection, by Pat Griffin, as she discusses (1) the political functions of homophobia in a sexist and heterosexist culture, (2) the manifestations of homophobia in women's sport, (3) the beliefs that support homophobia in women's sport, and (4) strategies for confronting homophobia in women's sport.

The second selection, by Brian Pronger, focuses on gay men and sport. Pronger's thesis is that since sport for men is overwhelmingly masculine and heterosexual, gay men are often estranged from sport. Team sports are especially difficult for gay men because of the male bonding rituals including "gay bashing" and contrived machismo with its emphasis on toughness and the sexual conquest of women.

Another dimension to minority group status is agency. That is, rather than acting as passive victims, minority group members individually or collectively resist, shape, and challenge existing structures. The goal is to change a society that disadvantages them. Gay men and lesbian women have challenged discriminatory arrangements through court cases and efforts to pass legislation favorable to them. They have organized protests to highlight their oppression and to fight for equal rights policies. As an example of this in sport, the homosexual community protested the location of the volleyball events in the 1996 Olympics in Cobb County, a suburb of Atlanta, because the Cobb County Commissioners had passed a resolution (unrelated to the Olympic Games) condemning homosexuality.[5] A number of individuals and organizations protested to the Olympic Organizing Committee. One organization, the Olympics Out of Cobb Coalition (OOCC), threatened to hold a demonstration at the Atlanta games. As a result, the Olympic Organizing Committee moved volleyball sixty miles away, to Athens, Georgia.

Another strategy employed by homosexuals is to identify themselves openly. Rather than evade the efforts of straights to stigmatize them, they challenge society in an effort to transform it. To encourage this among athletes, organizers created the Gay Games. Mike Messner, paraphrasing Tom Waddell, the leading organizer of the Gay Games, said this of the activity: "The games offer an alternative structure in which gay men, lesbians, bisexuals, and even heterosexuals can forge their own definitions of athleticism, unfettered by the often oppressive stereotypes of the dominant sports world."[6] Gay Games IV was held in New York City in 1994 with 10,879 competitors from forty-three countries. The nine-day event generated an estimated $100,000,000 for the local economy. The third selection in this unit, by John Gallagher, describes Gay Games IV, indicating, most important, that these games make a significant contribution to the gay rights movement.

NOTES

1. D. Stanley Eitzen and Maxine Baca Zinn, *Social Problems*, 6th ed. (Boston: Allyn & Bacon, 1994), p. 305.
2. Ibid., p. 311.
3. Messner, Michael A., "AIDS, Homophobia, and Sports." In Michael A. Messner and Donald F. Sabo, *Sex, Violence & Power in Sports: Rethinking Masculinity* (Freedom, California: The Crossing Press, 1994), p. 121.
4. See Debra E. Blum, "College Sports' L-Word," *Chronicle of Higher Education* (March 9, 1994): A35-A36.
5. Chris Bull, "They Shoot, They Score," *The Advocate* (September 6, 1994):24-25.
6. Messner, op. cit., p. 126.

34. *Changing the Game:*
Homophobia, Sexism,
and Lesbians in Sport

PAT GRIFFIN

Throughout the history of Western culture, restrictions have been placed on women's sport participation. These restrictions are enforced through sanctions that evolved to match each successive social climate. Women caught merely observing the male athletes competing in the early Greek Olympic Games were put to death. When Baron DeCoubertin revived the Olympic tradition in 1896, women were invited as spectators but barred from participation. Even in the present-day Olympic Games, women may compete in only one third of the events.

Although the death penalty for female spectators was too extreme for the late 19th and early 20th centuries, an increasingly influential medical establishment warned white upper-class women about the debilitating physiological effects of vigorous athleticism, particularly on the reproductive system. Women were cautioned about other "masculinizing effects" as well, such as deeper voices, facial hair, and overdeveloped arms and legs. The intent of these warnings was to temper and control women's sport participation and to keep women focused on their "natural" and "patriotic" roles as wives and mothers (Lenskyj, 1986).

During the 1920s and 1930s, as the predicted dire physical consequences proved untrue, strong social taboos restricting female athleticism evolved. Instead of warnings about facial hair and displaced uteruses, women in sport were intimidated by fears of losing social approval. Close female friendships, accepted and even idealized in the 19th century, became suspect when male sexologists like Freud "discovered" female sexuality in the early 20th century (Faderman, 1981, 1991; Katz, 1976). In the 1930s, as psychology and psychiatry became respected subfields in medicine, these doctors warned of a new menace. An entire typology was created to diagnose the "mannish lesbian," whose depraved sexual appetite and preference for masculine dress and activity were identified as symptoms of psychological disturbance (Newton, 1989). Social commentators in the popular press warned parents about the dangers

SOURCE: "Changing the Game: Homophobia, Sexism, and Lesbians in Sport" by Pat Griffin. From *Quest* 44(2), pp. 251–265. Copyright © 1992 by National Association for Physical Education in Higher Education. Reprinted by permission.

of allowing impressionable daughters to spend time in all-female environments (Faderman, 1991; Smith-Rosenberg, 1989).

As a result, women's colleges and sports teams were assumed to be places where mannish lesbians lurked. Women in sport and physical education especially fit the profile of women to watch out for: they were in groups without men, they were not engaged in activities thought to enhance their abilities to be good wives and mothers, and they were being physically active in sport, a male activity. Because lesbians were assumed to be masculine creatures who rejected their female identity and roles as wives and mothers, athletic women became highly suspect.

The image of the sick, masculine lesbian sexual predator and her association with athleticism persists in the late 20th century. The power of this image to control and intimidate women is as strong today as it was 60 years ago. What accounts for the staying power of a stereotype that is so extreme it should be laughable except that so many people believe it to be accurate? Whose interests are served by stigmatizing lesbians and accusing women in sport of being lesbians? Why does sport participation by women in the late 20th century continue to be so threatening to the social order? How have women in sport responded to associations with lesbians? How effective have these responses been in defusing concern about lesbians in sport?

The purpose of this article is to discuss the issue of lesbians in sport from a feminist perspective that analyzes the function of socially constructed gender roles and sexual identities in maintaining male dominance in North American society. I share the perspective taken by other sport feminists that lesbian and feminist sport participation is a threat to male domination (Bennett, Whitaker, Smith, & Sablove, 1987; Birrell & Richter, 1987; Hall, 1987; Lenskyj, 1986; Messner & Sabo, 1990). In a sexist and heterosexist society (in which heterosexuality is reified as the only normal, natural, and acceptable sexual orientation), women who defy the accepted feminine role or reject a heterosexual identity threaten to upset the imbalance of power enjoyed by white heterosexual men in a patriarchal society (Bryson, 1987). The creation of the mannish lesbian as a pathological condition by early 20th-century male medical doctors provided an effective means to control all women and neutralize challenges to the sexist status quo.

To understand the social stigma associated with lesbian participation in sport, the function of homophobia in maintaining the sexist and heterosexist status quo must be examined (Lenskyj, 1991). Greendorfer (1991) challenged the traditional definition of homophobia as an irrational fear and intolerance of lesbians and gay men. In questioning how irrational homophobia really is, Greendorfer highlighted the systematic and pervasive cultural nature of homophobia. Fear and hatred of lesbians and gay men is more than individual prejudice (Kitzinger, 1987). Homophobia is a powerful political weapon of sexism (Pharr, 1988). The lesbian label is used to define the boundaries of acceptable female behavior in a patriarchal culture: When a woman is called a lesbian, she knows she is out of bounds. Because lesbian identity carries the extreme negative social stigma created by early 20th-century sexologists, most women are loathe to be associated with it. Because women's sport has been labeled a lesbian activity, women in sport are particularly sensitive and vulnerable to the use of the lesbian label to intimidate.

HOW IS HOMOPHOBIA MANIFESTED IN WOMEN'S SPORT?

Manifestations of homophobia in women's sport can be divided into six categories: (a) silence, (b) denial, (c) apology, (d) promotion of a heterosexy image, (e) attacks on lesbians, and (f) preference for male coaches. An exploration of these manifestations illuminates the pervasive nature of prejudice against lesbians in sport and the power of the lesbian stigma to control and marginalize women's sport.

Silence

Silence is the most consistent and enduring manifestation of homophobia in women's sport. From Billie Jean King's revelation of a lesbian relationship in 1981 to the publicity surrounding Penn State women's basketball coach Rene Portland's no-lesbian policy (Lederman, 1991; Longman, 1991), the professional and college sports establishment responds with silence to eruptions of public attention to lesbians in sport. Reporters who attempt to discuss lesbians in sport with sport organizations, athletic directors, coaches, and athletes are typically rebuffed (Lipsyte, 1991), and women in sport wait, hoping the scrutiny will disappear as quickly as possible. Women live in fear that whatever meager gains we have made in sport are always one lesbian scandal away from being wiped out.

Even without the provocation of public scrutiny or threat of scandal, silent avoidance is the strategy of choice. Organizers of coaches' or athletic administrators' conferences rarely schedule programs on homophobia in sport, and when they do, it is always a controversial decision made with fear and concern about the consequences of public dialogue (Krebs, 1984; Lenskyj, 1990). Lesbians in sport are treated like nasty secrets that must be kept locked tightly in the closet. Lesbians, of course, are expected to maintain deep cover at all times. Not surprisingly, most lesbians in sport choose to remain hidden rather than face potential public condemnation. Friends of lesbians protect this secret from outsiders, and the unspoken pact of silence is maintained and passed on to each new generation of women in sport.

Silence has provided some protection. Keeping the closet door locked is an understandable strategy when women in sport are trying to gain social approval in a sexist society and there is no sense that change is possible.

Maintaining silence is a survival strategy in a society hostile to women in general and lesbians in particular. How effectively silence enhances sport opportunities for women or defuses homophobia, however, is open to serious question.

Denial

If forced to break silence, many coaches, athletic directors, and athletes resort to denial. High school athletes and their parents often ask college coaches if there are lesbians in their programs. In response, many coaches deny that there are lesbians in sport, at least among athletes or coaches at *their* schools (Fields, 1983). These denials only serve to intensify curiosity and determination to find out who and where these mysterious women are. The closet, it turns out, is made of glass: People know lesbians are in sport despite these denials.

In some cases, parents and athletes who suspect that a respected and loved coach is a lesbian either deny or overlook her sexual identity because they cannot make sense of the apparent contradiction: a lesbian who is competent, loved, and respected. In other instances, a respected lesbian coach is seen as an exception because she does not fit the unflattering lesbian stereotype most people accept as accurate. The end result in any case is to deny the presence of lesbians in sport.

Apology

The third manifestation of homophobia in sport is apology (Felshin, 1974). In an attempt to compensate for an unsavory reputation, women in sport try to promote a feminine image and focus public attention on those who meet white heterosexual standards of beauty. Women in sport have a tradition of assuring ourselves and others that sport participation is consistent with traditional notions of femininity and that women are not masculinized by sport experiences (Gornick, 1971; Hicks, 1979; Locke & Jensen, 1970). To this end, athletes are encouraged, or required in some cases, to engage in the protective camouflage of feminine drag. Professional athletes and college teams are told to wear dresses or attend seminars to learn how to apply makeup, style hair, and select clothes ("Image Lady," 1987). Athletes are encouraged to be seen with boyfriends and reminded to act like ladies when away from the gym (DePaul University's 1984 women's basketball brochure).

The Women's Sports Foundation (WSF) annual dinner, attended by many well-known professional and amateur female athletes, is preceded by an opportunity for the athletes to get free hairstyling and makeup applications before they sit down to eat with the male corporate sponsors, whose money supports many WSF programs. The men attending the dinner are not offered similar help with their appearance. The message is that female athletes in their natural state are not acceptable or attractive and therefore must be fixed and "femmed up" to compensate for their athleticism.

Femininity, however, is a code word for heterosexuality. The underlying fear is not that a female athlete or coach will appear too plain or out of style; the real fear is that she will look like a dyke or, even worse, is one. This intense blend of homophobic and sexist standards of feminine attractiveness remind women in sport that to be acceptable, we must monitor our behavior and appearance at all times.

Silence, denial, and apology are defensive reactions that reflect the power of the lesbian label to intimidate women. These responses ensure that women's sport will be held hostage to the *L* word. As long as questions about lesbians in sport are met with silence, denial, and apology, women can be sent scurrying back to our places on the margins of sport, grateful for the modicum of public approval we have achieved and fearful of losing it.

NEW MANIFESTATIONS OF HOMOPHOBIA IN WOMEN'S SPORT

In the last 10 years, three more responses have developed in reaction to the persistence of the association of sport with lesbians. These manifestations have developed at the same time that women's sport has become more visible, potentially marketable, and increasingly under the control of men and men's sport organizations. Representing an intensified effort to purge the lesbian image, these new strategies reflect a new low in mean-spirited intimidation.

Promotion of a Heterosexy Image

Where presenting a feminine image previously sufficed, corporate sponsors, professional women's sport organizations, some women's college teams, and individual athletes have moved beyond presenting a feminine image to adopting a more explicit display of heterosex appeal. The Ladies Professional Golf Association's 1989 promotional material featured photographs of its pro golfers posing pin-up style in swimsuits (Diaz, 1989). College sport promotional literature has employed double entendres and sexual innuendo to sell women's teams. The women's basketball promotional brochure from Northwestern State University of Louisiana included a photograph of the women's team dressed in Playboy bunny outfits. The copy crowed "These girls can play, boy!" and invited basketball fans to watch games in the "Pleasure Palace" (Solomon, 1991).

Popular magazines have featured young, professional female athletes, like Monica Seles or Steffi Graf, in cleavage-revealing heterosexual glamour drag (Kiersh, 1990).

In a more muted attempt to project a heterosexual image, stories about married female athletes and coaches routinely include husbands and children in ways rarely seen when male coaches and athletes are profiled. A recent nationally televised basketball game between the women's teams from the University of Texas and the University of Tennessee featured a half-time profile of the coaches as wives and mothers. The popular press also brings us testimonials from female athletes who have had children claiming that their athletic performance has improved since becoming mothers. All of this to reassure the public, and perhaps ourselves as women in sport, that we are normal despite our athletic interests.

Attacks on Lesbians in Sport

Women in sport endure intense scrutiny of our collective and individual femininity and sexual identities. Innuendo, concern, and prurient curiosity about the sexual identity of female coaches and athletes come from coaches, athletic directors, sports reporters, parents of female athletes, teammates, fans, and the general public (South, Glynn, Rodack, & Capettini, 1990). This manifestation of homophobia is familiar to most people associated with women's sport. Over the last 10 to 12 years, however, concern about lesbians in sport has taken a nasty turn.

Though lesbians in sport have always felt pressure to stay closeted, coaches and athletic directors now openly prohibit lesbian coaches and athletes (Brownworth, 1991; Figel, 1986; Longman, 1991). In a style reminiscent of 1950s McCarthyism, some coaches proclaim their antilesbian policies as an introduction to their programs. Athletes thought to be lesbian are dropped from teams, find themselves benched, or are suddenly ostracized by coaches and teammates (Brownworth, 1991). Coaches impose informal quotas on the number of lesbians, or at least on the number of athletes they think look like lesbians, on their teams (Brownworth, 1991). At some schools, a new coach's heterosexual credentials are scrutinized as carefully as her professional qualifications (Fields, 1983). Coaches thought to be lesbians are fired or intimidated into resigning. These dismissals are not the result of any unethical behavior on the part of the women accused but simply because of assumptions made about their sexual identity.

Collegiate and high school female athletes endure lesbian-baiting (name-calling, taunting, and other forms of harassment) from male athletes, heterosexual teammates, opposing teams, spectators, classmates, and sometimes their own coaches (Brownworth, 1991; Fields, 1983; Spander, 1991; Thomas, 1990). Female coaches thought to be lesbians endure harassing phone calls and antilesbian graffiti slipped under their office doors. During a recent National Collegiate Athletic Association (NCAA) women's basketball championship, it was rumored that a group of male coaches went to the local lesbian bar to spy on lesbian coaches who might be there. Another rumor circulated about a list categorizing Division I women's basketball coaches by their sexual identity so that parents of prospective athletes could use this information to avoid schools where lesbians coach. Whether or not these rumors are true doesn't matter: The rumor itself is intimidating enough to remind women in sport that we are being watched and that if we step out of line, we will be punished.

Negative recruiting is perhaps the most self-serving of all the attacks on lesbians in sport. Negative recruiting occurs when college coaches or athletic department personnel reassure prospective athletes and their parents not only that there are no lesbians in this program but also that there *are* lesbians in a rival school's program (Fields, 1983). By playing on parents' and athletes' fear and ignorance, these coaches imply that young women will be safe in their programs but not at a rival school where bull dykes stalk the locker room in search of fresh young conquests.

Fears about lesbian stereotypes are fueled by a high-profile Christian presence at many national championships and coaches' conferences. The Fellowship of Christian Athletes, which regularly sponsors meal functions for coaches at these events, distributes a free antihomosexual booklet to coaches and athletes. Entitled *Emotional Dependency: A Threat to Close Friendships,* this booklet plays into all of the stereotypes of lesbians (Rentzel, 1987). A drawing of a sad young woman and an older woman on the cover hints at the dangers of close female friendships. Unencumbered by any reasonable factual knowledge about homosexuality, the booklet identifies the symptoms of emotional dependency and how this "leads" to homosexual relationships. Finally, the path out of this "counterfeit" intimacy through prayer and discipline is described. The booklet is published by Exodus, a fundamentalist Christian organization devoted to the "redemption" of homosexuals from their "disorder."

By allowing the active participation of antigay organizations in coaches' meetings and championship events, sport governing bodies like the NCAA and the Women's Basketball Coaches' Association are taking an active role in the perpetuation of discrimination against lesbians in sport and the stigmatization of all friendships among women in sport. In this intimidating climate, all women in sport must deal with the double burden of maintaining high-profile heterosexual images and living in terror of being called lesbians.

Preference for Male Coaches

Many parents, athletes, and athletic administrators prefer that men coach women's teams. This preference reflects a lethal mix of sexism and homophobia. Some people believe, based on gender and lesbian stereotypes, that men are better coaches than women. Although a recent NCAA survey of female athletes (NCAA, 1991) indicated that 61% of the respondents did not have a gender preference for their coaches, respondents were concerned about the images they thought male and female coaches had among their friends and family: 65% believed that female coaches were looked upon favorably by family and friends whereas 84% believed that male coaches were looked on favorably by family and friends.

Recent studies have documented the increase in the number of men coaching women's teams (Acosta & Carpenter, 1988). At least part of this increase can be attributed to homophobia. Thorngren (1991), in a study of female coaches, asked respondents how homophobia affected them. These coaches identified hiring and job retention as problems. They cited examples where men were hired to coach women's teams specifically to change a tarnished or negative (read *lesbian*) team image. Thorngren described this as a "cloaking" phenomenon, in which a team's lesbian image is hidden or countered by the presence of a male coach. Consistent with this perception, anecdotal reports from other female head coaches reveal that some believe it essential to hire a male assistant coach to lend a heterosexual persona to a women's team. The coaches in Thorngren's study also reported that women (married and single) leave coaching because of the pressure and stress of constantly having to deal with lesbian labels and stereotypes. Looking at the increase in the number of men coaching women's teams over the last 10 years, it is clear how male coaches have benefited from sexism and homophobia in women's sport.

SUSPICION, COLLUSION, AND BETRAYAL AMONG WOMEN IN SPORT

The few research studies addressing homophobia or lesbians in sport, as well as informal anecdotal information, have revealed that many women have internalized sexist and homophobic values and beliefs (Blinde, 1990; Griffin, 1987; Guthrie, 1982; Morgan, 1990; Thorngren, 1990, 1991; Woods, 1990). Blinde interviewed women athletes about the pressures and stress they experienced. Many talked about the lesbian image women's sport has and the shame they felt about being female athletes because of that image. Their discomfort with the topic was illustrated by their inability to even say the word *lesbian*. Instead, they made indirect references to *it* as a problem. Athletes talked in ways that clearly indicated they had bought into the negative images of lesbians, even as they denied that there were lesbians on their teams. These athletes also subscribed to the importance of projecting a feminine image and were discomforted by female athletes who didn't look or act feminine.

Quotes selected to accompany the NCAA survey and the Blinde study illustrate the degree to which many female athletes and coaches accept both the negative stigma attached to lesbian identity and the desirability of projecting a traditionally feminine image:

> The negative image of women in intercollegiate sport scares me. I've met too many lesbians in my college career. I don't want to have that image. (NCAA, 1991)

> Well, if you come and look at our team, I mean, if you saw Jane Doe, she's very pretty. If she walks down the street, everybody screams, you know, screams other things at her. But because she's on the field, it's dykes on spikes. If that isn't a stereotype, then who knows what is. (Blinde, p. 12)

> Homosexual females in this profession (coaching) definitely provide models and guidance in its worst for female athletes. I'd rather see a straight male coach females than a gay woman. Homosexual coaches are killing us. (NCAA, 1991)

> I don't fit the stereotype. I mean the stereotype based around women that are very masculine and strong and athletic. I wouldn't say I'm pretty in pink, but I am feminine and I appear very feminine and I act that way. (Blinde, p. 12)

These attempts to distance oneself from the lesbian image and to embrace traditional standards of femininity set up a division among women in sport that can devastate friendships among teammates, poison coach-athlete relationships, and taint feelings about one's identity as an athlete and a woman. Some women restrict close friendships with other women to avoid the possibility that someone might think they are lesbians. Other women consciously cultivate high-profile heterosexual images by talking about their relationships with men and being seen with men as often as possible. As long as our energy is devoted to trying to fit into models of athleticism, gender, and sexuality that support a sexist and heterosexist culture, women in sport can be controlled by anyone who chooses to use our fears and insecurities against us.

UNDERLYING BELIEFS THAT KEEP WOMEN IN SPORT FROM CHALLENGING HOMOPHOBIA

The ability to understand the staying power of the lesbian stigma in sport is limited by several interconnected beliefs. An examination of these beliefs can reveal how past responses in dealing with lesbians in sport have reinforced the power of the lesbian label to intimidate and control.

A Woman's Sexual Identity Is Personal

This belief is perhaps the biggest obstacle to understanding women's oppression in a patriarchal culture (Kitzinger, 1987). As long a women's sexual identity is seen as solely a private issue, how the lesbian label is used to intimidate all women and to weaken women's challenges to male-dominated institutions will never be understood. The lesbian label is a political weapon that can be used against any woman who steps out of line. Any woman who defies traditional gender roles is called a lesbian. Any woman who chooses a male-identified career is called a lesbian. Any woman who chooses not to have a sexual relationship with a man is called a lesbian. Any woman who speaks out against sexism is called a lesbian. As long as women are afraid to be called lesbians, this label is an effective tool to control all women and limit women's challenges to sexism. Although lesbians are the targets of attack in women's sport, all women in sport are victimized by the use of the lesbian label to intimidate and control.

When a woman's lesbian identity is assumed to be a private matter, homophobia and heterosexism are dismissed. The implication is that these matters are not appropriate topics for professional discussion. As a result, the fear, prejudice, and outright discrimination that thrive in silence are never addressed. A double standard operates, however, for lesbians and heterosexual women in sport. Although open acknowledgment of lesbians in sport is perceived as an inappropriate flaunting of personal life (what you do in the privacy of your home is none of my business), heterosexual women are encouraged to talk about their relationships with men, their children, and their roles as mothers.

Magazine articles about such heterosexual athletes as Chris Evert Mill, Florence Griffiths Joyner, Jackie Joyner Kersey, Joan Benoit, Nancy Lopez, and Mary Decker Slaney have often focused on their weddings, their husbands, or their children. Heterosexual professional athletes are routinely seen celebrating victories by hugging or kissing their husbands, but when Martina Navratilova went into the stands to hug *her* partner after winning the 1990 Wimbledon Championship, she was called a bad role model by former champion Margaret Court. Although heterosexual athletes and coaches are encouraged to display their personal lives to counteract the lesbian image in sport, lesbians are intimidated into invisibility for the same reason.

Claiming to Be Feminist Is Tantamount to Claiming to Be Lesbian

Claiming to be feminist is far too political for many women in sport. To successfully address the sexism and heterosexism in sport, however, women must begin to understand the necessity of seeing homophobia as a political issue and claim feminism as the unifying force needed to bring about change in a patriarchal culture. Part of the reluctance to embrace the feminist label is that feminists have been called lesbians in the same way that female athletes have and for the same reason: to intimidate women and prevent them from challenging the sexist status quo. Women in sport are already intimidated by the lesbian label. For many women, living with the athlete, lesbian, and feminist labels is stigma overload.

By accepting the negative stereotypes associated with these labels, women in sport collude in our own oppression. Rather than seeking social approval as a marginal part of sport in a sexist and heterosexist society, we need to be working for social change and control over our sport destinies. The image of an unrepentant lesbian feminist athlete is a patriarchal nightmare. She is a woman who has discovered her physical and political strength and who refuses to be intimidated by labels. Unfortunately, this image scares women in sport as much as it does those who benefit from the maintenance of the sexist and heterosexist status quo.

The Problem Is Lesbians in Sport Who Call Attention to Themselves

People who believe this assume that as long as lesbians are invisible, our presence will be tolerated and women's sport will progress. The issue for these people is not that there are lesbians in sport but how visible we are. Buying into silence this way has never worked. Other than Martina Navratilova, lesbians in sport are already deeply closeted (Bull, 1991; Muscatine, 1991). This careful camouflage of lesbians has not made women's sport less suspect or less vulnerable to intimidation. Despite efforts to keep the focus on the pretty ones or the ones with husbands and children, women in sport still carry the lesbian stigma into every gym and onto every playing field.

Women in sport must begin to understand that it wouldn't matter if there were no lesbians in sport. The lesbian label would still be used to intimidate and control women's athletics. The energy expended in making lesbians invisible and projecting a happy heterosexual image keeps women in sport fighting among ourselves rather that confronting the heterosexism and sexism that our responses unintentionally serve.

Lesbians Are Bad Role Models and Sexual Predators

This belief buys into all the unsavory lesbian stereotypes left over from the late 19th-century medical doctors who made homosexuality pathological and the early 20th-century sexologists who made female friendships morbid. In reality, there are already numerous closeted lesbians in sport who are highly admired role models. It is the perversity of prejudice that merely knowing about the sexual identity of these admired women instantly turns them into unfit role models.

The sexual-predator stereotype is a particularly pernicious slander on lesbians in sport (South et al., 1990). There is no evidence that lesbians are sexual predators. In fact, statistics on sexual harassment, rape, sexual abuse, and other forms of violence and intimidation show that these offenses are overwhelmingly heterosexual male assaults against women and girls. If we need to be concerned about sexual offenses among coaches or athletes, a better case could be made that it is heterosexual men who should be watched carefully. Blinde (1989) reported that many female athletes, like their male counterparts, are subjected to academic, physical, social, and emotional exploitation by their coaches. When men coach women in a heterosexist and sexist culture, there is the additional potential for sexual and gender-based exploitation when the unequal gender dynamics in the larger society are played out in the coach-athlete relationship.

It is difficult to imagine anyone in women's sport, regardless of sexual identity, condoning coercive sexual relationships of any kind. Even consensual sexual relationships between coaches and athletes involve inherent power differences that make such relationships questionable and can have a negative impact on the athlete as well as on the rest of the team. This kind of behavior should be addressed regardless of the gender or sexual identity of the coaches and athletes involved instead of assuming that lesbian athletes or coaches present a greater problem than others.

Being Called Lesbian or Being Associated with Lesbians Is the Worst Thing That Can Happen in Women's Sport

As long as women in sport buy into the power of the lesbian label to intimidate us, we will never control our sport experience. Blaming lesbians for women's sports' bad image and failure to gain more popularity divides women and keeps us fighting among ourselves. In this way, we collude in maintaining our marginal status by keeping alive the power of the lesbian label to intimidate women into silence, betrayal, and denial. This keeps our energies directed inward rather that outward at the sexism that homophobia serves. Blaming lesbians keeps all women in their place, scurrying to present an image that is acceptable in a sexist and heterosexist society. This keeps our attention diverted from asking other questions: Why are strong female athletes and coaches so threatening to a patriarchal society? Whose interests are served by trivializing and stigmatizing women in sport?

Women in sport need to redefine the problem. Instead of naming and blaming lesbians in sport as the problem, we need to focus our attention on sexism, heterosexism, and homophobia. As part of this renaming process, we need to take the sting out of the lesbian label. Women in sport must stop jumping to the back of the closet and slamming the door every time someone calls us dykes. We need to challenge the use of the lesbian label to intimidate all women in sport.

Women's Sport Can Progress without Dealing with Homophobia

If progress is measured by the extent to which we, as women in sport, control our sporting destinies, take pride in our athletic identities, and tolerate diversity among ourselves, then we are no better off now than we ever have been. We have responded to questions about lesbians in sport with silence, denial, and apology. When these responses fail to divert attention away from the lesbian issue, we have promoted a heterosexy image, attacked lesbians, and hired male coaches. All of these responses call on women to accommodate, assimilate, and collude with the values of a sexist and heterosexist society. All require compromise and deception. The bargain struck is that in return for our silence and our complicity, we are allowed a small piece of the action in a sports world that has been defined by men to serve male-identified values.

We have never considered any alternatives to this cycle of silence, denial, and apology to the outside world while policing the ranks inside. We have never looked inside ourselves to understand our fear and confront it. We have never tried to analyze the political meaning of our fear. We have never stood up to the accusations and threats that keep us in our place.

What do we have to pass on to the next generation of young girls who love to run and throw and catch? What is the value of nicer uniforms, a few extra tournaments, and occasional pictures in the back of the sports section if we can't pass on a sport experience with less silence and fear?

STRATEGIES FOR CONFRONTING HOMOPHOBIA IN WOMEN'S SPORT

What, then, are the alternatives to silence, apology, denial, promoting a heterosexy image, attacking lesbians, and hiring male coaches? How can women in sport begin confronting homophobia rather than perpetuating it? If our goal is to defuse the lesbian label and to strip it of its power to intimidate women in sport, then we must break the silence, not to condemn lesbians but to condemn those who use the lesbian label to intimidate. Our failure to speak out against homophobia signals our consent to the fear, ignorance, and discrimination that flourishes in that silence. If our goal is to create a vision of sport in which all women have an opportunity to proudly claim their athletic identity and control their athletic experience, then we must begin to build that future now.

Institutional Policy

Sport-governing organizations and school athletic departments need to enact explicit nondiscrimination and antiharassment policies that include sexual orientation as a protected category. This is a first step in establishing an organizational climate in which discrimination against lesbians (or gay men) is not tolerated. Most sport governing organizations have not instituted such policies and, when asked by reporters if they are planning to, avoid taking a stand (Brownworth, 1991; Longman, 1991). In addition to nondiscrimination policies, professional standards of conduct for coaches must be developed that outline behavioral expectations regardless of gender or sexual orientation. Sexual harassment policies and the procedures for filing such complaints must be made clear to coaches, athletes, and administrators. As with standards of professional conduct, these policies should apply to everyone.

Education

Everyone associated with physical education and athletics must learn more about homophobia, sexism, and heterosexism. Conferences for coaches, teachers, and administrators should include educational programs focused on understanding homophobia and developing strategies for addressing homophobia in sport.

Athletic departments must sponsor educational programs for athletes that focus not only on homophobia but on other issues of social diversity as well. Because prejudice and fear affect the quality of athletes' sport experience and their relationships with teammates and coaches, educational programs focused on these issues are appropriate for athletic department sponsorship and should be an integral part of the college athletic experience.

Visibility

One of the most effective tools in counteracting homophobia is increased lesbian and gay visibility. Stereotypes and the fear and hatred they perpetuate will lose their power as more lesbian and gay people in sport disclose their identities. Although some people will never accept diversity of sexual identity in sport or in the general population, research indicates that, for most people, contact with "out" lesbian and gay people who embrace their sexual identities reduces prejudice (Herek, 1985).

The athletic world desperately needs more lesbian and gay coaches and athletes to step out of the closet. So far only a handful of athletes or coaches, most notably Martina Navratilova, have had the courage to publicly affirm their lesbian or gay identity (Brown, 1991; Brownworth, 1991; Bull, 1991; Burke, 1991; Muscatine, 1991). The generally accepting, if not warm, reaction of tennis fans to Martina's courage and honesty should be encouraging to the many closeted lesbian and gay people in sport. Unfortunately, the fear that keeps most lesbian and gay sportspeople in the closet is not ungrounded: Coming out as a lesbian or gay athlete or coach is a risk in a heterosexist and sexist society (Brown, 1991; Brownworth, 1991; Burton-Nelson, 1991; Hicks, 1979; Muscatine, 1991). The paradox is that more lesbian and gay people need to risk coming out if homosexuality is to be demystified in North American society.

Another aspect of visibility is the willingness of heterosexual athletes and coaches, as allies of lesbian and gay people, to speak out against homophobia and heterosexism. In the same way that it is important for white people to speak out against racism and for men to speak out against sexism, it is important for heterosexual people to object to antigay harassment, discrimination, and prejudice. It isn't enough to provide silent, private support for lesbian friends. To remain silent signals consent. Speaking out against homophobia is a challenge for heterosexual women in sport that requires them to understand how homophobia is used against them as well as against lesbians. Speaking out against homophobia also requires that heterosexual women confront their own discomfort with being associated with lesbians or being called lesbian, because that is what will happen when they speak out: The lesbian label will be used to try and intimidate them back into silence.

Solidarity

Heterosexual and lesbian women must understand that the only way to overcome homophobia, heterosexism, and sexism in sport is to work in coalition with each other. As long as fear and blame prevent women in sport from finding common ground, we will always be controlled by people whose interests are served by our division. Our energy will be focused on social approval rather than on social change, and on keeping what little we have rather than on getting what we deserve.

Pressure Tactics

Unfortunately, meaningful social change never happens without tension and resistance. Every civil and human rights struggle in the United States has required the mobilization of political pressure exerted on people with power to force them to confront injustice. Addressing sexism, heterosexism, and homophobia in women's sport will be no different. Taking a stand will mean being prepared to use the media, collect petitions, lobby officials, picket, write letters, file official complaints, and take advantage of other pressure tactics.

CONCLUSION

Eliminating the insidious trio of sexism, heterosexism, and homophobia in women's sport will take a sustained commitment to social justice that will challenge much of what has been accepted as natural about gender and sexuality. Addressing sexism, heterosexism, and homophobia in women's sport requires that past conceptions of gender and sexuality be recognized as social constructions that confer privilege and normalcy on particular social groups: men and heterosexuals. Other social groups (women, lesbians, and gay men) are defined as inferior or deviant and are denied access to the social resources and status conferred on heterosexual men.

Sport in the late 20th century is, perhaps, the last arena in which men can hope to differentiate themselves from women. In sport, men learn to value a traditional heterosexual masculinity that embraces male domination and denigrates women's values (Messner & Sabo, 1990). If sport is to maintain its meaning as a masculine ritual in a patriarchal society, women must be made to feel like trespassers. Women's sport participation must be trivialized and controlled (Bennett et al., 1987). The lesbian label, with its unsavory stigma, is an effective tool to achieve these goals.

If women in sport in the 21st century are to have a sport experience free of intimidation, fear, shame, and betrayal, then, as citizens of the 20th century, we must begin to reevaluate our beliefs, prejudices, and practices. We must begin to challenge the sexist, heterosexist, and homophobic status quo as it lives in our heads, on our teams, and in our schools. A generation of young girls—our daughters, nieces, younger sisters, and students—is depending on us.

REFERENCES

Acosta, V., & Carpenter, L. (1988). Status of women in athletics: Causes and changes. *Journal of Health, Physical Education, Recreation & Dance, 56*(6), 35-37.

Bennett, R., Whitaker, G., Smith, N., & Sablove, A. (1987). Changing the rules of the game: Reflections toward a feminist analysis of sport. *Women's Studies International Forum, 10*(4), 369-380.

Birrell, S., & Richter, D. (1987). Is a diamond forever? Feminist transformations of sport. *Women's Studies International Forum, 10*(4), 395-410.

Blinde, E. (1989). Unequal exchange and exploitation in college sport: The case of the female athlete. *Arena Review, 13*(2), 110-123.

Blinde, E. (1990, March). *Pressure and stress in women's college sports: Views from athletes.* Paper presented at the annual convention of the American Alliance for Health, Physical Education, Recreation and Dance, New Orleans.

Brown, K. (1991). Homophobia in women's sports. *Deneuve, 1*(2), 4-6, 29.

Brownworth, V. (1991, June 4). Bigotry on the home team: Lesbians face harsh penalties in the sports world. *The Advocate,* pp. 34-39.

Bryson, L. (1987). Sport and the maintenance of male hegemony. *Women's Studies International Forum, 10*(4), 349-360.

Bull, C. (1991, December 31). The magic of Martina. *The Advocate,* pp. 38-40.

Burke, G. (1991, September 18). Dodgers wanted me to get married. *USA Today,* p. 10C.

Burton-Nelson, M. (1991). *Are we winning yet?* New York: Random House.

Diaz, J. (1989, February 13). Find the golf here? *Sports Illustrated,* pp. 58-64.

Faderman, L. (1981). *Surpassing the love of men: Romantic friendship and love between women from the Renaissance to the present.* New York: Morrow.

Faderman, L. (1991). *Odd girls and twilight lovers: A history of lesbian life in twentieth-century America.* New York: Columbia University Press.

Felshin, J. (1974). The triple option . . . for women in sport. *Quest,* **21**, 36-40.

Fields, C. (1983, October 26). Allegations of lesbianism being used to intimidate, female academics say. *Chronicle of Higher Education,* pp. 1, 18-19.

Figel, B. (1986, June 16). Lesbians in the world of athletics. *Chicago Sun-Times,* p. 119.

Gornick, V. (1971, May 18). Ladies of the links. *Look,* pp. 69-76.

Greendorfer, S. (1991, April). *Analyzing homophobia: Its weapons and impacts.* Paper presented at the annual convention of the American Alliance for Health, Physical Education, Recreation and Dance, San Francisco.

Griffin, P. (1987, August). *Lesbians, homophobia, and women's sport: An exploratory analysis.* Paper presented at the annual meeting of the American Psychological Association, New York.

Guthrie, S. (1982). *Homophobia: Its impact on women in sport and physical education.* Unpublished master's thesis, California State University, Long Beach.

Hall, A. (Ed.) (1987). The gendering of sport, leisure, and physical education [Special issue]. *Women's Studies International Forum,* **10**(4).

Herek, G. (1985). Beyond "homophobia": A social psychological perspective on attitudes toward lesbians and gay men. In J. DeCecco (Ed.), *Bashers, baiters, and bigots: Homophobia in American society* (pp. 1-22). New York: Harrington Park Press.

Hicks, B. (1979, October/November). Lesbian athletes. *Christopher Street,* pp. 42-50.

Image lady. (1987, July). *Golf Illustrated,* p. 9.

Katz, J. (1976). *Gay American History.* New York: Avon.

Kiersh, E. (1990, April). Graf's dash. *Vogue,* pp. 348-353, 420.

Kitzinger, C. (1987). *The social construction of lesbianism.* Newbury Park, CA: Sage.

Krebs, P. (1984). At the starting blocks: Women athletes' new agenda. *Off our backs,* **14**(1), 1-3.

Lederman, D. (1991, June 5). Penn State's coach's comments about lesbian athletes may be used to test university's new policy on bias. *Chronicle of Higher Education,* pp. A27-28.

Lenskyj, H. (1986). *Out of bounds: Women, sport, and sexuality.* Toronto: Women's Press.

Lenskyj, H. (1990). Combatting homophobia in sports. *Off our backs,* **20**(6), 2-3.

Lenskyj, H. (1991). Combatting homophobia in sport and physical education. *Sociology of Sport Journal,* **8**(1), 61-69.

Lipsyte, R. (1991, May 24). Gay bias moves off the sidelines. *New York Times,* p. B1.

Locke, L., & Jensen, M. (1970, Fall). Heterosexuality of women in physical education. *The Foil,* pp. 30-34.

Longman, J. (1991, March 10). Lions women's basketball coach is used to fighting and winning. *Philadelphia Inquirer,* pp. 1G, 6G.

Messner, M., & Sabo, D. (Eds.) (1990). *Sport, men, and the gender order: Critical feminist perspectives.* Champaign, IL: Human Kinetics.

Morgan, E. (1990). *Lesbianism and feminism in women's athletics: Intersection, bridge, or gap?* Unpublished manuscript, Brown University, Providence.

Muscatine, A. (1991, November/December). To tell the truth, Navratilova takes consequences. *Women's SportsPages,* pp. 8-9. (Available from Women's SportsPages, P.O. Box 151534, Chevy Chase, MD 20825)

National Collegiate Athletic Association. (1991). *NCAA study on women's intercollegiate athletics: Perceived barriers of women in intercollegiate athletic careers.* Overland Park, KS: Author.

Newton, E. (1989). The mannish lesbian: Radclyffe Hall and the new woman. In M. Duberman, M. Vicinus, & G. Chauncey (Eds.), *Hidden from history: Reclaiming the gay and lesbian past* (pp. 281-293). New York: New American Library.

Pharr, S. (1988). *Homophobia: A weapon of sexism.* Inverness, CA: Chardon Press.

Rentzel, L. (1987). *Emotional dependency: A threat to close friendships.* San Rafael, CA: Exodus International.

Smith-Rosenberg, C. (1989). Discourses of sexuality and subjectivity: The new woman, 1870–1936. In M. Duberman, M. Vicinus, & G. Chauncey (Eds.), *Hidden from history: Reclaiming the gay and lesbian past* (pp. 264-280). New York: New American Library.

Solomon, A. (1991, March 20). Passing game. *Village Voice,* p. 92.

South, J., Glynn, M., Rodack, J., & Capettini, R. (1990, July 31). Explosive gay scandal rocks women's tennis. *National Enquirer,* pp. 20-21.

Spander, D. (1991, September 1). It's a question of acceptability. *Sacramento Bee,* pp. D1, D14-15.

Thomas, R. (1990, December 12). Two women at Brooklyn College file rights complaint. *New York Times,* p. 22.

Thorngren, C. (1990, April). *Pressure and stress in women's college sport: Views from coaches.* Paper presented at the annual convention of the American Alliance for Health, Physical Education, Recreation and Dance, New Orleans.

Thorngren, C. (1991, April). *Homophobia and women coaches: Controls and constraints.* Paper presented at the annual convention of the American Alliance for Health, Physical Education, Recreation and Dance, San Francisco.

Woods, S. (1990). The contextual realities of being a lesbian physical education teacher: Living in two worlds (doctoral dissertation, University of Massachusetts, Amherst, 1989). *Dissertation Abstracts International,* **51**(3), 788.

35. Sport and Masculinity: The Estrangement of Gay Men

BRIAN PRONGER

Athletics is a traditional theater for the acting out of myths. The ancient Olympic Games were religious celebrations in which the central myths of Hellenic culture were dramatized. Class and patriarchy, as well as the religious belief that fame (which can be achieved by winning at the Olympics) bestows immortality, were the cultural focus of the ancient games. The similarity between the ancient Olympics and modern-day athletics is limited to the more abstract fact that both are dramatizations of myth. Notions that we take for granted, such as fair play, the virtue of participation in sport for its own sake, and the importance of personal bests, were unknown to the ancients. The ancient games could be quite violent, sometimes being fought to the death, and winning was the only thing that mattered. In fact, if an athlete could intimidate his opponents to the point of their withdrawing from the competition, he was considered successful without even participating in the event.

Sport in contemporary Western culture also dramatizes myths; preeminent among them is the myth of masculinity. One of the men I interviewed said:

> Our culture has definitely rewarded those who are very masculine and perform well, and men over women. Male tennis players, male golf players make more money than female golfers do. So there is a reward for masculinity and a punishment, in some way, for femininity. . . . I think also there's an intimidating factor to athletics and the way the program's run: gym teachers calling kids sissies if they can't run laps.

Another, who likes lifting weights and wrestling, said:

> The way it's currently constituted in terms of the commercial basis that most sport depends on, and certainly the way it was taught to me in school, sport as it exists now parallels closely the individual, aggressive qualities that are seen as masculine by most people today, so I think that the connection is quite clear.

SOURCE: "Rookies and Debutantes: Estranged Athletes" by Brian Pronger. From *The Arena of Masculinity: Sports, Homosexuality and the Meaning of Sex,* by Brian Pronger. Copyright © 1990 by St. Martin's Press. Reprinted by permission.

And in team sports, it's not a feminist quilting-bee type group, but rather a bunch of behemoths who, instead of not being aggressive and choosing to be cooperative, are in fact simply pooling their collective aggressiveness and channeling it in one way. So I think there's quite a clear connection between sports and masculinity. . . .

For boys, sport is an initiation into manhood, a forum in which they can realize their place in the orthodoxy of gender culture. Sport gives them a feel for masculinity, a sense of how they are different from girls. For those who wish to emphasize their masculine sense of place, the masculinity of sport is a happy discovery, a way of expressing and exploring an important sense of themselves. But not all boys are comfortable with this rookie masculinity. For some, becoming adult men is more a matter of learning how they are estranged from masculine culture than it is one of becoming snug in its orthodoxy. For these boys, the sporting rights of masculine passage make them poignantly aware of their unease. Sport is a masculine obligation that they may fulfill, sometimes at great psychic and physical cost. And there are some boys who just see sports as a hostile world that is to be avoided. One of my interviewees said:

> My experience was that there was no place for me in the conventional sports structure, either ones that my peers had devised for playing ball hockey in the streets, or in the standard high-school or junior-high-school structure.

Athletics, as an expression of orthodox masculinity, can be typified in three categories: violence, struggle, and aesthetics. The most masculine sports are the violent ones—boxing, football, and hockey. Less masculine are those in which struggle is a dominant characteristic: one struggles with one's opponents and with oneself without perpetrating violence. Baseball, wrestling, tennis, swimming, and track are sports in which nonviolent struggle with one's opponent(s) is integral to the sport. Typical sports where the struggle is primarily with oneself are field events, golf, archery, and weight lifting. The least masculine sports are those where success is determined by the marriage of skill and aesthetic expression. Such sports are figure skating, diving, gymnastics, and body building. These aesthetic sports are the least masculine because they involve the lowest degree of aggression. . . .

Contrary to the popular opinion that aggressive combative sports like football and hockey are an outlet for the diffusion of natural aggressive energies, it has been found that these sports actually contribute to the development of aggressive behavior. "Research with high-school and college athletes finds they are more quick to anger than nonathletes and that those who participate in combative sports, such as hockey and football, respond to frustration with a greater degree of aggression when compared to athletes in noncontact sports and nonathletes."[1] Combative sports are really a training ground for aggressive violent masculinity.

The physical and psychic pain that is at the heart of this kind of masculinity is an imposition. According to Gary Shaw, Dave Meggyesy, and other commentators on football, vulnerable young men are pushed to the limits of physical and psychic abuse by coaches and athletic bureaucracies whose only interest is in winning, regardless of the long- and short-term damage it may cause the athletes.[2] Shaw points out that Darrell Royal, the famous head coach of the University of Texas Longhorns, was successful because of his ability to manipulate "the fears of boys in their late adolescence. Their fears of masculinity, their fears of acceptance, their fears of not being good enough—in short, their need to feel like acceptable men."[3] I interviewed a national track coach (who is heterosexual) who said:

> I played football and hockey because it was masculine. My fear that I would be discovered being afraid was greater than my fear of being hurt, and I was getting hurt all the time because I was much smaller than most everyone else. It hurt a lot to hit and get hit. But I was aggressive. It was part of being male and defining your masculinity and toughness. It's a dehumanizing process.

He also described the perverse attitude that one learns to take to injury and pain, not only that that one experiences oneself, but also among one's teammates.

> When I was coaching high-school football one of the kids broke his leg; he was screaming in pain; his femur was sticking out through his pant leg. We carried him off in a stretcher and went on with the game. It was terrible; a human tragedy had happened there and no one let on that anything bad had happened. They just pushed down their emotions and went on with the game.

Boys and men who are willing to put themselves through such violence do so out of an attachment to the meaning of orthodox masculinity. The pain is worth it because masculinity is worth it. Stressing the importance of masculinity, Vince Lombardi said, "when a football player loses his supreme confidence in his super-masculinity, he is in deep trouble."[4] Homosexual boys can be quite apprehensive about the status of their masculinity. Some may go through the horrors of football in an attempt to counteract suspicions of their extremely vulnerable masculinity. The former American pro football player David Kopay said: "[Football] also provided a convenient way for me— and who can say how many of my teammates?—to camouflage my true sexual feelings for men."[5] Others, and I think the majority, avoid violent sports because they feel no need to pursue an inappropriate world of masculinity.

Homosexual men and boys often feel estranged from sport because of its masculinity. Said one man:

> I didn't have a great predilection for sports. I didn't like competition. I really felt uncomfortable with my male peers. Even before I knew I was homosexual, I

knew that I had sexual feelings for men. I was also aware that people were categorizing me as nelly or sissy. And I knew that I just wouldn't enjoy going out and playing football in that kind of atmosphere. I was more comfortable reading.

I very often saw myself as less masculine than the boys who were doing [sports]. I suffered a lot because of that; I really think I undervalued myself because of that and never really felt comfortable being a gentle person, which I feel is the best way to categorize the way I was then.

I was very intimidated by sports then; I felt it was very ungentle. I'm not so intimidated anymore. The moment I was able to drop athletics as a subject, I did, and I didn't go near a gym again until university.

The estrangement that many homosexual boys and men feel can be very intense in team sports, especially those characterized by violence and aggression. Of the thirty-two gay men I interviewed, two had played some football in high school and three had played hockey as children—none had continued playing hockey after puberty. That they did not play hockey after puberty is significant, for it is at puberty that hockey playing becomes truly violent[6] and a serious manifestation of masculinity. Although there is evidence that some particularly ambitious parents encourage their prepubescent boys to play a rough game of hockey, it is at puberty and the onset of adolescence that some boys play rough on their own initiative and take it as an expression of their masculinity. (I personally remember well the difference between older adolescent boys and myself—they would hit and roughhouse in earnest; you could tell that it meant something important to them. Whereas it struck me as an unpleasant and alien kind of behavior.) Only one of the men I interviewed found these sports satisfying. He lived on an air force base where everyone played hockey and his father was the coach. His sisters and even his mother played hockey. When his father was transferred to another base, where hockey was not the major social institution, he stopped playing. Another, who became a competitive swimmer, came from a hockey-playing family—his uncle was in the NHL. He said, "My father's idea of sports is very traditional—camaraderie between the men, the physical contact. . . . I gave up hockey; I did it for a few years. I pretended I was going to block people. I went through the motions but didn't believe in what I was doing, so I walked away from it. I got involved in swimming and really enjoyed it." One man who played football quit because "they always want you to play when you're injured and tough it out. 'It doesn't hurt *that* much.' After sophomore year, when I broke my foot playing football, I lost my trust in playing football anymore after that. It wasn't worth it. My big event was track, and the broken foot put my track career back, so I said, 'It's not worthwhile for me in the long run.'"

Not one of the men I spoke to had laudatory things to say about football. Regarding football and hockey, one said:

I would say that there's something masculine about certain sports. Football and hockey. I think these sports are much more red-necked because they are violent. I don't like them as sports, they are noisy, boisterous, based on the desire to see people hit, be hit, and if that's masculine, I don't want any part of it.

A competitive swimmer said:

Homosexuality and football just do not mix—I don't know why. Maybe it's the homophobic tendency of men that they are not comfortable with the idea of doing anything else but massacring one another on the football field.

Many of the men I interviewed said they were uncomfortable with team sports. As a member of a team it's important that one identify with the team, that one see one's goals as being in common with the team. Now, if team goals were simply athletic, then homosexual men and boys would probably have no problem identifying with them. But athleticism is often not the only theme in team sports; orthodox masculinity is usually an important subtext if not *the* leitmotif. Coaches demand that their athletes play like men, even if they are just boys; it's boys' concern about masculinity that is played upon to motivate more aggressive performances. Team dynamics depend on a common commitment to orthodox masculinity. With that commitment go assumptions, not the least of which is the heterosexuality of team members. In such a setting where heterosexuality is assumed, homosexuality is more of an insult than a sexual disposition—football coaches are well known for berating their players with insults: "ladies," "faggots," "pansies." Such childish pejoratives are effective because there is a tacit understanding on the team that no one is homosexual or would want to be known as such. Needless to say, gay men or boys who do not share this contempt for homosexuality will feel uncomfortable with its use as a "motivating" insult. More importantly, because they may not share the same view of orthodox masculinity as others on the team, they will feel estranged from its role in sport and find it difficult to join in the chorus of its masculine leitmotif. Consequently, gay men often avoid team sports. Comments from gay men such as, "I had to play baseball and soccer in school and I didn't like team sports," are not uncommon.

Adding to their estrangement in athletics is the not exceptional experience of gay men being the last picked for teams. One man recalled field day at his public school. "They divided each class into teams and there were six kids on each team. We all stood there and the team leaders decided who they wanted. Finally, I was the last one standing and I had to join a team. When the teacher asked the team leaders how many they had, my leader said, 'Five and a half, 'cause we have Palmer.'" Rather than an intrinsic lack of physical ability, this athletic ineptitude is probably a reflection of the indifference some homosexual boys feel toward sports because of its orthodox masculine leitmotif.

There's the whole nightmare about baseball—trying to be as far out in left field as you could possibly get and then every now and then a ball coming your way and having to pick it up, throw it, run after it, pick it up again, throw it until it finally got back to the starting post, or whatever it is in baseball.

A man who is now quite muscular and a good swimmer said:

I was a real klutz. I was always the last one picked to be in anything. You didn't throw the ball right, you couldn't skate properly, and you were afraid of playing hockey. You didn't want to play hockey. I would say that a lot of gays would be in that category. Mostly, I hated going to [gym classes in high school]. I couldn't stand it. Volleyball, basketball—I didn't understand the rules and [had] no desire to do any of that either.

Even gay men who were in fact fine athletes in individual sports would sometimes be the last picked for teams. Myles Pearson, who swam as an international competitor, recalls how he felt in gym class. "I was a little sissy kid, so in gym classes you'd be the last one chosen on the team to play soccer or dodge ball, or whatever, and the same in high school. I went to a private boy's high school where the ultimate insult was 'you faggot.' And I didn't fit in well there. I don't remember high school warmly. It was the worst time."

Most athletic activities, with the exception of those that are by nature violent, have little or no *intrinsic* connection with orthodox masculinity. But orthodox masculinity often becomes associated with athletics nonetheless. Gay men and boys who are involved in athletics are often aware of the orthodox masculine leitmotif that can make them feel that they are outsiders in sports. Myles, the swimmer, said he felt like an outsider "in the locker room, but not in the pool. In the pool everyone was friends, and swim meets were fine. In the locker room, I think maybe I pulled away rather than was pushed away. Just because locker rooms are a boisterous kind of place; they were telling dirty jokes and talking about the girls in the locker room next to them, and I wasn't interested in participating. I would just be on the sidelines." His experience emphasizes the fact that from a purely athletic point of view, the experience of homosexual men and boys in sports cannot always be distinguished from their heterosexual counterparts. But when the orthodox masculine, and therefore heterosexual, leitmotif comes into play in the athletic environment, a sense of not being part of the action, of being outside, of estrangement, is amplified for homosexual men and boys.

While uncomfortable in team sports, many gay men and boys find individual athletic activity more satisfying.

Being from the north, certain kinds of physical activity were very central and very enjoyable to me—canoeing, rowing, hiking, backpacking, snowshoeing, skiing, these were all part of the regular activity. And I think I've always enjoyed individual performance. I've always got a great deal of enjoyment of this kind out of paddling, being able to do so many miles a day, and doing a real long portage, and the great physical satisfaction of the whole thing, and the sense of well-being. But it's always been individual sports, or sports of that kind, that I shared with two or three other people, I never enjoyed team sports, very much. I never enjoyed hockey, I liked skating. I never enjoyed baseball. I liked hitting the ball. The game at which I was best was tennis. I liked fencing too. These were things that I did by myself as opposed to being a member of a team.

This man found the physical activities themselves, for example, skating and hitting the ball, enjoyable, but it was the team dynamics he found distasteful.

A university-level competitive swimmer said that, unlike his friends, he didn't play team sports much.

I never did play hockey or baseball, which is what all my friends were doing. I swam; started when I was eight. In school, I was very into sports—track—I excelled in sports. Volleyball, badminton, gymnastics. I wasn't seriously into basketball, even though I'm tall. The only team sports were volleyball and curling.

Eilert Frerichs, who grew up on a farm and enjoyed the hard physical labor of farming, hated team sports.

[Team sports] scared me. It may have had to do with comparison with other children, and then in organized sports, in athletics at school, marks were assigned, which is gross. I probably could work in the fields longer than most boys who weren't from the farm, but no marks are assigned to that kind of activity.

And Myles Pearson:

I can remember when we played team sports in elementary school and maybe high school. If you did something wrong the whole team would turn on you, sometimes it was your fault, sometimes it wasn't. That really pissed me off. But I found with track (which I did for one year too), and with swimming, it's a lot more individual. I was a lot more proud of individual medals than I was of relay medals. That's part of why I didn't like team things when I was younger. But later on, I was never really interested in team sports because the boys grew up and were tougher and it was this macho thing that I didn't fit in with and that didn't feel a part of me.

One of the reasons Myles didn't like team sports was that he was aware of the orthodox masculine or "macho" leitmotif that at adolescence becomes the métier for boys in sports. Sensing this leitmotif in team sports, some gay men, even though they are participating on a team, prefer to think of the sport as individual. John Goodwin, once an internationally competitive oarsman, said he thought of rowing as an individual sport even if he was rowing in sixes or eights. "It's a team sport only because you are together in the boat, but you have to go beyond that."

Commenting on the seeming predilection that gay men have for individual sports over team sports, former runner Jim Pullen said:

> I think there are more gay people who are swimmers, runners, and skaters than there are football players and baseball players, partly because it's something you can do on your own. I think if you are uncomfortable being part of the mainstream heterosexual thing, if you are a little different, if you are a little effete, shall we say, and you're interested in sports or you're led to sports, then it's easier to do something on your own, where you don't have eighty people in the locker room together, which is intimidating anyway, I would think. When I talk to my gay friends now, for them, gym class was always a dreaded thing. They would always find some illness or something, anything to avoid going to gym and going through this team thing and playing ball and playing football. So if you were athletically talented you probably got into figure skating or swimming. I think that there are probably more natural things than football where you have to learn to knock people over. You can just go out for a run or a swim. If you are insecure, even the slightest bit, about being involved in any big group thing, especially with a bunch of heterosexual men thumping each other, then, at the very first practice when you've got eighty of them all doing it [trying to make the team] you'd probably avoid it. You'd have to really want to do it in order to suffer through that.

A former varsity swimmer, John Argue, said, "The difference between running, skiing, and swimming and team sports is that you are dealing with your own body in order to get it into as good shape as possible in order to excel, so that it is between you and nature, so to speak. It's an expression of pleasure and well-being. Whereas in team sports, the point is domination over others. . . . In team sports it is quite frightening; one wins by fighting, beating, and pummeling—I don't like that." A university phys ed instructor said, "The gay men I know around here are swimmers, divers, gymnasts. I don't know any gay football players."

* * *

The orthodox masculine leitmotif can also be heard in sports that fall into the "struggle" category. The volume at which the leitmotif is played depends not so much on the nature of the sport as it does on the attitude of the athletes and coaches. Some gay men think of swimming and similar sports as very masculine. A varsity-level swimmer told me:

> I think swimming is a very masculine sport. I think people who swim are some of the hardest-trained athletes, just because of the element of water. I think your body goes through more. You have to be tough mentally. . . . Swimmers aren't bulky so some people may tend to think they aren't as masculine, but I'm biased. I guess the most masculine to me are the sports like running . . . anything by itself . . . biking, track.

Another man, a volleyball player, agreed.

> I think, probably, athletes in individual sports like skiing would be more masculine, only because the challenge is so much greater and nobody relies on other people, you're doing it all yourself.

These men consider the attributes of strength, mental toughness, and independence, which are required in the individual sports, to be masculine and, therefore, see these sports as more masculine than violent team sports. But this equation of toughness and masculinity is unsatisfactory because it ignores the importance of violent aggression as the quintessential expression of masculine power. The desire to cast less violent sports as equally masculine as more violent ones reflects a wish to maintain a sort of masculine credibility, a credibility that, ultimately, is dubious.

A swimmer, Gerry Oxford, said he sees nothing particularly masculine about his sport.

> Swimming isn't up there with football; it isn't associated in most people's minds with a traditional masculine kind of image. Being a good swimmer just earns you scorn in the weight room of Hart House [a university athletic facility]. You are probably a faggot if you are a good swimmer. They'd have trouble saying about a football team, 'You don't play with that *fag* football team, do ya?' Swimming is not a butch enough sport to discredit accusations that you're queer. Athletes, however, wouldn't have this attitude about swimming because they know how hard it is to swim. People have more trouble with a football player being queer; there's something gentle about swimmers—they don't go around beating each other up.

The swimming world was horrified when at the Commonwealth Games, in the presence of the Queen, the world record holder in breast stroke, Victor Davis, kicked over a chair because he was upset that his relay team had been disqualified from a race. Such masculine expression of anger pales next to football players breaking each other's legs or hockey players smashing each other into the boards, knocking themselves unconscious.

Another competitive swimmer said he thought orthodox masculinity was expressed in sports not so much through the sport itself but through a more peripheral machismo. "The camaraderie that borderlines on macho, the bum patting sort of locker-room stuff, is macho. There's a lot of contrived machismo as the trappings of the sport—the image goes with the sport but it's not in the sport. . . . There's nothing particularly macho about swimming; both men and women do it and they do it the same way." He thinks the level of orthodox masculinity depends on the coach and other athletes. "The coach didn't try to motivate the team by references to fags. . . . My coach was a professor of child psychology—so that he was concerned about the development of his athletes as people, not just as swimmers. There were a couple of assholes [on the team] but I think that everyone thought they were ridiculous brutes. . . ."

Being in the midst of the machismo of sports can be estranging. One man said, "Doing basic jock stuff with the guys in the swim club, the 'all-for-one-and-one-for-all' sort of thing, I felt that I was a hypocrite, that I was playing along, doing the team, macho thing, talking about women, and you know it's not your natural thing, and you really are different, and you think absolutely nobody understands me."

The social side of athletics, especially for teenagers and college athletes, is overwhelmingly heterosexual. For most boys, their relationship with girls is a preoccupation of their adolescence. One's teammates form a boys-wanting-girls club. Weekend nights, the club goes out together in Dad's car. With the radio blaring, they cruise the town's main drag, looking for girls. There is a lot of hooting, and many rude comments are hurled at the female passersby. Boys "hanging moons" is de rigueur on such occasions. To most of the boys in the car, this playful baring of posteriors is both funny and "kinda gross." Who, after all, would want to look at a guy's ass? For the homosexually inclined, this teenage experience may be read in several ways. Out with their friends, they *are* members of the boys-wanting-girls club. But secretly, often unconsciously, they are more interested in the *boys* than the girls. And when one of the guys "hangs a moon," the homosexually inclined teenager's laughter is probably a response to more than one interpretation of the significance of a boy's bared bum. But he knows that he must not let on that he is aware of any other significance. And so he hides behind the facade of being a member of the club. The other boys in the club, unaware of the homosexually inclined boy's inclinations, assume that everyone is a member in good standing. That experience of seeming to belong when one senses that one really does not, the experience of keeping one's life a secret, amplifies the feeling of estrangement.

The athletic world is organized under the ironic assumption that everyone is heterosexual. It's a setup that few in that world question. Males and females, for example, are always given separate change and shower facilities; the assumption being, if they were to change and shower together, their heterosexual desires would overwhelm their sense of propriety. Women's teams that have male coaches do not allow them in the showers or changing rooms with the athletes. A male coach of a men's or boy's team, on the other hand, is automatically accorded the privilege of seeing his athletes naked in the locker room and showers.

Frequently, boys on the team will go out together on dates with girls. While the other boys have their arms around the girls, feeling this to be advantageous to the fulfillment of their sexual destiny, the homosexual boy is aware that the situation has somewhat less potential. John Goodwin told me that he remembered such dates:

> And girls, although I liked them, weren't doing the same to me that boys were doing. So there'd be a gang that was going out on dates and I'd be with my

girlfriend and this boy who I had a crush on and his girlfriend, and what I really wanted was to be with him, not the girl. It got to be awkward at that point.

In situations such as this, a young homosexual man knows that as far as everyone else is concerned he is like them. It makes him poignantly aware, however, that he is not.

The irony of being with girls when one is interested in boys can be intense. Novelist John Fox writes of a young swimmer who, while dancing with a girl at a high-school dance, finds himself fantasizing about having sex with a man in a movie he had seen.

> I liked this brother of Paul Newman in this sort of western movie I saw that took place in the present. There I was dancing this slow dance with Sue, thinking about this guy in the movie and my head was on her neck and I could smell perfume but in my mind this guy is on a rumpled bed in his underwear in the ranch house that's in the movie and it's late in the morning. I, also in my underwear, sit on the bed and reach out, put my hand on his crotch and his cock jumps into my hand and he smiles out one side of his mouth and I have a hard-on and I tried to grind up against Sue but there was nothing *down* there to grind up *against* and her tits were all mushed up against my chest. I lifted my head, looked up at the band playing on the stage and kind of choked, "I'm thirsty."[7]

Having had girlfriends all through high school, wanting to be a member in good standing of the boys-wanting-girls club, when I went to university I thought it was appropriate to continue doing so. Several months into a relationship with a woman, whom I was seeing almost daily, we still hadn't had sex; we hadn't even kissed each other. She was getting frustrated. One night when we were out drinking with the gang, she decided to show her dissatisfaction with my seemingly inactive libido: she put her arms around one of the other fellows at the table and he responded gratefully to her advances. It hit me like a ton of bricks. I was jealous. But it was *my girlfriend* I was jealous of. For weeks, I had had a crush on the guy she was coming on to, although until that moment I hadn't realized it. I remember I couldn't take my eyes off his strong, hairy forearms. My girlfriend was watching me. When she realized what was going on, she started to laugh. Still watching me, she ran her fingers up and down his arms, playing with those brown hairs. Then, with an incredibly devious look in her eyes, she turned her attention from me, said something to him I couldn't hear, and deep-kissed him. I was devastated. My girlfriend was getting the man I wanted. I looked around our table; everyone was drunk. It was boy/girl all the way around and they were all over each other. I couldn't stand it; I grabbed my coat and ran out of the bar.

As time passes, membership in the boys-wanting-girls club becomes more of a strain; it becomes more difficult to reconcile with one's homosexual desires. Eventually some men with homosexual desires, but by no means all of them, relinquish their membership. While they are in the club, they find themselves in a heterosexual world, a world in which they don't belong. Some homosexual boys make a point of avoiding the club, one manifestation of which is the social world of athletics. Others live with the duality of being outsiders on the inside.

The experience of being a "sissy," or at least being known as one, is not uncommon for gay boys and men. A sissy is a man or boy who does not subscribe to the orthodox myth of masculinity; he doesn't think like a "real man." Sissiness isn't necessarily the description of behavior; it's a personal disposition. The word "sissy" is derived from "sister" (*Concise Oxford Dictionary*), hence the "girlish" connotation. "Sissy" is usually considered a pejorative expression, especially when it is hurled as an accusation. But when employed by gay men as self-description, its pejorative sense is undermined. Gay men who have eschewed orthodox masculinity have no problem considering themselves as sissies—they do not, after all, subscribe to orthodoxy in gender and don't, therefore, feel compelled to establish a nonsissy status for themselves. One exercise club very popular with gay men in Toronto was well known as "Sissy Fitness." Certainly, not all gay men welcome the application of sissiness to themselves—some are uncomfortable with their estranged place in gender culture; they prefer to think of themselves as just as masculine as their heterosexual counterparts. Like David Kopay, they may go out of their way to "prove" their orthodox masculinity.

Whereas one might behave in a certain way because one is a sissy, one is not confined to that behavior; a sissy may behave effeminately or masculinely. A number of the men I interviewed, even though some of them were fine high-performance athletes, referred to themselves and their gay teammates as "sissies." One man talked about the juxtaposition of fine athletic ability and markedly gay self-expression.

> In gay sports, the sports I play, there are some athletes that are absolutely superb. These people could have played on any state university team and they are in fine physical shape. So it's a very competitive sport, especially the North American Gay Volleyball Association, but those wonderful, superb athletes are the most outrageous screamers you've ever seen and they'll do it right there on the court.[8]

A very fashionable young man, who used to be a gymnast and a certified gymnastics coach, joined a gay baseball team. Although many of the men on the team were very good baseball players, many of them did not behave in the traditionally masculine manner of baseball players.

> In baseball this summer I've never seen so many nelly boys. There's a lot of nelly boys and they can be just amazing athletes. They may not have a masculine bone in their bodies but put a baseball bat in their hands and they'll show you how to play baseball. I think that surprises a lot of people—it surprised me. But I surprised a lot of people too. They expected this trendy little fag to not know what

to do with a baseball bat; but, you know, I got up there and did a good job and I helped my team. . . . Everyone always associates sports with being a butch man and the idea of fags playing baseball. . . . Playing baseball with gay people was really interesting; it was a lot of fun.

Commenting on the juxtaposition of fine athletic ability and sissy-like effeminate manners, a former college basketball player said:

> I have friends who are effeminate, and athletically speaking, I know of some very good volleyball players, who are among the best in North America, who are very effeminate, drag-queen types, and that opened my eyes a long time ago. How could this person possibly be better than me when they have long hair, long finger nails, every time he gets a spike he screams, and then I realized that your level of masculinity or femininity really doesn't have a hell of a lot to do with your athletic ability.

It's important to note that these three examples referred to the experience that these men had with gay community sports. When gay men are involved in mainstream sports organizations, they usually do not feel free to express sissy sensibilities. The orthodox masculine leitmotif, although it is most severely expressed in violent team sports, reverberates throughout the athletic world, albeit in varying degrees.

Not surprisingly, it is the aesthetic sports that are the most gay sports. A gymnast I spoke to said that being a gymnast in high school made his peers suspect that he was gay. Figure skating is dominated by gay men. A former figure skater who is now a policeman told me:

> Figure skating was called "fairy skating." Figure skating is very close to ballet; it's a feminine sport. I was a figure skater. Everyone automatically assumed you were gay if you were a figure skater. Straight men were so far in a minority in figure skating—I can remember sitting at the 1980 national men's championship, and of the eight senior men at the national level, seven of them were gay. And that's probably a fairly accurate projection of the numbers in figure skating. Eighty or ninety percent of the men in figure skating are gay. My suspicion is that it's because of the artistic component in figure skating. I've also heard that there are a lot more gay men in gymnastics than there are in other sports. I don't know whether it's overgeneralizing to say that gay men are attracted to a sport that involves some sort of artistic expression, but it seems to be that there are more gay gymnasts and figure skaters than football players.

Although figure skating is dominated by gay men on the ice, the rules and traditions of the sport belie that fact somewhat. The pairs competition is the only sport that requires the competitors to ape heterosexual relations—it is ironic indeed that the sport with the highest proportion of homosexual men employs the most blatantly heterosexual signs. Even in football men don't have to feign an interest in women in order to score points. The rules do not allow two men to skate the pairs event together. Most of the time, the men wear pseudo-masculine outfits—tight-fitting little military uniforms are de rigueur on the ice. But these uniforms are not without irony; invariably their masculinity is elegantly undermined by glittering accents in sequins and gold lamé.

Because most male figure skaters are gay, the sport can feel like home for gay men and boys. Nevertheless, there are at least shadows of the experience of estrangement in this sport. The inherently romantic heterosexual significance of the pairs competition is at odds with the proclivities of gay men and boys. And famous figure skaters try to keep their homosexuality a secret. Whereas most sports heroes like to feature their wives and children when the media does personal profiles, gay figure skaters hide their "significant others" from the press. So, hiding homosexuality and the sense of estrangement that comes with it is a feature of even the most homosexual (mainstream) sport.

* * *

By showing that homosexual men tend to gravitate to individual, nonviolent sports, I am not suggesting that there are no homosexual men and boys in violent team sports. There certainly are homosexual men who pursue these sports, David Kopay being a well-known case in point. In fact, that there are homosexual men in such sports, given the overwhelmingly orthodox and heterosexual significance of those sports, is very important; it speaks of the multifaceted nuances of homosexuality. . . .

Sports for homosexual men is a place of estrangement. It is an orthodox masculine world that emphasizes the unusual relationship homosexuals have with our culture in general.

NOTES

1. J. Goldstein, "Sports Violence." In D. S. Eitzen (ed.), *Sport in Contemporary Society: An Anthology,* 2nd ed. (New York: St. Martin's Press, 1984), p. 92.
2. Gary Shaw, *Meat on the Hoof: The Hidden World of Texas Football* (New York: St. Martin's Press, 1972). See also sports psychologist Thomas Tutko, *Winning is Everything and Other American Myths* (New York: Macmillan, 1976).
3. Shaw, op. cit., p. 207.
4. David Kopay with P. Young, *The David Kopay Story: An Extraordinary Self-Revelation* (New York: Donald I. Fine, 1977), p. 152.
5. Ibid., p. 53.
6. See Edmund Vaz, "The Culture of Young Hockey Players: Some Initial Observations." In Albert W. Taylor (ed.), *Training: Scientific Basis and Application: A Symposium* (Springfield, Illinois: Charles C. Thomas, 1972), pp. 222-234.
7. John Fox, *The Boys on the Rock* (New York: St. Martin's Press, 1984), pp. 19-20.
8. "Screamers" refers to "screaming queens," which is an expression for gay men who make a point of their gayness by behaving in blatantly effeminate ways—it often entails a lot of shrieking.

36. Fun and Games: The Gay Games 1994

JOHN GALLAGHER

The jury is still out on whether Gay Games IV was a financial success, but organizers said they're confident the event enhanced the public image of gays and lesbians and improved their ability to obtain corporate backing for future events.

"It was everything we hoped for," said Jay Hill, executive director of the games. "We wanted to educate people out there to let them know that gays and lesbians are everywhere including places they wouldn't expect."

The event, which also included a cultural festival, is said to have attracted 10,879 athletes from 43 countries to New York City the week of June 19. The athletes ranged in age from a 13-year-old Belgian boy whose parents allowed him to compete in swimming matches to men and women in their 80s.

At the games' opening ceremonies, New York City mayor Rudolph Giuliani told an audience of 25,000 that "the Gay Games are about more than athletic competition. They offer a deeper understanding of America, where tolerance and skills overcome stereotypes and prejudice."

Among the other participants in the opening ceremonies was diver Greg Louganis, who won two gold medals in both the 1984 and the 1988 Olympic Games. In a video, Louganis—who has repeatedly refused to discuss reports that he is gay—told the athletes, "It's great to be out and proud." Gay Games spokesman Marlin Collingwood said the diver will not talk to reporters or discuss his sexual orientation until after his autobiography, *Breaking the Surface,* is published later this year.

Gay Games IV was notable for the concerted effort of organizers to attract a variety of corporate sponsors, including AT&T, Miller beer, and Continental Airlines. Organizers of the Gay Games in previous years had not sought such backing. "The fact that people like AT&T were happy afterward bodes well for our community and for future projects," Hill said. Nonetheless, he added, games organizers would not know until late July whether the event had turned a profit.

In many ways the games were as noteworthy for what did not happen as for what did. No incidents of antigay violence were reported, even though many events were held in traditionally conservative neighborhoods outside Manhattan. And no foreign athletes apparently attempted to seek asylum in the United States, even though Attorney General Janet Reno had said twice in the days immediately preceding the games that she is inclined to begin granting asylum claims to refugees who can demonstrate that they are victims of antigay persecution in their homelands.

Hill said games officials had consulted lawyers about handling defections, but senior staff attorney Evan Wolfson of Lambda Legal Defense and Education Fund said he—unlike some members of the media—did not anticipate defections. "We felt it was all media hype," he said. "We didn't put that much stock in it."

HIV-positive athletes were allowed to enter the United States for the games after Reno waived the federal ban on issuance of tourist visas for HIV-positive people. However, Gay Games officials estimated that only a few dozen of the 2,500 foreign athletes identified themselves to immigration officials as HIV-positive.

Athletes may have been reluctant to seek waivers for fear of revealing their HIV-positive status and having their passports stamped with a notation disclosing it, Wolfson said. "The waiver is certainly not price-free," he observed. "People identify themselves. It has consequences."

Although the games received considerable attention from the mainstream media, a series of faulty communications most likely kept the event from receiving more. Organizers were unable to promptly provide a complete list of medal winners for reporters, forcing the Associated Press (AP) to advise editors that it would be unable to post daily results on its wire service. Instead, AP could post a list only after the games ended, when media attention had waned.

In addition, the list of medalists was too long to be accommodated in most publications, including *The Advocate*. Although the games included 31 sports, there were numerous categories based on type of event, participant gender, and participant age. As a result, a total of 5,500 medals were awarded, with some participants winning in uncontested events. (Game organizers had said their intention was to honor as many athletes as possible.) In addition, some medal winners were reportedly reluctant to have their names released to the media.

Organizers released a partial list of world and United States records that they alleged had been broken at the competition, but many publications, including *The Advocate*, could not publish it because of its incomplete nature and because games organizers could not specify the previous records.

Hill said the organizers had not anticipated the media interest in results. "We hadn't planned to do anything" with the results, he said. "We had to very quickly develop a system to get results out. It wasn't perfect." Instead,

Hill said, the organizers devoted their energy to stressing "the great individual dignity of people out there achieving what they could."

By presenting such individual stories, he said, the games made a significant political contribution to the gay rights movement. "When I started out with this job, a lot of people asked, 'Why the Gay Games?'" Hill said. "I hope this week answered that question."

■ FOR FURTHER STUDY

Birrell, Susan, and Cheryl L. Cole, "Double Fault: Renee Richards and the Construction and Naturalization of Difference," *Sociology of Sport Journal* 7 (March 1990):1-11.

Blum, Debra E., "College Sports' L-Word," *Chronicle of Higher Education* (March 9, 1994):A35-A36.

Cahn, Susan K., *Coming on Strong: Gender and Sexuality in Twentieth Century Women's Sport* (New York: The Free Press, 1994).

Lenskyj, Helen, *Out of Bounds: Women, Sport, and Sexuality* (Toronto: Women's Press, 1986).

Lenskyj, Helen, "Sexuality and Femininity in Sport Contexts: Issues and Alternatives," *Journal of Sport & Social Issues* 18 (November 1994):356-375.

Messner, Michael A., "AIDS, Homophobia, and Sports." Pp. 120-126 in Michael A. Messner and Donald F. Sabo (eds.), *Sex, Violence & Power in Sports: Rethinking Masculinity* (Freedom, California: The Crossing Press, 1994).

Pronger, Brian, *The Arena of Masculinity: Sports, Homosexuality, and the Meaning of Sex* (New York: St. Martin's Press, 1990).

Sabo, Donald, "The Myth of the Sexual Athlete." Pp. 36-41 in Michael A. Messner and Donald F. Sabo (eds.), *Sex, Violence & Power in Sports: Rethinking Masculinity* (Freedom, California: The Crossing Press, 1994).

Sabo, Donald, "The Politics of Homophobia in Sport." Pp. 101-112 in Michael A. Messner and Donald F. Sabo (eds.), *Sex, Violence & Power in Sports: Rethinking Masculinity* (Freedom, California: The Crossing Press, 1994).